Preface

When we initially conceived the idea of writing a statistics book, our first thought was that it must be entertaining enough to keep students reading, relevant enough to maintain their interest, and comprehensible enough to ensure that students would understand the concepts. Yet it needed to be so extensive in coverage and exacting in detail that it would stand as a comprehensive, rigorous textbook, one that would be treasured as a reference book when students went on to conduct experiments of their own or analyze research done by others. We hoped to write a book that would help students grasp that critical connection between behavioral science research and the study of statistics. We wanted to help them understand not only the *how* of conducting statistical tests but also, even more important, the *why*—why it is necessary to show statistical significance and why any particular test is used in a given situation.

As we began writing the text, we found that it was easy to maintain my ideals. It was easy to write in an entertaining manner. We truly enjoyed writing about Mark Twain, the effect of television on the behavior of children, the Stroop effect, and automobile crashes. We felt that if we were having so much fun writing it, readers would doubtlessly have fun reading it. Writing about topics relevant to students was also easy. Our students and college-age children continually reveal their interests in casual conversation, so it was easy to write about topics relevant to them. As for being comprehensible, we have written this book in a light, conversational tone so that students can and will actually read it. We have been careful to include all the topics and concepts necessary for a comprehensive introduction to statistics, thanks in part to the expert reviewers of the original manuscript. However, underlying the extensive coverage, painstaking explanations, and engaging examples has been our compulsion to infuse the logic behind the methods, concepts, and procedures described in the textbook. It is through grasping the logic behind the concepts and procedures that students come to truly comprehend what the various statistics are all about.

This is a book intended for use in an introductory behavioral science statistics class. Students taking this course are interested in pursuing their interests in education, psychology, sociology, anthropology, or any other field of behavioral science. Examples pertaining to those interests are found throughout the text. This book is intended for all students, not only those who grasp math concepts readily, but also those who have traditionally had trouble learning math, even those who may be a little math phobic. In some of the chapter openers and in many of the examples, a little levity breaks up the intensity of the text. With all students in mind, we have designed a book that is full of helpful pedagogy to facilitate success. The pedagogical aids to student success revolve around the SQ4R study technique.

As behavioral scientists, we know that learning is most effective when the student is an active participant in the learning process. To enable students to actively participate in learning statistics, the book is structured around the SQ4R (**S**urvey, **Q**uestion, **R**ead, w**R**ite, **R**ecite, **R**eview) technique. When students use the technique on their own, it becomes tedious and they tend to stop using it. However, this text helps them use the technique with minimum effort by involving them in the study and use of statistical concepts in the course of reading each chapter.

Incorporated in the book are several features that are designed to support SQ4R. Each chapter begins with a **chapter outline** that encourages students to *survey* the major topics that will be presented in that chapter. **Student questions** are found throughout each chapter that help develop a questioning attitude in the students. Our experience in teaching statistics has enabled us to anticipate many student questions. These questions are embedded within the text, and the answers follow them.

An informal writing style facilitates *reading* of the chapters. **Chapter openers** introduce each chapter with a provocative research question. Each opener is integrated into the text and in most cases is used as the basis for many examples within that chapter. Although this is a statistics book, we have tried to keep the reading at an easy level and have tried to include extensive applications of statistical concepts and methods. Students should find that reading the text is enjoyable and that the writing style facilitates ease of learning.

Students are encouraged to *write* as they read. As much as possible, they should jot notes in the margins and summaries written in their own words next to new concepts as they are presented. They should have scratch paper available as they read so that they can work the samples presented in the text. In addition, they should be encouraged to work the **problems** at the end of each chapter to practice concepts presented in that chapter. Professors can assign only odd- or only even-numbered problems for homework and be assured that all main concepts will be covered by an adequate number of problems. Answers to odd-numbered problems can be found in Appendix B, and even-numbered answers are included in the Instructor's Manual.

Even more than learning how to perform statistical procedures, learning the logic behind statistical concepts—the rationale behind each concept, test, or procedure and why one is used over another—is the core of the statistics course. To help students evaluate their understanding of the concepts covered in the text, students find **concept quizzes** periodically throughout each chapter. These learning checks are in the form of short questions that invite each student to *recite* the conceptual content of the material just covered.

At the end of each chapter there is a **chapter summary,** a list of the **key terms** in the chapter, and a list of all new **formulas.** Defining each of the key terms provides an additional opportunity for students to *recite* the material covered in the chapter, and reading the summaries and formulas enables them to *review* the material. A significant new feature that also provides a chance for *review* are the **visual summaries** of major statistical procedures in the form of a flow chart found where applicable throughout the chapters. These visual summaries enable students to review the procedures at a glance without having to wade through the explanations and examples after they have already internalized the logic behind the procedures. They can be especially helpful as handouts or as the basis of review sessions.

Acknowledgments

The writing and publishing of any college textbook is a group effort involving the input and support of many people. We would like to thank our families, our friends, and our colleagues. In addition there are several persons who deserve special recognition.

We would first like to thank our editors. Frank Graham who brought the book to Mayfield and Ken King whose wisdom, insight, and commitment to excellence greatly enhanced the project. We thank Linda Ward who orchestrated the final editing and production of the third edition. Thanks also to Robin Mouat, Marty Granahan, Helen Walden, and Stan Loll for their contributions. To the following reviewers we offer our sincere appreciation: Gregory Burton, Seton Hall University; James F. Juola, University of Kansas, Lawrence; Daniel G. Mossler, Hampden-Sydney College; and David Wallace, Ohio University.

Finally, we would like to express our continuing appreciation to our students. They are our inspiration, and we wrote this book for them.

Contents

Preface   iii

1

An Introduction to Statistics   1

- Features of the Book   2
- Tips for Doing Well in Statistics   4
- A Note About Notation and Rounding   6
- Hypotheses   7
- Variables   8
- Scales of Measurement   11
  Nominal Scales   11
  Ordinal Scales   12
  Interval Scales   12
  Ratio Scales   13
  VISUAL SUMMARY: Scales of Measurement   14
  Populations and Samples   14
- Summary   16
- Key Terms   17
- Problems   17
  Problems From the Literature   19
- References   21

2

Frequency Distributions   22

- Ranked Distributions   23
- Frequency Distributions   24

■ Grouped Frequency Distributions   24
Constructing the Class Intervals: How Big and How Many?   *26*
*Constructing the Class Intervals and Determining Frequency: Setting
Limits and Counting Raw Scores*   *27*

■ Apparent Limits and Real Limits:
What You See Versus What Is Meant   29

■ Midpoint: The Center of the Class Interval   30
VISUAL SUMMARY: Creating a Grouped Frequency Distribution   32

■ Cumulative Frequency   34

■ Relative Frequency and Cumulative Relative Frequency   36

■ Cumulative Percent   39

■ Summary   42

■ Key Terms   42

■ Formulas   42

■ Problems   43
Problems From the Literature   *46*

■ References   48

3

Graphs   49

■ Basics in Constructing a Graph   51
The Axes   *52*
Plotting the Data: Histograms and Polygons   *55*

■ Frequency Histogram   55

■ Frequency Polygon   58

■ Relative Frequency Polygon   59

■ Cumulative Frequency Polygon   63

■ Cumulative Relative Frequency Polygon   64

■ Cumulative Percent Polygon   65

■ Stem-and-Leaf Diagrams   66

■ Changing the Shape of a Graph   67

■ Summary   70

■ Key Terms   70

■ Problems   71
Problems From the Literature   *73*

■ References   76

4

Measures of Central Tendency   77

- The Mean   79
  VISUAL SUMMARY: Computing the Mean From Raw Scores   81
- The Median   82
  Quartiles   84
- The Mode   86
- Mean, Median, or Mode: A Question of Skew   89
  Boxplots   92
- Frequency Distributions   95
  The Mean   95
  VISUAL SUMMARY: Computing the Mean of a Frequency Distribution   98
  The Median   99
  The Mode   100
  VISUAL SUMMARY: Finding the Median in a Grouped Frequency Distribution   101
- Summary   103
- Key Terms   104
- Formulas   104
- Problems   105
  Problems From the Literature   108
- References   110

5

Measures of Variability   111

- The Range   113
- Mean Deviation   114
  Average Mean Deviation: It All Adds Up to Nothing   114
- The Variance: The Mean of the Squared Deviations   117
- Standard Deviation: The Square Root of the Variance   118
  VISUAL SUMMARY: Computing the Variance and Standard Deviation   120
- Computational Formulas   120
  VISUAL SUMMARY: Computational Formulas for the Variance and Standard Deviation   122

▪ Calculating Variability From Grouped Frequency Distributions   124
    VISUAL SUMMARY: Finding the Variance and Standard Deviation
    of a Grouped Frequency Distribution   127

▪ Summary   129
▪ Key Terms   129
▪ Formulas   129
▪ Problems   130
    Problems From the Literature   *133*
▪ References   135

Scaled Scores and Standard Scores: How to Change Apples Into Oranges   136

▪ Scaled Scores   137
    Adding or Subtracting a Constant: No Change in Variability   *138*
    *Multiplying or Dividing by a Constant: A Concurrent Change
    in Mean and Standard Deviation*   *139*
    Standard Scores (z Scores)   *144*
    VISUAL SUMMARY: Coverting *X* to *z*   146

▪ Summary   148
▪ Key Terms   149
▪ Formulas   149
▪ Problems   149
    Problems From the Literature   *151*
▪ References   153

The Normal Curve   154

▪ Characteristics of the Normal Curve   155
▪ Finding Proportions and Percentages   159
    Using Table Z: Finding Areas Under the Normal Curve   *159*
    Area Above: Finding Proportions Above Positive and Negative z Scores   *162*
    Area Below: Finding Proportions Below Positive and Negative z Scores   *164*
    VISUAL SUMMARY: Finding Areas Under the Normal Curve   166

Area Between: Finding Proportions Lying Between Two z Scores   *168*
VISUAL SUMMARY: Finding the Area Between Two z Scores   171

■ Finding Percentiles   172
Using Table P: Finding Distinct Scores   *173*
VISUAL SUMMARY: Finding Percentiles   175

■ Summary   176
■ Key Terms   177
■ Formulas   177
■ Problems   177
Problems From the Literature   *178*
■ References   179

8

Correlation   180

■ The Nature of Correlation   181
Types of Correlation: How Are Variables Related?   *181*
Degree of Correlation: How Strongly Are Variables Related?   *182*

■ The Correlation Coefficient   184
The Covariance   *184*
VISUAL SUMMARY: Computing the Covariance   187
Computing the Correlation Coefficient   *188*
VISUAL SUMMARY: Computing the Correlation Coefficient Using the
Covariance   189
*Computational Formulas for the Covariance and Correlation
Coefficient*   *191*

■ The Significance of the Correlation Coefficient   193
Interpreting the Correlation Coefficient: What Do the Numbers Mean?   *193*

■ The Coefficient of Determination   197
■ Summary   199
■ Key Terms   199
■ Formulas   199
■ Problems   200
Problems From the Literature   *203*
■ References   205

9

Regression   206

- Making Predictions via Linear Regression   207
  The z-Score Method: Using Y *to Predict* X   *208*
  The z-Score Method: Using X *to Predict* Y   *210*
  VISUAL SUMMARY: Using *z* Scores to Make Predictions   212
- The Regression Line: Faster Predictions   213
- The Standard Error of the Estimate   221
  VISUAL SUMMARY: Using Regression Equations to Make Predictions   223
- Summary   224
- Key Terms   225
- Formulas   225
- Problems   225
  Problems From the Literature   *227*
- References   230

10

Probability Theory and Sampling   231

- Probability Theory   232
- Sampling   238
- The Standard Error of the Mean   241
- The Central Limit Theorem   243
- The *z* Test   244
  VISUAL SUMMARY: The *z* Test   246
- Summary   248
- Key Terms   248
- Formulas   248
- Problems   249
  Problems From the Literature   *250*
- References   253

11

Experimental Design   254

- Developing a Hypothesis   255
- Identifying Variables   256
- Factors in Experimental Design   259
  Between-Subjects, Within-Subjects, and Mixed Designs   259
  One-Group Experimental Designs   263
  Completely Randomized Designs   263
- Important Aspects of Experimental Design   265
  The Necessity for Control   265
  Experimenter Bias and Demand Characteristics   267
- Statistical Significance   269
- Power   275
- Summary   278
- Key Terms   279
- Problems   279
  Problems From the Literature   282
- References   284

12

t Tests   285

- *z* Tests (A Review)   287
- *t* Tests   290
- Single-Sample *t* Tests   290
  VISUAL SUMMARY: Single-Sample *t* Tests   294
- *t* Tests Between Two Independent Sample Means   296
  VISUAL SUMMARY: *t* Tests Between Two Independent Sample Means   300
- *t* Tests for Correlated Samples   302
  VISUAL SUMMARY: *t* Tests for Correlated Samples   308
- Power and *t* Tests   309
  VISUAL SUMMARY: Choosing the Proper *t* Test   313
- Summary   313
- Key Terms   314

- Formulas   314
- Problems   315
  Problems From the Literature   320
- References   324

13

One-Way Analysis of Variance   326

- Analysis of Variance: One Test Is Better Than Many   328
- Hypothesis Testing and Analysis of Variance   328
- Conducting an Analysis of Variance   329
  Two Methods for Estimating the Population Variance   330
  Computation of the Mean Square Between Groups   333
  Computation of the Mean Square Within Groups   335
  The F Test   336
  VISUAL SUMMARY: One-Way Analysis of Variance   337
  Computational Formula for F   339
  VISUAL SUMMARY: One-Way Analysis of Variance—Computational Formulas   343
- Summary   345
- Key Terms   346
- Formulas   346
- Problems   347
  Problems From the Literature   351
- References   353

14

Two-Way Analysis of Variance   354

- Main Effects   358
- Interaction   359
- Computation of Sums of Squares for Two-Way Analysis of Variance   363
- Computation of Degrees of Freedom for Two-Way Analysis of Variance   369
- Computation of the Mean Squares for Two-Way Analysis of Variance   370

- Computation of the *F* Ratios for Two-Way Analysis of Variance   372
    VISUAL SUMMARY: Two-Way Analysis of Variance   373
- Significance of the Main Effects   375
- Significance of the Interaction   376
- Summary   378
- Key Terms   379
- Formulas   379
- Problems   380
    Problems From the Literature   *383*
- References   385

15

Chi-Square and Other Nonparametric Statistics   386

- Chi-Square   387
    VISUAL SUMMARY: Chi-Square   393
- The Mann–Whitney *U* Test   395
    VISUAL SUMMARY: The Mann–Whitney *U* Test   402
- The Wilcoxon *T* Test   404
    VISUAL SUMMARY: The Wilcoxon *T* Test   409
- The Kruskal–Wallis Test   411
    VISUAL SUMMARY: The Kruskal–Wallis Test   414
- Summary   415
    VISUAL SUMMARY: Chi-Square and Other Nonparametric Statistics   416
- Key Terms   416
- Formulas   417
- Problems   417
    Problems From the Literature   *423*
- References   427

APPENDIX  A

Tables   429

- Table F: The *F* Distribution   430
- Table N: Random Numbers   431
- Table P: Values of *z* Corresponding to the Larger or Smaller Proportion   432

- Table Q: The Studentized Range Statistic   434
- Table R: Critical Values of the Correlation Coefficient   435
- Table T: Critical Values of the t Distribution   437
- Table U: Critical Values of the Mann–Whitney U Test   438
- Table W: Critical Values of the Wilcoxon T Test   439
- Table X: The χ^2 Distribution   440
- Table Z: Areas Under the Normal Curve   441

APPENDIX **B**

Solutions to Odd-Numbered Problems   447

Index   523

An Introduction to Statistics

- Features of the Book
- Tips for Doing Well in Statistics
- A Note About Notation and Rounding
- Hypotheses
- Variables

- Scales of Measurement
  Nominal Scales
  Ordinal Scales
  Interval Scales
  Ratio Scales
  VISUAL SUMMARY: Scales of Measurement

Populations and Samples
- Summary
- Key Terms
- Problems
  Problems From the Literature
- References

A child watches a film of a woman repeatedly kicking and hitting a "Bobo" doll, one of those blow-up clowns that pop back up after being knocked down. The woman not only punches the doll, but she also absolutely batters it, flinging it up into the air and even pouncing on it to thrash it as much as she can. After watching her, the child, alone in the room with the Bobo doll, jumps up, whacks the doll around, and abuses it in precise imitation of the adult in the film. Another child watches a different film of the same woman in the same room with the same toys, including the Bobo doll, but in this film the woman sits passively, ignoring the inflatable doll. At the end of the film, this second child exhibits a similar passive behavior, quite different from the full-blown aggression demonstrated by the first child.

Media violence has been a research concern for over 50 years (see MacCoby, 1954) and continues to be a concern of researchers, parents, and politicians. Children spend thousands of hours in front of the television; it has been estimated that by age 18 the average young person has viewed over 200,000 acts of TV violence (American Academy of Pediatrics, 1995). Around 40 years ago, Albert Bandura and Richard Walters (1963) wrote a fascinating book exploring how people learn a repertoire of behaviors through watching and imitating others. One of their research projects, described in the opening vignette, was a study of how children's aggressive behavior can be shaped by watching aggressive models on film. The design of their experiment was relatively simple. One group of children was shown the film described previously of an adult model hitting and kicking a Bobo doll; another group was shown a film of the passive model; and still another group, the control group, was shown no film. When left alone in the room with the inflatable doll and other toys, the children who had seen the violent film viewed the nonaggressive film and the children in the control group rarely committed aggressive acts. Indeed, the children who watched the passive models in the film were even more inhibited than those in the control group.

Having read about the Bandura and Walters experiment, what can you conclude? Is watching violence on television or in the movies bad for children? Should violent TV programs be banned? Given the limited amount of information you have about the experiment, you really should not come to any definite conclusions. Before making judgments based on this research project, you might want to have answers to such questions as these:

1. How many children were in each group?
2. What were the ages of the children?
3. How many aggressive acts were seen by the children who watched the film?
4. How many aggressive acts, on the average, were performed by the children who watched the aggressive film?
5. How many aggressive acts, on the average, were performed by the children who watched the passive film?
6. How long was the film?

As you may have noticed, all of the preceding questions ask for numbers. Behavioral scientists who read or conduct research are constantly bombarded with numbers: "30 children in each group," "ages 4 to 7 years," "21 aggressive acts," "28.7 minutes long." These numbers are meant to convey important information about the research. Whenever we use these types of numbers, we are using statistics. **Statistics** is a branch of applied mathematics that scientists use to plan research; to gather, organize, and analyze data; to present data in research papers; and to make inferences about data. Ultimately, behavioral scientists use statistics to support or refute predictions concerning the behavior of humans and animals.

Features of the Book

This book should be easy to understand. The goal of the book is to introduce you to the uses of behavioral science statistics in a friendly, interesting way, using provocative and sometimes amusing examples. Several features should greatly help you learn statistics if you take advantage of them. These features are

- chapter outlines
- chapter openers or vignettes
- student questions
- visual summaries
- concept quizzes
- chapter summaries
- key terms
- formulas
- problems

The **chapter outline** at the beginning of each chapter provides an overview of that chapter. Reading the outline will let you know what topics will be covered in each chapter, help you keep the material you read in perspective, and aid you in reviewing the chapter.

The short stories and research examples that open each chapter are also an integral part of that chapter. Each **chapter opener** introduces the initial statistical concept and/or serves as an example that is referred to extensively through the chapter. The chapter openers also illustrate the interrelationship between statistics and experimental design, as well as highlight the importance of statistics in the study of behavior.

Student questions are used throughout the text. How many times have you been listening to a lecture or reading a textbook when a question about the material being covered pops into your mind? Sometimes you need a point clarified, an important concept repeated, or confirmation of whether you are right about an inference you have made or about the way the new concept relates to previous material. Whatever the case, these questions are an important part of the learning process. During a lecture, you and your classmates can ask these questions and your professor can answer them. However, when you are reading, it is impossible to get immediate answers. Questions that are frequently asked by students appear at critical points throughout the text. The number and types of questions vary from chapter to chapter and topic to topic, but each question and answer will enhance your comprehension of the section you're reading.

A course in statistics has two main objectives: (1) to teach you the mathematical formulas for computing statistics, and (2) to teach you the logic underlying the computation and use of those statistics. To reinforce both computational and logical statistical concepts, visual summaries and concept quizzes have been added to each chapter.

After the discussion of most statistical procedures or computations, you will find a visual summary. The **visual summary** is essentially a flowchart or figure that shows you the step-by-step procedure you need to follow in order to compute the statistic. The visual summaries will be especially helpful when reviewing the chapter before an exam.

To reinforce and apply both computational and logical statistical concepts, there are **concept quizzes** at vital points in each chapter. These quizzes, based on examples from research studies, are short-answer fill-ins that review and reinforce critical concepts covered in the chapter. They will also enable you to quickly check whether you know the material you have just finished reading. Of course, for answers you don't know or get wrong, you should reread the section covering those concepts or skills.

A **chapter summary** at the end of each chapter reviews the major mathematical and logical concepts covered in the chapter.

Following each chapter summary are the key terms, a list of formulas, and problems. The **key terms** will help you quickly identify and review the important terms and topics covered in the chapter. All new **formulas** used in the chapter are collected and restated after the summary for quick reference. Finally, each chapter ends with **problems,** including a separate section of problems based on research studies from the scientific literature, that were carefully designed to give you practice and to reinforce the material covered in the chapter. The solutions to the odd-numbered problems can be found in Appendix B at the end of the book.

Tips for Doing Well in Statistics

Doing well (i.e., getting good grades) in any college-level class requires a lot of work, and statistics is no exception. Learning statistics and getting a good grade in this course will require a great deal of study and organization on your part. No one can force you to study, but suggestions for ways to go about it and help with the organization can make your study more efficient and productive.

1. Statistics is cumulative. This statistics class, like most of your classes, consists of a specific body of knowledge. Your job as a student is to master that knowledge. Unlike the content of many other psychology or sociology courses, however, the information you learn in statistics is *cumulative.* Thorough comprehension of topics and concepts covered at the beginning of the course is imperative for the understanding of topics and concepts presented later. Missing only one lecture or one page in the textbook may cause you to have difficulty with the rest of the course. First and foremost, you must keep up with the work, attend all lectures, do the homework problems, and read the book consistently.

2. Your professor is there to help. As a student you have at least four sources for information about statistics: your professor, the book, fellow students, and the Internet. All four can be helpful, but your professor can be extremely so. Don't be afraid to approach the professor. Ask for help when you first detect you need it, clear up questions as they arise, ask questions in class if you don't quite understand something. Not only do statistics professors know the material backward and forward, but they also have lots of experience in pinpointing the causes of students' confusion. Your professor dictates the topics you will cover and the speed at which you will cover them, and your feedback will help him or her adjust the rate of coverage. Take careful notes in class, work all demonstration problems along with your professor, and when you don't understand something, ask questions, either in class or in your professor's office.

3. Make friends quickly. Other students in your class are another significant source of help in statistics. If you must miss a lecture or don't understand a small point, a fellow student can often provide the notes or information that will solve your problem. In turn, helping other students will benefit you because as you shed light on specific concepts for your friends, you further clarify them for yourself. Take time to get to know your fellow students, exchange telephone numbers and e-mail addresses, and set up study groups.

4. Read the book. This book is an extremely important part of your statistics course. Think of it as an additional set of lecture notes or a knowledgeable friend. The book is designed to teach you statistics as well as serve as a reference for later years. The main features of the book were described earlier in the chapter. Now you will see how to use them effectively.

As you might have guessed, reading a statistics book is not like reading a novel. Always have a pencil, paper, and a calculator handy when you start a new chapter. Before you begin to read the body of the chapter, take time to read the outline so that (a) you can get an idea of what topics will be discussed and (b) you can gain some notion of the chapter's general organization. As you read the chapter, be sure you understand each new concept or statistical procedure before going on to the next section. Also, as you're reading, don't be afraid of underlining, highlighting, and writing in the margins. After all, this is your book that you will refer to again and again, maybe even throughout graduate school.

Make sure you work all the numerical examples in the text. By working the examples using your own paper and calculator, you will get invaluable guided practice. Don't take the text's word for a sum or computed value; compute it yourself. Take time to study the visual summaries. You might want to see whether you can create your own visual summaries and compare them to the ones in the book. Take time to complete the concept quizzes at the end of each major section. These quizzes are quick checks to let you know whether you understand the concepts sufficiently to proceed to the next section. Once you have finished a chapter, try to summarize it, and then read the chapter summary to see whether you got it right. Next, try to define each of the key terms. Finally, to reinforce your comprehension, work the problems at the end of the chapter. By utilizing this study system for each chapter, you will maximize your understanding of statistics.

5. Practice helps. This is a fundamental psychological law that is especially applicable to statistics. The best way to improve your skill is to practice. You practice statistics by working problems. Copy and rework the problems demonstrated by your professor in class. Solve the numerical examples while you are reading the book. Work the problems at the end of each chapter. Make sure you do any homework as soon as it is assigned. You can also make up problems, by yourself or with your study group, and attempt to solve them. The study guide that accompanies this text also has hundreds of solved problems for you to use in your studies.

6. Calculators are necessary. Statistics involves a lot of computation. Computing the sums of columns of numbers, squares, and square roots can be extremely time consuming without an electronic calculator. To do the computations required for this course, you will need the assistance of an electronic calculator or possibly a computer. Before purchasing any calculator, computer, or software that you are buying expressly for this course, it is wise to talk with your professor. He or she can tell you exactly what is required and which calculators or computers meet those requirements. At the very least, you will need a calculator that does addition, subtraction, multiplication, division, and square roots. For a little additional cost, you can purchase a statistical or scientific calculator that can be programmed to calculate many of the statistical procedures discussed in this textbook. Before you buy any scientific or statistical calculator, however, take time to read the instruction booklet to confirm that the calculator will do what you want it to do. Make sure the calculator will compute at least the mean and the standard deviation. It will also be helpful if your calculator computes correlation coefficients. Once you have purchased your calculator, make sure you are thoroughly familiar with it by working the sample problems in the booklet for a particular statistic before you discuss it in class.

7. Get a "feel" for statistics. As you are learning statistics, try to do more than memorize the formulas: *try to understand the concepts behind the formulas.* At the end of this course you should know whether a computed value is reasonable. *Think* about the problem you are working or the experiment you are trying to analyze. You already have a feel for some kinds of statistics. For instance, you know that the mean (average) for the numbers 51, 56, 55, 54, and 59 cannot be greater than 60 or less than 50. You *should* know that if a friend tells you the average age of people frequenting bars in your town is 16.5, he or she has to be pulling your leg. Similarly, after having learned that a correlation coefficient can never be more than $+1.00$ or less than -1.00, you should know that when you compute a correlation of $+23$, you must have made a mistake. Use your knowledge of mathematics, statistics, and the problem you are working on to decide whether each sum or statistic you compute is reasonable. If there is any doubt, recompute the value. (Just because your calculator gives you a number, it does not mean it is correct.) As you work more and more problems, you should get a better feel for statistics. The next section begins to build the foundation you will need to develop this statistical sense and to comprehend the whys and wherefores of statistics.

A Note About Notation and Rounding

Statistics, like algebra or any other form of mathematics, has its own notation. Mathematical or statistical notation is merely a type of shorthand, much of which you already know because statistics shares many of its symbols with algebra, such as $+, -, \cdot, \div$, and $=$. However, some of the notation you encounter will be new. The new notation, as well as how to use it, is discussed in detail when it is introduced, and sufficient examples are given to allow you to master it. For example, in later chapters you will encounter subscripted variables such as S_x or S_y. Remember that the subscripts serve to differentiate one value from another and that they are not the same. For example, S_x is a value for Sample X and S_y is a value for Sample Y.

Careful attention to mathematical notation is vital in statistical work, and so is computational accuracy. Take out your calculator (yes, right now) and divide 1 second by 7 (1 second $\div$ 7). What answer did you get? Your calculator might read 0.142857143 seconds, which is the value in billionths of a second. Did your calculator give you more digits? Fewer digits? Different calculators have different memory and display capacity. To remedy this problem of large decimals and differing display capacity, you can round off the quotient to tenths, hundredths, or thousandths of a second. However, there is an inherent problem in rounding because if one person always rounds to the nearest tenth and another person rounds to the nearest thousandth, there will often be a discrepancy in their answers. To prevent this, there must be some agreement, some ground rules, for rounding numbers. These "rounding rules" are described next.

For most statistical calculations, rounding to the thousandths place (three digits to the right of the decimal point) provides sufficient accuracy. To do this, it is customary to use the following round-off procedure:

1. Calculate your answer to at least four decimal places.
2. If the fourth digit is less than 5 (0, 1, 2, 3, or 4), report the first three digits without change.
3. If the fourth digit is 5 or greater (5, 6, 7, 8, or 9), report the first two digits and increase the third digit by 1.

This procedure is the one used throughout the book. To practice, work the two examples that follow.

As mentioned earlier, dividing 1 second by 7 results in 0.142857143. To round off this result to the thousandths place, or the third digit to the right of the decimal point, you need to consider the fourth digit: 0.142<u>8</u>. Because this digit is greater than 5, you report the first two digits and add 1 to the third digit to get 0.143. For another example, divide 1 by 3 on your calculator. The result is something like 0.333333333. Again, look at the fourth digit: 0.333<u>3</u>. Because 3 is less than 5, you need report only the original three digits, 0.333. Now consider some factors more specifically related to behavioral science research.

Hypotheses

All behavioral science research begins with a question about behavior: What happens to a certain behavior if . . . ? What causes people to . . . ? Can a person's behavior be influenced by . . . ? In the scientific study of behavior, such a question must be restated in the form of a **hypothesis,** a possible explanation for the behavior being studied that is based on previously gathered facts and theories. Expressed as a prediction, a scientific hypothesis is not always true, but it is stated in such a way that it can be proved false if indeed it is false. For example, Bandura and Walters might have one day noticed that there seems to be a lot of violence on television and in movies, and then wondered, Do television and film actors actually serve as models for children? From this question, they might have generated the following hypothesis: Children who view a film depicting aggressive adult models will exhibit more aggressive acts than children who see a film depicting passive models. This hypothesis makes a prediction that should be easy to verify.

Because the concept of developing a hypothesis is an important one, here is one more example of how this is done. Everyone knows that "two eyes are better than one." Are they really? (We will look into this in more detail in Chapter 14.) How would you state a hypothesis designed to answer the question, Are two eyes better than one? Take a few minutes, or seconds, and write down your hypothesis. You want to create a hypothesis that is testable and that investigates the differences in visual perception between two eyes and one eye, but what differences do you want to test? Color, shape, size, or distance perception? How will you measure these differences? Each of these must go into your hypothesis. If you are interested in testing distance perception, you would need to measure distance perception under each of the two conditions, one eye or two. A reasonable hypothesis might be: Participants will be more accurate at estimating the relative distances of objects when viewing the objects with two eyes than when viewing with one eye.

In most experiments, there are two mutually exclusive hypotheses (which means that if one is true, the other can't be). A **research hypothesis** is one that the researcher wishes to support. The two hypotheses stated in the preceding paragraph are both research hypotheses. The **null hypothesis,** on the other hand, is the one the researcher wants to reject because it proposes that there will be no change in behavior, no difference between the groups being measured. In the case of the Bandura and Walters experiment, the null hypothesis might be: The number of aggressive acts performed by children who view a film portraying aggressive adult models will be no greater than the number of aggressive acts performed by children who see a film portraying passive models. Because of the way statistical tests are designed, *it is actually the null hypothesis that is tested in a research study.* If the null hypothesis can be shown to be false, then the research hypothesis is supported.

Variables

After generating a hypothesis, a researcher needs to decide how to test it. Often, the test is conducted via an experiment in which the researcher takes great care to hold everything constant (keep everything the same), except for the factors being investigated. These factors are manipulated, or systematically altered, to see whether they cause any change in the participants' behavior. By doing this, the researcher can attribute any change in the behavior directly to the factors being manipulated because all other factors have been held constant.

Factors in an experiment are known as variables. **Variables** are events or qualities that can vary—they can assume more than one value. Variables include such factors as reaction time, number of participants in a group, number of aggressive acts, age of the participants, length of a video program, and distance. When researchers decide to conduct an experiment, one of the first things they do is to decide which variable(s) will be manipulated and which variable(s) will be measured for changes that result from the manipulation. These two distinct types of variables are known as *independent* and *dependent variables.*

An **independent variable** is a factor that is selected and manipulated, or controlled, by the experimenter. It is totally independent of anything the participant does. In the Bandura and Walters experiment, the independent variable was the type of film viewed by the child—the aggressive or passive version. Because the experimenters were solely responsible for determining which film the child viewed, this variable was totally independent of the child's response. In the depth perception experiment, the independent variable was the number of eyes used by the participant to view the display.

In contrast to the independent variable, a **dependent variable** is a measurable behavior exhibited by the *participant.* It is a result of, or is dependent on, the independent variable. Thus, in an experiment we expect that with any change in the independent variable, there will be a corresponding change in the dependent variable. Because the dependent variable is a measure of each participant's behavior, it is the source of the numbers used in statistics. In the Bandura and Walters experiment, the dependent variable was the number of aggressive acts performed by each child after seeing the film. As it turned out, the children who viewed the violent film performed many aggressive acts, and the children who viewed the passive film performed few, if any, aggressive acts. Thus, the children's behavior was dependent on which film they viewed (the independent variable).

A good way to determine which variable is the independent variable and which is the dependent variable is to reword the research question in the form, What is the effect of (independent variable) on (dependent variable)? In the Bandura and Walters experiment, the question could be stated, What is the effect of the type of film viewed by the child on the number of aggressive acts performed by each child?

In any experiment, researchers also need to control **extraneous variables,** or "extra" variables, that may affect the outcome of the experiment but are not directly related to the study. For example, if there had been an obnoxious noise from a jackhammer outside the window during or after the children's viewing of the violent film, then their subsequent aggression might actually have been due to the noise rather than to the aggressive behavior of the models in the film. Presumably, Bandura and Walters controlled extraneous variables such as noises, personal interruptions, and excessively bright lights.

To research and collect information about human or animal behavior, it is necessary to measure the dependent variable and record the measurement using the same type of scale so that participants' responses can be compared objectively. The next section describes the kinds of measurement scales.

Concept Quiz

Do you think people will tip differently depending on whether or not a food server innocently touches their hand or shoulder compared to not touching them at all? Interpersonal touch communicates a variety of messages and, in some contexts, may have positive effects on an experience. Researchers Crusco and Wetzel (1984) speculated that the percentage of tip would be higher if the waitress innocently touched a diner either on the hand or shoulder compared to no touch at all. In a natural setting, restaurant diners were randomly assigned to receive a brief shoulder touch, hand touch, or no touch when the waitress returned with their change from paying the food bill. After data were collected and analyzed, it was revealed that the percentage of tip didn't differ between the two touch conditions. However, when the touch data were combined, it was found that the average percentage tip was larger when diners were touched than when they were not touched.

1. Round off the following percentage of tips to the third digit after the decimal:
   a. 13.234473%   d. 21.92375%
   b. 15.77377%   e. 24.9999999%
   c. 23.3333%

2. The possible explanation for the effect of interpersonal touch on tipping behavior that Crusco and Wetzel expressed as a prediction is called a _____.

3. Crusco and Wetzel want the results of their study to support the _____ hypothesis and reject the _____ hypothesis.

4. Explain why the null and research hypotheses must be mutually exclusive.

5. The _____ variable manipulated by Crusco and Wetzel was _____.

6. The _____ variable was the _____ and measured the effect of interpersonal touch.

7. Interpersonal touch, for example, is called a variable because _____.

8. Suppose Crusco and Wetzel wanted to conduct another study and examine whether a food server's facial expression (smile or no smile), might influence customers' ratings of their dining experience. Identify the independent and dependent variables.

Answers

1. a. 13.234%
   b. 15.774%
   c. 23.333%
   d. 21.924%
   e. 25.000%
2. hypothesis
3. research; null
4. If the null hypothesis is not rejected (which means there are no differences) then the research hypothesis (stating there are differences) can't be true.
5. independent; interpersonal touch
6. dependent; percentage of tip
7. characteristics or qualities can vary, such as shoulder touch, hand touch, and no touch
8. The food server's facial expression is the independent variable, and the rating of customers' dining experience is the dependent variable.

Scales of Measurement

Because there are countless types of dependent variables, from heartbeats per minute to rankings of tennis players, all kinds of data can be collected to measure them. However, no matter what kind of data you collect, they will be recorded on one of four measurement scales: *nominal, ordinal, interval,* or *ratio.* These scales differ in complexity according to how the relationships are described between various points on the scales.

Nominal Scales

Are you an introvert or an extrovert? Are you rich or poor? Are you tall or short? Do you have green, blue, or brown eyes? Is your hair black, brown, red, or yellow? Are you a Democrat, an Independent, or a Republican? What is your favorite type of music? Often, people are placed or place themselves in a particular category based on a name, a color, a belief, or a preference. When data are collected based on a name or a category, a nominal scale of measurement is being used.

A **nominal scale** is the simplest form of measurement and is used when the variable being measured (the dependent variable) is qualitative as opposed to quantitative. The word *nominal* means *name,* so when researchers use a nominal scale, they assign participants to a category based on the name of some physical or psychological quality or characteristic rather than some numerical score. In their study of the effect of television violence, for instance, Bandura and Walters could have used such categories as male–female, aggressive–passive, and tall–short. If they had used the passive–aggressive categories, they could have observed each child during the experiment and assigned him or her to either the passive or aggressive category. Children who exhibited few aggressive acts would be placed in the passive category, and those with lots of aggressive acts would be placed in the aggressive category. If one child was only mildly aggressive and another was extremely aggressive, both would have been assigned to the aggressive category. Countless other behavioral variables can be measured using a nominal scale. Examples are intellectual ability (above normal, normal, below normal) and personality type (extroverted, introverted).

The problem with a nominal scale of measurement is that it cannot be used to record anything but qualitative comparisons. Knowing that a child is passive or aggressive does not allow you to make quantitative comparisons. If a child is passive, you don't know whether he or she is bordering on aggressive or is almost asleep. Thus, nominal scales of measurement allow for only the crudest types of comparisons among participants. If more precision is needed, you must use a more accurate scale of measurement reflecting more quantitative comparisons. The ordinal scale is one of these.

Ordinal Scales

Of the quantitative scales, the ordinal scale of measurement is the simplest. An **ordinal scale** requires that you order, or rank, the data from the highest to lowest. This ordering tells you whether any one participant ranks higher or lower than any other participant, although it does not tell you how much higher or lower. For example, all the children who participated in the Bandura and Walters experiment could be ranked according to aggressiveness of their behavior after viewing the film. If there are only seven children in the experiment, the most aggressive child might get a rank of 7, the next most aggressive a rank of 6, and so on.

Ordinal scales of measurement show relative rankings but reveal nothing about the extent of the differences between the rankings. Equal distances on an ordinal scale do not necessarily represent equal differences between the participants' qualities. Using an ordinal scale of measurement, you can tell that a child with a rank of 7 is more aggressive than one with a rank or 5, but you cannot determine the difference in the degrees of aggressiveness between the two children. The change in aggressiveness between a child with a rank of 1 and a child with a rank of 2 is not necessarily the same as the change between a child with the rank of 3 and a child with the rank of 4. For more distinct comparisons, you need to use an interval scale of measurement.

Interval Scales

An **interval scale** of measurement indicates not only relative ranks of scores but also equal distances or degrees of difference between the scores. Thus, the distance between scores of 1 and 2 is the same as the distance between scores of 3 and 4. For example, Bandura and Walters might have asked their assistants to use an interval scale to rate the aggressiveness of the children that ranged from 1 (least aggressive) to 7 (most aggressive). Had they done so, they would have made sure that the difference in aggressiveness between scores of, say, 1 and 2 was equal to the difference between scores of 4 and 5. In another example, IQ scores compare the intellectual attributes of different people on an interval scale. The distance on a typical IQ scale between scores of 100 and 120 is presumed to equal the distance between scores of 70 and 90. Quantitative comparisons can readily be made using an interval scale. Differences between any two participants are in standard increments, so if on a scale of 1 to 7 one child is rated a 6 in aggressiveness, you know that he or she is as close to the "most aggressive" rating as another child rated a 2 is to the "least aggressive" rating.

The major disadvantage of the interval scale is that it does not allow you to make ratio types of comparisons. You cannot say that a child who is rated a 6 in aggressiveness is twice as aggressive as a child who is rated a 3. You also cannot say that a person who has an IQ score of 120 is twice as intelligent as a person with an IQ score of 60.

> **Question:** Wait a minute: 120 is twice the size of 60, so why isn't a person with an IQ of 120 twice as smart as a person with an IQ of 60?

The difficulty arises because interval scales of measurement have no real meaningful zero point. In the case of the aggressiveness ratings, it is impossible to set a meaningful zero point: Everyone is capable of at least a mild amount of aggression. Therefore, a rating of zero is not meaningful. Likewise, because of the way IQ tests are scored, it is impossible for a person to have an IQ of zero. Without a meaningful zero point, ratio comparisons cannot be made. A ratio scale of measurement must be used to make ratio comparisons.

Ratio Scales

A **ratio scale** of measurement has all the properties of the scales just mentioned, but in addition it has a meaningful zero point—a point at which there is a total absence of the variable being measured. This meaningful zero point makes ratio comparisons possible. If you were to record the number of aggressive acts performed by each child in the Bandura and Walters experiment, you would be using a ratio measurement scale. A child who exhibits 10 aggressive acts performs twice as many as a child who exhibits only 5. This makes sense because there is a base point, zero, at which no aggressive acts are performed.

Although most of the examples in this book use interval scales or ratio scales of measurement, it is extremely important in the real world of research to be able to identify the measurement scale being used. The reason for this is that nominal and ordinal scales require different types of statistical analyses than do interval and ratio scales of measurement. Chapter 15, "Chi-Square and Other Nonparametric Statistics," is devoted to the analysis of nominal and ordinal data sets.

VISUAL SUMMARY

Scales of Measurement

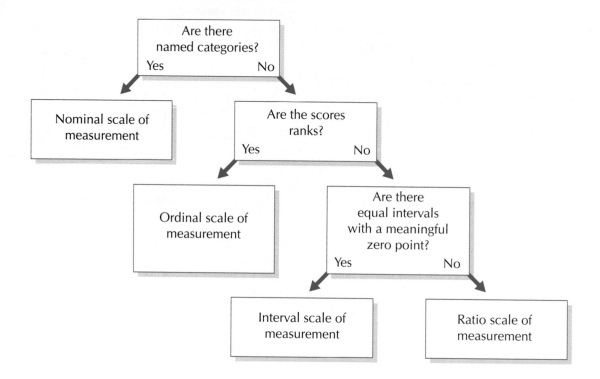

Populations and Samples

No matter which measurement scale is used, they all offer a way of measuring some type of behavior. In most cases, a single piece of data represents some behavior or characteristic about an individual person or animal. Although it is sometimes intriguing to know how one particular person behaves in a certain situation, the purpose of most behavioral science inquiry is to determine how *everyone* should behave in that situation. Here *everyone* refers to all the people in a certain population. A **population** includes *all* members of a certain group. It may be large or small, but it must contain all the members of a defined group. All the people in the world make up a population. All the people in the United States of America are a population. All the people in California, all the people in San Diego County, all the students who attend Palomar College, all the students who take behavioral science statistics at Palomar College—all groups, whether extremely large or relatively small—are separate populations. Most often, the attempt in behavioral science research is to learn about relatively large populations because the results are applicable to more people. In statistical notation, a capital italic *N* is used to denote the number of members in a population.

When a population is large, it is difficult, perhaps even impossible, to measure everyone in that population. To illustrate, suppose you wanted to determine the average IQ of all the people in the United States of America. To do so, you would have to give an IQ test to every person living in the United States. Currently, according to the U.S. Census Bureau, the population of the United States is over 270 million people (in statistical notation, $N > 270,000,000$). It is literally impossible to give an IQ test to every one of these people. Assuming that you could locate everyone in the entire population, it would take years to administer the tests, even if you hired droves of assistants, costing millions of dollars.

> **Question:** Couldn't it be done by choosing about 1,000 people or so, measuring their IQs, figuring out the average IQ, and then projecting that average to the entire U.S. population?

Yes, it could, but then you would not be measuring the population; you would be estimating the population via a sample. A **sample** is a relatively small representative group selected from a population. The statistical notation for the number of participants in a sample is a lowercase italic n. Quite often, researchers conduct their experiments with a smaller sample and then generalize their results to a larger population. You could certainly give an IQ test to 1,000 people ($n = 1,000$) and use the average of this sample to estimate the average of the population. When it is too time consuming or too expensive to collect information from the entire population, the only alternative is to select and measure a sample of the population and use that information to estimate population values.

Statistics that describe population values, such as the mean (average), are called **parameters.** Statistics collected from samples and used to describe population values are called **estimates.** As you work your way through this book, you will learn how to compute both population parameters and population estimates. Obviously, parameters are more accurate than estimates; therefore, if you have access to both population parameters and population estimates, you should rely on the parameters to give you the most accurate view of the population.

Learning statistics is like learning to play the piano. Almost no one enjoys the initial lessons and the long hours of practice, but everyone appreciates the results. Knowing how to analyze data and use statistics is a skill that will always be in demand. During your learning period, remember that when you have mastered the material in this book, you will possess fundamental skills that will serve you for the rest of your professional and personal life.

Concept Quiz

Recall the Crusco and Wetzel (1984) study that examined the effects of interpersonal touch on restaurant tipping. In addition to restaurant tipping, Crusco and Wetzel were also interested in the effects of interpersonal touch on the customers' dining experience. Diners were asked to complete a restaurant survey and leave it in a sealed envelope on the table. The results revealed that interpersonal touch had no effect on dining experience in general. However, when male and female ratings were separated and analyzed, it was discovered that after interpersonal touch, male diners rated the restaurant much more favorably than did female diners.

1. Restaurant dining experience can be measured using each scale of measurement. Using the examples that follow, identify the scale of measurement the data represent:
   a. the number of positive words used to describe the meal
   b. the ranking of the restaurant's food quality
   c. whether the dining atmosphere was pleasant or unpleasant

2. All diners at the restaurant are called the _____ because it represents all the members of a defined group.

3. In this study, the smaller group of diners is called a _____ because they were selected from the entire defined group that was studied.

4. **Used as a _____, statistics refers to the methods and procedures of organizing and analyzing data, but when it is used as an _____ it refers to interpreting data.**

5. Statistics that are used to describe population values are called _____, and statistics that are used to describe population values from samples are called _____.

6. N is the number of participants in a _____; n is the number of participants in a _____.

Answers

1. a. ratio	2. population	5. parameters; estimates
b. ordinal	3. sample	6. population; sample
c. nominal	4. **verb; adjective**	

Summary

Statistics is a branch of applied mathematics that uses numbers to describe and analyze data collected by researchers. Although beginning students are often apprehensive about the mathematics of statistics, anyone who has a solid knowledge of algebra should be successful in the study of statistics.

All behavioral science research begins with some kind of hypothesis. The research hypothesis expresses the idea that the researcher wants to prove true, whereas the null hypothesis usually states that the research will uncover no new findings. In the design of an experiment, the researcher must identify the independent and dependent variables. The independent variable is a factor selected and manipulated by the experimenter; it is independent of anything the participant does. The dependent variable is a measurable behavior exhibited by the participant. It is the dependent variable measurements that become the data for the statistical analysis.

There are four different types of measurement scales. A nominal scale of measurement involves assigning participants to a category based on some physical or psychological assessment. An ordinal scale involves the ranking of data from highest to lowest. An interval scale guarantees equal distances between scores on the scale. Finally, a ratio scale has a meaningful zero point that allows ratio judgments between scores on the scale.

Most research is performed to determine what behavior is typical for any particular population. A population consists of all the members of a particular group, whereas a sample is a relatively small representative group selected from a population. Statistical properties of populations are called parameters. Statistics collected from samples that are used to describe population values are called estimates.

Key Terms

statistics	problems	nominal scale
chapter outline	hypothesis	ordinal scale
chapter opener	research hypothesis	interval scale
student questions	null hypothesis	ratio scale
visual summary	variable	population
concept quiz	independent variable	sample
chapter summary	dependent variable	parameters
key terms	extraneous variable	estimates
formulas		

Problems

Round off the numbers in Problems 1–6 to three digits to the right of the decimal point.

1. 23,345.5678

2. 890,389.24745

3. 0.2398

4. 2.9921354

5. 2.9999254

6. 93.2345789

Generate both a research hypothesis and a null hypothesis for the research described in Problems 7–12.

7. Suppose you are a psychologist studying how children acquire language, and you want to see whether a new teaching technique will help children learn faster.

8. You have been assigned to test whether the job proficiency of National Guard soldiers is as high as that of soldiers in the Army.

9. You are a health psychologist interested in knowing whether patients who have undergone knee surgery recover faster if they are released from the hospital 3 days after surgery rather than the customary 5 days.

10. You are the personnel director of a large multinational manufacturing company, and you are interested in measuring the relative effectiveness of two different management training programs.

11. You are interested in studying the romantic differences between couples that are married and unmarried couples that are living together.

12. You are a sociologist who is interested in studying the difference in the level of happiness between groups of people at different socioeconomic levels.

Identify both the independent and dependent variables in the experiments described in Problems 13–15.

13. A researcher has two groups of identical nerve cells living in separate dishes. He proposes to apply different concentrations of a nerve-blocking agent to the groups of nerve cells and to measure any change in the number of nerve impulses generated by the nerve cells.

14. A psychologist interested in the use of imagery in memory teaches one group of participants to make mental images of things they are trying to remember. She compares their memories for a list of words to the memories of a group that does not receive imagery training.

15. A school psychologist for a large urban school district believes that temporary forced withdrawal of a student from school (suspension) is more effective than physical punishment in improving the behavior of a disruptive student. She assigns 50 disruptive students to the suspension group and 50 to the physical punishment group and then counts the number of disruptive acts the children exhibit on the 3 days following their return to the classroom.

Identify the examples in Problems 16–28 as representing the nominal, ordinal, interval, or ratio scales of measurement.

16. Time

17. Skin temperature in degrees centigrade

18. The number of statistics questions answered correctly on a test

19. Class rank

20. The position of a chicken in the current pecking order

21. The name of the EEG tracing exhibited by a sleeping patient (alpha, beta, theta, delta, . . .)

22. The number of errors a rat makes while running a maze

23. The number of errors made on a color vision test

24. The total number of words recalled from a list of 50 words

25. The number of stressful events you have experienced during the past 6 months

26. Your rankings of the 10 best movies of last year

27. The number of trials necessary for a pigeon to learn how to press a key

28. The number of people in your class who have red, blond, black, and brown hair

Problems From the Literature

The following problems refer to actual results from research studies that are cited at the end of the chapter. However, the data used to generate the problem sets are hypothetical.

Read the following research example and solve Problems 29–33.

Kyle and Mahler (1996) conducted an experiment to examine whether a female job applicant's hair color might influence judgments of her capability. They expected the applicant would be judged more capable when depicted with brunette hair than with red or blonde hair. Participants were randomly assigned to review a professional resume with an attached photograph of the female applicant, depicted with brunette, red, or blonde hair. Afterward, participants evaluated the applicant's capability for an accounting position and then recommended a beginning salary. The findings revealed that evaluations of capability significantly differed depending on the applicant's hair color. She was judged most capable and assigned the highest salary when depicted with brunette hair color and the least capable and assigned the lowest salary when depicted with blonde hair.

29. Identify the null hypothesis and the research hypothesis.

30. Identify the independent and dependent variables.

31. Determine whether the data came from a population or a sample.

32. Suppose participants in Kyle and Mahler's study answered the following questions. Identify whether the data represent nominal, ordinal, interval, or ratio data.

   a. How capable is this job applicant? (circle one)

1	2	3	4	5	6	7
Not capable						Very capable

   b. Would you hire this applicant? (circle one)   Yes   No

   c. Rank the quality of work you expect from this applicant. (circle one)

Excellent	Above average	Average	Below average

   d. The beginning salary for this position ranges from $22,000 to $40,000 annually. What is the beginning salary you would assign this applicant?

   _____.

33. The researchers used the same photograph of the same woman in all conditions and mechanically altered her hair color to one of the three colors. Explain what type of variable(s) was being controlled and why.

Read the following research example and solve Problems 34–38.

Many people experience apprehension and anxiety when they need dental surgery, but some people are dental phobic. Thom, Sartory, and Johren (2000) believed that a single psychological treatment would have more long-term benefits in reducing dental anxiety than benzodiazepine medication. Fifty dental phobic patients were allocated to one of three treatment conditions: a psychological treatment of stress management and imaginary exposure to phobic stimuli 1 week prior to dental surgery, the medication benzodiazepine 30 minutes prior to dental surgery, or no treatment at all prior to dental surgery. Patients reported less anxiety in both treatment conditions than with no treatment. However, only patients in the psychological treatment condition showed continued reduction in anxiety several weeks later.

34. Identify the null hypothesis and the research hypothesis.

35. Identify the independent and dependent variables.

36. Determine whether the data came from a population or a sample.

37. Suppose participants in this study were asked the questions that follow. Identify whether the data represent nominal, ordinal, interval, or ratio data.

   a. How much pain did you feel after surgery? (circle one)

   Extreme   Reasonable   Minimal   No
    pain   pain   pain   pain

   b. How comfortable do you feel about dental treatments? (circle one)

   1   2   3   4   5   6   7
   Not   Very
   comfortable   comfortable

   c. How many times have you had dental surgery? _____

   d. Of the following dental treatments, indicate the order of your apprehension, with the number 1 indicating the procedure that makes you feel the most apprehensive and 4 the procedure that makes you feel the least apprehensive.

   Oral surgery ____   Root canal ____

   Routine filling ____   Gum-scraping ____

38. Identify three extraneous variables these researchers may have controlled.

Read the following research example and solve Problems 39–43.

   Many medical procedures are stressful and often involve pain to some degree. Fishman, Turkheimer, and DeGood (1995) conducted a study to see whether people reported less pain and had a decrease in blood pressure and heart rate if they were incidentally touched (pulse palpation) compared to no touch during a cold pressor test. Sixty college students participated in this lab study, and results indicated that incidental touch produced a significant reduction in blood pressure, heart rate, and the amount of pain reported. However, in a second session 1 month later, the findings indicated that individual responses to physical contact were not stable over time.

39. Identify the null hypothesis and the research hypothesis.

40. Identify the independent and dependent variables.

41. Determine whether the data came from a population or a sample.

42. Compose four questions, one for each of the four measurement scales (nominal, ordinal, interval, and ratio) that might be used in data collection for this study.

43. Suppose you conduct a study involving interpersonal touch; generate both research and null hypotheses.

Read the following research example and solve Problems 44–48.

   Studies have shown that drawing a smiling face on a restaurant bill may increase the percentage of tip left for food servers. Gueguen and Legoherel (2000) wanted to see whether something similar might take place in a coffee bar if the barman drew a sun on the coffee bill. They conducted an experiment in local coffee bars with clients that ordered an espresso coffee and measured the frequency and amount of tips left the barman. The data showed that when a sun was drawn on the coffee bill, clients left a tip more frequently and the tips were higher than when the sun was not drawn on the bill.

44. Identify the null hypothesis and the research hypothesis.

45. Identify the independent and dependent variables.

46. Determine whether the data came from a population or a sample.

47. Compose four questions, one for each of the four measurement scales (nominal, ordinal, interval, and ratio), that might be used to collect data in this study.

48. Suppose you conduct a study on tipping behavior; generate both research and null hypotheses.

References

American Academy of Pediatrics (1995). Media violence. *Pediatrics, 95,* 949–951.

Bandura, A., & Walters, R. H. (1963). *Social learning and personality development.* New York: Holt, Rinehart & Winston.

Crusco, A. H., & Wetzel, C. G. (1984). The effects of interpersonal touch on restaurant tipping. *Personality and Social Psychology Bulletin, 10,* 512–517.

Fishman, E., Turkheimer, E., & DeGood, D. E. (1995). Touch relieves stress and pain. *Journal of Behavioral Medicine, 18,* 69–79.

Gueguen, N., & Legoherel, P. (2000). Effect on tipping of barman drawing a sun on the bottom of customers' checks. *Psychological Reports, 87,* 223–226.

Kyle, D. J., & Mahler, H. I. M. (1996). The effects of hair color and cosmetic use on perceptions of a female's ability. *Psychology of Women Quarterly, 20,* 447–455.

MacCoby, E. E. (1954). Why do children watch television? *Public Opinion Quarterly, 18,* 239–244.

Thom, A., Sartory, G., & Johren, P. (2000). Comparison between one-session psychological treatment and benzodiazepine in dental phobia. *Journal of Consulting and Clinical Psychology, 68,* 378–387.

2

Frequency Distributions

- Ranked Distributions
- Frequency Distributions
- Grouped Frequency Distributions
  Constructing the Class Intervals: How Big and How Many?
  Constructing the Class Intervals and Determining Frequency: Setting Limits and Counting Raw Scores
- Apparent Limits and Real Limits: What You See Versus What Is Meant
- Midpoint: The Center of the Class Interval
  VISUAL SUMMARY: Creating a Grouped Frequency Distribution
- Cumulative Frequency
- Relative Frequency and Cumulative Relative Frequency
- Cumulative Percent
- Summary
- Key Terms
- Formulas
- Problems
  Problems From the Literature
- References

$\mathbf{M}$ost high school seniors who plan to enter a 4-year college the following year take the Scholastic Achievement Test, commonly known as the SAT. The SAT has become extremely controversial because certain subgroups of students tend to score higher than others. For example, on the average, male students tend to score higher than female students. This can be a real problem because the lower scoring subgroups can be at an obvious disadvantage when the SAT is used to rank students for college admission or for granting merit scholarships. Researchers at the College Board, the company that publishes the SAT, are constantly revising the exam in an attempt to address this problem.

Suppose you are one of those researchers and you are conducting a pilot study for a new SAT, which will be called the SAT-R (Revised). Your job is to make some sense out of the data that others have gathered. You have been handed the list of test scores in Table 2.1. Take a look at the list and then answer the following questions: How many numbers are in the table? What do the numbers represent? Are there more numbers in the 500s or the 600s? What is the highest score? The lowest score? The answers to the preceding questions should be: 100, scores from the Scholastic Aptitude Test-Revised, more in the 500s, 799, and 218.

Virtually no one would look at the unorganized list of numbers in Table 2.1 and experience any immediate sense of joy (except perhaps accountants and statisticians). The emotions experienced by most people range from indifference to

Table 2.1   Scores From the Scholastic Aptitude Test-Revised (SAT-R),
Verbal Subtest

540	432	345	673	740	444	456	732	665	442
437	498	510	522	734	614	623	413	719	750
523	479	463	390	440	457	392	498	685	631
463	442	505	621	577	554	623	444	345	300
496	345	675	620	744	790	562	441	497	472
521	533	667	532	578	599	621	429	468	542
554	476	766	721	645	298	277	346	499	512
512	297	479	505	401	622	771	702	621	234
443	345	489	592	523	532	578	606	432	654
218	799	245	776	523	550	492	472	561	552

utter shock and panic. Long lists or large tables of numbers are often like lists of foreign words: They have little or no meaning. Because they have no meaning, they are difficult to understand and almost impossible to remember. Yet as a well-informed psychologist, teacher, sociologist, anthropologist, or other professional, you must be able to understand and evaluate the results of any research study. This means being able to make some sense out of this seemingly endless list of SAT-R scores.

In this chapter, you will learn the basic methods used to decipher the jumble of raw data obtained from research studies, surveys, tests, or other measures employed in gathering information in the behavioral sciences. The term **raw data** refers to scores or numbers that have been collected but not yet organized or summarized. In your role as a researcher, the first thing you would want to do is to get a "feel" for the data. The way to do this is to *organize* the data in some meaningful way.

Question: But how can such a long list of numbers be organized?

You can begin organizing the raw data by creating a **ranked distribution,** which will be described next.

Ranked Distributions

A ranked distribution is created by ordering the scores, which means simply rearranging or listing the data so that the highest number is at the top of the list and the lowest is at the bottom. Your ranked distribution of the SAT-R scores should look like Table 2.2, which shows an ordered distribution of the same data that appear in Table 2.1. Now it is easier to answer such questions as what the highest and lowest scores are and whether there are more scores in the 500s or 600s. However,

Table 2.2   Ranked Distribution of the SAT-R Scores in Table 2.1

799	721	631	599	550	521	496	463	437	345
790	719	623	592	542	512	492	457	432	345
776	702	623	578	540	512	489	456	432	345
771	685	622	578	533	510	479	444	429	300
766	675	621	577	532	505	479	444	413	298
750	673	621	562	532	505	476	443	401	297
744	667	621	561	523	499	472	442	392	277
740	665	620	554	523	498	472	442	390	245
734	654	614	554	523	498	468	441	346	234
732	645	606	552	522	497	463	440	345	218

a listing of 100 numbers is still difficult for most people to interpret at a glance. For instance, without actually counting, can you tell whether more students scored in the lower or in the upper 500s? (It's hard, isn't it?) Thus, there is another tool for organizing and summarizing of large amounts of data: the frequency distribution.

Frequency Distributions

Simple frequency distributions are created by listing all the possible score values in any distribution and then indicating their frequency (how often each score occurs). After exams, your professors have probably drawn simple frequency distributions on the board to show the distribution of grades, like the one in Table 2.3. As you can see, the number of people who received each score, the **frequency,** is listed after the actual score. Scores that are not listed are assumed to have a zero frequency; it is assumed that no one received those scores. Clearly, it is much easier to find out how well you did on an exam by looking at a frequency distribution than by looking at a long list of raw data. However, if you were to make a frequency distribution of the 100 SAT-R scores in Table 2.1, it would be more than two pages long. As such, it might be just as hard to read as the ranked distribution because only a few scores occur more than once and therefore have a frequency greater than 1. Simple frequency distributions are useful only if they simplify the data; when they don't simplify the data because of the high number of unique scores, it's a good idea to use a *grouped* frequency distribution to summarize the data.

Grouped Frequency Distributions

In a **grouped frequency distribution,** the raw data are combined into equal-sized groups, which are called **class intervals.** Table 2.4 is a grouped frequency distribution of the SAT-R scores in which the 100 scores have been grouped into 13

Table 2.3 Simple Frequency Distribution of Grades on a Test

Grade	Score	Frequency
	95	1
	93	1
A	92	4
	91	2
	90	4
	89	2
	87	2
B	86	3
	84	4
	82	1
	80	1
	79	3
	78	3
	77	4
C	74	6
	73	7
	72	3
	71	4
	68	2
D	64	1
	63	1
	62	1
F	54	1

Table 2.4 Grouped Frequency Distribution of the SAT-R Scores in Table 2.1

Class Interval	Frequency
750–799	6
700–749	7
650–699	6
600–649	11
550–599	11
500–549	15
450–499	17
400–449	13
350–399	2
300–349	6
250–299	3
200–249	3

class intervals. When the raw data are summarized in this way, it is easy to see that most of the scores fall between 400 and 600, with the middle of the distribution near 500. Grouped frequency distributions, therefore, can be quite useful in "getting the whole picture" at a glance, which is your goal with the scores from the SAT-R.

Question: How does someone go about making a grouped frequency distribution?

Constructing the Class Intervals: How Big and How Many?

When creating a grouped frequency distribution, you begin by determining the number, as well as the size, of the class intervals. The number of class intervals is related to their size, and both are related to the range of scores in the raw data distribution. So first you must compute the **range,** which is the full extent of the scores, from the highest to the lowest. To compute the range, subtract the lowest score from the highest score.

$$\text{Range} = \text{highest score} - \text{lowest score} \tag{2.1}$$

$$= 799 - 218 = 581$$

Having computed the range, you can now select an interval size. Over the years, experience with hundreds of different data sets has shown that it is best to choose an interval size that produces between 10 and 20 class intervals. Fewer than 10 intervals result in a loss of information about the original raw data (as would have been the case if your professor had just reported how many As, Bs, etc. from Table 2.3); more than 20 make it difficult to readily comprehend the information. The following two formulas show how to approximate the interval size and the number of class intervals. The class *interval* size is represented by i.

$$i \approx \frac{\text{range}}{\text{number of class intervals}} \tag{2.2}$$

$$\text{Number of class intervals} \approx \frac{\text{range}}{i} \tag{2.3}$$

The squiggly equal sign ($\approx$) means "approximately equals." If you use Formula 2.2 to compute i, often you will have to round off the result to a more appropriate number before constructing the grouped frequency distribution. If the range of the raw data in Table 2.1 is 581, and if you decide to have about 12 class intervals, you need to make the following calculations.

$$i \approx \frac{581}{12} \approx 48.417$$

Because 48.417 is not an easy number to work with, you should choose a number close to 48.417 that is easier to count by. Using a higher number would lead to fewer class intervals than the 12 you had originally planned on, and using a lower number would lead to more intervals. One possibility is to choose 50 for the class interval size. In general, it is best to use numbers like 2, 5, 10, 20, 25, 50, or 100 for the interval size because most people know how to count successive numbers and thereby construct successive intervals by 2s, 20s, 50s, and so on.

Now Formula 2.3 can be used to determine the approximate number of class intervals for an interval size of 50.

$$\text{Number of class intervals} \approx \frac{581}{50} \approx 11.62$$

Because it is impossible to have a fractional class interval, you will have at least 12 intervals. If you count the number of class intervals in Table 2.4, you will find that using 50 as an interval size actually produces 12 class intervals. (Keep in mind that Formulas 2.2 and 2.3 are approximations only; the actual class interval size is chosen by you, and the number of class intervals depends on where the class intervals start and the actual highest and lowest scores. Do not panic if you get one more class interval than predicted by the formula.) After selecting an appropriate interval size, you can begin to construct the class intervals.

Constructing the Class Intervals and Determining Frequency: Setting Limits and Counting Raw Scores

Each class interval is represented by a lower limit and an upper limit. In Table 2.4, you can see that the first column of numbers is labeled "class interval." The lower limit of the top class interval is 750; the upper limit of the top class interval is 799. Because each class interval is the same size (50), the top class interval is constructed so that it contains the highest score in the distribution (799) and the bottom class interval contains the lowest score (218). (Although it happens once in a while, there is no rule that says that the highest score or the lowest score in the distribution must be at one of the limits.)

It is usually best to establish a lower limit that is a multiple of the interval size because this makes the table easier to understand and often simplifies the construction of the grouped frequency distribution. For instance, because $i = 50$, each lower limit should be a multiple of 50. The choices for lower limits, then, are 0, 50, 100, 150, 200, and so on. If you had selected 25 for our interval size, the choices for lower limits would have been 0, 25, 50, 75, and so on.

After the class intervals have been constructed, the frequency for each interval needs to be counted. To do this, tally how many raw scores fall within the limits of each class interval. Then count the tallies and record the frequency, or the number of scores, for each class interval, as shown in Table 2.4. It is important that you pay close attention when counting the frequencies; one mistake can cause severe problems later. It is wise to total the frequency column after tallying all the frequencies because the sum of the frequencies must equal the total number of scores in the distribution (n). (Σ is a summation sign, and denotes "the sum of.")

$$\sum \text{Frequencies} = n \tag{2.4}$$

Here is another example to illustrate the entire process of organizing raw data into class intervals. Suppose you invented a driving simulator that enables you to study simple reaction time. A television monitor shows a toddler dashing into the middle of the street. The simulator measures the amount of time that elapses between the instant the child is first shown on the screen and the point when the driver slams his or her foot on the brake. You recruit 150 Introductory Psychology students to participate in the study. The fastest student responds in 182 milliseconds and the slowest in 433 milliseconds. (A millisecond is one one-thousandth of a second.)

In constructing a grouped frequency distribution of these scores, you need to decide what interval size to use and how many class intervals there should be. What do you need to do first? (Try to remember, then read on.) First, compute the range.

$$\text{Range} = \text{highest score} - \text{lowest score}$$

$$= 433 - 182 = 251$$

Now use either Formula 2.2 or 2.3 to select the interval size. If you want about 10 class intervals, then, from Formula 2.2,

$$i \approx \frac{\text{range}}{\text{number of class intervals}} \approx \frac{251}{10} \approx 25.100$$

Thus, an interval size of approximately 25 will produce about 10 class intervals. You can now use Formula 2.3 to confirm this:

$$\text{Number of class intervals} \approx \frac{\text{range}}{i} \approx \frac{251}{25} \approx 10.040$$

Actually, an interval size of 25 will give 11 class intervals because any fractional class interval will necessitate the addition of an entire additional interval. Remembering that the lower limit of each class interval must be a multiple of 25, you can begin to construct the class intervals. The top class interval must contain the highest score in the distribution, which is 433; therefore, the highest class interval will be 425–449. Each succeeding lower class interval will have a lower limit that is 25 milliseconds less than that of the preceding interval. Now that you have determined the class intervals, you are ready to tally the raw scores that fall within each class interval and record the frequency next to each interval. You don't have all the scores, but if you did, your frequency distribution would end up looking like Table 2.5.

Before moving on to the next section, remember the advantage of choosing an interval size that is easy to work with. It is much easier and faster to figure out successive lower limits with an interval size of 25 or 50 than with an interval size of 27 or 48. Make it easy on yourself and choose an interval size that makes sense and is easy to work with.

Table 2.5 Grouped Frequency Distribution for the Driving Simulator Data

Class Interval	Frequency
425–449	5
400–424	11
375–399	7
350–374	15
325–349	6
300–324	32
275–299	24
250–274	21
225–249	17
200–224	9
175–199	3

Apparent Limits and Real Limits: What You See Versus What Is Meant

Question: In the list of class intervals in Table 2.5, it looks as if the limits don't include all possible scores. For instance, where would a time like 274.2 milliseconds be put?

In this experiment, you could not obtain a score of 274.2 milliseconds because your scores are all measured in milliseconds, not tenths of milliseconds. In your grouped frequency distribution, your upper and lower limits are listed in the actual measurements, which in this case are whole milliseconds. However, if in another study there *were* a score of 274.2, it would fall into the 250–274 class interval. The limits normally listed for a grouped frequency distribution are called the **apparent limits,** which are always in the same units as the original scores. However, each class interval *really* extends from 0.5 unit below the lower apparent limit to 0.5 unit above the upper apparent limit. Thus, the **real limits** are the lower apparent limit minus 0.5 unit and the upper apparent limit plus 0.5 unit. Table 2.6 shows the apparent limits and the real limits for the driving simulator data. You can easily see that a score of 274.2 milliseconds belongs in the class interval with the real limits 249.5–274.5. Now take a look at Table 2.7, which shows the grouped frequency distribution, including real limits, for the 100 SAT-R scores. After examining the table, can you tell where a score of 499.8 would be placed? Answer: In the interval with the real limits 499.5–549.5.

Although grouped frequency distributions are helpful, they do have one major limitation: They are only a *summary* of the raw data. As you can see in Table 2.4 or 2.7, there are 17 scores in the class interval 450–499, but the precise scores are not listed, so all 17 scores could be in the 450s, all in the 490s, or all spread evenly throughout the entire class interval. The only accurate way of knowing

Table 2.6   Real and Apparent Limits for the Driving Simulator Data

Real Limits	Apparent Limits	Frequency
424.5–449.5	425–449	5
399.5–424.5	400–424	11
374.5–399.5	375–399	7
349.5–374.5	350–374	15
324.5–349.5	325–349	6
299.5–324.5	300–324	32
274.5–299.5	275–299	24
249.5–274.5	250–274	21
224.5–249.5	225–249	17
199.5–224.5	200–224	9
174.5–199.5	175–199	3

Table 2.7   Grouped Frequency Distribution of SAT-R Scores Showing Real Limits and Apparent Limits

Real Limits	Apparent Limits	Frequency
749.5–799.5	750–799	6
699.5–749.5	700–749	7
649.5–699.5	650–699	6
599.5–649.5	600–649	11
549.5–599.5	550–599	11
499.5–549.5	500–549	15
449.5–499.5	450–499	17
399.5–449.5	400–449	13
349.5–399.5	350–399	2
299.5–349.5	300–349	6
249.5–299.5	250–299	3
199.5–249.5	200–249	3

how the scores are actually distributed is by examining the raw data. If the raw data are not available, then one recourse is to specify the center of the class interval to represent all the scores in that class interval.

Midpoint: The Center of the Class Interval

The exact center of the class interval is called the **midpoint.** The midpoint is easy to calculate because it is merely the average of the lower and the upper limits of the class interval:

$$\text{Midpoint} = \frac{\text{lower limit} + \text{upper limit}}{2} \qquad (2.5)$$

Regardless of whether the apparent or the real limits are summed, they both add to the same number. Table 2.8 shows the grouped frequency distribution of the SAT-R scores with the midpoint calculated for each class interval. Note that all the midpoints end in .5. When the interval size (i) is even, all the midpoints end in .5.

If you wish to avoid fractional midpoints, you must select an interval size that is an odd number (e.g., 5 or 25) if it is appropriate for your particular data. An interval size of 25 was appropriate for the driving simulator data, and the midpoints for that data set are shown in Table 2.9. If you have to choose between interval sizes

Table 2.8   Grouped Frequency Distribution of SAT-R Scores Showing the Midpoint of Each Class Interval

Real Limits	Apparent Limits	Frequency	Midpoint
749.5–799.5	750–799	6	774.5
699.5–749.5	700–749	7	724.5
649.5–699.5	650–699	6	674.5
599.5–649.5	600–649	11	624.5
549.5–599.5	550–599	11	574.5
499.5–549.5	500–549	15	524.5
449.5–499.5	450–499	17	474.5
399.5–449.5	400–449	13	424.5
349.5–399.5	350–399	2	374.5
299.5–349.5	300–349	6	324.5
249.5–299.5	250–299	3	274.5
199.5–249.5	200–249	3	224.5

Table 2.9   Midpoints for the Driving Simulator Data

Real Limits	Apparent Limits	Frequency	Midpoint
424.5–449.5	425–449	5	437
399.5–424.5	400–424	11	412
374.5–399.5	375–399	7	387
349.5–374.5	350–374	15	362
324.5–349.5	325–349	6	337
299.5–324.5	300–324	32	312
274.5–299.5	275–299	24	287
249.5–274.5	250–274	21	262
224.5–249.5	225–249	17	237
199.5–224.5	200–224	9	212
174.5–199.5	175–199	3	187

VISUAL SUMMARY

Creating a Grouped Frequency Distribution

Before You Begin: Rank the scores.

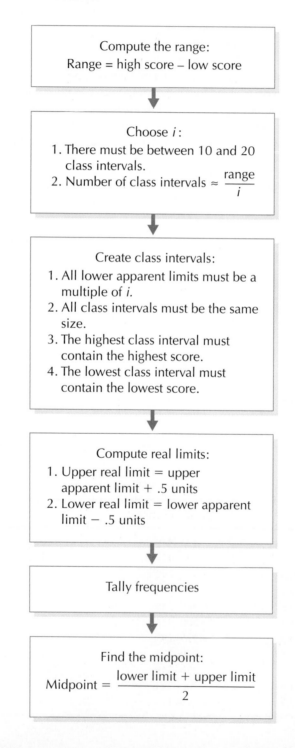

Compute the range:
Range = high score – low score

Choose i:
1. There must be between 10 and 20 class intervals.
2. Number of class intervals $\approx \dfrac{\text{range}}{i}$

Create class intervals:
1. All lower apparent limits must be a multiple of i.
2. All class intervals must be the same size.
3. The highest class interval must contain the highest score.
4. The lowest class interval must contain the lowest score.

Compute real limits:
1. Upper real limit = upper apparent limit + .5 units
2. Lower real limit = lower apparent limit − .5 units

Tally frequencies

Find the midpoint:
$$\text{Midpoint} = \dfrac{\text{lower limit} + \text{upper limit}}{2}$$

of 20 and 25, then 25 is the logical choice because, as well as being easy to work with, it is odd. However, if you must choose between interval sizes of 45 and 50, then choose 50 because it is much easier to work with—everyone is much more familiar with multiples of 50 than with multiples of 45. Never choose an interval size simply because it is odd.

Concept Quiz

The relationship of college students' health behaviors and their perceived level of stress were assessed in a survey done by Hudd (2000). Stressed students reported eating more unhealthy foods and exercising less than their counterparts. Suppose you decide to conduct a similar study about the time of midterm examinations on your campus. You ask 30 students how many times they ate fast foods, such as hamburgers and pizzas, during the previous 2-week period. The data you collected are listed here.

12	20	2	15	4	8	24	6	34	3
14	5	10	1	28	10	37	15	41	5
4	8	6	14	2	41	8	19	7	5

1. The study data, not yet organized or summarized, are called _____ data.

2. The first step in summarizing data is to rearrange the data in order from highest to lowest scores, which is called a _____.

3. To create a _____ distribution, you organize data by listing all of the possible fast-food scores in the distribution with a tally of the number of times each score occurs in the distribution.

4. To get the whole picture of the fast-food data at a glance, sometimes it is best to present it in a grouped frequency distribution in which data are divided into groups called _____.

5. Before you choose the number and size of the class intervals, compute the _____ by subtracting the lowest from the highest number of fast foods reported.

6. In this study, what is the range? _____

7. To display the data in approximately 10 class intervals, you would use an interval size of _____.

8. How many class intervals will you have if you choose an interval size equal to 3? _____

9. Grouped frequency distribution tables are easier to understand if the lower limit of each class interval is a multiple of the _____.

10. In a grouped frequency distribution, the highest class interval must contain the _____ score and the lowest class interval must contain the _____ score.

11. Using an interval size of 3, the apparent limits of the highest class interval are _____ and the real limits are _____.

12. Using an interval size of 4, the value of the lower real limit of the highest class interval is _____.

13. The midpoint of the class interval 36–39 is equal to _____.

Answers

1. raw	6. 40	10. highest; lowest
2. rank distribution	7. 4	11. 39–41; 38.5–41.5
3. simple frequency	8. 14	12. 39.5
4. class intervals	9. interval size	13. 37.5
5. range		

At this point, you should be able to answer easily all the questions in the Concept Quiz, and you should know how to construct a simple and a grouped frequency distribution. You should also understand that frequency distributions are created to organize data into tables that summarize large numbers of data points. If you are still unclear on any of the concepts in the Concept Quiz, now is the time to review the concepts. Aside from the frequency and midpoint, there are other types of helpful information that you can get from a frequency distribution: cumulative frequency, relative frequency, cumulative relative frequency, and cumulative percent.

Cumulative Frequency

Frequency, as previously explained, is the total number of scores that fall within a class interval. **Cumulative frequency** is the total number of scores that fall *below* the upper real limit of the class interval. Cumulative frequency can be particularly helpful when you need to know how many scores in a distribution happen to fall below a particular score. Table 2.10 shows the cumulative frequencies for the SAT-R data. You will need to refer to this table several times as you read the rest of this paragraph. To generate the cumulative frequency, begin with the lowest class interval. In Table 2.10, the lowest class interval is the one that has an upper real limit of 249.5. Now find all the scores in the distribution that are below 249.5. There are 3 of these scores (the 3 in the lowest class interval). Now go to the next highest class interval, the one with an upper real limit of 299.5. Find the number of scores in the distribution that are below 299.5. These will include the 3 scores in the class interval with the upper real limit of 299.5 plus the 3 scores in the class interval below, for a total of 6 scores. Continue in the same way for each of the class intervals until you reach the highest, which has an upper real limit of 799.5 and a cumulative frequency of 100. Note that 100 is also the total number of scores in the distribution (n). All of the scores in the distribution must be below the upper real limit of the highest class interval.

Question: Why would anyone ever need to know this?

Imagine that you are a school counselor. At your school there is a special program called SMART (**S**tudents with **M**agnificently **A**stute **R**are **T**alents), in which only a small, academically elite group of students who score 700 or higher on the SAT-R may participate. As a counselor, you want to establish a similar program for the remainder of the students—those who score below 700 on the SAT-R. You plan to call the second program SMART 2B (**S**tudents with **M**agnificently **A**stute **R**are **T**alents who need **2 B**e stimulated). The first step in setting up the program is to determine how many students are eligible, which you can do by

Table 2.10   Grouped Frequency Distribution of SAT-R Scores Showing Cumulative Frequency

Real Limits	Apparent Limits	Frequency	Cumulative Frequency
749.5–799.5	750–799	6	100
699.5–749.5	700–749	7	94
649.5–699.5	650–699	6	87
599.5–649.5	600–649	11	81
549.5–599.5	550–599	11	70
499.5–549.5	500–549	15	59
449.5–499.5	450–499	17	44
399.5–449.5	400–449	13	27
349.5–399.5	350–399	2	14
299.5–349.5	300–349	6	12
249.5–299.5	250–299	3	6
199.5–249.5	200–249	3	3

calculating the cumulative frequencies of the SAT-R scores shown in Table 2.10. (Remember that the cumulative frequency is the total number of scores below the upper real limit of each class interval.) The cumulative frequency for the interval with its upper real limit equal to 699.5 is 87. Therefore, you find that 87 students score below 700 and are eligible for the SMART 2B program.

At times, people will want to compare the frequencies in one distribution with those in another. Such a comparison is valid only when the number and the range of scores in both distributions are the same. If the number of scores is different, it is necessary to compute *relative frequency* or *cumulative relative frequency* to make the comparison. In the next section, you will see why you cannot simply make direct comparisons among grouped frequency distributions.

Relative Frequency and Cumulative Relative Frequency

Imagine that in an analysis of the SAT-R you want to compare scores from your pilot study involving 100 high school seniors with data from an all girls' school that has 450 seniors. Although the range of scores in the two distributions is similar, the total number of scores is quite different; thus, any differences between frequencies may be due to the different sizes of the samples. In order to make a meaningful comparison, you can convert all the frequencies in each sample to relative frequencies. **Relative frequency** is the proportion of scores from the distribution that fall within the class interval. Relative frequency is computed simply by dividing the frequency in the class interval by the total number of scores in the distribution. Because frequency distributions are almost always created from samples, the total number of scores in the distribution is denoted by n.

$$\text{Relative frequency} = \frac{\text{frequency}}{n} \qquad (2.6)$$

For example, the relative frequency for the class interval 500–549 in Table 2.7 is computed as follows:

$$\text{Relative frequency} = \frac{\text{frequency}}{n} = \frac{15}{100} = .15$$

It may help you comprehend relative frequency as a proportion of the scores if you keep in mind that relative frequency is much like a percentage. The difference is that when denoting a percentage, you go one step further and multiply the proportion by 100. For instance, in the preceding example you would multiply .15 by 100 to get 15%. If you take a moment to consider this idea, you'll see that a percentage is a proportion: 15% of all the scores means 15 scores per 100 scores. Relative frequency is merely expressed differently; in terms of hundredths, it is .15 of all scores.

To compare the SAT-R scores of the students in the girls' school with those in your pilot study, you will need to calculate the relative frequency for each group. (This has been done in Tables 2.11 and 2.12.) Even though the relative frequency distributions are not identical, you can draw meaningful comparisons from the corresponding intervals in each distribution. For example, look at the

Table 2.11 Grouped Frequency Distribution of SAT-R Scores for Pilot Group Showing Relative Frequency

Real Limits	Apparent Limits	Frequency	Relative Frequency
749.5–799.5	750–799	6	.06
699.5–749.5	700–749	7	.07
649.5–699.5	650–699	6	.06
599.5–649.5	600–649	11	.11
549.5–599.5	550–599	11	.11
499.5–549.5	500–549	15	.15
449.5–499.5	450–499	17	.17
399.5–449.5	400–449	13	.13
349.5–399.5	350–399	2	.02
299.5–349.5	300–349	6	.06
249.5–299.5	250–299	3	.03
199.5–249.5	200–249	3	.03

Table 2.12 Grouped Frequency Distribution of SAT-R Scores for 450 Girls' School Seniors Showing Relative Frequency

Real Limits	Apparent Limits	Frequency	Relative Frequency
749.5–799.5	750–799	29	.06
699.5–749.5	700–749	30	.07
649.5–699.5	650–699	26	.06
599.5–649.5	600–649	45	.10
549.5–599.5	550–599	53	.12
499.5–549.5	500–549	66	.15
449.5–499.5	450–499	75	.17
399.5–449.5	400–449	50	.11
349.5–399.5	350–399	20	.04
299.5–349.5	300–349	27	.06
249.5–299.5	250–299	20	.04
199.5–249.5	200–249	9	.02

class interval 500–549 for each of the samples. Even though there are only 15 scores from the pilot group and 66 scores from the girls' school for the same class interval, they both have the same relative frequency, .15.

Question: Is there some simple check to determine whether the relative frequencies have been calculated correctly?

There is no way to determine whether each of the individual relative frequencies is correct, short of recalculating each one a second time. However, you can make a quick check by adding up all the relative frequencies. Their sum should equal 1.00. If you take a few seconds to add the relative frequency columns in Tables 2.11 and 2.12, you will see that both of them add up to 1.00. Don't be surprised if the sum is off by a hundredth or a few thousandths; small roundoff errors are unavoidable. However, if the sum is a few hundredths above or below 1.00, you'll need to recheck your calculations to find your error.

If the SMART 2B program were available to both the pilot group and the girls' school, you could calculate the *cumulative relative frequency* to compare the cutoff points for the two groups. **Cumulative relative frequency** is the total proportion of scores that lie below the upper real limit of the class interval. The formula for cumulative relative frequency follows:

$$\text{Cumulative relative frequency} = \frac{\text{cumulative frequency}}{n} \tag{2.7}$$

Table 2.13 Grouped Frequency Distribution of SAT-R Scores for Pilot Group Showing Cumulative Relative Frequency

Real Limits	Apparent Limits	Frequency	Cumulative Frequency	Relative Frequency	Cumulative Relative Frequency
749.5–799.5	750–799	6	100	.06	1.00
699.5–749.5	700–749	7	94	.07	.94
649.5–699.5	650–699	6	87	.06	.87
599.5–649.5	600–649	11	81	.11	.81
549.5–599.5	550–599	11	70	.11	.70
499.5–549.5	500–549	15	59	.15	.59
449.5–499.5	450–499	17	44	.17	.44
399.5–449.5	400–449	13	27	.13	.27
349.5–399.5	350–399	2	14	.02	.14
299.5–349.5	300–349	6	12	.06	.12
249.5–299.5	250–299	3	6	.03	.06
199.5–249.5	200–249	3	3	.03	.03

Table 2.14 Grouped Frequency Distribution of SAT-R Scores for 450 Girls' School Seniors Showing Cumulative Relative Frequency

Real Limits	Apparent Limits	Frequency	Cumulative Frequency	Relative Frequency	Cumulative Relative Frequency
749.5–799.5	750–799	29	450	.06	1.00
699.5–749.5	700–749	30	421	.07	.94
649.5–699.5	650–699	26	391	.06	.87
599.5–649.5	600–649	45	365	.10	.81
549.5–599.5	550–599	53	320	.12	.71
499.5–549.5	500–549	66	267	.15	.59
449.5–499.5	450–499	75	201	.17	.45
399.5–449.5	400–449	50	126	.11	.28
349.5–399.5	350–399	20	76	.04	.17
299.5–349.5	300–349	27	56	.06	.12
249.5–299.5	250–299	20	29	.04	.06
199.5–249.5	200–249	9	9	.02	.02

Cumulative relative frequencies for the girls' school students and for the pilot group are shown in Tables 2.13 and 2.14, where you can see that .87 of the students in both groups scored below 700 (actually, below 699.5).

Cumulative Percent

To indicate the percentage of students involved, you can multiply the cumulative relative frequency by 100 and thereby determine what is known as the **cumulative percent,** or the *percentile.* Standardized achievement test results from tests given to public school children are often reported in terms of percentiles. These tests are being utilized more and more in the push for teacher accountability, so if you're planning on becoming a public school teacher, percentiles will have a particularly significant meaning to you in the years ahead. Cumulative percent for the SAT-R scores for the pilot project are shown in Table 2.15, and the formula for cumulative percent is shown next.

$$\text{Cumulative percent} = \text{cumulative relative frequency} \cdot 100 \qquad (2.8)$$

Table 2.15   Grouped Frequency Distribution of SAT-R Scores for Pilot Group Showing Cumulative Percent

Real Limits	Apparent Limits	Frequency	Relative Frequency	Cumulative Relative Frequency	Cumulative Percent
749.5–799.5	750–799	6	.06	1.00	100
699.5–749.5	700–749	7	.07	.94	94
649.5–699.5	650–699	6	.06	.87	87
599.5–649.5	600–649	11	.11	.81	81
549.5–599.5	550–599	11	.11	.70	70
499.5–549.5	500–549	15	.15	.59	59
449.5–499.5	450–499	17	.17	.44	44
399.5–449.5	400–449	13	.13	.27	27
349.5–399.5	350–399	2	.02	.14	14
299.5–349.5	300–349	6	.06	.12	12
249.5–299.5	250–299	3	.03	.06	6
199.5–249.5	200–249	3	.03	.03	3

Concept Quiz

In a study similar to Hudd's (2000) study, in addition to assessing college students' eating habits and stressful times, you also asked participants the extent they exercised during the 2-week period prior to midterm examinations. The grouped frequency distribution for the number of minutes students exercised during this 14-day period are shown in the table.

1. The cumulative frequency is the total number of participants who exercised _____ the _____ real limit of the class interval.

2. The proportion of scores from the distribution that fall within the class interval is called the _____ frequency.

3. The highest proportion of scores was _____ in the class interval _____.

4. The total proportion of scores that fall below the upper real limit of the class interval is called the _____ frequency.

5. What was the total proportion of participants who exercised below the upper real limit of 224.5 minutes?

6. Explain why the relative frequency is used to compare the exercise time in this study with the exercise data Hudd collected with a different number of participants.

Grouped Frequency Distribution of Number of Minutes Exercised in Minutes

Real Limits	Apparent Limits	Frequency	Midpoint	Cumulative Frequency	Relative Frequency	Cumulative Relative Frequency	Cumulative Percent
224.5–229.5	225–249	1	237	30	.033		
199.5–224.5	200–224	1	212	29	.033		
174.5–199.5	175–199	2	287	28	.067		
149.5–174.5	150–174	3	262	26	.100		
124.5–149.5	125–149	5	237	23	.167		
99.5–124.5	100–124	1	212	18	.033		
74.5–99.5	75–99	2	187	17	.067		
49.5–74.5	50–74	4	162	15	.133		
24.5–49.5	25–49	6	137	11	.200		
0–24.5	0–24	5	112	5	.167		

7. To find the percentage of participants scoring below the upper real limit of a class interval, you need to compute the _____ percent.

8. The percentage of participants scoring below 174.5 minutes is _____ and is calculated by _____.

9. In a grouped frequency distribution, the cumulative frequency, cumulative relative frequency, and cumulative percent below the upper real limit of the highest class interval equal _____, _____, and _____, respectively.

10. Half of the participants in your study exercised less than _____ minutes for the 2-week period.

Answers

1. below; upper
2. relative
3. .167; 125–149
4. cumulative relative
5. .967
6. When the total number of scores is

unequal, it is best to compare the proportion of scores in each class interval rather than the actual number of scores.

7. cumulative

8. 86.67%; multiplying the relative cumulative frequency by 100
9. n (N), 1.00, 100%
10. 74.5

Summary

The first step in summarizing raw data is to create a ranked distribution. If the distribution has a relatively small range, you can further summarize the data by creating a simple frequency distribution where each score that occurs is represented, along with its frequency. If the range is larger, you can create a grouped frequency distribution. In a grouped frequency distribution, the data are represented by the number of scores that fall within the limits of each class interval. You begin by creating the apparent limits for each class interval, and then you tally the frequencies for each class interval. The real limits and the midpoint can be computed from the apparent limits. Using the frequency in each class interval, you can compute the relative frequency, cumulative relative frequency, cumulative frequency, and cumulative percent.

Key Terms

raw data	grouped frequency	midpoint
ranked distribution	distribution	cumulative frequency
simple frequency	class interval	relative frequency
distribution	range	cumulative relative
frequency	apparent limits	frequency
	real limits	cumulative percent

Formulas

$$\text{Range} = \text{highest score} - \text{lowest score} \tag{2.1}$$

$$i \approx \frac{\text{range}}{\text{number of class intervals}} \tag{2.2}$$

$$\text{Number of class intervals} \approx \frac{\text{range}}{i} \tag{2.3}$$

$$\sum \text{Frequencies} = n \tag{2.4}$$

$$\text{Midpoint} = \frac{\text{lower limit} + \text{upper limit}}{2} \tag{2.5}$$

$$\text{Relative frequency} = \frac{\text{frequency}}{n} \tag{2.6}$$

$$\text{Cumulative relative frequency} = \frac{\text{cumulative frequency}}{n} \tag{2.7}$$

$$\text{Cumulative percent} = \text{cumulative relative frequency} \cdot 100 \tag{2.8}$$

Problems

1. Create a ranked distribution for the following numbers of third-born children who graduated from 25 high schools in Escuela Nueva County last year:

   67 54 39 77 54 46 54 59 86 34
   55 61 49 43 71 56 63 77 70 52
   50 46 33 41 55

2. Create a ranked distribution for the following 30 scores on a test of artistic ability:

   97 74 45 21 21 78 12 42 92 64
   88 32 21 35 39 63 13 35 77 52
   72 88 89 67 54 99 58 89 73 32

3. A military psychologist collected scores on the number of targets missed by 20 radar operators over a 5-day period. Create a ranked distribution for the following 20 scores:

   5 23 17 5 3 16 18 0 2 4
   7 2 13 21 16 6 5 6 7 8

4. The IQ scores of students at Random High School vary from a low of 72 to a high of 151. Compute the range.

5. The price of new automobiles at a local dealer varies from a low of $10,023 to a high of $52,298. Compute the range.

6. If the high score in a distribution is 289 and the low score is 16, what is the range?

7. The reaction time for the fastest participant in an experiment was 197 milliseconds, and the time for the slowest was 876 milliseconds. What is the range?

8. If the range of a distribution of scores is 75, list all the possible interval sizes that will result in no fewer than 10 class intervals and no more than 20. State which of these

possible class intervals is the best choice, and why.

9. Given that the range of scores on an Introduction to Psychology test is 60, what class interval size would produce 12 class intervals?

10. What would be a good class interval size for a distribution of scores that had a range of 262?

11. A cognitive psychologist was measuring the time it took for her participants to mentally rotate an object. She found that the fastest person could do it in 235 milliseconds and the slowest person could do it in 623 milliseconds. Given this range of scores, approximately how many class intervals would the psychologist obtain if she decided to make a grouped frequency distribution with each of the following class interval sizes?
    a. 25
    b. 15
    c. 20
    d. 50

12. In a distribution of IQ scores, the high score is 132 and the low score is 65. Compute the range, then choose an appropriate class interval size and create the apparent limits of the class intervals of a grouped frequency distribution that could be used to represent these scores.

13. A clinical psychologist recorded the number of negative statements made during 1-hour conversations with 45 people who were depressed. Using the following data, create a grouped frequency distribution using 3 as an interval size. Make sure that your table includes the real limits, apparent limits, frequency, and midpoint for each class interval.

```
 3  12  19  25  11  25   4  13   9   3
 1   6  22  21  13  21  14  11  29  32
18  19   7  28  14  29  16   1   2   8
15  19  16  19  22  15  29  31   3  18
21  29  22  31  12
```

14. A sociologist recruited 60 people for a study on personal space, which is the amount of space people need between themselves and others in order to feel comfortable. He asked each person to tell him when to stop as he walked toward him or her. The distances, in centimeters, at which he was told to stop are listed here. Generate a grouped frequency distribution with 12 class intervals that includes the real limits, apparent limits, frequency, midpoint, cumulative frequency, relative frequency, cumulative relative frequency, and cumulative percent for each class interval.

```
119  100  92  81  69  54  50  40  21  14
114  100  90  74  69  52  47  39  19  12
112   98  87  72  68  52  46  38  17  10
106   97  85  71  64  52  45  37  15   9
103   97  85  71  60  51  44  34  15   9
100   95  84  70  57  50  41  33  14   8
```

15. A neuropsychologist was testing the safety of a new drug by injecting it into 40 rats and then monitoring their average heart rates over the next hour. Using the heart rates listed here, generate a grouped frequency distribution with 15 class intervals. Make sure you include the real limits, apparent limits, frequency, midpoint, cumulative frequency, relative frequency, cumulative relative frequency, and cumulative percent for each class interval.

```
229  220  210  195  184  176  170  164  160  157
228  217  207  193  182  176  169  162  159  157
222  214  201  190  181  174  165  161  159  156
221  210  198  184  180  173  164  161  158  155
```

16. A developmental psychologist studying nail-biting behavior in small children counted the number of times each child placed at least one finger in his or her mouth during a 1-hour play period. Use the following data to create a grouped frequency distribution, including the real limits, apparent limits, frequency, midpoint, cumulative frequency, relative frequency, cumulative relative frequency, and cumulative percent for each class interval.

```
1  5  7  10  11  13  14  16  19  22
2  6  8  10  11  14  14  16  19  22
2  6  9  10  12  14  15  17  20  22
4  6  9  10  12  14  15  18  20  23
4  6  9  11  13  14  15  19  21  23
```

17. A child psychologist studied the aggressive behavior of 30 three-year-old children by counting the number of aggressive acts they displayed over a 2-week period. The results of her research follow. Use the data to create a frequency distribution with 10 as the class interval size. Include in your frequency distribution the real limits, apparent limits, frequency, midpoint, cumulative frequency, relative frequency, cumulative relative frequency, and cumulative percent for each class interval.

```
17  35  40  55  68  92   99  107  110  117
23  37  40  57  70  94  101  107  111  122
29  38  42  61  77  97  101  109  114  123
```

18. Another child psychologist also studied the aggressive behavior of 3-year-olds, but he observed only 25 children. Use the data to create a frequency distribution with 10 as the class interval size. Include in your frequency distribution the real limits, apparent limits, frequency, midpoint, cumulative frequency, relative frequency, cumulative relative frequency, and cumulative percent for each class interval.

```
14  27  30  37  44  54  67  89   97  117
17  27  34  39  45  55  75  96  115  127
22  29  35  40  46
```

19. Problems 17 and 18 are based on research projects studying aggressive behavior in children. How can you compare the two studies, given that there are different numbers of children in the two distributions? What can you conclude from this comparison?

20. A psychologist interested in chess began to collect data on the amount of time a chess player needs to make a decision on a particular chess move. The time for the decision, in seconds, for each of the 40 chess players in the study follow. Use the data to create a frequency distribution with 12 class intervals. Include in your frequency distribution the real limits, apparent limits, frequency, midpoint, cumulative frequency, relative frequency, cumulative relative frequency, and cumulative percent for each class interval.

26	59	88	109	154	209	265	294	304	321
42	64	96	121	155	224	267	294	304	322
54	77	97	129	164	248	275	299	306	323
57	85	107	136	179	249	287	299	309	324

21. A researcher interested in the types of things that frighten toddlers presents 14-month-old infants with a variety of items and records the number of items feared by each child. The numbers of items feared by 50 children follow. Use the data to create a grouped frequency distribution with a class interval size equal to 2. Include in your frequency distribution the real limits, apparent limits, frequency, midpoint, cumulative frequency, relative frequency, cumulative relative frequency, and cumulative percent for each class interval.

1	3	5	7	8	10	12	15	18	21
2	4	5	7	8	10	12	15	18	21
2	4	6	7	9	10	12	17	19	22
2	4	7	7	9	11	13	17	19	22
2	4	7	7	9	11	14	17	21	23

22. A developmental psychologist interested in smile production in infants measures the total numbers of smiles produced by 30 infants during a 30-minute play period, in a room full of toys. Using the following data, create a grouped frequency distribution with a class interval size of 3 smiles. Include in your frequency distribution the real limits, apparent limits, frequency, midpoint, cumulative frequency, relative frequency, cumulative relative frequency, and cumulative percent for each class interval.

2	4	6	11	15	21	22	29	30	34
2	4	9	11	16	22	24	29	30	35
3	5	10	12	17	22	27	29	33	37

23. Sixty people were shown a list of 100 words and asked later to recall the list. Use their scores to generate a grouped frequency distribution with a class interval size equal to 5. Include in your frequency distribution the real limits, apparent limits, frequency, midpoint, cumulative frequency, relative frequency, cumulative relative frequency, and cumulative percent for each class interval.

7	10	15	21	27	29	32	38	51	60
8	10	17	21	27	29	32	39	51	62
8	12	18	22	28	30	33	40	52	64
9	12	18	23	28	30	33	44	53	68
9	14	18	24	28	31	34	45	57	69
9	15	20	25	29	31	36	49	58	74

24. A researcher studying the reading process recorded the number of eye fixations made by 24 research participants as they read a 100-word passage of prose. From this list, create a frequency distribution using a class interval size of 25. Include in your frequency distribution the real limits, apparent limits, frequency, midpoint, cumulative frequency, relative frequency, cumulative relative frequency, and cumulative percent for each class interval.

100 114 132 135 183 198 223 252 334 423
102 122 132 156 189 207 245 278 387 446
110 128 133 164

Problems From the Literature

The following problems refer to actual results from research studies that are cited at the end of the chapter. However, the data used to generate the problem sets are hypothetical.

Read the following research example and solve Problems 25–28.

Gauggel, Wietasch, Bayer, and Rolko (2000) *investigated the effect of positive and negative feedback on the reaction time of brain-injured patients with low or high depression and a control group of orthopedic patients. The study measured reaction time for a computer task that involved hitting as fast as possible one of four response buttons matching a directional arrow displayed on the computer monitor. One minute after the task began, patients saw on the computer screen written instructions stating either "Very good, you are very fast" (positive feedback) or "Not good, you are too slow" (negative feedback). Among their findings, these researchers found that brain-injured patients with both low and high depression had shorter reaction times when they received negative feedback. In contrast, negative feedback had no influence on the reaction time of orthopedic patients. Positive feedback did not influence the reaction times of either group of patients. Gauggel and colleagues suggest that motivational factors may be responsible for the quicker response among the brain-injured patients.*

25. Suppose you conducted a similar study and randomly assigned brain-injured patients to see either a happy face (positive feedback) or sad face (negative feedback) after they worked on the computer task 1 minute. The following reaction time data (in milliseconds) are from the total 60 brain-injured patients in your study. Generate a grouped frequency distribution with 16 class intervals that includes the real limits, apparent limits,

frequency, midpoint, cumulative frequency, relative frequency, cumulative relative frequency, and cumulative percent for each class interval.

558	664	611	632	531	520
607	645	531	631	546	650
532	511	635	602	630	540
649	546	551	515	642	590
599	635	614	549	524	618
529	659	548	518	548	659
649	523	555	622	642	556
623	623	539	539	574	640
550	648	542	633	634	533
540	642	633	517	551	511

26. The reaction time data for the 30 brain-injured patients in the sad face (negative feedback) condition follow. Generate a grouped frequency distribution with 6 as the class interval size. Include the real limits, apparent limits, frequency, midpoint, cumulative frequency, relative frequency, cumulative relative frequency, and cumulative percent for each class interval.

546	558	540	531	523	551
533	548	539	517	548	539
574	520	551	511	546	529
524	511	555	542	515	556
549	550	531	518	540	532

27. The reaction time data for the 30 patients in the happy face (positive feedback) condition follow. Generate a grouped frequency distribution with 13 class intervals. Include the real limits, apparent limits, frequency, midpoint, cumulative frequency, relative frequency, cumulative relative frequency, and cumulative percent for each class interval.

664	632	645	623	630	650
642	640	623	633	649	635
622	590	659	614	607	659
599	631	648	618	635	611
634	649	602	633	642	642

28. Look at the grouped frequency distributions generated in Problems 25, 26, and 27 and answer the following questions.
    a. Which class interval of all 60 brain-injured patients had the highest frequency?
    b. According to the grouped frequency distribution of all 60 brain-injured patients, the top 20% of reaction times ranged between _____ and _____ milliseconds.
    c. Refer to the grouped frequency distribution for brain-injured patients that received negative feedback. What percentage of patients scored below 533 milliseconds?
    d. Refer to the grouped frequency distribution for brain-injured patients that received positive feedback. One third of the participants had a reaction time of _____ milliseconds or slower.

Read the following research example and solve Problems 29–32.

According to a study done by Marian and Neisser (2000), autobiographical memories of birthdays, holidays, friends, and so on may be more accessible for bilingual individuals if the language used to ask or cue the retrieval of such memories is matched to the language environment when the memory was originally encoded. Language-dependent recall was examined among Russian-English bilingual individuals. The results indicated that participants retrieved more experiences from their Russian-speaking period and English-speaking period when they were interviewed in the matching language.

29. You conduct a study among 100 middle-age Italian-English bilingual individuals in which you ask participants about specific life experiences. Half are asked these questions in the matching-language used when the experience was encoded, and the other half are asked in the nonmatching language. The number of events recalled was recorded. Following are data collected for the 50 participants in the matching-language group. Generate a grouped frequency distribution using a class interval size of 3. Include the real limits, apparent limits, frequency, midpoint, cumulative frequency, relative frequency, cumulative relative frequency, and cumulative percent for each class interval.

33	16	5	9	16	11	21	2	4	10
8	9	7	14	5	31	2	16	10	16
16	14	21	27	15	19	33	14	3	11
12	17	6	18	17	9	13	17	20	15
10	26	13	12	22	24	20	34	15	8

30. A colleague of yours conducts a similar study among a different group of Spanish-American bilingual individuals. Data for the number of events recalled for the 50

participants in the matching-language condition for this study follow. Generate a grouped frequency distribution with 10 class intervals. Include the real limits, apparent limits, frequency, midpoint, cumulative frequency, relative frequency, cumulative relative frequency, and cumulative percent for each class interval.

38	18	22	9	3	21	16	11	16	2
11	37	28	17	10	17	15	15	27	16
6	33	15	15	8	20	19	33	24	14
9	27	14	26	12	34	17	5	10	21
24	21	19	20	36	8	16	13	18	9

31. In Problem 30, how many participants recalled more than 14 events? What proportion of participants recalled fewer than 12 events?

32. In Problem 31, what proportion of participants recalled more than 23 events? How many participants recalled fewer than 15 events?

References

Gauggel, S., Wietasch, A., Bayer, C., & Rolko, C. (2000). The impact of positive and negative feedback on reaction time in brain-damaged patients. *Neuropsychology, 14,* 125–133.

Hudd, S. (2000, June). Stress at college: Effects on health habits, health status and self-esteem. *College Student Journal,* 6–9.

Marian, V., & Neisser, U. (2000). Language dependent recall of autobiographical memories. *Journal of Experimental Psychology: General, 129,* 361–368.

Graphs

- Basics in Constructing a Graph
  The Axes
  Plotting the Data: Histograms and Polygons
- Frequency Histogram
- Frequency Polygon
- Relative Frequency Polygon
- Cumulative Frequency Polygon
- Cumulative Relative Frequency Polygon
- Cumulative Percent Polygon
- Stem-and-Leaf Diagrams
- Changing the Shape of a Graph
- Summary
- Key Terms
- Problems
  Problems From the Literature
- References

Y ou are curled up in a corner of your couch, your fingernails nearly bitten to the bone, agonizing as your hero dangles barely a foot above the snapping jaws of the alligators in the pit below, when your tension is relieved by a box of aspirin appearing on the TV screen. Next to it is a graph comparing this product, which gives the "most effective relief," to the other leading brand. Sound familiar? Graphs are used in marketing, research, sports, and industry to convey visually some type of information, but do you always understand what the graphs are trying to say? Are all the graphs you see accurate? Are they useful? This chapter is designed to help you understand the properties of common types of graphs, to read graphs effectively, to critically evaluate other people's graphs, and to construct your own graphs from raw data and grouped frequency distributions.

Graphs are essentially pictures of numerical data; as such, they tell a story about the data. These "data pictures" can assume various forms, a few of which can be seen in Figures 3.1–3.4. Figure 3.1 is typical of the graphs we see in newspaper and magazine ads and in TV commercials. Truthful or not, it tells quite a tale about the effectiveness of aspirin: Brand A definitely *appears* to be more effective than Brand B. However, several important facts were omitted from this graph:

1. The title doesn't communicate the true intent of the graph, to sell you Brand A. Does the graph really show aspirin effectiveness over time, as it implies?

2. The vertical direction on the graph apparently represents effectiveness, but there are no numbers or labels for comparing the two types of aspirin. Is one type significantly more effective than the other?

Figure 3.1 Typical graph seen in media ads.

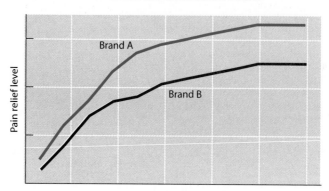

3. What were the dosages of the two types of aspirin? Were they equal?

4. What is the time period depicted in this graph? A few minutes? Several hours?

These types of questions should be asked about *all* graphs because some graphs, intentionally or not, are designed in ways that mislead the viewer.

Figure 3.2 shows a graph that contrasts not only in form to the one just discussed but also, and particularly, in merit. The title tells you what kind of information is being conveyed; the labels tell you precisely what is being measured; the numbers along the vertical axis tell in what increments the measurements are being reported; and the vertical bars make it easy to determine the tuition for each of the universities.

The graph depicted in Figure 3.3 is called a pie graph or pie chart. This type of graph is helpful for portraying any kind of population distribution or budget allowances. Figure 3.3 illustrates how much tuition at MONYU is apportioned to instruction, administration, and student services. Consider how effective such a chart would be if a MONYU faculty member used it in an appeal for a salary raise. No administrator would want the university's benefactors to suspect that the amount of money spent on direct instruction is only 10% more than the amount spent on administration.

Graphs are often used to illustrate trends and to help predict the future. Figure 3.4 shows the history of the price of a single automobile model from 1991 to 2001. As you can see, the price increased from about $13,000 in 1991 to nearly $28,000 in 2001. If this trend continues, you can expect to pay over $40,000 in another 10 years.

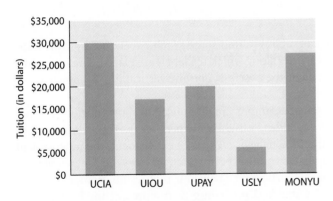

Figure 3.2   Yearly tuition at five different universities.

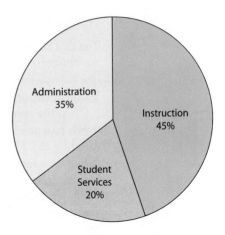

Figure 3.3
Apportionment of tuition at MONYU.

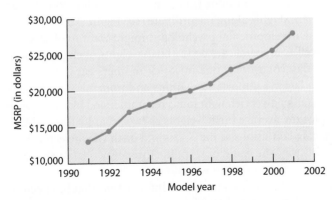

Figure 3.4   Manufacturer's suggested retail price (MSRP) of a single automobile model from 1991 to 2001.

Basics in Constructing a Graph

If you've never made a graph and want to graph your own data, it is important to know where to start.

The Axes

The first step in creating a graph is to find some graph paper and draw the **axes,** the horizontal and vertical lines along which the labels are placed. The horizontal line is known as the **X axis** or the **abscissa,** and the vertical line is known as the **Y axis** or the **ordinate.**

In the behavioral sciences, graphs are often used to show relationships between independent and dependent variables. Remember from the discussion of variables in Chapter 1 that in a behavioral science experiment, the independent variable is a factor manipulated by the experimenter, whereas the dependent variable is some measure of the participant's behavior that results from, or *depends on,* the manipulation. The standard procedure is to represent the independent variable along the abscissa, or *X* axis, and the dependent variable along the ordinate, or *Y* axis. For example, suppose a developmental psychologist is interested in the effect of prenatal care on the birth weight of infants. She could assign several mothers to one of three prenatal care conditions: no prenatal care, occasional prenatal care, and regular prenatal care. Then she could average the birth weights from each group and display the results in a graph. To graph the data, she would plot the prenatal care conditions (independent variable) along the abscissa and the average birth weights along the ordinate (see Figure 3.5).

The same developmental psychologist might want to observe the effects of nutrition as well as prenatal care on the birth weights of children. She could have two different diet conditions: one in which mothers eat unhealthy diets full of junk food and lacking important vitamins and minerals, and another in which mothers eat healthy diets rich with foods recommended by nutrition experts. She could then plot the average birth weights as two separate lines on the graph that has prenatal care conditions as the *X* axis and birth weight as the *Y* axis (see Figure 3.6). In this way, she could observe the three-way relationship among prenatal care, maternal diet, and birth weight.

Graphs can also be used to display information that has been summarized in a frequency distribution, in which case it is customary to represent the dependent variable (the scores) along the abscissa and the frequency along the or-

Figure 3.5
Average birth weights for three different prenatal care conditions.

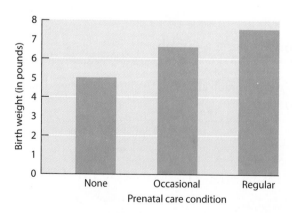

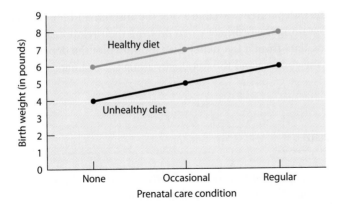

Figure 3.6
Average birth weights
for two different diets
and three different
prenatal care
conditions.

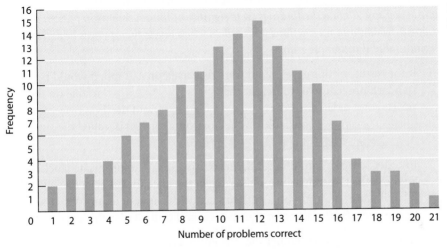

Figure 3.7
Statistics exam scores.

dinate. (Because it is easy to illustrate graphing procedures by using information from frequency distributions, frequency distributions are used in the examples throughout the remainder of the chapter. Other types of graphs are discussed in Chapters 9 and 14.) Take a look at Figure 3.7. Each possible score (dependent variable) is represented along the abscissa, with the lower scores on the left and the higher scores on the right. The frequency of each score is represented along the ordinate, with the low frequencies at the bottom and the high frequencies at the top. Frequency is thereby represented by the height of the bar. If you received a score of 11 on the exam, you could refer to the graph to find that a total of 14 students, including you, scored 11.

In review, a few major points are important to remember in the initial stages of setting up a graph:

- Give the graph a clear, unambiguous title or figure caption.
- Assign appropriate labels and meaningful numbers to each axis.

▪ Plot the independent variable along the abscissa and the dependent variable along the ordinate when plotting their relationships. When plotting data from a frequency distribution, plot the dependent variable along the abscissa and the frequency along the ordinate.

Concept Quiz

Nayak, Wheeler, Shiflett, and Agostinelli (2000) wanted to see whether music therapy might be an effective technique to help improve the mood of patients with traumatic brain injuries. In their experiment, patients were assigned to either the standard rehabilitation program or the standard rehabilitation program with music therapy. Among the findings were significant improvements in patient's cooperativeness and interactions with others when music therapy was added to the regular rehabilitation program.

1. If the results of this experiment were displayed on a graph, it would be standard procedure to represent the _____ variable on the vertical or *Y* axis, called the _____, and the _____ variable on the horizontal or *X* axis, called the _____.

2. In order to make a graph useful, the axes must have appropriate labels. Suppose the researchers wanted to depict the effect of the type of rehabilitation program on a patient's cooperation with others. What would be the appropriate labels for the abscissa and ordinate for this experiment?

3. It is important to remember that the entire graph itself must have an _____ title, such as _____ for this experiment.

4. Suppose you constructed a frequency distribution of the number of times patients were cooperative with hospital staff after their rehabilitation with music therapy program. If you graphed this frequency distribution, it would be customary to represent the _____ along the abscissa and the _____ along the ordinate.

Answers

1. dependent; ordinate; independent; abscissa
2. Type of Rehabilitation Program (abscissa); Patient's Cooperation (ordinate)
3. unambiguous; The Effect of Music Therapy on Improving Mood Among Brain-Injured Patients
4. dependent variable; frequency

Plotting the Data: Histograms and Polygons

The next step in graph construction is transferring the data to the graph. The data used to illustrate this procedure were collected last summer in a visit to San Diego's Qualcomm Stadium. At a charity booth set up just outside the stadium, baseball fans could test their throwing arms against a radar gun. For $1.00, a person could throw three baseballs at a target, and the radar gun would measure their speeds. The average speeds of the baseballs thrown by 200 San Diego Padres fans (in miles per hour) are listed in the grouped frequency distribution in Table 3.1. The most common graphs representing this type of data are a *histogram* (a type of bar graph) and a *polygon* (a type of line graph).

Frequency Histogram

A **frequency histogram** consists of a number of bars placed side by side, similar to those in Figure 3.2, where the width of each bar indicates the class interval size and the height of each bar indicates the frequency of the class interval. Here is how to plot a histogram of the baseball speed data. First, determine that the frequency will be indicated along the ordinate, and the baseball speeds, the dependent variable, will be indicated along the abscissa. You need to determine the size and scale of the axes. The ordinate should be labeled so that all possible frequencies are represented. Referring to Table 3.1, note that the frequencies range from a low of 4 to a high of 36, so by labeling the ordinate from 0 to 40, all possible frequencies are covered. Also from Table 3.1, you see that the abscissa labels need to extend from 39.5 miles per hour, the lower real limit of the lowest class interval, to 94.5, the upper

Table 3.1 Speeds of Baseballs Thrown by 200 Padres Fans

Real Limits (mph)	Apparent Limits (mph)	Frequency	Cumulative Frequency	Relative Frequency	Cumulative Relative Frequency	Cumulative Percent	Midpoint
89.5–94.5	90–94	4	200	.020	1.000	100.0	92
84.5–89.5	85–89	10	196	.050	.980	98.0	87
79.5–84.5	80–84	15	186	.075	.930	93.0	82
74.5–79.5	75–79	16	171	.080	.855	85.5	77
69.5–74.5	70–74	25	155	.125	.775	77.5	72
64.5–69.5	65–69	36	130	.180	.650	65.0	67
59.5–64.5	60–64	35	94	.175	.470	47.0	62
54.5–59.5	55–59	27	59	.135	.295	29.5	57
49.5–54.5	50–54	18	32	.090	.160	16.0	52
44.5–49.5	45–49	9	14	.045	.070	7.0	47
39.5–44.5	40–44	5	5	.025	.025	2.5	42

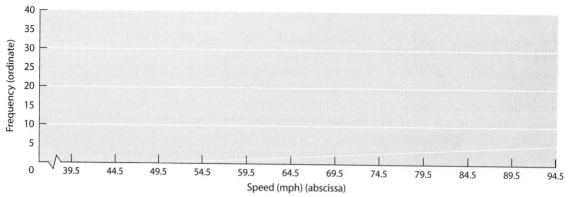

Figure 3.8   The labeling of the axes for a frequency histogram of the data in Table 3.1.

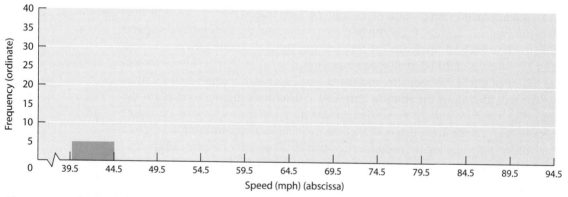

Figure 3.9   The first bar in the frequency histogram for the data in Table 3.1.

real limit of the highest class interval. It is important to do this because each class interval begins at the lower real limit and continues to the upper real limit; therefore, if a bar is to represent the entire class interval, it must extend from the lower real limit to the upper real limit. Typical frequency histograms such as those published in journals or books normally display apparent limits as labels along the abscissa rather than real limits because, as you can see in Figure 3.8, using real limits makes the abscissa particularly hard to read. However, real limits are used in Figure 3.8 to help you remember to actually plot real limits even though your labels will be in apparent limits when you build your own graphs.

Once the axes have been labeled, the next step is to draw in the bars of the histogram. Beginning at the lower real limit of the lowest class interval (39.5 mph), draw a vertical line up to a frequency of 5, then draw a horizontal line equal to the width of the class interval (5 mph) so that it extends to 44.5 mph, and then draw a vertical line down to the abscissa. This single bar represents the class interval 39.5–44.5 with a frequency of 5 (see Figure 3.9). The next bar is drawn in the same fashion, beginning at its lower real limit of 44.5, with a height of 9 and

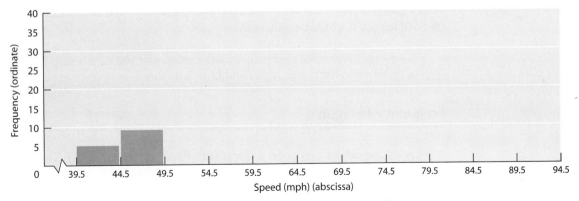

Figure 3.10   The second bar in the frequency histogram for the data in Table 3.1.

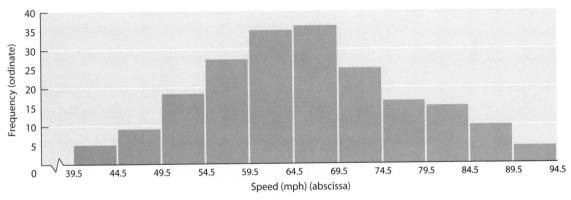

Figure 3.11   The entire frequency histogram for the data in Table 3.1.

a width of 5 mph, and extending out to 49.5 (see Figure 3.10). Note that in Figure 3.10 there is no gap between the two bars because the upper real limit of the first class interval is the same as the lower real limit of the second class interval: Both are 44.5 mph. Each successive class interval is represented by a bar having the appropriate frequency and sharing its limits with the adjacent class intervals.

The completed frequency histogram illustrating the data from Table 3.1 is shown in Figure 3.11. Take a few minutes to compare the table with the figure. Look at each class interval in the table and compare it with the corresponding bar in the figure. Note that the information for exact limits and frequency presented in the table is exactly the same as that presented in the graph.

Just as you can generate a frequency histogram from a grouped frequency distribution, you can also create a grouped frequency distribution from a histogram. The histogram is labeled such that each bar reveals the real limits, the class interval size, and the frequency of each class interval. If you were given a properly labeled frequency histogram, you could readily regenerate the grouped frequency distribution from which it was created. For this reason, you never find both a grouped frequency table and a frequency graph of that table in the same research report; it would be redundant.

> **Question:** As mentioned before, data can be graphed as a histogram or a polygon. What is a polygon and how is it made?

Frequency Polygon

A polygon consists of points on a graph with lines connecting them. The lines form an actual geometric polygon when they are connected to the abscissa at the extreme left and right ends of the graph. Although there are several types, the simplest is the frequency polygon, which portrays the same information found in a frequency histogram, but in graphic form. A **frequency polygon** uses a single point rather than a bar to represent a class interval on a graph.

> **Question:** If only a single point represents an entire class interval, how do you decide where to put the point?

The best place is the midpoint of the class interval because it is the most representative of all the scores within any class interval. If you were to use one of the lower limits, you would consistently *under*estimate the scores in that interval, whereas if you were to use one of the upper limits, you would consistently *overesti*mate the scores. If you assume that, on average, half the scores fall above the midpoint and half fall below, the best decision is definitely the midpoint. To create a frequency polygon, determine the midpoint of each class interval, plot the midpoint at the height of the frequency, and connect the points with straight lines (Figure 3.12). To complete the polygon, bring the lines down to the abscissa (zero frequency). The normal practice is to *begin the graph at the midpoint of the interval just below the lowest class interval in the grouped frequency distribution* and to *end the graph at the midpoint of the class interval just above the highest class interval*. Because there are no scores in either of these extra class intervals, the frequency is

Figure 3.12
An incomplete frequency polygon for the data in Table 3.1.

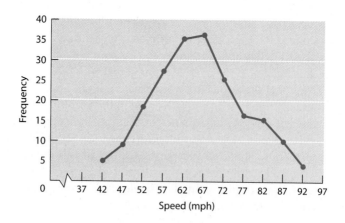

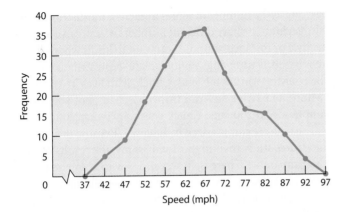

Figure 3.13
A completed frequency polygon for the data in Table 3.1.

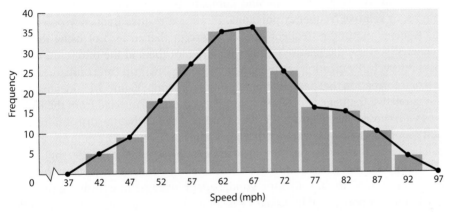

Figure 3.14
A combination of the frequency histogram and frequency polygon for the data in Table 3.1.

zero in each. The lowest class interval for the baseball speed information is 40–44; if there was a class interval below that, it would have apparent limits of 35–39 and a midpoint of 37. You would then plot a point at 37 with a frequency of zero. Remember to leave space for this extra class interval to the left of the rest of the graph. The interval above the highest class interval would have apparent limits of 95–99, with a midpoint of 97 and a frequency of zero. Figure 3.13 shows the completed frequency polygon of the baseball data.

The baseball speed information depicted in the frequency histogram (Figure 3.11) is the same as that depicted in the frequency polygon (Figure 3.13). This is illustrated in Figure 3.14, which is a combination of the two figures. Note that the shapes of the two graphs are the same, which is to be expected because the same frequencies were used to plot both of them.

Relative Frequency Polygon

Question: Can frequency polygons of two different distributions be compared?

Yes, they can, as long as the number of scores in each of the distributions is the same. However, if the distributions have different numbers of scores, you should not compare them directly. For instance, suppose you want to know whether Padres fans are unique in their baseball-throwing ability or are representative of baseball fans throughout the country. You ask a friend, Chuck, who lives in Minneapolis, to find out how fast Minnesota Twins fans can throw baseballs, but you forget to tell him to limit his sample size to 200 fans. Chuck goes to a Twins game and collects data from 250 fans. The data are summarized in Table 3.2. Because there are 50 fewer participants in the Padres study than in the Twins study, the results of the two studies are not directly comparable. There is, however, a way to compare them.

As discussed in Chapter 2, you can compare two distributions that have different numbers of participants by computing *relative* frequency rather than mere frequency. Similarly, you can compute and graph the relative frequency for the Padres and Twins distributions and compare the resulting relative frequency graphs, or **relative frequency polygons.** Plotting a relative frequency polygon is the same as plotting a frequency polygon, except that instead of using the frequencies, you use the relative frequencies and plot them at the midpoints of the class intervals. By creating relative frequency polygons, you can compare similar sets of information that have different numbers of scores. Figure 3.15 does just this. Using relative frequency polygons, it compares the data collected from the Padres fans with those collected from the Twins fans and shows that the distributions are quite similar. Most fans, whether they are Padres or Twins fans, can throw a baseball between 60 and 70 mph, but only a few can throw it faster than 90 mph.

Suppose that when you threw the baseball, the radar gun registered an average speed of 67 mph. Is 67 mph good, bad, or average? In examining the relative frequency polygon, it looks like 67 is somewhere in the average range. On the other hand, if you look at a cumulative frequency polygon or a cumulative relative frequency polygon, which are discussed in the next two sections, you can tell at a glance how your baseball speed compares with others.

Table 3.2   Speeds of Baseballs Thrown by 250 Twins Fans

Apparent Limits	Frequency	Relative Frequency	Midpoint
90–94	5	.020	92
85–89	18	.072	87
80–84	23	.092	82
75–79	24	.096	77
70–74	30	.120	72
65–69	39	.156	67
60–64	37	.148	62
55–59	33	.132	57
50–54	26	.104	52
45–49	12	.048	47
40–44	3	.012	42

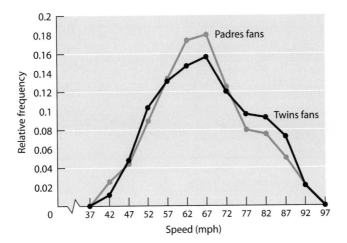

Figure 3.15
A comparison of
relative frequency
graphs for the data
from San Diego and
Minneapolis.

Concept Quiz

*The Concept Quiz from Chapter 2 looked at Hudd's (2000) investigation of college
students' stress level and exercise behaviors and then used data from a similar but
hypothetical study to construct the grouped frequency distribution of exercise data
shown here.*

Grouped Frequency Distribution of Exercise Data

Real Limits	Apparent Limits	Frequency	Midpoint	Relative Frequency
224.5–249.5	225–249	1	237	.033
199.5–224.5	200–224	1	212	.033
174.5–199.5	175–199	2	187	.067
149.5–174.5	150–174	3	162	.100
124.5–149.5	125–149	5	137	.167
99.5–124.5	100–124	1	112	.033
74.5–99.5	75–99	2	87	.067
49.5–74.5	50–74	4	62	.133
24.5–49.5	25–49	6	37	.200
−0.5–24.5	0–24	5	12	.167

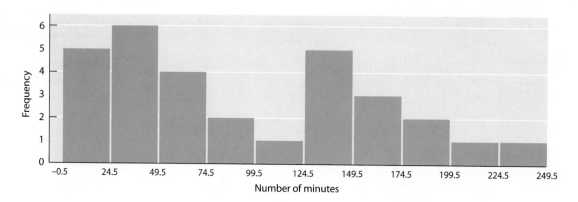

1. The type of bar graph shown here is called a _____, in which the height of the bar represents the _____ and the width of the bar represents the _____ of an interval in a grouped frequency distribution.

2. When the frequency histogram of exercise data was drawn, the ordinate was labeled with numbers ranging from _____ to _____ to reflect the range of all possible _____ and the abscissa was labeled with the number of minutes exercised to include the entire range of scores on the _____ measure.

3. Because the width of a bar in a frequency histogram represents the width of the entire class interval, the right edge of each bar was plotted at the _____ and the left edge was plotted at the _____ of the class interval.

4. The highest bar in the frequency histogram represents the class interval _____ and its frequency of _____.

5. To create a frequency polygon of the grouped frequency exercise data, the _____ of the class interval is the _____ point used to represent a class interval instead of a bar on the graph.

6. According to the frequency distribution of exercise data, what would be the single point used to represent the class interval 149.5–174.5?

7. The height along the ordinate of each point in a frequency polygon represents the _____ of the class interval, and the position of each point along the abscissa represents the _____ of the class interval.

8. The most effective way to graphically compare two distributions with different numbers of participants is to use a _____.

9. Plotting a relative frequency polygon is the same as plotting a frequency polygon, except that instead of plotting the frequency at the midpoint, you plot the _____ at the _____.

10. To draw a relative frequency polygon from the grouped frequency exercise data, the ordinate should be labeled with numbers from _____ to _____ that reflect all possible _____ frequencies.

Answers

1. frequency histogram; frequency; size
2. 0; 6; frequencies; dependent
3. upper real limit; lower real limit
4. 24.5–49.5; 6
5. midpoint; single
6. 162
7. frequency; midpoint
8. relative frequency polygon
9. relative frequency; midpoint
10. 0; .20; relative

Cumulative Frequency Polygon

In Chapter 2, cumulative frequency was defined as the total number of scores that fall below the upper real limit of the class interval. If you graph cumulative frequency in the form of a polygon, the result is a picture of how many participants score below a particular score, and you can see how one person compares to others in the study. In the case of your throwing speed, a cumulative frequency polygon helps to readily see how many people throw slower than you do. In drawing this graph, the points are not plotted in quite the same way as in a frequency polygon. True, cumulative frequency is plotted along the ordinate and speed in miles per hour along the abscissa, and the height of each point is determined by cumulative frequency. However, you do not plot the points at the midpoints of the class intervals.

> **Question:** Why aren't the points at the midpoint plotted? Isn't that the most representative place?

Look again at the definition of cumulative frequency. Cumulative frequency is the total number of scores that fall *below the upper real limit* of the class interval. Therefore, when you construct a **cumulative frequency polygon,** the upper real limit is the most representative place to plot each point.

There are a few other rather technical factors to remember about constructing a cumulative frequency polygon. (It will be helpful to refer to Figure 3.16 during this discussion.)

1. The first point should be plotted at the upper real limit of the class interval below the lowest class interval on the cumulative frequency

Figure 3.16
A cumulative
frequency polygon
for the data in Table
3.1.

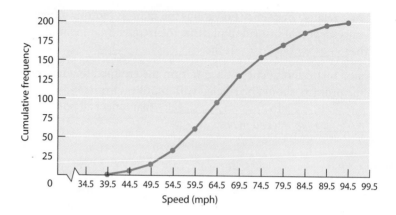

Figure 3.16
A cumulative
frequency polygon
for the data in Table
3.1.

distribution where there is a cumulative frequency of zero. (In Figure 3.16, this is a speed of 39.5 mph with a cumulative frequency of 0.)

2. The last point represents the cumulative frequency of the highest class interval, which is always equal to *n*, the total number of scores in the distribution.

3. The cumulative frequency line is *not* brought back down to the abscissa after the last point but is allowed to hang in the air because all class intervals above the highest class interval have the same cumulative frequency; they are all equal to *n*.

4. The *S* shape of this curve is called an *ogive* (pronounced "oh-jive").

After studying Figure 3.16, you should be able to readily determine whether a baseball-throwing speed of 67 mph is good or bad. You can see on the graph that the cumulative frequency for 67 mph is approximately 110. That is, of the 200 fans whose speeds were measured, you threw the baseball faster than 110 of them. To make the comparison even clearer, you could convert the cumulative frequency to a proportion by dividing by 200 and then display the data as a cumulative relative frequency polygon.

Cumulative Relative Frequency Polygon

The **cumulative relative frequency polygon** is a graph that enables proportions to be read directly. It is plotted in a similar fashion to the cumulative frequency polygon: Cumulative relative frequency is plotted at the upper real limit of the class interval. Figure 3.17 is the cumulative relative frequency polygon generated from the data in Table 3.1. By using the same procedure as for the cumulative frequency polygon, you can look up your score of 67 on this graph and find that the proportion of fans that threw baseballs more slowly than you is .55.

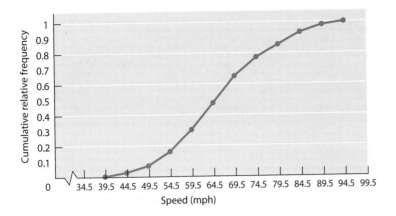

Figure 3.17
A cumulative relative frequency polygon for the data in Table 3.1.

Cumulative Percent Polygon

The **cumulative percent polygon** is a graph that enables percentiles to be read directly. **Percentile** tells the *percentage* of scores below the score of interest. The cumulative percent polygon is plotted in a similar fashion to the cumulative frequency polygon and the cumulative relative frequency polygon: Cumulative percent is plotted at the upper real limit of the class interval. Figure 3.18 is the cumulative percent polygon generated from the data in Table 3.1. By using the same procedure as for the cumulative frequency polygon, you can look up the score of 67 on this graph and find that the percentage of fans that threw baseballs more slowly than you is 55%.

> **Question:** All these graphs use frequency distributions. Is there some kind of graph that displays raw data?

All these graphs can be used with a simple frequency distribution, which is essentially the same as raw data. In addition, there is a technique similar to a graph, called a stem-and-leaf diagram, that allows us to display raw data visually.

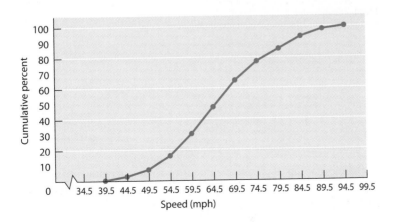

Figure 3.18
A cumulative percent polygon for the data in Table 3.1.

Table 3.3   Speeds (in miles per hour) of Baseballs Thrown by 50 Padres Fans

35	38	39	39	44	44	45	47	48	49
50	53	54	55	56	57	59	59	61	61
63	64	66	67	68	68	68	69	69	69
70	70	71	71	72	76	78	78	79	83
84	84	86	87	89	91	92	92	93	93

Stem-and-Leaf Diagrams

In a **stem-and-leaf diagram,** each raw score is divided into two parts, a stem and a leaf. The leaf is normally the last digit of the score, and the stem is the remaining digit(s) of the score. For example, a raw score of 37 would have a leaf of 7 and a stem of 3. A raw score of 736 would have a leaf of 6 and a stem of 73.

To make a stem-and-leaf diagram from the raw data in Table 3.3, first create a vertical column that contains all the possible stems in the data:

Stem	Leaf
3	
4	
5	
6	
7	
8	
9	

Next, take each score and list its leaf next to the corresponding stem. For example, the first number in Table 3.3 is 35. Thirty-five has a stem of 3 and a leaf of 5. Therefore, put the 5 leaf next to the 3 stem in the diagram:

Stem	Leaf
3	5
4	
5	
6	
7	
8	
9	

Then continue placing all the leaves next to their corresponding stems. Table 3.4 shows the completed stem-and-leaf diagram for all 50 scores in Table 3.3. As you can see, all the scores are represented in the diagram without the loss of any information.

Table 3.4   Stem-and-Leaf Diagram for the Data in Table 3.3

Stem	Leaf
3	5 8 9 9
4	4 4 5 7 8 9
5	0 3 4 5 6 7 9 9
6	1 1 3 4 6 7 8 8 8 9 9 9
7	0 0 1 1 2 6 8 8 9
8	3 4 4 6 7 9
9	1 2 2 3 3

Table 3.5   Rotated Stem-and-Leaf Diagram

				9			
				9			
				9			
				8	9		
			9	8	8		
			9	8	8		
Leaf		9	7	7	6	9	
		8	6	6	2	7	3
	9	7	5	4	1	6	3
	9	5	4	3	1	4	2
	8	4	3	1	0	4	2
	5	4	0	1	0	3	1
Stem	3	4	5	6	7	8	9

If you rotate the stem-and-leaf diagram 90 degrees counterclockwise, as in Table 3.5, the resulting diagram is very similar to a histogram.

Changing the Shape of a Graph

Usually, a graph gives you a picture of data that has been presented by another person in some particular manner for some particular reason. Most often, that reason is to convince people of some belief or conclusion held by the person who created the graph. Just as any two professors, conveying the same subject matter, can give two entirely different lectures infused with their own beliefs and opinions, so can any two researchers, using the same data, devise two different graphs infused with their distinctive biases.

   Question: Isn't that lying?

No, it is not lying. If you were given a certain set of data, you could, without altering the data, vary the type of graph (histogram or polygon), vary the scale along the abscissa, or vary the scale along the ordinate. By modifying any or all of these factors, you could change the appearance of the entire graph, and such a change might influence the opinions of its viewers. For instance, look at the graphs in Figure 3.19. The way the Padre fans' data are presented in Figure 3.19(a) seems to be saying that there is a spread of abilities. It looks like many people throw about the same as others, and only a few throw either exceedingly fast or

Figure 3.19
Three different frequency polygons for the data in Table 3.1. (a) The graph shows a relatively normal spread of abilities; (b) the data appear to cluster tightly; (c) the data appear to be widely dispersed.

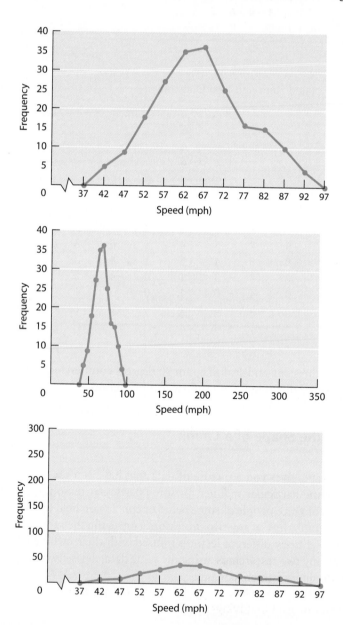

embarrassingly slow. Figure 3.19(b) represents the same data, but the abscissa has been lengthened to make the data appear to cluster in the center of the graph. This shape gives the viewer the impression that everyone has similar throwing abilities. The opposite impression is produced by Figure 3.19(c), in which the ordinate has been distorted to make the data appear flat. In this figure, it appears that few people are alike in their throwing abilities.

When you read someone else's graph, be aware of the point just made and take care not to be misled; take the time to study the labels on the axes. If the axes are labeled properly, you can read any graph accurately. Even though the three graphs in Figure 3.19 look different, they all depict the same information, and the original grouped frequency distribution can be precisely reconstructed from any one of them. If you are constructing your own graph, you are free to present it in any way you wish, as long as you remember to label it properly so that viewers can see the true picture.

Concept Quiz

The following is a cumulative frequency polygon drawn from grouped frequency distribution exercise data that were discussed earlier.

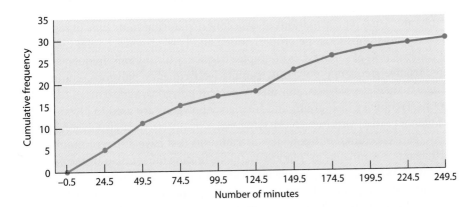

1. If the cumulative frequency of the grouped frequency distribution of exercise data are plotted in the form of a polygon, the result is a picture of how many people in the distribution exercised _____ a particular number of minutes compared to others in the distribution.

2. In the cumulative frequency polygon, the height of each point is determined by the _____ of the class interval represented by that point.

3. According to the cumulative frequency polygon, the number of people that exercised less than the _____ real limit of the class interval of _____ is 15.

4. A _____ polygon is plotted in the same way as a cumulative frequency polygon except that the height of each point represents the proportion of scores that fall below the upper real limit of the class interval.

5. A _____ polygon can be used to find percentiles.

6. Because graphs can be misleading, you should always make sure you understand how the graphs are _____ before you attempt to interpret the information displayed in the graph.

7. According to the cumulative frequency polygon, _____ people exercised less than 99.5 minutes during the 2-week period prior to midterm exams.

Answers

1. below
2. cumulative frequency
3. upper; 49.5–74.5
4. cumulative relative frequency
5. cumulative percent
6. labeled
7. 17

Summary

Graphs are visual representations of data collected during some type of research. To be useful, graphs must be properly titled and labeled. This chapter discussed the construction of seven types of graphs: frequency histograms, frequency polygons, relative frequency polygons, cumulative frequency polygons, cumulative relative frequency polygons, cumulative percent polygons, and stem-and-leaf diagrams. Frequency histograms and frequency polygons are used to illustrate the number of participants in each class interval. A relative frequency polygon is used to compare two different frequency distributions that have different numbers of participants. Cumulative graphs are useful for finding the number or the proportion, or the percentage, of participants who score below a certain value in the distribution. Although all of the above-mentioned graphs could be constructed from a simple frequency distribution, a stem-and-leaf diagram can be used to graphically display raw data distributions. Because the height and width of a graph can be easily modified by changing the scale of the numbers along the ordinate or the abscissa, it is important to read and understand the numbers and labels along the axes before trying to interpret the graph.

Key Terms

axes	abscissa	ordinate
X axis	*Y* axis	frequency histogram

frequency polygon
relative frequency
    polygon
cumulative frequency
    polygon

cumulative relative
    frequency polygon
cumulative percent
    polygon

percentile
stem-and-leaf diagram

Problems

One hundred students at the University of
Perfectly Average Yahoos (UPAY) were asked to
swim as many laps of the pool as possible in 60
minutes. The raw data on the numbers of laps are
listed here.

8	20	35	40	45	55	59	65	68	70
9	20	36	41	45	55	61	65	68	71
9	22	36	42	45	56	63	65	69	71
11	27	38	42	45	56	63	66	69	74
14	29	38	42	46	56	63	66	69	74
16	31	39	42	46	57	63	67	69	75
18	33	39	43	48	58	64	67	69	75
18	34	40	43	50	58	64	67	70	76
19	34	40	44	51	58	64	67	70	77
20	34	40	44	54	59	64	68	70	83

1. Using the UPAY data, generate a grouped
   frequency distribution with a class interval
   size of 5 laps. In your grouped frequency
   distribution, include real limits, apparent
   limits, frequency, relative frequency,
   cumulative frequency, cumulative relative
   frequency, cumulative percent, and
   midpoints.

Use the frequency distribution that you created in
Problem 1 to plot the following.

2. A frequency histogram

3. A frequency polygon

4. A cumulative frequency polygon

5. A cumulative relative frequency polygon

6. A cumulative percent polygon

7. Create a stem-and-leaf diagram of the
   UPAY data.

The same swimming test is given at Big State
University (BSU), but only 50 students
participate. The number of laps swum in 60
minutes is as follows:

9	20	29	40	49	55	60	65	69	72
9	23	33	44	50	56	61	66	69	73
14	27	34	44	51	57	62	68	70	75
17	29	34	46	52	59	62	67	70	77
17	29	35	48	53	59	64	69	71	82

8. Using the BSU data, generate a grouped
   frequency distribution with a class interval
   size of 5 laps. In your grouped frequency
   distribution, include real limits, apparent
   limits, frequency, relative frequency,
   cumulative frequency, cumulative relative
   frequency, cumulative percent, and midpoints.

Use the frequency distribution that you created in
Problem 8 to plot the following.

9. A frequency histogram

10. A frequency polygon

11. A cumulative frequency polygon

12. A cumulative relative frequency polygon

13. A cumulative percent polygon

14. Use the relative frequency information from
    Problems 1 and 8 to compare the swimmers
    from UPAY and BSU.

15. Create a stem-and-leaf diagram of the BSU
    data.

Use the following frequency distribution of scores
on a personality questionnaire to solve Problems
16–20.

Apparent Limits	Frequency	Cumulative Frequency	Relative Frequency	Cumulative Relative Frequency	Cumulative Percent
550–599	17	500	.034	1.000	100.0
500–549	25	483	.050	.966	96.6
450–499	37	458	.074	.916	91.6
400–449	56	421	.112	.842	84.2
350–399	73	365	.146	.730	73.0
300–349	94	292	.188	.584	58.4
250–299	82	198	.164	.396	39.6
200–249	49	116	.098	.232	23.2
150–199	38	67	.076	.134	13.4
100–149	22	29	.044	.058	5.8
50–99	7	7	.014	.014	1.4

16. Plot a frequency histogram of the data.

17. Plot a frequency polygon of the data.

18. Plot a cumulative frequency polygon of the data.

19. Plot a cumulative relative frequency polygon of the data.

20. Plot a cumulative percent polygon of the data.

21. Compare the table of personality questionnaire data with the following table of personality questionnaire data from a different group of participants by plotting the relative frequency polygons of both on the same axes.

Apparent Limits	Frequency	Relative Frequency
550–599	130	.033
500–549	220	.055
450–499	317	.079
400–449	423	.106
350–399	545	.136
300–349	684	.171
250–299	516	.129
200–249	422	.106
150–199	386	.097
100–149	222	.056
50–99	135	.034

Two hundred fifty students were asked to rate the level of student services at their college or university. Students who thought that their student services were the best in the nation were to rate their school a 100; those who believed their student services to be virtually nonexistent were to rate their school a 0. The results of this survey are given in the following grouped frequency distribution. Use this information to solve Problems 22–25.

Apparent Limits	Frequency
90–99	10
80–89	16
70–79	28
60–69	34
50–59	49
40–49	25
30–39	39
20–29	32
10–19	17

22. Using the data, generate the real limits and then plot a frequency histogram.

23. Using the data, generate the midpoints and then plot a frequency polygon.

24. Using the data, generate a cumulative frequency column and then plot a cumulative frequency polygon.

25. Using the data, generate a cumulative percent column and then plot a cumulative percent polygon.

26. Using the data, plot a frequency polygon that makes it appear all the ratings are grouped at the low end of the graph.

27. Use the accompanying frequency polygon of test scores to re-create the frequency distribution that was used to generate the graph. You need only re-create the apparent limits and the frequency for each class interval.

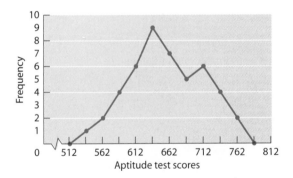

28. Use the accompanying frequency polygon of reaction times to re-create the frequency distribution that was used to generate the graph. Re-create the real limits, the apparent limits, the frequency, and the midpoint for each class interval.

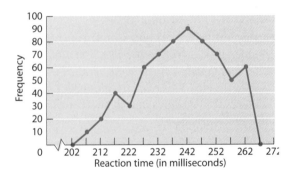

29. Use the following grades on a statistics exam to create a stem-and-leaf diagram.

20	29	39	44	49	58	67	84	89	94
21	30	39	45	50	58	72	84	89	95
22	35	40	47	54	61	76	87	91	96
29	36	41	48	54	63	77	88	92	97
26	39	42	49	56	65	78	88	93	99

30. Use the following scores from a personality inventory to create a stem-and-leaf diagram.

372	384	399	408	412	414	419	427	437	450
374	397	401	409	413	415	420	428	440	459
378	398	407	411	414	418	424	432	442	467

Problems From the Literature

The following problems refer to actual results from research studies that are cited at the end of the chapter. However, the data used to generate the problem sets are hypothetical.

Zadra and Donderi (2000) investigated the prevalence of bad dreams and nightmares to participants' psychological well-being. Participants completed a number of questionnaires assessing psychological well-being. They also recorded the frequency and content of their bad dreams and nightmares in a sleep journal for a 4-week period. They found a stronger relationship between nightmare frequency and well-being than between bad dreams and well-being. After reading these findings, researchers Dr. Good and Dr. Night want to see how prevalent nightmares are among college students on their campus. They had students record their nightmares in a sleep journal during the 18-week semester. The results of this study are shown in the following grouped frequency distribution. Use the data to solve Problems 31–35.

| | | | | Cumulative | |
Apparent Limits	Frequency	Cumulative Frequency	Relative Frequency	Relative Frequency	Cumulative Percent
50–54	10	345	.029	1.000	100.0
45–49	5	335	.014	.971	97.1
40–44	14	330	.041	.957	95.7
35–39	12	316	.035	.916	91.6
30–34	23	304	.067	.881	88.1
25–29	47	281	.136	.814	81.4
20–24	38	234	.110	.678	67.8
15–19	59	196	.171	.568	56.8
10–14	62	137	.180	.397	39.7
5–9	75	75	.217	.214	21.7

Grouped Frequency Distribution of Nightmare Data

31. Plot a frequency histogram of the nightmare data.

32. Plot a frequency polygon of the nightmare data.

33. Plot a cumulative frequency polygon using the nightmare data.

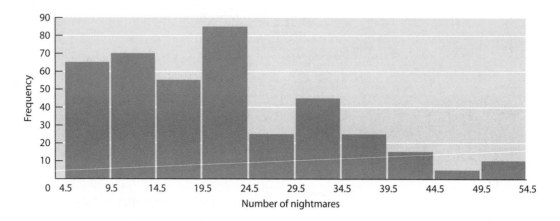

34. Plot a cumulative relative frequency polygon using the nightmare data.

35. If Dr. Good and Dr. Night wanted to compare the data from their study to Zadra and Donderi's nightmare data, which type of graph should they use and why?

Suppose Drs. Good and Night wanted to assess the prevalence of nightmares among high school students. Use the frequency histogram of nightmare data shown in the graph above to solve Problems 36 and 37.

36. Re-create the grouped frequency distribution that was used to generate the graph. You need only to recreate the apparent limits, frequency, midpoints, and the relative frequency for each interval.

37. Recall that Drs. Good and Night collected nightmare prevalence data first from a sample of college students and then from a sample of high school students. Suppose you heard students saying that they used histograms to see whether the distributions of reported nightmares were similar for the two student samples. Explain why this decision was not correct.

Sankis, Corbitt, and Widiger (1999) investigated the extent to which the English language contained more male-valued or female-valued terms. Ratings of 1,710 trait terms were provided by 1,390 undergraduate students. Twenty-nine to 37 students evaluated each term. Findings from this study suggest the English language may have more female-valued terms than male-valued terms. Suppose another researcher investigated this question differently and asked participants to list as many female-valued terms or male-valued terms as possible. The number of male- and female-valued words recalled were counted and used to create the grouped frequency distributions that follow. Use these to solve Problems 38–40.

Female-Valued Words		Male-Valued Words	
Apparent Limits	Frequency	Apparent Limits	Frequency
52–55	7	44–47	4
48–51	19	40–43	20
44–47	11	36–39	27
40–43	34	32–35	41
36–39	47	28–31	34
32–35	19	24–27	26
28–31	28	20–23	14
24–27	12	16–19	6
20–23	4	12–15	12
16–19	2	8–11	7
12–15	6	4–7	5
8–11	2		

38. Plot a frequency histogram using the data.

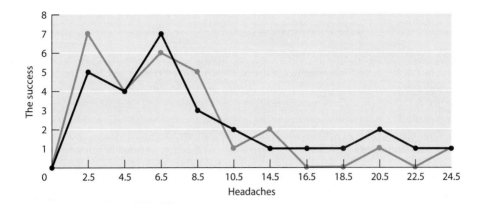

39. Generate a relative frequency column for each grouped frequency distribution.

40. Using the relative frequencies from both grouped frequency distributions, plot a single relative frequency polygon to compare the number of male-valued and female-valued words listed by the participants.

Given the popularity of the Internet, researchers are examining the potential benefits of self-help treatments via this medium. Strom, Pettersson, and Andersson (2000) carried out a 6-week controlled trial to see whether self-help treatment over the Internet and through e-mail might reduce people's headaches. Over half of the participants dropped out of the study. Of those remaining, participants in the treatment group reported significantly fewer headaches than those in the control group. Because the high drop-out rate was a concern, suppose researchers redid this study and only 25% dropped out of this study. The data collected are presented on the graph above. Use the graph to solve Problems 41–43.

41. Evaluate the construction of this graph by listing all errors and the needed corrections.

42. Discuss whether you would or would not agree with the researchers' suggestion that their self-help intervention was a success.

43. Explain which type of graph you would recommend and why this is the best choice to present the data.

Instead of examining the effects of music therapy on mood among brain-injured patients as studied by Nayak et al. (2000), Dr. E. Clapton conducted a study to see whether this type of therapy would improve the cooperativeness of prison inmates. The prison guards recorded the number of times each inmate was cooperative 1 week before and 1 week after the 6-week program. These cooperation data were used to construct the graph. Use this graph to solve Problems 44–46.

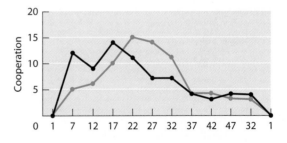

44. Evaluate the construction of this graph by listing all errors and the needed corrections.

45. Discuss whether you would or would not agree with the researcher's suggestion that music therapy did not affect prisoners' cooperation much.

46. Explain which type of graph you would recommend and why this is the best choice to present the data.

References

Hudd, S. (2000, June). Stress at college: Effects on health habits, health status and self-esteem. *College Student Journal,* 6–9.

Nayak, S., Wheeler, B. L., Shiflett, S. C., & Agostinelli, S. (2000). Effect of music therapy on mood and social interaction among individuals with acute traumatic brain injury and stroke. *Rehabilitation Psychology, 45,* 274–283.

Sankis, L. M., Corbitt, E. M., & Widiger, T. A. (1999). Gender bias in the English language? *Journal of Personality and Social Psychology, 77,* 1289–1295.

Strom, L., Pettersson, R., & Andersson, G. (2000). A controlled trial of self-help treatment of recurrent headache conducted via the Internet. *Journal of Consulting and Clinical Psychology, 68,* 722–727.

Zadra, A., & Donderi, D. C. (2000). Nightmares and bad dreams—their prevalence and relationship to well-being. *Journal of Abnormal Psychology, 109,* 273–281.

4

Measures of Central Tendency

- The Mean
  VISUAL SUMMARY: Computing
  the Mean From Raw Scores
- The Median
  Quartiles
- The Mode
- Mean, Median, or Mode: A
  Question of Skew
  Boxplots

- Frequency Distributions
  The Mean
  VISUAL SUMMARY: Computing
  the Mean of a Frequency
  Distribution
  The Median
  The Mode
  VISUAL SUMMARY: Finding the
  Median in a Group Frequency
  Distribution

- Summary
- Key Terms
- Formulas
- Problems
  Problems From the Literature
- References

Because he would be graduating in a couple of weeks from the University of Popular and Easy Programs (UPEP), Roy Babbins had been interviewing for a job with a number of companies. His current interview was with a recruiter from RatStuff.com, which sells over the Internet Skinner boxes, rat mazes, and other equipment used in psychological animal research. Roy felt that the interview was going remarkably well. Having worked in the psychology lab at UPEP, he was well versed in the uses of the products sold by RatStuff.com, and he was sure that he was conveying his knowledge to the recruiter. In turn, Roy was quite impressed with the company. Toward the end of the interview, Roy asked, "What is the average salary at RatStuff.com?"

The recruiter replied, "The average is quite high, more than $5,000 per month. Of course, new employees begin at the bottom and work up. We are willing to pay you $1,000 per month to start, and if you work hard, you can expect that to increase after you have been with us for a short while."

The beginning salary was more than a thousand dollars a month lower than those of other similar companies, but the average monthly salary was much higher. After some consideration, Roy accepted a position at RatStuff.com because of the promised potential for rapid salary advancement.

Although Roy worked hard, after nearly a year his salary had risen to only $1,250 a month, still thousands of dollars away from the average of $5,000. Aware

Table 4.1   Monthly Salaries for All Employees at RatStuff.com

Employee	Position	Monthly Salary ($)
RBJ	President	30,000
BJ	Vice president	25,000
TBJ	Vice president	25,000
TBQ	Recruiter	20,000
MMP	Manager	2,000
CAF	Manager	2,000
DUD	Worker	1,500
MOG	Worker	1,500
DDP	Worker	1,500
MNN	Worker	1,500
MNP	Worker	1,500
KMD	Worker	1,500
OFT	Worker	1,500
DGA	Worker	1,500
CST	Worker	1,500
ZAS	Worker	1,500
KIP	Worker	1,500
DUN	Worker	1,500
RGB	Worker	1,500
TLC	New worker	1,000
MBD	New worker	1,000
MFP	New worker	1,000
DDK	New worker	1,000
POP	New worker	1,000
MIP	New worker	1,000
	Total	129,500

that fellow employees seldom discussed their paychecks with one another, Roy patiently kept to himself until one day, out of desperation, he began asking his colleagues how much they received each month. The more employees he approached, the angrier he became, until he finally stormed into the office of the recruiter who had convinced him to come to RatStuff.com.

"You told me at my interview a year ago that the average salary here was more than $5,000 a month." Roy bellowed. "I've talked to most of my fellow workers, and not one of them makes more than $2,000 a month."

"Nearly everyone makes exactly $1,500 a month," the recruiter calmly replied.

"Then why did you lie to me and tell me that the average salary was $5,000 a month?" blared Roy.

"I never lied to you," said the recruiter. "The average salary at RatStuff.com *is* more than $5,000 a month. Here take a look at my computer screen. We'll list all the employees in this company along with their salaries and then compute the average salary. As you can see, the average salary is actually $5,180 a month." (See Table 4.1.)

"Sure, the average is more than $5,000 a month because you included the salary of the company president and a few other bigwigs, and each of them makes around $25,000 a month!" Roy was furious. "You yourself admitted that most employees make only $1,500 a month."

"That's true," agreed the recruiter, "and if you had asked me for the median salary, I would have told you it was $1,500 a month. That's the reason I like to recruit employees from UPEP—they aren't required to take a statistics class before graduating."

Obviously, the recruiter *had* taken a statistics course and had chosen to use his statistical knowledge to deceive Roy and probably many other recruits. By asking for the "average" salary, what Roy really wanted to know was the most representative salary. The recruiter was aware of this, but he was also aware that there were several salary figures he could provide to denote the "average" salary; he decided to furnish Roy with the one that best suited his recruiting purposes.

Every day people refer to a single number falling somewhere around the center of a distribution that best represents the distribution: "The typical weight of a 5′5″ woman is . . . ," "The average number of college students who achieve their BA degree is . . . ," "The Dow Jones Average is. . . ." Scores that represent the center of the distribution are called **measures of central tendency.** In this chapter, the three most common measures are discussed: the arithmetic mean (hereafter referred to as the *mean*), the median, and the mode. As illustrated by Mr. Babbins's unfortunate employment decision, it is important for you to know which measure best represents your data and best serves your purposes.

The Mean

The mean is the most commonly used measure of central tendency. People often ask about the *average* of a certain group of scores. Almost invariably, what they really want to know is the mean. The **mean** of any set of raw scores is the sum of all the scores divided by the total number of scores. The formulas for calculating the mean of a sample and the mean of a population follow. To understand the formulas, you need to know a few things. First, Σ (the Greek capital letter *sigma*) tells you to add all the scores represented by the symbol following it. Second, because the symbols X and Y are typically used as variable names throughout the text, the symbol X represents the scores in either a sample or a population that were collected by the researcher.

Thus, ΣX means to add all the scores represented by X in the sample or the population. Finally, you need to remember that n represents the total number of scores in a sample and N represents the total number of scores in a population.

Now let's take a look at the formulas. First, the formula for the mean of a sample, which is usually designated by the symbol $\overline{X}$, known as "X-bar":

$$\text{Mean of a sample} = \overline{X} = \frac{\Sigma X}{n} \tag{4.1}$$

Next, the formula for the mean of a population, which is designated by the Greek letter μ (mu):

$$\text{Mean of a population} = \mu = \frac{\Sigma X}{N} \tag{4.2}$$

As you can see, the formulas for the mean of a sample and the mean of a population are nearly identical. The only difference is that the sample mean is computed by summing all the scores in the sample and dividing by the total number of scores in the sample, whereas the population mean is computed by summing all the scores in the entire population and dividing by the total number of scores in the population.

Suppose you want to calculate the sample mean of the numbers 1, 2, 3, 4, and 5. (Remember that these numbers are called Xs.) You would first sum the numbers: $\Sigma X = 1 + 2 + 3 + 4 + 5 = 15$. Counting the number of scores gives $n = 5$. Then you can use Formula 4.2 to calculate the mean:

$$\overline{X} = \frac{\Sigma X}{n} = \frac{15}{5} = 3$$

To see whether the RatStuff.com recruiter was telling the truth, you need to compute the mean salary at his company. The salaries of all 25 employees are listed in Table 4.1. Use Formula 4.2 because you are dealing with a population—the population of people who work for RatStuff.com. According to the formula, first sum all 25 salaries. As you can see at the bottom of Table 4.1, the total for all salaries is $129,500. Then divide this sum by the total number of salaries, 25:

$$\mu = \frac{\Sigma X}{N} = \frac{\$129,500}{25} = \$5,180$$

Thus, the recruiter was absolutely correct. The mean salary at RatStuff.com is more than $5,000 per month.

VISUAL SUMMARY

Computing the Mean From Raw Scores

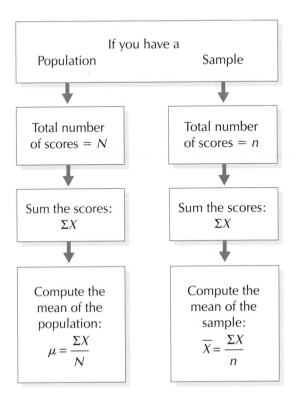

Concept Quiz

Cupal and Brewer (2001) conducted a study at a sports medicine clinic to determine whether relaxation and guided imagery sessions might increase knee strength and also reduce reinjury anxiety among knee surgery patients. Twenty-four weeks after surgery, they found that patients assigned to the relaxation and guided imagery sessions had significantly greater knee strength and reported less pain and reinjury anxiety than those in both the placebo and control conditions. Suppose another researcher decided to replicate this study and collected the following data on reinjury anxiety (1 = not worried about reinjury and 7 = very worried about reinjury).

Treatment Condition		
Relaxation and Guided Imagery (Experimental)	Support and Encouragement (Placebo)	No Intervention (Control)
1	3	3
3	4	4
3	5	3
2	3	4
1	4	5

1. The scores that represent the center of the distribution are called

   _____.

2. Because these are data collected from a sample of knee surgery patients, the symbol to represent the mean is _____. If these were population data, the symbol for the mean would be _____.

3. The mean of any set of raw data is the _____ of all the scores divided by the _____ of scores.

4. The mean of the three treatment conditions are as follows: (1) experimental group _____; (2) placebo group _____; and (3) control group _____.

5. The overall mean of all scores in the knee surgery study is _____.

Answers

1. measures of central tendency

2. $\overline{X}$; μ

3. total; number

4. 2; 3.8; 3.8

5. 3.2

The Median

The **median** is the middle score, with half the scores above and half the scores below, when all the scores have been ranked, or placed in numerical order. If there are 5 ranked scores, the middle score is the 3rd score; if there are 25 ranked scores, the median is the 13th score. The monthly salaries for the 25 RatStuff.com employees are listed here. Note that the 13th salary is the median.

1. $30,000	8. $1,500	14. $1,500	20. $1,000
2. $25,000	9. $1,500	15. $1,500	21. $1,000
3. $25,000	10. $1,500	16. $1,500	22. $1,000
4. $20,000	11. $1,500	17. $1,500	23. $1,000
5. $2,000	12. $1,500 ← Median	18. $1,500	24. $1,000
6. $2,000	13. $1,500	19. $1,500	25. $1,000
7. $1,500			

Question: Picking the middle score is easy when the number of scores is odd because there is a middle score, but how do you pick the median when there are an even number of scores?

When there are an even number of scores, the median is the average of the two middle scores. This means, of course, that there is no actual "middle score" in the data; the median is merely the value halfway between the two middle scores. Following are the heights of the eight players on the local college basketball team. Because there are an even number of players, the median is the average between the two middle heights.

79 inches
78 inches
76 inches
76 inches ◀— Middle score
74 inches ◀— Middle score
72 inches
72 inches
69 inches

$$\text{Median} = \frac{76 + 74}{2} = 75$$

The challenge in determining the median lies in finding the middle score(s). In smaller distributions, the middle score is obvious by inspection, but in large distributions it is not so obvious. For instance, suppose you had to find the median of a distribution with 327 scores, or 214 scores, or 533 scores. Fortunately, when faced with distributions that have large numbers of scores, you can rely on the following formulas, one for odd numbers of scores and one for even numbers, to help determine the median:

$$\text{Median}_{\text{odd number of scores}} = \left[\frac{n + 1}{2}\right]\text{th score} \tag{4.3}$$

$$\text{Median}_{\text{even number of scores}} = \frac{\left[\frac{n + 2}{2}\right]\text{th score} + \left[\frac{n}{2}\right]\text{th score}}{2} \tag{4.4}$$

The median for a distribution with 327 scores can be computed using Formula 4.3 because there are an odd number of scores.

$$\text{Median}_{\text{odd number of scores}} = \left[\frac{n+1}{2}\right]\text{th score} = \left[\frac{327+1}{2}\right]\text{th score} = 164\text{th score}$$

The median for a distribution with 762 scores is the average of the two middle scores because there are an even number of scores. Using Formula 4.4, gives

$$\text{Median}_{\text{even number of scores}} = \frac{\left[\dfrac{n+2}{2}\right]\text{th score} + \left[\dfrac{n}{2}\right]\text{th score}}{2}$$

$$= \frac{\left[\dfrac{762+2}{2}\right]\text{th score} + \left[\dfrac{762}{2}\right]\text{th score}}{2}$$

$$= \frac{382\text{nd score} + 381\text{st score}}{2}$$

In this example, the median is not the 381.5th score. It is the average of the 382nd score and the 381st score, whatever they are.

In summary, to find the median score in all but the smallest distributions, you will need to rank all scores, determine the middle score using either Formula 4.3 or 4.4, and then count down to that score.

Quartiles

Quartiles are closely related to the median. Whereas the median is the middle score when the scores are ranked, the quartiles divide the distribution into quarters. The first quartile is one quarter the way up through the distribution, the second quartile is halfway through the distribution, and the third quartile is three quarters of the way through the distribution. The quartiles are designated Q_1, Q_2, and Q_3. To find the quartiles, begin by ranking the scores and then finding Q_2. Because Q_2 is halfway through the distribution, it is equal to the median. To find Q_2, use the procedure described above for finding the median: If you have an odd number of scores you count to the middle score, and if you have an even number of scores you find the two middle scores and then find their mean. Therefore, to find where Q_2 is you use Formula 4.3 or 4.4:

$$\text{Median}_{\text{odd number of scores}} = \left[\frac{n+1}{2}\right]\text{th score} \tag{4.3}$$

$$\text{Median}_{\text{even number of scores}} = \frac{\left[\dfrac{n+2}{2}\right]\text{th score} + \left[\dfrac{n}{2}\right]\text{th score}}{2} \tag{4.4}$$

These formulas will tell you how far into the rank distribution you must count to find the median or Q_2. If n equals 15, then you must count to the 8th score to find Q_2. If n equals 20, you must count to the 10th and 11th scores, the 10.5th score, and average them to find Q_2.

Finding Q_1 and Q_3 is as easy as finding Q_2. First, use Q_2 to find out how far down from the top of the distribution you have to count to locate Q_1, and this in turn will tell you how far up from the bottom you will have to count to find Q_3. To find Q_1, take the number of scores that you need to count to get to the median, add 1, and then divide that number by 2:

$$Q_1 = \left[\frac{\left(\dfrac{n+1}{2}\right)+1}{2}\right]\text{th score} \tag{4.5}$$

For example, suppose you asked 25 women to list as many stereotypes of men they could think of, such as "likes sports" and "hides his emotions." The number of stereotypes that each woman listed in rank order appears in the table titled "Number of Stereotypes Mentioned." Because there are 25 scores, $n = 25$, Q_2 is equal to the median, which is 25 + 1 divided by 2, or the 13th score. Counting to the 13th score, you find that Q_2 equals *8 stereotypes*. Next, using Formula 4.5, you need to count to find Q_1:

$$Q_1 = \left[\frac{\left(\dfrac{n+1}{2}\right)+1}{2}\right]\text{th score} = \left[\frac{\left(\dfrac{25+1}{2}\right)+1}{2}\right]\text{th score}$$

$$= \left[\frac{\left(\dfrac{26}{2}\right)+1}{2}\right]\text{th score} = \left[\frac{13+1}{2}\right]\text{th score}$$

$$= \left[\frac{14}{2}\right]\text{th score} = \text{7th score}$$

Therefore, Q_1 is the 7th score in the distribution, *6 stereotypes.* To find Q_3, start at the highest score and count to the 7th score from the highest, which is *10 stereotypes.*

Number of Stereotypes Mentioned

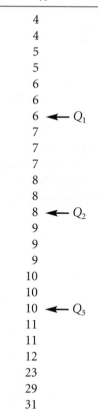

This procedure can then be used to find Q_1, Q_2, and Q_3 for any distribution of raw scores.

The Mode

The easiest to compute of all the measures of central tendency is the **mode,** which is simply the most frequent score. To determine the mode, you need only look at the ranked distribution of scores and find the most frequent one. Look at the following simple distribution. The score 9 is represented three times, whereas all the other scores are represented only once; therefore, the mode is equal to 9.

9 ←
9 ← Mode
9 ←
8
6
1

Take a look at Table 4.1. Can you pick out the mode? Thirteen of the 25 workers make $1,500 a month, so $1,500 is the mode for the salaries at RatStuff.com.

> **Question:** What if there are two scores that have the highest frequency? Or what if there is only one of each score in the distribution?

In cases where two different scores tie for the most frequent score, there are two modes. Although most distributions are unimodal, having only one mode, it is not uncommon for distributions to be bimodal with two modes or multimodal with more than two modes. A bimodal distribution often occurs in tests that are exceedingly difficult because there are typically some people who know the material very well, resulting in a cluster of high scores, and others who know the material barely at all, resulting in a separate cluster of low scores. This situation is illustrated in the following data from a highly challenging mechanical aptitude test given to a sample of 25 college freshmen.

95	87	75	45 ←	10
90 ←	86	73	45 ← Mode	9
90 ← Mode	84	70	45 ←	9
90 ←	77	60	45 ←	8
90 ←	76	53	25	8

A distribution that consists of only one of each score has n modes. In other words, there are as many modes as there are scores.

Concept Quiz

According to a study done by North, Hargreaves, and McKendrick (1999), you might want to pay attention to the music playing when you are selecting a wine to buy. These researchers conducted a field study in a supermarket to see whether a customer's decision to buy either French or German wine would be influenced by hearing either German or French music. The type and number of bottles of wine purchased during each of the music conditions was recorded. Results revealed that when French music was played, the French wines outsold the German wines, and when German music was played, German wines outsold French wines. Suppose another researcher designed a similar study using American and Italian music and wines and collected the data shown here.

Bottles of Wine Purchased

American Music		Italian Music	
American	Italian	American	Italian
31	9	11	28
10	8	9	19
7	5	8	10
6	4	7	9
6	3	7	5
6	2	1	4
2	1		

1. After data are placed in numerical order, the median is the
   _____ score.

2. When there are an even number of scores, the median is the
   _____ of the _____ middle scores.

3. When there are an odd number of scores, the median is the score with
   _____ the scores above and _____ it.

4. The median number of Italian wine bottles purchased when American
   music was playing is _____, which is the _____
   score.

5. The median number of American wine bottles purchased when Italian
   music was playing is _____, which is the average of the
   _____ and _____ score.

6. Whereas the median is the middle score when scores are ranked, the
   _____ divide the distribution into quarters.

7. Q_2 is the same as the _____.

8. The mode is the most _____ score in a distribution of raw
   scores.

9. When two scores tie for the most frequent score, there are
   _____ modes and it is called _____.

10. Which of the wine and music conditions have n modes?

Answers

1. middle
2. average; two
3. half; below
4. 4; fourth
5. 7.5; third; fourth

6. quartiles
7. median
8. frequent
9. two; bimodal

10. American music/Italian wine and Italian music/Italian wine

Mean, Median, or Mode: A Question of Skew

You are now familiar with the three measures of central tendency, but how do you know which one to use in any one circumstance? How do you avoid a problem like the one faced by Roy Babbins when you need to know which "average" score best represents a particular set of data? For the most part, the answer lies in knowing the *skew* of the distribution.

The term **skew** refers to the general shape of a distribution when it is graphed as a frequency polygon. A distribution is *not* skewed when it is symmetrical; a distribution *is* skewed when it has most of the scores at one end and very few at the other. Figure 4.1 illustrates the three types of skew: Figure 4.1(a) shows a symmetrical distribution with no, or zero, skew; Figure 4.1(b) shows a distribution with a positive skew; and Figure 4.1(c) shows a distribution with a negative skew.

> **Question:** The scores in Figure 4.1(b) are all clustered at the low end of the graph, and low scores are generally considered to be closer to negative. Why is this distribution said to have a positive skew?

The skew of a distribution has nothing to do with the area that contains the most scores; it has to do with the direction in which the tail is pointing. Tails of distributions are the areas at the extreme high or extreme low end where the data frequency tapers off to zero—where the graph approaches the abscissa. When the tail is to the right of the distribution [pointing in the positive direction as in Figure 4.1(b)], the skew is positive; when the tail is to the left of the distribution [pointing in the negative direction as in Figure 4.1(c)], the skew is negative. Another way to remember positive and negative skew is to imagine yourself standing on the tail (the flat part) of the distribution getting ready to climb to the top of the curve. If, as you face the steep curve, your back is to the ordinate, then the curve has a negative skew; if you are facing in the direction of the ordinate, the curve has a positive skew. As you climb up the curve from the tail, you will first encounter the mean, then the median, and then the mode (note the alphabetical order.) A symmetrical distribution has two tails and, as previously mentioned, is not skewed. Note that in a perfectly symmetrical distribution with absolutely no skew [see Figure 4.1(a)], the mean, median, and mode are all equal. On the other

Figure 4.1
Graphs indicating the three different types of skew: (a) zero skew (the distribution is symmetrical); (b) positive skew (the tail points in the positive direction); and (c) negative skew (the tail points in the negative direction).

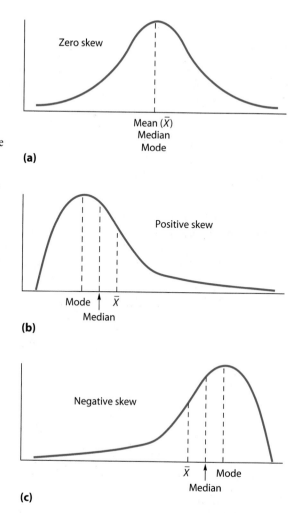

hand, in a skewed distribution, the mean, median, and mode are all different. In fact, you can determine the skew of any distribution by comparing the measures of central tendency. When they are the same, there is no skew; when the mean is greater than the median and the median is greater than the mode, the distribution has a positive skew; and when the mean is less than the median and the median is less than the mode, the distribution has a negative skew.

Question: How can you tell which measure of central tendency to use?

In distributions without skew, the mean is the most commonly used measure for a number of reasons. The mean can be readily calculated without having to rank the data, which can be time consuming when there are many scores; its mathematical properties lend themselves well to use in statistical formulas, as you will see in future chapters, and it is the measure that most people immediately think of when referring to the center of the distribution, or the average. When the data are skewed, the median or the mode best represents the center of the distribution because extreme scores at the upper or lower end of the distribution can heavily influence the mean. Such influence is evidenced by the RatStuff.com example at the beginning of the chapter and is clearly illustrated by the following example.

Suppose you measure a person's reaction time to the same stimulus on seven consecutive trials and obtain the following results (in milliseconds):

$$
\begin{array}{r}
300 \\
275 \\
250 \\
250 \\
250 \\
225 \\
200 \\
\hline
\end{array}
$$

$$\overline{X} = 250$$
$$\text{Median} = 250$$
$$\text{Mode} = 250$$

This distribution of reaction times is symmetrical—the mean, the median, and the mode are all equal to 250 milliseconds. Because this distribution is not skewed, the mean is the best choice to represent the central score. Now suppose the participant in your research became distracted on one of her trials, and one of her reaction times was 2,050 milliseconds rather than 300 milliseconds.

$$
\begin{array}{r}
2,050 \\
275 \\
250 \\
250 \\
250 \\
225 \\
200 \\
\hline
\end{array}
$$

$$\overline{X} = 500$$
$$\text{Median} = 250$$
$$\text{Mode} = 250$$

The change to the new high score, 2,050 milliseconds, has no effect on the median or the mode—they both remain 250 milliseconds—but the mean has changed drastically, doubling from 250 milliseconds to 500 milliseconds. Obviously, the measure that best represents the center of this revised distribution is the median or the mode. In such cases, the median is typically selected over the mode because there can only be one median but more than one mode. Also, in small distributions, the mode can be unstable: It can change significantly whenever a score that happens to duplicate another score is added.

You also must consider the scale of measurement being used. The only valid measure of central tendency for nominal scales of measurement is the mode. The best measure of central tendency for an ordinal scale is the median. Also, as mentioned above, either the mean, the median, or the mode might be the most appropriate score for an interval or ratio scale of measurement. In general, however, choose a measure of central tendency that best represents the distribution and the scale of measurement. In most cases, the most representative score is the mean.

Boxplots

Another way to view the distribution, and to see the skew, is to create a boxplot of the data. (Sometimes this is called a box-and-whisker plot.) A boxplot is a simple graph based on the three quartiles, Q_1, Q_2, and Q_3, that were discussed earlier in the chapter. To create the boxplot, you need to know the three quartiles (Q_1, Q_2, and Q_3) and the interquartile range ($Q_3 - Q_1$), and you need to compute values that designate the inner fence. An inner fence is a point that falls 1.5 times the interquartile range below Q_1 and 1.5 times the interquartile range above Q_3. Reprinted here is the table on male stereotypes that was used to demonstrate the computation of quartiles earlier in the chapter, now labeled Table 4.2.

With Q_1 equaling 6 and Q_3 equaling 10, the interquartile range is $10 - 6$, or 4. Therefore, the lower inner fence is $Q_1 - (1.5 \cdot 4) = 6 - 6 = 0$. The upper inner fence is $Q_3 + (1.5 \cdot 4) = 10 + 6 = 16$. Finally, you need to identify those scores that are either below the lower inner fence or above the upper inner fence. These scores are called outliers. The outliers for the data in Table 4.2 are 23, 29, and 31. Now you are ready to create the boxplot using the following information:

$Q_1 = 6$
$Q_2 = 8$
$Q_3 = 10$
Lower inner fence $= 0$
Upper inner fence $= 16$
Outliers $= 23, 29, 31$

The procedure for creating boxplots is as follows:

1. Label the abscissa in the appropriate units from the lowest score, or the lower inner fence, to the highest score, or the higher inner fence.
2. Draw an ordinate without a scale high enough to accommodate the boxplot.
3. Draw a rectangular box that stretches between the first quartile (Q_1) and the third quartile (Q_3).
4. Within the box, draw a vertical line at the median (Q_2).

Table 4.2   Quartiles, Inner Fence, and Outliers
for Data on Number of Male Stereotypes
Mentioned by 25 Female Participants

Number of Stereotypes Mentioned

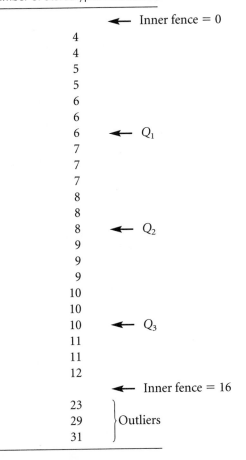

5. Draw horizontal lines (the whiskers) in each direction from the box to the inner fence.
6. Locate each outlier, if any, with an $\times$ and label that case if necessary.

Figure 4.2 shows the completed boxplot.

Examination of the boxplot can allow you to pick out the outliers and to see whether the distribution is skewed in one direction or another. Boxplots also give you a feel for the spread of the scores in the distribution. There are several different statistical measures of the spread of the scores, and these are discussed in Chapter 5.

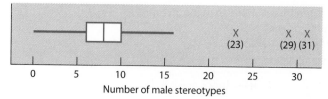

Figure 4.2   Completed Boxplot for the Data on Number of Male Stereotypes Mentioned by 25 Female Participants.

Concept Quiz

Psychologists have studied the relationship of chronic noise exposure to physiological responses for some time. In a 2-year field study of children living near an airport, Evans, Bullinger, and Hygge (1998) found that chronic exposure to aircraft noise was related to an elevation of children's psychophysiological stress (resting blood pressure and overnight epinephrine and norephinephrine). Suppose another group of researchers extended this area of research and investigated the relationship of chronic aircraft noise exposure and aggressive behavior among children living near airports. Among the data collected were the number of aggressive acts, such as hitting, kicking, punching, biting, and so on, observed and reported by parents and their teachers during the 3-week study. The aggression data are shown in the frequency histogram shown here.

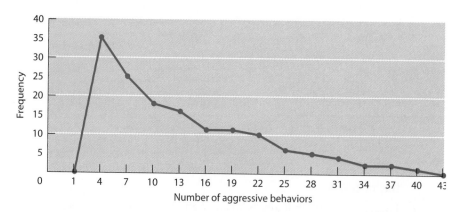

1. The term _____ refers to the general shape of a distribution when it is graphed as a frequency polygon.

2. If the distribution of aggression data were _____, the mean, the median, and the mode would be the same.

3. There are three different types of skew: _____ skew, _____ skew, and _____ skew.

4. The aggression data has a _____ skew because the
    _____ points in the _____ direction.

5. Measures of _____ can be compared to determine the skew.

6. The skew of the aggression data reveals that the _____ is
    greater than the _____ and the _____ is greater
    than the _____.

7. Explain which measure of central tendency best represents the aggression
    data.

8. The best measure of central tendency for nominal data is the
    _____ and for ordinal data it is the _____.

9. A _____ is based on the three _____ and is
    another way to view the distribution of scores within the distribution.

10. The inner _____ of a boxplot is _____ times the
    interquartile range _____ Q_1 and _____ Q_3.

Answers

1. skew
2. symmetrical
3. zero; positive; negative
4. positive; tail; positive
5. central tendency

6. mean; median;
    median; mode
7. the median, because it
    isn't affected by
    extreme scores

8. mode; median
9. boxplot; quartiles
10. fence; 1.5; below;
    above

Frequency Distributions

The Mean

Often, raw data are not available. In research reports and newspaper articles, for
instance, experimental results are often reported in graphs or in frequency distributions. Suppose you run across a study having to do with personal space—the
amount of space people need between themselves and another person in order to
feel comfortable. You become interested in the results of this experiment because
you think they might be helpful in a project of your own that involves interpersonal exchanges. Specifically, you want to know the mean interpersonal distance
with which people feel comfortable, but the only data reported were in a frequency distribution, like the one in Table 4.3.

> **Question:** Can the mean be found even if no raw data are included in
> the report?

Table 4.3   Interpersonal Distance (in centimeters) for 75 College Sophomores

Apparent Limits	Frequency	Midpoint
150–164	6	157
135–149	6	142
120–134	5	127
105–119	7	112
90–104	9	97
75–89	12	82
60–74	15	67
45–59	7	52
30–44	6	37
15–29	1	22
0–14	1	7

Sure, if you are willing to settle for an estimate that, though not exact, will often be very close to the mean of the raw data. When no raw data are reported, you merely have to reconstruct them. Of course, without serious ESP powers, it is impossible to reconstruct the actual raw data; however, it *is* possible to make some well-founded guesses. For example, take the class interval 15–29, which has only one score. If you had to select a number within this interval to represent that score, what would you choose? The midpoint, 22? Yes; in general, the midpoint is always your best choice. By computing the midpoint for each class interval and then recording that midpoint once for each frequency in the class interval (six 157s for the class interval 150–164, nine 97s for the class interval 90–104, and so on), you can effectively reconstruct a "raw" distribution for the data (see Table 4.4).

Now that the "raw" data have been reconstructed, you can sum the scores and use the raw-data formula (Formula 4.1) to compute the mean:

$$\overline{X} = \frac{\Sigma X}{n} = \frac{6,690}{75} = 89.200$$

Table 4.4   Midpoints Representing the Data in Table 4.2

157	142	127	97	97	82	67	67	52	37
157	142	112	97	82	82	67	67	52	37
157	142	112	97	82	82	67	67	52	37
157	142	112	97	82	82	67	67	52	37
157	127	112	97	82	82	67	67	52	37
157	127	112	97	82	67	67	67	52	22
142	127	112	97	82	67	67	52	37	7
142	127	112	97	82					

Question: Isn't there an easier way to do this? Wouldn't this be very time consuming if there were 1,000 scores?

Yes. It is quite time consuming with only 75 scores; it would be extremely so if there were 1,000. Fortunately, there is a faster, simpler method. Take a look at Table 4.5, which is made up of 1,000 people's estimates of the length (in meters) of the painted dashed lane-divider lines on highways. These lines produce a re-markably potent modern-day illusion—nearly everyone greatly underestimates their length. (Most lane lines are well over 250 centimeters, or longer than 8 feet. See Harte, 1975.) To determine the mean of these estimates, you could proceed as earlier and list the midpoints according to their frequency. However, this would be rather ridiculous considering that you would have to write down the midpoint for the class interval 200–224 (which is 212) 247 times. It makes much more sense to multiply the midpoint of each class interval by the number of *scores* (the fre-quency) in that interval and then sum the resulting values over all the class inter-vals. This has been done (the frequency of each class interval has been multiplied by its midpoint) in the "Frequency · Midpoint" column in Table 4.5.

With this method, the formula for obtaining the mean of a frequency dis-tribution is

$$\text{Mean of a frequency distribution} = \overline{X} = \frac{\Sigma\left(\text{frequency} \cdot \text{midpoint}\right)}{n} \quad (4.6)$$

A note of caution: Make sure you use the total number of scores for *n*, not the number of class intervals.

Table 4.5   Estimated Lengths of Highway Divider Lines (in centimeters)

Apparent Limits	Frequency	Midpoint	Frequency · Midpoint
300–324	10	312	3,120
275–299	25	287	7,175
250–274	69	262	18,078
225–249	146	237	34,602
200–224	247	212	52,364
175–199	206	187	38,522
150–174	147	162	23,814
125–149	104	137	14,248
100–124	32	112	3,584
75–99	14	87	1,218
$n = \Sigma F = 1{,}000$			$\Sigma(\text{frequency} \cdot \text{midpoint}) = 196{,}725$

Using Formula 4.3, you can compute the mean of the frequency distribution in Table 4.5:

$$\overline{X} = \frac{\Sigma(\text{frequency} \cdot \text{midpoint})}{n} = \frac{196{,}725}{1{,}000} = 196.725$$

Thus, the average, or mean, estimate for the length of the highway divider lines from the sample is 196.725 centimeters.

Formula 4.3 is an easy one that can be used to compute the mean of any grouped frequency distribution. Keep in mind, however, that when you are dealing with data that have been summarized into a grouped frequency distribution, you no longer know the original raw data. Because the mean of the grouped frequency distribution has not been computed from the raw data, it is often slightly different from the mean of the actual raw data. The point to remember is that the mean of the raw data is more accurate and should be used if at all possible.

VISUAL SUMMARY

Computing the Mean of a Frequency Distribution

Before You Begin: Create a frequency distribution, including apparent limits frequency and midpoints.

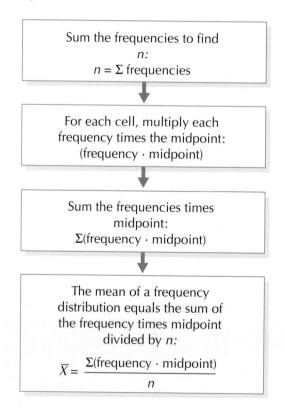

The Median

Take a look at Table 4.6, which has the same distribution as Table 4.5. Can you tell which score is the median? Probably not, although you may be able to figure out which class interval contains the median (particularly because that class interval is in boldface type). You know that the median is the middle score and that the number of scores in the distribution is 1,000. You also know from Chapter 2 that the definition of cumulative frequency is the total number of scores below the upper real limit of the class interval. Therefore, starting with the lowest class interval in the cumulative frequency column, scan each successively higher cumulative frequency until you find the first value that is greater than or equal to 500. In the example, it is 503 in the class interval 175–199.

> **Question:** Couldn't an educated guess be made that the median score would be the midpoint of the class interval?

There is a much more accurate way of estimating the median from a grouped frequency distribution. Even though you do not know the exact median, you do know several things. You know the real limits of the class interval (174.5–199.5), the size of the class interval (25), and the number of scores within the class interval (206), and you can compute how far up into the class interval the median resides if you assume all 206 scores are evenly distributed within the class interval. Given this information, the following formula can be used to estimate the median from a grouped frequency distribution.

$$\text{Median} = L + \left[\frac{(n/2) - CF_b}{F_i} \right] \cdot i \tag{4.7}$$

where

L = the lower real limit of the class interval that contains the median

n = the number of scores in the entire distribution

CF_b = the cumulative frequency in the class interval *below* the class interval that contains the median

F_i = the frequency in the class interval that contains the median

i = the class interval size

Table 4.6   Estimated Lengths of Highway Divider Lines (in centimeters)

Real Limits	Apparent Limits	Frequency (F)	Cumulative Frequency (CF)
299.5–324.5	300–324	10	1,000
274.5–299.5	275–299	25	990
249.5–274.5	250–274	69	965
224.5–249.5	225–249	146	896
199.5–224.5	200–224	247	750
L ➞ **174.5–199.5**	**175–199**	**206** ◀ F_i	**503**
149.5–174.5	150–174	147	297 ◀ CF_b
124.5–149.5	125–149	104	150
99.5–124.5	100–124	32	46
74.5–99.5	75–99	14	14

$$\text{Median} = 174.5 + \left[\frac{(1{,}000/2) - 297}{206}\right] \cdot 25$$

$$= 174.5 + \left[\frac{500 - 297}{206}\right] \cdot 25$$

$$= 174.5 + \left[\frac{203}{206}\right] \cdot 25$$

$$= 174.5 + 0.985 \cdot 25 = 174.5 + 24.625$$

$$= 199.125$$

The most critical factor in obtaining the median of a grouped frequency distribution is locating the class interval that contains the median. Once you have found the class interval, you can readily locate the necessary information to "plug into" the formula and then proceed to estimate the median.

The Mode

The mode in a grouped frequency distribution is the midpoint of the class interval with the highest frequency. Take a look at Table 4.5 (estimated lengths of highway divider lines) and find the class interval that has the highest frequency; then determine the midpoint of that class interval. You should have selected the class interval with apparent limits equal to 200–224 and found a midpoint of 212. Thus, the mode for Table 4.5 is 212 centimeters. For more practice, look at Table 4.7, a repeat of Table 4.3, and see whether you can figure out the mode. Do you see that the mode is 67?

VISUAL SUMMARY

Finding the Median in a Grouped Frequency Distribution

Before You Begin: Create a grouped frequency distribution with the real limits, apparent limits, frequency, and cumulative frequency; identify the class interval size (i); and tally the number of scores (n).

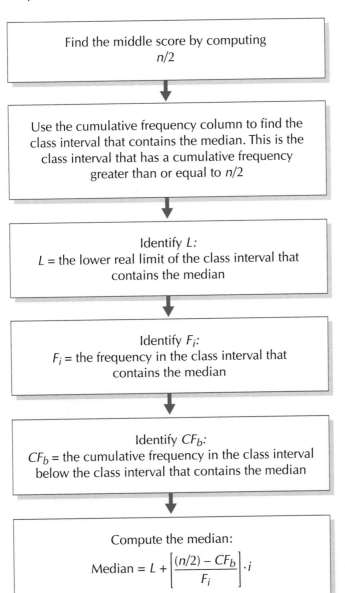

Find the middle score by computing
$n/2$

Use the cumulative frequency column to find the class interval that contains the median. This is the class interval that has a cumulative frequency greater than or equal to $n/2$

Identify L:
L = the lower real limit of the class interval that contains the median

Identify F_i:
F_i = the frequency in the class interval that contains the median

Identify CF_b:
CF_b = the cumulative frequency in the class interval below the class interval that contains the median

Compute the median:
$$\text{Median} = L + \left[\frac{(n/2) - CF_b}{F_i}\right] \cdot i$$

Table 4.7   Interpersonal Distance (in centimeters) for 75 College Sophomores

Apparent Limits	Frequency	Midpoint
150–164	6	157
135–149	6	142
120–134	5	127
105–119	7	112
90–104	9	97
75–89	12	82
60–74	15	67
45–59	7	52
30–44	6	37
15–29	1	22
0–14	1	7

Concept Quiz

Recall the chronic noise and aggression study discussed in the previous Concept Quiz. The grouped frequency distribution of the aggression data is shown here.

Grouped Frequency Distribution of Aggression Data

Real Limits	Apparent Limits	Frequency	Cumulative Frequency	Midpoint
25.5–27.5	26–27	1	146	26.5
23.5–25.5	24–25	2	145	24.5
21.5–23.5	22–23	2	143	22.5
19.5–21.5	20–21	4	141	20.5
17.5–19.5	18–19	5	137	18.5
15.5–17.5	16–17	6	132	16.5
13.5–15.5	14–15	10	126	14.5
11.5–13.5	12–13	11	116	12.5
9.5–11.5	10–11	11	105	10.5
7.5–9.5	8–9	16	94	8.5
5.5–7.5	6–7	18	78	6.5
3.5–5.5	4–5	25	60	4.5
1.5–3.5	2–3	35	35	2.5

1. When raw data are not available, frequency distribution data can be used to _____ the measures of central tendency.

2. To calculate the mean estimate from the frequency distribution of aggression data, first multiply the _____ and _____ of each class interval and then divide the total by _____ .

3. The mean estimate for the aggression data is _____ .

4. The most critical factor in obtaining the _____ from a grouped frequency distribution is locating the _____ that contains the median.

5. In order to calculate the median estimate from the grouped frequency distribution of aggression data, we use the lower real limit of _____ and the frequency in the class interval that contains the median, the cumulative frequency of _____ located just below the class interval containing the median, and the class interval size.

6. The mode estimated from a grouped frequency distribution is the _____ of the class interval with the _____ frequency.

7. The mode estimate from the grouped frequency distribution of aggression data is _____ .

Answers

1. estimate
2. frequency; midpoint; n
3. 14.229

4. median; class interval
5. 5.5; 60

6. midpoint; highest
7. 2.5

Summary

This chapter discusses the computation of three measures of central tendency: the mean, the median, and the mode. Although all three measures of central tendency can be called averages, the mean is the value that most people associate with the average. The mean is computed by summing all the scores and then dividing by the total number of scores. The mean is the score that, by weight, is in the center of the distribution. The actual middle score in the distribution is the median. When there are an odd number of scores, the median is the middle score if the scores are ranked. If there are an even number of scores, the median is the mean of the two middle scores if the scores are ranked. Quartiles are related to the median because the first quartile (Q_1) is the score that is halfway between the lowest score in the distribution and the median, the second quartile (Q_2) is equal to the median, and the third quartile (Q_3) is halfway between the median and the highest score in the distribution. The mode is the most frequent score. Most distributions have only one mode, but it is possible to have multiple modes. In symmetrical, bell-shaped distributions, the mean, the median, and the mode are the same score. In skewed distributions, the mean, the median, and the mode are usually different. Boxplots can give you a visual representation of the symmetry or skew in a distribution.

Key Terms

measures of central   mean   mode
    tendency   median   skew

Formulas

$$\text{Mean of a sample} = \overline{X} = \frac{\Sigma X}{n} \tag{4.1}$$

$$\text{Mean of a population} = \mu = \frac{\Sigma X}{N} \tag{4.2}$$

$$\text{Median}_{\text{odd number of scores}} = \left[\frac{n+1}{2}\right]\text{th score} \tag{4.3}$$

$$\text{Median}_{\text{even number of scores}} = \frac{\left[\frac{n+2}{2}\right]\text{th score} + \left[\frac{n}{2}\right]\text{th score}}{2} \tag{4.4}$$

$$Q_1 = \left[\frac{\left(\frac{n+1}{2}\right)+1}{2}\right]\text{th score} \tag{4.5}$$

$$\text{Mean of a frequency distribution} = \overline{X} = \frac{\Sigma(\text{frequency}\,.\,\text{midpoint})}{n} \tag{4.6}$$

$$\text{Median}_{\text{grouped}} = L + \left[\frac{(n/2) - CF_b}{F_i}\right] \cdot i \tag{4.7}$$

where

L = the lower real limit of the class interval that contains the median

n = the number of scores in the entire distribution

CF_b = the cumulative frequency in the class interval below the class interval that contains the median

F_i = the frequency in the class interval that contains the median

i = the class interval size

Problems

1. Find the mean, the median, and the mode of the following IQ scores:

120	134	74	79	98	88
124	129	106	143	106	92
134	119	111	76	128	96
129	97	85	89	100	92

2. Find the mean, the median, and the mode of the following welding aptitude test scores:

23	25	27	22	35	45
29	26	33	34	25	27
25	29	33			

3. Find the mean, the median, and the mode of the following sample of the number of items answered correctly on a memory test:

49	46	43	40	38	37
48	45	43	39	38	37
48	44	42	38	38	36
47	44	41	38	37	34
46	43	41	38	37	33

4. Find the mean, the median, and the mode of the following sample of the annual salaries (in dollars) of 15 college professors:

55,000	50,000	40,000	30,000	25,000
54,000	49,000	38,000	29,000	24,000
52,000	49,000	33,000	27,000	22,000

5. These 11 scores are the result of a simple reaction time experiment (reported in milliseconds). Compute the mean, the median, and the mode.

240	356	277	835	277	354
456	789	923	235	456	

6. The following data represent the number of times that 15 patients of a psychoanalyst used the defense mechanism of regression over the last year of therapy. Compute the mean, the median, and the mode.

23	7	11	21	6
6	17	45	23	67
25	22	11	56	6

7. A cognitive psychologist interested in short-term working memory has measured the capacity of the short-term memory for 18 students. Compute the mean, the median, and the mode.

9	3	5	6	7	7	7	6	8
9	10	13	5	6	4	7	7	7

8. A neuropsychologist has been studying the density of neurons in a structure called the hippocampus in the brain of the rat and has found that the density of neurons vary from rat to rat. The following data represent the

numbers of neurons found in equal-sized tissue samples from the brains of 13 rats. Compute the mean, the median, and the mode.

88	93	65	77	77	106	123
139	142	190	97	143	88	

9. A drug rehabilitation center has kept records of the number of days that 20 former patients have remained drug free. Compute the mean, the median, and the mode.

21	35	78	90	78	121	88	17	19	123
45	45	67	123	72	89	78	122	180	87

10. As the pressure to publish increases at colleges and universities, many psychologists meet this pressure by working with coauthors on more and more papers. The following scores are the numbers of authors for all research reports published in the journal *Psychological Science* for the year 1990. Compute the mean, the median, and the mode.

3	4	2	3	1
2	4	5	4	3
3	2	4	3	1
5	2	1	1	
4	2	5	2	

11. The work performance ratings for 18 employees of a small business follow. Compute the mean, the median, and the mode.

2	4	5	5	6	6	6	6	6
6	7	7	8	9	9	9	9	10

12. A psychologist studying the sensation of touch uses a vibrator to stimulate the nerve endings in the fingers of 11 participants. Because the rate of vibration can be changed, she is able to find the number of vibrations per second to which each participant is most sensitive. Compute the mean, the median, and the mode of the following data.

234	254	266	250	231	245
300	222	250	245	231	

13. Compute the mean, the median, and the mode of the frequency distribution of the following IQ scores.

Apparent Limits	Frequency	Cumulative Frequency	Midpoint
150–159	3	173	154.5
140–149	5	170	144.5
130–139	9	165	134.5
120–129	18	156	124.5
110–119	26	138	114.5
100–109	36	112	104.5
90–99	34	76	94.5
80–89	23	42	84.5
70–79	13	19	74.5
60–69	5	6	64.5
50–59	1	1	54.5

14. Compute the mean, the median, and the mode of the grouped frequency distribution of the following welding aptitude test scores.

Apparent Limits	Frequency	Cumulative Frequency	Midpoint
45–47	3	88	46
42–44	5	85	43
39–41	10	80	40
36–38	14	70	37
33–35	22	56	34
30–32	15	34	31
27–29	10	19	28
24–26	7	9	25
21–23	1	2	22
18–20	1	1	19

15. Compute the mean, the median, and the mode of the following grouped frequency distribution of the numbers of items answered correctly on a memory test.

Apparent Limits	Frequency
48–49	2
46–47	4
44–45	5
42–43	9
40–41	13
38–39	11
36–37	8
34–35	3
32–33	2
30–31	1

16. Compute the mean, the median, and the mode of the following grouped frequency distribution of student rankings of student services at a small college.

Apparent Limits	Frequency
90–99	10
80–89	16
70–79	28
60–69	34
50–59	49
40–49	25
30–39	39
20–29	32
10–19	11
0–9	6

17. Compute the mean, the median, and the mode of the following grouped frequency distribution of professors' annual salaries (in dollars):

Apparent Limits	Frequency
56,000–59,999	2
52,000–55,999	5
48,000–51,999	11
44,000–47,999	14
40,000–43,999	27
36,000–39,999	35
32,000–35,999	29
28,000–31,999	18
24,000–27,999	14
20,000–23,999	6

18. The following midterm exam scores for 500 statistics students at a major university are shown in a grouped frequency distribution. Compute the mean, the median, and the mode.

Apparent Limits	Frequency
95–99	6
90–94	9
85–89	55
80–84	67
75–79	189
70–74	47
65–69	29
60–64	22
55–59	21
50–54	22
45–49	13
40–44	9
35–39	7
30–34	3
25–29	1

19. The following grouped frequency distribution summarizes the numbers of errors made by 294 new student drivers in their first attempt at a driving simulation test. Compute the mean, the median, and the mode.

Apparent Limits	Frequency
70–76	12
63–69	23
56–62	24
49–55	43
42–48	56
35–41	54
28–34	44
21–27	23
14–20	12
7–13	3

20. The chairs of 117 psychology departments in the United States were asked how many students were currently employed by their departments as undergraduate research assistants. A grouped frequency distribution of the data follows. Compute the mean, the median, and the mode.

Apparent Limits	Frequency
22–23	1
20–21	3
18–19	3
16–17	4
14–15	4
12–13	6
10–11	8
8–9	13
6–7	14
4–5	17
2–3	20
0–1	24

21. Given that the mean, the median, and the mode of a distribution of 10 scores all equal 15, what would be the effect on the mean, the median, and the mode of adding an additional score of 37 to the distribution?

22. Suppose you have a distribution with the high score of 250 and a low score of 150, and the mean, median, and mode all equal 200. What would be the effect on the mean, median, and mode if you added an additional score of 12 to the distribution?

23. Suppose you have a distribution with a mean equal to 34, the median equal to 50, and the mode equal to 75. What is the skew of this distribution: positive, negative, or zero? Which measure of central tendency would you choose to best represent this distribution?

24. Suppose you have a distribution with a mean equal to 34, the median equal to 30, and the mode equal to 22. What is the skew of this distribution: positive, negative, or zero? Which measure of central tendency would you choose to best represent this distribution?

25. Suppose you have a distribution with the mean equal to 123, the median equal to 124, and the mode equal to 125. Which measure of central tendency best represents this distribution? How would you describe the skew of this distribution?

26. Suppose you have a distribution with the mean equal to 123, the median equal to 84, and the mode equal to 22. Which measure of central tendency best represents this distribution? How would you describe the skew of this distribution?

27. A distribution with most of the scores at the low end and very few scores at the high end has what kind of skew?

28. How would you describe the relationship between the mean, the median, and the mode in a distribution that has no skew?

Problems From the Literature

The following problems refer to actual results from research studies that are cited at the end of the chapter. However, the data used to generate the problem sets are hypothetical.

Doyle's (2001) examination of cross-racial bias in the criminal justice system suggests that a person's own-race bias might increase the likelihood of cross-racial errors in criminal identification or recognition. Suppose you conduct a study exploring this issue. A video is created depicting a person wearing a baseball cap stealing an unattended backpack in the college library. The video appears to be of poor quality with inadequate lighting so that participants see only a brief glimpse of the culprit, making it extremely difficult to distinguish ethnicity. Thirty different and culturally diverse classrooms of 30–35 students are shown the video and complete a questionnaire about the identification of the thief. The number of cross-racial identification errors for each classroom are shown here. Use the data to solve Problems 29–33.

22	17	13	19	17	21	14	9	12	18
16	8	21	17	14	19	22	23	16	11
21	15	12	16	21	11	17	24	17	9

29. Find the mean, median, and mode for the identification error data.

30. Calculate the quartiles for the identification error data.

31. Use the three measures of central tendency to determine the skew of the distribution of identification error data.

32. Suppose the researcher sampled 35 classrooms instead of 30 and the following new data points were added: 30, 32, 33, 34, and 35. Calculate the new mean, median, and mode. Discuss the impact of these additional scores on the representativeness of the mean, median, and mode.

33. Suppose another researcher ran a study like this and the mean, median, and mode of her sample data were 22, 17, and 14, respectively.

Discuss the skew of the distribution of scores in this researcher's study. The researcher also plans to conduct a sensitivity program in the classes with identification errors above the average. What measure of central tendency would you recommend this researcher use as a cutoff point for a new cultural sensitivity program? Why?

Recall Crusco and Wetzel's (1984) study examining interpersonal touch and restaurant tipping discussed in Chapter 1. Suppose you wanted to run a similar study. Waitresses and waiters were randomly assigned to either briefly touch or not touch the hand of the diner when they returned with the change from the food bill payment. The average percentages of tip per diner are shown here. Use the data to solve Problems 34–38.

Briefly Touch		No Touch	
34	35	15	25
10	24	13	19
25	38	13	21
31	35	16	15
28	39	13	35

34. Find the mean, median, and mode for the data for each of the conditions separately.

35. Calculate the quartiles for the data for each of the conditions separately.

36. Use the three measures of central tendency to determine the skew of the distribution of the data for each condition.

37. If a new server wanted to know the average percentage of tip per diner, which measure of central tendency would be the best answer for each condition? Which measure of central tendency would underestimate the average percentage of tip per diner for each condition?

38. The data that follow are the average percentage of tips for both conditions

separated between waitresses and waiters. Find the mean, median, and mode for the average percentage of tip for each group. Compare the measures of central tendency for both groups and determine the skew of the distributions of both sets of data. Which measure of central tendency would be best to use for the average percentage of tip for waitresses and waiters separately? Explain why. How do these measures compare to the overall measures of central tendency?

| Waitresses | 35 | 24 | 38 | 35 | 39 | 25 | 19 | 21 | 15 | 35 |
| Waiters | | 34 | 10 | 25 | 31 | 28 | 35 | 24 | 38 | 35 | 39 |

Benjamin and Bjork (2000) conducted several experiments examining the effect of recognition time pressure on learning new words using either rote or elaborative rehearsal. They found that when participants were under time pressure during recognition, there was a decrease in the accessibility to words learned via elaborative rehearsal compared to those learned via rote rehearsal. Suppose the following data were collected from a similar study done by another researcher. Participants learned 35 new words, and the total numbers of words recognized under time pressure are presented. Use the frequency data to solve Problems 39–42.

Frequency Distribution of Word Recognition Data	
Apparent Limits	Frequency
22–23	18
20–21	4
18–19	3
16–17	6
14–15	5
12–13	5
10–11	5
8–9	5
6–7	7
4–5	6
2–3	7

39. Find the estimated mean, median, and mode from the frequency data of words recognized.

40. Create a boxplot from the frequency data of the words recognized.

41. Using the estimated measures of central tendency, identify the skew of the distribution of the data.

42. Which of the estimated measures of central tendency best represents these data, and why?

References

Benjamin, A. S., & Bjork, R. A. (2000). On the relationship between recognition speed and accuracy for words rehearsed via rote versus elaborative rehearsal. *Journal of Experimental Psychology: Learning, Memory, and Cognition, 26,* 638–648.

Crusco, A. H., & Wetzel, C. G. (1984). The effects of interpersonal touch on restaurant tipping. *Personality and Social Psychology Bulletin, 10,* 512–517.

Cupal, D. D., & Brewer, B. W. (2001). Effects of relaxation and guided imagery on knee strength, reinjury anxiety, and pain following anterior cruciate ligament reconstruction. *Rehabilitation Psychology, 46,* 28–43.

Doyle, J. M. (2001). Discounting the error costs. Cross-racial false alarms in the culture of contemporary criminal justice. *Psychology, Public Policy, and Law, 7,* 253–262.

Evans, G. W., Bullinger, M., & Hygge, S. (1998). Chronic noise exposure and physiological response. A prospective study of children living under environmental stress. *Psychological Science, 9,* 75–77.

Harte, D. B. (1975). Estimates of the length of highway guidelines and spaces. *Human Factors, 17,* 455–460.

North, A. C., Hargreaves, D. J., & McKendrick, J. (1999). The influence of in-store music on wine selections. *Journal of Applied Psychology, 84,* 271–276.

5

Measures of Variability

- The Range
- Mean Deviation
  Average Mean Deviation: It All Adds Up to Nothing
- The Variance: The Mean of the Squared Deviations
- Standard Deviation: The Square Root of the Variance
  VISUAL SUMMARY: Computing the Variance and Standard Deviation

- Computational Formulas
  VISUAL SUMMARY: Computational Formulas for the Variance and Standard Deviation
- Calculating Variability From Grouped Frequency Distributions
  VISUAL SUMMARY: Finding the Variance and Standard Deviation of a Grouped Frequency Distribution

- Summary
- Key Terms
- Formulas
- Problems
  Problems From the Literature
- References

Humans seem to have a built-in need for competition. The legendary Green Bay Packers coach Vince Lombardi once said, "Winning isn't everything; it's the only thing." Many people agree wholeheartedly with his statement, and even the most noncompetitive find themselves acceding to it in at least some circumstances. We compete in many aspects of our lives: in business to earn a living, in research to make the first discovery, in school to get the highest grades, in shopping to find the shortest line, in sports to have fun.

Even though humans spend much of their lives competing, it is not clear that competition always brings out the best in people. Indeed, most of the psychological literature on games stresses the need for cooperation rather than competition to improve performance (Buskist & Morgan, 1988). Still, there is something about competition that incites some people to new heights of performance, particularly in sports. What makes competition so compelling is that even heavily favored people or teams often lose. They lose because people's behavior, whether academic, athletic, or cooperative team behavior, is not always the same; it varies. With this in mind, see if you can answer the following question.

Ami Chin, with a diving average of 9.5, and Jamie Fowler, who averages 9.3, are vying for the world diving championship. Who will win? An academic college bowl team that averages 150 points per game is competing against a team that averages 140 points. Which team do you think will win? The water polo teams from Cucamonga College and Buckaroo University both average 6 points a match. Do you think that the match will end in a 6-6 tie? To predict the outcomes of these matches, it is certainly helpful to know the competitors' averages. However, just because Ami averages 9.5 does not mean that she always gets exactly 9.5. Just because a team averages 6 points per match does not mean that they score six goals every time they take to the pool. People aren't perfect, and they certainly aren't perfectly consistent. Some, however, are more consistent than others. For example, let's look at the Cucamonga and Buckaroo water polo teams.

Knowing the average scores of the Cucamonga and Buckaroo water polo teams leads you to assume that the game will be a close one, but look at their scores in Table 5.1. Cucamonga College unfailingly scores just about six goals in every contest, whereas Buckaroo University scores either a lot of goals or none at all, and it has never scored exactly six. Knowing the point spread for each team, now what do you think about the possibility of a 6-6 tie?

There are statistical tools that can be used to measure the spread of scores in such distributions as the water polo teams' performances; they are called *measures of variability*. When used in conjunction with measures of central tendency, they disclose additional information about any distribution.

Measures of central tendency yield a single average score that represents the center of the distribution. **Measures of variability** give an idea of how much scores in the distribution vary from that one average score. For instance, by knowing that Ami Chin averages 9.5 on her dives, you know that she is an overall better diver than Jamie Fowler, who averages 9.3. Also, if each diver's scores almost never vary by more than 0.1 point, you can safely assume that Chin will have a better chance of winning the diving championship. Thus, measures of variability can reveal the consistency or similarity of the scores in a distribution. They can

Table 5.1   Goals Scored in the Past 10 Games by the Cucamonga College and Buckaroo University Water Polo Teams

Game	Cucamonga College (X_1)	Buckaroo University (X_2)
1	6	0
2	5	11
3	6	13
4	7	0
5	6	12
6	6	0
7	6	0
8	8	14
9	5	10
10	5	0
	$\Sigma X_1 = 60$	$\Sigma X_2 = 60$
	$\overline{X}_1 = 6$	$\overline{X}_2 = 6$

also indicate how much the average score truly represents all the scores in the distribution. If there is a large spread among the scores, as with Buckaroo's water polo scores, there is quite a different picture of the team's performance than there would be if the scores clustered around the average, as do Cucamonga's. In some cases, especially cases that involve planning for the future, it is more important to know the spread of the distribution than the center of the distribution. Examples are determining peak electrical loads for power companies, designing treatments for patients with mental disorders, and staffing for colleges and universities.

In this chapter, four basic measures of variability are discussed: the range, the average mean deviation, the variance, and the standard deviation. The range, though by far the easiest to compute, is quite unstable because one extreme score can have a radical effect on it. Therefore, it is seldomly used as a measure of variability. By comparison, the variance and the standard deviation, though more complicated than the range, are less affected by extreme scores and are much more widely used.

The Range

The **range** is a measure of the full extent of the scores in a distribution, from the highest to the lowest. It is computed by subtracting the low score from the high score.

$$\text{Range} = \text{high score} - \text{low score} \tag{5.1}$$

The range is extremely easy to compute. Quite often, in fact, you can compute it in your head. For example, look at the data in Table 5.1 and calculate the range for the Cucamonga and Buckaroo water polo teams. If you need help, use Formula 5.1:

$$\text{Range}_{\text{Cucamonga}} = 8 - 5 = 3$$

$$\text{Range}_{\text{Buckaroo}} = 14 - 0 = 14$$

Even if you didn't have access to the actual scores, knowing the range would tell you that Cucamonga's team must be fairly consistent because all its final scores vary within only 3 points of one another. Buckaroo's team is much more unpredictable because its scores are highly scattered and vary quite a bit. However, what if Cucamonga played the worst team in the league, and that team had an exceptionally bad day, resulting in Cucamonga scoring 19 points on that day? Then its distribution of points would vary from a low of 5 to a high of 19. All the other scores in the distribution are the same as before, but note that Cucamonga's range has increased from 3 to 14, which is the same as Buckaroo's. If you were now shown the means and the range for each of the teams, you would assume that their performances were quite similar. It is clear that even though the range is easy to compute, it is severely affected by extreme scores; even one score can alter the range to a large degree. Thus, although the range is sometimes used to gain a quick and easy picture of the data, it is not used as a reliable measure of variability.

> **Question:** Is there some measure of variability that takes into account each of the scores so that one extreme score doesn't have so much influence?

Yes, the other measures of variability do just this: They incorporate all the scores in their calculations. Using the mean as a sort of reference point, they determine how much the other scores differ from the mean.

Mean Deviation

Average Mean Deviation: It All Adds Up to Nothing

The **average mean deviation (*AMD*)** is the average deviation of each score from the mean of the distribution. To compute the average mean deviation, first find the mean, then subtract the mean from each score. This will give you the **deviation scores,** or the mean deviations, which are represented by the symbol x (we call them "little xs"). Next, sum the deviation scores (Σx) and divide that by the total number of scores (n). Thus, you compute the average mean deviation as you would any average, but instead of computing an average of several scores, you are computing an average of the deviations from the mean. Here is the formula:

$$\text{Average mean deviation } (AMD) = \frac{\Sigma(X - \overline{X})}{n} = \frac{\Sigma x}{n} \tag{5.2}$$

To illustrate the calculation of the average mean deviation, let's pretend you are conducting a preliminary study on conformity. In conformity experiments, it is customary to place participants in situations where a group of confederates (people hired by the experimenter) try to convince the participant to give a response that he or she knows is wrong or false. Suppose that there are five groups, each group consisting of one participant and three confederates. The task of each participant is to determine which of three lines displayed on a computer screen is the same length as a line previously displayed. Everyone in the group sees the same computer screen, and the experimenter asks each person in turn which of the lines on the screen matches the line previously displayed. The confederates are always asked their opinion before the participant, and the confederates always agree on the same line. During eight of the trials, the critical trials, the confederates name the wrong line as matching the previous line. The dependent variable in this research project is the number of conforming trials: the number of times the participant agrees with the confederates on the critical trials. Table 5.2 lists the number of conforming trials for each of the five participants in the study.

Table 5.2 Computation of the Deviation Scores and Average Mean Deviation for the Study on Conformity

X	$X - \bar{X}$	x
1	1 − 3	−2
2	2 − 3	−1
3	3 − 3	0
4	4 − 3	1
5	5 − 3	2

$\Sigma X = 15$ $\Sigma x = 0$

$\bar{X} = 3$

Average mean deviation $= \dfrac{\Sigma x}{n} = \dfrac{0}{5} = 0$

As you can see, the average mean deviation is equal to zero. Compare this to the average mean deviation for the two water polo teams, which is computed in Table 5.3. Do you notice the similarity? These are not special cases. *The average mean deviation is always equal to zero.* Because you are computing the average

Table 5.3 Computation of the Deviation Scores and the Average Mean Deviation for the Cucamonga College and Buckaroo University Water Polo Teams

Game	Cucamonga College			Buckaroo University		
	X_1	$X_1 - \bar{X}_1$	x_1	X_2	$X_2 - \bar{X}_2$	x_2
1	6	6 − 6	0	0	0 − 6	−6
2	5	5 − 6	−1	11	11 − 6	5
3	6	6 − 6	0	13	13 − 6	7
4	7	7 − 6	1	0	0 − 6	−6
5	6	6 − 6	0	12	12 − 6	6
6	6	6 − 6	0	0	0 − 6	−6
7	6	6 − 6	0	0	0 − 6	−6
8	8	8 − 6	2	14	14 − 6	8
9	5	5 − 6	−1	10	10 − 6	4
10	5	5 − 6	−1	0	0 − 6	−6

$\Sigma X_1 = 60$ $\Sigma x_1 = 0$ $\Sigma X_2 = 60$ $\Sigma x_2 = 0$

$\bar{X}_1 = 6$ $\bar{X}_2 = 6$

$AMD = \dfrac{\Sigma x_1}{n_2} = \dfrac{0}{5} = 0$ $AMD = \dfrac{\Sigma x_2}{n_2} = \dfrac{0}{5} = 0$

deviation, about half the deviations are positive. These are counterbalanced by the other half, which are negative. When added together, they equal zero.

The basic idea of finding the average amount each score deviates from the mean is quite sound. However, when the end result always equals zero, the procedure is worthless as a measure of variability because it does not allow for any meaningful comparisons between different distributions. If all distributions have the same average mean deviation, then another way must be found to compute the variability of scores within a distribution. The way out of this dilemma is to eliminate the minus signs of the deviation scores, but how can you do this? One way is to use absolute value: Sum the absolute values of the mean deviations, then divide by the total number of scores. Although this method does get rid of the minus signs, this absolute mean deviation method is not as useful as the method that is discussed after the Concept Quiz. After completing the Concept Quiz, try to think of another way to get rid of those minus signs in front of half the deviation scores.

Concept Quiz

Personal injury damage awards are made to help alleviate people's pain and suffering when they are harmed in some way. Among the findings of Marti and Wissler's (2000) study was the discovery that the amount of money people are awarded could be influenced by the presence and size of the minimum and maximum award people thought was reasonable. In this study, mock jurors' perception of the severity of the injury did not differ, but the size of the award varied depending on the boundaries of the request. Awards increased as the requested amounts increased and decreased when the requests were extreme.

1. The distribution of all monetary awards from the lowest award to the highest award is called the _____.

2. The problem with using the range as a measure of variability is that it can be unduly influenced by _____ scores.

3. If the lowest award was $5,000 and the highest award was $90,000, the range is _____.

4. Subtracting the mean from each score creates _____ scores.

5. The average mean deviation for any distribution is equal to

   _____.

Answers

1. range
2. extreme
3. $85,000
4. deviation
5. zero

The Variance: The Mean of the Squared Deviations

Question: How about squaring the deviation scores? When you square negative numbers, the results are positive.

This is exactly what you do when you compute the variance and the standard deviation. Both measures take advantage of the fact that whenever any number, positive or negative, is squared, the resulting value is positive. The variance, in fact, is simply the mean of the squared deviations. The variance of the entire population is represented by σ^2 (lowercase Greek letter sigma squared), and the variance of a sample is represented by S^2.

The formula for the population variance is shown in Formula 5.3.

$$\text{Variance of a population} = \sigma^2 = \frac{\Sigma(X - \mu)^2}{N} = \frac{\Sigma x^2}{N} \qquad (5.3)$$

The **variance** of a population is the actual computed variance of the population, whereas the sample variance is an estimate of the population variance using only the values in the sample. Because samples rarely contain all the extreme scores of a population, their variances are generally smaller than those of the population. In other words, the scores in the sample are likely to be more closely packed around the mean. Therefore, the variance of a sample cannot be considered a good estimate of the variance of the population unless there is some kind of correction. The usual correction for this underestimation is to divide by $n - 1$ rather than n. The effect of this change from n to $n - 1$ is to increase the size of the variance. The amount of this increase varies depending on the size of n. If n is small, subtracting 1 may make a large difference in the computed value of the variance; if n is large, subtracting 1 may make no noticeable difference. For example, if $n = 5$, then dividing by 4 ($n - 1$), rather than 5 (n) will create a 25% increase in the size of the variance. On the other hand, if $n = 100$, then dividing by 99 ($n - 1$) rather than by 100 (n) will create only a 1% increase. Because it is rare to have access to scores for an entire population, the variance of the sample is more widely used than the variance of the population. Thus, when the term *variance* is used in the rest of this chapter, it means the variance of the sample, as in Formula 5.4. The formula and the procedure for computing the variance of a sample are shown here.

$$\text{Variance of a sample} = S^2 = \frac{\Sigma(X - \overline{X})^2}{n - 1} = \frac{\Sigma x^2}{n - 1} \qquad (5.4)$$

In Table 5.4, the variance is computed from the distribution of scores from the conformity study. In Table 5.5, the variance for the water polo data is calculated.

Table 5.4   Computation of the Variance in the Study on Conformity

Participant	X	$X - \overline{X}$	x	x^2
A	1	1 − 3	−2	4
B	2	2 − 3	−1	1
C	3	3 − 3	0	0
D	4	4 − 3	1	1
E	5	5 − 3	2	4

$$\Sigma X = 15 \qquad\qquad \Sigma x^2 = 10$$

$$\overline{X} = 3$$

$$S^2 = \frac{\Sigma x^2}{n - 1} = \frac{10}{5 - 1} = \frac{10}{4} = 2.5$$

Although you may not have noticed, there is a problem with the variance: It is not in the same units as the original scores. Because all the deviations are squared, the variance is in squared units; this fact can be quite misleading when you try to relate the variance to the raw scores. The solution to this dilemma is quite simple: Compute the square root of the variance. The result of this is known as the standard deviation.

Standard Deviation: The Square Root of the Variance

The **standard deviation** is the square root of the variance, and it is represented by either σ or S. Thus, the standard deviation is in the same units as the original scores. The formula for the standard deviation of a population is

$$\sigma = \sqrt{\frac{\Sigma(X - \mu)^2}{N}} = \sqrt{\frac{\Sigma x^2}{N}} \text{ or } \sigma = \sqrt{\sigma^2} \tag{5.5}$$

The formula for the standard deviation of a sample is

$$S = \sqrt{\frac{\Sigma(X - \overline{X})^2}{n - 1}} = \sqrt{\frac{\Sigma x^2}{n - 1}} \text{ or } S = \sqrt{S^2} \tag{5.6}$$

To find the standard deviation of the conformity distribution from Table 5.4, you merely calculate the square root of the variance:

$$S = \sqrt{S^2} = \sqrt{2.5} = 1.581$$

Table 5.5 Computation of the Variance and the Standard Deviation for the Cucamonga College and Buckaroo University Water Polo Teams

Game	Cucamonga College			Buckaroo University		
	X_1	x_1	x_1^2	X_2	x_2	x_2^2
1	6	0	0	0	−6	36
2	5	−1	1	11	5	25
3	6	0	0	13	7	49
4	7	1	1	0	−6	36
5	6	0	0	12	6	36
6	6	0	0	0	−6	36
7	6	0	0	0	−6	36
8	8	2	4	14	8	64
9	5	−1	1	10	4	16
10	5	−1	1	0	−6	36

$$\Sigma X_1 = 60 \qquad \Sigma x_1^2 = 8 \qquad\qquad \Sigma X_2 = 60 \qquad \Sigma x_2^2 = 370$$

$$\overline{X}_1 = 6 \qquad\qquad\qquad\qquad\qquad \overline{X}_2 = 6$$

$$S_1^2 = \frac{\Sigma x_1^2}{n_1 - 1} = \frac{8}{10 - 1} = \frac{8}{9} = .889 \qquad S_2^2 = \frac{\Sigma x_2^2}{n_2 - 1} = \frac{370}{10 - 1} = \frac{370}{9} = 41.111$$

$$S_1 = \sqrt{S_1^2} = \sqrt{.889} = .943 \qquad\qquad S_2 = \sqrt{S_2^2} = \sqrt{41.111} = 6.412$$

Table 5.5 shows the calculation of the standard deviation for the water polo scores.

Question: I still don't really understand the variance and the standard deviation. Without using formulas, can you tell me what they are?

Both the standard deviation and the variance are essentially averages. The variance is the average of the squared deviations from the mean. Because the standard deviation is the square root of the variance, it represents an average measure of the amount each score deviates from the mean.

Question: Computing the variance and standard deviation is so complicated and time consuming! Isn't there an easier way to calculate them?

There are several alternative methods for computing the variance and standard deviation. One of these is to use computational formulas rather than the deviation score formulas we gave earlier. These are discussed in the next section.

VISUAL SUMMARY

Computing the Variance and Standard Deviation

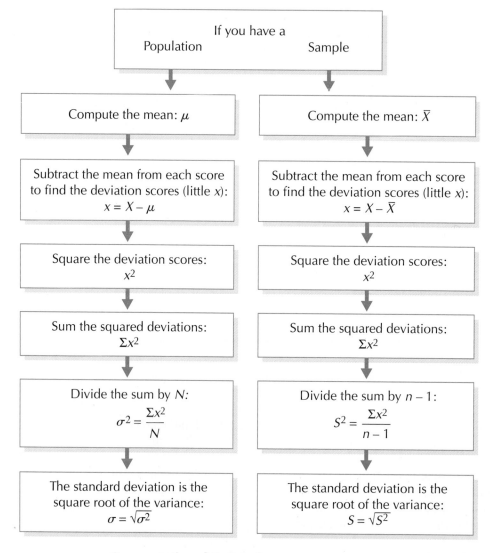

If you have a	
Population	Sample

Compute the mean: μ | Compute the mean: $\bar{X}$

Subtract the mean from each score to find the deviation scores (little x):
$$x = X - \mu$$
| Subtract the mean from each score to find the deviation scores (little x):
$$x = X - \bar{X}$$

Square the deviation scores:
$$x^2$$
| Square the deviation scores:
$$x^2$$

Sum the squared deviations:
$$\Sigma x^2$$
| Sum the squared deviations:
$$\Sigma x^2$$

Divide the sum by N:
$$\sigma^2 = \frac{\Sigma x^2}{N}$$
| Divide the sum by $n - 1$:
$$S^2 = \frac{\Sigma x^2}{n - 1}$$

The standard deviation is the square root of the variance:
$$\sigma = \sqrt{\sigma^2}$$
| The standard deviation is the square root of the variance:
$$S = \sqrt{S^2}$$

Computational Formulas

Computational formulas are designed to take advantage of the features of pocket calculators to make calculations faster. However, computational formulas can be dreadfully tedious when done with paper and pencil because of the large numbers involved in the computations. Therefore, the answer to the preceding question is yes, there are formulas that can make your life easier, *if* you have an electronic calculator. The following are the computational formulas for the variance and standard deviation.

$$\text{Variance} = S^2 = \frac{\Sigma X^2 - \dfrac{(\Sigma X)^2}{n}}{n-1} \tag{5.7}$$

$$\text{Standard deviation} = S = \sqrt{\frac{\Sigma X^2 - \dfrac{(\Sigma X)^2}{n}}{n-1}} \tag{5.8}$$

These formulas introduce a new term: ΣX^2. This term is read as "the sum of the X squares," and it equals $X_1^2 + X_2^2 + X_3^2 + \cdots + X_n^2$. It means that you should square each original score and then compute the sum of these squared scores. (Remember that this is the *sum of the X squares*, not the sum of the "little x" squares. "Little x" squares are deviation scores; X squares are the squares of the original scores.) In Table 5.6, the variance and the standard deviation for the scores from the conformity study are computed using Computational Formula 5.7.

Table 5.7 illustrates how the computational formulas can be used to calculate the variance and standard deviation of the water polo data for Cucamonga College and Buckaroo University.

The easiest alternative to computing any statistic is to use a computer program or a calculator that will compute the values for you. However, before you use computer programs or calculators to compute the variance or standard deviation, make sure you know which formulas the machine uses. The formulas shown here

Table 5.6 Computation of the Variance Using the Computational Formula for the Study on Conformity

Participant	X	X^2
A	1	1
B	2	4
C	3	9
D	4	16
E	5	25
	$\Sigma X = 15$	$\Sigma X^2 = 55$

$$S^2 = \frac{\Sigma X^2 - \dfrac{(\Sigma X)^2}{n}}{n-1} = \frac{55 - \dfrac{(15)^2}{5}}{5-1} = \frac{55 - \dfrac{225}{5}}{4} = \frac{55 - 45}{4} = \frac{10}{4} = 2.5$$

$$S = \sqrt{S^2} = \sqrt{2.5} = 1.581$$

VISUAL SUMMARY

Computational Formulas for the Variance and Standard Deviation

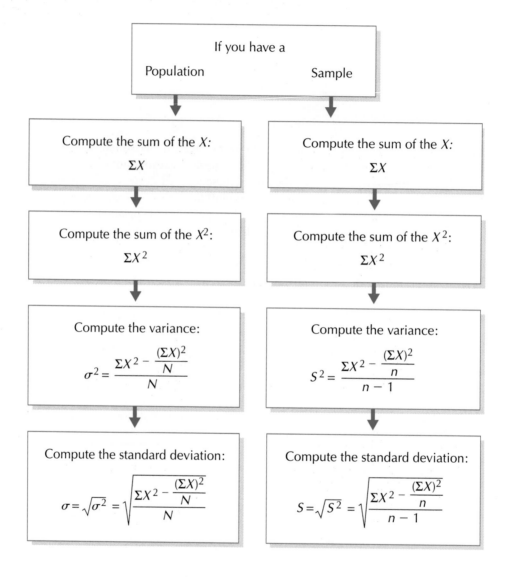

for the population variance and the sample variance are different. The population variance and standard deviation use only N in the denominator, whereas the sample standard deviation uses $n - 1$. Because there are two similar but very different formulas, most calculators are designed to display both a population value and a sample value. You will need to read the instruction manuals that come with your calculator or computer to determine which value is the one you want.

Table 5.7 Computation of the Variance and the Standard Deviation for the Cucamonga College and Buckaroo University Water Polo Teams

Game	Cucamonga College X_1	X_1^2	Buckaroo University X_2	X_2^2
1	6	36	0	0
2	5	25	11	121
3	6	36	13	169
4	7	49	0	0
5	6	36	12	144
6	6	36	0	0
7	6	36	0	0
8	8	64	14	196
9	5	25	10	100
10	5	25	0	0

$$\Sigma X_1 = 60 \qquad \Sigma X_1^2 = 368 \qquad\qquad \Sigma X_2 = 60 \qquad \Sigma X_2^2 = 730$$

$$S_1^2 = \frac{638 - \dfrac{60^2}{10}}{10 - 1} = \frac{368 - 360}{9} = \frac{8}{9} = .889 \qquad S_2^2 = S_1^2 = \frac{730 - \dfrac{60^2}{10}}{10 - 1} = \frac{730 - 360}{9} = \frac{370}{9} = 41.111$$

$$S_1 = \sqrt{S_1^2} = \sqrt{.889} = .943 \qquad\qquad S_2 = \sqrt{S_2^2} = \sqrt{41.111} = 6.412$$

Concept Quiz

Suppose a group of personal injury attorneys hired you to conduct a study similar to the study done by Marti and Wissler (2000). In your study, you ask mock jurors to read a scenario involving a person seriously injured on a construction job and to award monetary damages between a minimum of $1,000 and a maximum of $100,000.

1. The variance in monetary awards is simply the _____ of the squared deviations from the sample mean.

2. If the variance is $300,000, the standard deviation is the _____ of the variance, or $_____.

3. Suppose the following were the monetary awards separated for mock jurors in three different age groups. Which age group had the greatest variance?
   a. Senior jurors: $20,000, $30,000, $40,000, $50,000, $60,000
   b. Middle-age jurors: $20,000, $20,000, $20,000, $30,000, $60,000
   c. Young jurors: $20,000, $60,000, $60,000, $60,000, $60,000

4. Why is the standard deviation typically preferred over the variance when describing the variability of a distribution of scores?

5. If Billy Bob was injured on the job and had a choice of juries, which would you recommend if you knew the means and standard deviations of the monetary awards of Jury A and Jury B in a similar injury case? Why?

   a. Jury A: $\overline{X}$ = $70,000, s = $1,550
   b. Jury B: $\overline{X}$ = $70,000, s = $18,000

6. What is the difference between the computation of the value ΣX^2 and the value $(\Sigma X)^2$?

Answers

1. mean
2. square root; $547.72
3. c; The variance equals 17,888.544 (the variance of a equals 15,811.368; the variance of b equals 17,320.508).
4. The standard deviation is in the same units as the scores in the original distribution, whereas the variance is in squared units.
5. Jury A, because there is more consistency in their award
6. To compute the ΣX^2, you first square each score in the distribution then add the squared scores. To compute $(\Sigma X)^2$, you first add all the scores in the distribution and then square that sum.

Question: Is it possible to compute the variance and standard deviation from a grouped frequency distribution?

It is always preferable to use raw data to compute means, variances, and standard deviations. Nevertheless, it is possible to compute these values from a grouped frequency distribution if the raw data are not available. You will look at that procedure next.

Calculating Variability From Grouped Frequency Distributions

The procedure for computing the variance and standard deviation from a grouped frequency distribution is similar to that used to compute the mean from a grouped frequency distribution. In that procedure, you assume that the scores within each class interval are represented by the midpoint of that interval and use the following formula:

$$S^2 = \frac{\Sigma\left(F \cdot x^2\right)}{n - 1}$$

(5.9)

where

F = the frequency in the class interval

x^2 = the squared deviation for the class interval (to compute this you subtract the mean from the midpoint of the class interval and then square the result)

n = the total number of scores in the entire frequency distribution

Because the standard deviation is the square root of the variance, the formula for the standard deviation of a grouped frequency distribution is

$$S = \sqrt{S^2} = \sqrt{\frac{\Sigma(F \cdot x^2)}{n-1}}$$ (5.10)

In Table 5.8, the variance and standard deviation from a simplified grouped frequency distribution have been computed using Formulas 5.9 and 5.10. Table 5.9 uses these formulas to compute the variance and standard deviation from the frequency distribution of the highway divider line estimates discussed in Chapter 4.

Question: It's so easy to get caught up in the mathematical formulas and calculations for the variance and standard deviation that you lose sight of what they are all about. Can you explain why we would use them without using mathematical jargon?

In plain terms, the variance and the standard deviation are statistics that measure how much the scores in the distribution deviate from the mean, and they

Table 5.8 Computation of the Variance and Standard Deviation From a Simplified Grouped Frequency Distribution

Apparent Limits	Frequency (F)	Midpoint	F · Midpoint	x	x^2	$F \cdot x^2$
12–14	1	13	13	6	36	36
9–11	2	10	20	3	9	18
6–8	4	7	28	0	0	0
3–5	2	4	8	−3	9	18
0–2	1	1	1	−6	36	36
	$n = 10$		$\Sigma(F \cdot \text{midpoint}) = 70$			$\Sigma(F \cdot x^2) = 108$

$$\overline{X} = \frac{70}{10} = 7$$

$$S^2 = \frac{\Sigma(F \cdot x^2)}{n-1} = \frac{108}{10-1} = \frac{108}{9} = 12$$

$$S = \sqrt{S^2} = \sqrt{\frac{\Sigma(F \cdot x^2)}{n-1}} = \sqrt{12} = 3.464$$

Table 5.9   Computation of the Variance and Standard Deviation From Estimated Line Lengths of Highway Divider Lines (in centimeters)

Apparent Limits	Frequency (F)	Midpoint	F · Midpoint	x	x^2	$F \cdot x^2$
300–324	10	312	3,120	115.275	13,288.326	132,883.26
275–299	25	287	7,175	90.275	8,149.576	203,739.40
250–274	69	262	18,078	65.275	4,260.826	293,996.99
225–249	146	237	34,602	40.275	1,622.076	236,823.10
200–224	247	212	52,364	15.275	233.326	57,631.52
175–199	206	187	38,522	−9.725	94.576	19,482.66
150–174	147	162	23,814	−34.725	1,205.826	177,256.42
125–149	104	137	14,248	−59.725	3,567.076	370,975.90
100–124	32	112	3,584	−84.725	7,178.326	229,706.43
75–99	14	87	1,218	−109.725	12,039.576	168,554.06

$$n = 1,000 \qquad \Sigma(F \cdot \text{midpoint}) = 196,725 \qquad \Sigma(F \cdot x^2) = 1,891,049.74$$

$$\overline{X} = \frac{196,725}{1,000} = 196.725$$

$$S^2 = \frac{\Sigma(F \cdot x^2)}{n-1} = \frac{1,891,049.74}{1,000 - 1} = \frac{1,891,049.74}{999} = 1,892.942$$

$$S = \sqrt{S^2} = \sqrt{\frac{\Sigma(F \cdot x^2)}{n-1}} = \sqrt{1,892.942} = 43.508$$

enable you to determine the extremes of the distribution. They indicate whether the scores are clustered close to the mean, as were the Cucamonga water polo team's, or spread out far from the mean, as were Buckaroo's. As standards, the variance and the standard deviation can be readily used to compare the variability of different distributions. For example, you could use them to compare the variability of a conformity study involving a heterogeneous sample of people with a separate study involving a sample of high-anxiety people.

The difference between the variance and the standard deviation is that the latter is the square root of the former. This difference is quite helpful when you are discussing the characteristics of various distributions because the standard deviation is in the same units as the original scores, whereas the variance is in squared units. For instance, suppose you were scouting out information to help you predict the outcome of the water polo match and someone told you that the variance of Buckaroo's scores was 41. This wouldn't help you much, especially in light of the fact that Buckaroo's scores range from 0 to 14. However, if you were told that the standard deviation was about six and a half compared to a standard deviation of close to one for Cucamonga, it would be easy to compare the two distributions, and you would almost certainly not bet on a 6-6 tie.

Finding the Variance and Standard Deviation of a Grouped Frequency Distribution

Before You Begin: Compute the mean of the grouped frequency distribution.

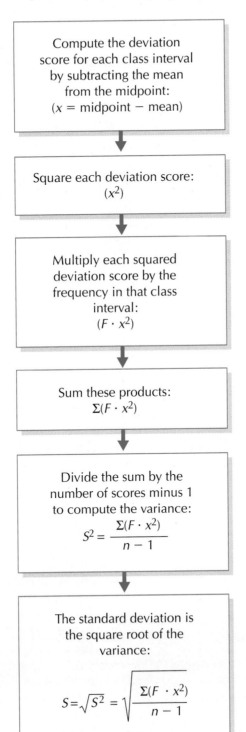

Compute the deviation score for each class interval by subtracting the mean from the midpoint:
$(x = \text{midpoint} - \text{mean})$

Square each deviation score:
(x^2)

Multiply each squared deviation score by the frequency in that class interval:
$(F \cdot x^2)$

Sum these products:
$\Sigma(F \cdot x^2)$

Divide the sum by the number of scores minus 1 to compute the variance:
$$S^2 = \frac{\Sigma(F \cdot x^2)}{n - 1}$$

The standard deviation is the square root of the variance:
$$S = \sqrt{S^2} = \sqrt{\frac{\Sigma(F \cdot x^2)}{n - 1}}$$

Concept Quiz

Recall the personal injury awards discussed in the previous Concept Quizzes. The grouped frequency distribution of these data is shown here.

Grouped Frequency Distribution of Monetary Award Data in Dollars

Apparent Limits	Frequency	Midpoint
90,000–99,000	2	94,500
80,000–89,000	5	84,500
70,000–79,000	5	74,500
60,000–69,000	10	64,500
50,000–59,000	12	54,500
40,000–49,000	16	44,500
30,000–39,000	20	34,500
20,000–29,000	25	24,500
10,000–19,000	25	14,500

1. Calculating estimates of variance and standard deviation from a grouped frequency distribution is similar to computing the estimated _____ from a grouped frequency distribution.

2. The best single score used to represent each class interval in the grouped frequency distribution is the _____, and it is used to calculate variance and standard deviation.

3. To calculate the variance from the grouped frequency distribution of monetary award, we first must compute the deviation score of each interval by subtracting the _____ from the midpoint of each class interval. The deviation score for the class interval 60,000–69,000 is _____.

4. After calculating the deviation scores, _____ each score and multiply it by the _____ in that interval.

5. The final step in calculating the variance is _____ the products of deviation scores times the frequency of the class intervals and dividing by _____.

Answers

1. mean
2. midpoint

3. mean ($38,833.33);
   $25,666.67

4. square; frequency
5. summing; $n - 1$

Summary

This chapter has focused on the measures of variation: the range, the average mean deviation, the variance, and the standard deviation. The range is simply the difference between the highest and lowest scores. Although it is easily computed, the range can be overly influenced by extreme scores.

The computation of the other measures of variation begins with the calculation of deviation scores. The variance and standard deviation are the most widely used measures of variability.

The variance is computed by squaring each deviation score, adding up all the squared deviations, and then dividing that sum by $n - 1$. The standard deviation is the square root of the variance. The major advantage of the standard deviation over the variance is that the standard deviation is in the same units as the original scores.

It is also possible to compute the variance and standard deviation from a grouped frequency distribution.

Key Terms

measures of variability
range
average mean
  deviation

deviation scores
variance

standard deviation

Formulas

Range = high score − low score   (5.1)

$$\text{Average mean deviation } (AMD) = \frac{\Sigma(X - \overline{X})}{n} = \frac{\Sigma x}{n} \qquad (5.2)$$

Deviation Formulas

$$\text{Variance of a population} = \sigma^2 = \frac{\Sigma(X - \mu)^2}{N} = \frac{\Sigma x^2}{N} \qquad (5.3)$$

$$\text{Variance of a sample} = S^2 = \frac{\Sigma(X - \overline{X})^2}{n - 1} = \frac{\Sigma x^2}{n - 1} \qquad (5.4)$$

$$\sigma = \sqrt{\frac{\Sigma(X - \mu)^2}{N}} = \sqrt{\frac{\Sigma x^2}{N}} \quad \text{or} \quad \sigma = \sqrt{\sigma^2} \qquad (5.5)$$

$$S = \sqrt{\frac{\Sigma(X - \overline{X})^2}{n - 1}} = \sqrt{\frac{\Sigma x^2}{n - 1}} \quad \text{or} \quad S = \sqrt{S^2} \qquad (5.6)$$

Computational Formulas

$$\text{Variance} = S^2 = \frac{\Sigma X^2 - \dfrac{(\Sigma X)^2}{n}}{n - 1} \qquad (5.7)$$

$$\text{Standard deviation} = S = \sqrt{\frac{\Sigma X^2 - \dfrac{(\Sigma X)^2}{n}}{n - 1}} \qquad (5.8)$$

Grouped Frequency Distributions

$$S^2 = \frac{\Sigma(F \cdot x^2)}{n - 1} \qquad (5.9)$$

$$S = \sqrt{S^2} = \sqrt{\frac{\Sigma(F \cdot x^2)}{n - 1}} \qquad (5.10)$$

Problems

1. Find the mean, the variance, and the standard deviation of the following IQ scores:

120	134	74	79	98	88
124	129	106	143	106	92
134	119	111	76	128	96
129	97	85	89	100	92

2. Find the mean, the variance, and the standard deviation of the following welding aptitude test scores:

23	25	27	22	35	45
29	26	33	34	25	27
25	29	33			

3. Find the mean, the variance, and the standard deviation of the following sample of the number of items answered correctly on a memory test:

49	46	43	40	38	37
48	45	43	39	38	37
48	44	42	38	38	36

47	44	41	38	37	34
46	43	41	38	37	33

4. Find the mean, the variance, and the standard deviation of the following sample of the annual salaries of 15 college professors:

55,000	50,000	40,000	30,000	25,000
54,000	49,000	38,000	29,000	24,000
52,000	49,000	33,000	27,000	22,000

5. These 11 scores are the result of a simple reaction time experiment (in milliseconds). Compute the mean, the variance, and the standard deviation.

240	356	277	835	277	354
456	789	923	235	456	

6. The following data represent the number of times that 15 patients of a psychoanalyst used the defense mechanism of regression over the last year of therapy. Compute the mean, the variance, and the standard deviation.

23	7	11	21	6
6	17	45	23	67
25	22	11	56	6

7. A cognitive psychologist interested in short-term working memory has measured the capacity of the short-term memory for 18 students. Compute the mean, the variance, and the standard deviation.

9	3	5	6	7	7	7	6	8
9	10	13	5	6	4	7	7	7

8. A neuropsychologist has been studying the density of neurons in a structure called the hippocampus in the brain of the rat and has found the density of neurons vary from rat to rat. The following data represent the numbers of neurons found in equal-sized tissue samples from the brains of 13 rats. Compute the mean, the variance, and the standard deviation.

88	93	65	77	77	106	123
139	142	190	97	143	88	

9. A drug rehabilitation center has kept records of the number of days that 20 former patients have remained drug free. Compute the mean, the variance, and the standard deviation.

21	35	78	90	78	121	88	17	19	123
45	45	67	123	72	89	78	122	180	87

10. As the pressure to publish increases at colleges and universities, many psychologists meet this pressure by working with coauthors on more and more papers. The following scores are the numbers of authors for all research reports published in the journal *Psychological Science* for the year 1990. Compute the mean, the variance, and the standard deviation.

3	4	2	3	1
2	4	5	4	3
3	2	4	3	1
5	2	1	1	
4	2	5	2	

11. The work performance ratings for 18 employees of a small business are listed here. Compute the mean, the variance, and the standard deviation.

2	4	5	5	6	6	6	6	6
6	7	7	8	9	9	9	9	10

12. A psychologist studying the sensation of touch uses a vibrator to stimulate the nerve endings in the fingers of 11 participants. Because the rate of vibration can be changed, she is able to find the number of vibrations per second to which each participant is most sensitive. Compute the mean, the variance, and the standard deviation.

234	254	266	250	231	245
300	222	250	245	231	

13. Compute the mean, the variance, and the standard deviation of the frequency distribution of the following IQ scores.

Apparent Limits	Frequency	Cumulative Frequency	Midpoint
150–159	3	173	154.5
140–149	5	170	144.5
130–139	9	165	134.5
120–129	18	156	124.5
110–119	26	138	114.5
100–109	36	112	104.5
90–99	34	76	94.5
80–89	23	42	84.5
70–79	13	19	74.5
60–69	5	6	64.5
50–59	1	1	55.5

14. Compute the mean, the variance, and the standard deviation of the group frequency distribution of the following welding aptitude test scores.

Apparent Limits	Frequency	Cumulative Frequency	Midpoint
45–47	3	88	46
42–44	5	85	43
39–41	10	80	40
36–38	14	70	37
33–35	22	56	34
30–32	15	34	31
27–29	10	19	28
24–26	7	9	25
21–23	1	2	22
18–20	1	1	19

15. Compute the mean, the variance, and standard deviation of the following grouped frequency distribution of the numbers of items answered correctly on a memory test.

Apparent Limits	Frequency
48–49	2
46–47	4
44–45	5
42–43	9
40–41	13
38–39	11
36–37	8
34–35	3
32–33	2
30–31	1

16. Compute the mean, the variance, and the standard deviation of the following grouped frequency distribution of student rankings of student services at a small college.

Apparent Limits	Frequency
90–99	10
80–89	16
70–79	28
60–69	34
50–59	49
40–49	25
30–39	39
20–29	32
10–19	11
0–9	6

17. Compute the mean, the variance, and the standard deviation of the following grouped frequency distribution of professors' annual salaries (in dollars):

Apparent Limits	Frequency
56,000–59,999	2
52,000–55,999	5
48,000–51,999	11
44,000–47,999	14
40,000–43,999	27
36,000–39,999	35
32,000–35,999	29
28,000–31,999	18
24,000–27,999	14
20,000–23,999	6

18. The midterm exam scores for 500 statistics students at a major university are shown here in a grouped frequency distribution. Compute the mean, the variance, and the standard deviation.

Apparent Limits	Frequency
95–99	6
90–94	9
85–89	55
80–84	67
75–79	189
70–74	47
65–69	29
60–64	22
55–59	21
50–54	22
45–49	13
40–44	9
35–39	7
30–34	3
25–29	1

19. The following grouped frequency distribution summarizes the numbers of errors made by 294 new student drivers in their first attempt at a driving simulation test. Compute the mean, the variance, and the standard deviation.

Apparent Limits	Frequency
70–76	12
63–69	23
56–62	24
49–55	43
42–48	56
35–41	54
28–34	44
21–27	23
14–20	12
7–13	3

20. The chairs of 117 psychology departments in the United States were asked how many students were currently employed by their departments as undergraduate research assistants. A grouped frequency distribution of the data is given here. Compute the mean, the variance, and the standard deviation.

Apparent Limits	Frequency
22–23	1
20–21	3
18–19	3
16–17	4
14–15	4
12–13	6
10–11	8
8–9	13
6–7	14
4–5	17
2–3	20
0–1	24

Problems From the Literature

The following problems refer to actual results from research studies that are cited at the end of the chapter. However, the data used to generate the problem sets are hypothetical.

Sometimes college students dislike group projects, especially when they believe the grading is not fair. This may hinder some students from enrolling in courses requiring group work. Hoffman and Rogelberg (2001) examined this issue and randomly assigned students to evaluate 1 of 12 versions of a hypothetical college syllabus from a course that required group projects. They found that students reported the highest intentions to enroll in courses and had the most positive perceptions of the grading procedure when both individual and group performance in the group project were evaluated. Suppose students were asked to evaluate two course syllabi at their college. One course graded group projects using the preferred grading method found in Hoffman and Rogelberg's study, and the other course did not. The evaluations of syllabi were made on a 1 (poor syllabus) to 7 (excellent syllabus) scale. Use the following data to solve Problems 21–25.

Course 1: Preferred Grading Method

3	5	4	6	7	1	4	6	6	5
2	7	4	5	1	6	7	5	4	7
4	6	2	7	3	3	6	5	7	7

Course 2: Nonpreferred Grading Method

1	3	2	5	6	3	4	4	6	1
4	5	3	4	1	1	1	2	4	5
4	5	6	4	3	3	3	5	4	2

21. What is the mean evaluation of the course syllabus for each course?

22. Compute the range of the evaluation scores for each course.

23. Compute the variance of the evaluation scores for each course.

24. Compute the standard deviation of evaluation scores for each course.

25. Evaluate the mean evaluation score relative to the size of the standard deviation.

In close relationships, people may be biased in their perceptions of each other. They may think their partner sees the world as they do. This may be because they assume their partners are similar to them. Researchers Kenny and Acitelli (2001) examined these issues, among others, in their study of a sample of heterosexual dating and married couples. Participants answered many questions, including those relating to feelings of closeness, feelings of caring, enjoyment of sex, and job satisfaction. Among their findings, the researchers discovered evidence for bias particularly when the topic was related to the relationship. Suppose another researcher decides to study perceived similarity among intimate heterosexual couples and collects evaluations of the partners' similarity using a similarity scale. Higher scores indicate more perceived similarity. Use the following data to solve Problems 26–30.

22	31	34	28	47	36	9	18	15
16	25	43	41	39	35	48	30	44

26. What is the mean of the scores?

27. Compute the range of the scores.

28. Compute the variance of the scores.

29. Compute the standard deviation of the scores.

30. Evaluate the mean relative to the size of the standard deviation of the scores.

Recall Benjamin and Bjork's (2000) study discussed in the Problems of Chapter 4. These researchers conducted several experiments examining the effect of recognition time pressure on learning new words using either rote or elaborative rehearsal. They found that time pressure during recognition decreased the accessibility to words learned via elaborative rehearsal compared to those learned via rote rehearsal. The frequency distribution from another researcher's similar study is shown here. Participants learned 35 new words. The total numbers of words recognized under time pressure were measured. Use the frequency data to solve Problems 31 and 32.

31. Find the estimated mean from the grouped frequency data.

32. Use the estimated mean to calculate the estimation of variance from the grouped frequency.

Frequency Distribution of Word Recognition Data

Apparent Limits	Frequency
22–23	18
20–21	4
18–19	3
16–17	6
14–15	5
12–13	5
10–11	5
8–9	5
6–7	7
4–5	6
2–3	7

References

Benjamin, A. S., & Bjork, R. A. (2000). On the relationship between recognition speed and accuracy for words rehearsed via rote versus elaborative rehearsal. *Journal of Experimental Psychology: Learning, Memory, and Cognition, 26,* 638–648.

Buskist, W., & Morgan, D. (1988). Method and theory in the study of human competition. In G. Davey & C. Cullen (Eds.), *Human operant conditioning and behavior modification* (pp. 167–195). New York: Wiley.

Hoffman, J. R., & Rogelberg, S. G. (2001). All together now? College students' preferred project group grading procedures. *Group Dynamics: Theory, Research, and Practice, 5,* 33–40.

Kenny, D., & Acitelli, L. K. (2001). Accuracy and bias in the perception of the partner in a close relationship. *Journal of Personality and Social Psychology, 80,* 439–448.

Marti, M. W., & Wissler, R. L. (2000). Be careful what you ask for. The effect of anchors on personal injury damage awards. *Journal of Experimental Psychology: Applied, 6,* 91–103.

6

Scaled Scores and Standard Scores: How to Change Apples Into Oranges

- Scaled Scores
  - *Adding or Subtracting a Constant: No Change in Variability*
  - *Multiplying or Dividing by a Constant: A Concurrent Change in Mean and Standard Deviation*
- Standard Scores (*z* Scores)
  - VISUAL SUMMARY: Converting *X* to *z*
- Summary
- Key Terms
- Formulas
- Problems
  - *Problems From the Literature*
- References

One of the major uses of statistics is for making comparisons. Indeed, we are constantly making comparisons. Employees compare their salaries to coworkers' salaries to see whether they are being paid fairly. Students compare their exam grades to other students' to see how they are doing in their classes. Parents compare the age their child first said "Momma" to the age at which other babies accomplished this common but victorious feat.

The preceding comparisons are simple because similar things are being compared. In a figurative sense, apples are being compared to apples. However, what if the things you want to compare are dissimilar? Remember back to your elementary school days. Your arithmetic teachers told you it is quite all right to add, subtract, or in some way compare apples to apples; but woe to the pupil who attempts to compare apples to oranges. If you have to work with different fractions or different scales, you must find a common denominator. Finding a common denominator is easy when you are comparing fractions, but it is much more difficult when you are comparing an IQ test score to an SAT test score. You can easily convert thirds to twelfths and fourths to twelfths and then make the comparison. However, it is a little different when you try to convert IQ test scores to the same thing as SAT test scores. What would you use as a common denominator, IQSAT scores? It seems impossible. Well, in the world of statistics, such conversions are totally possible. In this chapter, first you'll walk through the rationale, and then through the procedures, for changing distributions in such a way that they can be compared with other previously dissimilar distributions.

Scaled Scores

Before looking at how to convert different scales to a common denominator, first you will see how to change the mean and standard deviation of a distribution. Suppose that the professor for your advanced personality course, Dr. Easyone, is subpoenaed to testify about the personality of a defendant in a murder trial and she is replaced for 2 weeks by Dr. Ardtest. At the end of the 2 weeks, you are tested on the material covered by Dr. Ardtest, and the entire class does very poorly. The scores on this exam for the five students in your class are listed in Table 6.1. The mean is 35 out of 100, which is 45 points below the typical mean for this class. The standard deviation is 7.906, which is exactly the same as that for Dr. Easyone's tests. Because Dr. Easyone always grades on a straight percentage ($90 = A$, $80 = B$, etc.), this one test is likely to cause some of the students to fail the course, or at least fall a couple of grade points when this score is combined with the tests given earlier in the semester. Faced with this situation, what do you do if you are a student in this class?

> **Question:** Couldn't the students just try to convince the professor to change her grading scale and give more A's?

Yes, that's possible. You would need to get her to adjust the scores so that you will not be penalized for this overly difficult and unfair test. She can do this by converting the test scores to **scaled scores.** These are scores that are adjusted via

Table 6.1   Test Scores

Student	X	x	x^2
Matt	45	10	100
Judy	40	5	25
Karen	35	0	0
Dennis	30	-5	25
Oscar	25	-10	100

$$\Sigma X = 175 \qquad\qquad \Sigma x^2 = 250$$

$$\overline{X} = 35$$

$$S^2 = \frac{250}{5 - 1} = 62.5$$

$$S = \sqrt{62.5} = 7.906$$

some type of scale, through applying (adding, subtracting, multiplying, or dividing) the same constant to all the scores in the distribution. Be aware that when raw scores are transformed to scaled scores, the distribution is invariably modified in some way. The mean, the variance, and the standard deviation may change depending on how the scores are modified. First you will look at the effect of adding or subtracting a constant to each score in the distribution.

Adding or Subtracting a Constant: No Change in Variability

If a constant is added to each score in any distribution, in effect a new distribution based on the original one is created. Because the scores on Dr. Ardtest's exam were 45 points below the typical mean for this class, Dr. Easyone could just add 45 points to each student's test score to make up the difference. If she does this, it will result in the distribution shown in Table 6.2. The new distribution has a new mean that is 45 points higher than in the original distribution; thus, this new mean is increased by exactly the same number of points as the constant that was added to each score. The variance and the standard deviation have not changed.

Question: Why does the mean change and not the standard deviation?

It is easy to see that adding a constant to each score will raise the value of each score; therefore, the sum of the scores will be increased, as will the mean. However, adding the constant does not affect the spread of the scores. The highest score is still 20 points higher than the lowest score. The range has not changed.

Table 6.2 Test Scores With 45 Points Added to Each Score

Student	$X_{original}$	$(X_{original} + 45)$ X_{new}	x_{new}	x^2_{new}
Matt	45	90	10	100
Judy	40	85	5	25
Karen	35	80	0	0
Dennis	30	75	−5	25
Oscar	25	70	−10	100

$$\Sigma X_{original} = 175 \qquad \Sigma X_{new} = 400 \qquad \Sigma x^2 = 250$$

$$\bar{X}_{original} = 35 \qquad \bar{X}_{new} = \frac{400}{5} = 80$$

$$S^2_{original} = \frac{250}{5-1} = 62.5 \qquad S^2_{new} = \frac{250}{5-1} = 62.5$$

$$S_{original} = \sqrt{62.5} = 7.906 \qquad S_{new} = \sqrt{62.5} = 7.906$$

Because the general spread of all the scores is not affected by adding a constant to each score, this simple transformation does not change the variance or the standard deviation.

Question: Is the same thing true when you subtract a constant from each score?

Yes. When you subtract a constant from each score, you again change the mean without affecting the variance or the standard deviation. Table 6.3 shows the scores for 25 college students on a test measuring their need for affiliation. A high score (25) indicates that the student has personality traits associated with people who like to be with other people, whereas a low score (2) indicates that the student is a loner. The mean affiliation score for this group of college students is 15. Rather than subtract a random constant from each of these scores, you can subtract 15, the mean. It is clear from an inspection of Table 6.3 that when 15 is subtracted from each score, the mean decreases by the same amount, whereas the variance and the standard deviation remain the same. To summarize, *if you add or subtract a constant from each score in the distribution, the mean changes by the amount that is added or subtracted, and the variance and the standard deviation remain the same.* Stated more succinctly:

$$\overline{X}_{new} = \overline{X}_{original} \pm constant \tag{6.1}$$

and

$$S_{new} = S_{original} \tag{6.2}$$

Multiplying or Dividing by a Constant: A Concurrent Change in Mean and Standard Deviation

Question: If each score is multiplied by the same number—say, 2— what happens to the mean and standard deviation?

If each score is doubled, the sum of the scores will of course double, resulting in a change in the mean. Multiplying each score by 2 will also change the spread of the scores, thus affecting the variance and the standard deviation. Table 6.4 shows what happens when you double each score in the sample of five test scores. If you compare both the original mean and standard deviation to the new mean and standard deviation, it is evident that the new mean is twice the original mean and the new standard deviation is twice the original standard deviation. The variance also changes, but it is multiplied by the square of the constant rather than only the constant itself.

Table 6.5 shows the effect of dividing each score in the distribution by a constant. In Table 6.5, which uses the same scores as Table 6.3, each original score is divided by the original standard deviation. This results in a new mean that equals

Table 6.3   Need for Affiliation Scores for 25 Students Minus a Constant

$X_{original}$	$(X_{original} - \overline{X}_{original})$ X_{new}	x_{new}	x^2_{new}
7	−8	−8	64
10	−5	−5	25
25	10	10	100
21	6	6	36
9	−6	−6	36
2	−13	−13	169
13	−2	−2	4
25	10	10	100
15	0	0	0
17	2	2	4
15	0	0	0
11	−4	−4	16
7	−8	−8	64
19	4	4	16
23	8	8	64
8	−7	−7	49
17	2	2	4
17	2	2	4
22	7	7	49
21	6	6	36
12	−3	−3	9
24	9	9	81
10	−5	−5	25
10	−5	−5	25
15	0	0	0

$\Sigma X_{original} = 375$ $\Sigma X_{new} = 0$ $\Sigma x^2 = 980$

$\overline{X}_{original} = 15$ $\overline{X}_{new} = \dfrac{0}{25} = 0$

$S^2_{original} = \dfrac{980}{25-1} = 40.833$ $S^2_{new} = \dfrac{980}{25-1} = 40.833$

$S_{original} = \sqrt{40.833} = 6.390$ $S_{new} = \sqrt{40.833} = 6.390$

Table 6.4   Test Scores Multiplied by 2

Student	$X_{original}$	$(X_{original} \cdot 2)$ X_{new}	x_{new}	x^2_{new}
Matt	45	90	20	400
Judy	40	80	10	100
Karen	35	70	0	0
Dennis	30	60	-10	100
Oscar	25	50	-20	400

$$\Sigma X_{original} = 175 \qquad \Sigma X_{new} = 350 \qquad \Sigma x^2 = 1,000$$

$$\overline{X}_{original} = 35 \qquad \overline{X}_{new} = \frac{350}{5} = 70$$

$$S^2_{original} = \frac{250}{5-1} = 62.5 \qquad S^2_{new} = \frac{1,000}{5-1} = 250$$

$$S_{original} = \sqrt{62.5} = 7.906 \qquad S_{new} = \sqrt{250} = 15.811$$

the original mean divided by the original standard deviation and a new standard deviation that equals the original standard deviation divided by itself, 1. From these two examples, it is easy to see that if you multiply or divide each score in the distribution by the same constant, then

$$\overline{X}_{new} = \overline{X}_{original} \times \text{ or } \div \text{ constant} \tag{6.3}$$

and

$$S_{new} = S_{original} \times \text{ or } \div \text{ constant} \tag{6.4}$$

Table 6.5   Need for Affiliation Scores Divided by a Constant

$X_{original}$	$(X_{original} \div \overline{X}_{original})$ X_{new}	x_{new}	x^2_{new}
7	1.095	−1.252	1.568
10	1.565	−0.782	0.162
25	3.912	1.565	2.449
21	3.286	0.939	0.882
9	1.408	−0.939	0.882
2	0.313	−2.034	4.137
13	2.034	−0.313	0.098
25	3.912	1.565	2.449
15	2.347	0.000	0.000
17	2.660	0.313	0.098
15	2.347	0.000	0.000
11	1.721	−0.626	0.392
7	1.095	−1.252	1.568
19	2.973	0.626	0.392
23	3.599	1.252	1.568
8	1.252	−1.095	1.199
17	2.660	0.313	0.098
17	2.660	0.313	0.098
22	3.443	1.096	1.201
21	3.286	0.939	0.882
12	1.878	−0.469	0.220
24	3.756	1.409	1.985
10	1.565	−0.782	0.612
10	1.565	−0.782	0.612
15	2.347	0.000	0.000

$\Sigma X_{original} = 375$ $\Sigma X_{new} = 58.679$ $\Sigma x^2 = 24.002$

$\overline{X}_{original} = 15$ $\overline{X}_{new} = \dfrac{58.679}{25} = 2.347$

$S^2_{original} = \dfrac{980}{25 - 1} = 40.833$ $S^2_{new} = \dfrac{24.002}{25 - 1} = 1.000$

$S_{original} = \sqrt{40.833} = 6.390$ $S_{new} = \sqrt{1} = 1$

Concept Quiz

Poole and Lindsay (2001) investigated factors such as parental misinformation that might impact memory and the accuracy of information provided by young children. Young children, ranging from 3 to 8 years old, participated in a science fair where they listened to their parents read a story that described experienced and nonexperienced events. Later, in several interviews, the children discussed and answered questions about their science fair experience. The children often described false events, and the accuracy of their reports declined when they were asked direct questions. Suppose these researchers suspected the stories parents read were especially difficult for the 3-year-olds. Thus, it might be a good idea to adjust the children's scores on the direct questions before comparing them to the scores of older children.

1. When you add, subtract, multiply, or divide each score in the distribution by the same constant, you create a new distribution of _____ scores.

2. If you added 10 points to the accuracy score of each child in the distribution of scores for the 3-year-olds, you would create a new mean equal to the old mean _____ and a new standard deviation equal to _____ standard deviation.

3. Instead of adding points to each of the 3-year-old's accuracy scores, suppose you decide to subtract 10 points from the accuracy score of each child in the distribution of scores for the 8-year-olds. What effect would subtracting a constant have on the mean and standard deviation of the distribution of scores for the older children?

4. If you create a new distribution by dividing all the scores in the distribution by 3, the mean of this new distribution is equal to the old mean _____ and the new standard deviation equal to the old standard deviation _____.

5. Suppose the mean of the 8-year-olds is 24 with a standard deviation of 4. If you divide all the scores in the distribution by 2, the new distribution would have a new mean of _____ and a new standard deviation of _____.

6. When each score is multiplied or divided by a constant, what is the effect on the mean and standard deviation?

Answers

1. scaled
2. plus 10; the old
3. It reduces the mean of the distribution by the amount subtracted

   from each score, but the standard deviation stays the same.
4. divided by three; divided by three

5. 12; 2
6. It either multiplies or divides both the mean and standard deviation by the constant.

Standard Scores (z Scores)

If Dr. Ardtest's exam had produced a distribution similar to Dr. Easyone's distribution with the same mean and standard deviation, Dr. Ardtest's scores could be considered comparable to the scores on the other tests. Unfortunately, when you want to compare two distributions, the means and standard deviations are often *not* the same. Fortunately, it is possible to create scaled scores for each distribution that do have the same mean and standard deviation. These are called **standard scores** or **z scores.** *z* scores make it possible to compare different distributions like apples and oranges, SAT scores and ACT scores, dollars and euros by converting the original distributions to yet another distribution. It is, in effect, converting apples and oranges into pears, or *z* scores. *z* scores are standard, uniform values to which any raw-score value can be converted. The **z-score distribution** has a mean of 0 and a standard deviation of 1. Any distribution, regardless of its original mean and standard deviation, can be converted to the *z*-score distribution through a simple transformation of the scores using the rules given in Formulas 6.1–6.4.

To transform a distribution of scores into *z* scores, the first step is to create a new distribution with a mean of 0. Take a look at Formula 6.1. It states that the new mean is equal to the original mean plus or minus the constant used to transform the scores. Thus, if the original mean was 35, what value must be subtracted for the new mean to equal 0? Of course: 35, the original mean. And because you must subtract 35 from the mean, you must also subtract 35 from each score in the distribution. If you think of *z* as representing "zero," it will remind you that you must bring the mean down to 0 by subtracting the mean from each score in the distribution.

If Dr. Easyone were to devise a *z*-score distribution for the low test scores, she would first subtract the original mean, 35, from each score and obtain the distribution listed in Table 6.6.

Table 6.6   Test Scores With 35 Points Subtracted

Student	$X_{original}$	$(X_{original} \cdot 2)$ X_{new}	x_{new}	x^2_{new}
Matt	45	10	10	100
Judy	40	5	5	25
Karen	35	0	0	0
Dennis	30	− 5	−5	25
Oscar	25	−10	−10	100

$$\Sigma X_{original} = 175 \qquad \Sigma X_{new} = 0 \qquad \Sigma x^2_{new} = 250$$

$$\overline{X}_{original} = 35 \qquad \overline{X}_{new} = \frac{0}{5} = 0$$

$$S^2_{original} = \frac{250}{5 - 1} = 62.5 \qquad S^2_{new} = \frac{250}{5 - 1} = 62.5$$

$$S_{original} = \sqrt{62.5} = 7.906 \qquad S_{new} = \sqrt{62.5} = 7.906$$

To review: A *z*-score distribution has a mean of 0 and a standard deviation of 1. You have just learned how to transform a group of scores so that their mean is 0; now you will learn how to transform their standard deviation so that it equals 1. Recall from Formula 6.4 that the new standard deviation equals the original standard deviation multiplied or divided by a constant. The second step in creating *z* scores requires that you change the spread of the scores by multiplying or dividing each score by a constant such that the standard deviation of the resulting scores equals 1. What constant do you use? If the original standard deviation is 7.906, by what number do you divide it to make 1? The answer is: You divide it by itself. Thus, *subtracting the original mean from each score in the distribution, then dividing each of those resulting scores by the original standard deviation, produces z scores.* The formula using the sample mean and sample standard deviation is

$$z = \frac{X - \overline{X}}{S} \qquad (6.5)$$

The formula for *z* using the population mean and the population standard deviation is

$$z = \frac{X - \mu}{\sigma} \qquad (6.6)$$

Although *z* scores can be computed using the population mean and population standard deviation, these are often not available. Thus, the mean and the standard deviation of the *sample* are most commonly used. (If you were fortunate enough to have the population values, you would definitely use them because your computations would be more accurate.) In the following table, Dr. Ardtest's scores have been converted to *z* scores by using Formula 6.5.

Student	X	z
Matt	45	1.265
Judy	40	0.623
Karen	35	0.000
Dennis	30	−0.623
Oscar	25	−1.265

To prove to you that these are true *z* scores and to illustrate that *z* scores do indeed have a mean of 0 and a standard deviation of 1, the mean and standard deviation for the preceding scores have been computed in Table 6.7.

Because all *z* scores are in the same units (actually *z* scores are all in standard deviation units), you now can appreciate that once a distribution has been converted to *z* scores, it can be compared to any other distribution that has also been converted to *z* scores. Thus, it really is possible to compare apples to oranges as long as you first convert them to *z* scores.

Table 6.7   Computation of the Mean and Standard Deviation of z Scores

Student	z	x_z	x_z^2
Matt	1.265	1.265	1.600
Judy	0.632	0.632	0.399
Karen	0.000	0.000	0.000
Dennis	−0.632	−0.632	0.399
Oscar	−1.265	−1.265	1.600

$$\Sigma z = 0.000 \qquad\qquad\qquad\qquad \Sigma x_z^2 = 3.998$$

$$\bar{z} = 0.000$$

$$S_z^2 = \frac{3.998}{5 - 1} = 1.000$$

$$S_z = \sqrt{1.000} = 1.000$$

VISUAL SUMMARY

Converting X to z

Before You Begin: Compute $\overline{X}$ and S.

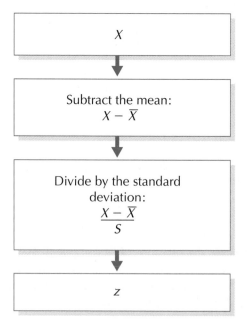

Question: It still isn't clear what a z score actually represents. What does a z score tell you?

The next chapter is dedicated to discussing the normal curve, and after reading that chapter you'll have a much clearer comprehension of the value of z scores. Basically, however, a z score tells you how many standard deviation units above or below the mean your original score lies. A z score of +2 means that the original score is two standard deviations above the original mean. A z score of −1 means that the original score is one standard deviation unit below the original mean. A z score of +0.27 means that the raw score is 27/100 of a standard deviation above the mean.

Here is an example to clarify this point. Suppose you want to compare the IQ scores of two people. This may seem simple until you realize that there are several types of IQ tests and the two people took different tests. Mark took the Stanford–Binet Intelligence Scale and scored 145, and Diana took the Wechsler Adult Intelligence Scale and scored 144. Mark's score was higher than Diana's, but if you assume that IQ tests actually do measure intelligence (and this is an extremely controversial subject right now), who is *really* more intelligent?

The way to answer this question is to find the mean and standard deviation of each test, convert each IQ score to a z score, and then determine who has the higher z score. Assume that Mark's test has a mean of 100 and a standard deviation of 16 points; the mean of Diana's test is 100 and the standard deviation is 15. Because these are standardized tests, the means and standard deviations are population values and Formula 6.6 can be used to compute the z scores needed for this comparison.

$$z_{Mark} = \frac{X - \mu}{\sigma} = \frac{145 - 100}{16} = \frac{45}{16} = 2.813$$

$$z_{Diana} = \frac{X - \mu}{\sigma} = \frac{144 - 100}{15} = \frac{44}{15} = 2.933$$

These calculations show that Diana has a slightly higher z score than Mark. Diana's IQ score was 2.933 standard deviations above the mean; Mark's IQ score was only 2.813 standard deviations above the mean. Both of these IQ scores are very high, but assuming that these IQ tests do measure intelligence, Diana's score on the Wechsler test indicates a slightly higher intelligence than Mark's score on the Stanford–Binet. Converting to z scores can allow you to compare apples to oranges.

Concept Quiz

Students often seem to feel anxiety to some degree when they begin a statistics course. Many researchers have studied math anxiety. For example, Zettle and Raines (2000) examined the relationship of math anxiety to trait and test anxiety among students who had identified themselves as math anxious. Students completed a number of anxiety measures, and the results demonstrated a significant relationship between math anxiety and both trait and test anxiety.

1. Suppose another researcher asked a different group of math students to complete anxiety questions different from those used in Zettle and Raines's study. If this researcher wanted to compare the anxiety scores of the two disparate distributions, he would first need to transform each distribution into _____ scores or _____ scores.

2. The *z* distribution has a mean of _____ and a standard deviation equal to _____.

3. To transform a score to a *z* score, _____ the original mean from the original score and then divide by the _____.

4. Once a distribution has been converted to *z* scores, it can be compared to any distribution that has also been _____.

5. If the mean of the distribution of anxiety scores is 6 and the standard deviation is 2, a raw score of 12 would be converted to a *z* score of
_____.

6. A *z* score of 2.0 indicates a raw score that is two standard deviation units _____ the mean and a *z* score of -2.0 indicates a raw score that is two standard deviation units _____ the mean.

Answers

1. standard; *z*
2. 0; 1
3. subtract; original standard deviation

4. converted to *z* scores
5. 3

6. above; below

Summary

It is possible to transform scores in several ways. The simplest is to merely add or subtract a constant from each score in the distribution, which causes the mean to change without affecting the variance or the standard deviation. It is also possible to multiply or divide each score by a constant, which results in a change in both the mean and standard deviation.

Knowing these rules of transformation, you can create a new distribution that has a mean of 0 and a standard deviation of 1. This new distribution is called a *z*-score distribution, and the scores that make up this distribution are known as standard scores or *z* scores. *z* scores are computed by subtracting the mean of the distribution from the original score and then dividing that result by the standard deviation.

Key Terms

scaled scores   *z* scores   *z*-score distribution
standard scores

Formulas

$$\overline{X}_{new} = \overline{X}_{original} \pm constant \tag{6.1}$$

$$S_{new} = S_{original} \tag{6.2}$$

$$\overline{X}_{new} = \overline{X}_{original} \times \text{ or } \div constant \tag{6.3}$$

$$S_{new} = S_{original} \times \text{ or } \div constant \tag{6.4}$$

$$z = \frac{X - \overline{X}}{S} \tag{6.5}$$

$$z = \frac{X - \mu}{\sigma} \tag{6.6}$$

Problems

Use the following information to solve Problems 1–18.

Suppose you were examining the lengths of positive interactions between siblings in various environments during a 3-hour period and you found that the mean length of time for a positive interaction was 100 minutes, with a standard deviation of 20 minutes.

Calculate the new mean and the new standard deviation after making each of the following changes.

1. Add 10 minutes to each score.

2. Add 20 minutes to each score.

3. Add 25 minutes to each score.

4. Add 200 minutes to each score.

5. Subtract 10 minutes from each score.

6. Subtract 100 minutes from each score.

7. Subtract 25 minutes from each score.

8. Subtract 33 minutes from each score.

9. Multiply each score in the old distribution by 7.

10. Multiply each score in the old distribution by 10.

11. Multiply each score in the old distribution by 5.

12. Multiply each score in the old distribution by 22.

13. Divide each score in the old distribution by 7.

14. Divide each score in the old distribution by 25.

15. Divide each score in the old distribution by 10.

16. Divide each score in the old distribution by 3.

17. What is the effect on the mean and the standard deviation if you divide each score by the standard deviation?

18. What is the effect on the mean and the standard deviation if you first subtract the mean from each score and then divide those resulting scores by the standard deviation?

19. In a duplication of Pavlov's classic conditioning experiment, the following amounts of saliva were obtained when dogs were presented with meat powder. Compute the mean and standard deviation for this distribution, and then convert all the scores to z scores.

Dog	Amount of Saliva (in milliliters)	z score
Spot	250	_____
Rover	240	_____
Blackie	280	_____
Ginger	190	_____
Gus	300	_____
Scruffy	200	_____
Digger	230	_____
Muffin	180	_____
Amber	160	_____
Tiger	280	_____

20. A psychiatrist who was particularly interested in the use of defense mechanisms recorded the numbers of defense mechanisms used by her clients during their sessions with her over a 1-month period. Find the mean and standard deviation for her distribution, and then convert the individual clients' scores to z scores.

Client	Number of Defense Mechanisms	z score
L. V.	0	_____
P. D.	3	_____
O. S.	6	_____
T. J.	7	_____
T. V.	11	_____
M. W.	18	_____
S. I.	21	_____
B. J.	26	_____
K. S.	28	_____
L. B.	30	_____

21. Given that the mean of a statistics test is 84 and the standard deviation of this test is 4, convert the following test scores to z scores.

94   97   88   84   80   77   74   76

22. Given that the mean number of secondary reinforcements each day in a psychiatric hospital token economy is 10 tokens and the standard deviation is 4.5 tokens, convert the following to z scores.

16 tokens	8 tokens	10 tokens
19 tokens	9 tokens	7 tokens

23. If the mean response time to a very complex visual display is 825 milliseconds (ms) with a standard deviation of 186 ms, convert the following response times to z scores.

700 ms	850 ms	975 ms
1,000 ms	623 ms	832 ms
1,200 ms	245 ms	469 ms

24. The following are key pecking rates for eight pigeons at the local psychology lab. Compute the mean and the standard deviation for the eight pigeons, and then convert each pigeon's rate to a z score.

Client	Number of Defense Mechanisms	z score
A	22	_____
B	23	_____
C	20	_____
D	24	_____
E	21	_____
F	21	_____
G	24	_____
H	25	_____

Problems From the Literature

Adolescents and young adults were surveyed in a study of risk judgments (Halpern-Felsher et al., 2001). Participants were asked to judge their risk of natural disasters, such as dying in an earthquake, being killed by lightening, and so on, and behavior-linked risks, such as the chance of being in a car accident if they drove under the influence of alcohol. It was found that when participants had personal experience in a natural disaster or behavior risk, they estimated their chance of experiencing a negative outcome from these risks in the future as less likely than those people who had not experienced a disaster. Thus, it seems that risk judgments are reflective of one's personal experience in these matters. Suppose that in a related study, health educators from two colleges asked smokers to estimate their chance of developing lung cancer on a scale of 0 (no chance I will get lung cancer) to 100 (I will get lung cancer). The mean estimate of risk at College One was 43.2 with a standard deviation of 11.7, and the mean estimate of risk at College Two was 57.1 with a standard deviation of 22.4. Use the data to solve Problems 25–29.

25. Calculate the new means and standard deviation of these distributions if you added 15 to each score. What is the effect on the means and standard deviations of these distributions?

26. Calculate the new means and standard deviations of these distributions if you divided each score by 5. What is the effect on the means and standard deviations?

27. Convert to z scores the following risk scores of students at College One.

College One

Student	Estimated Risk	z score
Puff	23	
Cough	31	
Gasp	33	
Smokie	27	
Flick	15	

28. Convert to z scores the following risk scores of students at College Two.

College Two

Student	Estimated Risk	z score
Choke	28	
Huffy	18	
Croaker	35	
Weeze	9	
Sneezy	41	

29. Suppose Flossy Mae, a participant in the College Two study, had an estimated risk score of 31 and her brother Billy Bob, a participant in the College One study, had an estimated risk score of 31. Compare their risk estimations.

Approximately 22–26% of the participants in the Halpern-Felsher et al. (2001) study of risk judgments reported one of the negative outcomes associated with drinking alcohol examined in the study. For example, one of the risk judgment scenarios asked participants to imagine being at a party for 3 hours and drinking six beers. Among the negative alcohol-related outcomes, participants were asked to estimate the likelihood (0–100%) of getting sick from the beer and throwing up. Suppose you conducted a study and asked students in two different classes to read this same scenario and estimate their chances of throwing up. Use the means and standard deviations shown here to solve Problems 30–34.

Class A | $\overline{X}$ = 39.9 and s = 17.1
Class B | $\overline{X}$ = 39.9 and s = 21.9

30. Calculate the new means and standard deviation of these distributions if you subtracted 8 from each score. What is the effect on the means and standard deviations of these distributions?

31. Calculate the new means and standard deviations of these distributions if you multiplied each score by 4. What is the effect on the means and standard deviations?

32. Convert the following scores to z scores.

Class A

Student	Estimated Risk (%)	z score
A. L.	29	
G. F.	41	
D. K.	67	
C. M.	10	
B. B.	3	

Class B

Student	Estimated Risk (%)	z score
L. A.	54	
T. Q.	25	
X. A.	10	
C. D.	62	
M. V.	0	

33. Suppose two students, one in class A and the other in class B, estimated their risk of getting sick and throwing up at 45%. Based on the two different distributions of scores, which student had a lower risk estimation?

34. Explain why it is necessary to convert raw scores to standard scores if you want to compare distributions with the same means but different standard deviations.

References

Halpern-Felsher, B. L., Millstein, S. G., Ellen, J. M., Adler, N. E., Tschann, J. M., & Biehl, M. (2001). The role of behavioral experience in judging risks. *Health Psychology, 20,* 120–126.

Poole, D. A., & Lindsay, D. S. (2001). Children's eyewitness reports after exposure to misinformation from parents. *Journal of Experimental Psychology: Applied, 7,* 27–50.

Zettle, R. D., & Raines, S. J. (2000). The relationship of trait and test anxiety with mathematics anxiety. *College Student Journal, 34,* 246–258.

7

The Normal Curve

- Characteristics of the Normal Curve
- Finding Proportions and Percentages
  Using Table Z: Finding Areas Under the Normal Curve
  Area Above: Finding Proportions Above Positive and Negative z Scores
  Area Below: Finding Proportions Below Positive and Negative z Scores

VISUAL SUMMARY: Finding Areas Under the Normal Curve
Area Between: Finding Proportions Lying Between Two z Scores
VISUAL SUMMARY: Finding the Area Between Two z Scores
- Finding Percentiles
  Using Table P: Finding Distinct Scores

VISUAL SUMMARY: Finding Percentiles
- Summary
- Key Terms
- Formulas
- Problems
  Problems From the Literature
- References

I n 1884, Mark Twain observed:

We should be careful to get out of an experience only the wisdom that is in it—and stop there, lest we be like the cat that sits down on a hot stove lid. She will never sit down on a hot stove lid again—and that is well; but also she will never sit down on a cold one any more.

Mark Twain earned acclaim through his exceptional ability to fathom human and, in this case, animal behavior and then write about it in a way that prompts us to laugh at our shortcomings and ponder our antics. Observations similar to Mark Twain's about the cat learning not to sit on hot stove lids have been scientifically explored in psychological research on classical conditioning, which was begun about 100 years ago by Ivan Pavlov. Any stimulus, such as heat, that causes a reflex response can be paired with a neutral stimulus, such as a stove lid, so that eventually the neutral stimulus will cause the response. In this way, the cat is conditioned—it learns—to avoid hot stove lids.

Mark Twain notes not only the conditioning but also an interesting phenomenon associated with classical conditioning. He admonishes us to beware of our tendency to generalize. Once a person or an animal has learned a conditioned response to a conditioned stimulus, stimuli similar to the conditioned stimulus may also cause that same response. Through generalization, the cat learns to avoid not only hot stove lids but cold stove lids as well. Likewise, as much as Mark Twain warned against it, through generalization some of us learn to stereotype some people and to fear all things in a group even though only a few are dangerous. We learn to fear all snakes, not only those with rattles on their tails, and we react to all bells as if they are attached to phones or doors that need to be answered.

Speaking of bells, Ivan Pavlov first used bells and then tones to study conditioning. While conditioning his dogs to salivate to a specific tone—for example, a tone with a pitch of 1,000 cycles per second—he noticed that he could also cause salivation in the dogs if he used a slightly lower pitch, such as 900 cycles per second, or a slightly higher pitch, such as 1,100 cycles per second. As a matter of fact, the amount of salivation was directly related to the similarity between the tone presented and the original tone. The more closely the tone resembled the original tone, the more the dogs salivated. When Pavlov graphed the amount of salivation on the Y axis and the tone on the X axis, he noticed a bell-shaped curve with its center at the original 1,000-cycle tone.

Typical of most generalization experiments, the results of Pavlov's experiments illustrate the **normal curve,** which is in essence a graphic picture of the bell-shaped normal distribution. In a **normal distribution,** most of the scores are clustered around the middle, around the mean/median/mode (as you recall, these measures are all equal in a normal distribution), with the frequency of the other scores gradually lessening on either side. When the normal distribution is graphed, it takes on the shape of a bell, with a large center hump where the highest frequency of scores is located. The curve gradually descends on either side and flattens out as it approaches either end, indicating that there are progressively fewer scores at the extremes. (See Figure 7.1 for examples of normal curves.) Much of the data collected in any scientific discipline—such as chemistry, biology, or psychology—tend to be normally distributed and can be described by the normal curve. For instance, if during Pavlov's experiment he had measured the activity level of each dog and graphed the numbers of times the dogs moved, he would have inevitably graphed a normal curve. A few dogs would have made a few movements, most of them would have made a moderate number of movements, and a few would have moved around a lot. Likewise, if he had measured the dogs' eating behavior by counting the number of bits of dog chow each dog consumed and then graphed these data, the resulting graph would probably have approximated a normal curve. When working with the normal curve, remember that real data can only approximate the normal curve because the perfect normal distribution exists in theory only.

Characteristics of the Normal Curve

The shape of the normal curve reflects the fact that most behavior is "normal," with the extremes of behavior being rare and found at either end of the curve. This is evident when graphing any behavioral variable, from scores on personality tests to

Figure 7.1
Examples of three normal curves: (a) the heights of male students in a psychological statistics class, (b) scores on the Stanford–Binet IQ scale, and (c) the ages at which children took their first steps at the midtown Child Care Center.

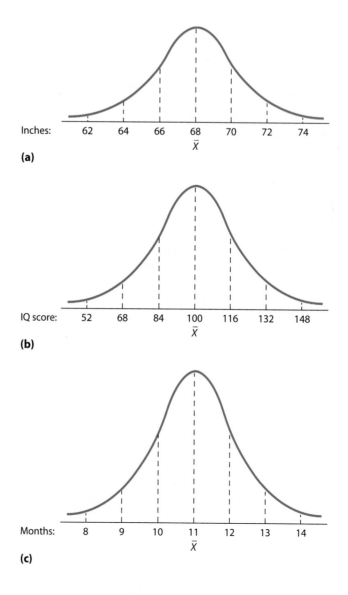

(a)

(b)

(c)

reaction times to numbers of nonsense words remembered in a memory task. For the most part, behavior tends to be normally distributed across most populations. Depending on the behavior being measured and the individual performances of the members of the population or sample, normal curves can assume various shapes with an endless variety of means and standard deviations, as illustrated in Figure 7.1. Nevertheless, all normal curves share some common characteristics:

1. The curve is bell-shaped and symmetrical.
2. The mean, median, and mode are all equal.

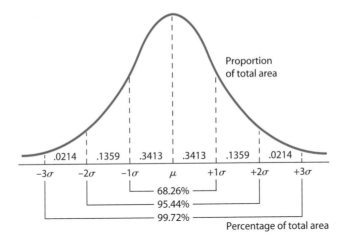

Figure 7.2
Areas under the
normal curve.

3. The highest frequency is in the middle of the curve.

4. The frequency gradually tapers off as the scores approach the ends of the curve.

5. The curve approaches, but never meets, the abscissa at both the high and low ends.

The normal curve can be envisioned as a picture of the proportion of the total number of scores lying under the curve. The entire area under the curve is equal to 1. Imagine a line drawn from the precise center at the top of the curve straight down to the horizontal axis. Exactly .50 (50%) of the total number of scores in the distribution lie above or to the right of this line, and the other .50 lie below or to the left of the line. As you can see in Figure 7.2, 34.13% of the scores (a little more than one third) can be found from the mean to the point that is one standard deviation *above* the mean ($+1\sigma$). The same amount, 34.13%, can be found from the mean to one standard deviation unit *below* the mean (-1σ), so it follows that 68.26% of the scores (a little more than two thirds) lie between -1σ and $+1\sigma$. Figure 7.2 illustrates the proportions of scores lying under the entire normal curve. Note that the curve never touches the horizontal axis. This is because, conventionally, normal curves are used to describe populations, and they must be open ended to allow for the rare scores that do not fall within three standard deviation units of the mean.

> **Question:** But what if the mean is 100 and the standard deviation is 16? The figure shows only three standard deviation units; it doesn't go up to 16.

When the standard deviation is equal to 16, one standard deviation unit (1σ) equals 16 points. Remember that one standard deviation unit is also equal to a z score of 1. Thus, one standard deviation unit *above* the mean would be equal to the mean, 100, plus (1 · 16), or 116; two standard deviation units *below* the mean would equal 100 minus (2 · 16), or 68. As an illustration, consider an IQ test. One of the most widely used IQ tests, the Stanford–Binet Intelligence Scale, has a mean IQ score of 100 and a standard deviation equal to 16 IQ points. By looking at Figure 7.2, you can see that slightly more than two thirds of the people who take the test score within one standard deviation unit above the mean, which is 116, and one standard deviation unit below the mean, which is 84. Therefore, about two thirds of the people who take the Stanford–Binet test score between 84 and 116. Moreover, if your IQ is 132 (132 is 2σ above the mean), then only 2.28% of the population has an IQ higher than yours.

This normal curve information can have highly practical applications. For instance, a teacher had a student who seemed particularly bright but was unable to read at grade level, subtract double-digit numbers, or spell even simple words. The teacher referred the student for testing in order to confirm or deny her impressions of his basic intelligence. Was he intelligent enough to do well in school, or did he in fact lack the intellectual capacity to perform at grade level? Assuming that the tests used were valid, the teacher could answer the following questions merely by knowing her student's score: Is the student about average in intelligence? Is he above average, as she had suspected? What percentage of the population scores higher than this student? Lower? Even if the teacher were not told the student's exact scores but only that he scored, say, in the top 20% of the population, she could find out the exact minimum score that the child must have achieved to be in the top 20%.

> **Question:** Does this mean that there is a way to find out a child's exact score just by knowing the percentage?

Yes, by knowing the percentage, as well as knowing the mean and the standard deviation of the test. In fact, a great many questions can be answered about how an individual's behavior compares to a population by using the normal curve. These questions are answered next.

Concept Quiz

According to the National Center for Health Statistics (1998), the height of American women between the ages of 20 and 29 years is normally distributed, $\mu = 64$ inches, $\sigma = 2.7$ inches. Using this information, answer the following questions.

1. Because the heights are normally distributed across this population, it is called a normal curve and the shape is _____.

2. According to the common characteristics of normal curves, the mean, the median, and the mode of women's heights are all _____.

3. In the normal curve of women's heights, the highest frequency of heights is in the _____ of the distribution and tapers off as the frequency (scores) move farther from the mean and approach the _____ of the curve.

4. In a normal curve, _____ of the scores lie above the mean and _____ of the scores lie below the mean.

5. Approximately what percentage of scores lie between one standard deviation unit above and one standard deviation unit below the mean?

6. Among this population, what percentage of women measure between 58.6 inches and 69.4 inches in height?

7. Based on the height population data, use Figure 7.2 to determine what heights (in inches) represent the limits of the middle 68.26% of the women in this population.

Answers

1. symmetrical or bell-shaped
2. equal or the same or 64 inches
3. center; ends
4. 50% or one half; 50% or one half
5. 68.26
6. 95.44
7. 61.3 and 66.7

Finding Proportions and Percentages

As mentioned, normal curves have countless shapes and sizes, depending on the data collected and how the scores are distributed. Their means, as well as their standard deviations, can vary widely. In Chapter 6, you learned that in order to compare two completely different sets of scores, you can create standardized scores by converting both sets to z scores. Two separate tables based on z scores, Table Z and Table P, have been devised to help people answer questions about proportions of scores. Tables Z and P are found in Appendix A at the end of the book.

Using Table Z: Finding Areas Under the Normal Curve

You should use Table Z when you know a particular score or scores and you want to determine the proportion or percentage of scores lying above or below that one score or between two known scores. Table Z is divided into three columns. So that you won't have to turn back to the appendix each time it is discussed, a section of Table Z is excerpted in Figure 7.3. Refer to Figure 7.3 while reading the discription.

- **Column 1** lists positive z scores from 0 to 3.70 in hundredths. (Note that to enter this table you will need to compute your z score and then

Figure 7.3
A portion of Table Z
in Appendix A.

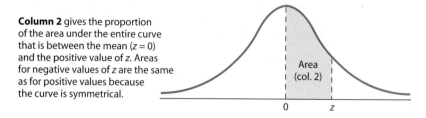

Column 2 gives the proportion
of the area under the entire curve
that is between the mean ($z = 0$)
and the positive value of z. Areas
for negative values of z are the same
as for positive values because
the curve is symmetrical.

Column 3 gives the proportion
of the area under the entire curve
that falls beyond the stated positive
value of z. Areas for negative values
of z are the same because the curve
is symmetrical.

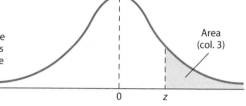

z 1	Area Between Mean and z 2	Area Beyond z 3	z 1	Area Between Mean and z 2	Area Beyond z 3
1.25	.3944	.1056	1.30	.4032	.0968
1.26	.3962	.1038	1.31	.4049	.0951
1.27	.3980	.1020	1.32	.4066	.0934
1.28	.3997	.1003	1.33	.4082	.0918
1.29	.4015	.0985	1.34	.4099	.0901

round it to hundredths.) The normal curve is symmetrical, so to find a
negative z score, you need only look up the corresponding positive
score.

▪ **Column 2** lists the area between the mean (which corresponds to a
z score of 0) and the z score listed in column 1. If the z score is positive,
this area is just to the right of the mean [see Figure 7.4(a)]; if the z score
is negative, the area is just to the left of the mean [see Figure 7.4(b)].

▪ **Column 3** lists the area beyond the z score in column 1. If the z score is
positive, this is the area of the entire remainder of the normal curve
above the z score [see Figure 7.5(a)]; if the z score is negative, then
column 3 represents the entire remainder of the normal curve below the
z score [see Figure 7.5(b)].

The areas given in columns 2 and 3 are proportions of the total area under
the normal curve; as such, they are listed in ten thousandths of the total area. It is
important to understand that when discussing the normal curve, because the areas listed in Table Z are proportions, these proportions can easily be converted to
percentages or probabilities. To convert the areas to percentages, simply multiply

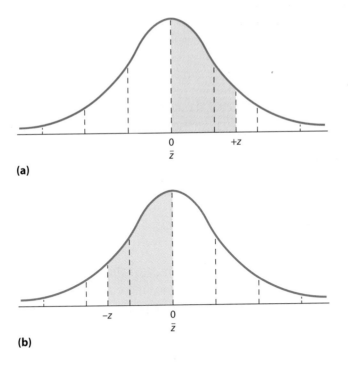

Figure 7.4
Areas in column 2
for (a) positive
z scores and
(b) negative z scores.

(a)

(b)

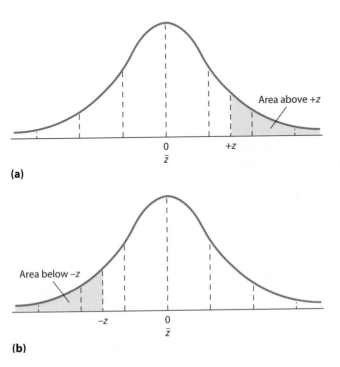

Figure 7.5
Areas in column 3
for (a) positive
z scores and
(b) negative z scores.

Area above +z

(a)

Area below −z

(b)

the figures by 100. The proportions are exactly equal to the probability. As mentioned previously, the normal curve is symmetrical, so .50, or 50%, of the scores lie above the mean and .50 lie below the mean. Knowing this, you should be able to add any column 2 area to its corresponding column 3 area, and the result should always equal .50. Try it: From columns 2 and 3, add both areas that correspond to a z score of +1.25. They should add up to .50. If you did this for +1.25 and then for −1.25, you would get .50 and .50, and these add up to 1.00, or 100% of the total area. Now add together both areas that correspond to a z score of −1.32. (Remember that because the table is symmetrical, the areas for −1.32 are the same as for +1.32.) Again, the area between the mean and −1.32 plus the area beyond −1.32 should total .50.

Area Above: Finding Proportions Above Positive and Negative z Scores

Suppose you're that teacher with the student who had trouble with reading, arithmetic, and spelling, and suppose you find out that he scored 120 on the Stanford–Binet Intelligence Scale. To get a better idea of how he compares to other children, you want to determine what percentage of children score above 120. Because IQ scores are normally distributed, we can use the normal curve and Table Z to solve this problem. *First, convert the IQ score of 120 to a z score.* With the population mean of the Stanford–Binet Intelligence Scale of 100 and the population standard deviation of 16, the z score is computed as follows:

$$z = \frac{X - \mu}{\sigma} = \frac{120 - 100}{16} = \frac{20}{16} = 1.25$$

Thus, the z score that corresponds to an IQ of 120 is 1.25. (Remember that you must always compute or be given both the mean and standard deviation in order to compute a z score.) Next, make a rough drawing of a normal curve, marking the mean and standard deviations and shading the portion of the curve that you want to find. This is an invaluable aid to help you estimate your answer and avoid making mistakes. (If you shade approximately 25% of the curve and your answer is 78%, you know that you must have made an error.) Returning to the IQ problem, note that the area of the curve corresponding to the percentage of scores above a z score of 1.25 in the positive tail of Figure 7.6 has been shaded. To find the exact percentage of scores in this area, you need to refer to column 3 in Table Z because it corresponds to the area beyond the z score:

Area above a positive z score = column 3   (7.1)

Locate 1.25 in the partial table shown in Figure 7.3 and read across to column 3. You should find the value .1056. Multiply by 100 to convert to a percentage and you get 10.56%. Your student is very intelligent if only 10.56% of the population scored better than he. Knowing this will help you make a more responsible recommendation concerning his education.

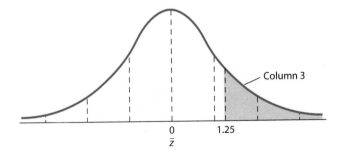

Figure 7.6
The area above a
z score of +1.25.

Question: What if the student's score were low, such as 76? Would the same procedure be used to find the percentage of scores above this low score?

No; the procedure for finding the area above this score is slightly different. Because 76 is below the mean, resulting in a negative *z* score, you will need to find the area between the *z* score and the mean, column 2, and then add to it the entire area above the mean, which is .5000 (half of the total distribution):

Area above a negative *z* score = column 2 + .5000   (7.2)

As with all procedures involving the normal curve, the first step is to convert the original score, in this case an IQ score, to a *z* score:

$$z = \frac{X - \mu}{\sigma} = \frac{76 - 100}{16} = \frac{-24}{16} = -1.50$$

Next, sketch a normal curve and shade the portion you're trying to determine (this is done in Figure 7.7). Then refer to Table Z in Appendix A. Because Table Z does not list negative *z* scores, ignore the minus sign for the moment and look up a *z* score of 1.50 in column 1. Now look across to column 2, which lists the area between the *z* score and the mean. Add this value, .4332, to .5000 and you will find that the area above an IQ score of 76 equals .9332.

Area above a *z* score of −1.50 = .4332 + .5000 = .9332

Converting to a percentage, you find that 93.32% of the population scored above an IQ of 76 on the Stanford–Binet test. Had your student actually scored a 76 on the test, your impression of him as a bright child would not have been supported.

Determining the proportion of people who score above a particular value is particularly helpful if you need to set a cutoff score and you want to know how many people, or what percentage of the people in your population, will score above your cutoff. Researchers in human factors are often confronted with this type of problem. For example, suppose you are part of a team that is designing a new automatic teller machine (ATM) for banks, and you need to determine the appropriate height for the video screen. The screen is to be angled down to prevent glare; consequently, customers who are shorter than midscreen will be able to see the image

Figure 7.7
The area above a
z score of −1.50.

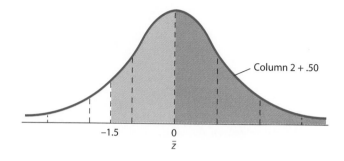

Column 2 + .50

−1.5

0
z̄

easily, but those who are taller will have to stoop to see it. Assuming that the height is normally distributed, knowing the mean and standard deviation of the population, and knowing how to use Table Z, you should be able to determine what proportion of the population is too tall to use the machine comfortably at any height.

Area Below: Finding Proportions Below Positive and Negative *z* Scores

Question: Is finding the area below the *z* score the same as finding the area above?

Yes and no. The procedures are similar: You must convert the original score to a *z* score and then find the area. However, finding the area below a *z* score is the reverse of finding the area above it. Suppose you live in Tyrannia, a totalitarian state where the government has decreed that all graduating eighth-graders who have an IQ of less than 108 must enter a blue-collar training program. Your job is to find out what percentage of the children this involves. In short, you need to find the area below the IQ score of 108. What do you do first? Convert the IQ score to a *z* score, as follows:

$$z = \frac{X - \mu}{\sigma} = \frac{108 - 100}{16} = \frac{8}{16} = .50$$

Then (don't forget this step!) sketch the normal curve to be sure you know what area to look up in Table Z in Appendix A. Try doing this first, and then check what you did by referring to Figure 7.8. From your sketch, it should be evident that in order to calculate the area below a *z* score of .50, you must first look up the area between the mean and the *z*, listed in column 2, and then add .5000, which is the area below the mean:

$$\text{Area below a positive } z \text{ score} = \text{column 2} + .5000 \tag{7.3}$$

Thus,

$$\text{Area below } .50 = .1915 + .5000 = .6915$$

Therefore, .6915, or 69.15%, of the eighth-graders will score below 108 and will be required to enter Tyrannia's training program.

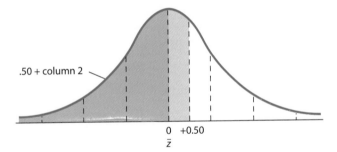

Figure 7.8
The area below a
z score of .50.

.50 + column 2

0 +0.50
z̄

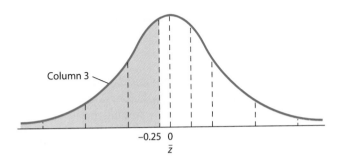

Figure 7.9
Area below a z score
of −.25.

Column 3

−0.25 0
z̄

By inspection, it is evident that the procedure for finding the area above a negative z score is the same as the one for finding the area below a positive z score. Correspondingly, finding the area below a negative z score is similar to finding the area above a positive z score. Suppose the minister of Tyrannia's Department of Education confers with the Secretary of the Treasury and finds that there are not enough funds to train nearly 70% of the children. The Minister of Education then arbitrarily lowers the cutoff score to 96 and asks you to determine the percentage of eighth-graders who score below 96. To begin this problem, you must first convert the IQ score to a z score:

$$z = \frac{X - \mu}{\sigma} = \frac{96 - 100}{16} = \frac{-4}{16} = -.25$$

Then make your sketch of the area below −.25, as in Figure 7.9, and find the area below (beyond z) in Table Z by locating −.25 (remember to ignore the minus sign when looking in the table) and referring to column 3:

Area below a negative z score = column 3   (7.4)

Area below −.25 = .4013, or 40.13%

Because there are ample funds for training 40.13% of the children, the Minister of Education gives the go-ahead for the program.

For an example of how this procedure can be used for measures other than IQ scores, recall the human factors project to determine the optimum height for the ATM video screen. Let's suppose that after reviewing your report, your superior

Table 7.1   Computation of the Area Below the Height of the ATM Machine

Mean height of ATM users $= \mu = 68$ inches

Standard deviation of ATM users $= \sigma = 4$ inches

Midscreen height of ATM $= X = 70$ inches

z score for 70 inches $= z = \dfrac{X - \mu}{\sigma} = \dfrac{70 - 68}{4} = \dfrac{2}{4} = .50$

Area between mean and z of .50 $\left(\text{from Table Z}\right) = .1915$

Area below 70 inches $= .1915 + .5000 = .6915$

stated that it was too negative because it emphasized the percentage of people who *could not* use the machine comfortably. Your solution: Report the percentage of people who *could* use the machine comfortably by finding the area below the height of the screen. This area is calculated in Table 7.1.

VISUAL SUMMARY

Finding Areas Under the Normal Curve

Before You Begin: Compute the mean and standard deviation.

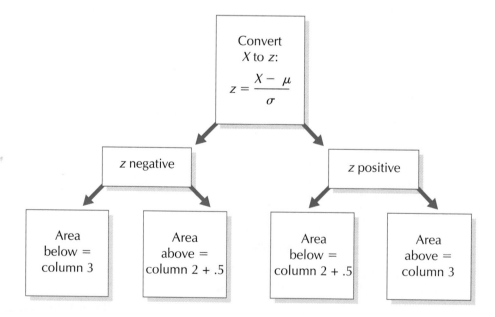

Concept Quiz

According to the National Center for Health Statistics (1998), the height of American men between the ages of 20 and 29 years is normally distributed, $\mu = 69.2$ inches, $\sigma = 2.9$ inches. Using this information, answer the following questions.

1. In order to use the normal curve to find the proportion or percentage of men above or below varied heights, Table _____ must be used.

2. Table Z in Appendix A is divided into three columns: Column 1 lists the _____, column 2 lists the area _____, and column 3 lists the area _____.

3. To convert the areas in Table Z to percentages, you must multiply the values by _____.

4. Suppose you are interested in knowing the percentage of men taller than 74 inches (6 ft. 2 in.). The first thing you must do before you can use Table Z is convert 74 inches to a _____ score.

5. The percentage of men above a positive z score of 1.69 is _____% and is found by locating the z score in Table Z, then reading across to the value under column _____, and multiplying by 100.

6. To determine the proportion of men above a negative z score of -1.45 (5 ft. 5 in.), first find the z score in Table Z, then find the value under column _____ and add _____. The proportion of men taller than 5 ft. 5 in. is _____.

7. The proportion of men below a positive z score of .97 (6 ft.) is _____ and is found by locating the z score in Table Z, then reading across to the value under column _____, and adding _____.

8. The percentage of men below a negative z score of -1.10 (5 ft. 6 in.) is _____% and is found by locating the z score in Table Z, then reading across to the value under column _____, and multiplying by 100.

9. Describe how to find the areas for a negative z score in Table Z.

Answers

1. Z
2. z score; between the mean and z; beyond z
3. 100
4. z
5. 4.55; 3
6. 2; .5000; .9265
7. .8340; 2; .5000
8. 36.43; 3
9. Table Z lists only positive values for z, but because the z-score distribution is symmetrical, you can use Table Z to find areas for negative z scores. To find an area for a negative z score, you enter the table using the absolute value of z. (Drop the negative sign.) Also remember that column 2 still represents the area between the mean and the z score, and column 3 represents the area out in the tail beyond z.

Area Between: Finding Proportions Lying Between Two z Scores

Question: Suppose that you want to know something more complicated, like what percentage of people score between 92 and 120 on the Stanford–Binet IQ test. How can that be done?

Finding the area between two scores is as easy as finding the area above or below a single score. First, convert both of the scores to z scores.

$$z_{92} = \frac{92 - 100}{16} = \frac{-8}{16} = -.50$$

$$z_{120} = \frac{120 - 100}{16} = \frac{20}{16} = 1.25$$

Now sketch the problem, as shown in Figure 7.10. It is easy to see that the area between the two z scores is simply the area between the mean and $-.50$ plus the area between the mean and 1.25. You need only look up the column 2 values for both z scores and then add the column 2 values:

Area between $-z$ score and $+z$ score $= (\text{column } 2)_{-z} + (\text{column } 2)_{+z}$ (7.5)

Now refer to Table Z and look up the z scores just computed to find their corresponding column 2 values:

Column 2 value of $-.50$ z score $= .1915$

Column 2 value of $+1.25$ z score $= .3944$

The sum of these column 2 values is

$.1915 + .3944 = .5859$

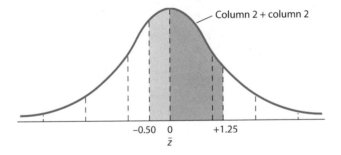

Figure 7.10
Area between *z*
scores of −.50 and
+1.25. (One *z* score
is negative and one
z score is positive.)

Column 2 + column 2

−0.50 0   +1.25
       $\bar{z}$

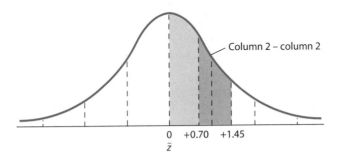

Figure 7.11   Area
between *z* scores of
+.70 and +1.45.
(Both *z* scores are
positive.)

Column 2 − column 2

0   +0.70   +1.45
$\bar{z}$

(Remember that you only add the proportions you find in Table Z; you *never* add *z* scores together.) Multiplying this result by 100 to express the percentage indicates that 58.59% of the people who take the Stanford–Binet Intelligence Scale test will score between 92 and 120.

> **Question:** Is the procedure the same if both *z* scores have the same sign—both negative or both positive?

To find the area between two *z* scores that have the same sign, you must still find the column 2 values for each score, but you subtract—rather than add—the column 2 values. Figure 7.11 illustrates this clearly: To find the area between the *z* scores of +.70 and +1.45, you need to subtract the area between the mean and the *z* score of +.70 from the area between the mean and the *z* score of +1.45. The column 2 area for a score of +.70 is .2580, and the column 2 area for a *z* score of +1.45 is .4265. The difference between the two areas is .1685, or 16.85%. The general formula for computing the area between two *z* scores that have the same sign is as follows:

$$\text{Area between } (+z_1 \text{ and } +z_2) \text{ or } (-z_1 \text{ and } -z_2) =$$
$$(\text{column 2})z_1 - (\text{column 2})z_2 \qquad (7.6)$$

where z_1 is the *z* score farther from the mean than z_2.

To see how to calculate the area between two negative z scores, find the percentage of people who score between 88 and 96 on the Stanford–Binet test. First, convert each IQ score to a z score:

$$z_{96} = \frac{96 - 100}{16} = \frac{-4}{16} = -.25$$

$$z_{88} = \frac{88 - 100}{16} = \frac{-12}{16} = -.75$$

Sketch the z scores on a normal curve graph as in Figure 7.12. Find the column 2 values for each of these z scores:

Column 2 value for a z of $-.25 = .0987$

Column 2 value for a z of $-.75 = .2734$

Finally, find the difference between these two areas, which is .1747. Consequently, 17.47% of the people who take this IQ test are expected to score between 88 and 96. The following formulas summarize this part of the chapter:

- Area above:

  $+z =$ column 3
  $-z =$ column 2 + .5000

- Area below:

  $+z =$ column 2 + .5000
  $-z =$ column 3

- Area between:

  $+z$ and $-z =$ column 2 + column 2
  $+z$ and $+z =$ column 2 − column 2
  $-z$ and $-z =$ column 2 − column 2

Figure 7.12
Area between z scores of $-.75$ and $-.25$. (Both z scores are negative.)

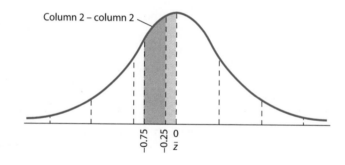

Column 2 – column 2

VISUAL SUMMARY

Finding the Area Between Two *z* Scores

Before You begin: Compute the mean and standard deviation.

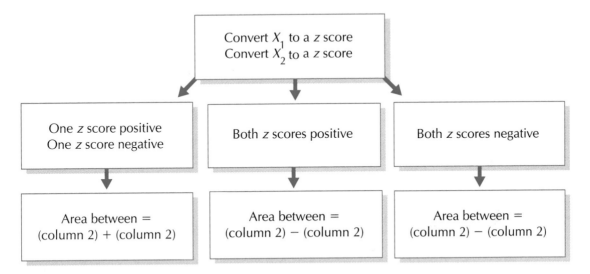

Before moving on to the next section on finding percentiles, it is important to realize that because you are always adding areas, or subtracting a smaller area from a larger area, the result is always positive. *You never get a normal curve result that is negative.*

Concept Quiz

According to the National Center for Health Statistics (2001), there were 3,959,417 births in 1999. The weights of newborns were $\mu = 3,400$ grams with an estimated $\sigma = 600$ grams. Assuming this birth data are normally distributed, answer the following questions.

1. To find the proportion of births between 4,000 and 2,800 grams, first convert the raw scores to _____, then use Table Z.

2. To find the proportion of births between a positive *z* score of 1.50 (4,300 grams) and a negative *z* score of -1.50 (2,500 grams), find the column 2 values that correspond to $z = 1.50$ (_____) and $z = -1.50$ (_____), and then _____ these areas.

3. What is the proportion of births between 3,800 grams and 3,300 grams?

4. To find the area between two positive *z* scores or two negative *z* scores, you must first find the column 2 values that correspond to the *z* scores and then

_____ .

5. What is the proportion of births between 2,700 and 3,150 grams?

6. Using the information calculated in Question 5, how many babies were born in 1999 weighing between 2,700 and 3,150 grams? (Round to the nearest whole number.)

7. The area between any two *z* scores is always a positive value. True or false?

Answers

1. *z* scores	4. subtract the smaller	5. .2142 (.3770 − .1628)
2. .4332; .4332; add	area from the larger	6. 848,107
3. .3161 (.2486 + .0675)	area	7. True

Finding Percentiles

So far in this chapter you have seen ways to use a normal curve to determine proportions or percentages. These procedures involve knowing a particular score or scores and then finding the area above, below, or between these scores. The procedure for finding the percentage below a particular score (*X*) is summarized here:

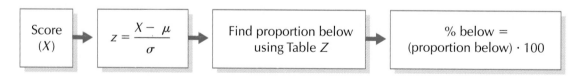

But what if the situation is reversed? What if you know the percentage below and want to find that score. For example, suppose the Tyrannian Minister of Education decrees that only the lower 25% of the graduating eighth-graders are required to enter the training program and she wants you to calculate which score will be the cutoff. This situation, which is shown in Figure 7.13, involves a known area but unknown raw and *z* scores. The score you want to find is referred to as the *percentile*.

A **percentile** is a score that has a certain percentage of scores below it. For instance, if you score at the 25th percentile, 25% of the scores fall below your score; if you score at the 75th percentile, 75% of the scores fall below your score. Finding the percentile, then, is the exact opposite of finding the percentage below a score because rather than knowing a score and trying to find the percentage, you know the percentage and are trying to find the score. To find the raw score that corresponds to the 25th percentile for the Tyrannian government, look at Figure 7.13 again. The figure shows that the 25th percentile has an area below the score equal

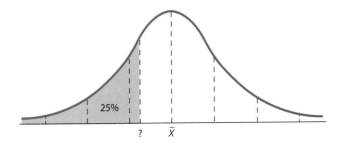

Figure 7.13
Diagram of the known area below a score equal to 25% but an unknown *z* score.

to .2500, an area that is obviously in the left tail of the distribution. What should you do with this information?

Suppose you try to find .2500 in column 3 of Table Z. Column 3 gives that area in the tail beyond the *z* score listed in column 1. Consequently, if you find an area in column 3, you find its corresponding *z* score in column 1 at the same time. The only problem with this approach is that Table Z is designed to be entered from column 1 instead of from column 2 or 3. Therefore, there is no guarantee that the area you are looking up will be listed in column 3. If you have already looked at the table, you have found that .2500 is in fact not listed. The closest value in column 3 is .2514.

> **Question:** Can't the figures listed on either side of .2500 be used to estimate the *z* score?

There is quite a problem with estimating areas and *z* scores accurately in Table Z because the frequency for adjacent *z* scores on the normal curve is not uniform. Thus, even a slight movement in one direction or another can mean a large difference in respect to the frequency of scores, and therefore the proportion. The solution to this difficulty is not to estimate using Table Z but to use Table P, which is designed so you can look up an area above or below a score in order to find a corresponding *z* score.

Using Table P: Finding Distinct Scores

To use Table P in Appendix A, first you must convert a known percentage into a proportion (an area) by dividing the percentage by 100. Then you find the known area in either column 1 or column 3 of Table P and read the *z* score from column 2. Your new assignment for the Tyrannian minister is to find the 25th percentile, the score below which 25% of the eighth-graders scored. To do this, divide 25 by 100 to find the area, .250. Next, find .250 in column 3 of Table P and read the *z* score from column 2, .6745. Before continuing, remember that some *z* scores are positive and some are negative. All *z* scores that correspond to percentiles less than 50 are negative, and all *z* scores that correspond to percentiles greater than 50 are positive. (Another way of saying this is: If you enter Table P from column 1, the *z* score is positive, but if you enter Table P from column 3, the *z* score is negative.) Therefore, the percentile, 25, is less than 50—you entered Table P from column 3—and that makes the z score from column 2 negative, $-.6745$. If you were looking for the 90th percentile, the z score would be a positive 1.2816.

Question: Once you know how to find the z score, how do you convert the z score back into an IQ score?

To do this, plug the values of the z score, the mean, and the standard deviation into Formula 7.7, which is derived from the z score formula via a little algebraic maneuvering:

$$X = \mu + (z \cdot \sigma) \tag{7.7}$$

So to find the raw IQ score that represents the 25th percentile, substitute the known values into Formula 7.7:

$$X = 100 + (-.6745 \cdot 16)$$

$$= 100 - 10.792$$

$$= 89.208$$

Thus, the IQ score of 89.208 is the raw score that represents the 25th percentile.

A note of caution is necessary here: Always remember to make sure that you assign the proper sign to the z score after you find it in Table P. To repeat: A z score is negative when the percentile is less than 50 and positive when the percentile is greater than 50.

Before ending this section on percentiles, here is one more example. Find the IQ score that represents the 90th percentile. This is illustrated in Figure 7.14. The first step is to convert the percentage to an area by dividing it by 100: .900. The next step is to determine the z score. To do this, you locate the area .900 in Table P. (Because it is greater than .5000, it is found in column 1.) The corresponding z score is 1.2816. Finally, substitute the known values into Formula 7.7 and solve for the IQ score:

$$X = 100 + (1.2816 \cdot 16)$$

$$= 100 + 20.5056$$

$$= 120.5056$$

Figure 7.14
Diagram of the known area below a score equal to 90% with an unknown z score.

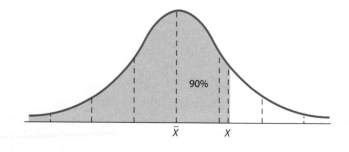

An IQ score of just over 120 represents the 90th percentile; this means that 90% of the people who take the test will score less than 120.5056.

VISUAL SUMMARY

Finding Percentiles

Before You Begin: Compute the mean and standard deviation.

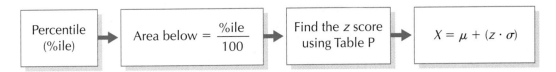

Percentile (%ile) → Area below $= \dfrac{\%ile}{100}$ → Find the z score using Table P → $X = \mu + (z \cdot \sigma)$

Question: School principals sometimes talk about a proportion of their students scoring in certain quartiles—the first quartile, the third quartile, and so on. What is the difference between a percentile and a quartile?

Percentiles and quartiles are quite similar. A percentile is the raw score that has a certain percentage of scores falling below it. Typically, percentiles are stated as whole integers. If you find out that you scored in the 83rd percentile on a standardized test, that means you scored higher than 83% of the people who took the test. **Quartiles** are the raw scores that divide the distribution into four equal parts, as shown in Figure 7.15. Normally, the quartiles are designated Q_1, Q_2, and Q_3. Q_1 is equivalent to the 25th percentile and is the cutoff for the bottom quarter of the distribution. Q_2 is equivalent to the 50th percentile (the median) and divides the distribution into halves. Q_3 is the 75th percentile. Thus, 50% of the scores in a distribution fall between Q_1 and Q_3. When principals receive their schools' scores from a state achievement test, they are very happy if most of their scores fall above Q_3.

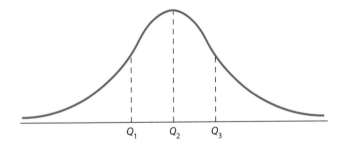

Figure 7.15
Quartiles (Q_1, Q_2, and Q_3) for the normal curve.

Concept Quiz

The Scholastic Aptitude Test (SAT) was designed to measure developed verbal and mathematical reasoning ability and is widely used to predict success in college for high school students. Thus, it is an important influence on the educational and career opportunities of thousands of students each year. According to the National College Board (2001), the 2000 SAT I math scores, $\mu = 514$, $\sigma = 113$, were slightly higher than the scores for several previous years. Assume the data are normally distributed, and answer the following questions.

1. The 30th percentile of SAT math scores is the score with 30% of the scores
   _____.

2. The z score that represents the 45th percentile is _____; the z score for the 73rd percentile is _____.

3. The z score will be negative if the percentile is _____; the z score will be positive if the percentile is _____.

4. A percentile must be converted to a(n) _____ before you can find the z score in Table _____.

5. What is the formula for converting a z score to a raw score?

6. If a college sets the 77th percentile as the minimum SAT math score required for admission to their college, then what is the minimum score they will accept? (Round to the nearest whole number.)

7. If an educational company offers students with SAT scores below the 30th percentile a free remedial math course, what is the cutoff score for the free deal? (Round to the nearest whole number.)

Answers

1. below
2. $-.1257$; $+.6128$
3. less than 50; greater than 50
4. proportion or area; P
5. $X = \mu + (z \cdot \sigma)$
6. 597
7. 455

Summary

The normal curve is a bell-shaped, symmetrical curve that graphically illustrates any normal distribution. It is often assumed that most scientific data, and particularly data collected in the behavioral sciences, are normally distributed. In all normal curves, the mean, median, and mode are all equal. The highest frequency of scores lies in the middle of the curve, with the frequency gradually tapering off as the scores approach the ends of the curve. The normal curve is a graphic picture of the proportion of scores in a distribution. With the aid of either Table Z or Table P, it is possible to answer questions such as the area above, below, and between scores as well as find percentiles and quartiles.

Key Terms

normal curve   percentile   quartile
normal distribution

Formulas

Area above a positive z score $=$ column 3   (7.1)

Area above a negative z score $=$ column 2 $+$ .5000   (7.2)

Area below a positive z score $=$ column 2 $+$ .5000   (7.3)

Area below a negative z score $=$ column 3   (7.4)

Area between $-z$ score and $+z$ score $=$ (column 2)$_{-z}$ $+$ (column 2)$_{+z}$ (7.5)

Area between $(+z_1$ and $+z_2)$ or $(-z_1$ and $-z_2) =$
(column 2)z_1 $-$ (column 2)z_2 (7.6)

$X = \mu + (z \cdot \sigma)$ (7.7)

Problems

1. Use Table Z to find the areas beyond the following z scores:

   3.00   1.00   .50   −.25   −1.37   −2.75

2. Use Table Z to find the areas beyond the following z scores:

   2.35   .72   1.68   −.37   −2.37   −1.75

3. Use Table Z to find the area between the mean and the following z scores:

   3.00   1.00   .50   −.25   −1.37   −2.75

4. Use Table Z to find the area between the mean and the following z scores:

   2.74   1.29   .48   −.77   −1.84   −2.91

Use the following information to solve Problems 5–22. You have administered a reaction time test to thousands of people and have found that the population mean is 150 milliseconds and the population standard deviation is 25 milliseconds. What proportion of the people who take this test have a reaction time

5. Longer than 140 milliseconds?

6. Longer than 127 milliseconds?

7. Longer than 115 milliseconds?

8. Longer than 100 milliseconds?

9. Shorter than 99 milliseconds?

10. Shorter than 119 milliseconds?

11. Shorter than 127 milliseconds?

12. Shorter than 132 milliseconds?

13. Between 128 and 112 milliseconds?

14. Between 132 and 115 milliseconds?

15. Between 113 and 105 milliseconds?

16. Between 121 and 117 milliseconds?

17. Between 137 and 142 milliseconds?

18. Between 141 and 133 milliseconds?

What reaction time represents

19. The 75th percentile?

20. The 88th percentile?

21. The 45th percentile?

22. The 23rd percentile?

Suppose that you are a designer for the world's largest manufacturer of toy dinosaur cars. You have just designed a toy intended for 3- to 6-year-olds that will safely accommodate a child who is no shorter that 36 inches and no taller than 48 inches. The mean height for children of this age group is 42 inches, and the standard deviation is 5 inches. Use these data to solve Problems 23–27.

What proportion of the target sales population

23. Can safely use your product?

24. Is too tall to safely use your product?

25. Is too short to safely use your product?

26. What is Q_1 for this population of children?

27. What is Q_3 for this population of children?

For Problems 28–38, the mean family income in Uppityton is $68,000 per year, with a standard deviation of $17,000 per year. What proportion of the families in Uppityton make

28. More than $100,000 per year?

29. More than $43,000 per year?

30. Less than $97,000 per year?

31. Less than $54,000 per year?

32. Between $75,000 and $100,000 per year?

33. Between $80,000 and $70,000 per year?

34. Between $35,000 and $62,000 per year?

35. Between $47,000 and $58,000 per year?

What is the family income that represents

36. The 43rd percentile?

37. The 15th percentile?

38. The 73rd percentile?

Problems From the Literature

The following problems refer to actual results from research studies that are cited at the end of the chapter. However, the data used to generate the problem sets are hypothetical.

Sports psychologists are trained in physical education, sport and exercise science, psychology, and counseling. The professional opportunities vary from teaching and research to working with athletes. The question of annual earnings for sports psychologists was surveyed by Myers, Coleman, Whelan, and Mehlenbeck (2001). They found that the mean total gross income for 407 respondents was $70,617 with a standard deviation of $41,373. The range of salaries was $0–$300,000. Use this information to solve Problems 39–48.

What proportion of the sports psychologists make

39. More than $150,000 per year?

40. Less than $100,000 per year?

41. Less than $35,000 per year?

42. Between $60,000 and $100,000 per year?

43. Between $150,000 and $200,000 per year?

44. Between $25,000 and $50,000 per year?

What is the income that represents

45. The 25th percentile?

46. The 85th percentile?

47. The 10th percentile?

48. The 90th percentile?

In a study examining memory of names, Morris and Fritz (2000) used a technique called the name game *to introduce students to one another. The technique began with the teaching assistant writing on the board the name of the first person to be introduced. After the spelling was checked and confirmed, the name was erased. The next person to be introduced had to say the full name of the first person before saying his or her own full name aloud. Then the teaching assistant wrote the name on the board, confirmed spelling, and erased the name. The third person had to say the full name of the first two people before saying his or her own name aloud, and so the routine continued until all people in the group were introduced. Results demonstrated that this technique improved the recall of names compared to simply saying and using the name in some manner. Morris and Fritz suggest that this useful memory strategy is simple compared to the more complex mnemonics or*

other techniques. Suppose you did a similar study and asked participants to use the name game to remember the names of the other students in their statistics class the first day of the semester. There were 38 students in the statistics class. After all of the participants were finished playing the name game, they were asked to recall as many first names as possible. The mean number of names recalled was 19.41 with a standard deviation of 3.17. Use this information to solve Problems 49–58.

What proportion of the participants recalled

49. Less than 15 names?

50. Less than 25 names?

51. More than 30 names?

52. Between 25 and 35 names?

53. Between 10 and 20 names?

54. Between 25 and 38 names?

What number of names recalled represents

55. The 20th percentile?

56. The 65th percentile?

57. The 90th percentile?

58. The 75th percentile?

References

Morris, P. E., & Fritz, C. O. (2000). The name game: Using retrieval practice to improve the learning of names. *Journal of Experimental Psychology: Applied, 6,* 124–129.

Myers, A. W., Coleman, J. K., Whelan, J. P., & Mehlenbeck, R. S. (2001). Examining careers in sports psychology: Who is working and who is making money? *Professional Psychology: Research and Practice, 32,* 5–11.

National Center for Health Statistics (1998). *Healthy People 2000 Review, 1998–99* [Online]. Hyattsville, MD: Public Health Service. Maryland June 1999 DHHS Public. Available: http://www.cdc. gov/nchs (visited April 14, 2001).

National Center for Health Statistics (2001). *Births: Final Data for 1999.* Vol. 49 (1), 2001–1120 [Online]. Available: http://www.cdc.gov/nchs (visited April 14, 2001).

National College Board (2001). 2000 SAT I test performance: Comparing students who took the SAT I [Online]. Available: http://www.collegeboard.org/sat/html/students/scrpt000.html (visited April 16, 2001).

8

Correlation

- The Nature of Correlation
  Types of Correlation: How Are Variables Related?
  Degrees of Correlation: How Strongly Are Variables Related?
- The Correlation Coefficient
  The Covariance
  VISUAL SUMMARY: Computing the Covariance
  Computing the Correlation Coefficient

VISUAL SUMMARY: Computing the Correlation Coefficient Using the Covariance
Computational Formulas for the Covariance and Correlation Coefficient
- The Significance of the Correlation Coefficient
  Interpreting the Correlation Coefficient: What Do the Numbers Mean?

- The Coefficient of Determination
- Summary
- Key Terms
- Formulas
- Problems
  Problems From the Literature
- References

Daily life is full of hassles. The car needs gas, the rent is due, your boss wants you to work overtime for the next couple of weeks, there is a statistics test tomorrow, you need to make some kind of dinner out of the stuff that is beginning to smell in your refrigerator (maybe it is too late already), and on top of this you are starting to get a cold. These are all sources of stress. Health psychologists have long been interested in stress, and especially in the relationship between stress and illness. Thomas Holmes and Richard Rahe (1967) conjectured that exposure within a short time to several stressful major life events, such as the death of a family member or a change in residence, may have a detrimental effect on health. Over the years, several researchers have studied the relationship between health and minor events or hassles.

One of these studies, conducted by Rod Martin and James Dobbin (1998), measured the relationship between the number of daily hassles and the amount of immunoglobulin A in a person's bloodstream. Whereas high levels of immunoglobulin A indicate a strong immune system and consequent higher resistance to illness, low levels indicate a weaker immune system. Martin and Dobbin found a significant relationship between the number of daily hassles and the levels of immunoglobulin A in their participants' saliva. The more hassles a participant reported, the lower the level of immunoglobulin A in his or her saliva. Through awareness of this relationship, health care professionals can target which people are at risk for illness, and they can work with them to develop strategies for coping with their hassles and the resultant stress.

You have probably noticed that a great variety of other factors are related in one way or another, such as mood swings being related to the weather, or height being related to weight. There is a game that illustrates how, once a relationship between two factors has been established, that relationship can be used to make predictions. The setting for the game: the college union, or cafeteria. The object of the game: to guess the height of the next man to walk through the entrance. The winner: the person whose guess is within an inch of the man's true height three times in a row. The loser has to buy lunch. It is now your turn. What height do you guess? You can use a variety of strategies: Choose the height of a male friend, the height of your favorite actor, or the height of the last man to walk into the cafeteria. Of course, the best strategy, over time, is to choose the mean height of the men on campus.

By some stroke of luck, you just happen to have a list of the heights for all the men who attend your college. Hurriedly, you enter the heights into your calculator and compute the mean: 70 inches. Guessing 70 inches each time may not be as much fun as making random guesses, but you will probably be more likely to win. Suppose a friend changes the game slightly and asks another friend to stand outside the cafeteria with a scale. She is to weigh each man before he enters the cafeteria, stick her head inside, and tell you the person's weight. You're still supposed to guess the man's height, but now you have the advantage of knowing his weight. Let's imagine that your friend opens the door and shouts, "120 pounds." What would you guess? The mean height, 70 inches? It's more likely that you would guess a height much less than 70 inches.

Your guess would be lower than 70 inches because over the years you have learned that height and weight are related to each other. In most instances, taller people weigh more than shorter people. Of course, there are exceptions: some people are like beanpoles—tall and thin—and others are short and round. In general, however, as height goes up, so does weight. Many other interesting variables are also related to one another: grades and the amount of time spent studying, athletic success and practice time, ice cream sales and temperature, calories consumed and weight gained, and, as previously noted, level of immunoglobulin A and number of daily hassles. When factors are related in some *systematic* way, they are said to be *correlated*. A **correlation** is a relationship between two variables whereby a change in one variable is associated with a concurrent change in the other. In statistics, we not only establish the existence of certain correlations but also measure the direction and degree of correlation.

The Nature of Correlation

Types of Correlation: How Are Variables Related?

Variables can be correlated in any one of three ways. If both factors vary in the same direction—as one goes up, the other goes up—the relationship is described as *positive.* For instance, yearly income and years of education are positively correlated because the people who have the highest income tend to be the ones who have gone to school the longest. Conversely, if two factors vary in the opposite direction—as one goes up, the other goes down—the relationship is *negative*. For example, the number of daily hassles and the amount of immunoglobulin A in a person's saliva are negatively correlated because as the number of hassles goes up, the amount of immunoglobulin A in a person's saliva goes down. Finally, variables that are not at all related have a *zero correlation*. The relationship between personality fluctuations and the movement of distant stars has a zero correlation. (Contrary to strong beliefs in astrology held by a surprising number of people, no scientific study has found a correlation between these two factors.)

Degrees of Correlation: How Strongly Are Variables Related?

Question: Aren't some things more closely related than others?

Absolutely. Some things are closely related, whereas others are only loosely related. One way to display the degree of correlation between two variables is to generate a **scatterplot,** which is a graph with plotted values for two variables that are being compared, such as height and weight or IQ score and grade point average. Look at the scatterplots in Figures 8.1(a)–(e). In each one, two sets of data are

Figure 8.1
Five scatterplots indicating (a) a positive correlation between weight and height, (b) a positive correlation between IQ and GPA, (c) a negative correlation between weight loss and calories consumed, (d) number of hallucinations and the blood level of an antipsychotic drug, and (e) a zero correlation between height and GPA.

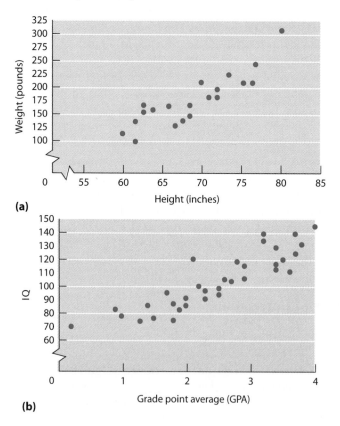

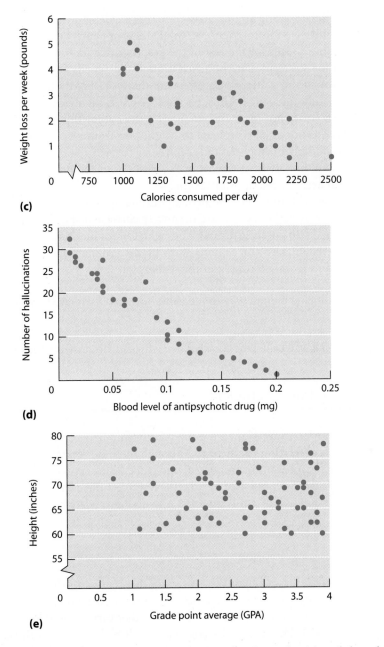

Figure 8.1
(continued)

(c)

(d)

(e)

displayed, one (such as height) along the abscissa (horizontal axis) and the other (such as weight) along the ordinate (vertical axis). The points are plotted where corresponding X and Y values intersect (for example, if you are 70 inches tall and you weigh 190 pounds, plotting a point at 70 and 190 would represent you on the scatterplot).

By merely glancing at the scatterplots, you can often see correlational trends. These trends can be illustrated by laying a pencil, with its tip pointing away from the ordinate, along an imaginary line running lengthwise through the center of the points. Do this for Figure 8.1(a). Does your pencil point up to the right? It should. Now do this for the rest of the graphs in Figure 8.1. Note how closely the dots in the scatterplot are bunched around the pencil. The more closely the two variables in the scatterplot are related, the more tightly the points will be bunched around the pencil. Thus, because weight is highly correlated to height [see Figure 8.1(a)], the points are bunched together along this imaginary line, but because GPA is not at all correlated to height [see Figure 8.1(e)], the points are scattered randomly throughout the graph.

By examining the scatterplots in Figure 8.1, you should also be able to see positive and negative relationships. Variables that are positively correlated show a positive slope, with the tip of the pencil pointing up to the right, away from the abscissa, whereas variables that are negatively correlated show a negative slope, with the pencil's tip pointing down to the right, toward the abscissa. Variables that are not correlated (zero correlation) show no discernible slope at all; the points are scattered randomly throughout the scatterplot.

> **Question:** Is there a way to measure how closely related two variables are?

> There is a way, called the correlation coefficient, discussed in the next section.

The Correlation Coefficient

The most common way to measure the relationship between two variables is to compute the **correlation coefficient.** Although there are several measures of correlation, the most common and useful one is the Pearson product moment correlation coefficient, represented here by the lowercase italic letter r. Before beginning the computation of r, it is useful first to discuss a related measure called the covariance.

The Covariance

The **covariance** (cov_{XY}) is basically a number that represents the degree to which two different variables change together. For example, if high scores on one variable tend to be paired with high scores on the other variable, and low scores tend to be paired with low scores, the covariance will be large and positive. On the other hand, if high scores on one variable tend to be paired with low scores on the other variable, then the covariance will be negative. This is easy to see when computing the covariance for a couple of different sets of numbers. The formula for the covariance is

$$\text{cov}_{XY} = \frac{\Sigma\left[(X - \overline{X}) \cdot (Y - \overline{Y})\right]}{n - 1} \tag{8.1}$$

As you can see from this equation, the numerator is computed by calculating the mean deviation scores for X and multiplying each of those by their corresponding mean deviation scores for Y. The covariance is the sum of these products divided by $n - 1$. (Remember that the covariance measures how two variables change together. The formula for covariance reflects this by treating each pair of scores as just that: a pair. Until this point, n has been used as the symbol for the number of scores in a sample. Because pairs of scores are used in computing the covariance and correlation coefficient, n designates the number of pairs in the covariance formula.) For example, if you ask five men their height and weight, you might get the responses listed in Table 8.1. For clarity, the height variable is labeled X and the weight variable Y. Also given are the mean for X, the standard deviation for X, the mean for Y, and the standard deviation for Y. Note that there are two scores, a height score and a weight score, for each man. If you scrutinize the data, you may be able to tell that there is a positive relationship between height and weight. In general, the taller men are heavier and the shorter men are lighter. However, this relationship is much easier to see when you compute the mean deviations for both X and Y, as in Table 8.2.

Table 8.1   Heights and Weights for Five Men

Man	Height (X)	Weight (Y)
M. P.	72	190
T. D.	66	135
C. Q.	69	155
C. Y.	72	165
D. P.	71	155
	$\overline{X} = 70$	$\overline{Y} = 160$
	$S_X = 2.550$	$S_Y = 20$

Table 8.2   Mean Deviations of the Heights and Weights for Five Men

Man	Height (X)	$X - \overline{X}$	Weight (Y)	$Y - \overline{Y}$
M. P.	72	+2	190	+30
T. D.	66	−4	135	−25
C. Q.	69	−1	155	−5
C. Y.	72	+2	165	+5
D. P.	71	+1	155	−5
	$\overline{X} = 70$		$\overline{Y} = 160$	
	$S_X = 2.550$		$S_Y = 20$	

By comparing the mean deviations for height to the mean deviations for weight, you can see that in four of the five pairs of scores, both have the same sign—both are either positive or negative. This is what you expect in a distribution that has a positive covariance and a positive correlation. Next, if you take a look at the *signs* of the products of the paired deviation scores in Table 8.3, you will notice that if both deviation scores are positive, the product is positive; if both deviation scores are negative, the product is positive. It is only when the signs of the mean deviations are different that the product is negative. In this example, most of the products are positive, so you could expect that their sums will probably also be positive. If the pairs of scores tended to have opposite signs, you could expect a negative covariance and negative correlation. (Table 8.5 demonstrates

Table 8.3   The Sign of the Products of the Mean Deviations of the Heights and Weights for Five Men

Man	Height (X)	$X - \overline{X}$	Weight (Y)	$Y - \overline{Y}$	Sign of Product
M. P.	72	+2	190	+30	+
T. D.	66	−4	135	−25	+
C. Q.	69	−1	155	−5	+
C. Y.	72	+2	165	+5	+
D. P.	71	+1	155	−5	−
	$\overline{X} = 70$		$\overline{Y} = 160$		
	$S_X = 2.550$		$S_Y = 20$		

Table 8.4   The Products of the Mean Deviations of the Heights and Weights for Five Men

Man	Height (X)	$X - \overline{X}$	Weight (Y)	$Y - \overline{Y}$	$(X - \overline{X}) \cdot (Y - \overline{Y})$
M. P.	72	+2	190	+30	60
T. D.	66	−4	135	−25	100
C. Q.	69	−1	155	−5	5
C. Y.	72	+2	165	+5	10
D. P.	71	+1	155	−5	−5
	$\overline{X} = 70$		$\overline{Y} = 160$		$\Sigma[(X - \overline{X}) \cdot (Y - \overline{Y})] = 170$
	$S_X = 2.550$		$S_Y = 20$		

count. You will return to Table 8.5 after computing the covariance for the height and weight data.) To finish the computation of the covariance, you need to compute the products of the mean deviations and then sum those products, as in Table 8.4. Now using Formula 8.1, you can compute the covariance.

$$\text{cov}_{XY} = \frac{\Sigma\left[(X - \overline{X}) \cdot (Y - \overline{Y})\right]}{n - 1} = \frac{170}{5 - 1} = \frac{170}{4} = 42.5$$

The procedure for computing the covariance is summarized next.

VISUAL SUMMARY

Computing the Covariance

Before You Begin: Compute $\overline{X}, \overline{Y}, n$.

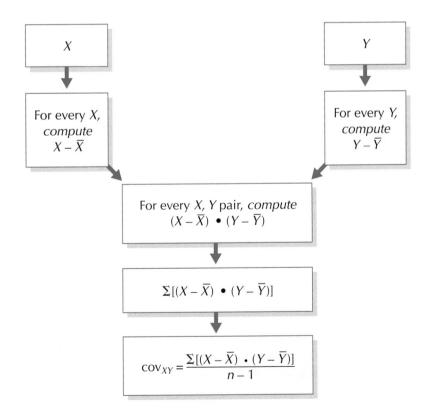

Table 8.5 Computation of the Correlation Coefficient for Number of Hassles and Immunoglobulin A (IA) Counts for 10 Women

Women	Daily Hassles (X)	$X - \bar{X}$	IA Count (Y)	$Y - \bar{Y}$	$(X - \bar{X}) \cdot (Y - \bar{Y})$
C. D.	12	−2.8	1.72	.52	−1.456
P. M.	15	.2	1.15	−.05	−.010
R. R.	20	5.2	.15	−1.05	−5.460
M. D.	12	−2.8	2.00	.80	−2.240
J. L.	17	2.2	.25	−.95	−2.090
M. F.	16	1.2	1.33	.13	+.156
J. P.	10	−4.8	2.10	.90	−4.320
H. S.	12	−2.8	1.75	.55	−1.540
M. H.	15	.2	1.35	.15	+.030
M. V.	19	4.2	.20	−1.00	−4.200

$$\bar{X} = 14.8 \qquad \bar{Y} = 1.2 \qquad \Sigma\left[(X - \bar{X}) \cdot (Y - \bar{Y})\right] = -21.130$$

$$S_X = 3.293 \qquad S_Y = .751$$

$$\text{cov}_{XY} = \frac{\Sigma\left[(X - \bar{X}) \cdot (Y - \bar{Y})\right]}{n - 1} = \frac{-21.130}{10 - 1} = \frac{-21.130}{9} = -2.348$$

$$r_{XY} = \frac{\text{cov}_{XY}}{S_X \cdot S_Y} = \frac{-2.348}{3.293 \cdot .751} = \frac{-2.348}{2.473} = -.949$$

Although the covariance is useful when describing the relationship between two variables, its usefulness is limited because it is in the same units as the original scores. This limits its usefulness because it is impossible to compare the covariance of heights and weights to the covariance of hassles and immunoglobulin A. Computing the correlation coefficient corrects for this problem.

Computing the Correlation Coefficient

The computation of the correlation coefficient is relatively simple once you have computed the covariance. The covariance formula for the correlation coefficient is

$$r_{XY} = \frac{\text{cov}_{XY}}{S_X \cdot S_Y} \qquad (8.2)$$

(You can see that dividing by the product of the standard deviations will cause the units to cancel, thereby resulting in r having no units.) You can now use Formula 8.2 to compute the correlation coefficient for the height and weight data:

$$r_{XY} = \frac{\text{cov}_{XY}}{S_X \cdot S_Y} = \frac{42.500}{2.550 \cdot 20.000} = \frac{42.500}{51} = .833$$

The correlation between height and weight for the five men is a positive .833, which is a relatively high correlation.

> **Question:** Is +.833 high? It seems awfully small. Shouldn't it be larger, like 100 or 1,000?

Correlation coefficients are never greater than +1.000 or less than −1.000. (This occurs because the covariance can never be outside plus or minus S_X times S_Y.) So the answer to the question is no, +.833 is not small, it is relatively high. You also need to remember that the sign of the correlation coefficient, minus or plus, indicates the *direction* of the relationship, and the number represents the *size*

VISUAL SUMMARY

Computing the Correlation Coefficient Using the Covariance

Before You Begin: Compute $\overline{X}$, S_X, $\overline{Y}$, S_Y, n.

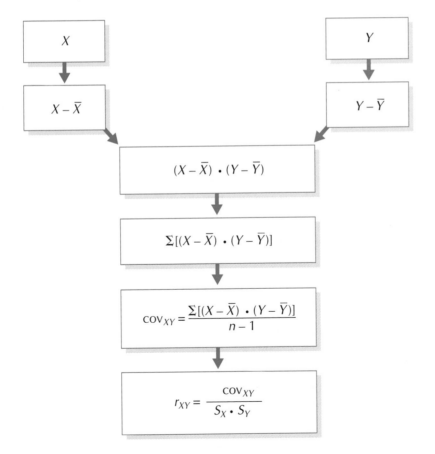

of the relationship. A positive correlation represents the situation where both X and Y vary in the same direction, whereas a negative correlation indicates a situation where X and Y vary in opposite directions. Therefore, a correlation coefficient near $+1$ or -1 is a large correlation, whereas a correlation close to 0 is small. Table 8.5 shows the computation of a negative correlation coefficient between the number of daily hassles and the amount of immunoglobulin A in the saliva of 10 different participants.

The procedure for computing the correlation coefficient using the covariance is summarized here.

Concept Quiz

In a study examining the relationship of variables in new marital relationships to the quality, success, and length of marriages in their later years, researchers Huston, Caughlin, Houts, Smith, and George (2001) found that the amount of overt romantic affection displayed by newlyweds was related to their level of marital satisfaction much later in the relationship.

1. In a scatterplot, positive correlation of the amount of romantic affection and couple's ratings of marital satisfaction 10 years later would be shown by a _____ slope to the plotted points.

2. The most common way to measure the linear relationship between two variables, such as romantic affection and marital satisfaction, is to compute the _____.

3. When computing the covariance or the correlation coefficient, n represents the number of _____ of scores.

4. The covariance is basically a number that represents the degree to which two different variables, such as the amount of affectionate expression and marital satisfaction scores, _____.

5. The covariance can never be larger than $+$ or $-$ _____.

6. The correlation coefficient is the covariance divided by _____.

7. Correlation coefficients are never greater than _____ or less than _____.

8. A negative correlation between romantic affection and marital satisfaction would indicate that scores on one variable increased as scores on the other variable _____.

9. A positive correlation between romantic affection and marital satisfaction would indicate that scores on one variable increased as scores on the other

variable _____, or scores on one variable decreased as scores
on the other variable _____.

10. Which of the following are valid correlation coefficients: $+.83$, $+100$, $+10$, -105, -90, $-.85$, $+.08$? Which is the largest? Which is the smallest?

Answers

1. positive
2. Pearson product
   moment correlation
   coefficient
3. pairs

4. change together
5. $S_X \cdot S_Y$
6. $S_X \cdot S_Y$
7. $+1$; -1
8. decreased

9. increased; decreased
10. $+.83$, $-.85$, $+.08$;
    $-.85$ is the largest;
    $+.08$ is the smallest

Computational Formulas for the Covariance and Correlation Coefficient

Question: Computing the covariance and correlation coefficient is a lot of work. You have to compute the mean for X, the standard deviation for X, the mean for Y, the standard deviation for Y, the mean deviations for X and the mean deviations for Y, and then you have to multiply the mean deviations and then add them. Isn't there a simpler, faster way to do this?

The answer to this question really depends on your sense of humor. Several alternative formulas for computing the covariance and correlation coefficient may save you a little time, but none is simple. The alternative formulas presented next in the text are called computational formulas because they take advantage of the capabilities of scientific calculators and do not require the computation of means, standard deviations, or mean deviations. However, as you will see, they are not simple.

The covariance can be computed by using the following computational formula:

$$\text{cov}_{XY} = \frac{\Sigma XY - \dfrac{\Sigma X \cdot \Sigma Y}{n}}{n - 1} \tag{8.3}$$

The only value in Formula 8.3 that hasn't yet been discussed is the ΣXY. To compute the ΣXY, you need to multiply each X by its paired Y and then sum the products. (Note that this value is different from $\Sigma X \cdot \Sigma Y$, where you add up all the Xs and then multiply that total by the sum of all the Ys.) The computation of the covariance using the computational formula is presented in Table 8.6.

Table 8.6 Computation of the Covariance Using the Computational Formulas for Men's Heights and Weights

Man	Height (X)	X^2	Weight (Y)	Y^2	XY
M. P.	72	5,184	190	36,100	13,680
T. D.	66	4,356	135	18,225	8,910
C. Q.	69	4,761	155	24,025	10,695
C. Y.	72	5,184	165	27,225	11,880
D. P.	71	5,041	155	24,025	11,005

$$\Sigma X = 350 \quad \Sigma X^2 = 24,526 \quad \Sigma Y = 800 \quad \Sigma Y^2 = 129,600 \quad \Sigma XY = 56,170$$

$$\text{cov}_{XY} = \frac{\Sigma XY - \frac{\Sigma X \cdot \Sigma Y}{n}}{n-1} = \frac{56,170 - \frac{350 \cdot 800}{5}}{5-1} = \frac{56,170 - \frac{280,000}{5}}{4}$$

$$= \frac{56,170 - 56,000}{4} = \frac{170}{4} = 42.5$$

You may be thinking, "These numbers are huge and it really seems like a lot of work." Well, the numbers are large, but your calculator does not care how large the numbers are. And it really does take less time than using the deviation formulas, especially if you use the functions of your scientific calculator to compute all the sums. If you check with the covariance computed earlier in the chapter using the values in Table 8.4, you will find it is also 42.5.

You could now use the covariance in Formula 8.2 to compute the correlation coefficient, but there is also a computational formula for the computation of the correlation coefficient:

$$r_{XY} = \frac{(n \cdot \Sigma XY) - (\Sigma X \cdot \Sigma Y)}{\sqrt{[(n \cdot \Sigma X^2) - (\Sigma X)^2] \cdot [(n \cdot \Sigma Y^2) - (\Sigma Y)^2]}} \tag{8.4}$$

Table 8.7 shows the computation of the correlation coefficient using Formula 8.4 for the men's height and weight data. It is clear that these computational formulas are not real shortcuts, but they are not difficult to use, and they will save you a little time in the calculation of the covariance or the correlation coefficient. In addition, the deviation formulas are easier to memorize, but they require several additional calculations and, because of this, are more prone to errors. The computational formulas are more difficult to memorize and can result in large numbers during the calculations, but they require fewer calculations and are therefore less likely to be affected by calculation and roundoff errors. However, remember that both the mean deviation formulas and the computational formulas are mathematically equivalent, and both will give you the same values for the covariance and the correlation coefficient.

Table 8.7 Computation of the Correlation Coefficient Using the Computational Formulas for Men's Heights and Weights

Man	Height (X)	X^2	Weight (Y)	Y^2	XY
M. P.	72	5,184	190	36,100	13,680
T. D.	66	4,356	135	18,225	8,910
C. Q.	69	4,761	155	24,025	10,695
C. Y.	72	5,184	165	27,225	11,880
D. P.	71	5,041	155	24,025	11,005

$$\Sigma X = 350 \quad \Sigma X^2 = 24{,}526 \quad \Sigma Y = 800 \quad \Sigma Y^2 = 129{,}600 \quad \Sigma XY = 56{,}170$$

$$r_{XY} = \frac{(n \cdot \Sigma XY) - (\Sigma X \cdot \Sigma Y)}{\sqrt{\left[(n \cdot \Sigma X^2) - (\Sigma X)^2\right] \cdot \left[(n \cdot \Sigma Y^2) - (\Sigma Y)^2\right]}}$$

$$= \frac{(5 \cdot 56{,}170) - (350 \cdot 800)}{\sqrt{\left[(5 \cdot 24{,}526) - 350^2\right] \cdot \left[(5 \cdot 129{,}600) - 800^2\right]}}$$

$$= \frac{280{,}850 - 280{,}000}{\sqrt{\left[122{,}630 - 122{,}500\right] \cdot \left[648{,}000 - 640{,}000\right]}}$$

$$= \frac{850}{\sqrt{130 \cdot 8{,}000}} = \frac{850}{\sqrt{1{,}040{,}000}} = \frac{850}{1{,}019.804} = .833$$

The Significance of the Correlation Coefficient

Interpreting the Correlation Coefficient: What Do the Numbers Mean?

Obviously, a correlation coefficient of .25 is not the same as a correlation coefficient of .90, but how are they different? What do they mean? As mentioned, some variables are related more closely than others, and the more closely they are related, the closer the correlation will be to +1.000 or −1.000. A correlation coefficient of 0 indicates no relationship at all between the two variables. The relationship between height and weight ($r = +.833$) results in a much higher correlation coefficient (closer to +1.000) than the relationship between the IQs of married couples ($r = +.45$). And the correlation between the number of hassles and the level of immunoglobulin A (−.949) is higher than the correlation between grade point average and the amount of time spent watching television (−.680). Using the preceding formulas, you can compute a correlation coefficient between any two interval or ratio variables. You can compute the correlation between the scores on two different tests, the temperature and the number of people at a beach, manual dexterity score and typing speed, and so on.

Question: If some things are correlated and some things are not, isn't it possible to get a high correlation coefficient just by chance? How do you know when a correlation is real and not due to coincidence?

Detecting whether a correlation is real or is due to chance can present quite a problem. Even if you are sampling from two populations that have absolutely no relationship, it is possible to obtain a group of scores that will return a large correlation coefficient. Look at the correlation between two very important human variables: shoe size and number of friends. There is no psychological theory or common sense reason to suggest that there is any relationship at all between these two variables. If you sampled the entire population of college students and computed the correlation coefficient, you would expect it to be 0. But if you sample only a small number of students, it is possible that simply by chance you could end up with a sample in which big-footed people have the most friends. Consider Table 8.8. The correlation coefficient is positive and small (near 0), but it is not 0. However, it is so close to 0 that the difference could easily be due to chance.

Question: How can you tell when it is a chance deviation from 0 and when it is a true correlation?

The answer to this question involves a discussion of the concepts of hypothesis testing, statistical significance, statistical inference, and degrees of freedom. These topics are discussed in detail in Chapters 10, 11, and 12, so a detailed explanation will be reserved until then. For now, you will be given a little background and will see how to use Table R to determine whether the correlation coefficient is

Table 8.8   Correlation Coefficient for Shoe Size and Number of Friends for Five Students

Student	Shoe Size (X)	X^2	Number of Friends (Y)	Y^2	XY
B. D.	12	144	3	9	36
J. C.	10	100	1	1	10
B. W.	9	81	2	4	18
K. T.	7	49	1	1	7
K. H	6	36	3	9	18
	$\Sigma X = 44$	$\Sigma X^2 = 410$	$\Sigma Y = 10$	$\Sigma Y^2 = 24$	$\Sigma XY = 89$

$$r_{XY} = \frac{(n \cdot \Sigma XY) - (\Sigma X \cdot \Sigma Y)}{\sqrt{\left[(n \cdot \Sigma X^2) - (\Sigma X)^2\right] \cdot \left[(n \cdot \Sigma Y^2) - (\Sigma Y)^2\right]}} = \frac{(5 \cdot 89) - (44 \cdot 10)}{\sqrt{\left[(5 \cdot 410) - 44^2\right] \cdot \left[(5 \cdot 24) - 10^2\right]}}$$

$$= \frac{445 - 440}{\sqrt{\left[2{,}050 - 1{,}936\right] \cdot \left[120 - 100\right]}} = \frac{5}{\sqrt{114 \cdot 20}} = \frac{5}{\sqrt{2{,}280}} = \frac{5}{47.749} = .105$$

likely to be a real correlation, or whether it is likely that the correlation coefficient is only a chance deviation from 0. First, you will begin with something called a critical value. The term **critical value** refers to a numerical value that is used as a decision point. For example, suppose your professor decided that students scoring 90 and above on the next statistics test would receive a grade of A on the test. A score of 90 would then be the critical value because students scoring at or above this score would get an A, and students scoring below 90 would not get an A. Your professor, based on his or her grade standards, sets the critical value. Critical values in statistical analyses are based on the probability of a certain outcome occurring merely by chance. Critical values for the correlation coefficient can be found in Table R in Appendix A.

To find a critical value in Table R, first compute a value called **degrees of freedom** (df). For the correlation coefficient, degrees of freedom are always equal to the number of pairs (n) minus two:

$$df = n - 2 \tag{8.5}$$

Then find the row in Table R that is headed by the appropriate df and move across to the column that is labeled .05 for a two-tailed test to find the critical value of the correlation coefficient. (Two-tailed and one-tailed tests are discussed later in Chapter 11.)

For example, you previously computed a correlation coefficient equal to +.833 for the height and weight data for five men. To find the critical value for this correlation coefficient, you need to first compute the degrees of freedom. Using Formula 8.5, with an n of 5,

$$df = n - 2 = 5 - 2 = 3$$

Using $df = 3$, go to Table R and move down to 3 in the df column and over to the .05 column, where you find a critical value equal to .878. Because correlation coefficients can be either positive or negative, compare the computed correlation coefficient to the critical value found in the table using absolute value. Therefore, the absolute value of any computed correlation coefficient with three degrees of freedom that is greater than or equal to .878 can be considered a real correlation. Any correlation coefficient with three degrees of freedom that is less than .878 might be only a random departure from 0. The height/weight correlation of .833 is obviously less than the critical value of .878, so you are unable to say that this is a real correlation; it might only be a chance deviation from 0. In this case, even though the correlation appears to be close to +1, it is not greater than the critical value and will be treated as if it were actually 0.

> **Question:** This seems awfully strange; .833 is almost 1, but it has to be treated as if it were 0?

Yes, because it was not greater than the critical value. The critical value is quite large due to the small sample size. If you take a look at Table R, you will notice that if there were 10 people in the sample rather than 5, the degrees of freedom would have been 8 and the critical value would have been .632. In small samples, the chances of making chance errors are much higher than in large samples, so the critical values are higher.

Before moving on, take a look at the correlation coefficient between the number of hassles and the level of immunoglobulin A that was computed in Table 8.5. The correlation coefficient was $-.949$. There were 10 pairs of scores in this sample, making n equal to 10. The degrees of freedom, $n - 2$, equals 8. The critical value from Table R is .632. Before you compare this correlation to the critical value, you need to know that all the critical values in Table R can be used with both positive and negative correlation coefficients. To compare a negative correlation coefficient to the critical value, compare the absolute value of the correlation coefficient to the critical value and proceed as if the correlation were positive. The absolute value of $-.949$ is .949, and .949 is greater than the critical value, .632. Therefore, there is reason to believe that the correlation between hassles and the level of immunoglobulin A is real; it is significantly greater than 0.

> **Question:** When there is a high correlation that is greater than the critical value, like hassles and the level of immunoglobulin A, does that mean that one thing, hassles, causes the other, the level of immunoglobulin A?

No! The correlation coefficient is a measure of whether or not the two variables are related. It does *not* indicate whether one variable causes the other. It is very important to understand that *correlation does not mean causation.* Just because there is a correlation between skin cancer and the number of times that a person wears a bathing suit, it does not mean that bathing suits cause skin cancer. Consider the following example. There is a positive correlation between the number of migrating whales passing Point Loma (in San Diego) and the number of migrating birds passing the same point. Even if this correlation were very high, no rational person would claim that the whale migration is caused by the bird migration or, conversely, that the bird migration is caused by the whale migration. (Only in a cartoon would you see a whale breaching and calling to a group of birds nesting nearby, "Yo, birds. Better get a move on; it's time to migrate.") Often, two variables are correlated with each other because they are both caused by a third variable. In the case of the migrations, this variable might be a seasonal change in temperature that in turn affects the availability of food or nesting opportunities. In the skin cancer example, the variable might be hot weather that causes people to wear bathing suits, which results in an increased exposure to the sun, which in turn causes skin cancer. Whatever the cause, it cannot be determined with correlational studies. The only way to determine the cause of any phenomenon is through experimental procedures.

Another important thing to note about correlational studies is that both variables of interest (height and weight, number of whales and number of birds, bathing suits and skin cancer, etc.) are measured by the researcher, but neither is manipulated or controlled by the researcher, as is done in a true experiment. This lack of manipulation or control is the reason that no determination of causation can be made using the correlational statistical method. Only by conducting an experiment can a researcher determine that one variable causes a change in another.

The Coefficient of Determination

Correlations cannot be used to explain whether or not one variable causes another, but they can be used for predictive purposes, nonetheless. For instance, if the correlation were high quite high in the preceding example, you might predict that because the birds were 2 weeks late in the beginning of their migration, the whales might also be late. But how accurate is such a prediction? Should the companies that organize whale-watching trips postpone the trips for 2 weeks? There is a statistical tool to measure the accuracy of correlational predictions. Known as the **coefficient of determination,** it is the part of the variance of one variable that can be explained by, or attributed to, the variance of a related variable. Often, the variance explained is called the *effect size* of the statistic. It is important to know not only that your statistic is significant but also whether that significance is meaningful. The more of the variance in the data that is explained by the statistic, the more meaningful is the statistic.

Because this is a difficult concept to grasp, the following additional explanation may help. You know from previous chapters that there is always some variability in any group of scores. For example, you know that the scores for height and the scores for weight are distributed around their means. The amount that these scores differ from the mean can be measured by the variance. You also know that these variances are due to, or can be explained by, several different factors. The variability in weight, for example, can be explained by how much a person eats, what he eats, his genetics, how much he exercises, his height, and many more factors. Therefore, one of the reasons that people vary in weight is because they also vary in height. If people were all the same height, there would be less variability in weight. By using the coefficient of determination, you can determine how much of the variance of one factor (weight) can be explained by the variability of a factor with which it is correlated (height). Easy to calculate, the coefficient of determination is the square of the correlation coefficient:

$$\text{Coefficient of determination} = r^2 \tag{8.6}$$

As an illustration, suppose that the bird and whale migrations were correlated with an *r* of .50. Using the coefficient of determination, .25 ($.50^2$) of the variance in the time of whale migrations can be explained by the variance in the time of bird migrations. .75, or 75%, of the variance can be explained by other factors. Therefore, even if the birds were 2 weeks late in their migration, you would not necessarily expect the whales to be 2 weeks late because 75% of the variation in whale migration is explained by factors other than bird migration.

Question: Considering the formula for the coefficient of determination, is it correct to assume that a correlation coefficient of +.40 is not actually half as good as a correlation coefficient of +.80?

That is exactly right. With a correlation coefficient of +.40, only .16, or 16%, of the variance of one variable is predictable from the other variable. A correlation coefficient of .80 explains 64% of the variance. Actually, through comparison it is evident that a correlation coefficient of +.80 explains *4 times* the variance of a correlation coefficient of +.40. The coefficient of determination for +.80, which is .64, is 4 times that of +.40, which is .16. Correlation cannot explain causation—only an experiment can do that—but correlation is the basis of most predictions that are made using behavioral science data, and the coefficient of determination tells you how accurate those predictions are likely to be. The use of the correlation coefficient to make predictions is called regression analysis, which is the topic of Chapter 9.

Concept Quiz

Clinical studies suggest a strong positive relationship between eating and alcohol use disorders (Holderness, Brooks-Gunn, & Warren, 1994). Suppose you assessed the eating and alcohol behaviors of 20 women on your campus. Answer the following data analysis questions.

1. The computational formulas allow you to compute the covariance and the correlation coefficient without using _____.

2. How are the terms ΣXY and $\Sigma X \cdot \Sigma Y$ different?

3. In this study, what are the degrees of freedom and the critical value of r?

4. If there is a relationship between eating and alcohol behaviors ($r = .68$), does this suggest that the women's eating behavior caused them to increase their use of alcoholic beverages?

5. Explain why the critical value of r increases if sample size decreases.

6. The coefficient of determination is equal to _____.

7. If the correlation coefficient in this study was $-.5$, approximately _____% of the variance of one variable could be explained by the variance of the other variable.

Answers

1. means, mean deviations, or standard deviations

2. To compute ΣXY, you multiply each X by its paired Y value, then sum those products. To compute $\Sigma X \cdot \Sigma Y$, you add all the Xs, add

all the *Y*s, and then multiply the sums.

3. 18; critical $r = .378$
4. No. Correlation does not imply causation.

5. As the sample size gets smaller, there is more possibility of a correlation by chance.

6. r^2
7. 25

Summary

A scatterplot is a graph in which individual pairs of scores are plotted as points in order to view the relationship between two variables. If the general slope of the points in a scatterplot is positive, then the relationship is positive; if the general slope of the points in the scatterplot is negative, then the relationship is negative. If there is no general slope—that is, the points are totally random—there is no relationship.

This chapter describes two statistics that measure the relationship between two variables. The covariance (cov_{xy}) is basically a number that represents the degree to which two different variables change together. The correlation coefficient is a measure of the relationship between two variables that can be no lower than -1 and no greater than $+1$. The closer the correlation coefficient is to $+1$ or to -1, the stronger is the relationship. A correlation equal to 0 indicates no relationship between the two variables.

The coefficient of determination, computed by squaring the correlation coefficient, tells the proportion of the variability of one variable that can be explained by the other variable. It is extremely important to remember that no matter how large the correlation coefficient or how large the coefficient of determination, correlation does not imply causation.

Key Terms

correlation
scatterplot
correlation coefficient

covariance
degrees of freedom
(*df*)

coefficient of
determination

Formulas

$$cov_{XY} = \frac{\Sigma\left[(X - \overline{X}) \cdot (Y - \overline{Y})\right]}{n - 1} \tag{8.1}$$

$$r_{XY} = \frac{cov_{XY}}{S_X \cdot S_Y} \tag{8.2}$$

$$\text{cov}_{XY} = \frac{\Sigma XY - \dfrac{\Sigma X \cdot \Sigma Y}{n}}{n-1} \tag{8.3}$$

$$r_{XY} = \frac{(n \cdot \Sigma XY) - (\Sigma X \cdot \Sigma Y)}{\sqrt{[(n \cdot \Sigma X^2) - (\Sigma X)^2] \cdot [(n \cdot \Sigma Y^2) - (\Sigma Y)^2]}} \tag{8.4}$$

$$df = n - 2 \tag{8.5}$$

$$\text{Coefficient of determination} = r^2 \tag{8.6}$$

Problems

Past research has suggested a correlation between a person's verbal score on the SAT and his or her birth order. (Birth order is a measure of the order in which you are born into a family. If you are the first child, your birth order equals 1, etc.) You want to see whether this trend has changed in recent years, so you ask 10 of your friends their birth orders and their verbal SAT scores. Use the data in the following table to solve Problems 1–4.

Participant	Birth Order (X)	Verbal SAT Score (Y)
1	1	650
2	2	550
3	4	450
4	1	500
5	3	475
6	4	425
7	2	565
8	2	525
9	6	400
10	3	480

1. Using the scores in the table, draw a scatterplot and state whether you think the correlation between birth order and SAT score is positive, negative, or zero.

2. Compute the covariance of the scores in the table.

3. Using the scores in the table, compute the correlation coefficient, compute the degrees of freedom, find the critical value in Table R, and state whether or not the correlation coefficient is significantly greater than 0.

4. Compute the coefficient of determination and explain what it represents.

The following table lists the typing speed as measured by a standardized typing test for 12 college students, along with the number of pages they had to type for their Sociological Research Methods class. Use the data to solve Problems 5–8.

Student	Number of Pages Typed	Typing Speed
Chris	37	73
Mary	6	24
Paul	12	36
Juan	24	72
Marcel	16	50
Olga	7	19
Ni	22	49
Nima	4	6
Sari	34	48
Jarrod	32	59
Kevin	17	38
Lisa	8	16

5. Compute the covariance of the scores in the table.

6. Using the scores in the table, compute the correlation coefficient, compute the degrees of freedom, find the critical value in Table R, and state whether or not the correlation coefficient is significantly greater than 0.

7. Given the correlation coefficient that you computed in Problem 6, what proportion of the variance of typing speed can be explained by the variance in the number of pages typed?

8. Using the scores in the table, draw a scatterplot and state whether you think the correlation between number of pages typed and typing speed is positive, negative, or zero.

Use the following test data to solve Problems 9–12.

Participant	Test A	Test B
T. K.	700	35
D. M.	772	38
S. T.	605	36
B. P.	721	39
S. M.	695	34

9. Using the scores in the table, draw a scatterplot and state whether you think the correlation between test A and test B is positive, negative, or zero.

10. Compute the covariance of the scores in the table.

11. Using the scores in the table, compute the correlation coefficient, compute the degrees of freedom, find the critical value in Table R, and state whether or not the correlation coefficient is significantly greater than 0.

12. Compute the coefficient of determination and explain what it represents.

An industrial psychologist has collected data consisting of on-the-job aptitude scores and the numbers of assembly line errors for five of his workers. The data are listed in the following table. Use the data to solve Problems 13–16.

Worker	Aptitude Test Score	Errors
P. K.	13	22
M. D.	7	48
L. S.	24	5
T. D.	19	12
M. P.	25	6

13. Compute the covariance of the scores in the table.

14. Using the scores in the table, compute the correlation coefficient, compute the degrees of freedom, find the critical value in Table R, and state whether or not the correlation coefficient is significantly greater than 0.

15. Given the correlation coefficient that you computed in Problem 14, what proportion of the variance of assembly errors can be explained by the variance in the aptitude test scores?

16. Using the scores in the table, draw a scatterplot and state whether you think the correlation between number of pages typed and typing speed is positive, negative, or zero.

A survey was conducted by a human sexuality research laboratory on the use of birth control by newly married couples. One of their striking findings was that the couples who owned the most electrical appliances were more likely to use birth control. The data for seven couples are given here. Use these data to solve Problems 17–21.

Couple	Birth Control Use	Electrical Appliances Owned
A	85	9
B	80	7
C	66	7
D	50	4
E	40	3
F	20	1
G	0	2

17. Compute the covariance of the scores in the table.

18. Using the scores in the table, compute the correlation coefficient, compute the degrees of freedom, find the critical value in Table R, and state whether or not the correlation coefficient is significantly greater than 0.

19. Given the correlation coefficient you computed in Problem 18, what proportion of the variance of birth control use can be explained by the variance in the electrical appliances owned?

20. Using the scores in the table, draw a scatterplot and state whether you think the correlation between birth control use and the number of electrical appliances owned is positive, negative, or zero.

21. Given the data, does it make statistical sense for the government to begin giving toasters to teenage girls to help in the fight against teen pregnancy? Please explain your answer in a few sentences.

Use the following values to solve Problems 22–24.
   .73 1.77 −.77 106 −23 −.23 −.75 .45

22. Which of these values are possible correlation coefficients?

23. Which of these values is the highest of the possible correlation coefficients?

24. Which of these values is the lowest of the possible correlation coefficients?

The following are personality test scores for 10 pairs of male and female fraternal twins. Use these data to solve Problems 25–28.

Male Twin	Female Twin
88	86
76	65
96	84
36	47
54	48
66	66
73	65
85	72
90	99
23	18

25. Using the scores in the table, draw a scatterplot and state whether you think the correlation between the male twin and the female twin is positive, negative, or zero.

26. Compute the covariance of the scores in the table.

27. Using the scores in the table, compute the correlation coefficient, compute the degrees of freedom, find the critical value in Table R, and state whether or not the correlation coefficient is significantly greater than 0.

28. Compute the coefficient of determination and explain what it represents.

29. If you know that the correlation coefficient between two tests is +.79, you expect a person who gets a high score on one of the tests to get a _____ score on the other test.

30. If you know that the correlation coefficient between two tests is −.79, you expect a person who gets a high score on one of the tests to get a _____ score on the other test.

31. Explain why a high correlation between two variables does not mean that one variable causes the other.

32. Give an example not used in this book or in your class lectures of two variables that are positively correlated, and give an example not used in this book or your class lectures of two variables that are negatively correlated.

33. What is the critical value for a correlation coefficient that was computed using 15 scores?

34. What is the critical value for a correlation coefficient that was computed using 30 scores?

Student	Grip Strength	Introversion/Extroversion
Jamie	3	16
Carrie	4	21
Bob	7	35
Jorge	5	30
Olga	3	19
Robin	6	36
Linso	2	15
Nima	3	11
Yukari	6	28
Mark	8	36
Harrison	9	32
Anna	9	27

35. Compute the covariance of the scores in the table.

36. Using the scores in the table, draw a scatterplot and determine whether there is a linear relationship between these variables.

37. If the linearity assumption is met, compute the correlation coefficient, compute the degrees of freedom, find the critical value in Table R, and state whether or not the correlation coefficient is significantly greater than 0.

38. If the relationship is significant, what proportion of the variance in grip strength can be explained by the variance in introversion/extroversion scores?

39. The findings, according to Dr. Strong, revealed that extroversion is a personality characteristic that makes people have a stronger handshake. Do you agree? Why or why not?

Problems From the Literature

The following problems refer to actual results from research studies that are cited at the end of the chapter. However, the data used to generate the problem sets are hypothetical.

Chaplin, Phillips, Brown, Clanton, and Stein (2000) found that the characteristics of one's handshake, particularly grip strength, were related to first impressions. Suppose another researcher, Dr. Strong, examined grip strength and extroversion. At the time of recruitment, he set up appointments to meet participants in the lab. When participants arrived for the appointment, they were introduced and shook hands with a friendly six-person research team. Members of the research team were trained to independently score grip strength using a 1 to 9 scale with 1 = very weak grip and 9 = very strong grip. After the introductions, each participant was asked to complete a personality inventory that included an introversion/extroversion scale. The data for this study follow. (Note: Higher scores indicate higher extroversion.) Use this information to solve Problems 35–39.

Iwata (2001) investigated relationships between proenvironmental attitudes and 20 concepts of nature. As expected, proenvironmental attitudes were related to several of the concepts of nature measured. However, further analyses revealed the 20 concepts were part of two overarching concepts: (1) positive evaluation of nature and (2) rejection of manipulation of human life. Suppose you assessed the relationship between knowledge of the environment and proenvironmental behavior, such as recycling and using biodegradable products, on your campus. Data from your study follow. (Note: Higher numbers indicate more positive evaluations of nature and more proenvironmental behaviors.) Use this information to solve Problems 40–44.

Student ID number	Positive Evaluation of Nature	Proenvironmental Behaviors
1	7	12
2	6	8
3	7	5
4	5	11
5	8	19
6	6	9
7	4	6
8	9	11
9	6	2
10	8	16
11	5	7
12	8	19
13	7	10
14	7	13
15	3	8

40. Compute the covariance of the scores in the table.

41. Using the scores in the table, draw a scatterplot and determine whether there is a linear relationship between these variables.

42. If the linearity assumption is met, compute the correlation coefficient, compute the degrees of freedom, find the critical value in Table R, and state whether or not the correlation coefficient is significantly greater than 0.

43. If the relationship is significant, what proportion of the variance in proenvironmental behaviors can be

accounted for by knowledge of the environment?

44. Use the variables in this study to explain why correlation is not causation.

McCullough, Hoyt, Larson, Koenig, and Thoresen's (2000) meta-analysis involved examining data from many studies connecting religious involvement and mortality. Their work provided further support for a strong positive relationship between the length of life and involvement in religion. Thus, identifying factors related to religious involvement could be quite useful in understanding its relationship to mortality. Suppose another researcher conducted a new study among participants who identified themselves as religiously active and assessed the relationship between the number of friends they have and the number of times they were sick in a year. The data collected from this study are shown in the following table. Use the data and the information about the study to solve Problems 45–49.

Participant ID Number	Friends	Times Sick
1	7	5
2	11	1
3	13	0
4	5	3
5	19	0
6	28	1
7	6	3
8	21	0
9	17	1
10	20	2
11	17	0
12	9	2
13	9	1
14	16	0
15	22	1
16	14	0
17	12	1
18	10	1

45. Does the researcher expect a positive or negative relationship between the numbers of friends a person has and the frequency they are sick?

46. Compute the covariance of the scores in the table.

47. The researcher has done a scatterplot and confirmed a linear relationship between number of friends and number of times sick. Compute the correlation coefficient, compute the degrees of freedom, find the critical value in Table R, and state whether or not the correlation coefficient is significantly greater than 0.

48. If the relationship is significant, what proportion of the variance in the number of friends participants reported can be accounted for by the number of times they said they were sick?

49. Did the number of friendships buffer participants from illness? Explain why or why not.

References

Chaplin, W. F., Phillips, J. B., Brown, J. D., Clanton, N. R., & Stein, J. L. (2000). Handshaking, gender, personality, and first impressions. *Journal of Personality and Social Psychology, 110*–117.

Holderness, C. C., Brooks-Gunn, J., & Warren, M. P. (1994). Comorbidity of eating disorders and substance abuse review of literature. *International Journal of Eating Disorders, 16(1)*, 1–34.

Holmes, T. H., & Rahe, R. H. (1967). The social readjustment rating scale. *Journal of Psychosomatic Research, 11*, 213–218.

Huston, T. L., Caughlin, J. P., Houts, R. M., Smith, S. E., & George, L. J. (2001). The connubial crucible: Newlywed years as predictors of marital delight, distress, and divorce. *Journal of Personality and Social Psychology, 80*, 237–252.

Iwata, O. (2001). Relationships between proenvironmental attitudes and concepts of nature. *Journal of Social Psychology, 141*, 75–83.

Martin, R. A., & Dobbin, J. P. (1998). Sense of humor, hassles, and Immunoglobulin A: Evidence of a stress-moderating effect of humor. *International Journal of Psychiatry in Medicine, 18(2)*, 93–105.

McCullough, M. F., Hoyt, W. T., Larson, D. B., Koenig, H. G., & Thoresen, C. (2000). Religious involvement and mortality: A meta-analytic review. *Health Psychology, 19*, 211–222.

Regression

- Making Predictions via Linear Regression
  The z-Score Method: Using Y to Predict X
  The z-Score Method: Using X to Predict Y
  VISUAL SUMMARY: Using *z* Scores to Make Predictions
- The Regression Line: Faster Predictions
- The Standard Error of the Estimate
  VISUAL SUMMARY: Using Regression Equations to Make Predictions
- Summary
- Key Terms
- Formulas
- Problems
  Problems From the Literature
- References

 magine that you are back in the college cafeteria playing the same guessing game described at the beginning of Chapter 8. Once again, you are trying to guess the height of the next man who enters the cafeteria, and your friend is still outside weighing each man before he comes through the door. However, this time you have more information. Now you know not only the mean height of all men who attend your college but also the mean weight and the standard deviations for both height and weight:

Height (X)	Weight (Y)
$\overline{X} = 70$ inches	$\overline{Y} = 160$ pounds
$S_X = 2.550$ inches	$S_Y = 20.000$ pounds

This time, when your friend outside sticks her head in the door and shouts "120 pounds," what will you do? You know from Chapter 8 that height and weight are positively correlated. You also know that because 120 pounds is well below the mean for weight, you should guess a height that is proportionally as far below the mean as is the weight. But how far below the mean should you guess? See if you can figure out a way to use this new information to calculate a guess that will be a realistic estimate based on what you know. Compute the new guess and then continue reading.

Question: Can the weight just be converted to a *z* score and then the corresponding *z* score for height be found?

This sounds like a good idea, and it will work if the height and weight are perfectly correlated. Suppose that height and weight *are* perfectly correlated, with $r = +1.000$. Assuming this, you can predict that the man's height should lie proportionally the same distance from the mean as his weight. Consequently, each pair of height/weight scores should have the same z score. Because you know the means and the standard deviations, you can find a specific z score for weight, use this to find the z score for height, and then convert the z score to a raw score.

First you compute the z score for a weight of 120 pounds:

$$z_Y = \frac{Y - \overline{Y}}{S_Y} = \frac{120 - 160}{20.000} = \frac{-40}{20.000} = -2.000$$

Then, because of your assumption that height and weight are perfectly correlated, the z score for X should equal the z score for Y. So $z_x = -2.236$. You can then use a variant of Formula 7.7 to convert this z score to a raw score:

$$X = \overline{X} + (z_X \cdot S_X) = 70 + (-2.000 \cdot 2.550) = 70 - 5.100 = 64.900 \text{ inches}$$

You can thereby predict that the man who weighs 120 pounds is probably about 65 inches tall.

As hinted earlier, there is one huge flaw in this approach: Behavioral science variables are never perfectly correlated. It's true that taller people tend to weigh more than shorter people, students who spend a lot of time studying tend to get higher grades, and people who wear bathing suits more often tend to get more skin cancers. But when it comes to human and animal behavior, there are always so many fluctuations and irregularities that there is little chance of a *perfect* correlation ever occurring between two behavioral variables. For instance, have you ever been on a diet and actually *gained* weight? If you doubt that this can happen, just attend a couple of Weight Watchers meetings. It is extremely unlikely to come across a study involving two behavioral variables where the correlation is equal to $+1.000$ or -1.000, and almost as unlikely to see a correlation coefficient above $+.900$ or below $-.900$. In fact, the preceding example explaining how to predict height based on a z score of weight is completely bogus because we assumed a perfect correlation between height and weight. Such correlation is nonexistent. (Just look around a room full of people and count how many exceptions there are to the "perfect" figure or physique.)

Question: How do you make predictions when the relationship is not perfect?

Making Predictions via Linear Regression

The simplest way to make predictions is to use linear regression, and making accurate predictions through linear regression is what the rest of this chapter is all about. In using this type of prediction, a vital assumption is made: that the variables used

Figure 9.1
Examples of types of
relationships: (a) and
(b) are linear
relationships,
whereas (c) and
(d) are curvilinear
relationships.

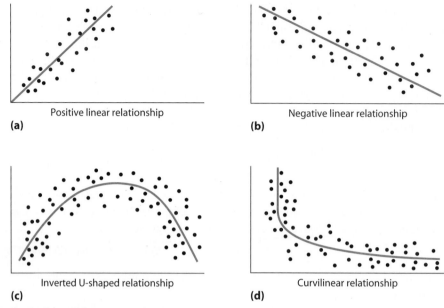

Positive linear relationship

(a)

Negative linear relationship

(b)

Inverted U-shaped relationship

(c)

Curvilinear relationship

(d)

to make the prediction are linearly related. Linear relationship are illustrated in Figures 9.1(a) and (b), where the line that best fits the set of data points in a scatterplot is a *straight line*. Data distributed in a *non*linear fashion, such as those in Figures 9.1(c) and (d), do not satisfy this assumption and cannot be used in linear regression.

The *z*-Score Method: Using *Y* to Predict *X*

Height and weight are related in a linear fashion, so linear regression can be used to make height/weight predictions. In the preceding example, z scores were used to predict a man's height when his weight is known. To make such a prediction valid, you must take into consideration the *value of the correlation* between the two variables. The correlation between the two variables is used to adjust your prediction and make it more accurate. If the variables were perfectly correlated, with r equal to $+1.000$, the preceding method would be acceptable; when the two variables are not perfectly correlated, this fact must be reflected in the prediction. To make a more accurate prediction of one factor, (X) from another factor (Y) when there is a known correlation between the two, you need only multiply the z score of the known factor by the correlation coefficient (r_{XY}) to predict the z score of the other factor:

$$\hat{z}_X = z_Y \cdot r_{XY} \qquad\qquad (9.1)$$

[*Note:* The symbol $\hat{z}_X$ (pronounced z hat sub x) is used to designate the predicted value of the z score of X. The predicted value of a variable or a z score is indicated by a ^, called a "hat," above the symbol. ($\hat{Y}$ and $\hat{X}$ are called "Y-hat" and "X-hat.")]

For the height/weight data used in Chapter 8, there is the following information:

Height (X)	Weight (Y)
$\overline{X} = 70$ inches	$\overline{Y} = 160$ pounds
$S_X = 2.550$ inches	$S_Y = 20.000$ pounds
$r_{XY} = .833$	

A valid prediction of the height of a 120-pound man can be made by first computing the z score of his weight:

$$z_Y = \frac{Y - \overline{Y}}{S_Y} = \frac{120 - 160}{20.000} = \frac{-40}{20.000} = -2.000$$

Then you can use Formula 9.1 to predict the z score of his height:

$$\hat{z}_X = z_Y \cdot r_{XY} = -2.000 \cdot .833 = -1.666$$

Finally, you can use a modification of Formula 7.7 to convert the z score of his height into the raw score, in inches:

$$\hat{X} = \overline{X} + (\hat{z}_X \cdot S_X) = 70 + (-1.666 \cdot 2.550) = 70 - 4.248 = 65.752 \text{ inches}$$

Thus, you can predict that a man who weighs 120 pounds will be about 65 3/4 inches tall.

As you may have noticed, 65.752 inches is slightly taller and slightly closer to the mean (70 inches) than the height predicted using z scores alone, which was 64.902 inches. When making predictions, predicted values are always a little closer to the mean than the known values. Consider the task of predicting the height of the daughter of a 7-foot 5-inch woman. Even though we know that tallness tends to run in families, we have to admit that the height of this woman is atypical and that her daughter's height will almost certainly be between the mean and her mother's incredible height. This is what happens when any unknown variable is predicted from one that is known. The predicted value always *regresses,* or goes back toward the mean. The term *regression* indicates a movement back toward something. Psychoanalysts use the term *regression* to indicate a backward personality shift toward a more infantile coping strategy. Statisticians use the term **regression** to indicate a backward shift toward the mean when they are predicting an unknown value from a known value when the two values are correlated.

The amount of regression toward the mean depends on the value of the correlation coefficient, r. If r is equal to 0, if there is no correlation, the predicted value will always be a z score of 0, which is the mean; if r is equal to $+1.000$, the predicted value will be equal to the value of the known variable (remember, $\hat{z}_X = z_Y \cdot r_{XY}$). So if r is low, or close to 0, the predicted value will be closer to the value of the mean than it would be if r were closer to $+1$ or -1. One way to think of this is to consider the coefficient of determination (r^2). A high r will have a high coefficient of determination, and more of the variance of one variable will be explained by the variance in the other variable, thus allowing a prediction farther from the mean and resulting in a more accurate overall prediction.

The z-Score Method: Using X to Predict Y

Question: What if the cafeteria game is once again changed so that now the men's heights are given but their weights must be predicted. Can the same formula be used?

No; you can't use the same formula because you can't plug in a known X value and solve backward to predict Y. However, there is a similar formula for predicting Y values. The two regression equations are shown here. One is used for predicting X, the other for predicting Y:

$$\hat{z}_X = z_Y \cdot r_{XY} \tag{9.1}$$

$$\hat{z}_Y = z_X \cdot r_{XY} \tag{9.2}$$

In the guessing game, you know that the next man who will enter the room is 72 inches tall. His known height is the X value; what you want to predict is the Y value, his weight. You can use Formula 9.2 to predict the man's weight. The first step is to convert the height of 72 inches to a z score:

$$z_X = \frac{X - \overline{X}}{S_X} = \frac{72 - 70}{2.550} = \frac{2}{2.550} = .784$$

Next, predict the z score of Y using Formula 9.2:

$$\hat{z}_Y = z_X \cdot r_{XY} = .784 \cdot .833 = .653$$

Now convert the predicted z score into a raw score by using the equivalent of Formula 7.7.

$$\hat{Y} = \overline{Y} + (\hat{z}_Y \cdot S_Y) = 160 + (.653 \cdot 20.000) = 160 + 13.060$$

$$= 173.060 \text{ pounds}$$

Now apply prediction via linear regression to a more productive situation: Step into the future a few years and imagine yourself as an industrial psychologist who needs to predict job performance from a job aptitude test. You give several current employees the aptitude test and compute the correlation between these test scores and their monthly job performance scores. The results of your research are shown in Table 9.1 and are summarized as follows:

Job Aptitude Test (X)	Job Performance Score (Y)
$\overline{X} = 54$	$\overline{Y} = 77$
$S_X = 8.110$	$S_Y = 12.009$
$r_{XY} = .792$	

Table 9.1 Computation of Mean, Standard Deviation, and Correlation Coefficient for Job Aptitude Test (X) and Job Performance (Y) Data

Worker	X	X^2	Y	Y^2	XY
M. P.	65	4,225	90	8,100	5,850
T. D.	60	3,600	95	9,025	5,700
C. Q.	62	3,844	82	6,724	5,084
C. Y.	59	3,481	87	7,569	5,133
D. P.	58	3,364	80	6,400	4,640
J. D.	53	2,890	75	5,625	3,975
Q. R.	50	2,500	60	3,600	3,000
N. N.	48	2,304	69	4,761	3,312
M. O.	45	2,025	60	3,600	2,700
Y. T.	40	1,600	72	5,184	2,880

$$\Sigma X = 540 \quad \Sigma X^2 = 29,752 \quad \Sigma Y = 770 \qquad \Sigma XY = 42,274$$

$$\overline{X} = 54 \qquad\qquad\qquad \overline{Y} = 77$$

$$S_X = 8.110 \qquad\qquad\qquad S_Y = 12.009$$

$$r_{XY} = \frac{(n \cdot \Sigma XY) - (\Sigma X \cdot \Sigma Y)}{\sqrt{\left[(n \cdot \Sigma X^2) - (\Sigma X)^2\right] \cdot \left[(n \cdot \Sigma Y^2) - (\Sigma Y)^2\right]}}$$

$$= \frac{(10 \cdot 42,274) - (540 \cdot 770)}{\sqrt{\left[(10 \cdot 29,752) - 540^2\right] \cdot \left[(10 \cdot 60,588) - 770^2\right]}}$$

$$= \frac{422,740 - 415,800}{\sqrt{\left[297,520 - 291,600\right] \cdot \left[605,880 - 592,900\right]}}$$

$$= \frac{6,940}{\sqrt{5,920 \cdot 12,980}} = \frac{6,940}{\sqrt{76,841,600}} = \frac{6,940}{8,765.934} = .792$$

A correlation coefficient of $+.792$ indicates that the aptitude test is a pretty good predictor of job performance, so you decide to use it for screening job applicants. The first applicant who takes the test scores 57. From this you want to predict her job performance. What do you do first? Convert the test score to a z score:

$$z_X = \frac{X - \overline{X}}{S_X} = \frac{57 - 54}{8.110} = \frac{3}{8.110} = .370$$

Next, use Formula 9.2 to compute the predicted z score for job performance:

$$\hat{z}_Y = z_X \cdot r_{XY} = .370 \cdot .792 = .293$$

Then use Formula 7.7 to find the predicted raw score for job performance:

$$\hat{Y} = \overline{Y} + (\hat{z}_Y \cdot S_Y) = 77 + (.293 \cdot 12.009) = 77 + 3.519 = 80.519$$

Should you recommend hiring this applicant? Because her predicted job performance is very high, you would certainly want to hire her if you are basing your decision solely on the outcome of this job aptitude test.

VISUAL SUMMARY

Using z Scores to Make Predictions

Before You Begin: Compute $\overline{X}$, $\overline{Y}$, S_X, S_Y, r.

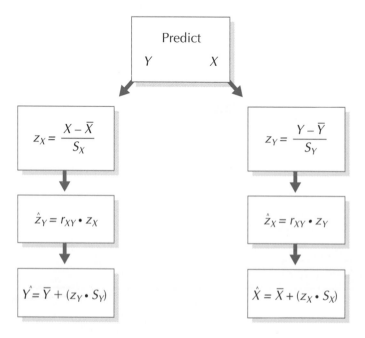

Concept Quiz

Researchers Wright and Cropanzano (2000) conducted several field studies among human service workers and compared the relative contributions of both their job satisfaction and psychological well-being as predictors of job performance. They found that psychological well-being (X), not job satisfaction, was a predictor of job performance (Y).

1. The simplest way to make accurate predictions based on means, standard deviations, and the correlation coefficient is to use _____.

2. To use linear regression, there must be a _____ line relationship between psychological well-being and job performance, the two variables involved in the prediction.

3. To use the z-score method of linear regression for predicting an X value from a Y value, you must first convert the _____ value to a _____.

4. The predicted z score of psychological well-being (X) is equal to the _____ times the _____.

5. The predicted z score value always _____ toward the mean.

6. The smaller the correlation coefficient, the _____ the predicted value will be to the mean.

7. The symbol "$\hat{Y}$" is called _____ and represents _____.

Answers

1. linear regression
2. straight
3. Y; z score
4. z score of job performance (Y);

correlation coefficient between X and Y
5. regresses
6. closer

7. Y-hat; the predicted value of job performance (Y)

The Regression Line: Faster Predictions

Question: Do three separate formulas always have to be used to make a prediction?

No, they don't. Remember that when the discussion of regression first began, the point was made that only variables with a straight-line relationship are candidates for linear regression. Therefore, it is possible to use one equation to make a prediction, the equation for a straight line. Think back to your algebra class. The equation for a straight line is $Y = bX + a$. (You may have used different letters in place of a and b, but these are the letters that are used by most statisticians.) Because you will be using this formula to make predictions, you should write the **regression equation** like this:

$$\hat{Y} = bX + a \tag{9.3}$$

where

$\hat{Y}$ = the predicted value of Y

b = the slope of the regression line (the amount of change in Y associated with a one-unit change in X)

a = the Y intercept (the predicted value of Y when $X = 0$)

X = the value of X used to predict Y

In your algebra class, you were able to create this formula using any two points to compute b and a. The case of linear regression is a bit more complicated. Typically, there are many points that tend in one direction, but they are not all on a single straight line. Therefore, your task is to find the straight line that is the *best* fit for all those points. [See Figures 9.1(a) and (b).] There are several approaches you could take to find the *best* fitting straight line. The most useful approach is to find the line that minimizes the sum of the squared errors made when predicting from the line—that is, the line that minimizes $\Sigma(Y - \hat{Y})^2$. The formulas for b and a are

$$b = \frac{\text{cov}_{XY}}{S_X^2} = r_{XY} \cdot \frac{S_Y}{S_X} \tag{9.4}$$

$$a = \overline{Y} - (b \cdot \overline{X}) \tag{9.5}$$

Because they are used in a regression equation, the values of a and b are called **regression coefficients.** Note that the formula for b can be computed using either the covariance or the correlation coefficient, depending on which you have available. In addition, the formula for a requires that you have first computed b. It might seem like a lot of work to create the equation for a straight line, but these formulas use values that are available after computing the covariance or the correlation coefficient. Once you have computed b and a, making a prediction or multiple predictions is quite easy.

As an example, use the height and weight data to predict the weight of a man who is 73 inches tall. The height/weight data are repeated here:

Height (X)	Weight (Y)
$\overline{X} = 70$ inches	$\overline{Y} = 160$ pounds
$S_X = 2.550$ inches	$S_Y = 20.000$ pounds
$r_{XY} = .833$	

To use Formula 9.3, you will need to first compute a and b using Formulas 9.4 and 9.5. First, compute b using Formula 9.4:

$$b = r_{XY} \cdot \frac{S_Y}{S_X} = .833 \cdot \frac{20}{2.550} = .833 \cdot 7.843 = 6.533$$

Use Formula 9.5 to compute a:

$$a = \overline{Y} - (b \cdot \overline{X}) = 160 - (6.533 \cdot 70) = 160 - 457.310 = -297.310$$

Now you can create the regression equation using Formula 9.3:

$$\hat{Y} = bX + a = 6.533X - 297.310$$

Finally, substituting 73 inches for X, you get the predicted weight:

$$\hat{Y} = bX + a = 6.533X - 297.310 = (6.533 \cdot 73) - 297.310$$
$$= 476.909 - 297.310 = 179.599 \text{ pounds}$$

To predict X instead of Y, you can use a similar formula, but remember that to predict X, you must use different values for a and b:

$$\hat{X} = bY + a \tag{9.6}$$

where

$\hat{X}$ = the predicted value of X

b = the slope of the regression line (the amount of change in X associated with a one-unit change in Y)

a = the X intercept (the predicted value of X when $Y = 0$)

Y = the value of Y used to predict X

$$b = \frac{\text{cov}_{XY}}{S_Y^2} = r_{XY} \cdot \frac{S_X}{S_Y} \tag{9.7}$$

$$a = \overline{X} - (b \cdot \overline{Y}) \tag{9.8}$$

Therefore, if you want to use the data from Table 9.1 to predict the job aptitude test score of a person who got a job performance score of 69, you would need to follow these steps:

First, compute b:

$$b = r_{XY} \cdot \frac{S_X}{S_Y} = .792 \cdot \frac{8.110}{12.009} = .792 \cdot .675 = .535$$

Then compute a:

$$a = \overline{X} - (b \cdot \overline{Y}) = 54 - (.535 \cdot 77) = 54 - 41.195 = 12.805$$

Then use Formula 9.6 to compute $\hat{X}$:

$$\hat{X} = bY + a = .535 \cdot 69 + 12.805 = 36.915 + 12.805 = 49.720$$

Question: This is supposed to be a faster way to make predictions than using z scores. It seems to take as long, if not longer. Exactly how is this faster?

If you are *only* going to make *one* prediction, then both methods will take about the same amount of time. However, if you are going to make more than one prediction using the same correlated variables, computing the regression coefficients and then using them in a regression equation will save a lot of time. After having calculated all the values necessary for the regression equation, it should take only a few seconds to make multiple predictions. Another even quicker but less accurate way to make predictions is to graph the regression line. Look at Figure 9.2. You see a graph with a diagonal line on it. This line is known as a **regression line** because a regression equation was used to plot the line. This particular regression line can be used only to predict height from weight because it was plotted using the regression equation for predicting height from weight. As discussed in the previous section, there are two separate regression equations for each pair of correlated variables, one for predicting Y from X and another for predicting X from Y. Therefore, there are also two regression lines for each pair of correlated variables.

Because you need two points to plot a straight line, you need to choose only two different values for X, given that you have X values, and find their corresponding values for Y in order to plot the regression line for predicting Y, and you need to do likewise for predicting X. Suppose that you want to predict a person's height from his weight. First you would need to generate the appropriate regression equation using the information in the following table:

Height (X)	Weight (Y)
$\overline{X} = 70$ inches	$\overline{Y} = 160$ pounds
$S_X = 2.550$ inches	$S_Y = 20.000$ pounds
$r_{XY} = .833$	

Then you need to compute the necessary regression coefficients using Formulas 9.7 and 9.8:

$$b = r_{XY} \cdot \frac{S_X}{S_Y} = .833 \cdot \frac{2.550}{20.000} = .833 \cdot .128 = .107$$

$$a = \overline{X} - (b \cdot \overline{Y}) = 70 - (.107 \cdot 160) = 70 - 17.120 = 52.880$$

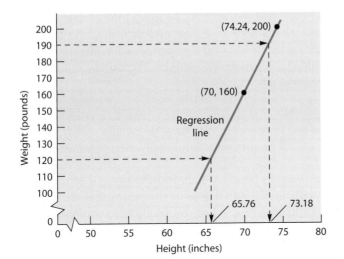

Figure 9.2
A regression line for predicting height from weight.

Now complete the regression equation:

$$\hat{X} = bY + a = .107Y + 52.880$$

Finally, use this regression equation to predict the heights (X) from two different weights (Y) of men. Suppose that one man weighs 200 pounds and the other weighs 160 pounds, which is the mean weight. Given these two Y values, you can use the following formula to compute the two corresponding values for X:

If $Y = 200$ pounds, then

$$\hat{X} = bY + a = .107Y + 52.880 = .107 \cdot 200 + 52.880 = 21.400 + 52.880$$

$$= 74.28 \text{ inches}$$

If $Y = 160$ pounds, then

$$\hat{X} = bY + a = .107Y + 52.880 = .107 \cdot 160 + 52.880 = 17.120 + 52.880$$

$$= 70.000 \text{ inches}$$

(You probably noticed that when we used the mean for weight, 160 pounds, the regression equation predicted the mean for height, 70 inches. This should always happen, and it is one way to check the accuracy of your regression equation.)

Now that you have the two points, (74.28, 200) and (70, 160), you are ready to plot the points and draw the regression line through them. Your graph should look like the one in Figure 9.2, which you can now use to speedily predict as many heights as you wish. But remember that because the points used to plot this straight line were generated from a regression equation designed only for predicting X, *the graph is accurate only for predicting height (X) from weight (Y).* You must draw a separate line for predicting weight (Y) from height (X). To use Figure 9.2, you first need a known weight. For instance, if a man weighs 120 pounds, to predict his height you would find 120 along the ordinate, move horizontally across the graph to the regression line, and then drop vertically to the X axis, where you can read the height of the person, which is about 65 3/4 inches. If you do the same thing for a person who weighs 190 pounds, you should predict that he is about 73 inches tall.

> **Question:** Can it be assumed that in order to predict a man's weight when his height is known, the same procedure would be used but with the formula for predicting Y rather than the one for predicting X?

Yes. If you want to predict weight from height, you need to plot the regression line for predicting Y. Again, one of the points that you choose can be the mean for X and the mean for Y, but you will have to compute a second point to plot the regression line. As an example, let's say that you want to predict the weight of a man who is 60 inches tall. Remember that you will need to use the formula for predicting Y this time.

Begin by computing b and a (this was already done earlier in the chapter but is being shown again for review and practice):

$$b = r_{XY} \cdot \frac{S_Y}{S_X} = .833 \cdot \frac{20.000}{2.550} = .833 \cdot 7.843 = 6.533$$

$$a = \overline{Y} - (b \cdot \overline{X}) = 160 - (6.533 \cdot 70) = 160 - 457.31 = -297.31$$

The regression equation is

$$\hat{Y} = bX + a = 6.533X - 297.310$$

If $X = 60$, then the predicted value of Y is

$$\hat{Y} = bX + a = 6.533X - 297.310 = 6.533 \cdot 60 - 297.310$$

$$= 391.980 - 297.310 = 94.67 \text{ pounds}$$

Because the point given by the means is (70, 160) and the computed point is (60, 94.67), you can now plot the regression line. A completed regression line for predicting the weight of any man from his height is plotted in Figure 9.3. Thus, you can predict that the weight of a man who is 65 inches tall will be between 127 and 128 pounds, and the weight of a man who is 75 inches tall will be between 192 and 193 pounds. As you can see, you can use these regression lines to make predictions, but you must use the regression equations if you want to be perfectly accurate.

Remember that the two different regression equations result in different regression lines. The difference can readily be seen if both regression lines are plotted on the same axes. Figure 9.4 shows both regression lines for the height and weight data plotted on the same axes. As you can see, the two regression lines cross at the means of height and weight, but they have slightly different slopes and intercepts.

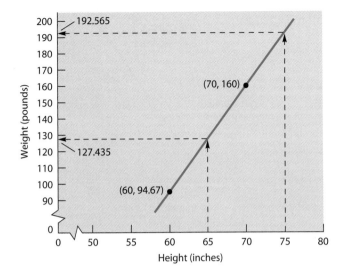

Figure 9.3
A regression line for predicting weight from height.

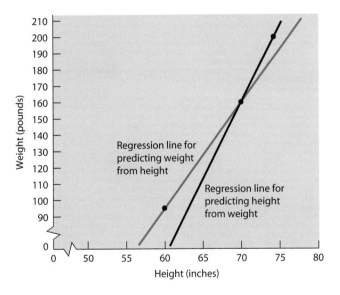

Figure 9.4
Regression lines for predicting height and weight plotted on the same axes.

To plot regression lines for the data from the job aptitude test and job performance scores in Table 9.1, you can use the identical procedure. You may want to construct your own regression lines for practice—one for predicting aptitude test scores from job performance and another for predicting job performance scores from the aptitude test—and compare yours with the ones plotted in Figure 9.5. Note that the lines again cross at the mean for X and the mean for Y, and the lines have different slopes. Figure 9.6 illustrates that as the correlation coefficient between two variables grows smaller, or closer to 0, the two regression lines tend to diverge more and more.

Figure 9.5
Regression lines for predicting job aptitude test scores and for predicting job performance plotted on the same axes.

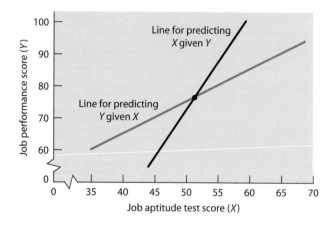

Figure 9.6
The relationship between the two regression lines when (a) $r = 1$, (b) $r = .5$, and (c) $r = 0$.

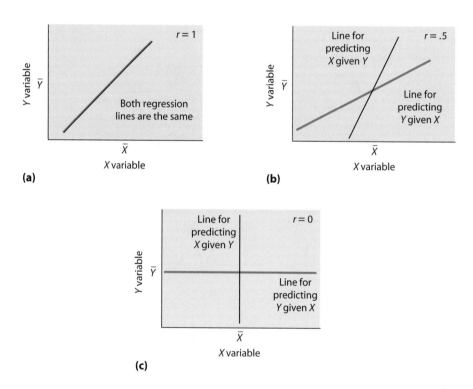

Question: Again, why plot two regression lines? Why not just draw the best-fitting straight line through the points and use that to make both types of predictions?

The easiest way to answer this question is to refer to Figure 9.6. This figure shows regression lines for three hypothetical situations, where the means and standard deviations remain constant for X and Y but the correlation coefficient changes from $+1.0$ to $+.5$ to 0. Let us assume that we have two types of psychological tests, Test X and Test Y, and we would like to be able to predict scores on one test based on scores from the other. If we know that there is no measurable relationship between the two tests, $r = 0$, then no matter what a person scores on Test Y, the best estimate of that person's score on Test X will always be the mean for X $(\overline{X})$, as represented by the vertical black line in Figure 9.6(c). Conversely, if we wish to predict a person's score on Test Y, it doesn't matter what score he or she receives on Test X, we would still predict the mean for Y $(\overline{Y})$, as shown by the horizontal colored line in Figure 9.6(c). It should be obvious that these two different lines are necessary when there is no correlation.

In Figure 9.6(b), the correlation coefficient is .5. The black line, the line for predicting X, has rotated away from the mean in light of the correlational information. The colored line, the one for predicting Y, has likewise rotated away from the mean. These lines still cross at the mean for X and the mean for Y. The best-fitting single line for Figure 9.6(b) is a line that goes between these two regression lines, but it cannot be used reliably for prediction purposes; as you can see, the lines still diverge by quite a bit. It is not until the correlation is 1.00, as depicted in Figure 9.6(a), that both of the regression lines are the same as the single line of best fit.

The Standard Error of the Estimate

Using the regression equations paid off in the cafeteria game: Your friend treated you to lunch. In fact, you felt so assured of your predictive proficiency that the next day you proposed playing the same game with another friend, but with higher stakes. This time, the loser would take the winner out to dinner at a fancy restaurant. You used the same formulas that won you a lunch the day before, but instead of winning a dinner, you ended up buying one for your friend.

> **Question:** What went wrong? Isn't it more accurate to use regression equations than to guess?

Yes, regression equations are more accurate than guessing. But even if you are using a regression equation, you should not fall into the trap of thinking these equations will give you predictions that are 100% accurate. As long as the correlation coefficients you are using are not perfect, your predictions will not be perfect. Remember the discussion about the correlation between height and weight: some people are tall and thin, and some are short and stout. In all populations of living things, some unexplained variance will cause inaccuracies in predictions that are made using regression equations. As you may recall, the coefficient of determination expresses the amount of variance in one variable that is explained by the other variable. Whenever the coefficient of determination is less than 1.00, the unexplained variance will always cause some error in prediction. This error of prediction is called the *standard error of the estimate*.

The **standard error of the estimate** is the standard deviation of the actual values of a variable from the predicted values. For example, suppose you had a sample of 100 men who all weighed 150 pounds. You would not expect all of these men to be exactly the same height. If you used the formula generated above for predicting height from weight, $\hat{X} = .107Y + 52.880$, you would predict that a man who weighs 150 pounds should be 68.930 inches tall. But of course not all, perhaps even none, of the 100 men in the sample would be exactly that height. The heights of these 150-pound men would form a normal distribution around the mean height of 68.930 inches, and the standard deviation of this distribution would be the standard error of the estimate. The smaller the standard error of the estimate, the closer the actual scores are to the predicted value.

Just as there are two separate regression equations, there are also two equations for the standard error of the estimate: one for the prediction of X from Y,

$$S_{XY} = S_X \cdot \sqrt{1 - r^2} \tag{9.9}$$

and one for the prediction of Y from X,

$$S_{YX} = S_Y \cdot \sqrt{1 - r^2} \tag{9.10}$$

To compute the standard error of the estimate for the height prediction made previously, you would use Formula 9.9.

$$S_{XY} = S_X \cdot \sqrt{1 - r^2} = 2.550 \cdot \sqrt{1 - .833^2} = 2.550 \cdot \sqrt{1 - .694}$$
$$= 2.550 \cdot \sqrt{.306} = 2.550 \cdot .553 = 1.410 \text{ inches}$$

Because the standard error of the estimate is the standard deviation of the actual scores from the predicted regression line, you can use the logic discussed in Chapter 6 (on the normal curve) to find the proportion of the people who fall within a certain distance of the regression line. In the preceding example, think of 1.410, which is the standard error of the estimate when predicting height from weight, as a standard deviation. Thus, you can say that approximately 68%, or about two thirds, of the people in the sample population who all weighed 150 pounds will have heights between 70.34 and 67.52 inches (68.930 ± 1.410). This type of analysis is valid only if the standard deviation of the Y values is the same for every value of X. This assumption of equal standard deviations is referred to as **homoscedasticity.**

In this chapter, you saw how to make predictions about one variable from another known variable. The formulas in this chapter will allow you to make accurate predictions if the correlation between the two factors is high and their relationship is linear. If the variables are not linearly related, or if it might be more accurate to make predictions based on several variables rather than only one, other types of regression analysis need to be used. If you need to perform a more complicated regression analysis, you will need to consult a more advanced statistics book.

As you leave this chapter, remember that correlation and regression are helpful in measuring the relationship between variables and in making predictions. However, keep in mind that the correlation coefficient you compute and the predictions you make are only as good as the data you use to make those measurements. In addition, all predictions are subject to some error. *You must always state the standard error of the estimate along with your prediction.* Without the standard error of the estimate, your prediction is incomplete and cannot be used reliably. Whenever you hear of a new prediction—an earthquake will destroy half of California sometime during July, the Yankees will win the pennant, or one candidate will get more votes than the other—try to look for the data used in making those predictions. Remember that anyone can make a prediction or hold an opinion, but accurate predictions come from accurate scientific data collection and analysis, not ESP, horoscopes, or guesswork. Also remember that correlation will never pinpoint the causal relationships between variables; only an experiment can do that.

VISUAL SUMMARY

Using Regression Equations to Make Predictions

Before You Begin: Compute $\overline{X}$, $\overline{Y}$, S_X, S_Y, r_{XY}, and cov_{XY}.

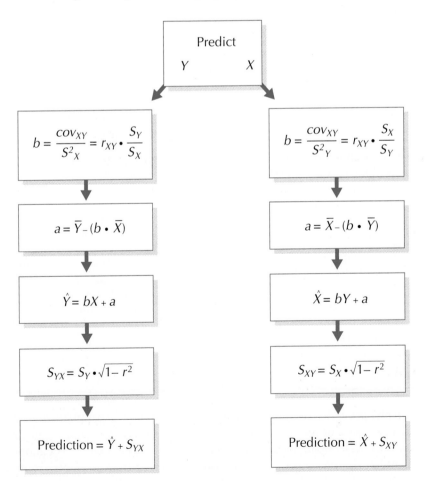

Predict

Y   X

$$b = \frac{\text{cov}_{XY}}{S^2_X} = r_{XY} \cdot \frac{S_Y}{S_X}$$

$$b = \frac{\text{cov}_{XY}}{S^2_Y} = r_{XY} \cdot \frac{S_X}{S_Y}$$

$$a = \overline{Y} - (b \cdot \overline{X})$$

$$a = \overline{X} - (b \cdot \overline{Y})$$

$$\hat{Y} = bX + a$$

$$\hat{X} = bY + a$$

$$S_{YX} = S_Y \cdot \sqrt{1 - r^2}$$

$$S_{XY} = S_X \cdot \sqrt{1 - r^2}$$

$$\text{Prediction} = \hat{Y} + S_{YX}$$

$$\text{Prediction} = \hat{X} + S_{XY}$$

Concept Quiz

Recall from the previous concept quiz that Wright and Cropanzano (2000) compared the relative contributions of employee job satisfaction and psychological well-being as predictors of job performance. Psychological well-being (X) was found to be a predictor of job performance (Y) in both of their field studies.

1. In this study, there is one pair of correlated variables and there is (are) _____ regression line(s).

2. The regression line used to predict Y (job performance) from X (psychological well-being) cannot be used to predict X (psychological well-being) from Y (job performance). True or false?

3. In the regression line $\hat{Y} = bX + a$,
   $\hat{Y} = $ _____
   $b = $ _____
   $a = $ _____
   $X = $ _____

4. Because the correlation coefficient in this study is $r = .32$ and not a perfect relationship ($+1.00$ or -1.00), there is unexplained error in the prediction called _____.

5. Using the following information, psychological well-being $\overline{X} = 3.6, s = 1.4$; job satisfaction $\overline{Y} = 3.3, s = .9$; $r_{XY} = .32$, predict an employee's job satisfaction score when his or her psychological well-being score is 4.

6. The assumption that the standard deviation of all Y values is the same as every value of X is referred to as _____.

Answers

1. two
2. True
3. $\hat{Y} = $ The predicted value of Y
   $b = $ The slope of the regression line (the amount of change in Y

associated with a 1-unit change in X)
$a = $ The Y intercept (the predicted value of Y when $X = 0$)

$X = $ The value of X used to predict Y
4. standard error of the estimate
5. $\hat{Y} = 3.384 \pm .853$
6. homoscedasticity

Summary

This chapter presented two different approaches to making linear predictions using the covariance or the correlation coefficient between two variables. The first approach uses z scores to make the prediction, and the other uses the equation of a straight line. In the z-score approach, you first convert the known variable to a z score and then multiply that z score by the correlation coefficient to obtain the z score of the other variable. Then you convert the predicted z score to a predicted value for X or Y. In the second approach, you use the formula for a straight line to make your predictions. To do this, you must first compute the regression coefficients and then substitute these coefficients into the regression equation.

Because all predictions involve some error, all predictions must be accompanied by the standard error of the estimate. The smaller the standard error of the estimate, the more accurate your predictions will be.

Key Terms

regression   regression line   homoscedasticity
regression equation   standard error of the
regression coefficients   estimate

Formulas

$$\hat{z}_X = z_Y \cdot r_{XY} \tag{9.1}$$

$$\hat{z}_Y = z_X \cdot r_{XY} \tag{9.2}$$

$$\hat{Y} = bX + a \tag{9.3}$$

$$b = \frac{\text{cov}_{XY}}{S_X^2} = r_{XY} \cdot \frac{S_Y}{S_X} \tag{9.4}$$

$$a = \overline{Y} - (b \cdot \overline{X}) \tag{9.5}$$

$$\hat{X} = bY + a \tag{9.6}$$

$$b = \frac{\text{cov}_{XY}}{S_Y^2} = r_{XY} \cdot \frac{S_X}{S_Y} \tag{9.7}$$

$$a = \overline{X} - (b \cdot \overline{Y}) \tag{9.8}$$

$$S_{XY} = S_X \cdot \sqrt{1 - r^2} \tag{9.9}$$

$$S_{YX} = S_Y \cdot \sqrt{1 - r^2} \tag{9.10}$$

Problems

Each year millions of babies are born in the United States. Some are firstborns, some are second born, and so on. Using available data, we can compute the average birth order of all children born in any one year. A researcher is interested in seeing whether there is a relationship between birth order average and SAT verbal average. The corresponding birth order average and SAT average for 10 years are listed in the following table. Use the data to solve Problems 1–10. (Remember that you must attach the appropriate standard error of the estimate to each prediction.)

Birth Order Average (X)	SAT Verbal Average (Y)
2.5	485
2.6	480
2.6	480
2.6	475
2.7	475
2.7	470
2.8	470
2.8	465
2.8	460
2.9	455

1. Compute the means, standard deviation, covariance, and correlation coefficient for the data in the table.

2. Compute the standard error of the estimate for predicting Y from X.

3. Compute the standard error of the estimate for predicting X from Y.

4. Using the z-score regression equations, predict the average SAT verbal score for a year that has a corresponding birth order average of 2.4.

5. Using the z-score regression equations, predict the birth order average for a year that has an average SAT verbal score of 495.

6. Compute the regression coefficients for the data.

7. Write the regression equation for predicting Y.

8. Write the regression equation for predicting X.

9. Using the regression equation for predicting Y, predict the average SAT verbal score for a year that has a birth order equal to 3.0.

10. Using the regression equation for predicting X, predict the birth order average for a year that has an average SAT verbal score of 400.

Twenty-five mothers, along with their daughters, were asked to participate in a test of manual dexterity. The means and the standard deviations for each group, along with the correlation coefficient for the mothers' and daughters' scores, are listed here. Use these data for Problems 11–21.

	Mothers (X)		Daughters (Y)
Mean	45		52
Standard deviation	4.5		6.5
Correlation coefficient		+.55	

11. Compute the standard error of the estimate for predicting Y from X.

12. Compute the standard error of the estimate for predicting X from Y.

Predict the mother's score from the following daughter's score.

13. A score of 44

14. A score of 46

15. A score of 52

16. A score of 54

17. A score of 53

Predict the daughter's score when the mother has the following score.

18. A score of 50

19. A score of 46

20. A score of 43

21. A score of 39

22. A graduate school selection committee has filled all but one of its openings for next year's psychology class. The committee is having difficulty deciding between two applicants, Sigmund F., who attended Psychoanalytic U., and Carl R., who attended Client-Centered U. The committee decides that both candidates are equally desirable, so they will pick the student whose undergraduate grade point average predicts the highest grade point average in graduate school. Sigmund F. graduated with a 3.9 GPA, and Carl R. graduated with a 3.6 GPA. Using the data in the following table, predict the graduate school GPA for each applicant, and remember to attach the appropriate standard error of the estimate to each prediction.

School	Mean	Standard Deviation	Correlation With Graduate School Grades
Graduate school	3.5	.3	—
Psychoanalytic U.	3.7	.2	.50
Client-Centered U.	3.4	.1	.90

A researcher interested in the study habits of college freshmen computed a correlation coefficient between the average number of hours a student spends watching television each day and his or her GPA. The correlation coefficient and the means and standard deviations can be found in the following table.

	Daily Hours Spent Watching Television (X)		GPA (Y)
Mean	1.700		2.950
Standard deviation	.580		1.836
Correlation coefficient		−.880	

For the following predictions, remember that every prediction must be accompanied by the standard error of the estimate. Given the following GPAs, how many hours does the student spend watching television each day?

23. A GPA of 2.8

24. A GPA of 1.7

25. A GPA of 3.2

26. A GPA of 3.1

27. A GPA of 2.95

Predict the GPA of a student who spends the following amount of time watching television each day.

28. 2.7 hours

29. 3 hours

30. 1 hour

31. 1.5 hours

Problems From the Literature

The following problems refer to actual results from research studies that are cited at the end of the chapter. However, the data used to generate the problem sets are hypothetical.

Stress reactions to traumatic experiences can differ among trauma survivors. In some cases, the survivor's stress response may meet the DSM-IV criteria for acute stress disorder (ASD), which may facilitate an early prediction and therapeutic intervention of posttraumatic stress disorder (PTSD). Bryant, Harvey, Guthrie, and Moulds (2000) examined survivors of traumatic motor vehicle accidents and found that 78% of trauma survivors who met the symptom requirement for ASD developed PTSD 6 months later. They also discovered that approximately 60% of the trauma survivors who failed to meet the ASD criteria and had symptoms of acute stress also displayed PTSD later. Based on their findings, the researchers think there may be more than a single pathway to PTSD. Suppose another researcher conducted a related study and found a negative relationship between the number of acute stress symptoms and perceived control of life events. (Note: Perceived control was measured on a scale of 1 = low control to 9 = high control.) Use this information to solve Problems 32–39.

	Number of Acute Stress Symptoms (X)		Perceived Control (Y)
Mean	12.700		2.88
Standard deviation	1.76		1.15
Correlation coefficient		−.680	

For the following predictions, remember that every prediction must be accompanied by the standard error of the estimate. Given that a trauma survivor has this number of symptoms of ASD, predict the extent of perceived control the person has over his or her life events.

32. 13 symptoms of ASD

33. 8.2 symptoms of ASD

34. 5 symptoms of ASD

35. 9.5 symptoms of ASD

36. 2 symptoms of ASD

Predict the number of ASD symptoms of a trauma survivor who reported the following for perceived control over his or her life events.

37. A score of 6

38. A score of 4

39. A score of 2

Giuliano, Popp, and Knight (2000) recruited a sample of college women varsity athletes and nonathletes to see whether these groups differed in the types of children's games or childhood experiences and whether these games related to their subsequent participation in college sports. Among the many findings, they found that athletes played more masculine games, such as "Army," as children than nonathletes. Yet, there were no differences between the athletes and nonathletes in their tendency to play with masculine toys, such as cars and trucks. Presume that another researcher wanted to extend this line of inquiry. She asked a sample of college women athletes to complete a questionnaire to see whether there was a relationship between the extent each enjoyed masculine games as a child and her need for competitive activity. (Note: Enjoyment of games and need for competition were measured on 7-point scales with 1 = enjoyed a little/low need and 7 = enjoyed a lot/high need.) Use this information to solve Problems 40–47.

	Enjoyment of Masculine Games (X)		Need for Competitive Activity (Y)
Mean	5.33		4.15
Standard deviation	2.15		1.79
Correlation coefficient		.811	

For the following predictions, remember that every prediction must be accompanied by the standard error of the estimate. Given that a college woman athlete has the following score for enjoyment of masculine childhood games, predict the extent of her need for competitive activity.

40. A score of 4

41. A score of 6

42. A score of 7

43. A score of 2

Given that a college woman athlete had the following need for competitive activity score, predict her enjoyment of masculine games score.

44. A score of 2

45. A score of 3

46. A score of 4

47. A score of 6

Selection of organ transplant recipients is a difficult task. However, the selection of organ donors may also be difficult. Sometimes the choice is made because the surgeon cannot be reached in a reasonable amount of time. At other times, surgeons are more likely to reject poor-quality organs if the patient to whom the organ was offered is healthy (Howard, 2000). This pattern highlights the tendency of urgent patients to undergo transplantation before nonurgent patients and leads to a positive correlation between patient health and organ quality.

Suppose researchers studied this issue relative to kidney transplants and found a similar pattern of findings as Howard (2000). Researchers evaluated patient's health status (1 = not urgent to and 7 = very urgent) and the doctor's notes concerning the quality of the accepted kidney (1 = poor quality to and 7 = excellent quality). The data are listed here. Use this information to solve Problems 48–55.

	Patient's Health Status (X)		Quality of Accepted Kidney (Y)
Mean	4.92		2.64
Standard deviation	2.39		.83
Correlation coefficient		−.591	

48. Given that the health status score of a patient was 7, predict the quality of the kidney accepted for transplant.

49. Given that the health status score of a patient was 6, predict the quality of the kidney accepted for transplant.

50. Given that the health status score of a patient was 4, predict the quality of the kidney accepted for transplant.

51. Given that the health status score of a patient was 1, predict the quality of the kidney accepted for transplant.

52. Given that the health status score of a patient was 2, predict the quality of the kidney accepted for transplant.

53. Predict the quality of the liver accepted for transplant for a patient who has a health status score of 2.

54. Predict the quality of the liver accepted for transplant for a patient who has a health status score of 4.

55. Predict the quality of the liver accepted for transplant for a patient who has a health status score of 6.

References

Bryant, R. A., Harvey, A. G., Guthrie, R. M., & Moulds, M. L. (2000). A prospective study of psychophysiological arousal, acute stress disorder, and posttraumatic stress disorder. *Journal of Abnormal Psychology, 109,* 341–344.

Giuliano, T. A., Popp, K. E., & Knight, J. L. (2000). Footballs versus Barbies: Childhood play activities as predictors of sports participation by women. *Sex Roles, 42,* 159–181.

Howard, D. H. (2000). *The Economics of Organ Allocation.* Doctoral dissertation. Cambridge, MA: Harvard University.

Wright, T. A., & Cropanzano, R. (2000). Psychological well-being and job satisfaction as predictors of job performance. *Journal of Occupational Health Psychology, 5,* 84–94.

Probability Theory and Sampling

- Probability Theory
- Sampling
- The Standard Error of the Mean
- The Central Limit Theorem

- The z Test
  VISUAL SUMMARY: The z Test
- Summary
- Key Terms

- Formulas
- Problems
  Problems From the Literature
- References

In the movie *Ghostbusters*, Bill Murray plays the unorthodox psychologist, Dr. Peter Venkman, who in one of the opening scenes is showing a set of "Zener cards" to two participants in his ESP experiment. Zener cards are used in real-life experiments to investigate extrasensory perception (ESP). A Zener deck consists of 100 cards, each showing one of five symbols: a circle, a square, a star, a set of wavy lines, or a plus. In the movie, we see Dr. Venkman holding up the cards one by one, with the symbols facing away from the participants, and asking them to guess which symbol is on each card. Whenever the male participant responds, Dr. Venkman invariably gives him an electrical shock, whether or not he answers correctly; whenever the attractive female participant responds, the good doctor smiles, congratulates her, and administers no electrical shock, whether or not she is correct. It is obvious that the unethical Venkman is more concerned with courting the woman's favors than with obtaining objective, scientific data.

Suppose that you are more serious about investigating ESP, and you set up a research project to determine whether people actually possess mental telepathy, the ability to read another person's mind. Your materials consist solely of a Zener deck of 100 cards, 20 of each of the five types. Like Dr. Venkman, you shuffle the deck, hold up each card, and ask the participants to guess what symbol is on the card. Now comes the critical question: How many cards must each participant guess correctly before you can legitimately declare the person to have mental telepathy? 50? 75? All 100? The participant must consistently score higher than a person who does not have ESP and is merely guessing.

Question: How many cards out of 100 will people guess correctly if they do not have ESP?

231

To compute the answer, you need to know something about probability. Nearly all scientific research is reported in terms of probabilities, as are many scientific "facts" and "laws." Thus, studying or working with behavioral research requires at least a basic understanding of probability theory.

Probability Theory

Question: What do you mean by probability? How are scientific results reported as probabilities?

Probability is a measure of how likely it is that a given event or behavior will happen. Take psychology, for example. Isn't probability what psychological research is all about? What psychologists want to determine in their studies is how probable it is that the behavior they are studying is actually the behavior typical of most people under the same circumstances. In one experiment, they may determine the probability of an enriched environment producing brighter children than a deprived one. In another, they may determine the probability of a behavior therapy program increasing the life span of high-risk patients who have cancer.

Probability is measured in terms of numbers between 0 and 1. If the probability of an event occurring is 0, it means that the event will never happen. If the probability is 1, it means that the event will definitely happen. If the probability is somewhere between 0 and 1, it means that the event *may* happen, and the closer it is to 1, the more likely the event will occur. Let's illustrate this with an example.

Suppose you are taking your Introduction to Psychology midterm exam. What is the probability of getting question 10 correct? Well, you say, that depends on the question. Here it is:

10. Which of the following men is generally known as the "father of psychology"?
    a. Herman Ebbinghaus
    b. Wilhelm Wundt
    c. Sigmund Freud
    d. B. F. Skinner

Now that you know the question, it is easier to determine the probability of getting it correct. If you are absolutely sure of the answer, the probability is 1.00. If you don't have a clue and must make a wild guess, the probability of your getting the correct answer is 1 out of 4, or .25. If you are certain that the answer is *not* B. F. Skinner but are not sure of the other three, the probability is 1 out of 3, or .33, and so on. (By the way, for those of you who have repressed all the information from your Psychology 100 class, the answer is Wilhelm Wundt.)

Sometimes it is easy to tell the probability of an event occurring. The probability of getting heads when tossing an evenly balanced coin is .5. The probability of drawing any spade from a typical deck of playing cards is .25. In short, the probability of any one event occurring is the number of possible ways it can occur divided by the total number of all possible events relating to that one event.

$$\text{Probability of event A} = \frac{\text{number of events in A}}{\text{total number of all events}} \text{ or } p(A) = \frac{n(A)}{n} \qquad (10.1)$$

Using this formula, you can test the accuracy of the probabilities just mentioned. Every fair coin has two sides, one head and one tail. The probability of getting a head on a single toss of a coin is the number of possible heads, which is 1, divided by the number of possible outcomes, a head or a tail, which is 2:

$$p(\text{head}) = \frac{1}{2} = .5$$

The probability of drawing a spade from a deck of 52 cards is the number of spades in the deck, 13, divided by the number of cards in the deck, 52:

$$p(\text{spade}) = \frac{13}{52} = .25$$

The same thing can be done with the deck of ESP cards discussed previously. Suppose you want to know the probability of the first card drawn from the deck being a plus. You know that there are 20 pluses in the deck and 100 total cards. Therefore, the probability of the first card being a plus is

$$p(\text{plus}) = \frac{20}{100} = .20$$

If a participant in your ESP experiment guesses that a card shows a plus, he or she has a .2 chance of being correct. Extending this formula to every guess, as long as you do not tell the participant what cards have been drawn, each participant would have a .2 chance of being correct on each trial. With 100 cards in the deck, each participant should, simply by chance, guess correctly 20 times out of 100.

> **Question:** It's easy to figure out probabilities when you're just choosing cards or tossing coins, but how about figuring out the probability that someone will develop schizophrenia or that someone is color-blind?

Finding these probabilities is not as easy as finding the probability of getting heads or a spade, but it *may be* possible if you collect the appropriate data for estimating these probabilities. Suppose you want to figure out the probability that any one individual will develop schizophrenia. How should you proceed? One way is to interview several thousand people—say, 10,000—and create a frequency distribution. Suppose you did this and came up with the following data:

Label	Frequency	Relative Frequency
Schizophrenia	108	.0108
No disorder	9,027	.9027
Other psychological disorders	865	.0865
Total	10,000	1.0000

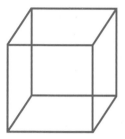

Figure 10.1   The Necker cube is an ambiguous figure that can be seen as a cube with its front square face either toward the top right of the page or toward the bottom left of the page.

Using Formula 10.1 and the preceding data, you can compute the probability of a person having schizophrenia. (Remember that these are not actual real-life data.)

$$p(\text{schizophrenia}) = \frac{\text{number of occurrences of schizophrenia}}{\text{total number of people}} = \frac{108}{10,000} = .0108$$

Thus, based on the preceding sample, the probability of a person having schizophrenia is .0108, or about 1 out of every 100. Take another look at the frequency distribution. Do you notice that the relative frequency for schizophrenia is the same as the computed probability? Another way to think of the probability of a behavior or event happening is to think of the relative frequency of that behavior or event occurring in the population. Any time the data of an event can be displayed in a frequency distribution, the probability of that event can be estimated by computing its relative frequency. To carry this idea further, once you know the probabilities of single events, you can compute the probabilities of multiple events. Look at the Necker cube in Figure 10.1. Which square forms its front face? Close your eyes for a few seconds, then look at the cube again, and this time try to see the other square as the one in front. Because the Necker cube ignores perspective, people are typically able to perceive either the right square or the left square as being the front of the cube. Here is a probability question: What is the probability that either the square on the right or the square on the left is seen in front? The answer is 1.00. There are only two perceptual organizations possible, either the right square in front or the left square in front, and the probability of seeing at least one of them is 1.00.

Question: Does this mean that when figuring out the probability of one event or another event, we need only sum the probabilities of the two events?

Yes, *if* the two events are **mutually exclusive**—that is, if the two events cannot occur simultaneously. This is an important point. In the Necker cube example, you perceive either the right square or the left square in front; you never see a combination of the two. Similarly, the probability that the next animal you see is a dog or a cat is merely the sum of the individual probabilities because no animal can be both a dog and a cat. This relationship is often called the **addition rule of probability** or the **addition theorem of probability,** and it is expressed by the following formula:

$$p(A \text{ or } B) = p(A) + p(B) \qquad\qquad (10.2)$$

Remember that Formula 10.2 holds true only if the two events are mutually exclusive. Of course, many events are not mutually exclusive. For instance, you might ask the question, "What is the probability of drawing a jack or a heart from a typical deck of cards?" or "What is the probability that the next person I meet will be a man or someone who has schizophrenia?" The answers to these are a bit more complicated because a card can be both a jack and a heart, and a person can be both a man and have schizophrenia.

To answer these probability questions, first focus on the card problem. You know that 4 of the cards in the deck are jacks. You also know that 13 of the cards are hearts, but you must keep in mind that one of these hearts is also a jack. So rather than 17 cards (4 jacks + 13 hearts) being either a jack or a heart, there are really only 16: the 4 jacks plus the 12 hearts that are not jacks. From Formula 10.1, the probability of drawing a jack or a heart is the number of cards that are either jacks or hearts divided by the total number of cards in the deck:

$$p(\text{jack or heart}) = \frac{16}{52} = .308$$

Often the probabilities associated with individual events are known rather than the number of events themselves. For example, you might know that the probability of drawing a heart is .25 without knowing how many hearts there actually are. If this is the case, there is a general probability formula you can use to compute the probability of event A or event B:

$$p(A \text{ or } B) = p(A) + p(B) - p(A \text{ and } B) \qquad\qquad (10.3)$$

The formula can be used whether or not events A and B are mutually exclusive: If they are mutually exclusive, the probability of A and B—$p(A$ and B)—equals 0, and Formula 10.3 will lead to the same result as Formula 10.2.

Formula 10.3 can be applied to determine the probability of drawing a jack or a heart. To do this, use Formula 10.1 to compute the separate entries of Formula 10.3:

$$p(\text{jack}) = \frac{4}{52} = .077$$

$$p(\text{heart}) = \frac{13}{52} = .250$$

$$p(\text{jack and heart}) = \frac{1}{52} = .019$$

Now plug all these values into Formula 10.3:

$$p(\text{jack or heart}) = p(\text{jack}) + p(\text{heart}) - p(\text{jack and heart}) =$$
$$.077 + .250 - .019 = .308$$

This value is identical to the one computed earlier for the same problem.

You can do a similar analysis to determine the probability of the next person you meet being a man or someone who has schizophrenia. Here you must make some assumptions: (1) that the population is half men and half women, (2) that 1% of the population has schizophrenia, and (3) that men and women are equally likely to have schizophrenia. If these assumptions are true, then the probability of meeting a man is .5, the probability of meeting a person who has schizophrenia is .01, and the probability of meeting a man who has schizophrenia is .005. From Formula 10.3,

$$p(\text{man or schizophrenia}) = .5 + .01 - .005 = .505$$

Question: How did you figure the probability of being a man and a person who has schizophrenia?

If two events are independent, the probability of both of them occurring together is the product of their separate probabilities:

$$p(\text{A and B}) = p(\text{A}) \cdot p(\text{B}) \tag{10.4}$$

This is often called the **multiplication rule of probability** or the **multiplication theorem of probability.** So if the probability of being a man is .5 and the probability of being a person who has schizophrenia is .01, then the probability of being a man who also has schizophrenia is

$$p(\text{man and schizophrenia}) = p(\text{man}) \cdot p(\text{schizophrenia}) = .5 \cdot .01 = .005$$

Similarly, if the probability of a card being a heart is .25 and the probability of a card being a jack is .077, the probability of a card being a heart that is a jack is the product of their probabilities:

$$p(\text{heart and jack}) = p(\text{heart}) \cdot p(\text{jack}) = .25 \cdot .077 = .019$$

In Chapter 7, another means of computing probability, the normal curve, was discussed. If a population variable is normally distributed and if you know the mean and the standard deviation of the population, you can readily make probability computations using the normal curve tables. For example, the probability of getting a score of 130 (X) or higher on the Wechsler Adult Intelligence Scale is equal to the area under the normal curve above 130. To compute the probability of your getting a score of 130 or higher, you convert the test score to a z score and then look up the probability in Table Z. If the population mean (μ) for this test is 100 and the population standard deviation (σ) is 15, then the z score equals

$$z = \frac{X - \mu}{\sigma} = \frac{130 - 100}{15} = \frac{30}{15} = 2$$

Now look up the area above a *z* score of 2 in Table Z. It equals .0228. Therefore, the probability of getting a test score equal to or higher than 130 is .0228. As you can see, the normal curve can be helpful for making probability statements about populations, which is the primary goal of behavioral science research. Unfortunately, population means and population standard deviations are not always available for various reasons. Sometimes populations are so large that it is financially impossible to gather data from every member of the population. At other times, it may be too difficult or too dangerous (collecting data from every ice cream parlor in the country could be detrimental to your waistline). Due to such problems, researchers frequently sample a small portion of the population and then estimate population values from their sample.

Concept Quiz

The following table presents selected characteristics of the 70.5 million Internet users in 1998 (Neilsen/NetRatings, 2000).

Internet Users in 1998: Selected U. S. Population Characteristics
(in millions)

Number of Internet users who are female	30.30
Number of Internet users who are male	40.20
Number of Internet users who are full-time students	9.52
Total number of Internet users (male + female)	70.50

1. The _____ of an event occurring is the number of possible ways the event can occur divided by the total number of all possible events relating to that one event.

2. To find the probability of an Internet user being male, the total number of _____ is divided by the total number of _____.
   Thus, *p*(male) = _____.

3. Any time data can be displayed in a simple frequency distribution, you can estimate the probability of any particular event by computing the _____ frequency of that event.

4. If two events are mutually exclusive, such as *p*(male Internet user or female Internet user), the probability that one or the other will occur is the

_____ of the probabilities for each event. Therefore, p(male Internet user or female Internet user) = _____.

5. When two events are not mutually exclusive, such as p(female Internet user or full-time college student Internet user), the probability that one or the other will occur is the _____ of the probabilities for each event _____ the probability of both occurring at the same time. Calculate p(female Internet user or full-time college student Internet user).

6. For two independent events, such as p(female Internet user or full-time college student Internet user), the probability of both of them occurring at the same time is the _____ of their separate probabilities, and p(female Internet user or full-time college student Internet user) = _____.

7. Probabilities can also be determined by computing _____ and then finding the corresponding area under the normal curve.

Answers

1. probability	3. relative	6. product; .058
2. male users; all users; .57	4. sum; 1.000	7. a z score
	5. sum; minus; .507	

Sampling

There are several ways to collect a sample from a population, but no matter what method you use, one consideration is paramount. *The sample collected must be as representative of the target population as possible.* Obtaining a **representative sample** means that all significant subgroups of the population must be represented in the sample. If you were hired to assess how people would vote on a critical national issue, you would certainly not restrict your sample to college sophomores. Opinions and voting patterns are often influenced by factors such as age, years of schooling, and geographic location, so limiting your survey to only college sophomores would severely restrict your sample.

On the other hand, if you were investigating how people perceive depth in motion pictures, a sample of college sophomores might be quite representative of the general population because no research indicates any difference between college sophomores and the general population in perceiving depth. It is critically important to be aware of all relevant population characteristics before taking a sample. Unfortunately, this is often difficult, if not impossible, so researchers frequently resort to **random sampling** to increase the chances of obtaining a representative sample.

Random sampling is much like picking a name from a hat. It assumes that everyone in the population of interest is equally likely to be chosen as a participant and that all participants are chosen by some completely random process.

> **Question:** To estimate the grade point average of an entire college student body, how would you go about collecting a random sample of 25 students?

There are many ways to collect a random sample. One of the easiest is to find a list of all the students who attend your college and then randomly select 25 names from the list. You could put the name of each student on a card, place the cards in a box, mix them up, and then draw out 25 cards. Of course, this could be quite time consuming if the list were long, and you would have to take great care to mix the cards thoroughly before your drawing. Even with a lot of mixing, the sample might not be very random; if you put the cards in the box alphabetically, the As through Gs would probably tend to remain toward the bottom, with the Ts through Zs tending to stay at the top.

A more efficient and accurate way of generating a random sample is to assign each member of the student body a number and then select numbers at random. For a number to be totally random, it must have the same probability of occurring as any other number. Because people are almost never completely impartial, the best generator of totally random numbers is a computer. A computer-generated **random number table** can be found in most statistics books. To illustrate their use, suppose that 1,000 students are enrolled at your college. You assign each of the 1,000 students a three-digit number (from 000 to 999) and then refer to a random number table like Table N in Appendix A (N stands for Number), which contains 2,000 random digits. Turn to this table, choose a starting place—anywhere—and read the three-digit number that you fix your eyes on. If the number is the same as one you have assigned to a student, that student will be part of your sample. Continue reading down the table and choose all 25 students in this way. In modern laboratories, random assignment is more likely to be done by a random number generator in a computer than by an experimenter using a random number table, but the procedure is similar and the results are the same.

After selecting a random sample, you can collect whatever information you need (in this case, GPAs) and reasonably assume that this information can safely be used to make inferences about your general population (the college student body). Table 10.1 lists the grade point average data for the 25 students in your sample. From these data, you can compute a mean and standard deviation for the sample: The mean GPA is 2.601 and the standard deviation is .852.

> **Question:** But this information pertains to the sample only. How do you know that the mean and the standard deviation of the sample are the same as the mean and standard deviation for the population?

Table 10.1   Grade Point Averages for 25 Randomly Selected Students

3.95	2.13	1.11	0.87	1.92
3.33	2.01	1.90	2.84	3.44
3.33	2.25	1.88	2.10	2.82
3.45	3.77	1.67	2.75	3.86
3.25	3.24	2.00	2.18	2.98

$n = 25$
$\Sigma X = 65.03$
$\Sigma X^2 = 186.561$
$\overline{X} = 2.601$
$S = 0.852$

If the sample is completely random, then the sample mean should be a good estimate of the population mean. This follows from the fact that random sampling, if truly random, should produce scores that are above, below, and close to the population mean. The larger the sample, the greater the chance that the sample mean will approximate the population mean. When the sample is small, it may happen that, by coincidence, most or even all of the scores may fall at one end of the scale; they may all be high or all low. Such a case results in an especially high or low sample mean. When the sample is large, this is much less likely to happen. For instance, suppose that in the previous example you sampled only 5 students out of the 1,000 who attend the school, rather than 25. The 5 you sampled may all be friends that are on academic probation, or they may all be on the Dean's List. By enlarging the sample, you increase the likelihood that some of the students in the sample will be on probation, some will be at the top of their class, and most will be somewhere in between. Thus, the larger the sample, if it is random, the more likely it will be representative of the population. However, whether the sample is large or small, the mean of the sample is the best estimate of the population mean.

Question: How big does a sample have to be in order to be representative of the population?

The general rule is: The bigger, the better. Researchers should try to collect samples that are as large as possible, given their resources of time and money. This concept may be even clearer if you examine estimates of the variance and standard deviation rather than the mean.

In Chapter 5, you examined the standard deviation as a standard of measurement that indicates how much the scores in a distribution deviate from the mean. With this in mind, compare again the standard deviation of a sample with that of a population. The standard deviation of a population is calculated using all the scores in the population, including the most extreme scores. Because a sample is smaller than the population, it is likely that the sample will not include all the extreme scores. For example, it is unlikely that your sample of 25 students will contain the student with the highest GPA as well as the student with the lowest. It is possible, but highly unlikely. That is the reason, remember, for using $n - 1$ in the denominator when computing the standard deviation of a sample. $n - 1$ is a correction for the small size of the sample. As long as you use $n - 1$ in the formula for the standard deviation of the sample, this value will be your best estimate of the standard deviation of the population. As a reminder, the formula for standard deviation is repeated here:

$$\text{Standard deviation} = S = \sqrt{\frac{\Sigma X^2 - \frac{(\Sigma X)^2}{n}}{n - 1}}$$

Any time a sample is taken from a population, that sample is only one of many, sometimes countless, samples that *could* be taken from that same population. Therefore, if you take several samples, all the same size, from one particular population, it is quite possible that each sample will be different from all of the others. Some samples may have means similar to the mean of the population, most will have means a little different from the population mean, and a few may have means far below or above the population mean.

> **Question:** Can't these sample means be averaged to come up with a mean that's pretty close to the population mean?

Yes. In fact, from any population, you can create a distribution made up of an unlimited number of sample means from that population. This is known as the **distribution of sample means.** In such a distribution, if all samples are the same size, the mean of the sample means ($\mu_{\bar{X}}$) will equal the population mean (μ):

$$\mu_{\bar{X}} = \mu \tag{10.5}$$

How about the standard deviation of this distribution? For a distribution of sample means with an n greater than 1, will its standard deviation be the same as that of the population? Take a few minutes to think this through. The answer is that it will be smaller than the standard deviation for the population.

The Standard Error of the Mean

The standard deviation of the distribution of sample means is known as the **standard error of the mean** $(\sigma_{\bar{X}})$. The standard error of the mean is equal to the standard deviation of the population divided by the square root of the sample size:

$$\sigma_{\bar{X}} = \frac{\sigma}{\sqrt{n}} \tag{10.6}$$

As Formula 10.6 reflects, the standard error of the mean decreases as n increases. You can see this graphically in Figure 10.2.

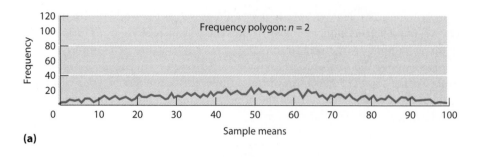

(a)

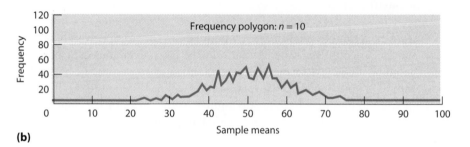

(b)

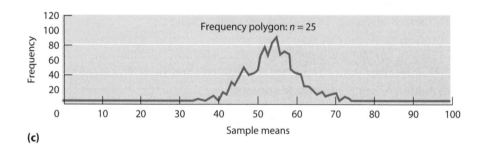

(c)

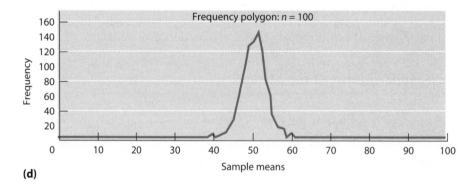

(d)

Figure 10.2 Frequency polygons of four distributions of 1,000 sample means. Each distribution differs only in the number of participants (*n*) used to generate each sample: (a) *n* = 2, (b) *n* = 10, (c) *n* = 25, and (d) *n* = 100.

Figure 10.2 shows the frequency polygons of four sampling distributions involving 1,000 samples that were taken from the same population ($\mu = 50.5$ and $\sigma = 28.866$). The only difference in the sampling distributions is the sizes of the samples, which are 2, 10, 25, and 100. Note in the figure that when the samples are small, the polygon is flat because the means of the samples are spread apart. When the samples are large, the polygon has a definite peak near the population mean because the means of the samples are concentrated toward the center. These patterns occur because with small samples it is more likely that the scores will be extreme and will tend to lie in the same direction (they may be greater or less than the population mean), but with large samples extreme scores in one direction tend to be offset by extreme scores in the other direction. Consequently, the standard error of the mean (which is essentially the standard deviation of the distribution of sample means) grows smaller as the sample size grows larger, and this is exactly what you want: the smallest possible standard error of the mean. A small standard error of the mean indicates that the distribution of sample means resulted in little error in estimating the true population mean, and this, of course, is what all research strives for.

The Central Limit Theorem

The **central limit theorem** states that the distribution of sample means approaches a normal distribution when n is large. Note that this theorem makes no mention of the shape of the original population distribution. No matter what its shape (skewed, flat, normal, or any other shape), the distribution of sample means becomes more normal as the sample size increases. The polygons in Figure 10.2 illustrate this: As the sample sizes increase from 2 to 100, the distributions grow to approximate more closely the normal curve. This is important for statistical inference because when the sample is sufficiently large, you can assume that the distribution of sample means is normal. It is therefore easy to compare the samples you have collected to the theoretical distribution of sample means. This can be illustrated by an experiment using a test of stress.

Suppose you have developed over a period of years the Stress Battery for College Students, 1st edition (SBCS-1 for short). You have previously administered this battery to a large population of college students, and you know that the population mean is 25 and the population standard deviation is 5. You have a theory that intercollegiate athletes are better able to handle stress and will thereby have a lower score on the SBCS-1 than will the population of other college students. You run a small research project and give the SBCS-1 to a random sample of 100 intercollegiate athletes. You find that their mean score is 24.

Question: The hypothesis must be correct because the mean score for the athletes was less than the population mean of 25, so the athletes do experience less stress than other college students. Right?

Not necessarily. Twenty-four is indeed lower than the population mean of 25, but it is possible that this difference is due entirely to sampling error or to chance. To confirm your hypothesis, you must establish that there is a true difference between the population mean and the sample mean—that the athletes actually scored *significantly* lower on the stress battery than the population of other students. You must show, using the normal curve, that the sample mean of 24 is extremely unlikely to have occurred strictly by chance.

What you need to do is to compare the mean of the sample to the mean of a theoretical distribution of sample means that has an *n* of 100. The mean of the sample means, as you may remember from Formula 10.5, is equal to the mean of the original population. The standard deviation of the distribution of sample means—the standard error of the mean—is equal to the population standard deviation divided by the square root of *n* (Formula 10.6). By now you know that the distribution of sample means approaches a normal distribution when the sample size is large. The sample size of 100 is fairly large, so you can use the sample mean as well as the mean and standard deviation of the sampling distribution to determine how likely it is that a sample drawn from the general college population will have a mean of 24. To do this, you need only compute a *z* test.

The *z* Test

A **z test** is used to compare the mean of a particular sample to the mean of a population. To do this, you determine the *z* score for the sample mean and then find the area beyond the *z* score to see how it compares to the mean of the population. To compute a *z* test on the preceding example, you first compute a *z* score for a raw score of 24 (the mean of the sample) and then find the area beyond the *z* score.

The formula for a *z* score used previously is

$$z = \frac{X - \mu}{\sigma}$$

where X typically equals the score that is being converted to a *z* score, μ equals the population mean, and σ equals the standard deviation of the population. However, in the distribution of sample means, $\overline{X}$ represents each of the sample means that make up the distribution, $\mu_{\overline{X}}$ equals the mean of the distribution of sample means, and $\sigma_{\overline{X}}$ equals the standard error of the mean. The formula for converting a sample mean to a *z* score, then, is

$$z = \frac{\overline{X} - \mu_{\overline{X}}}{\sigma_{\overline{X}}} \tag{10.7}$$

Before computing the *z* score for your sample value, you need to compute the value for the standard error of the mean ($\sigma_{\overline{X}}$). You also need to compute the mean of the distribution of sample means ($\mu_{\bar{X}}$). Knowing that the standard deviation of the population is 5 and the sample size is 100, Formula 10.6 can be used to calculate the standard error of the mean:

$$\sigma_{\bar{X}} = \frac{\sigma}{\sqrt{n}} = \frac{5}{\sqrt{100}} = \frac{5}{10} = 0.5$$

Formula 10.5 can be used to compute the mean of the distribution of sample means:

$$\mu_{\bar{X}} = \mu = 25$$

Therefore, the *z* score for a sample mean of 24 from this population is

$$z = \frac{\bar{X} - \mu_{\bar{X}}}{\sigma_{\bar{X}}} = \frac{24 - 25}{.5} = \frac{-1}{.5} = -2.00$$

Now that you have a *z* score, what do you do with it? You use the procedures developed in Chapter 6 to look up the *z* score of −2.00 in Table Z to find out how extreme the score actually is. From Table Z, the area below a *z* score of −2.00 is .0228, or 2.28%, of all possible samples. This means that out of all possible samples with size 100 drawn from this college student population, you expect that only 2.28 out of 100 samples (2.28% of the samples) will have a mean of 24 or less. Your sample of athletes is among this 2.28% because its mean is 24. If you refer to a normal curve of the means of samples size 100 from this population, you will find that a mean of 24 is out in the tail and is not representative of the typical students in this population. So the sample of athletes *may* come from this population, but it is not likely.

> **Question:** So can it be concluded that intercollegiate athletes score lower on this stress test than other college students and that they therefore experience less stress?

The rationale behind the answer to this question is discussed in great detail in the next chapter. But briefly, most psychologists agree that if a sample mean has a probability of less than .05 (5%) of coming from a particular population, then the sample is probably not a part of that population, but is from another population. Applying this to the preceding example, the probability is .0228 that the sample is from the population of general college students, and because .0228 is less than .05, most behavioral science researchers would agree that the athlete sample probably does not belong to this general college student population. The athlete sample more likely belongs to a different population, a population of people who score lower than 25 on the stress test. Thus, in answer to the question: Yes, athletes probably do experience less stress than other college students.

Before ending this chapter, here is one more example of a z test. You are probably aware of the use of hypnosis as an aid to memory in certain legal cases. The theory behind this is that witnesses will remember more under hypnosis than they would otherwise. Have you ever wondered whether this premise is true? Does hypnosis really help people remember? Suppose you conduct a research project to determine whether people can remember a list of objects better when they are hypnotized than when they are not.

To begin the research, you ask a large population of people (several thousand) to attempt to remember a list of 100 items. Five days later, you ask them to write down all the items they remember. The mean number of items remembered by this population is 17, and the population's standard deviation is 7. Next, you recruit a random sample of 144 people and have them do the same thing, except that they are hypnotized before they are instructed to recall the list. The mean number of items recalled by this hypnotized sample is 17.75. This mean is higher than the population mean, but is it high enough that you can confidently state that memory under hypnosis is better than memory without hypnosis?

To make that determination, conduct a z test. First, compute the standard error of the mean:

$$\sigma_{\bar{X}} = \frac{\sigma}{\sqrt{n}} = \frac{7}{\sqrt{144}} = \frac{7}{12} = .583$$

Knowing the standard error of the mean, you can now complete the z test:

$$z = \frac{\bar{X} - \mu_{\bar{X}}}{\sigma_{\bar{X}}} = \frac{17.75 - 17}{.583} = \frac{.75}{.583} = 1.29$$

Now use Table Z to find the area of the normal curve that falls beyond a z score of 1.29. The area beyond is .0985, or 9.85%. Few, if any, behavioral scientists would state, based on this memory recall task, that recall under hypnosis is any better than with no hypnosis. It is certainly not clear from this research whether hypnosis has any effect on memory.

VISUAL SUMMARY

The z Test

Before You Begin: Compute $\bar{X}$, n, μ, σ.

$$\sigma_{\bar{X}} = \frac{\sigma}{\sqrt{n}} \quad\longrightarrow\quad z = \frac{\bar{X} - \mu}{\sigma_{\bar{X}}}$$

Concept Quiz

Deffenbacher, Huff, Lynch, Oetting, & Salvatore (2000) conducted a study designed to both explore emotional, behavioral, and accident-related characteristics of highly angry drivers and evaluate two anger-reducing treatment interventions. They found that the relaxation treatment intervention significantly reduced driver anger compared to a control group. Suppose you want to conduct a similar study to reduce the anger level of college students on your campus.

1. For the sample you select for your study to be useful, it must be _____ of the target population.

2. _____ sampling is the most common method used to create a representative sample.

3. A computer-generated _____ could be used to randomly select a random sample, if each student on campus is assigned a number.

4. The best estimate of the population mean is _____.

5. The standard deviations of samples are generally _____ than those of populations because they rarely include _____ scores.

6. In a distribution of sample means, all with the same n, the mean of the sample means will equal _____.

7. The standard deviation of the distribution of sample means is called the _____ and is computed by dividing the standard deviation of the population by _____.

8. The central limit theorem states that the distribution of sample means approaches a _____ distribution when the sample size (n) is _____.

9. To compare the mean of a sample to the mean of a population, you can use a _____ test.

Answers

1. representative
2. Random
3. random number table
4. the mean of the sample
5. smaller; extreme
6. the population mean
7. standard error of the mean; the square root of n
8. normal; large
9. z

Summary

Results of behavioral science research are reported in terms of probabilities. The probability of any event occurring can be computed by dividing the number of possible ways it can occur by the total number of all possible ways that related events can occur. The probability of an event occurring is also equal to the relative frequency of that event in the population. The probability of one or the other of two mutually exclusive events occurring is equal to the sum of their individual probabilities. Similarly, the probability of one or the other of any two events occurring, whether or not they are mutually exclusive, is the sum of their probabilities, minus the probability that both events will occur at the same time. The probability of two events occurring at the same time is equal to the product of their separate probabilities. It is also possible to compute the probabilities associated with populations by using the normal curve formulas discussed in Chapter 7.

Often samples are used to estimate population values. It is important for the sample to be representative of the population. If you have only one sample, the mean and standard deviation of the sample are your best estimate of the mean and standard deviation of the population.

A distribution of sample means can be created by computing the means of many samples taken from the same population. This distribution of sample means has a mean equal to the population mean and a standard deviation equal to the standard error of the mean. It is possible to use the sample mean, the population mean, and the standard error of the mean to conduct a z test to determine whether a particular sample is likely to have come from a particular population.

Key Terms

probability
mutually exclusive
addition rule of
    probability
addition theorem of
    probability
multiplication rule of
    probability

multiplication
    theorem of
    probability
representative sample
random sampling
random number table

distribution of sample
    means
standard error of the
    mean
central limit theorem
z test

Formulas

$$\text{Probability of event A} = \frac{\text{number of events in A}}{\text{total number of all events}} \quad \text{or} \quad p(A) = \frac{n(A)}{n} \quad (10.1)$$

$$p(A \text{ or } B) = p(A) + p(B) \qquad (10.2)$$

$$p(A \text{ or } B) = p(A) + p(B) - p(A \text{ and } B) \qquad (10.3)$$

$$p(A \text{ and } B) = p(A) \cdot p(B) \qquad (10.4)$$

$$\mu_{\bar{X}} = \mu \qquad (10.5)$$

$$\sigma_{\bar{X}} = \frac{\sigma}{\sqrt{n}} \qquad (10.6)$$

$$z = \frac{\bar{X} - \mu_{\bar{X}}}{\sigma_{\bar{X}}} \qquad (10.7)$$

Problems

1. If there are 900 psychology majors at a university with 12,000 students, what is the probability that the next student who comes through the library door will be a psychology major?

2. If there are 700 history majors at a university with 15,000 students, what is the probability that the next student who comes through the library door will be a history major?

3. If there are 900 psychology majors and 500 sociology majors (with no double majors) at a university with 12,000 students, what is the probability that the next student who comes through the library door will be a psychology major or a sociology major?

4. If there are 700 history majors and 200 English majors (with no double majors) at a university with 15,000 students, what is the probability that the next student who comes through the library door will be a history major or an English major?

5. If there are 900 psychology majors and 500 sociology majors, and 50 of those students are psychology/sociology double majors, at a university with 12,000 students, what is the probability that the next student who comes through the library door will be a psychology major or a sociology major?

6. If there are 700 history majors and 200 English majors, and 25 of those students are history/English double majors, at a university with 15,000 students, what is the probability that the next student who comes through the library door will be a history major or an English major?

Using the following frequency data in the table and assuming that these events are mutually exclusive, compute the probabilities in Problems 7–12.

Label	Frequency
Highly introverted	106
Average	798
Highly extroverted	213

7. What is the probability of being highly introverted?

8. What is the probability of being average?

9. What is the probability of being highly extroverted?

10. What is the probability of being either highly introverted or highly extroverted?

11. What is the probability of being highly introverted or average?

12. What is the probability of being highly extroverted or average?

Use the following probabilities to solve Problems 13–18.

	Probability
Having schizophrenia	.01
Extroverted	.10
Employed by the government	.25
Employed in the private sector	.65
Unemployed	.10
High sensation seeker	.20
Low sensation seeker	.10

13. What is the probability of being either employed by the government or unemployed?

14. What is the probability of being either a high sensation seeker or a low sensation seeker? What is the probability of being either employed in the private sector or employed by the government?

15. What is the probability of both being employed by the government and having schizophrenia?

16. What is the probability of both being employed by the private sector and having schizophrenia?

17. What is the probability of both being employed by the government and being a high sensation seeker?

18. What is the probability of both being a low sensation seeker and having schizophrenia?

Using the frequency data in the following table and assuming that these events are mutually exclusive, compute the probabilities in Problems 19–25.

Behavioral Type	Frequency
Type A	123
Type B	177
Average (not A or B)	200

19. The probability of being Type A

20. The probability of being Type B

21. The probability of being average

22. The probability of being either Type A or Type B

23. The probability of being either Type B or average

24. The probability of being either Type A or Type B or average

25. The probability of being either Type A or average

Problems From the Literature

How young children spend their time is an important developmental issue in learning and social skills, as well as attitudes. Huston, Wright, Marquis, and Green (1999) studied how two cohorts of young children (2- and 4-year-olds) from families with low to moderate incomes used their time over a 3-year period. Among the findings was a negative relationship of age and time watching weekday entertainment television. There was also a positive relationship of parent's education level and the time children spent watching educational television. Suppose another researcher conducted a survey that focused on the

Minutes Spent Per Day and Category for 4-year-old Children ($n = 250$)

Sample characteristics: Activities:

Girls	115	Chores	32
Boys	135	Educational activities	78
		Outside play	65
Ethnicity:		Personal care	60
White	95	Sleep	510
African American	89	Socializing	45
Hispanic/Latino	38	Television	
Other	28	Educational	66
		Noneducational	294
		Videos (entertainment)	65
		Video games	125
		Other	100

daily time 4-year-old children spent doing various activities and asked parents to do the time estimations. Results of the survey are shown here. Use this information to solve Problems 26–35.

26. What is the probability of a child being male?

27. What is the probability of a child being either White or African American?

28. What is the probability of a child being female and White?

29. Disregarding the time of day, what is the overall probability that a child is watching either noneducational or educational television?

30. Disregarding the time of day, what is the overall probability that a child is watching

either noneducational or educational television?

31. Disregarding the time of day, what is the overall probability that a child is either socializing or doing chores?

32. Disregarding the time of day, and assuming a child is engaged in only one activity, what is the probability of a child being male and watching television or being a male child and playing video games?

33. Disregarding the time of day, and assuming a child is engaged in only one activity, what is the probability of a child being female and socializing or being female and playing video games?

34. Disregarding the time of day, what is the probability that a child in this study is male

and either White or Latino/Hispanic and sleeping?

35. Discuss the importance of the sampling technique in this study.

As mentioned earlier, Howard (2000) found that the quality of organs selected for transplantation is related to the urgency of the patient's need for the organ. It seems that surgeons are more likely to reject poor-quality organs if the patient to whom the organ was offered is otherwise healthy (Howard, 2000). Suppose researchers collect the following organ and health status data for patients who received organ transplants within the past 3 months. Use this information to solve Problems 36–50.

36. What is the probability of a transplant recipient being female?

Quality of Organs and Patient Need at Time of Transplantation (*n* = 100)

Sample characteristics:

Patient's Transplantation Need Condition:

Women	32	Very urgent	57
Men	68	Semi-urgent	28
		Moderately urgent	15
Ethnicity:		**Kidneys Donated by Quality:**	
White	56	Excellent	21
African American	26	Average	48
Hispanic/Latino	10	Poor	31
Asian American	8		

37. What is the probability of a transplant recipient being male and in very urgent need condition?

38. What is the probability of a transplant recipient being female, in very urgent need condition, and receiving an average quality kidney?

39. What is the probability of a transplant recipient being either an Asian American woman or an Asian American man?

40. What is the probability of a transplant recipient being in semi-urgent need and receiving an excellent quality kidney?

41. What is the probability of a transplant recipient being in moderately urgent need and receiving a poor quality kidney?

42. What is the probability of a transplant recipient being in very urgent need and receiving an excellent quality kidney?

43. What is the probability of a transplant recipient being in semi-urgent need and receiving an excellent quality kidney or being in semi-urgent need and receiving an average quality kidney?

44. What is the probability of a transplant recipient being an African American woman and very urgently needing the kidney transplant?

45. What is the probability of a transplant recipient, in moderately urgent need, receiving either a poor quality or average quality kidney?

46. What is the probability of a transplant recipient being a Latino male and in semi-urgent need of the kidney?

47. What is the probability of a transplant patient being a Hispanic woman or African American woman or Asian American woman?

48. What is the probability of a donated kidney being excellent quality?

49. What is the probability of a donated kidney being either average or poor quality?

50. What is the probability of the transplant patient being either African American or Hispanic/Latino?

References

Deffenbacher, J. L., Huff, M. E., Lynch, R. S., Oetting, E. R., & Salvatore, N. F. (2000). Characteristics and treatment of high-anger drivers. *Journal of Counseling Psychology, 47,* 5–17.

Howard, D. H. (2000). *The economics of organ allocation.* Doctoral dissertation. Cambridge, MA: Harvard University.

Huston, A. C., Wright, J. C., Marquis, J., & Green, S. B. (1999). How young children spend their time: Television and other activities. *Developmental Psychology, 35,* 912–925.

Neilsen/NetRatings (2000). *Characteristics of WWW users* [Online]. Available: http://209.249.142.27/nnpm/owa/NRpublicreports.usageweekly (visited April 4, 2001).

11

Experimental Design

- Developing a Hypothesis
- Identifying Variables
- Factors in Experimental Design
  Between-Subjects, Within-Subjects, and Mixed Designs
  One-Group Experimental Designs

Completely Randomized Designs
- Important Aspects of Experimental Design
  The Necessity for Control
  Experimenter Bias and Demand Characteristics
- Statistical Significance

- Power
- Summary
- Key Terms
- Problems
  Problems From the Literature
- References

Put yourself in the following situation. You spent the last 2 weeks finishing up the semester and working overtime. When not attending classes or working, you were completing term papers or cramming for finals until long into the night. The last day of finals was the worst, with two exams back to back. The day after finals, instead of winding down and relaxing like the rest of your friends, you had to report for jury duty. What a way to spend your break!

At first, jury duty was so boring that it almost made you long for the History of Civilization lectures you slept through during your freshman year. But after the first few days, that changed. Now you're hearing a criminal case that is turning out to be quite intriguing.

The defendant is accused of robbing a convenience store at gunpoint. He maintains his innocence, but the store clerk has positively identified him as the person who robbed her. Although the gun and the money were never recovered and several people claim they were with the defendant at the time of the robbery, the prosecution insists that this is the person who robbed the store. Whom are you to believe?

The prosecution's case relies solely on the eyewitness testimony of the store clerk. But how dependable is her memory? How reliable in general are eyewitnesses? Should this man be sent to jail solely on the clerk's testimony?

Several researchers have examined these questions and, on the whole, have found that eyewitness testimony is not reliable. (For a detailed discussion of eyewitness testimony, see Egeth, 1993; Loftus, 1979; Penrod, Loftus, and Winkler,

1982; U.S. Department of Justice Office of Justice Programs, 1999; or Wells, Malpass, Lindsay, Fisher, Turtle, & Fulero, 2000.) As a juror, however, you know nothing of the available research on eyewitness testimony. Consequently, you spend much of your time agonizing over whether or not you should trust the store clerk or the defendant and his friends.

It is now a few months later, and you are reflecting on the course of the trial, particularly the problems the jury had in deciding whether to trust the clerk's testimony. In a flash of insight, you realize that the area of eyewitness testimony would be a fascinating research topic for your senior thesis. You want to begin working on your thesis, but how do you start? You know what you want to study, but how do you go about studying it? The best way is to conduct an experiment, which involves formulating a hypothesis (a possible explanation for some behavior) and testing it by following standardized procedures.

First, you need to survey the research literature to find out what previous researchers have discovered and how they have gone about obtaining their results. This literature search can be done in many different ways using a variety of sources available to you as a student and a researcher. In the area of eyewitness testimony and memory, some of the possible sources are textbooks or chapters in books on memory and cognition, current journals such as *Memory and Cognition,* journals of literature reviews such as *Psychological Bulletin* or the *Annual Review of Psychology* that cover specific topic areas in psychology, journals of abstracts such as *Psychological Abstracts* and *Sociological Abstracts,* and, of course, electronic databases such as *PsycInfo* and *ERIC,* which can be searched using computers. In addition to literature searches, you should attempt to make personal contact with other researchers who are currently working in the area by using the telephone, mail, fax, or, more preferably, e-mail.

Next, based on your research and personal observations and knowledge, you can formulate a **hypothesis,** a prediction concerning the behavior you are studying, which in this case is memory for faces. Once you have identified the relevant factors, you can get down to actually designing your experiment by establishing various experimental conditions and controls, deciding how to assign participants to the conditions, and so on. Keep in mind that the basic idea behind an experiment is to investigate the validity of a hypothesis by manipulating critical variables under rigidly controlled conditions. The purpose of this chapter is to teach you how to do this.

Developing a Hypothesis

To reiterate, the first step in developing a research project is to survey previous research relating to that field, not only to uncover any pertinent information but also to learn how other researchers have investigated similar topics. The next step is to define your hypothesis. A scientific research hypothesis is a prediction based predominantly on a scientific theory or body of knowledge. As first proposed by

Karl Popper in 1959, there is only one criterion that a scientific hypothesis must meet: The hypothesis must be falsifiable; that is, it must be logically possible to show the hypothesis false. The following two statements are examples of hypotheses you might consider in your research on eyewitness testimony. Only one is a true scientific hypothesis. Which is it?

Hypothesis 1:   Memory for faces declines rapidly with time.

Hypothesis 2:   We remember every face we see, but often we are unable to retrieve that information from long-term memory.

To test Hypothesis 1, you could set up an experiment that requires participants to identify previously shown faces after a set period of time. Results of such an experiment would show either that the participants do remember new faces after a set period of time or that they do not remember faces after a set period time. Thus, Hypothesis 1 might either be supported or falsified by research findings. Hypothesis 2, on the other hand, is stated in such a way that it is impossible to collect data showing it is false. However unlikely, you *could* obtain data showing support for the proposition that recall for faces is always perfect. However, there is no way to reach into people's brains to determine whether memories of faces actually perish after a short time or whether memories remain for the life of the individual but become unattainable after some period of time. Thus, Hypothesis 2 is not a scientific hypothesis because it cannot be falsified.

Identifying Variables

After you have generated a hypothesis, the next step is to identify the relevant variables. Based on your research and with your hypothesis in mind, you need to determine what factors—what variables, such as scores on a visual memory task—will best help you test your hypothesis and measure your results. There are basically three types of variables: independent variables, dependent variables, and subject variables.

Independent variables are those that are manipulated by the experimenter and applied to the participant in order to determine what effect they may have on behavior. These are the factors that the experimenter *varies* from one condition to another, such as the items in memory lists or the dosages of an experimental drug. In an experiment, a researcher may want to compare the effects of different independent variables or the effects of varying amounts (such as different dosages of drugs) or levels (such as low imagery or high imagery stimuli in a memory experiment) of one particular independent variable. Having determined the independent variable, the experimenter can randomly assign each participant to any level or condition of the independent variable.

Dependent variables are those that are used to assess or measure the effects of the independent variables. In behavioral science research, dependent variables are measures of the behavior being studied. Examples are scores on an interest survey, the number of visual images identified correctly, and the amount of time it takes to push a button. An easy way to remember the difference between an independent and a dependent variable is that the dependent variable *depends* on the independent variable; if the variables are causally related, the dependent variable will vary, or change, as the independent variable changes. Thus, dependent variables are measured by the experimenter to determine whether the experimental procedures result in any behavioral change.

Subject variables are those that describe characteristics or attributes of participants that cannot be manipulated by the experimenter. Examples of subject variables are gender, IQ, ethnicity, and age.

Question: Aren't subject variables just other kinds of independent variables?

No, they aren't. Subject variables are determined *before* the participants enter into the research project, so the experimenter cannot control these qualities and certainly cannot randomly assign the participants to the various conditions of the subject variable. (It is impossible to assign a person randomly to be a male or female, for example.) Control of the independent variable enables the researcher to determine whether or not the variable is the factor responsible for any change in a participant's behavior. Without this control, as when the factor is a subject variable rather than a true independent variable, the researcher cannot know whether the change is actually due to the subject variable or to some alternative explanation. An example will illustrate this point.

Suppose your research on eyewitness testimony leads you to believe that women are better at remembering faces than men (remember that gender is a subject variable), and you set up an experiment to test your hypothesis. Unfortunately, you cannot randomly assign participants—they are already either men or women—although you do keep other variables constant, such as stimulus materials and the room environment. Let's say your hypothesis is supported, that the female participants do indeed remember more faces than the male participants. Does this mean that being female *causes* a person to better remember faces, or can there be some alternative explanations? Perhaps women learn to notice facial details when applying makeup, or perhaps our society encourages women more than men to pay attention to bodily appearance. Your study may enable you to document a discrepancy between men and women, but this discrepancy is not necessarily due to an innate gender difference. It may be due solely to social or learned factors. And so it is with all subject variables. Because they allow the researcher no control, the researcher cannot tell whether subject variables actually cause the behavior being studied or whether the behavior is caused by related but alternative factors.

Question: Does this mean, then, that good research never involves subject variables?

No, not at all. Much of the research in the behavioral sciences is *nonexperi-mental* and uses subject variables. Nonexperimental research, particularly corre-lational research, is valuable because it allows you to identify relationships be-tween variables, and often those variables happen to be subject variables. For example, a large body of knowledge has been gathered involving gender differ-ences, and this knowledge has accumulated through valid research using subject variables. Do keep in mind that although nonexperimental research is quite valu-able in identifying relationships, it cannot be used to explain *causes* of behavior, as does experimental research. To reiterate: The major difference between exper-imental and nonexperimental research is that nonexperimental research lacks a true independent variable that can be controlled by the experimenter, whereas ex-perimental research requires an independent variable that the experimenter can control. Because subject variables are frequently analyzed as if they were inde-pendent variables, merely looking at the statistical test that is used to analyze the collected data can be misleading. Remember to be careful when you are tempted to make generalizations regarding subject variables.

Concept Quiz

Although the background music in retail stores may make shopping a more pleasurable experience for customers, the music may also influence the behavior of employees. Chebat, Vaillant, and Gelinas-Chebat (2000) predicted that the type of background music played would also affect salespersons' persuasive efforts within the store. The results of their experiment indicated that the salespeople communicated more and their persuasive arguments were accepted more when low and moderately interesting music was played than when other music was played.

1. A prediction based predominantly on a scientific theory or body of knowledge is called a scientific _____.

2. The hypothesis that "The type of background music played would affect the salespersons' persuasive efforts within the store" is a true scientific hypothesis because it is stated in such a way that it can be shown to be

   _____.

3. Variables that are manipulated by the experimenter, such as type of background music, and applied to the participant in order to determine their effect on the behavior of the participant are called _____ variables.

4. Variables that are used to measure the effects of experimenter-manipulated variables are called _____ variables.

5. Identify the independent and dependent variables in this study.

6. Variables such as the salesperson's gender, IQ, ethnicity, and age are called _____ variables.

Answers

1. hypothesis
2. false
3. independent
4. dependent

5. The independent variable is background music. The dependent variable is persuasive efforts.

6. subject

Factors in Experimental Design

Return to the memory for faces experiment, in which you have identified the variables in your project, taking care that your independent variable is not a subject variable. The next step is to design an experiment that effectively tests the validity of your hypothesis. Your experimental design depends on the number of independent variables investigated, the number of levels or manipulations of each independent variable, and the way in which you assign participants to the various experimental conditions. It is the experimental design that determines exactly how you will analyze the data collected in the experiment.

Between-Subjects, Within-Subjects, and Mixed Designs

One of the primary decisions to make when designing an experiment is how to assign participants to the various experimental conditions. The assignment depends on several factors; most important are the number of independent variables and the number of levels within each independent variable. Remember that the independent variable is manipulated by the experimenter. The levels are the different ways you manipulate that variable. For example, if you are studying the effects of differing amounts of alcohol on driving performance, the independent variable is the amount of alcohol. The levels of the independent variable might be the one-beer level, the two-beer level, the three-beer level, and the no-beer level. Each level is a separate group within the independent variable.

There are basically three ways of assigning participants to experimental conditions: a between-subjects design, a within-subjects design, and a mixed design. A **between-subjects design** (sometimes called an independent-group design) requires that each level of each independent variable has different participants; thus, there is a distinct difference *between* each level of the experiment because each person participates in one and only one level. A **within-subjects design** (also called a repeated-measures design) requires that each person participates in all levels of all independent variables; thus, each participant stays *within* the experiment for its entire run. A **mixed design** most often occurs when there are at least two independent variables and each person participates in all levels of one variable but not all levels of at least one of the other variables.

Here is a sports psychology example to illustrate these design differences. Suppose you know a judge who plays golf. She's not a particularly good golfer, but she relishes the game nonetheless. The judge offers you a grant to investigate possible

Figure 11.1
The general experimental design for the experiment to improve golf swings.

Independent Variable 1

No Imagery   Imagery

No Relaxation

Independent Variable 2

Relaxation

Figure 11.2
The participant assignment for a between-subjects design. Each person participates in only one experimental condition.

Independent Variable 1

No Imagery   Imagery

No Relaxation	P_1 P_4	P_7 P_{10}
	P_2 P_5	P_8 P_{11}
	P_3 P_6	P_9 P_{12}

Independent Variable 2

Relaxation	P_{13} P_{16}	P_{19} P_{22}
	P_{14} P_{17}	P_{20} P_{23}
	P_{15} P_{18}	P_{21} P_{24}

techniques to improve her golf swing. After a review of the sports literature, you find two techniques worth studying: mental imagery (visualizing each golf shot before you swing) and relaxation techniques (specifically, deep breathing). The general design of your experiment is shown in Figure 11.1. There are two independent variables, mental imagery and relaxation, and each of the independent variables has two levels: no imagery or imagery and no relaxation or relaxation. Thus, there are four possible conditions: no imagery/no relaxation, no imagery/relaxation, imagery/no relaxation, and imagery/relaxation. Depending on how you assign participants to groups, you can use one of the three experimental designs just discussed.

As mentioned before, in a *between-subjects design,* each person participates in only one of the experimental conditions, and therefore each condition is independent of the other groups (see Figure 11.2). The participants in the no imagery/no relaxation condition are different from the participants in the imagery/relaxation condition, and so forth. In this way, subject effects such as

		Independent Variable 1	
		No Imagery	Imagery
Independent Variable 2	No Relaxation	P_1 P_4 P_2 P_5 P_3 P_6	P_1 P_4 P_2 P_5 P_3 P_6
	Relaxation	P_1 P_4 P_2 P_5 P_3 P_6	P_1 P_4 P_2 P_5 P_3 P_6

Figure 11.3
The participant assignment for a within-subjects design. Each person participates in all experimental conditions.

innate athletic ability are randomized throughout all conditions. A major advantage of the between-subjects design is that it is not affected by order effects where, as people participate in several conditions, the participants tend to improve with practice until they are considerably more adept in the final condition than they were in the initial condition. Another advantage is that the between-subjects design is statistically the simplest and is therefore easier to analyze. The major drawback of this design is that it requires more participants than the within-subjects or the mixed design. If you want to use 6 participants in each condition, you will need 24 participants to complete your design.

At the other extreme is the *within-subjects design,* in which each person participates in every condition (see Figure 11.3). Thus, in order to have 6 participants in each condition, you need a total of only 6 participants in the entire experiment. You can appreciate the merit in this if you've ever had to recruit participants without an Introductory Psychology pool available. Another advantage is that subject effects, at least theoretically, may be eliminated or subtracted out. Still another advantage is that experiments using this design tend to be more sensitive to differences among experimental conditions. For example, in the golf improvement study, the same person participates in each of the conditions, so each group, or cell, will have participants of equally good or equally poor ability. The major problem with the within-subjects design is difficulty in controlling learning factors. Thus, the within-subjects design should not be used when the participant's behavior is likely to change with the practice or knowledge gained through previous conditions. For instance, by the time the people in the golfing study participate in the fourth condition, they may all score higher than they did in the first condition, merely because of practice. Another disadvantage is that after participating in a couple of conditions, the participants may figure out the purpose of the experiment and change their responses accordingly. This is sometimes a problem, especially in experiments that, by their nature, require a certain amount of deception.

Finally, a mixed design is used when it is necessary to have each person participate in all levels of one independent variable, while participating in only one level of another independent variable. For example, if we were to use a mixed design in the golfing study, we could assign a particular participant (P_1) to only the no relaxation condition, as shown in Figure 11.4(a). Then this person participates solely in the no relaxation/no imagery and the no relaxation/imagery conditions. Or we could assign the participant to only the two no imagery conditions, as shown in Figure 11.4(b). Mixed designs use fewer participants than between-subjects designs, but they are the most difficult to analyze statistically.

In the following chapters, these designs are discussed where appropriate. Most often, however, between-subjects designs are used as examples because they are the most common simple designs, and the statistics needed to analyze them are easier to compute and therefore more appropriate to an Introductory Statistics course.

Figure 11.4
Two possible participant assignments for a mixed design. Each person participates in all levels of one independent variable but in only one level of the other independent variable.

Independent Variable 1

	No Imagery		Imagery	
	P_1	P_4	P_1	P_4
No Relaxation	P_2	P_5	P_2	P_5
	P_3	P_6	P_3	P_6
	P_7	P_{10}	P_7	P_{10}
Relaxation	P_8	P_{11}	P_8	P_{11}
	P_9	P_{12}	P_9	P_{12}

Independent Variable 2

(a)

or

Independent Variable 1

	No Imagery		Imagery	
	P_1	P_4	P_7	P_{10}
No Relaxation	P_2	P_5	P_8	P_{11}
	P_3	P_6	P_9	P_{12}
	P_1	P_4	P_7	P_{10}
Relaxation	P_2	P_5	P_8	P_{11}
	P_3	P_6	P_9	P_{12}

Independent Variable 2

(b)

One-Group Experimental Designs

Another consideration in designing experiments is the number of samples you need to collect. The simplest experimental design, known as the **one-group experimental design,** involves comparing a single sample mean to the mean of a known population. Suppose you want to know whether convenience store clerks have better memories than people in the general population. If you have access to population data for a memory task, you can give that memory task to a sample of convenience store clerks and compare its mean to the mean of the population. Do you remember the *z* test in Chapter 10 where intercollegiate athletes' scores on a stress test were compared with those of the general population of college students? That is an example of a single-sample test with a one-group design.

Completely Randomized Designs

One of the simplest ways to compare more than one sample is to use the **completely randomized experimental design.** In this design, there is one independent variable with at least two different levels, and participants are selected and assigned to one of the groups in a completely random fashion. Suppose you are a human factors psychologist who has just been employed by a large computer manufacturer. If you have ever used more than one type of computer, you are probably aware that computers come equipped with a variety of keyboards, each with its own distinctive touch and key spacing. You have been hired by the computer firm to determine which of two keyboards is more efficient.

The easiest way to do this is to conduct an experiment comparing one keyboard to another by using a completely randomized design. First, you need to devise or acquire a typing test that will provide a fair assessment of the two keyboards. Scores on this test will be the dependent variable. The type of keyboard used during the typing test will be the independent variable. All other variables—room illumination, noise level, computer and monitor used, word-processing program, and so on—should remain constant. You select participants randomly from a population of possible computer users, and then randomly assign them to one of the two groups (see Figure 11.5). This two-group design will enable you to determine which of the two keyboards is more efficient. Analysis of this type of experiment is discussed in Chapter 12.

Independent Variable

Keyboard 1		Keyboard 2	
P_1	P_4	P_7	P_{10}
P_2	P_5	P_8	P_{11}
P_3	P_6	P_9	P_{12}

Figure 11.5
A two-group completely randomized design having one independent variable.

Figure 11.6
A completely randomized design with three levels of one independent variable.

Independent Variable

Keyboard 1		Keyboard 2		Keyboard 3	
P_1	P_4	P_7	P_{10}	P_{13}	P_{16}
P_2	P_5	P_8	P_{11}	P_{14}	P_{17}
P_3	P_6	P_9	P_{12}	P_{15}	P_{18}

Question: Does testing more than two keyboards increase the number of independent variables?

No, it doesn't. You can certainly test more than two keyboards by adding more groups—by randomly selecting more participants and assigning them in a random fashion to the additional groups. However, adding more keyboards simply extends the completely randomized design; it does not increase the number of independent variables. There is only one independent variable, the type of keyboard (see Figure 11.6). You have merely increased the number of *levels* (the number of different keyboards) of the single independent variable. If you decide to test an additional factor, such as various word-processing programs, you are adding another independent variable and need to use a factorial design.

In the **completely randomized factorial experimental design,** there are at least two independent variables—each having at least two levels—and participants are randomly assigned to the experimental conditions. If, as suggested earlier, you want to add two word-processing programs to your experiment on two keyboards, your study will have two independent variables, each having two levels. This is known as a 2 × 2 (read "two by two") factorial design. If you add still another keyboard and another word-processing program, you will have created a 3 × 3 factorial design.

Concept Quiz

Watkins, LeCompte, and Kyungmi (2000) conducted a series of experiments to examine study strategy and recall of common and rare words. In a memory recall task, they found that when participants were presented a mixed list of common and rare words, the common words were no more recallable than rare words. However, when the expectation of a memory test was removed, common words were more recallable than rare words from the mixed list. Suppose Dr. K wants to test word type (common, rare, mixed) on memory recall. Keep Dr. K's study in mind and answer the following design questions.

1. In Dr. K's experiment, there is _____ independent variable, and, if each person in the study participates in only one of the levels, it is a _____ design.

2. If each person participates in all levels of a single independent variable, it is a _____ design.

3. Suppose Dr. K adds test expectation (test versus no test) as a second independent variable. Each person participates in one level of test expectation and all three levels of word type. This experiment is called a _____ design.

4. The advantage of the between-subjects design compared to the within-subjects design is that it has _____.

5. A major advantage to Dr. K using a within-subjects compared to a between-subjects design is that _____.

6. In the _____ design, there is one independent variable with at least two different levels, and the participants are selected and assigned to one of the groups in a completely random fashion.

7. In the _____ design, there are at least two independent variables, each having at least two levels, and the participants are randomly assigned to the experimental conditions.

Answers

1. one; between-subjects
2. within-subjects
3. mixed
4. no order or practice effects

5. fewer participants are needed
6. completely randomized

7. completely randomized factorial

Important Aspects of Experimental Design

At this point, you may be wondering what experimental design has to do with statistics. The type of statistics used in any experiment depends on the design of that experiment. The chapters immediately following explain the statistical procedures necessary to analyze experiments using the various experimental designs. The purpose of *this* chapter is to introduce you to these designs and discuss their critical aspects. One of the most important aspects is the very critical need for control.

The Necessity for Control

A fact of life about science in general and behavioral science in particular is that it pays to be skeptical. A scientific skeptic is a person who does not accept a hypothesis to be true until there is proof that alternative hypotheses are extremely unlikely. The scientific technique used to rule out alternative hypotheses is **experimental**

control. Experimenters must not only ensure objective selection and assignment of participants, but they must also exercise stringent control over the design of the experiment and experimental situation in general. They need to make sure that each independent variable consists of one single factor. Furthermore, they must ensure that participants in all conditions receive identical treatment under identical circumstances. If a relevant factor, an extraneous variable, is introduced to one group but not to another, and if a behavior change is recorded for that group, then the experimenter cannot determine whether the change in behavior is due to the independent variable or to the extraneous variable. Thus, the experimental results will not be altogether valid.

The need for strict control is illustrated in the following example. Suppose, from your personal experience, you develop the hypothesis that eating chocolate improves memory for new faces. (If found to be true, the prosecutor from the convenience store trial could use the results to argue for the good memory of the store clerk!) You design an experiment to test your hypothesis. You find 30 people who eat an average of one chocolate bar each day. You find another 30 people who never eat chocolate. You give both groups a test of memory for new faces and find that the chocolate eaters are much better at remembering faces than the non-chocolate eaters. Does this prove that eating chocolate improves memory for faces? Not really. It may be that the elevated blood sugar level influences the metabolism of the brain and increases memory. It may be that the caffeine in the chocolate results in heightened alertness. It may be that for some reason, chocolate candy commercials particularly appeal to people who have good memories. As you may have gathered, this chocolate study is not a true experiment. The various groups are based on a subject variable: whether or not the participant regularly eats chocolate. No independent variable is manipulated by the experimenter, and the experimenter cannot randomly or otherwise assign participants to groups; the participants have already assigned themselves based on whether or not they regularly eat chocolate.

> **Question:** So how can an experiment be designed that will determine whether eating chocolate improves people's memories?

You design your experiment so that participants can be assigned to groups randomly, so that you can manipulate the independent variable. Also, you must control any relevant **extraneous variables** (those "extra" variables that may affect participants' responses but are not the ones being examined). Ideally, in the best of all experimental worlds, your revised experiment should be similar to that described next.

First, you randomly select 60 people and randomly assign them to one of two conditions, chocolate eating or nonchocolate eating. This eliminates the objection made earlier that perhaps it is merely people with good memories who like to eat chocolate. You require that all of your participants eat the same food at the same dining hall for every meal. The chocolate-eating group eats, every day, six chocolate chip cookies, each with a half ounce of chocolate chips. The non-chocolate-eating group eats six identical cookies minus the chocolate chips but with the same amounts of sugar, caffeine, and other ingredients as the chocolate chip cookies. At the same time, you restrict the diet of the participants to no other chocolate for the duration of the experiment. In this way, like all competent experimenters, you maintain control through the random selection and assignment of participants and through the control of extraneous variables. Any difference between the two groups will be due solely to the manipulation of the independent variable.

Experimenter Bias and Demand Characteristics

Experimenters are people, and people make mistakes. When researchers make mistakes, the mistakes tend toward favoring the experimental hypothesis. Occasionally, there are cases in which experimenters make conscious attempts to influence their participants. This is outright fraud, and, fortunately, it is relatively rare in behavioral science research. More common are cases of unintentional error, anything from simple mistakes in recording data to subtle, unintentional hints made to participants by experimenters. This latter error, known as **experimenter bias,** is a noteworthy problem. Because they know the research hypothesis and wish to prove it true (and want evidence to support their prediction), experimenters may inadvertently behave in a way that influences their results. For instance, suppose that in studying the recognition of new faces, you design an experiment in which you present participants with photographs of people's faces and ask them to memorize the faces. When the participants return 2 weeks later, you show them several groups of photos and you ask them to point to the faces in each group that they remember having seen before. It is highly likely that you will exhibit some kind of experimenter bias. Because you know the correct responses, you may without knowing it give your participants subtle cues as to which pictures are correct by making offhand comments, stressing certain words in the instructions, using certain facial expressions or body language when displaying the correct pictures, and so on. Thus, you may convey crucial information to your participants that increases, or perhaps even decreases, their accuracy in the task.

The best way to control experimenter bias is to somehow distance the participants from experimenters who know the hypothesis. This can be done in several ways, the most effective being (1) to hire assistants who are unaware of the hypothesis to conduct the experiment and (2) to completely automate the experiment. In many cases, researchers do both: They hire undergraduate or graduate research assistants to do such tasks as read instructions and answer questions, and they use computers to control the actual experimental procedures.

Closely associated with the problem of experimenter bias is the problem of demand characteristics. If experimenters, by knowing their research hypothesis, can unintentionally influence their participants' behavior, then it follows that participants, by figuring out the research hypothesis, may alter their behavior to meet the predictions of the hypothesis. **Demand characteristics** appear when participants change their responses based on knowledge of the experimental hypothesis. Participants tend to find even the most mundane research interesting, and they want to help in whatever way they can. If a participant can figure out the research hypothesis via the design of the experiment or via comments or instructions given by the experimenter, he or she may try to give the "correct" response whenever possible. This, of course, can work to support or not to support the research hypothesis, depending on whether the participant's guessed hypothesis is the same as the experimenter's actual hypothesis.

It is difficult to avoid demand characteristics. The most effective way to do so is to use deception, in which experimenters tell their participants that they are investigating one particular factor or behavior, but in reality they are studying another. An alternative is to discuss the experiment with the participants after collecting the necessary data and then discard the data from those who discovered the hypothesis. Be aware, however, that extreme deception and the discarding of data for no apparent reason are unethical. If you discard data, be sure to report that fact, as well as the reason why, in your experimental write-up. The best way to control demand characteristics is to run a pilot study and watch for indications of them. If such indications are detected, analyze the design of the experiment and redesign it so that participants will have a more difficult time figuring out the hypothesis.

In a nutshell: For an experiment to have merit, the experimenter must exert rigorous and thorough control over every aspect. He or she must maintain such rigid control over all extraneous variables that the only difference between experimental groups is the manipulation of the independent variable. Furthermore, the researcher must take special care to eliminate any experimenter bias and to minimize demand characteristics.

Concept Quiz

Recall Chebat, Vaillant, and Gelinas-Chebat's (2000) background music study mentioned in the first concept quiz. It was predicted that the type of background music played would influence the persuasive efforts of sales employees. Four different types of music were played in the store at random times during the experimental period and the behavior of salespeople recorded. It was found that low and moderately interesting music increased sales employees' communication efforts and the acceptability of their arguments more than the other music played.

1. Before beginning the experiment, Chebat and colleagues made sure the different types of music were equally pleasant sounding. This is an example of the scientific technique called _____ that is used to rule out alternative hypotheses.

2. _____ variables make it difficult to rule out alternative hypotheses.

3. Unintentional errors in the direction of the research hypothesis made by experimenters are called _____.

4. _____ arise when participants change their behavior based on their knowledge of the research hypothesis.

Answers

1. experimental control   3. experimenter bias   4. Demand
2. Extraneous   characteristics

Statistical Significance

Question: In a well-controlled and well-designed experiment, if a notable difference in behavior between the groups is observed, then it should be okay to generalize the findings to the entire population, right?

Wrong. You need to take one more step before generalizing, and that is to test your results for statistical significance. Any time you observe a difference in behavior between your groups, as indicated by the difference in the sample means, it may exist for one of two reasons: (1) there is no actual difference between the groups because both samples were taken from the same population—the observed difference is just a chance occurrence due to the error involved in sampling; or (2) a difference actually exists because each sample came from a different population and the difference is therefore real. Thus, in any experiment there are two distinct, mutually exclusive hypotheses regarding the data collected: the **null hypothesis** (H_0), which states that there is no real difference between the sample means or between the sample mean and the population mean, and the actual hypothesis, called the **research hypothesis** (H_1), or alternative hypothesis, which states that the difference between the sample means or between the sample mean and the population mean is real. The difference between these mutually exclusive hypotheses is illustrated next, using the facial memory study as an example.

Research Hypothesis (H_1):   When shown faces and given a test of facial memory 8 hours later, participants who rehearse the faces once an hour via mental imagery *score higher* than participants who do not rehearse. There is a real difference between participants who use mental imagery and those who do not.

Null Hypothesis (H_0):   When shown faces and given a test of facial memory 8 hours later, participants who rehearse the faces once an hour via mental imagery *score the same* as participants who do not rehearse. There is no real difference between participants who use mental imagery and those who do not. Any observed difference is due to *chance*—to the fact that participants in each group were not identically matched.

Figure 11.7
The four possible
outcomes of a
statistical decision.

True Situation

	Null Hypothesis True	Null Hypothesis False
Reject the Null Hypothesis	Type I Error α	Correct
Fail to Reject the Null Hypothesis	Correct	Type II Error β

Decision

Statistical tests are formulated in such a way that they test the null hypothesis. They are set up to test whether the difference between the groups' performances (the difference between the sample means) is significantly large enough for researchers to rule out the possibility that the difference occurred by chance. If the results of the tests indicate that the difference is real—that it is significant— then researchers can *reject the null hypothesis* and accept the research hypothesis. On the other hand, if the results indicate that the difference between the groups is not significant, researchers say that they *fail to reject the null hypothesis*. They cannot accept the null hypothesis; they can only fail to reject it because there is always a chance, however small, that the difference is real, but your experiment was not sensitive enough to confirm your research hypothesis.

Question: So how can it be determined whether the difference between samples is real or chance?

This determination is based on several important factors, such as the number of samples, the variances of the population and the sample, and the size of the risk taken by the experimenters that their conclusion will be wrong. Remember the preceding example involving mental imagery as an aid to remembering faces? H_0 stated that there is no difference between the sample mean of memory scores and the population mean; H_1 stated that there is an actual difference between the sample and population means. Suppose you are a researcher who has just conducted an experiment investigating these hypotheses and you need to decide which one is actually true. As you make this decision, there are two ways you can be correct and two ways you can be wrong (see Figure 11.7). Obviously, you will be correct if you reject the null hypothesis when it is in reality false or if you fail to reject it when it is in reality true. However, if you decide to reject the null hypothesis when it is actually true (you accept a false research hypothesis), you have

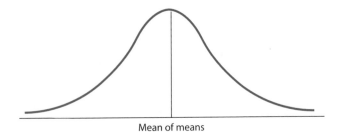

Mean of means

Figure 11.8
The distribution of
sample means.

committed a **Type I error.** If you fail to reject the null hypothesis when it is actually false (you fail to accept a true research hypothesis), you have committed a **Type II error.**

It is imperative that researchers take great pains to avoid making these errors, particularly Type I errors. When researchers accept research hypotheses that are false, they can mislead not only themselves and other researchers but also people who apply the research results to the real world. If Type I errors are committed in a series of learning studies and if the results are applied to the classroom, countless hours of learning time may be wasted. Thus, Type I errors are considered to be much more serious than Type II errors. When a Type II error is made because a researcher fails to reject the null hypothesis when the research hypothesis is actually true, the researcher or some other researcher may have to repeat the experiment, or a variation of it, sometime in the future. This may result in lost time, but it will not result in fallacious theories being implemented in the real world. Type II errors may slow down the progress of science, but they don't lead it down blind alleys.

Actually, if researchers select the appropriate statistical tests (the most widely used tests are explained in the following chapters) and apply their results to the tests correctly, the chance of committing a Type I error is very small (about .05, or 5 out of 100). The purpose of these tests is to determine whether the statistical differences recorded among the sample groups are significant. Figures 11.8 and 11.9 will help you understand the rationale underlying the success of the tests in determining significance.

Figure 11.8 shows a distribution of all possible sample means; any one particular sample mean will fall somewhere within this distribution. If that sample mean is near the population mean, as is $\overline{X}_1$ in Figure 11.9, it is likely that H_0 is true and that any difference between the experimental group receiving the independent variable and the rest of the population not receiving it is negligible and is due merely to a sampling error. In such a case, the researcher should accept the sample as being part of the greater population. On the other hand, if the sample mean lies in one of the tails of the distribution of sample means, as does $\overline{X}_2$ in Figure 11.9, it is quite unlikely that H_0 is true. In this case, the researcher should reject the null hypothesis and accept the research hypothesis. In other words, the experimental group receiving the independent variable is different enough from the population not receiving it that the researcher should consider the experimental group as part

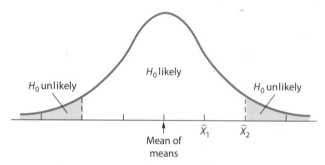

Figure 11.9   Sample mean 1 is near the mean of the distribution of sample means and therefore within the area where the null hypothesis is likely, whereas sample mean 2 is out in the tail of the distribution where the null hypothesis is unlikely.

of a separate population that behaves in a distinct manner because of the effects of the independent variable.

> **Question:** How far out in the tail should the sample mean lie before H_0 can be rejected?

The answer to this question is based on another question: How much of a chance do researchers want to take that they will not commit a Type I error? The probability of committing a Type I error is designated by alpha (α). Most behavioral scientists agree that an alpha level of .05 is reasonable, which means that the null hypothesis can reasonably be rejected if there is less than a .05 probability of committing a Type I error. Therefore, the alpha levels should be set at points in the tails where only .05, or 5%, of the distribution will yield more extreme scores. If a particular sample mean falls within these areas of the curve, you can reject H_0 (see Figure 11.10).

> **Question:** Because each sample has only one mean, it can lie on only one side of the curve. Why does Figure 11.10 show alpha areas in both tails?

The decision to spread the alpha areas between the two tails of the distribution or to concentrate all of the alpha area in only one tail of the distribution depends on the research hypothesis. If the research hypothesis specifies that the sample mean will be definitely above or definitely below the population mean, it is of course reasonable to look in only one tail of the theoretical sampling distribution to see whether the sample mean is significant. For example, if our research hypothesis states that eating chocolate will *improve* memory, then you need to look only in the tail above the population mean for significance. Research hypotheses that specify the direction of the experimental effect are called *one-tailed hypotheses* because you need to look only in one specified tail for significance. Tests of hypotheses such as these are called **one-tailed tests** (see Figure 11.11).

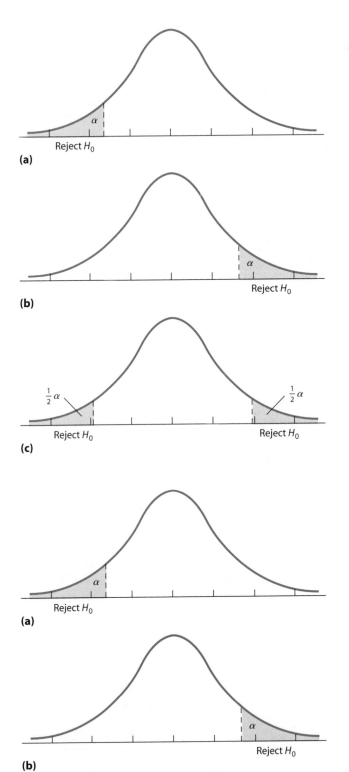

Figure 11.10
The placement of alpha areas for (a and b) a one-tailed test and (c) a two-tailed test. If a sample mean falls within the alpha area, you can reject the null hypothesis.

Figure 11.11
One-tailed statistical tests put all alpha (a) in the tail below the mean or (b) in the tail above the mean.

Many research hypotheses suggest merely that the sample mean will be different from the population mean without specifying the direction of the difference. Because the direction is not specified, it is necessary to look in both tails of the theoretical sampling distribution for significance (see Figure 11.12). Tests of hypotheses such as these are known as **two-tailed tests.** As an example, if your research hypothesis stated that a diet including chocolate changes a person's memory for faces, it is not clear whether this change is for the better or for the worse. Because the hypothesis does not specify the direction of the change, it is a *two-tailed hypothesis.*

Question: How do you know when to use a one-tailed test and when to use a two-tailed test?

The decision to use a one-tailed test or a two-tailed test begins with your literature search and the statement of your research hypothesis. If your knowledge of previous research leads you to believe that your experiment will result in the mean of one group or one level of the independent variable being greater than the mean of the other, then your research hypothesis should state this prediction and you will run a one-tailed test. If, on the other hand, it is not clear from your knowledge of previous research which group or level will have the larger mean, then your hypothesis will reflect this uncertainty and you will do a two-tailed test. Remember that to determine which type of test to conduct, you need only look at the research hypothesis. When it predicts a direction, do a one-tailed test; if it does not predict a direction, then do a two-tailed test. For example, if you know that caffeine aids memory, you can hypothesize that people who use caffeine before taking a memory test will perform better than people who do not use caffeine. This hypothesis leads to a one-tailed test because the prediction is that one group will perform better than the other group. In the real world of research, most researchers take the conservative approach and use the two-tailed test more often than the one-tailed.

Whenever you begin any research project, you are faced with many choices: whether to conduct an experiment, how many independent variables to investigate, how many participants to use and how to assign them to the various groups, and what controls to implement. Each of these choices has an impact on the experimental design and subsequently on the statistical analysis of the data you col-

Figure 11.12
Two-tailed statistical tests split alpha and put half of alpha in the tail below the mean and the other half in the tail above the mean.

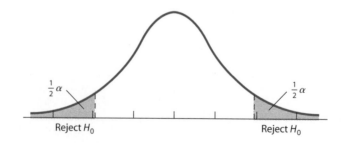

Reject H_0 Reject H_0

lect. Because of this close interrelationship between experimental design and statistics, it is to your advantage as a researcher to be knowledgeable about both. Often experimenters, especially those who are inexperienced, conduct research without considering the eventual analysis of the data. Mere possession of data does not mean that the data are useful or that the data will answer the questions you have posed. It is best to design all research projects with the statistical analyses of the data in mind.

Power

Another factor researchers need to consider is the power of the statistical test they will use to analyze their experiment. The more powerful the statistical test, the more likely it is that the test will yield a positive result for the experiment. In other words, the more powerful the test, the more likely it is that the test will reject the null hypothesis and allow the researcher to accept the research hypothesis. More technically, the **power** of a statistical test is the probability that the test will correctly reject the null hypothesis when the null hypothesis is in fact false. Beta (β) is used to indicate the probability of making a Type II error. The power of any statistical test is equal to 1 minus the probability of a Type II error, or $1 - \beta$ (see Figure 11.13):

$$\text{Power} = 1 - \beta$$

Several factors can affect the power of a statistical test: (1) the size of alpha, (2) the sample size, (3) the difference between the means of the two populations that the samples come from ($\mu_1 - \mu_2$), and (4) the type of statistical test used in the analysis.

As previously mentioned, when doing research you should try to choose an alpha (α) level that minimizes the chance of Type I errors. Doing this naturally leads to relatively small values for α. However, the smaller the α level, the more likely there will be a Type II error, β. This relationship between the size of α and the size of β is illustrated in Figure 11.14. Figure 11.14(a) shows that a small α will produce a relatively larger β, which results in lower power. An increase in the size of α, as shown in Figure 11.14(b), produces a smaller β and therefore results in higher power. Because the power of a test is equal to $1 - \beta$, you can increase the

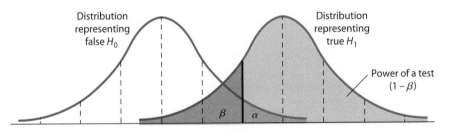

Figure 11.13
The probability of a Type I error, α, and the probability of a Type II error, β. The power of a statistical test is the shaded area, $1 - \beta$.

Figure 11.14
(a) A small α causes
a large β, which
decreases the power
of the test. (b) A
large α causes a
small β, which
increases the power
of the test.

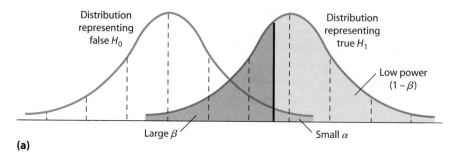

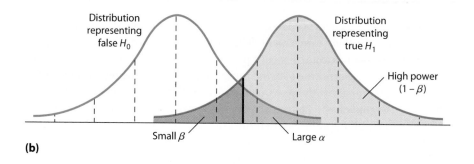

power of your test by choosing a larger value for α. For example, the power of the test increases if you change the α level from .01 to .05.

The power of a test also increases as you enlarge the size of your sample. An increase in the sample size decreases the standard deviation of the sampling distributions, which reduces the overlap between the two distributions and decreases β. Therefore, going to the trouble of recruiting lots of participants can pay off because a large sample increases the power of your statistical test. Given the same statistical test, you will more likely be correct in rejecting the null hypothesis when your sample size is 50 than when your sample size is 10.

It also follows that the power of the test increases as the means of the two populations that represent H_0 and H_1 move farther apart. As the distance between the means increases, there is less overlap and therefore a smaller β. Figure 11.15 illustrates the decrease in β as the means of the two populations move apart. Remember that any decrease in β increases the power of a test.

Finally, some statistical tests are simply more powerful than others. Tests that use interval or ratio data and require you to estimate population standard deviations and population means tend to be more powerful than tests without these features. Tests that involve accurate estimates of population parameters are called parametric tests; statistical tests that do not require the estimation of population parameters are called nonparametric tests. Parametric tests are generally more powerful than nonparametric tests. Chapters 12–14 describe the uses of the major parametric statistical tests. Nonparametric tests are covered in Chapter 15.

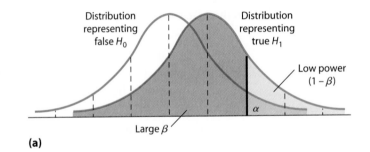

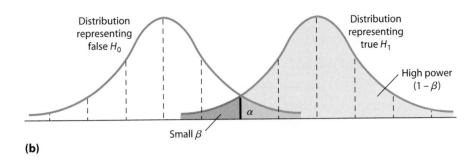

Figure 11.15
(a) If the means of
the two populations
are close together, β
is large and the
power is low. (b) If
the means of the two
populations are far
apart, β is small and
the power is high.

Concept Quiz

*Wells and Perrine (2001) investigated possible psychological benefits of employees
bringing their pets to work. They found that employees believed pets reduced stress
and brought positive benefits to the work environment. Based on this finding,
suppose Dr. Ohboy hypothesizes that participants will experience less physiological
stress watching a horror film holding a small pet than they will if they are alone.
Participants are randomly assigned to a condition, and their blood pressure is
recorded before the film begins. Their blood pressure is taken again 30 minutes after
the film begins.*

1. In any experiment there are two distinct, mutually exclusive hypotheses
   regarding the data collected: the _____ hypothesis and the
   _____ hypothesis.

2. The hypothesis predicting no differences in physiological stress between
   groups is called the _____ hypothesis.

3. The hypothesis predicting differences in physiological stress between
   groups is called the _____ hypothesis.

4. Statistical tests are formulated to test the _____ hypothesis.

5. If the difference in physiological stress in this experiment is significant, then
   Dr. Ohboy will reject the _____ hypothesis, but if the

difference is not significant, then Dr. Ohboy will _____ to reject the _____ hypothesis.

6. If there were real differences in physiological stress between the experimental conditions, and they weren't statistically detected, Dr. Ohboy would _____ the null hypothesis, but the null hypothesis was _____. This is called a Type _____ error.

7. If there were no real differences in physiological stress between the experimental groups, but a difference was statistically detected, Dr. Ohboy would _____ the null hypothesis, but the null hypothesis was _____. This is called a Type _____ error.

8. The probability of committing a Type I error is called _____ .

9. Tests of research hypotheses that specify the direction of the experimental effect are called _____ tests.

10. Tests of research hypotheses that do not specify the direction of the experimental effect are called _____.

11. Was Dr. Ohboy's research hypothesis one-tailed or two-tailed?

12. Power is equal to _____.

Answers

1. null; research
2. null
3. research
4. null

5. null; fail; null
6. fail to reject; false; II
7. reject; true; I
8. alpha (α)

9. one-tailed
10. two-tailed
11. one-tailed
12. $1 - \beta$

Summary

The three major classifications of variables are independent variables, dependent variables, and subject variables. The independent variable is the variable that is manipulated by the experimenter. The variable that is used to measure behavior, such as a test score, is the dependent variable. Subject variables are those that describe subjects' characteristics or attributes that cannot be manipulated by the experimenter.

Experiments are conducted to explain the causes of behavior by manipulating relevant independent variables and controlling extraneous variables. The two major types of experimental control are (1) randomly assigning participants to groups and (2) identifying relevant extraneous variables and holding them constant. Experimental designs are described by both the number and the type of independent variables, as well as by the way participants are assigned to the various conditions in the experiments.

Experiments can also be classified by the procedures used to assign participants to the experimental conditions. In a between-subjects design, each participant is randomly assigned to only one of the experimental conditions. In a within-subjects design, each randomly selected person participates in all experimental conditions for all independent variables. A mixed design occurs in factorial experiments when a person participates in all levels of one independent variable but participates in only one level of the other independent variables.

All experiments have a null hypothesis (H_0) and a research hypothesis (H_1). The null hypothesis states that the experimental manipulation has no effect. The research hypothesis states that the experimental manipulations have a significant effect on the experimental data that are collected.

The power of a statistical test is the probability the test will reject the null hypothesis when the null hypothesis is in fact false. Power can be increased by using a larger value for alpha, by increasing the sample size, by increasing the difference between the means of the populations being tested, or by using a more powerful statistical test.

Key Terms

hypothesis
independent variables
dependent variables
subject variables
between-subjects
   design
within-subjects design
mixed design
one-group
   experimental
   design

completely
   randomized
   experimental
   design
completely
   randomized
   factorial
   experimental
   design
experimental control
extraneous variable

experimenter bias
demand
   characteristics
null hypothesis (H_0)
research hypothesis
   (H_1)
Type I error
Type II error
one-tailed test
two-tailed test
power

Problems

1. A _____ is a statement based on a body of research knowledge or on a scientific theory that is in the form of a prediction.

2. Alison's adviser told her to revise her research proposal because her research hypothesis was so general that it was not _____.

3. Variables that are manipulated by the experimenter are called _____ variables.

4. _____ variables are those that are measures of the participants' behavior.

5. Reaction time, test scores, and heart rate are all examples of _____ variables.

6. Attributes or characteristics of participants that cannot be manipulated by the experimenter, such as eye color and athletic ability, are known as _____ variables.

7. Juan worked with people who had strokes and subsequent language impairment. They often became frustrated because they were unable to communicate their wants and needs. Some of the journal articles Juan read led him to believe that using sign language might be the answer. For his senior project, Juan decided to see whether these people might learn to communicate through sign language rather than oral speech.

   Juan divided his participants randomly into two groups, and each group received the following treatment on three separate days: A photograph was displayed on a computer screen along with either a spoken word or a gestured sign, depending on the condition. The participant was then asked to repeat the word or the sign. On the fourth day, Juan showed each participant the photograph and asked, "What is this?" He then recorded their answers and counted the number of correct responses for each group. In Juan's study, identify the following:
   a. The research hypothesis
   b. The independent variable
   c. The dependent variable

8. Dr. Peña is conducting research to see whether the severity of the chronic headaches suffered by her patients will be lessened through the use of biofeedback. Based on what she has read in medical journals and on her own observations, Dr. Peña has determined that the headaches are caused by muscle tension, so she feels that patients who learn to relax will have fewer or less severe headaches. To test her theory,

she attaches electrodes to the forehead of each of her patients. These tiny wires measure electrical activity in the muscles of the forehead. When her patients relax slightly, the electrical activity from their muscles drop and they receive feedback in the form of soothing music. Dr. Peña finds that compared to a separate control group of people to whom electrodes are attached but do not receive the feedback, the experimental group reports fewer and less severe headaches during the week following the biofeedback session. In this study, identify the following:
a. The research hypothesis
b. The independent variable
c. The dependent variable

9. Dr. Hilo developed a theory that tall people are more self-assured than short people. To test this theory, he recruited participants and placed them into three groups—tall, medium, and short—according to their height. Dr. Hilo then asked the participants to answer questions on the standardized Self-Assurance Rating Scale. What is wrong with Dr. Hilo's research design?

10. In Problem 8, Dr. Peña used a _____-subjects design in assigning participants to her two groups.

11. In a between-subjects experimental design, each person participates in _____ level(s) of the experiment.

12. In a within-subjects experimental design, each person participates in _____ level(s) of the experiment.

13. If Juan, in his study discussed in Problem 7, required that each person participate in both conditions, it would be a _____-subjects experimental design.

14. Ima Researcher is conducting an experiment with three independent variables, where each independent variable has two levels. Her participants are required to participate in both levels of one of the independent variables but in only one level of the other two independent variables. What kind of research design is this?

15. Between-subjects designs have many advantages. The major drawback for between-subjects designs is that they require _____.

16. Suppose you are interested in studying hearing loss caused by frequent exposure to moderate noises. You decide to compare the hearing of a group of men who have been randomly chosen to use an electric shaver for 1 month, and thus run a high-speed motor near their ears every day for a month, to a population of men who shave using a regular razor. You wish to determine whether the men who use the electric shaver are more hearing impaired than those men who shave using only a razor. The easiest statistical test for you to use to compare your sample of men to the population is a _____ test.

17. Dr. Bambino is doing research on pattern recognition in babies. He randomly selects and randomly assigns infants to two experimental groups. One group is presented with a card showing lines arranged in a random fashion; the second group is presented with a card showing horizontal lines arranged in a regular pattern. Dr. Bambino suspects that the infants will spend more time looking at the organized array of lines. Identify the following:
    a. The type of design
    b. The research hypothesis
    c. The independent variable
    d. The dependent variable

e. Some of the variables that need to be held constant

18. In a multilevel, completely randomized design, the number of _____ of the independent variable is increased, as opposed to the number of independent variables.

19. In another study, Dr. Bambino is investigating whether, in addition to organization, familiarity is a factor in the amount of time that infants look at a pattern. He randomly selects and randomly assigns infants to four groups. Group 1 is presented with a card showing a random arrangement of lines; Group 2 is presented with a card showing an organized arrangement of horizontal lines; Group 3 is presented with a card showing a drawing of a human face; Group 4 is presented with a card showing the same facial features as those on the Group 3 card but with the features arranged in a helter-skelter fashion. Dr. Bambino's design is a _____ experimental design, and it is in the form of a _____ × _____ factorial design.

20. A true scientist is unwilling to accept a hypothesis until all other alternative hypotheses can be ruled out. The way to rule out other possible hypotheses is through effective use of _____.

21. Whenever possible, all _____ should be held constant so that they don't interfere with the identification of the variables that are the true causes of the behavior being studied.

22. In Juan's study from Problem 7, he elicited and recorded the participants' responses himself. By so doing, he failed to control for

the effect of _____. To prevent this, what could he have done?

23. _____ occur when participants figure out the hypothesis and try to "help" by providing responses that they think support that hypothesis.

24. What should you do if you find that demand characteristics are cropping up in your experiment?

25. To determine whether observed differences in experimental samples are real or are due to chance, researchers need to test their results for _____.

26. The _____ states that there *is no* real difference between the sample means or between the sample mean and the population mean. The _____ states that there *is* a real difference between the sample means or between the sample mean and the population mean.

27. What is the null hypothesis in Dr. Peña's experiment in Problem 8 on the use of biofeedback to reduce headaches?

28. Suppose that biofeedback really does have some effect on reducing headache pain, but because of experimental error, Dr. Peña's results led her to the conclusion that it has no significant effect. This is a _____ error.

29. What is the null hypothesis in Juan's experiment from Problem 7 involving learning sign language versus oral speech?

30. Suppose that there is no actual difference between people who have had strokes learning to communicate through sign language and their learning to communicate through oral speech. However, because of experimenter bias, Juan's results led him to believe that learning sign language was significantly better. Juan has committed a _____ error.

31. It is generally agreed that _____ is an acceptable alpha level.

32. When the hypothesis states that there should be a difference between two samples but the direction of the difference is not stated, the hypothesis is _____-tailed.

33. Dr. Bambino's study on infant pattern recognition discussed in Problem 17 would use a _____-tailed test because he specifies that familiar, organized stimuli will hold infants' attention longer than unfamiliar, random stimuli.

34. What is the power of a test when beta (β) equals .75?

Problems From the Literature

The following problems refer to actual results from research studies that are cited at the end of the chapter.

In a study examining psychological and organization effects of pets in the workplace, Wells and Perrine (2001) found that employees believed pets reduced stress and brought positive benefits to the environment. Suppose another researcher, Dr. D, believes that the presence of pets will reduce speech anxiety in oral communication classes. To test his theory, participants were recruited from oral communication classes and randomly assigned to deliver a 10-minute persuasive speech either with or without a small older yet quiet dog resting near the podium. All speeches were videotaped, and trained observers scored the number of anxiety behaviors, such as shaking hands, wobbly legs, and cracking voice. Participants also completed a speech anxiety questionnaire when they finished their speech. As Dr. D expected, participants reported less anxiety when the dog was present than participants in the control condition. Use the information from the researcher's speech anxiety study to solve Problems 35–43.

35. Identify the null and research hypotheses for this experiment.

36. Identify the independent variable and state the different levels.

37. Identify the dependent variable.

38. What is the experimental design?

39. Name several extraneous variables that should be controlled.

40. Evaluate this study for experimenter bias and demand characteristics.

41. If the researcher examined differences in anxiety reduction between female and male participants, what kind of research design would this be?

42. If the difference in anxiety level between the experimental and control groups was due to chance, explain to the researcher why the results would change.

43. If true anxiety differences existed between the two experimental conditions, but they were not detected, what kind of error occurred?

When recognition or recall of words is better for those words presented at the beginning or end of a list or series, it is called a serial position effect. Reed (2000) wanted to see whether this might also happen with odors. Participants were presented a sequence of odors and then were asked to identify them from a list. Memory recognition for odors presented at the start and the end of the sequence was better than for those presented in the middle of the sequence. Suppose Dr. D did a memory recognition study using different types of sensory stimuli (odor only, sound only, and odor and

sound combined). Participants were seated in the lab and listened to a series of 10 sounds through headphones. After a 10-minute break, the same participants smelled a series of 10 odors. Again there was a 10-minute break before participants listened to 5 sounds and smelled 5 odors. The order in which the experimental stimuli were presented was randomly determined. To assess memory recognition, participants were asked to identify the stimuli on a list. Use the information about Dr. D's study to solve Problems 44–48.

44. Identify the null and research hypotheses in this experiment.

45. Identify the independent variable and state the different levels.

46. Identify the dependent variable.

47. a. What is the experimental design? b. Is it completely randomized?

48. What are some of the extraneous variables that need to be controlled in this experiment?

49. Suppose Dr. D wanted to see whether the lighting in the room made a difference in memory recognition. He proposed to keep the study the same and add the presence of light as an additional independent variable. With this modification, participants would be randomly assigned to either a lighted room or a room without light before the sensory stimuli were presented.
    a. Identify the experimental design of the proposed study.
    b. If Dr. D wanted 15 participants for each independent variable, what is the total number of participants he would need to recruit for this study?

50. If Dr. D said his findings were statistically significant, what did he mean?

References

Chebat, J., Vaillant, D., & Gelinas-Chebat, C. (2000). Does background music in a store enhance a salespersons' persuasiveness? *Perceptual and Motor Skills, 91,* 405–424.

Egeth, H. E. (1993). What do we not know about eyewitness identification? *American Psychologist, 48(5),* 577–580.

Loftus, E. (1979). *Eyewitness testimony.* Cambridge, MA: Harvard University Press.

Penrod, S., Loftus, E., & Winkler, J. (1982). The reliability of eyewitness testimony: A psychological perspective. In N. L. Kerr & R. M. Bray (eds.), *The psychology of the courtroom* (pp. 119–168). New York: Academic Press.

Popper, K. (1959). *The logic of scientific discovery.* New York: Basic Books.

Reed, P. (2000). Serial position effects in recognition memory for odors. *Journal of Experimental Psychology: Learning, Memory, and Cognition, 26,* 411–422.

U.S. Department of Justice Office of Justice Programs. (1999). *Eyewitness evidence: A guide for law enforcement.* Washington DC: Author.

Watkins, M. J., LeCompte, D. C., & Kyungmi, K. (2000). Role of study strategy in recall of mixed lists of common and rare words. *Journal of Experimental Psychology: Learning, Memory, and Cognition, 26,* 239–245.

Wells, G. L., Malpass, R. S., Lindsay, R. C. L., Fisher, R. P., Turtle, J. W., & Fulero, S. M. (2000). From the lab to the police station: A successful application of eyewitness research. *American Psychologist, 55(6),* 581–598.

Wells, M., & Perrine, R. (2001). Critters in the cube farm: Perceived psychological and organizational effects of pets in the workplace. *Journal of Occupational Health Psychology, 6,* 81–87.

t Tests

- *z* Tests (A Review)
- *t* Tests
- Single-Sample *t* Tests
  VISUAL SUMMARY: Single-Sample *t* Tests
- *t* Tests Between Two Independent Sample Means

VISUAL SUMMARY: *t* Tests Between Two Independent Sample Means
- *t* Tests for Correlated Samples
  VISUAL SUMMARY: *t* Tests for Correlated Samples
- Power and *t* Tests

VISUAL SUMMARY: Choosing the Proper *t* Test
- Summary
- Key Terms
- Formulas
- Problems
  Problems From the Literature
- References

Get out your stopwatch. If you don't have one, find a watch or a clock that measures time in seconds. Now look at the following 30 shapes and time how long it takes you to read the entire list out loud as fast as you can from left to right, top to bottom.

That was easy, wasn't it? You were probably pretty fast—about 20 seconds, plus or minus a little. Now try it again, but this time, see how long it takes you to say aloud the shapes in the list on the next page. Remember to read from left to right and top to bottom.

It took longer, didn't it? It might have taken even twice as long, and it was probably more than a little frustrating. This is a modified version of the "Stroop effect." It has fascinated psychologists since 1935 when J. Riddley Stroop first described it after using a list of color words as the stimulus in a learning experiment.

Question: Why is it so hard to read the shapes when the words above them are different from the shapes?

For most people, reading words is automatic by the time they become adults. They read every word presented to them without thinking about it. Consequently, *not* reading words that are put in front of them is extremely difficult. So when they look at a stimulus that contains printed words plus another attribute, they automatically read the words first, even if asked to attend to the other attribute. If a word and an attribute conflict with each other (as when the word *spade* is written above a diamond shape), naming the attribute usually takes longer because the brain processes the word before it processes the shape. Thus, the automaticity of reading the word interferes with the processing of the shape.

Spade ♠	Club ♣	Diamond ♦	Heart ♥	Club ♣	Spade ♠
Spade ♥	Heart ♣	Club ♦	Diamond ♣	Club ♥	Heart ♦
Diamond ♣	Club ♠	Spade ♥	Heart ♠	Spade ♦	Diamond ♣
Club ♥	Heart ♠	Spade ♦	Diamond ♥	Heart ♣	Club ♥
Heart ♠	Spade ♦	Diamond ♥	Heart ♠	Spade ♦	Diamond ♣

Many researchers have studied the Stroop effect and variations of it using various research designs. Suppose you conducted an experiment using the preceding lists as your stimuli. You used a between-subjects design and had one group of people name the symbols from one list, and then you compared the results to a second group who named the symbols from the other list. You observed a difference in speed similar to the difference in speed when you read the lists. As you have learned from the preceding two chapters, however, merely observing a difference between two groups is not sufficient; you must test the difference via statistical methods to determine whether the difference is statistically significant. The difference must be large enough to be considered unlikely to have happened by chance. The way to test for statistical significance is to conduct a statistical test on the data. The test you use depends on a number of factors, such as the availability of population data, the size of the sample, the number of independent variables, and whether the samples are correlated, to name only a few. The bulk of this chapter is devoted to examining *t* tests—one of the most widely used tests of significance in the behavioral sciences. You will learn when to use *t* tests, how to use them, and which one to use on what type of data. First, however, is a review of z tests—not only because you might benefit from a review, but also because understanding the rationale behind t tests is based on understanding z tests.

z Tests (A Review)

Suppose that by an amazing stroke of luck you came across some population data indicating that, on the average, it takes people in the general population 15 seconds to name all the shapes from the shapes-alone list at the beginning of this chapter. (Realistically, of course, it is probably impossible to find such population data because to find the true population mean, one must obtain a measurement from every member of the population, which would be very impractical.) You have decided to conduct an experiment to see whether people really do take longer to read the word-and-shapes list than the shapes-alone list. For your experiment, therefore, you need to randomly choose a group of people, time how long it takes to read the word-and-shapes list, and then compare the mean of this group to the population mean. Your research hypothesis (H_1) states: People will take longer to name the shapes when reading from a list of combined shapes and words than when reading from a list of shapes alone. The null hypothesis (H_0) states: People will take the same amount of time when reading from a list of combined shapes and words as they will take when reading from a list of shapes alone. To test these hypotheses, you ask a randomly chosen group of 25 people to name only the shapes for a combined list of conflicting words and shapes. Given what you know about the speed of the general population on the shapes-alone list, you can compare the mean from the single sample to the population mean. The results are as follows:

Population mean (μ) = 15
Sample mean ($\overline{X}$) = 18
Sample standard deviation (S) = 5
Number of participants (n) = 25

The sample mean of 18 seconds is indeed longer than the population mean of 15 seconds, but is this a true difference or merely a chance variation from the population mean? You can conduct a z test, which, as you remember from Chapter 10, can be used to determine the probability of the difference occurring by chance alone. This is done by computing the z score for the sample mean and finding the area beyond the z score to see how it compares to the population mean. Formula 10.7 states that

$$z = \frac{\overline{X} - \mu}{\sigma_{\overline{X}}} \qquad (10.7)$$

Because you know the sample mean and the population mean, you need only compute the standard error of the mean ($\sigma_{\bar{X}}$) to compute the *z*. For this you could use Formula 10.6, which is reprinted here:

$$\sigma_{\bar{X}} = \frac{\sigma}{\sqrt{n}} \qquad (10.6)$$

Question: How can the standard error of the mean be computed using this formula without knowing the standard deviation of the population?

If you know the standard deviation of the population, you should use it (Formula 10.6). If you do not, as is the case this time, you need to estimate the population standard deviation. Fortunately, the formula that you have been using to compute the standard deviation of the sample gives an unbiased estimate of the standard deviation of the population. So when you do not have access to the population standard deviation, you can use the standard deviation of the sample to estimate the standard error of the mean.

$$estimated\ \sigma_{\bar{X}} = \frac{S}{\sqrt{n}} \qquad (12.1)$$

Because you only have the sample standard deviation, you will use Formula 12.1 to estimate the standard error of the mean and then substitute the estimate of the standard error of the mean for the actual standard error of the mean in Formula 10.7 to compute the *z* score:

$$estimated\ \sigma_{\bar{X}} = \frac{S}{\sqrt{n}} = \frac{5}{\sqrt{25}} = \frac{5}{5} = 1$$

$$z = \frac{\bar{X} - \mu}{estimated\ \sigma_{\bar{X}}} = \frac{18 - 15}{1} = \frac{3}{1} = 3.00$$

Question: A *z* score of 3.00 is pretty large. How do you know that it is large enough not to have happened by chance?

As stated in Chapter 11, most psychologists agree that an alpha level of .05 is sufficient grounds for rejecting the null hypothesis. To test your null hypothesis proposing no differences between Stroop groups, you have computed a *z* score. Now you must look it up in the appropriate table to determine the probability of getting a score as extreme as the one obtained in your experiment. By looking up the *z* score of 3.00 in Table Z in Appendix A, you find that the probability of getting a *z* score as large as or larger than 3.00 is .0013, or much less than 1 out of 100. When using an alpha level of .05, any *z* score that results in a probability of less

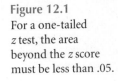

Figure 12.1
For a one-tailed
z test, the area
beyond the *z* score
must be less than .05.

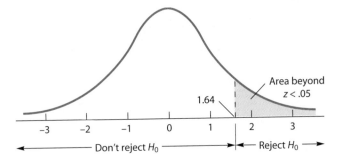

Figure 12.2
The *z* score must be
farther out in the tail
in order to reject the
null hypothesis when
using a two-tailed
test.

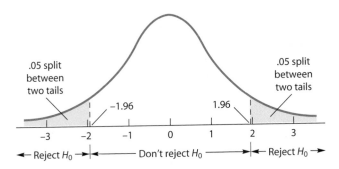

than .05 allows you to reject the null hypothesis and accept the research hypothesis. Your probability, .0013, is less than .05. Therefore, you can reject the null hypothesis and accept the research hypothesis. The difference between the sample mean and the population mean is significant, so you can assert that people do take longer to say the names of shapes when reading from a combined list of conflicting words and shapes than when reading from a list of shapes alone.

It is relatively simple to conduct a *z* test. You need only compute the *z* score and use Table Z to read the probability beyond the *z* score. If your research hypothesis is one-tailed, the area beyond the *z* score must be less than .05 (see Figure 12.1). If the research hypothesis is two-tailed, you must split the .05 probability between the two tails, with .025 in one tail and .025 in the other (see Figure 12.2). Thus, as explained in Chapter 11, a *z* score must be farther out in the tail in order to reject the null hypothesis when using a two-tailed test.

People who do a lot of research and run a lot of *z* tests don't continually refer to Table Z. They memorize two *z* scores that correspond with the level of significance required for their experiments. For one-tailed tests, they know that the *z* score necessary for a .05 level of probability is 1.645 or −1.645 (found in column 3, "Area Beyond *z*," in Table Z). For two-tailed tests, they know that the *z* score necessary for a .025 level of probability is −1.96 or less, or 1.96 or greater in order to reject the null hypothesis. Thus, if you compute several *z* scores and need to determine their significance, you don't have to keep referring to the table. All you need to know is the minimum *z* score necessary for significance.

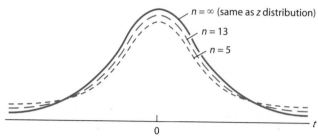

Figure 12.3   The *t* distribution for small samples is flatter than the *z* distribution, but as the sample size increases, the *t* distribution approaches the shape of the *z* distribution.

t Tests

The central limit theorem provides the justification for using sample data to run a *z* test. The central limit theorem states that any distribution of sample means approaches a normal distribution when the sample is infinitely large. (Review Chapter 10 for a more detailed discussion of the central limit theorem.) Therefore, when a sample is large (more than 1,000, for example), it is appropriate to conduct a *z* test because the distribution of sample means approaches a normal distribution. However, when the sample is relatively small (less than 1,000, for example), the distribution of sample means is best matched by the *t* distribution, not the *z* distribution.

The *t* distribution is similar to the *z* distribution in that both are symmetrical, bell-shaped sampling distributions. However, there is a noteworthy difference: The overall shape of the *t* distribution is influenced strongly by the size of the samples used to generate it. For very large samples, the *t* distribution approaches the *z* distribution, but for smaller samples, the *t* distribution is flatter. Figure 12.3 illustrates the differences between the two.

> **Question:** But in the example for the *z* test, the sample size was only 25. Why?

A small sample was used intentionally in order to lead into the *t* test. But also, it was done to call your attention to this fact: When the sample is large, you can use a *z* test; when the sample is small, you should use a **t test.** So instead of using a *z* test on your data, you should have used a *t* test.

Single-Sample *t* Tests

> **Question:** Is the *t* test anything like the *z* test?

It is, and that's why so much time has been spent reviewing the *z* test—because the *z* test and the *t* test are not much different. Both involve comparing the sample mean to the population mean. The formula for computing the *t* score is essentially the same as that for computing the *z* score:

$$t = \frac{\overline{X} - \mu}{\sigma_{\overline{X}}}$$

(12.2)

Not only is the formula similar, but also the procedure for computing a *t* score is identical to that for computing a *z* score. The sample mean, the population mean, and the standard error of the mean are all needed for the *t* score. If the standard deviation of the population is not available for computing the standard error of the mean, use the standard deviation of the sample to estimate the standard error of the mean, just as when computing the *z* score. In fact, the only difference between conducting a *z* test and conducting a *t* test is that after computing a *z* score, you look it up in Table Z, and after computing the *t* score, you look it up in Table T.

The following example will illustrate how to conduct a single-sample *t* test. Dr. Tee has developed a language training system that she claims significantly increases the number of new words acquired by infants. Typical children in this part of the world begin to speak a few basic words by the time they are 1 year old. By the time they are 2 years old, typical toddlers have a vocabulary of about 210 words. To test her system, Dr. Tee randomly selects 12 sets of parents who are willing to use her language training system with their newborn infants for 2 years. At the end of the 2-year test period, she tabulates the number of words in each toddler's vocabulary. The results are displayed in Table 12.1.

The mean number of words in the vocabularies of the infants in the experimental group is 223.083. This is obviously greater than the population mean of 210 words, but Dr. Tee wants to be certain that this difference is not due merely to chance. Because her sample was small, $n = 12$, she needs to conduct a *t* test, as opposed to a *z* test, to determine whether the observed difference between the means is significant. Because her statistics skills are a bit rusty, she engages your help to determine whether her results are significant. Before beginning, consider Dr. Tee's research and null hypotheses. The research hypothesis is: The language training system will increase the size of a child's vocabulary as measured at age 2 years. The null hypothesis is: The language training system will make no difference in the size of a child's vocabulary as measured at age 2 years.

To run a *t* test, you need to compute the *t* score using Formula 12.2. You already know the sample mean (223.083) and the population mean (210 words), but you still need to compute the standard error of the mean. You do not have access to the standard deviation of the population, so you are forced to estimate the standard error of the mean using the standard deviation of the sample. Using Formula 12.1, the estimate of the standard error of the mean is

$$estimated \; \sigma_{\overline{X}} = \frac{S}{\sqrt{n}} = \frac{29.740}{\sqrt{12}} = \frac{29.740}{3.464} = 8.585$$

Table 12.1   Number of Words in Vocabulary for 12 Toddlers Using the Language Training Program

Child	Number of Words in Vocabulary, X
C. W.	197
D. J.	223
P. V.	241
J. I.	183
T. B.	222
B. C.	231
R. A.	297
B. B.	220
D. T.	188
P. P.	231
C. D.	210
M. L.	234

$$\Sigma X = 2{,}677$$
$$\overline{X} = 223.083$$
$$S = 29.740$$

Now you can use Formula 12.2 to compute the *t* score for the group of toddlers:

$$t = \frac{\overline{X} - \mu}{\sigma_{\overline{X}}} = \frac{223.083 - 210}{8.585} = \frac{13.083}{8.585} = 1.524$$

If this *t* score were a *z* score, Dr. Tee would need a *z* of 1.645 or larger to reject the null hypothesis because her research hypothesis is one-tailed, so a score of 1.524 would fail to reject the null hypothesis. Because this is a *t* score instead of a *z* score, you need to look in a different table. The critical values for *t* are listed in Table T in Appendix A.

To find the critical value in this table for any particular *t*, you need to know the type of research hypothesis (one- or two-tailed) and the *degrees of freedom* (*df*) for your particular sample. The **degrees of freedom** vary with different types of *t* tests, but when used with the single-sample *t* test, the degrees of freedom equal the total number of scores in the sample minus 1:

$$df = n - 1 \tag{12.3}$$

Because there are 12 scores in Dr. Tee's sample, the degrees of freedom are 11:

$$df = n - 1 = 12 - 1 = 11$$

As indicated before, the *t* distribution changes with the sample size. This fact is taken into account in Table T because when entering the table, you must have already computed the degrees of freedom.

To find the critical value of *t* for Dr. Tee's sample at an alpha level of .05, you will use one of the two highlighted columns in Table T. The first highlighted column from the left lists the critical values for one-tailed research hypotheses, and the second highlighted column lists the critical values for two-tailed research hypotheses. Because Dr. Tee's original research hypothesis is one-tailed, you will use the one-tailed column. To begin, look down the *df* column until you find the row headed by the number 11. This row lists the critical values for the *t* statistic at several different possible alpha levels. (As previously mentioned, you are only interested in the .05 alpha level.) Then move across the row until you reach the first highlighted column (alpha equals .05 for a one-tailed test). Read from the table that the critical value for this particular one-tailed *t* test is 1.796. This means that the computed *t* must be greater than or equal to 1.796 to reject the null hypothesis and accept the research hypothesis. In this case, the computed value for *t* equals 1.524, which is less than the table value of 1.796. You therefore fail to reject the null hypothesis, so you can conclude that Dr. Tee's language training system will make no difference in the size of a child's vocabulary. Even though the mean of the sample was larger than the population mean, this difference could have occurred by chance.

Question: What exactly are "degrees of freedom"?

Degrees of freedom (*df*) is a statistical term used to denote the number of scores within any distribution that are free to vary without restriction. Every distribution has a mean, and so does every sample. Remember from Chapter 5 that the sum of all deviations from the mean, $\Sigma(X - \overline{X})$, is always equal to zero. Thus, in any sample with a fixed mean, the sum of the deviations from the mean is equal to zero. For example, suppose that a sample of five student grades has a mean of 87. Call these grades X_1, X_2, X_3, X_4, and X_5. Within reason, the first four of these scores can be anything; they are free to vary. Suppose, for example, that $X_1 = 89, X_2 = 84, X_3 = 100$, and $X_4 = 96$, and you are not sure what X_5 equals. Because you know that the mean of this sample equals 87 and that the sum of the mean deviations must be zero, you can do the following calculations to compute the correct value for X_5:

$$(X_1 - 87) + (X_2 - 87) + (X_3 - 87) + (X_4 - 87) + (X_5 - 87) = 0$$

Substituting the known values for X_1 through X_4, you get

$$(89 - 87) + (84 - 87) + (100 - 87) + (96 - 87) + (X_5 - 87) = 0$$

$$2 - 3 + 13 + 9 + (X_5 - 87) = 0$$

$$X_5 - 66 = 0$$

$$X_5 = 66$$

VISUAL SUMMARY

Single-Sample *t* Tests

Before You Begin: State H_0 and H_1.
Compute $\overline{X}$, μ, σ, or S.

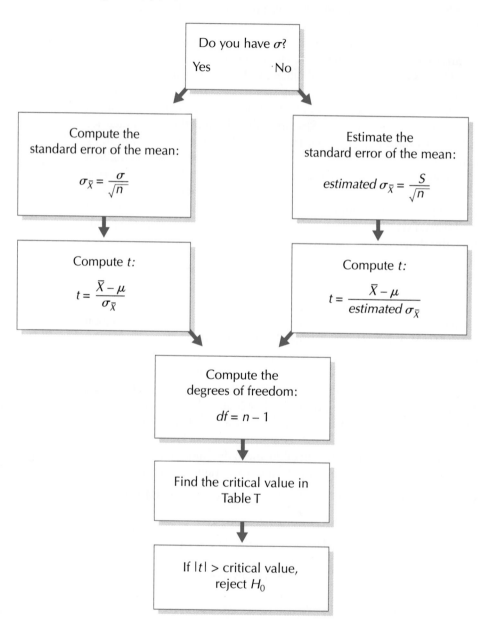

Given the first four scores, X_5 *must* be equal to 66. This last score is not free to vary. It is predetermined by the first four scores. Thus, the number of degrees of freedom in this sample is 4 because only four, $(n - 1)$, scores are free to vary. The concept of degrees of freedom appears again and again throughout the last several chapters of the book, but it is based on the fact that typically $n - 1$ scores in any sample are free to vary.

Concept Quiz

A recent survey of over 1,000 people reported that the population mean of time spent by people familiar with using the Internet was 10.5 hours per week (America Online/Roper Starch Worldwide, 2000). Researchers, concerned that students may be developing Internet addiction, collected the same information from a random sample of 30 students from MicroHard College and reported a sample mean of 9.8 hours with a standard deviation of .7 hours per week Internet use. Use this example to answer the following questions.

1. To estimate the standard error of the mean, you divide the
   _____ by the square root of n, and the calculated figure is
   _____ .

2. Explain what the estimated standard error of the mean represents in this study.

3. The formula for number of degrees of freedom for this single-sample t test is _____ , and the calculated degrees of freedom equals
   _____ .

4. If the researchers predicted that the mean for MicroHard students was more than the population, the hypothesis would be _____ -tailed, and using a significance level of .05, the critical value of t would be
   _____ .

5. To be significant, with an alpha level of .05, the absolute value of one-tailed z must exceed _____ , and a two-tailed z must exceed
   _____ .

6. The MicroHard sample is relatively small, and the distribution of sample means is best matched by the _____ distribution.

7. If the researchers predicted a nondirectional difference and using a .05 significance level, would MicroHard researchers reject or fail to reject their null hypothesis? Interpret this finding.

Answers

1. sample standard deviation (.7);

$$\frac{s}{\sqrt{n}} = \frac{.7}{\sqrt{30}} = .128$$

2. It is the estimated standard deviation of the mean number of hours spent on the Internet each week for a sample of means with the same *n*.

3. $n - 1; 30 - 1 = 29$

4. one-; 1.699

5. 1.64; 1.96

6. *t*

7. $t = \dfrac{9.8 - 10.5}{.128} = -5.469$, with $df = 29$, critical value is 2.045. Reject the null hypothesis and conclude that the MicroHard sample was not drawn from the population.

t Tests Between Two Independent Sample Means

Now that you know how to conduct single-sample *z* tests and *t* tests, it's important to know that most behavioral science research is designed to compare two sample means to one another rather than comparing one sample mean to the population mean. Although there are several reasons for this, the two main ones are that (1) the mean of the population is often not known, and (2) most experimenters like to use a control group in their research. Often, control groups are used as substitutes for population values. For example, in Dr. Tee's vocabulary learning experiment, you could have compared the 12 infants in the experimental group to a similar control group that did not go through the language training program. Then, instead of comparing the mean of the research sample to the mean of the population, you could have compared the mean of the research sample to the mean of the control sample. This is normally done by computing the difference between the two means and comparing this difference to the mean of the **sampling distribution of the differences between means.**

Yes, there is yet another distribution that you need to become familiar with: the distribution of differences between means, which is generated by taking two random samples and computing the difference between their means. By doing this a great number of times, a distribution is formed. If all the samples are selected from the same population or from populations with equal means, the mean of this distribution should be zero because the sum of all the differences between the sample means should be zero. On the other hand, if there are two independent samples from populations that have different means, with population 1 as the control population and population 2 as the research population, then the distribution of differences between sample means should have a mean equal to the difference between the two population means: $\mu_1 - \mu_2$. Thus, when two independent samples are being compared, the null hypothesis states that the two samples derive from populations with equal means ($\mu_1 - \mu_2 = 0$). The two-tailed research hypothesis states that the two samples derive from populations with different means ($\mu_1 - \mu_2 \neq 0$).

A *t* test can be used to test these hypotheses. Note that in this case, the score being tested is the difference between the two sample means. You then compare this difference to the difference between the means of the two population distributions used to create the independent samples. The following formula shows how to compute a *t* test for independent sample means:

$$t = \frac{(\overline{X}_1 - \overline{X}_2) - (\mu_1 - \mu_2)}{\sigma_{\text{diff}}} \qquad (12.4)$$

Question: How do you know the means of these two different populations, and what is σ_{diff}?

Unfortunately, there really is no way of knowing the population means, but luckily you don't need to know them because when you conduct a *t* test, you are testing the null hypothesis. To test the null hypothesis, you need to know only the value of $\mu_1 - \mu_2$. As previously stated, the null hypothesis predicts that $\mu_1 - \mu_2 = 0$. So you can substitute 0 for $\mu_1 - \mu_2$ in Formula 12.4:

$$t = \frac{(\overline{X}_1 - \overline{X}_2) - (\mu_1 - \mu_2)}{\sigma_{\text{diff}}} = \frac{(\overline{X}_1 - \overline{X}_2) - 0}{\sigma_{\text{diff}}}$$

$$t = \frac{(\overline{X}_1 - \overline{X}_2)}{\sigma_{\text{diff}}} \qquad (12.5)$$

The standard deviation of the distribution of the differences between sample means, which is drawn from two different independent populations (population 1 and population 2), is called the **standard error of the difference between independent sample means** (σ_{diff}). It is given by the following formula:

$$\sigma_{\text{diff}} = \sqrt{\sigma_{\overline{X}_1}^2 + \sigma_{\overline{X}_2}^2} \qquad (12.6)$$

The standard error of the difference between independent sample means is equal to the square root of the sum of the standard error of the mean, squared, for population 1 and the standard error of the mean, squared, for population 2. In most cases, the standard error of the mean must be estimated from the sample standard deviation rather than computed directly from the population values. This means that the standard error, or the difference between independent sample means, can be estimated by the following equivalent formulas:

$$\text{estimated } \sigma_{\text{diff}} = \sqrt{(\text{estimated } \sigma_{\overline{X}_1})^2 + (\text{estimated } \sigma_{\overline{X}_2})^2} \qquad (12.7)$$

$$\text{estimated } \sigma_{\text{diff}} = \sqrt{\frac{S_1^2}{n_1} + \frac{S_2^2}{n_2}} \qquad (12.8)$$

At this point, you are probably thoroughly bogged down with terms and formulas. Let's take some time to work an example and return to the analysis of

Dr. Tee's language training experiment. Suppose that instead of having you compare the sample mean to the population mean, Dr. Tee asks you to compare her experimental group to a control group of 12 similar children who did not receive language training. The data for both groups are listed in Table 12.2. Because you will compare the mean for the control sample to the mean of the research sample, you need to change the research hypothesis to: The mean number of the vocabulary words for the research sample is greater than the mean number of vocabulary words for the control sample. This implies that the research and control samples come from different populations with different means of μ_1 and μ_2, respectively, and that $\mu_1 > \mu_2$. The null hypothesis states that there is no difference between the means of the research and the control populations and that $\mu_1 - \mu_2 = 0$. Knowing this, you can now compute the *t* score. Use Formulas 12.5 and 12.8, starting with Formula 12.8 to compute the estimate of the standard error of the difference between means and then using Formula 12.5 to compute the *t* score.

$$\text{estimated } \sigma_{\text{diff}} = \sqrt{\frac{S_1^2}{n_1} + \frac{S_2^2}{n_2}} = \sqrt{\frac{29.740^2}{12} + \frac{15.699^2}{12}} = \sqrt{\frac{884.468}{12} + \frac{246.459}{12}}$$

$$= \sqrt{73.706 + 20.538} = \sqrt{94.244} = 9.708$$

Substituting the appropriate values in Formula 12.5, you get

$$t = \frac{\left(\overline{X}_1 - \overline{X}_2\right)}{\sigma_{\text{diff}}} = \frac{223.083 - 201.083}{9.708} = \frac{22.000}{9.708} = 2.266$$

Now you have computed the *t* score. Next, you need to calculate the degrees of freedom and then refer to Table T to determine whether the *t* score is significant.

Question: When looking up the critical value of *t* in Table T, which $n - 1$ should be used for the degrees of freedom?

When you conduct a *t* test between two independent samples, the total number of degrees of freedom is equal to the degrees of freedom in sample 1 plus the degrees of freedom in sample 2:

$$df = (n_1 - 1) + (n_2 - 1) \tag{12.9}$$

In the preceding example, the total number of degrees of freedom is

$$df = (n_1 - 1) + (n_2 - 1) = (12 - 1) + (12 - 1) = 11 + 11 = 22$$

By looking in Table T, you find that for a one-tailed research hypothesis with 22 degrees of freedom, the critical value of *t* equals 1.717. The computed *t* score of 2.266 is greater than the table value, so you can reject the null hypothesis and accept the research hypothesis. This means that the language training method does indeed lead to a more expanded vocabulary for 2-year-olds who participated in the program than for those in the control group.

Table 12.2   Number of Words in Vocabulary for Research Group of 12 Toddlers Using the Language Training System and Control Group of 12 Toddlers Without the Language Training System

Research Group Words in Vocabulary		Control Group Words in Vocabulary	
Child	X_1	Child	X_2
C. W.	197	P. J.	206
D. J.	223	D. M.	199
P. V.	241	O. C.	205
J. I.	183	M. V.	203
T. B.	222	B. T.	223
B. C.	231	Z. S.	189
R. A.	297	K. H.	221
B. B.	220	B. S.	195
D. T.	188	G. S.	218
P. P.	231	A. G.	177
C. D.	210	H. D.	203
M. L.	234	K. T.	174
$\Sigma X_1 = 2{,}677$		$\Sigma X_2 = 2{,}413$	
$\overline{X}_1 = 223.083$		$\overline{X}_2 = 201.0833$	
$S_1 = 29.740$		$S_2 = 15.699$	

t Tests Between Two Independent Sample Means

Before You Begin: State H_0 and H_1.

Compute $\overline{X}_1, S_1, n_1, \overline{X}_2, S_2, n_2$.

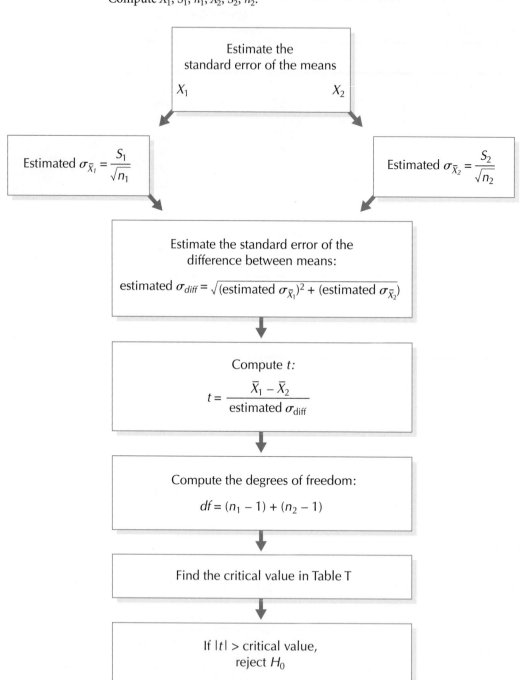

Estimate the
standard error of the means

X_1 X_2

Estimated $\sigma_{\overline{X}_1} = \dfrac{S_1}{\sqrt{n_1}}$

Estimated $\sigma_{\overline{X}_2} = \dfrac{S_2}{\sqrt{n_2}}$

Estimate the standard error of the
difference between means:

estimated $\sigma_{diff} = \sqrt{(\text{estimated } \sigma_{\overline{X}_1})^2 + (\text{estimated } \sigma_{\overline{X}_2})}$

Compute t:

$$t = \frac{\overline{X}_1 - \overline{X}_2}{\text{estimated } \sigma_{diff}}$$

Compute the degrees of freedom:

$$df = (n_1 - 1) + (n_2 - 1)$$

Find the critical value in Table T

If $|t| >$ critical value,
reject H_0

Concept Quiz

A recent lab experiment by Anderson and Dill (2000) found among other things that playing a video game with a violent content compared to a nonviolent content can prime aggressive thoughts. Suppose you want to extend this research and see whether people interpret the aggressiveness of another person's behavior differently after they play a video game with either a violent or nonviolent content. Thirty people are randomly selected and each is then randomly assigned to play a 15-minute video game with either a violent or nonviolent content and then read a short children's story. After reading the story, participants evaluated the extent of the main character's aggressive behavior on a 7-point scale (1 = not aggressive and 7 = very aggressive). The summary data are shown in the table. Use this research example to answer the following questions.

Condition	n	Mean	Standard Deviation
Violent content (X_1)	15	5.13	2.87
Nonviolent content (X_2)	15	3.41	2.13

1. This study involves comparing means from _____ groups of participants and is called a _____-subjects design.
   a. different; within
   b. single; between
   c. different; between
   d. single; within

2. Is this a one-tailed or two-tailed hypothesis? Would you expect the calculated *t*-value to be positive, negative, or either if you reject the null hypothesis?

3. The formula for standard error of the difference between independent sample means is the square root of the sum of the _____ for the violent content and nonviolent content video game samples?

4. The calculated standard error of the difference between two independent sample means for this study is _____.
   a. −.923
   b. 8.52
   c. .852
   d. .923

5. The number of degrees of freedom in a *t* test between independent sample means is equal to _____ and calculates to be _____ in this study.

6. According to Table T with a significance level of .05, the critical *t*-value is _____.

7. Given the *t* that you calculated, should you reject or fail to reject the null hypothesis?

8. If this was a one-tailed hypothesis, would the statistical conclusion change?

9. Can you change the hypothesis after data collection?

Answers

1. c

2. two-tailed; either a positive or negative *t*

3. standard error of the mean squared

4. c is correct;
   estimated $\sigma_{\text{diff}} =$
   $$\sqrt{\frac{2.87^2}{15} + \frac{2.13^2}{15}} = .923$$

5. the degrees of freedom in sample 1 $(n_1 - 1)$ plus the degrees of freedom in sample 2 $(n_2 - 1)$; 28

6. 2.04

7. Fail to reject H_0;
   $$t = \frac{(5.13 - 3.41)}{.923} = 1.86$$

8. The one-tailed critical *t* value is 1.70, and the conclusion changes to reject the null hypothesis.

9. No, the hypothesis is set before you do the statistical computations.

t Tests for Correlated Samples

Not all *t* tests are conducted between independent sample means. Frequently, the two samples are positively correlated with each other, as in a within-subjects design where each person participates in each of the experimental conditions. A case in point is the opening exercise for this chapter, where you were asked to time how long it takes you to name the shapes from the shapes-alone list, and then to time how long it takes you to name the shapes from the combined words-and-shapes list. If this were an experiment, you as a participant would have been in each condition and you would have been a member of two correlated samples. If you asked several friends to participate in the same experiment, you might obtain results similar to those in Table 12.3. From this table you can see that it takes longer, on average, for most people to name the shapes on the words-and-shapes list than on the shapes-alone list.

Now analyze the results to be sure that the observed difference is not due to mere chance. To do so, you need to conduct a *t* test. This *t* test, however, must be different from those previously described; these two samples are not independent because the same people participated in both conditions. Therefore, it must be a *t* test for *correlated samples*.

The major difference between a *t* test for *independent samples* and a *t* test for *correlated samples* is that in the latter the correlation or the covariance between the samples can be used to reduce the size of the standard error of the difference between the sample means. Reducing the standard error of the difference can be a real advantage because the smaller the standard error of the difference is, the larger is the *t*.

Because each participant is used twice, you can compute the amount of error that is due to the variability of each participant and use this to reduce the standard error of the difference, thereby increasing the size of *t*.

Table 12.3 The Time (in seconds) Needed for 10 Participants to Name the Shapes From Two Different Lists

Participant	List 1 (shapes only) X_1	List 2 (words and shapes) X_2
H. J.	22	27
T. B.	27	25
J. J.	23	32
M. V.	29	32
D. J.	32	51
P. T.	24	33
N. Z.	33	30
A. H.	23	29
K. L.	15	24
S. E.	12	20

$$\Sigma X_1 = 240 \qquad \Sigma X_2 = 303$$

$$\overline{X}_1 = 24.000 \qquad \overline{X}_2 = 30.3$$

$$S_1 = 6.749 \qquad S_2 = 8.354$$

$$\text{Estimated } \sigma_{\overline{X}_1} = 2.134 \qquad \text{Estimated } \sigma_{\overline{X}_2} = 2.642$$

$$r = .674$$

Another way of saying this is that the *t* should be allowed to be larger because by using each participant in each condition, it reduces the chance of other factors creeping in to influence the results. For example, by using the same people in naming the shapes, the participants are more evenly matched in general intelligence, speaking skills, and so on, than by using different people.

To illustrate this reduction, here are the formulas for computing the standard error of the difference for both independent and correlated samples. The formula for the standard error of the difference between *independent* sample means is

$$\sigma_{\text{diff}} = \sqrt{\sigma_{\overline{X}_1}^2 + \sigma_{\overline{X}_2}^2} \tag{12.9}$$

Now compare this to the following formulas for the **standard error of the difference between correlated sample means:**

$$\sigma_{\text{diff}} = \sqrt{\sigma_{\overline{X}_1}^2 + \sigma_{\overline{X}_2}^2 - (2 \cdot \text{cov})} \tag{12.10}$$

or

$$\sigma_{\text{diff}} = \sqrt{\sigma_{\overline{X}_1}^2 + \sigma_{\overline{X}_2}^2 - (2 \cdot r \cdot \sigma_{\overline{X}_1} \cdot \sigma_{\overline{X}_2})} \tag{12.11}$$

Note that the standard error of the difference between means is made smaller by subtracting twice the covariance between the two samples.

By examining Formula 12.10 or 12.11 closely, you can see that if the covariance or the correlation coefficient is zero, the entire expression within the parentheses equals zero and these formulas reduce to Formula 12.6. This makes sense because, as you may remember from the discussion of correlation in Chapter 8, samples that are totally independent from each other have a zero covariance and a zero correlation.

Unfortunately, these formulas are practical only when the population standard deviations of both distributions are known. When these population standard deviations are not known, which is most often the case, you must estimate these values and use Formula 12.12 or Formula 12.13 to estimate the standard error of the difference:

$$\text{Estimated } \sigma_{\text{diff}} = \sqrt{(\text{estimated } \sigma_{\bar{X}_1})^2 + (\text{estimated } \sigma_{\bar{X}_2})^2 - (2 \cdot \text{cov})} \quad (12.12)$$

or

$$\sigma_{\text{diff}} = \sqrt{(\text{estimated } \sigma_{\bar{X}_1})^2 + (\text{estimated } \sigma_{\bar{X}_2})^2 - (2 \cdot r \cdot \text{estimated } \sigma_{\bar{X}_1} \cdot \text{estimated } \sigma_{\bar{X}_2})} \quad (12.13)$$

Now you are ready to conduct a *t* test on the data in Table 12.3. First, compute the standard error of the difference. Use Formula 12.13 because Table 12.3 gives the correlation coefficient and you do not have the population standard deviations.

$$\sigma_{\text{diff}} = \sqrt{(\text{estimated } \sigma_{\bar{X}_1})^2 + (\text{estimated } \sigma_{\bar{X}_2})^2 - (2 \cdot r \cdot \sigma_{\bar{X}_1} \cdot \sigma_{\bar{X}_2})}$$

$$= \sqrt{2.134^2 + 2.642^2 - (2 \cdot .674 \cdot 2.134 \cdot 2.642)}$$

$$= \sqrt{4.554 + 6.980 - 7.600} = \sqrt{3.934} = 1.983$$

The formula for *t* remains the same as the formula for independent samples. Using the value just computed for the estimate of the standard error of the difference as well as the mean for 1 and the mean for 2 from Table 12.3, you can now compute the *t*:

$$t = \frac{\bar{X}_1 - \bar{X}_2}{\text{estimated } \sigma_{\text{diff}}} = \frac{24 - 30.3}{1.983} = \frac{-6.3}{1.983} = -3.177$$

Again, you need to compute the degrees of freedom before looking up the *t* score in Table T to tell whether it is significant. The number of degrees of freedom for a *t* test between two correlated means is equal to the number of pairs of scores minus 1:

$$df_{\text{correlated samples}} = \text{number of pairs} - 1 \quad (12.14)$$

There are 10 pairs of scores in the experiment, so

$$df = 10 - 1 = 9$$

Because the research hypothesis is one-tailed (you predicted that it would take longer to name the shapes when the words are present), you can look up the critical value of *t* in Table T for a one-tailed test with 9 degrees of freedom. That value is 1.833.

> **Question:** Should you fail to reject the null hypothesis because the computed value for *t*, −3.177, is less than the critical value in Table T, 1.833?

No, not in this case. If, as is true in this example, your hypothesis is one-tailed and it predicts that the second mean (naming the symbols with the words) will be greater than the first mean (naming the symbols alone), then your computed value *should* be negative. Before you even look up the *t*-value in the table, you need to analyze what your research hypothesis predicts. If it predicts that the second mean will be greater than the first mean, you should expect a negative *t*-value because the formula requires that you subtract the second mean from the first mean. If, on the other hand, your hypothesis predicts that the first mean will be greater than the second, you should expect a positive *t*-value. Remember: *When the research hypothesis predicts a negative t-value and your computed t-value is negative, or when the research hypothesis predicts a positive t-value and your computed t-value is positive, you can ignore the sign when comparing your computed t-value to the critical value from Table T and compare the absolute value of t to the critical value listed in the table.*

On the other hand, if the research hypothesis predicts a value in the opposite direction of your computed value (for instance, if it predicts a positive value for *t* and you compute a negative value), you don't even need to bother looking up the critical value because you know it is not significant and you must fail to reject the null hypothesis. In the example, because the hypothesis predicts that the second mean will be greater than the first and *t* should therefore be negative, ignore the minus sign and compare the absolute value of the negative *t* to the critical value in Table T. You will then find that the computed value is greater than the critical value in the table, so you can reject the null hypothesis and accept the research hypothesis. It does take longer to name the shapes when the conflicting words are present.

The above holds true for one-tailed hypotheses. With two-tailed, nondirectional hypotheses, it doesn't matter whether the computed *t*-value is positive or negative. If the absolute value of the computed *t* is larger than the value in Table T, then it is significant because the hypothesis doesn't specify the direction of the significance; it specifies only that there is a difference, no matter the direction.

It is important at this point to emphasize that one-tailed hypotheses and one-tailed tests are a bit tricky. A computed value for *t* is significant *only* if: (1) the

difference between the means is the same direction as that predicted by the research hypothesis *and* (2) the absolute value of *t* is greater than the critical value
found in Table T. You do not even need to compute a *t* or look up a critical value
when the difference between the means for the two samples lies in the wrong direction (if one is positive and the other is negative.)

> **Question:** Life is too short to have to compute the covariance or a
> correlation coefficient each time a *t* test must be done between
> correlated sample means. Isn't there a faster way?

Yes. When you don't already know the covariance or correlation coefficient
and the standard deviation for each sample, an alternative called the **difference
method** can save you considerable time. This method for computing *t* relies on
the differences between the paired scores rather than on the standard deviation
and the correlation coefficient to calculate the estimate of the standard error of
the difference between means. The formula for the estimated standard error of
the difference between means using difference scores is

$$\text{estimated } \sigma_{\text{diff}} = \sqrt{\frac{\dfrac{\Sigma D^2}{n} - \overline{D}^2}{n - 1}} \tag{12.15}$$

where $\overline{D}$ is the mean of the difference scores and ΣD^2 is the sum of the squared
differences.

In Table 12.4, the difference scores and the sum of their squares have been
calculated for the data in the shape task analyzed here. The differences were obtained by subtracting the X_2-value from the X_1-value in each pair. These differences were then added and the mean of the differences was computed. (The mean
of the differences, in this case -6.3 seconds, is equal to the difference between the
means of the two correlated samples, 24 seconds minus 30.3 seconds.) Next, each
of the difference scores was squared and then the squares of the differences were
added. With the data from Table 12.4, the estimate of the standard error of the difference between the means can be computed:

$$\text{estimated } \sigma_{\text{diff}} = \sqrt{\frac{\dfrac{\Sigma D^2}{n} - \overline{D}^2}{n - 1}} = \sqrt{\frac{\dfrac{751}{10} - (-6.3)^2}{10 - 1}} = \sqrt{\frac{75.1 - 39.69}{9}}$$

$$= \sqrt{\frac{35.41}{9}} = \sqrt{3.934} = 1.983$$

This value is identical to the one computed for the estimate of the standard error
of the difference between the means when the formula with the correlation coefficient was used.

Table 12.4   The Data Listed in Table 12.3, With Differences (*D*) and Differences Squared (D^2) Between the Time (in seconds) Needed for 10 Participants to Name the Shapes From Two Different Lists

Participant	List 1 (shapes only) X_1	List 2 (words and shapes) X_2	D	D^2
H. J.	22	27	−5	25
T. B.	27	25	2	4
J. J.	23	32	−9	81
M. V.	29	32	−3	9
D. J.	32	51	−19	361
P. T.	24	33	−9	81
N. Z.	33	30	3	9
A. H.	23	29	−6	36
K. L.	15	24	−9	81
S. E.	12	20	8	64
			$\Sigma D = -63$	$\Sigma D^2 = 751$
			$\overline{D} = -6.3$	

Because the mean of the difference scores is always equal to the difference between the means of the two samples, the following formula can be used to compute the *t* score:

$$t = \frac{\overline{D} - (\mu_1 - \mu_2)}{\text{estimated } \sigma_{\text{diff}}} \qquad (12.16)$$

Because the null hypothesis states that there is no difference between the two populations, $\mu_1 - \mu_2 = 0$. Knowing this, Formula 12.16 can be simplified as

$$t = \frac{\overline{D}}{\text{estimated } \sigma_{\text{diff}}} \qquad (12.17)$$

Now the *t* score can be calculated using the mean of the differences and the standard error or the difference between the means just computed:

$$t = \frac{\overline{D}}{\text{estimated } \sigma_{\text{diff}}} = \frac{-6.3}{1.983} = -3.177$$

This value is exactly the same as the *t* score previously computed for the same data using the correlation coefficient. As you have seen, the difference method can be much easier and faster than the method first described, which involved computing the standard deviations and the standard error of the means as well as the covariance or the correlation coefficient.

VISUAL SUMMARY

t Tests for Correlated Samples

Before You Begin: State H_0 and H_1.

Compute $\bar{X}_1$, S_1, n_1, $\bar{X}_2$, S_2, n_2, and covariance or r.

Or compute $\bar{D}$, ΣD^2, n.

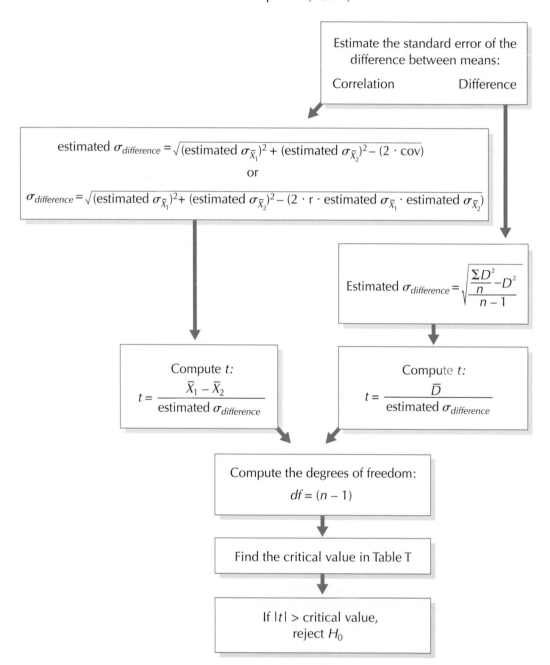

Estimate the standard error of the difference between means:

Correlation   Difference

$$\text{estimated } \sigma_{difference} = \sqrt{(\text{estimated } \sigma_{\bar{X}_1})^2 + (\text{estimated } \sigma_{\bar{X}_2})^2 - (2 \cdot cov)}$$

or

$$\sigma_{difference} = \sqrt{(\text{estimated } \sigma_{\bar{X}_1})^2 + (\text{estimated } \sigma_{\bar{X}_2})^2 - (2 \cdot r \cdot \text{estimated } \sigma_{\bar{X}_1} \cdot \text{estimated } \sigma_{\bar{X}_2})}$$

$$\text{Estimated } \sigma_{difference} = \sqrt{\frac{\frac{\Sigma D^2}{n} - \bar{D}^2}{n-1}}$$

Compute *t*:

$$t = \frac{\bar{X}_1 - \bar{X}_2}{\text{estimated } \sigma_{difference}}$$

Compute *t*:

$$t = \frac{\bar{D}}{\text{estimated } \sigma_{difference}}$$

Compute the degrees of freedom:

$$df = (n - 1)$$

Find the critical value in Table T

If $|t| >$ critical value, reject H_0

Power and *t* Tests

In Chapter 11, power was defined as the probability that the statistical test will correctly reject the null hypothesis when the null hypothesis is in fact false. Then four things were listed that can affect the power of a test: (1) the size of alpha, (2) the sample size, (3) effect size, and (4) the type of the statistical test used in the analysis. Alpha has been chosen to be equal to .05 for all examples in this statistics book, so therefore alpha remains constant. Begin your investigation of power by looking at the three formulas for *t* given in Table 12.5. As you can see, when the formulas are defined in more simplistic terms, the *t* statistic is simply the difference between two means divided by the estimated standard error of the mean or the estimated standard error of the difference between means.

If the difference between the two means (numerator) is held constant, then the only way *t* will change is by a change in the estimate of the standard error (denominator). If the estimate of the standard error gets larger, then *t* gets smaller, resulting in less of a chance that *t* will be greater than the critical value (fail to reject the null hypothesis). If the estimate of the standard error gets smaller, then *t* gets larger, resulting in more of a chance that *t* will be greater than the critical value (reject the null hypothesis). However, take a look at the formula for the estimate of the standard error of the mean used for the single sample *t*. Note that in this formula, you are dividing by the square root of *n*, not *n* itself. As shown in the example that follows, if you want to decrease the estimate of the standard error of the mean by $\frac{1}{2}$, you would need 4 times as many participants:

$$\text{estimated } \sigma_{\bar{X}} = \frac{S}{\sqrt{n}}$$

$$\text{estimated } \sigma_{\bar{X}} = \frac{12}{\sqrt{9}} = \frac{12}{3} = 4$$

$$\text{estimated } \sigma_{\bar{X}} = \frac{12}{\sqrt{36}} = \frac{12}{6} = 2$$

Table 12.5   Formulas for the Three Different *t* Tests

Single Sample	Independent Samples	Correlated Samples
$t = \dfrac{\bar{X} - \mu}{\text{estimated } \sigma_{\bar{X}}}$	$t = \dfrac{(\bar{X}_1 - \bar{X}_2)}{\text{estimated } \sigma_{\text{diff}}}$	$t = \dfrac{\bar{D}}{\text{estimated } \sigma_{\text{diff}}}$

This is not a problem if you had only 5 or 6 participants to begin with, but if you started out with 25 participants, you would need to find 75 more volunteers to decrease the standard error of the estimate by $\frac{1}{2}$. Because all *t* tests use the standard error of the mean in some form or another as the basis of the denominator in the *t* formula, increasing the sample size can increase the power for any *t* test. Sometimes, however, it is easier to increase the effect size—move the means farther apart by increasing the strength of the independent variable—than it is to increase the number of participants. Increasing the strength of the independent variable might involve extending the treatment program longer or making visual stimuli more noticeable.

Take, for example, the experiment used at the beginning of the chapter where you were asked to time how long it takes you to read the entire list of shapes out loud as fast as you can from left to right and top to bottom, and then you were asked to do the same thing with the list of combined words and shapes. For most people it takes a few seconds longer to say the combined shapes and words than it does to say only the shapes. If you wanted to increase the effect size, all you would have to do is to make the list longer. Rather than having 30 shapes, you could have 60 or 100. As the list gets longer, the difference in time between the shapes only and the combined words and shapes lists would get larger and larger, thus increasing the effect size. Rather than there being a difference of 6 seconds between the means of the two groups, the difference might be 12 or 20 seconds.

Finally, some tests are more powerful than other tests. As you might expect, *t* tests based on measured population parameters are more powerful than tests based on estimates of population values. Also, as mentioned in the section on correlated *t* tests, *t* tests between correlated samples are more powerful than *t* tests between independent samples.

Concept Quiz

A soft-drink company has hired you to start an aluminum can recycling program on your campus. You decide to implement a program similar to a study done by T. D. Ludwig, T. W. Gray, and A. Rowell (1998), in which researchers found that when recycling was made convenient by the placement of recycling receptacles in college classrooms, the percentage of cans thrown in the trash daily significantly decreased. To see if this program works on your campus, you count the number of cans in the trash daily for 2 weeks prior to and then 2 weeks after adding brightly colored recycling receptacles to five different classrooms. The data are shown next.

Classroom	Before Receptacles	After Receptacles
1	34	18
2	49	19
3	23	18
4	16	17
5	27	17

Use this example to answer the following questions:

1. This study involves comparing pairs of scores with each single count coming from a _____ classroom and is called a _____-subjects design.
   a. different; within
   b. different; between
   c. single; between
   d. single; within

2. Hypothesizing a difference in recycling behavior is a _____-tailed hypothesis, and the calculated $\overline{D}$ for this study is _____.

3. The standard error of the difference between two correlated means is the _____ of the sampling distribution of _____.

4. When two samples are correlated, you can still conduct a t test, but the formula for the _____ must take into account the _____.

5. To calculate the standard error of the difference between means for this study, the _____ formula should be used because the _____ and _____ are not available.

6. The calculated standard error of the difference between means is _____.
   a. 28.1
   b. 5.30
   c. −5.30
   d. −28.1

7. The degrees of freedom for a t test for correlated samples is equal to _____, and the critical value of t with alpha set at .05 is _____.

8. Briefly explain whether the standard error in the number of cans discarded in the trash is higher or lower in this study compared to another study that compared recycling behavior between different samples of classrooms and how that influences the size of *t*?

9. Calculate *t*, and determine if the recycling program at your school was consistent with the work of Ludwig et al. (1998).

10. The power of this *t* test would _____ if we added more classrooms to the study.

Answers

1. d

2. one; $\overline{D} = \dfrac{\Sigma D}{n} = 12$

3. standard deviation; $\overline{D}$

4. standard error of the difference between means; covariance or the correlation coefficient

5. difference; variance; correlation coefficient

6. b

$$\text{estimated } \sigma_{\text{diff}} = \sqrt{\dfrac{\dfrac{1{,}282}{5} - (12)^2}{4}} = 5.30$$

7. the number of pairs of scores − 1 = 4; 2.13

8. The standard error should be lower because fewer factors can creep in and affect the variability in cans being recycling, and this should increase the value of *t*.

9. $t = \dfrac{\overline{D}}{\text{estimated } \sigma_{\text{diff}}} = \dfrac{12}{5.3} = 2.26$

    Because *t* exceeds the critical value, conclude the recycling program was great and consistent with Ludwig et al. (1998).

10. increase

In this chapter, three different types of *t* tests have been discussed that can be used to analyze one-sample or two-sample experiments. You can use the following Visual Summary to help you choose the proper *t* test.

The statistical analyses described in this chapter apply to experiments that have only one independent variable and one or two samples. Obviously, many psychological experiments are not limited to this basic design. Experiments often involve more than one independent variable and three or more samples. To analyze these more complicated experimental designs, you might use different statistical tests such as the one- or two-way analysis of variance. These analyses are described in the next two chapters.

VISUAL SUMMARY

Choosing the Proper *t* Test

Before You Begin: Read your null hypothesis. Read your research hypothesis. Determine your research design.

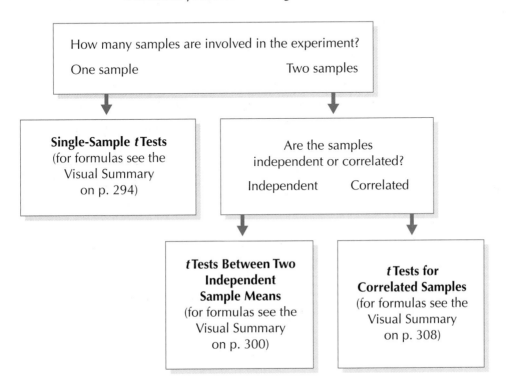

Summary

The three major types of *t* tests are single-sample *t* tests, *t* tests for independent samples, and *t* tests for correlated samples. A single-sample *t* test is similar to a *z* test, where a single-sample mean is compared to the mean of the population. The major difference between the *t* test and the *z* test is that when conducting a *t* test, you must use the degrees of freedom to look up the critical value in Table T.

When it is necessary to compare the means of two samples, you can also conduct a *t* test. First, however, you must determine whether the samples are independent or correlated. If the samples are independent, you can conduct a *t* test for independent samples. If the samples are correlated, you can conduct a *t* test for correlated samples.

Key Terms

t distribution

t test

degrees of freedom (*df*)

sampling distribution
of differences
between means

standard error of the
difference between
independent
sample means

standard error of the
difference between

correlated sample
means

difference method

Formulas

$$\text{Estimated } \sigma_{\bar{X}} = \frac{S}{\sqrt{n}} \tag{12.1}$$

$$t = \frac{\bar{X} - \mu_{\bar{X}}}{\sigma_{\bar{X}}} \tag{12.2}$$

$$df = n - 1 \tag{12.3}$$

$$t = \frac{(\bar{X}_1 - \bar{X}_2) - (\mu_1 - \mu_2)}{\sigma_{\text{diff}}} \tag{12.4}$$

$$t = \frac{(\bar{X}_1 - \bar{X}_2)}{\sigma_{\text{diff}}} \tag{12.5}$$

$$\sigma_{\text{diff}} = \sqrt{\sigma_{\bar{X}_1}^2 + \sigma_{\bar{X}_2}^2} \tag{12.6}$$

$$\text{Estimated } \sigma_{\text{diff}} = \sqrt{(\text{estimated } \sigma_{\bar{X}_1})^2 + (\text{estimated } \sigma_{\bar{X}_2})^2} \tag{12.7}$$

$$\text{Estimated } \sigma_{\text{diff}} = \sqrt{\frac{S_1^2}{n_1} + \frac{S_2^2}{n_2}} \tag{12.8}$$

$$df_{\text{independent samples}} = (n_1 - 1) + (n_2 - 1) \tag{12.9}$$

$$\sigma_{\text{diff}} = \sqrt{\sigma_{\bar{X}_1}^2 + \sigma_{\bar{X}_2}^2 - (2 \cdot \text{cov})} \tag{12.10}$$

$$\sigma_{\text{diff}} = \sqrt{\sigma_{\bar{X}_1}^2 + \sigma_{\bar{X}_2}^2 - (2 \cdot r \cdot \sigma_{\bar{X}_1} \cdot \sigma_{\bar{X}_2})} \tag{12.11}$$

$$\text{Estimated } \sigma_{\text{diff}} = \sqrt{\text{estimated } \sigma_{\overline{X}_1}^{\,2} + \left(\text{estimated } \sigma_{\overline{X}_2}\right)^2 - (2 \cdot \text{cov})} \qquad (12.12)$$

$$\sigma_{\text{diff}} = \sqrt{\text{estimated } \sigma_{\overline{X}_1}^{\,2} + \left(\text{estimated } \sigma_{\overline{X}_2}\right)^2 - \left(2 \cdot r \cdot \text{estimated } \sigma_{X_1} \cdot \text{estimated } \sigma_{X_2}\right)} \qquad (12.13)$$

$$df_{\text{correlated samples}} = \text{number of pairs} - 1 \qquad (12.14)$$

$$\text{Estimated } \sigma_{\text{diff}} = \sqrt{\dfrac{\dfrac{\Sigma D^2}{n} - \overline{D}^2}{n - 1}} \qquad (12.15)$$

$$t = \dfrac{\overline{D} - (\mu_1 - \mu_2)}{\text{estimated } \sigma_{\text{diff}}} \qquad (12.16)$$

$$t = \dfrac{\overline{D}}{\text{estimated } \sigma_{\text{diff}}} \qquad (12.17)$$

Problems

1. Suppose you are a military psychologist and know that the population of sonar operators has a mean identification rate of 82 targets out of 100, with a population standard deviation of 12 targets. You have just developed a new sonar training system that you claim will increase the number of targets correctly identified. Using 15 sonar trainees, you compute that they can, on average, identify 87 targets out of 100. Using these data, compute a t test to determine whether the trainees using your new system perform better than the population mean. Remember to include in your answer: (a) the null hypothesis, (b) the research hypothesis, (c) t, (d) the degrees of freedom, (e) the critical value from Table T, and (f) a brief statement about whether or not the t is significant.

2. Ms. Yonrev thinks that her class of fourth-grade students is exceptionally bright. To test this hypothesis, she decides to compare her students' IQ scores to the population that has a mean of 100 IQ points and a standard deviation equal to 16 IQ points. Using school records, she computes the mean IQ for her 25 students to be 110 IQ points. Using this data, state or find: (a) the null hypothesis, (b) the research hypothesis, (c) t, (d) the degrees of freedom, (e) the critical value from Table T, and (f) a brief statement about whether or not the t is significant.

3. Conduct a t test to determine whether a sample of 64 people with a mean of 82 and a standard deviation of 5.4 is significantly greater than a population mean of 80. Remember to include in your answer:

(a) the null hypothesis, (b) the research hypothesis, (c) *t*, (d) the degrees of freedom, (e) the critical value from Table T, and (f) a brief statement about whether or not the *t* is significant.

4. The "moon illusion" occurs when a person perceives the size of the moon as larger on the horizon than when it is at its zenith. To test this illusion, a researcher decides to ask 75 people to estimate the size of the moon when it is at the horizon and at the zenith, and then she computes the ratio of the two estimates. If there is no illusion, there should be a ratio of 1; if there is an illusion, the ratio should be greater than 1. (A ratio of 2.0 would mean that the horizon moon was judged twice as large as the zenith moon.) She finds that the mean ratio of her sample of 75 people is 1.4 with a standard deviation of .35. Use a *t* test to compare this sample mean to the population mean of 1. Remember to include in your answer: (a) the null hypothesis, (b) the research hypothesis, (c) *t*, (d) the degrees of freedom, (e) the critical value from Table T, and (f) a brief statement about whether or not the *t* is significant.

5. A psychologist studying the human factors of computer keyboards sets up an experiment to compare two different keyboard designs. Using two independent samples, he determines the number of words per minute typed by one group on keyboard A and the number typed on keyboard B. Use the results listed in the following table to compute *t*, and determine whether the two keyboards are significantly different. Remember to include in your answer: (a) the null hypothesis, (b) the research hypothesis, (c) *t*, (d) the degrees of freedom, (e) the critical value from Table T,

and (f) a brief statement about whether or not the *t* is significant.

| Words Typed per Minute ||
Keyboard A	Keyboard B
54	47
62	51
45	54
59	62
78	44
64	51
69	48
72	65
50	42
73	44
75	71
67	68

6. Herman Boncor, the local dogcatcher, thinks that the dogs at the pound tend to bark less when they are fed expensive brand-name dog food than when they are fed a cheaper generic brand of dog food. To test his hypothesis, he feeds one group of dogs the expensive brand for 1 week and records the number of barks during the 1-hour period following each feeding. The next week, he feeds *an entirely different group of dogs* the inexpensive dog food and records the number of barks during the 1-hour period after each feeding. The data for the dogs follow. Use the data to conduct a *t* test to determine whether the expensive dog food really does keep the dogs quieter. Remember to include in your answer: (a) the null hypothesis, (b) the research hypothesis, (c) *t*, (d) the degrees of freedom, (e) the critical value from Table T, and (f) a brief statement about whether or not the *t* is significant.

Number of Barks	
Brand Name Dog Food	Generic Dog Food
123	100
145	128
165	154
138	136
169	198
125	127
136	145
111	154
156	136
139	129
128	106
129	128

7. A researcher studying the effects of alcohol asks 25 people, who all weigh exactly 150 pounds, to take a reaction time test before and after drinking three beers. The results for the pretest and posttest, as well as the correlation between the two groups, are listed here. Use these results to compute the appropriate *t* test to tell whether there is a significant difference between the pretest and posttest results. Remember to include in your answer: (a) the null hypothesis, (b) the research hypothesis, (c) *t*, (d) the degrees of freedom, (e) the critical value from Table T, and (f) a brief statement about whether or not the *t* is significant.

Reaction Time	
Pretest X_1	Posttest X_2
$\overline{X}_1 = 235$ msec	$\overline{X}_2 = 342$ msec
$S_1 = 52$ msec	$S_2 = 85$ msec
Correlation $(r) = .77$	

8. An eyeglass manufacturer is interested in finding out whether people can read a computer screen *faster* using glasses with specially coated lenses as opposed to glasses with regular uncoated lenses. Sixteen people are asked to read a computer screen for 20 minutes with the coated lenses; on a separate day, the same 20 people are asked to read a computer screen for 20 minutes using lenses without the coating. The number of pages read by each participant for each condition was collected, and the results are summarized here. Compute a *t* test to determine whether the coating significantly improves the reading speed of these 16 people. Remember to include in your answer: (a) the null hypothesis, (b) the research hypothesis, (c) *t*, (d) the degrees of freedom, (e) the critical value from Table T, and (f) a brief statement about whether or not the *t* is significant.

Number of Pages Read	
With Coating X_1	Without Coating X_2
$\overline{X}_1 = 13.4$ msec	$\overline{X}_2 = 12.7$ msec
$S_1 = 2.6$ msec	$S_2 = 2.1$ msec
Correlation $(r) = .64$	

9. A human factors psychologist who works for an automobile manufacturer believes that it is possible to decrease the number of brake pedal errors by changing the location of the brake pedal in relation to the gas pedal in the best selling model, the Zoomer Special. He asks 10 participants to drive in a driving simulator with the old pedal arrangement. Later he asks the same 10 participants to drive in a simulator using the new pedal arrangement. The number of

errors for each participant using both pedal arrangements is listed here. Using the data, test his hypothesis by computing *t*. Remember to include in your answer: (a) the null hypothesis, (b) the research hypothesis, (c) *t*, (d) the degrees of freedom, (e) the critical value from Table T, and (f) a brief statement about whether or not the *t* is significant.

Participants	Number of Errors	
	New Pedal Arrangement	Old Pedal Arrangement
H. J.	3	5
G. M.	5	7
C. M.	3	4
J. P.	7	9
F. C.	10	14
M. G.	3	3
T. D.	7	9
H. A.	13	11
C. A.	4	6
T. C.	2	4

10. Twelve participants underwent an assertiveness training program. Before and after completing the program, they were asked to complete a check list of adjectives that describe their personality. The number of adjectives describing positive attributes were compiled in the "before" condition and in the "after" condition. Using the data in the following table, compute a *t*. Remember to include in your answer: (a) the null hypothesis, (b) the research hypothesis, (c) *t*, (d) the degrees of freedom, (e) the critical value from Table T, and (f) a brief statement about whether or not the *t* is significant.

Participants	Number of Positive Adjectives	
	Before	After
1	14	21
2	21	22
3	24	21
4	16	19
5	18	18
6	20	25
7	15	17
8	20	18
9	17	21
10	16	24
11	12	15
12	19	21

11. In your Introduction to Psychology class, you probably learned that short-term memory has a capacity of seven items, plus or minus two. But is this capacity the same for different categories of items? Might it not be possible to store more words than letters of numbers in short-term memory? The data in the following table are from an experiment comparing the short-term memory capacity of 24 participants who were randomly assigned to one of two conditions. In the first condition, the participants were asked to remember a list of words; in the other condition, the participants were asked to remember a list of numbers. Conduct a *t* test to determine whether there is a difference between short-term memory for words and numbers. Remember to include in your answer: (a) the null hypothesis, (b) the research hypothesis, (c) *t*, (d) the degrees of freedom, (e) the critical value from Table T, and (f) a brief statement about whether or not the *t* is significant.

Number Remembered	
Words	Numbers
5	4
7	6
5	6
4	3
3	7
8	5
3	8
7	9
8	7
8	7
5	4
7	9

12. A researcher who is an expert on proofreading has developed two ten-page manuscripts for an experiment. One manuscript has no errors on the first seven pages and then 20 errors on the last three pages. The other manuscript has an average of 5 errors per page on the first seven pages and the identical 20 errors on the last three pages. The dependent variable in this experiment is the number of errors participants find on the last three pages of the manuscript that they have been assigned to read. One group of participants is assigned one type of manuscript, and the other group is assigned the other manuscript. The researcher predicts that participants who are assigned the manuscript with errors throughout will catch more errors on the last three pages. Using the data in the following table, compute t and determine whether it is significant. Remember to include in your answer: (a) the null hypothesis, (b) the

research hypothesis, (c) t, (d) the degrees of freedom, (e) the critical value from Table T, and (f) a brief statement about whether or not the t is significant.

Number of Errors Found	
Errors in the First Seven Pages	No Errors in the First Seven Pages
13	10
18	12
7	6
15	10
14	6
12	8
17	3
19	9
15	10

13. A physiological psychologist has reason to expect that the blood level of a particular hormone will increase when an animal is under stress. To induce this stress, he places 25 rats in an ice-water bath and allows each rat to swim in the bath for 30 seconds. After the swim, he takes a blood sample and measures the hormone level. The population value for nonstressed rats is 250 micrograms of the hormone per milliliter of blood. The mean for the sample of stressed rats is 267 micrograms of the hormone per milliliter of blood, and the standard deviation of the sample is 25 micrograms. Using the appropriate t test, determine whether stressed rats do indeed have significantly increased hormone levels. Remember to include in your answer: (a) the null hypothesis, (b) the research hypothesis, (c) t, (d) the

degrees of freedom, (e) the critical value from Table T, and (f) a brief statement about whether or not the *t* is significant.

14. Is computer-synthesized speech as easy to understand as speech that is spoken by a human? To find an answer to that question, a researcher randomly assigned 20 people to one of two different groups. One group was asked to transcribe a 100-word statement "spoken" by a computer, and the other group was asked to transcribe the same 100-word statement spoken by a human. The mean number of errors made in the synthesized condition was 10 with a standard deviation of 4. The mean number of errors made in the human condition was 8 with a standard deviation of 3. Use the appropriate *t* to determine whether human speech is easier to understand than computer-synthesized speech. Remember to include in your answer: (a) the null hypothesis, (b) the research hypothesis, (c) *t*, (d) the degrees of freedom, (e) the critical value from Table T, and (f) a brief statement about whether or not the *t* is significant.

Problems From the Literature

The following problems refer to actual results from research studies that are cited at the end of the chapter. However, the data used to generate the problem sets are hypothetical. Unless stated otherwise, use the .05 significance level for all analyses.

15. A study reported by the U. S. Environmental Protection Agency (1999) found that the mean waste generated by American adults is 4.5 pounds per day. As an environmentalist, you think this amount is much too low. You randomly sample 60 adults and find that the mean waste generated each day per person is 4.9 pounds with a standard deviation of

1.3 pounds. Determine whether your prediction was supported. (a) State the null hypothesis and research hypotheses; (b) calculate the degrees of freedom and find the critical value from Table T; (c) calculate the appropriate *t*; (d) state whether to reject or fail to reject the null hypothesis; (e) write a brief interpretation of the results in the context of the original research question.

16. Dr. NyQuille's first-year college students fall asleep during lectures in his 10 A.M. Human Sexuality class. When NyQuille asked students if it was his teaching style, they replied that they fall asleep because college students get less sleep than others their age. Dr. NyQuille decided to examine their explanation. He surveyed his class and calculated a mean of 7.3 hours and a standard deviation of .8 hour of weekday sleep. He knows the college-age population mean is 6.8 hours of weekday sleep (National Sleep Foundation, 2000). What conclusions can be made from these data? (a) State the null hypothesis and research hypotheses; (b) calculate the degrees of freedom and find the critical value from Table T; (c) calculate the appropriate *t*; (d) state whether to reject or fail to reject the null hypothesis; (e) write a brief interpretation of the results in the context of the original research question.

17. Suppose you conduct a study similar to McCall and Belmont (1996), who discovered that restaurant patrons valued their dining experience more and subsequently left bigger tips when they were visually cued by a major credit card insignia on the bill tray. A random sample of 20 patrons at Food Makes U Drool restaurant were selected. Half of the patrons were randomly assigned to receive their dinner

bill on a tray with a MasterCard insignia, and the other half were assigned to receive their bill on a blank tray. The percentage of tips relative to the total food bill was recorded. The data follow:

Percentage of Tips	
With Insignia	Without Insignia
24.12	15.25
18.36	18.69
25.88	10.00
16.87	16.05
21.33	17.02
23.04	15.23
26.42	20.00
11.50	20.00
19.00	19.45
17.09	15.00

Determine whether your findings were consistent with McCall and Belmont's research. (a) State the null hypothesis and research hypotheses; (b) calculate the degrees of freedom and find the critical value from Table T; (c) calculate the appropriate t; (d) state whether to reject or fail to reject the null hypothesis; (e) write a brief interpretation of the results in the context of the original research question.

18. Researchers Drs. Beach and Bum conducted a study to examine the effectiveness among college students of a brochure designed to promote the use of waterproof sunscreen with a sun protection factor (SPF) of 15+. Based on the results of a study done by Detweiler, Bedell, Salovey, Pronin, and Rothman (1999), Beach and Bum's brochure included skin cancer statistics and a message about the increased chances of living a longer life with the use of sunscreen. They predicted that participants' intentions to use sunscreen would significantly increase after reading the brochure. To test this hypothesis, 10 students were randomly selected to participate in the study. Their intention to use sunscreen was measured prior to reading the brochure and then after reading the brochure. The data follow. Higher numbers indicate a stronger intention to use sunscreen in the future.

Participant	Intentions	
	Pretest	Posttest
A	5	7
B	6	9
C	7	7
D	8	7
E	6	6
F	4	5
G	3	8
H	6	7
I	2	5
J	2	3

(a) State the null hypothesis and research hypotheses; (b) calculate the degrees of freedom and find the critical value from Table T; (c) calculate the appropriate t; (d) state whether to reject or fail to reject the null hypothesis; (e) write a brief interpretation of the results in the context of the original research question; (f) because this concerns a serious health behavior, do you think researchers should set the significance level to a more conservative .01 a priori? Would the findings differ? Include the new critical value of t and statistical conclusion in your answer.

19. Cockle, Haller, Kimber, Dawe, and Hindmarch (2000) tested the influence of multivitamins (particularly B-2, B-6, and B-12) on cognitive functioning among healthy elderly people (ages 60–83 years). Although they found no significant effect in the 24-week vitamin program, they suggest that a longer program may enhance cognitive functioning. As a health-minded researcher, you decide to study their suggestion and randomly select 10 healthy elderly people from your community to participate in a 48-week multivitamin program. A puzzle task was used to measure cognitive functioning. The number of pieces from a 100-piece puzzle connected in a 5-minute period was recorded before and after the 48-week program. Both puzzles were pre-evaluated as equal in complexity and difficulty levels. Data are as follows:

	Number of Puzzle Pieces	
Participant	Before	After
I. A.	18	21
B. A.	9	10
C. V.	21	20
G. M.	32	29
T. R.	28	35
D. K.	42	60
M. V.	38	31
M. C.	26	28
H. A.	18	19
C. J.	33	39

(a) State the null hypothesis and research hypotheses; (b) calculate the degrees of freedom and find the critical value from Table T; (c) calculate the appropriate *t;* (d) state whether to reject or fail to reject the null hypothesis; (e) write a brief interpretation of the results in the context of the original research question.

20. Work by Dr. Frezza and colleagues (1990) reported that because women have less body water than men of similar body weight, they absorb and metabolize alcohol differently and achieve higher concentrations of alcohol in the blood after drinking equivalent amounts of alcohol. Women also tend to eliminate alcohol from the blood faster than men (Li et al., 1998). Suppose a researcher wanted to determine whether reaction times are immediately affected after drinking a small amount of alcohol. Twenty-five women, all weighing exactly 150 pounds, agreed to do a reaction time task before and after drinking one beer. The results for the pretest and posttest, as well as the correlation between the two, are listed here.

Reaction Time	
Pretest X_1	Posttest X_2
$\overline{X}_1 = 215$ msec	$\overline{X}_2 = 333$ msec
$S_1 = 48$ msec	$S_2 = 85$ msec
Correlation $(r) = .68$	

(a) State the null hypothesis and research hypotheses; (b) calculate the degrees of freedom and find the critical value from Table T; (c) calculate the appropriate *t;* (d) state whether to reject or fail to reject the null hypothesis; (e) write a brief interpretation of the results in the context of the original research question; (f) can the researcher conclude that the beer caused the observed difference or lack of difference in reaction time? Why or why not?

21. In our multitasking hectic lives, do you think our recall memory might differ depending on whether we encoded information while we were walking, standing, or sitting? Lindenberger, Marsiske, and Baltes (2000)

studied memory recall among different age groups during varied dual-task encoding contexts such as memorizing a word list while walking, standing, or sitting. Among their findings, the recall data revealed that recall was less efficient when participants encoded a word list while walking. The data in the following table are from another experiment comparing the memory performance of 24 statistics students randomly assigned to one of two encoding conditions. Participants were asked to try to memorize a list of words and at the same time either skip or hop on two feet.

Words Remembered	
Skipping	Hopping
5	4
7	6
5	6
4	3
3	7
8	5
3	8
7	9
8	7
8	7
5	4
7	9

(a) State the null hypothesis and research hypotheses; (b) calculate the degrees of freedom and find the critical value from Table T; (c) calculate the appropriate t; (d) state whether to reject or fail to reject the null hypothesis; (e) write a brief interpretation of the results in the context of the original research question.

22. Have you wondered whether you respond quicker to an auditory cue than to a visual one, especially in an emergency? In a study conducted by Abrams and Balota (1991), participants' foot pedal response was faster with an auditory signal than with a visual one. You decide to extend this area of research and recruit 20 people to participate in a study measuring reaction times to emergency vehicles. Participants are instructed to press a button when they see a flashing red light on the computer screen or hear an emergency siren. The signals are presented in random order. After 10 practice trials, their response times to each signal were recorded, and the results are summarized here.

Response Times in Seconds	
Auditory Signal X_1	Visual Signal X_2
$\overline{X}_1 = 13.4$	$\overline{X}_2 = 12.7$
$S_1 = 2.6$	$S_2 = 2.1$
Correlation (r) = .64	

(a) State the null hypothesis and research hypotheses; (b) calculate the degrees of freedom and find the critical value from Table T; (c) calculate the appropriate t; (d) state whether to reject or fail to reject the null hypothesis; (e) write a brief interpretation of the results in the context of the original research question.

23. Does music relax you? Although listening to music and silence were found to be effective in both reducing participants' anxiety and enhancing perceptions of relaxation, a music-assisted progressive muscle relaxation technique (MAPMRT) was found to be most effective in a study by Robb (2000). A Jitters University professor predicts that MAPMRT will be effective in reducing

dentist anxiety. Fourteen dental patients were selected from the dentist's clients and then randomly assigned to either a 1-hour MAPMRT session or 1 hour of silence before they saw the dentist. Just before they were called to meet with the dentist, they completed a dental anxiety questionnaire. Anxiety scores were tabulated (low scores indicate lower anxiety).

Anxiety Scores	
MAPMR Group	Control Group
9	15
11	11
5	10
7	8
11	10
8	13
7	9

(a) State the null hypothesis and research hypotheses; (b) calculate the degrees of freedom and find the critical value from Table T; (c) calculate the appropriate *t*; (d) state whether to reject or fail to reject the null hypothesis; (e) write a brief interpretation of the results in the context of the original research question.

24. Suppose the Jitters U. professor designed a different study than the one in Problem 23.

For this study, seven patients were randomly selected from the dentist's clients. The patients' dental anxiety was then measured before and after the 1-hour MAPMRT session. The data are listed here.

	Anxiety Scores	
Patient	Before MAPMRT	After MAPMRT
A	9	15
B	11	11
C	5	10
D	7	8
E	11	10
F	8	13
G	7	9

(a) State the null hypothesis and research hypotheses; (b) calculate the degrees of freedom and find the critical value from Table T; (c) calculate the appropriate *t*; (d) state whether to reject or fail to reject the null hypothesis; (e) write a brief interpretation of the results in the context of the original research question; (f) compare and evaluate any differences in the results of this study with those from Problem 23.

References

Abrams, R. A., & Balota, D. A. (1991). Mental chronometry: Beyond reaction time. *Psychological Science, 2,* 153–157.

America Online/Roper Starch Worldwide. (2000). *Second annual cyberstudy* [Online]. Available: http://cyberatlas.internet.com/big_picture/demographics/article/0,1323,5901_238221,000.html (visited March 3, 2001).

Anderson, C. A., & Dill, K. E. (2000). Video games and aggressive thoughts, feelings, and behavior in the laboratory and in life. *Journal of Personality and Social Psychology, 78,* 772–790.

Cockle, S. M., Haller, J., Kimber, S., Dawe, R. A., & Hindmarch, I. (2000). The influence of multivitamins on cognitive function and mood in the elderly. *Aging and Mental Health, 4,* 339–353.

Detweiler, J. B., Bedell, B. T., Salovey, P., Pronin, E., & Rothman, A. J. (1999). Message framing and sunscreen use: Gain-framed messages motivate beachgoers. *Health Psychology, 18,* 189–196.

Frezza, M., diPadova, D., Pozzato, G., Terpin, M., Baraon, E., & Lieber, C. S. (1990). High blood alcohol levels in women: The role of decreased gastric alcohol dehydrogenase activity and first-pass metabolism. *New England Journal of Medicine, 322,* 95–99.

Li, T. K., et al. (1998). Gender and ethnic differences in alcohol metabolism. *Alcohol Clinical Experimental Research, 22,* 771–772.

Lindenberger, U., Marsiske, M., & Baltes, P. B. (2000). Memorizing while walking increase in dual-task costs from young adulthood to old age. *Psychology and Aging, 15,* 417–436.

Ludwig, T. D., Gray, T. W., & Rowell, A. (1998). Increasing recycling in academic buildings: A systematic replication. *Journal of Applied Behavior Analysis, 31,* 683–686.

McCall, M., & Belmont, H. J. (1996). Credit card insignia and restaurant tipping: Evidence for an associative link. *Journal of Applied Psychology, 81,* 609–613.

National Sleep Foundation (2000). *2000 omnibus sleep in American poll* [Online]. Available: http://www.sleepfoundation.org/publications/2000poll.html (visited February 28, 2001).

Robb, S. L. (2000). Music assisted progressive muscle relaxation, progressive muscle relaxation, music listening, and silence: A comparison of relaxation techniques. *Journal of Music Therapy, 37,* 2–21.

U. S. Environmental Protection Agency (1999). Multiple solid waste fact book: An electronic reference manual [Online]. Available at: http://www.epa.gov/students/municipal_solid_waste_factbook.htm (visited March 2, 2001).

13

One-Way Analysis of Variance

- Analysis of Variance: One Test Is Better Than Many
- Hypothesis Testing and Analysis of Variance
- Conducting an Analysis of Variance
  Two Methods for Estimating the Population Variance
  Computation of the Mean Square Between Groups

Computation of the Mean Square Within Groups
The F Test
VISUAL SUMMARY: One-Way Analysis of Variance
Computational Formula for F
VISUAL SUMMARY: One-Way Analysis of Variance—Computational Formulas

- Summary
- Key Terms
- Formulas
- Problems
  Problems From the Literature
- References

I magine yourself sitting in the front seat of your brand-new Mercedes. You close the door, fasten the seat belt, insert the key in the ignition, and start the motor. After shifting into reverse, you look behind as you back out of the garage. Suddenly, the car begins to speed up. You jam your foot on the brake pedal, but instead of stopping, the car accelerates to more than 40 miles per hour before smashing into your neighbor's car on the other side of the street. Luckily, you are not seriously hurt, but your Mercedes and your neighbor's BMW roadster are a total loss. After hearing your explanation, both your insurance company and your neighbor insist that you have a mechanic inspect your car's brakes, engine, and throttle control linkage. Your mechanic, as well as a couple of others, is unable to detect any mechanical malfunction that might be responsible for your accident.

The phenomenon just described has become known as "unintended acceleration." It happens when automobiles accelerate out of control as their drivers press as hard as they can on what they think is the brake pedal, but the cars stop only when they hit something or when the ignition is turned off. Fortunately, this kind of accident is relatively rare. Nevertheless, several accidents of this type have been the basis of lawsuits against automobile manufacturers for faulty car design. Although the term unintended acceleration implies that it is due to some sort of intermittent mechanical malfunction, most researchers who have studied these accidents believe they are the result of driver error, not a malfunction of the automobile (Vernoy & Tomerlin, 1989).

Any time a person makes a movement, there is some possibility of making an error. Even highly practiced movements like writing your name, climbing stairs, or eating with a fork are not perfectly accurate *every time* because inevitably, at some time, you'll make an upsweep with your pen at the wrong time, trip on a step, or accidentally tilt food off your fork. Likewise, well-practiced drivers may happen to hit the accelerator rather than the brake pedal in a panic situation. Although driver mistakes are relatively rare, they do occur and can be measured and documented.

Suppose that as a result of your accident you decide to study unintended acceleration. First, you need to develop a viable hypothesis. After examining the related research and scrutinizing the positions of the pedals in various cars, you propose that the distance between the brake and the accelerator pedals may be a contributing factor in driver error. To test this hypothesis, you design an experiment in which participants use one of three driving simulators, each with a different pedal arrangement. In the close-pedal arrangement, the distance between pedals is only 1 inch; in the moderate-pedal arrangement, it's 2 inches; and in the far-pedal arrangement, 3 inches. You assign 10 participants to each condition and instruct them to drive their simulators for 4 hours. During this time, the number of errors made by each driver is recorded, as shown in Table 13.1. After gathering the data, you are faced with analyzing them. How do you do this with three groups of participants?

Question: Can't *t* tests simply be done among the different groups?

All *t* tests are conducted between only two samples, so if you want to run *t* tests for this experiment, you would have to conduct three separate tests to analyze

Table 13.1 Number of Pedal Errors With Three Pedal Arrangements in a Driving Simulator

Pedal Arrangement		
Type 1	Type 2	Type 3
3	4	6
2	3	4
4	4	3
1	3	4
0	5	7
2	4	6
3	2	5
2	5	8
1	4	5
2	4	6

these data: one between pedal arrangement types 1 and 2, one between types 1 and 3, and a third between 2 and 3. If there were four groups, you would have to conduct six t tests, and if there were five groups, you would have to conduct ten. Besides taking a lot of time, doing multiple t tests is statistically questionable because with every t test performed on the same data, the probability of making a Type I error increases. You know that the probability of a Type I error is equal to α, or .05, for each individual test, so you can use Formula 10.3 (because these events are mutually exclusive) to figure out the probability of either test A or test B being significant by chance alone when two tests are done at the same time:

$$p(A \text{ or } B) = p(A) + p(B) - p(A \text{ and } B) = .05 + .05 - [.05 \cdot .05]$$

$$= .10 - .0025 = .0975$$

Therefore, the probability of getting at least one significant result by chance alone when you do two simultaneous t tests is almost 1 in 10. If you expand this to the situation with three tests, as for the data in Table 13.1, you have

$$p[(A \text{ or } B) \text{ or } (C)] = p(A \text{ or } B) + p(C) - [p(A \text{ or } B) \cdot p(C)] = .0975 + .05 - [.0975 \cdot .05]$$

$$= .1475 - .0049 = .1426$$

The probability is about 1 in 7 that you will get at least one significant result by chance alone. As you can see, this error escalates as you do additional t tests. Therefore, conducting multiple t tests is not statistically valid. Fortunately, statisticians have developed a means of comparing multiple samples that *is* statistically valid: analysis of variance.

Analysis of Variance: One Test Is Better Than Many

When you want to compare the means of only two samples, the t test is the test of choice because it is designed to test hypotheses comparing only two samples. If you are testing hypotheses that require the comparison of three or more samples, then you should use analysis of variance. Analysis of variance allows you to determine whether there are any significant differences among three or more samples without increasing the size of alpha.

Hypothesis Testing and Analysis of Variance

Both the t test and the analysis of variance are tests of the null and research hypotheses. The difference between them is that the t test is used when the research design involves a comparison of two samples, whereas the **one-way analysis of variance** is used when the research design involves a comparison of three or more levels of one independent variable. The null hypotheses for the t test and the analysis of variance are similar. In a t test, the null hypothesis states that $\mu_1 = \mu_2$, meaning that the two samples both come from the same population, or from populations that have the same means, and there is no difference between them. In an analysis of variance, the null hypothesis states that $\mu_1 = \mu_2 = \mu_3 \ldots = \mu_k$, where k is the number of levels of the independent variable. This means that there is no difference between the sample means of any of the levels.

The research hypotheses for a t test and an analysis of variance are also similar. In a t test, the research hypothesis predicts that the two samples come from distributions with different population means. In an analysis of variance, the research hypothesis predicts that at least one of the sample means comes from a population different from that of the other sample means. As explained in Chapter 12, the point of running a t test is to determine whether the null hypothesis can be safely rejected. The same is true for an analysis of variance. If the null hypothesis is rejected, then at least part of the research hypothesis is supported because the null hypothesis and the research hypothesis are mutually exclusive. This is the reason for conducting an analysis of variance: to see whether the null hypothesis can be rejected.

Conducting an Analysis of Variance

Basically, an analysis of variance is an evaluation of the random differences between scores or participants. In any research involving three or more groups, with each group containing several participants, it is possible that any differences between the groups are due either to the experimental manipulation or to chance differences between the participants in the different groups. For example, the means of the three groups shown in Table 13.1 are all different from one another. The type 1 pedal arrangement has a mean of 2 errors, whereas the type 2 has a mean of 3.8 errors, and the type 3 has a mean of 5.4 errors. The explanation for these differences may be that increasing the separation between the pedals actually causes more errors, or that simply by chance the people who tend to make more pedal errors were assigned to the type 3 pedal arrangement. If the null hypothesis is true and the independent variable has no real effect, then the differences in the number of errors are due solely to chance differences in the drivers' abilities.

To test whether differences among sample groups are due to chance, you can conduct an analysis of variance. In an analysis of variance, you use the data gathered from the samples to make two separate estimates of the variance in the population. You arrive at these estimates using two very different methods, and then compare the two estimates to see whether they are similar.

> **Question:** Why estimate the variance in the population? How does that tell you whether the differences between the samples are due to chance?

Merely estimating the population variance tells you nothing. The key is in *comparing* two separate estimates that are arrived at using two distinctly different methods. If both estimates are similar or exactly the same, then it stands to reason that all the samples are probably from the same population and the null hypothesis is true. Most likely, the manipulation of the independent variable had no effect, and any difference between the groups is due to participant variability. On the other hand, if the estimates are very different, then at least one of the samples probably comes from a population different from the other samples, so the research hypothesis is true. Most likely, the manipulation of the independent variable was the cause of the difference between the sample groups.

> **Question:** What are the two methods used to estimate that population variance?

One of the methods estimates the population variance by using the variance *within* each sample or group. The other method uses the difference *between* the means of the samples, or groups. These methods will be discussed in detail after an explanation of the notation that will be used.

Thus far, the symbol S has been used for the sample standard deviation that is an unbiased estimate of the population standard deviation, and S^2 has been used for the variance of a sample that is the unbiased estimate of the population variance. In an analysis of variance, it is traditional to use a different term for the variance estimate: the **mean square,** abbreviated **MS.** The mean square is so called because it is the mean (the average) of the squared deviation scores used to calculate the variation. Furthermore, until this point in the book, n has been used to represent the number of scores in a sample. However, in calculating certain values for an analysis of variance, you will have three different n values, so you will need to denote each in a different way. Thus, lowercase n will be used to indicate the number of participants or scores in a sample, lowercase k to indicate the number of samples, and N_{total} to indicate the total number of participants or scores in all the samples combined. Next, you will see how the two approaches are used to estimate the population variance, or mean square.

Two Methods for Estimating the Population Variance

One approach is to examine the variation of the scores within each sample group. Remember that the variance of a sample is the sum of the squared deviation scores of the sample divided by $n - 1$. This gives an unbiased estimate of the population variance. The formula for S^2 is

$$S^2 = \frac{\Sigma(X - \overline{X})^2}{n - 1}$$

When there is more than one group, as in the pedal error experiment, you can generate several estimates of the population variance and then average them to obtain a combined estimate from the several groups. The formula for this combined estimate, if all the groups are the same size, looks like this:

$$MS_{wg} = \frac{\Sigma(X_1 - \bar{X}_1)^2 + \Sigma(X_2 - \bar{X}_2)^2 + \Sigma(X_3 - \bar{X}_3)^2 + \cdots + \Sigma(X_k - \bar{X}_k)^2}{(n_1 - 1) + (n_2 - 1) + (n_3 - 1) + \cdots + (n_k - 1)} \tag{13.1}$$

where n is the number of participants in each group and k is the total number of different groups. This is called the **mean square within groups,** or the within-groups variance estimate.

Now look at the other way to estimate the variance of the population, which involves examining the differences **between** the means of the sample groups. Do you remember the formula for the standard error of the mean? Here it is again:

$$\sigma_{\bar{X}} = \frac{\sigma}{\sqrt{n}}$$

Multiplying each side of the equation by the square root of n results in

$$\sigma = \sqrt{n} \cdot \sigma_{\bar{X}}$$

Thus, the population variance is equal to

$$\sigma^2 = n \cdot \sigma_{\bar{X}}^2 \tag{13.2}$$

Because the standard error of the mean is the same as the standard deviation of the distribution of sample means, the square of the standard error of the mean can be computed by using the following formula:

$$\sigma_{\bar{X}}^2 = \frac{\Sigma(\bar{X} - \bar{\bar{X}})^2}{k}$$

where k equals the number of samples and $\bar{\bar{X}}$ (pronounced X bar bar) equals the mean of all the sample means. If you estimate this from only a few sample means, then you must divide by $k - 1$ rather than k, as follows:

$$\text{Estimated } \sigma_{\bar{X}}^2 = \frac{(\bar{X}_1 - \bar{\bar{X}})^2 + (\bar{X}_2 - \bar{\bar{X}})^2 + (\bar{X}_3 - \bar{\bar{X}})^2 + \cdots + (\bar{X}_k - \bar{\bar{X}})^2}{k - 1}$$

Substituting this into Formula 13.2 results in the formula for the **mean square between groups:**

$$MS_{bg} = \frac{n_1(\bar{X}_1 - \bar{\bar{X}})^2 + n_2(\bar{X}_2 - \bar{\bar{X}})^2 + n_3(\bar{X}_3 - \bar{\bar{X}})^2 + \cdots + n_k(\bar{X}_k - \bar{\bar{X}})^2}{k - 1} \tag{13.3}$$

This formula is known as the mean square between groups because the differences between the group means and the mean of the means are used to calculate the variance estimate. The mean square between groups represents the variance that is due to the manipulation of the independent variable. It is a measure of the variance between the group means.

Question: Again, why do these two variance estimates need to be computed? What can be gained by estimating the same variance twice?

If there is no difference between the samples—if they are all taken from the same population—these two methods of estimating the population variance should return exactly the same values. That is, if the null hypothesis is true, then the mean square between-groups estimate and the mean square within-groups estimate should be the same. And the ratio of the mean square between to the mean square within, which is called the **F ratio,** will equal 1. On the other hand, if the research hypothesis is true, then it is reasonable to expect that the two mean squares will have two different values. In fact, if the research hypothesis is true, the mean square between groups will be much larger than the mean square within groups. This situation will then result in a ratio of the mean square between to the mean square within that is much greater than 1. This, then, is why you need to compute the two estimates: to determine whether the two values are the same. If their ratio, the F ratio, is significantly greater than 1, you can reject the null hypothesis.

To illustrate the procedure, after the Concept Quiz an analysis of variance for the driving simulator experiment is conducted using the data from Table 13.1.

Concept Quiz

Sometimes long-term therapy can restrict patients from psychological treatment. Addressing this concern, Clark et al. (1999) developed a brief cognitive therapy program that incorporated self-study modules and homework modified from the full therapy program. To test the therapy effectiveness, patients with panic disorder were assigned to one of three conditions: full therapy (12 sessions), brief therapy (5 sessions), or wait listed. The number of panic attacks and other measures were recorded. The results indicated that both types of therapy were equally effective and superior to the wait list.

1. Because *t* tests are used to test the significance of the differences between _____ means, researchers in this study would use a one-way analysis of variance because it tests the significance among _____ means.

2. When multiple *t* tests are performed on the same data, the probability of _____ error increases.

3. In this study, $\mu_1 = \mu_2 = \mu_3$ is the _____.

4. An analysis of variance consists of _____ the population _____ using two very different methods.

5. In an analysis of variance, the _____ is the equivalent of the estimate of the population variance.

6. The mean square between groups represents the variance that is due to
_____.

7. The differences between the group means and the mean of the means are used to compute the mean square _____ groups.

8. The mean square _____ groups is calculated by averaging the variance estimates of all groups in the analysis.

9. If the research hypothesis is true, you expect the mean square _____ to be greater than the mean square _____.

Answers

1. two; three or more
2. Type I
3. null hypothesis (H_0)
4. estimating; variance

5. mean square
6. the manipulated independent variable (type of therapy)

7. between
8. within
9. between; within

Computation of the Mean Square Between Groups

To compute the mean square between groups, use Formula 13.3:

$$MS_{bg} = \frac{n_1(\overline{X}_1 - \overline{\overline{X}})^2 + n_2(\overline{X}_2 - \overline{\overline{X}})^2 + n_3(\overline{X}_3 - \overline{\overline{X}})^2 + \cdots + n_k(\overline{X}_k - \overline{\overline{X}})^2}{k - 1}$$

Begin by calculating the mean for each sample, as well as the mean of the sample means. Remember that each sample represents a different level of the independent variable. Compute the mean of each sample as always: by summing all the scores in the sample and dividing by the number of scores in that sample. Then, because the samples are all the same size and thus have equal ns, you can do one of two things. You can compute the mean of the sample means by summing all the means and then dividing by the number of samples:

$$\overline{\overline{X}} = \frac{\Sigma \overline{X}}{k} = \frac{\overline{X}_1 + \overline{X}_2 + \overline{X}_3 + \cdots + \overline{X}_k}{k} \tag{13.4}$$

or you can compute the mean of the means by summing all the scores in all the samples and dividing by the total number of scores:

$$\overline{\overline{X}} = \frac{\Sigma(\Sigma X)}{N_{total}} = \frac{\Sigma X_1 + \Sigma X_2 + \Sigma X_3 + \cdots + \Sigma X_k}{N_{total}} \tag{13.5}$$

The means for the data in the pedal error experiment are computed in Table 13.2.

Table 13.2   Calculation of Sample Means and the Mean of the Means for the Number of Pedal Errors With Three Pedal Arrangements in a Driving Simulator

	Pedal Arrangement	
Type 1	Type 2	Type 3
3	4	6
2	3	4
4	4	3
1	3	4
0	5	7
2	4	6
3	2	5
2	5	8
1	4	5
2	4	6
$\Sigma X_1 = 20$	$\Sigma X_2 = 38$	$\Sigma X_3 = 54$
$\overline{X}_1 = 2$	$\overline{X}_2 = 3.8$	$\overline{X}_3 = 5.4$

$$\overline{\overline{X}} = \frac{\overline{X}_1 + \overline{X}_2 + \overline{X}_3}{k} = \frac{2 + 3.8 + 5.4}{3} = \frac{11.2}{3} = 3.733$$

or

$$\overline{\overline{X}} = \frac{\Sigma X_1 + \Sigma X_2 + \Sigma X_3 + \cdots + \Sigma X_k}{N_{total}} = \frac{20 + 38 + 54}{30} = \frac{112}{30} = 3.733$$

Using the computations in this table, the mean square between can be computed using Formula 13.3:

$$MS_{bg} = \frac{n_1(\overline{X}_1 - \overline{\overline{X}})^2 + n_2(\overline{X}_2 - \overline{\overline{X}})^2 + n_3(\overline{X}_3 - \overline{\overline{X}})^2 + \cdots + n_k(\overline{X}_k - \overline{\overline{X}})^2}{k - 1}$$

$$= \frac{10(2 - 3.733)^2 + 10(3.8 - 3.733)^2 + 10(5.4 - 3.733)^2}{3 - 1}$$

$$= \frac{10(-1.733)^2 + 10(.067)^2 + 10(1.667)^2}{2}$$

$$= \frac{10 \cdot 3.003 + 10 \cdot .004 + 10 \cdot 2.779}{2}$$

$$= \frac{30.030 + .040 + 27.790}{2} = \frac{57.860}{2} = 28.930$$

Computation of the Mean Square Within Groups

The computation of the mean square within groups involves the same procedures used in computing the standard deviation for each of the samples. You subtract the mean from each score and square the result. Then you sum these squares for each sample and use Formula 13.1 to compute the mean square within. Table 13.3 has the necessary calculations.

Using Formula 13.1, now substitute the appropriate sums to compute the mean square within groups:

$$MS_{wg} = \frac{\Sigma(X_1 - \overline{X}_1)^2 + \Sigma(X_2 - \overline{X}_2)^2 + \Sigma(X_3 - \overline{X}_3)^2 + \cdots + \Sigma(X_k - \overline{X}_k)^2}{(n_1 - 1) + (n_2 - 1) + (n_3 - 1) + \cdots + (n_k - 1)}$$

$$= \frac{12.00 + 7.60 + 20.40}{(10 - 1) + (10 - 1) + (10 - 1)} = \frac{40}{9 + 9 + 9} = \frac{40}{27} = 1.481$$

Question: Now the population variance has been estimated in two different ways with very different results. What does this mean? Is there a difference among these three samples?

Table 13.3   Calculation of Deviations and Squared Deviations for the Number of Pedal Errors With Three Pedal Arrangements in a Driving Simulator

				Pedal Arrangement				
	Type 1			Type 2			Type 3	
X_1	$X_1 - \overline{X}_1$	$(X_1 - \overline{X}_1)^2$	X_2	$X_2 - \overline{X}_2$	$(X_2 - \overline{X}_2)^2$	X_3	$X_3 - \overline{X}_3$	$(X_3 - \overline{X}_3)^2$
3	1	1	4	.2	.04	6	.6	.36
2	0	0	3	−.8	.64	4	−1.4	1.96
4	2	4	4	.2	.04	3	−2.4	5.76
1	−1	1	3	−.8	.64	4	−1.4	1.96
0	−2	4	5	1.2	1.44	7	1.6	2.56
2	0	0	4	.2	.04	6	.6	.36
3	1	1	2	−1.8	3.24	5	−.4	.16
2	0	0	5	1.2	1.44	8	2.6	6.76
1	−1	1	4	.2	.04	5	−.4	.16
2	0	0	4	.2	.04	6	.6	.36
$\Sigma(X_1 - \overline{X}_1)^2 = 12.00$			$\Sigma(X_2 - \overline{X}_2)^2 = 7.60$			$\Sigma(X_3 - \overline{X}_3)^2 = 20.40$		

The *F* Test

The way to decide whether to reject the null hypothesis or fail to reject it is to compare the two mean squares by using an **F test.** In a one-way analysis of variance, *F* is the ratio of the mean square between groups to the mean square within groups:

$$F = \frac{MS_{bg}}{MS_{wg}}$$

(13.6)

Theoretically, if the null hypothesis is true, then the mean square between and the mean square within will equal each other and the *F* ratio will equal 1. On the other hand, if the null hypothesis is false and the research hypothesis is true, the mean square between will be significantly larger than the mean square within. This difference in size will result in an *F* ratio that is significantly greater than l. Therefore, the next step is to compute the value of *F* using Formula 13.6:

$$F = \frac{MS_{bg}}{MS_{wg}} = \frac{28.930}{1.481} = 19.534$$

To find out whether the computed ratio is significant, you need to compare the computed value of *F* to the critical value of *F* given in Table F in Appendix A. Just as there are many different *t* distributions, there are also many *F* distributions, so you must use the degrees of freedom of both the numerator, mean square between, and the denominator, mean square within, to enter Table F. In a one-way analysis of variance, the number of **degrees of freedom for the mean square between** (df_{bg}) is equal to the number of samples in the experiment minus 1:

$$df_{bg} = k - 1$$

(13.7)

To calculate the degrees of freedom for the mean square within groups, you add together the degrees of freedom for all the samples' **degrees of freedom within groups** (df_{wg}) in the experiment:

$$df_{wg} = (n_1 - 1) + (n_2 - 1) + (n_3 - 1) + \cdots + (n_k - 1)$$

(13.8)

Thus, in the example, you compute the degrees of freedom between groups as follows:

$$df_{bg} = k - 1 = 3 - 1 = 2$$

and you compute the degrees of freedom within groups in the following way:

$$df_{wg} = (n_1 - 1) + (n_2 - 1) + (n_3 - 1) =$$
$$(10 - 1) + (10 - 1) + (10 - 1) = 9 + 9 + 9 = 27$$

Now you can see whether the computed *F* value is significant by looking in Table F. This table is arranged so that you look for the computed degrees of freedom between groups (which is 2 in the example) in the row at the top of the table. Then you look down that column until you reach the computed degrees of freedom within groups (which is 27 in the example). If you haven't already, find Table

VISUAL SUMMARY

One-Way Analysis of Variance

Before You Begin: State H_0 and H_1.

Compute $\overline{X}$ for each sample, $\overline{\overline{X}}$, and $\Sigma(X - \overline{X})^2$ for each sample.

Compute mean squares:

MS_{bg} $\qquad$ MS_{wg}

$$MS_{bg} = \frac{n_1(\overline{X}_1 - \overline{\overline{X}})^2 + n_2(\overline{X}_2 - \overline{\overline{X}})^2 + \cdots + n_k(\overline{X}_k - \overline{\overline{X}})^2}{k - 1}$$

$$MS_{wg} = \frac{\Sigma(X_1 - \overline{X}_1)^2 + \Sigma(X_2 - \overline{X}_2)^2 + \cdots + \Sigma(X_k - \overline{X}_k)^2}{(n_1 - 1) + (n_2 - 1) + (n_3 - 1) + \cdots + (n_k - 1)}$$

Compute the F ratio:

$$F = \frac{MS_{bg}}{MS_{wg}}$$

Compute the degrees of freedom:

df_{bg} $\qquad$ df_{wg}

$df_{bg} = k - 1$

$df_{wg} = (n_1 - 1) + (n_2 - 1) + \cdots + (n_k - 1)$

Use df_{bg} and df_{wg} to find the critical value in Table F.

If the computed value of the F ratio is greater than the critical value from Table F, then reject H_0.

F and do this. You will find that the critical value of F necessary to reject the null hypothesis with $\alpha = .05$ is 3.35. For the computed value of F to be significant, it must be *greater than or equal to* the critical value found in Table F. Because the critical value for F is 3.35 and your computed F ratio is 19.534, you can reject the null hypothesis, which states that there is no difference between the three pedal arrangements, and you can accept the research hypothesis. Thus, you can safely assume that there is a difference between at least two of the pedal arrangements, and the difference is significant.

Concept Quiz

Recall from the previous concept quiz that Clark et al. (1999) tested the effectiveness of a shorter version of a cognitive behavioral therapy for patients with panic disorder. They found that both the full therapy (12 sessions) and brief therapy (5 sessions) were equally effective in reducing panic attacks and other anxiety measures and that both therapy programs were superior to the wait-listed condition.

1. The way these researchers decided whether to reject or fail to reject the null hypothesis was by comparing the two _____ by computing an _____ .

2. F is the ratio of the _____ to the _____ .

3. Suppose that the mean square between groups was 16 and the mean square within was 4; what is the F ratio?

4. Theoretically, if the null hypothesis is true, the F ratio should equal _____ .

5. The degrees of freedom for the mean square between groups are equal to _____ .

6. The degrees of freedom for the mean square within are equal to _____ .

7. If there were 5 participants in each of the three therapy conditions, what are the degrees of freedom between groups and within groups?

8. If $df_{wg} = 12$ and $df_{bg} = 2$, would an F ratio of 5.66 at $\alpha = .05$ be significant?

Answers

1. mean squares; F ratio
2. mean square between; mean square within
3. 4
4. 1
5. the number of groups minus 1 ($k - 1$)
6. the sum of the degrees of freedom for all the groups in the experiment
7. $df_{wg} = 12$; $df_{bg} = 2$
8. Yes, the critical value $= 3.89$.

Computational Formula for *F*

Question: Is there a faster way to compute the *F* ratio?

Yes, there are computational formulas for computing the *F* ratio that are faster than the deviation formulas just presented. However, to use these formulas, it is necessary to break the variance estimates—the mean squares—into two parts: sum of squares and degrees of freedom. The sum of squares is similar to the sum of the deviation scores used in Chapter 5 to compute the variance of a sample; the degrees of freedom are identical to those used earlier to find the critical value of the *F* ratio. The sum of squares is always the numerator in the computation of the mean square, and the degrees of freedom are always the denominator. Consequently, the mean square between groups equals the sum of squares between divided by the degrees of freedom between:

$$MS_{bg} = \frac{SS_{bg}}{df_{bg}} \tag{13.9}$$

Likewise, the mean square within groups equals the sum of squares within divided by the degrees of freedom within:

$$MS_{wg} = \frac{SS_{wg}}{df_{wg}} \tag{13.10}$$

You already know how to compute the degrees of freedom both between and within from the discussion of Formulas 13.7 and 13.8. All you need to know is how to compute the sum of squares. The computation formulas for the **sum of squares between groups** (SS_{bg}) as well as **sum of squares within groups** (SS_{wg}) are given next:

$$SS_{bg} = \left[\frac{(\Sigma X_1)^2}{n_1} + \frac{(\Sigma X_2)^2}{n_2} + \cdots + \frac{(\Sigma X_k)^2}{n_k} \right] -$$

$$\left[\frac{(\Sigma X_1 + \Sigma X_1 + \cdots + \Sigma X_1)^2}{N_{total}} \right] \tag{13.11}$$

$$SS_{wg} = \left[\Sigma X_1^2 + \Sigma X_2^2 + \cdots + \Sigma X_k^2 \right] -$$

$$\left[\frac{(\Sigma X_1)^2}{n_1} + \frac{(\Sigma X_2)^2}{n_2} + \cdots + \frac{(\Sigma X_k)^2}{n_k} \right] \tag{13.12}$$

If you want to check your work, you can compute the **sum of squares total** (SS_{total}), which is equal to the sum of squares between plus the sum of squares within. Formula 13.13 is the computational formula for the sum of squares total. You can compute this and then check to see whether it equals the sum of the other two computed sums of squares:

$$SS_{total} = \left[\Sigma X_1^2 + \Sigma X_2^2 + \cdots + \Sigma X_k^2 \right] - \left[\frac{(\Sigma X_1 + \Sigma X_1 + \cdots + \Sigma X_1)^2}{N_{total}} \right] \tag{13.13}$$

Table 13.4 Calculation of the Sums Needed to Use the Computational Formulas for Sums of Squares in Analysis of Variance for the Number of Pedal Errors With Three Pedal Arrangements in a Driving Simulator

		Pedal Arrangement			
Type 1		Type 2		Type 3	
X_1	X_1^2	X_2	X_2^2	X_3	X_3^2
3	9	4	16	6	36
2	4	3	9	4	16
4	16	4	16	3	9
1	1	3	9	4	16
0	0	5	25	7	49
2	4	4	16	6	36
3	9	2	4	5	25
2	4	5	25	8	64
1	1	4	16	5	25
2	4	4	16	6	36
$\Sigma X_1 = 20$	$\Sigma X_1^2 = 52$	$\Sigma X_2 = 38$	$\Sigma X_2^2 = 152$	$\Sigma X_3 = 54$	$\Sigma X_3^2 = 312$

Now apply these formulas to the unintentional acceleration example. Before you begin any analysis of variance problem, it is best to first calculate all the sums that you will need for all your formulas. The necessary sums are calculated in Table 13.4.

Begin the analysis of variance by using Formula 13.11 to compute the sums of squares between groups:

$$SS_{bg} = \left[\frac{(\Sigma X_1)^2}{n_1} + \frac{(\Sigma X_2)^2}{n_2} + \cdots + \frac{(\Sigma X_k)^2}{n_k}\right] - \left[\frac{(\Sigma X_1 + \Sigma X_1 + \cdots + \Sigma X_1)^2}{N_{total}}\right]$$

$$= \left[\frac{20^2}{10} + \frac{38^2}{10} + \frac{54^2}{10}\right] - \left[\frac{(20 + 38 + 54)^2}{30}\right]$$

$$= \left[\frac{400}{10} + \frac{1{,}444}{10} + \frac{2{,}916}{10}\right] - \left[\frac{112^2}{30}\right]$$

$$= \left[40 + 144.4 + 291.6\right] - \left[\frac{12{,}544}{30}\right] = 476 - 418.133 = 57.867$$

This value is the same as computed for the numerator in Formula 13.3 earlier in the chapter. The slight difference is due entirely to roundoff error.

Having computed the sum of squares between, you can proceed to the computation of the sum of squares within groups using Formula 13.12.

$$SS_{wg} = \left[\Sigma X_1^2 + \Sigma X_2^2 + \cdots + \Sigma X_k^2\right] - \left[\frac{(\Sigma X_1)^2}{n_1} + \frac{(\Sigma X_2)^2}{n_2} + \cdots + \frac{(\Sigma X_k)^2}{n_k}\right]$$

$$= \left[52 + 152 + 312 \right] - \left[\frac{20^2}{10} + \frac{38^2}{10} + \frac{54^2}{10} \right]$$

$$= 516 - \left[\frac{400}{10} + \frac{1,444}{10} + \frac{2,916}{10} \right]$$

$$= 516 - \left[40 + 144.4 + 291.6 \right] = 516 - 476 = 40$$

Again, this value is the same as the numerator computed using Formula 13.1 earlier in the chapter.

The sum of squares within and the sum of squares between are the only sum of squares needed to compute the F ratio. However, because, when added together, the sum of squares within and the sum of squares between equal the sum of squares total, it is a good idea to use Formula 13.11 to compute the sum of squares total as a final check. This computation is relatively simple because you already computed the major terms of Formula 13.13 when you computed the sums of squares for between and within:

$$SS_{total} = \left[\Sigma X_1^2 + \Sigma X_2^2 + \cdots + \Sigma X_k^2 \right] - \left[\frac{(\Sigma X_1 + \Sigma X_1 + \cdots + \Sigma X_1)^2}{N_{total}} \right]$$

$$= \left[52 + 152 + 312 \right] - \left[\frac{(20 + 38 + 54)^2}{30} \right]$$

$$= 516 - \left[\frac{112^2}{30} \right] = 516 - \left[\frac{12,544}{30} \right]$$

$$= 516 - 418.133 = 97.867$$

Because the sum of squares between plus the sum of squares within equals the sums of squares total, you can check to see whether the previously computed values add to 97.867.

$$SS_{total} = SS_{bg} + SS_{wg} \tag{13.14}$$

$$= 57.867 + 40 = 97.867$$

This checks out. Now you can finish the analysis of variance by computing the mean squares and F.

The computation of the mean squares and F ratio are usually done with the aid of a **source table,** which displays the source of variation as well as the sums of squares, the degrees of freedom, the mean squares, the F ratio, and the p value. Table 13.5 is the source table for the pedal error data.

Here the number of degrees of freedom is computed using Formulas 13.7 and 13.8. The degrees of freedom between are equal to 2, and the degrees of freedom within are equal to 27. The result is a total number of degrees of freedom equal to 29. The sums of squares for between, within, and total are also listed here. The mean square is the sum of squares divided by the degrees of freedom, Formulas 13.9 and 13.10. You compute the values and enter them in the Mean Square column in the source table:

Table 13.5   Source Table for Analysis of Variance of Pedal Error Data

Source	Sums of Squares	df	Mean Square	F	p
Between	57.867	2	28.934	19.537	< .05
Within	40.000	27	1.481		
Total	97.867	29			

$$MS_{bg} = \frac{SS_{bg}}{df_{bg}} = \frac{57.867}{2} = 28.934$$

$$MS_{wg} = \frac{SS_{wg}}{df_{wg}} = \frac{40}{27} = 1.481$$

The F ratio is the mean square between divided by the mean square within.

$$F = \frac{MS_{bg}}{MS_{wg}} = \frac{28.934}{1.481} = 19.537$$

After comparing the computed F ratio to the critical value for the appropriate degrees of freedom, again, you have an F value that is significant, and you are able to reject the null hypothesis. Rejecting the null hypothesis means that there is less than a .05 probability that you have made a Type I error. This probability is referred to as the p value. In the source table, enter $< .05$ in the p column to indicate the p value. If the F ratio had been less than the critical value from Table F, then you would have failed to reject the null hypothesis, and the probability of making a Type I error would have been $> .05$.

> **Question:** There is significant F. This tells us that there is a significant difference among the groups in the experiment, but does it mean that all groups are significantly different from one another, that only two groups are different, or what?

The F test tells you that you can reject the null hypothesis. It indicates that there is some difference between at least two and possibly more of the groups, but it does not reveal where that difference lies. However, there are several tests that can do so. These are called **post-hoc tests.** *Post hoc* is Latin for "after the fact." These tests are only conducted after you have determined that you have an F ratio that is significant.

The post hoc test discussed next is called the **HSD,** which stands for honestly significant difference. The HSD is used to compare sample means when an analysis of variance leads to a significant F. It would not be used when the F ratio is not significantly large. It reveals how far apart the sample means must be in order to be significantly different. The HSD can be computed by using the following formula:

VISUAL SUMMARY

One-Way Analysis of Variance—Computational Formulas

Before You Begin: State H_0 and H_1.

Compute ΣX for each sample, ΣX^2 for each sample, n for each sample, and N_{total}.

Compute sums of squares:

SS_{bg} SS_{wg}

$$SS_{bg} = \left[\frac{(\Sigma X_1)^2}{n_1} + \frac{(\Sigma X_2)^2}{n_2} + \cdots + \frac{(\Sigma X_k)^2}{n_k} \right] - \left[\frac{(\Sigma X_1 + \Sigma X_2 + \cdots + \Sigma X_k)^2}{N_{total}} \right]$$

$$SS_{wg} = [\Sigma X_1^2 + \Sigma X_2^2 + \cdots + \Sigma X_k^2] - \left[\frac{(\Sigma X_1)^2}{n_1} + \frac{(\Sigma X_2)^2}{n_2} + \cdots + \frac{(\Sigma X_k)^2}{n_k} \right]$$

Compute degrees of freedom between:

$$df_{bg} = k - 1$$

Compute degrees of freedom within:

$$df_{wg} = (n_1 - 1) + (n_2 - 1) + \cdots + (n_k - 1)$$

Compute mean square between:

$$MS_{bg} = \frac{SS_{bg}}{df_{bg}}$$

Compute mean square within:

$$MS_{wg} = \frac{SS_{wg}}{df_{wg}}$$

Compute F ratio

$$F = \frac{MS_{bg}}{MS_{wg}}$$

$$\text{HSD} = q \cdot \sqrt{\frac{MS_{wg}}{n}} \qquad\qquad (13.15)$$

This formula contains two values that you have already used, MS_{wg} and n, and one value that you have not yet used, q. The mean square within groups, MS_{wg}, is 1.481, and n is the number of participants in each sample, 10. The value for q is the Studentized Range Statistic, which can be found in Table Q in Appendix A. To find the value for q, you must enter Table Q with the number of samples in the analysis of variance (k) and the number of degrees of freedom within (df_{wg}). This can be a problem because the table does not list all possible degrees of freedom. Thus, if your number of degrees of freedom is not listed, you must find the value in the table that is closest to yours without going over it. Try to find the q value in using the data from the pedal error experiment. Turn to Table Q, if you haven't done so already. In the pedal error problem, $k = 3$, so find the column for three groups. Now you need to look for the number of degrees of freedom, which is 27, but there is no listing for 27 degrees of freedom within groups. Therefore, you must find the value for the next lower number of degrees of freedom, which is 24. Look across to find q at an alpha level of .05, equal to 3.53. Having all the values you need, you can now compute the HSD:

$$\text{HSD} = q \cdot \sqrt{\frac{MS_{wg}}{n}} = 3.53 \cdot \sqrt{\frac{1.481}{10}} = 3.53 \cdot \sqrt{.1481} = 3.53 \cdot .385 = 1.359$$

This HSD value tells you that any difference between means of 1.359 pedal errors or greater is significant. Let's examine the differences between the means of the various pedal arrangement types. The means for types 1, 2, and 3, respectively, are 2 errors, 3.8 errors, and 5.4 errors. The difference between the means for types 1 and 2 is 1.8 errors, which is greater than the required 1.359. (Remember that you are only interested in the absolute value of the difference.) The difference between the means for types 1 and 3 is 3.4 errors, and the difference between types 2 and 3 is 1.6 errors, both of which are greater than the HSD of 1.359. Thus, in this experiment, all three pedal arrangements are significantly different from one another. Based on these results, automobile designers should choose pedal arrangement 1 because drivers who used it made significantly fewer errors.

Thus, an analysis of variance consists of three basic steps: (1) Compute the mean square between-groups, and the mean square within-groups. (2) Determine whether they are significantly different by computing the F ratio and comparing it to the critical value in Table F. (3) If the F ratio is significant, determine which sample(s) is significantly different from the others by conducting a post-hoc test, such as the HSD test.

Concept Quiz

Berman and Cutler (1996) studied the effects of inconsistencies in eyewitness testimony on the decisions of mock jurors. Participants were randomly assigned to watch one of four different versions of a videotaped court trial. Three of the versions had some form of inconsistency in the testimony. They found that jurors were significantly less likely to convict the defendant if exposed to any of the three conditions of inconsistent testimony.

1. Each mean square has two parts: the _____ and the

   _____.

2. Sum of squares total equals _____ plus _____.

3. In this study, the null hypothesis was _____, indicating a significant difference between the means in at least _____ of the experimental groups.

4. Only after rejecting the null hypothesis can researchers conduct a _____ to determine which condition means were significantly different.

5. The score that reveals how far apart the sample means must be in order for them to be significantly different is the _____.

6. Describe how you find q.

7. If the HSD value is 1.46, which of the condition means listed here significantly differ? Condition A = 4.21; Condition B = 5.67; Condition C = 3.52; Condition D = 4.99

Answers

1. sum of squares; degrees of freedom
2. sum of squares between; sum of squares within
3. rejected; two
4. post-hoc test
5. HSD
6. You look up q in Table Q in Appendix A using degrees of freedom within and k.
7. Conditions B and C; Conditions D and C

Summary

One-way analysis of variance is used when the research design involves one independent variable with three or more levels. The one-way analysis of variance tests the null hypothesis, which proposes that all the independent samples come from the same population. To conduct a one-way analysis of variance, you must first compute two different mean squares and then compute an F ratio. Once the F ratio is computed, you then use the degrees of freedom to find the critical value in Table F. If your computed F ratio is greater than the critical value from Table F, you can reject the null hypothesis. Once the null hypothesis is rejected, you can use a post-hoc test, the HSD, to determine which of the groups are significantly different from one another.

Key Terms

one-way analysis of variance

mean square (MS)

mean square within groups (MS_{wg})

mean square between groups (MS_{bg})

F ratio

F test

degrees of freedom between groups (df_{bg})

degrees of freedom within groups (df_{wg})

sum of squares between groups (SS_{bg})

sum of squares within groups (SS_{wg})

sum of squares total (SS_{total})

source table

post-hoc tests

HSD

Formulas

$$MS_{wg} = \frac{\Sigma(X_1 - \overline{X}_1)^2 + \Sigma(X_2 - \overline{X}_2)^2 + \Sigma(X_3 - \overline{X}_3)^2 + \cdots + \Sigma(X_k - \overline{X}_k)^2}{(n_1 - 1) + (n_2 - 1) + (n_3 - 1) + \cdots + (n_k - 1)} \tag{13.1}$$

$$\sigma^2 = n \cdot \sigma_{\overline{X}}^2 \tag{13.2}$$

$$MS_{bg} = \frac{n_1(\overline{X}_1 - \overline{\overline{X}})^2 + n_2(\overline{X}_2 - \overline{\overline{X}})^2 + n_3(\overline{X}_3 - \overline{\overline{X}})^2 + \cdots + n_k(\overline{X}_k - \overline{\overline{X}})^2}{k - 1} \tag{13.3}$$

$$\overline{\overline{X}} = \frac{\Sigma\overline{X}}{k} = \frac{\overline{X}_1 + \overline{X}_2 + \overline{X}_3 + \cdots + \overline{X}_k}{k} \tag{13.4}$$

$$\overline{\overline{X}} = \frac{\Sigma(\Sigma X)}{N_{total}} = \frac{\Sigma X_1 + \Sigma X_2 + \Sigma X_3 + \cdots + \Sigma X_k}{N_{total}} \tag{13.5}$$

$$F = \frac{MS_{bg}}{MS_{wg}} \tag{13.6}$$

$$df_{bg} = k - 1 \tag{13.7}$$

$$df_{wg} = (n_1 - 1) + (n_2 - 1) + (n_3 - 1) + \cdots + (n_k - 1) \tag{13.8}$$

$$MS_{bg} = \frac{SS_{bg}}{df_{bg}} \tag{13.9}$$

$$MS_{wg} = \frac{SS_{wg}}{df_{wg}} \tag{13.10}$$

$$SS_{bg} = \left[\frac{(\Sigma X_1)^2}{n_1} + \frac{(\Sigma X_2)^2}{n_2} + \cdots + \frac{(\Sigma X_k)^2}{n_k}\right] - \left[\frac{(\Sigma X_1 + \Sigma X_1 + \cdots + \Sigma X_1)^2}{N_{total}}\right] \tag{13.11}$$

$$SS_{wg} = \left[\Sigma X_1^2 + \Sigma X_2^2 + \cdots + \Sigma X_k^2\right] - \left[\frac{(\Sigma X_1)^2}{n_1} + \frac{(\Sigma X_2)^2}{n_2} + \cdots + \frac{(\Sigma X_k)^2}{n_k}\right] \qquad (13.12)$$

$$SS_{total} = \left[\Sigma X_1^2 + \Sigma X_2^2 + \cdots + \Sigma X_k^2\right] - \left[\frac{(\Sigma X_1 + \Sigma X_1 + \cdots + \Sigma X_1)^2}{N_{total}}\right] \qquad (13.13)$$

$$SS_{total} = SS_{bg} + SS_{wg} \qquad (13.14)$$

$$HSD = q \cdot \sqrt{\frac{MS_{wg}}{n}} \qquad (13.15)$$

Problems

All problems for Chapter 13 are hypothetical experiments that must be analyzed using one-way analysis of variance. For each problem, generate a null hypothesis and a research hypothesis and then create a source table that includes the following:

Source	Sums of Squares	df	Mean Square	F	p
Between	SS_{bg}	df_{bg}	MS_{bg}	F	> or < .05
Within	SS_{wg}	df_{wg}	MS_{wg}		
Total	SS_{total}	df_{total}			

Once you have created the source table, refer to Table F in Appendix A and find the critical value for the appropriate degrees of freedom and determine whether the F ratio is significant. If the F ratio is significantly large for you to reject the null hypothesis, then compute an HSD to determine which levels of the independent variable are significantly different from one another and state your conclusions in a sentence or two.

1. Much of an academic psychologist's professional success is based on his or her ability to conduct consequential research and publish that research. Suppose you, as a new assistant professor, have noticed that papers submitted with multiple authors are more likely to be accepted for publication than papers with only one author. You are also aware that one indicator of whether a paper will be published is the number of negative comments received when the paper is reviewed by the editors of the journal. Changing only the number of authors on the paper, you submit the same paper for publication to several journals. Your independent variable is the number of authors, and your dependent variable is the number of negative comments received. The numbers of negative comments are listed in the table.

Number of Authors			
1	2	3	4
16	24	13	15
23	20	9	5
28	16	17	19
23	14	19	17

2. The human nervous system is extremely sensitive to changes in the environment. Stimuli that remain the same do not demand the same amount of attention as those that are new. You are a human factors psychologist working for a large automobile manufacturer. You have been assigned the

task of determining what type of hot-engine warning system will be used on the next generation of small pickup trucks. The designers have given you three alternative systems: (a) a traditional temperature gauge that reads cold to the left, normal in the middle, and hot to the right; (b) a hot-engine warning light that flashes when the engine is about to overheat; and (c) a temperature gauge similar to (a), except that the entire gauge flashes on and off when the engine is about to overheat. You decide to test these three designs by having three separate groups of participants use the various warning systems in a driving simulator. The independent variable in this experiment is the type of warning system, and the dependent variable is the number of seconds it takes a driver to respond to the warning that the engine is about to overheat. The reaction times are given in the table.

Gauge	Flashing Light	Flashing Gauge
30	10	5
22	15	10
26	10	15
23	20	5

3. Scrooge McDuck has turned philanthropist and is itching to award scholarship money to deserving students. He feels that students who have full scholarships should get higher grades because they need to work only a minimum number of hours to support themselves and should therefore have abundant time to study. He has some doubts about his theory, however, and he doesn't want to part with his money if his hypothesis is false, so he hires you to conduct some research on the topic. You randomly assign 15 scholarship applicants to one of the following conditions: full scholarship, partial

scholarship, and no scholarship. At the end of 1 year, you compute the grade point average for each student. Using the grade point averages in the table, determine whether there is a difference between the different scholarship groups.

Full Scholarship	Partial Scholarship	No Scholarship
2.9	3.0	3.2
3.7	3.3	2.9
1.7	2.2	3.4
2.5	3.8	2.0
2.9	2.2	1.8

4. As a psychologist who works with people who have Down's syndrome, you design a study intended to determine which rewards are most effective for training your patients. You select four different groups of patients and record the number of days it takes to teach them the same task, with each group receiving one of four types of rewards: Reward A, Reward B, Reward C, and Reward D. The numbers of days are given in the table.

Reward A	Reward B	Reward C	Reward D
3	6	9	12
5	7	10	13
6	9	15	15
2	7	12	18
1	11	11	15
2	6	10	13

5. A good friend of yours is a teacher of medical doctors. Through her experience, she has come to feel that doctors in various specialties differ in their moral and ethical standards. She decides to test this hypothesis using some of her interns as participants. She randomly assigns them to one of three

specialties for a 3-month rotation, and at the end of that rotation she gives them a test that measures moral development. The moral development test returns a score on a 100-point scale, where a high score represents high moral development and a low score represents low moral development. The three different specialties are orthopedics (bones and joints), pediatrics (children), and oncology (cancer). The intern's scores are shown in the table.

Orthopedics	Pediatrics	Oncology
77	63	54
84	93	97
66	97	76
44	83	65
59	45	72
32	88	68
28	74	54

6. You are interested in the processes involved in solving anagrams. An anagram is a word with the letters *mdlcsarbe* (*scrambled*). You believe that an anagram is easier to solve if the word is familiar to the participant. Because of this, you choose four five-letter words that differ in familiarity and ask three different sets of participants to solve the anagrams. The dependent variable in this search project (with the values listed in the table) is the time in seconds for each participant to solve the anagram.

Very Familiar	Familiar	Not Very Familiar	Not Familiar
37	47	69	94
30	56	67	87
10	43	77	88
21	39	82	75
17	30	92	93
25	54	66	79

7. You are trying to determine whether there is a difference between four biofeedback methods for lowering blood pressure. You teach participants one of the methods and then measure the change in their blood pressure. The table values for decreases in blood pressure are for 20 participants who used only one of the four methods.

Method A	Method B	Method C	Method D
12	22	17	13
5	19	7	0
2	16	4	10
11	23	12	7
13	25	8	9

8. Everybody has taste preferences. Most people claim to be able to tell the difference between "their" brand and other nonpreferred brands. Suppose you put your taste buds to the test to see whether you can taste the difference between various brands of ice cream. Ice cream is usually sold as store-brand, premium, or super-premium, and the difference is supposed to be the quality of the ingredients. You buy several gallons of vanilla ice cream, place small scoops into plain paper cups, and then ask three different groups of people to rate the tastes of the ice cream using an interval rating scale from 1 (bad) to 7 (great). The data are in the table.

Store-Brand	Premium	Super-Premium
7	3	5
4	2	7
5	6	3
2	5	5
3	6	2

9. A psychologist interested in studying the effectiveness of subliminal perception (the

perception of a stimulus presented below threshold) asked participants to view a screen and identify a group of five letters flashed on it. Three separate groups were composed of 10 participants each: one was presented letters that were flashed at a rate above the participants' threshold, another was presented letters flashed at their threshold, and another was presented letters below their threshold. The dependent variable, given in the table, was the percentage of letters correctly identified.

Above Threshold	At Threshold	Below Threshold
90	50	20
95	55	25
85	55	15
90	45	20
80	40	20
90	45	25
85	50	20
90	55	15
80	50	20
95	45	20

10. The data in the accompanying table were gathered from 24 participants in an experiment on memory comparing short-term memory capacity for three different types of items: words, nonwords, and numbers.

Words	Nonwords	Numbers
8	5	6
9	4	6
7	5	5
10	6	7
9	3	5
8	5	6
8	4	7
7	3	7

11. A physiological psychologist knows that the blood level of a particular hormone increases when an animal is under stress. He decides to use the blood level of this hormone as a measure of stress in four situations: (a) having the animal swim in an ice water bath for 30 seconds, (b) administering a 5-second electric shock to the animal's feet, (c) dropping the animal from a height of 10 feet into a net, or (d) a control condition where the animal receives no stressor. Using the hormone blood levels from the table, use an analysis of variance to test whether there is a difference between any of the above stressful conditions.

Swimming	Shock	Drop	Control
265	260	265	250
266	271	267	245
267	268	266	250
268	266	265	252
272	269	268	253

12. Three separate groups of randomly assigned participants were asked to list the number of words that they recognized from a 100-word list spoken by a man, a woman, or a computer. Use the numbers of words listed in the table to conduct an analysis of variance.

Man	Woman	Computer
97	99	86
96	94	80
93	92	88
94	97	80
93	92	81
92	94	80
95	96	82
95	96	87
93	94	79

Problems From the Literature

The following problems refer to actual results from research studies that are cited at the end of the chapter. However, the data used to generate the problem sets are hypothetical. Unless stated otherwise, use the .05 significance level for all analyses.

13. Because traditional approaches to prevent accidents on the job usually fail to improve workers' safety beyond a certain level, Zohar (2000) conducted a study to see whether safety programs thought to originate either in managerial and supervisory levels might impact both workers' perceptions of the safety climate on the job and predict future accidents. Safety climate was measured in terms of how hurried or rushed workers felt with work, how physically demanding the jobs were, how likely they believed accidents would occur, and the hazard levels of the jobs. The results revealed that safety climate perceptions were predictive of minor accidents requiring medical attention. Suppose you were hired to evaluate the effectiveness of a safety awareness program in three different plant locations of a large corporation. The safety awareness program varied between locations in that employees in one location perceived the safety program was implemented by top-level management, those in another location perceived it was implemented by immediate supervisors, and the third location did not know the source of the safety program (control). The dependent variable was the number of accidents per month for the year. The results of the study are shown here. Use the data to solve the following problems.

Top-Level Management	Immediate Supervisors	Control
15	8	11
9	5	8
6	7	8
11	8	9
7	3	5
8	2	5
9	6	5
6	5	5
4	0	2
7	1	4
3	0	2
5	1	1

a. Generate a null hypothesis and a research hypothesis.
b. Perform the appropriate statistical test.
c. Generate the source table.
d. Refer to Table F in Appendix A and find the critical value for the appropriate degrees of freedom, and determine whether the F ratio is significant.
e. If the F ratio is significantly large for you to reject the null hypothesis, then perform the necessary post-hoc analysis.
f. Briefly interpret the results of this study relative to the research question. Be sure to include the means and standard deviations for each condition in the interpretation.

14. Based on the notion that thoughts of one's death would influence participants' desires to meet internalized (cultural) standards of self-worth, Goldenberg, McCoy, Pyszcyzynski, Greenberg, and Solomon (2000) examined the impact of reminders of death on self-esteem striving in the form of identification with one's body, interest in sex, and appearance monitoring. Among their findings, it was demonstrated that reminders of mortality increased people's striving for self-esteem in that participants with high

body esteem had increased identification with their physical body. Moreover, mortality salience also increased the appeal of physical sex for those participants with high body esteem. Participants with low body esteem decreased their appearance monitoring under conditions of mortality salience. Thus, it seems that when individuals are faced with mortality, they turn to behaviors that enhance self-esteem to buffer against this threat. Suppose a researcher conducted a study to see whether this finding might extend to other behaviors. The researcher recruited 36 women to participate in the study and asked each to complete a body esteem questionnaire and to indicate the number of times she engaged in sexual intercourse during the past 3-month period. The researcher separated the participants into three groups based on body esteem scores: high, medium, and low. It was predicted that those with the highest body esteem would have the highest frequency of sexual intercourse in the past 3 months compared to those with medium or low body esteem. Data from this study are listed here. Use this information to solve the following problems.

High Body Esteem	Medium Body Esteem	Low Body Esteem
30	22	18
24	19	21
29	14	16
65	42	36
70	27	2
21	18	14
15	37	16
54	7	28
33	20	7
19	13	4
60	2	15
27	39	1

a. Generate a null hypothesis and a research hypothesis.
b. Perform the appropriate statistical test.
c. Generate the source table.
d. Refer to Table F in Appendix A and find the critical value for the appropriate degrees of freedom, and determine whether the F ratio is significant.
e. If the F ratio is significantly large for you to reject the null hypothesis, then perform the necessary post-hoc analysis.
f. Briefly interpret the results of this study relative to the research question. Be sure to include the means and standard deviations for each condition in the interpretation.
g. Can researchers say the results of this study were caused by the body esteem of women living in high-crime areas? Explain why or why not.

15. Explain why the statistical results for Problems 13 and 14 should not be interpreted in causal terms.

16. Berman and Cutler (1996) looked at four different factors relative to eyewitness testimony to see how they might impact mock jurors' decisions. In this study, participants were randomly assigned to condition and viewed one of four versions of a videotaped trial. The key evidence against the defendant was the eyewitness testimony. The four versions differed in the types of inconsistent statements given by the eyewitness: (1) consistent testimony, (2) information given on the stand but not during the pretrial investigation, (3) contradictions between on-the-stand and pretrial statements, and (4) contradictions made on the stand. They found that when participants were exposed to any form of inconsistent testimony, the jurors were less likely to convict the defendant. Imagine that another researcher attempts to replicate this study and recruits

Consistent Testimony	Information Given on the Stand and Not Pretrial	Contradictions Between On-Stand and Pretrial Statements	Contradictions On Stand Only
6	4	3	5
4	4	4	4
5	3	2	4
6	2	1	4
4	4	2	2
7	3	3	1
6	2	4	5
7	4	1	3
5	3	1	2
4	6	3	4

40 participants. The researcher randomly assigns them to view one of the same four versions of a videotaped trial used by Berman and Cutler and then asks them to evaluate the level of the defendant's guilt on a 1 (not guilty) to 7 (guilty) scale. Data are shown here. Use this information to solve the following problems.

a. Generate a null hypothesis and a research hypothesis.

b. Perform the appropriate statistical test.

c. Generate the source table.

d. Refer to Table F in Appendix A and find the critical value for the appropriate

degrees of freedom, and determine whether the F ratio is significant.

e. If the F ratio is significantly large for you to reject the null hypothesis, then perform the necessary post-hoc analysis.

f. Briefly interpret the results of this study relative to the research question. Be sure to include the means and standard deviations for each condition in the interpretation.

g. Can researchers say the results of this study were caused by the differences in the consistency of the eyewitness testimony? Explain why or why not.

References

Berman, G. L., & Cutler, B. L. (1996). Effects of inconsistencies in eyewitness testimony on mock-juror decision-making. *Journal of Applied Psychology, 81,* 170–177.

Clark, D. M., Salkovskis, P. M., Hackmann, A., Wells, A., Ludgate, J., & Gelder, M. (1999). Brief cognitive therapy for panic disorder: A randomized controlled trial. *Journal of Consulting and Clinical Psychology, 67,* 583–589.

Goldenberg, J. L., McCoy, S. K., Pyszczynski, T., Greenberg, J., & Solomon, S. (2000). The body as a source of self-esteem: The effect of mortality salience on identification with one's body, interest in sex, and appearance monitoring. *Journal of Personality and Social Psychology, 79,* 118–130.

Vernoy, M. W., & Tomerlin, J. (1989). Pedal error and misperceived center line in eight different automobiles. *Human Factors, 31,* 369–375.

Zohar, D. (2000). A group-level model of safety climate. Testing the effect of group climate on microaccidents in manufacturing jobs. *Journal of Applied Psychology, 85,* 587–596.

14

Two-Way Analysis of Variance

- Main Effects
- Interaction
- Computation of Sums of Squares for Two-Way Analysis of Variance
- Computation of Degrees of Freedom for Two-Way Analysis of Variance
- Computation of the Mean Squares for Two-Way Analysis of Variance

- Computation of the *F* Ratios for Two-Way Analysis of Variance
  VISUAL SUMMARY: Two-Way Analysis of Variance
- Significance of the Main Effects
- Significance of the Interaction

- Summary
- Key Terms
- Formulas
- Problems
  Problems From the Literature
- References

You're late. You miscalculated the time it would take to drive to the university, and now you're going to be late for your final exam. You're going as fast as you dare, but you keep getting stuck behind slow trucks and hitting red lights, and now railroad crossing signals are flashing up ahead. Maybe you can beat the train across the tracks. You look for the train. You see it, but it seems pretty far away and it looks like it's going slowly. Should you chance it? You're late, and you have to take the final to pass the course. You go for it! You jam the accelerator to the floor and whiz toward the tracks, but when you look again, you see that *the train is on top of you!* How could you have made such a gross misjudgment?

Such miscalculations have cost people their lives. Researcher Herschel Leibowitz (1985) studied the perceptual errors people make in depth and motion detection—errors that lead to car–train accidents such as the imminent one just described. After careful study, Leibowitz found that people perceive large objects like locomotives as moving more slowly than smaller ones and that when people move their heads and eyes to track objects, they tend to perceive these objects as moving more slowly than when they keep their heads and eyes still. The combination of these factors may be at least partially responsible for car–train collisions. (If you are interested in other research regarding the behavior of motorists at railroad crossings, see Meeker, Fox, & Weber, 1997; Raslear, 1996; Tenkink & van der Horst, 1990; Witte & Donohue, 2000.)

Ever since psychology has been a science, psychologists have been interested in perception—the process of interpreting information sent from the sense organs to the brain. The perception of such things as sound, pain, taste, and smell has been the subject of thousands of psychological experiments. The study of visual perception has been especially alluring, particularly the perception of depth. How well people perceive depth and distance is of extreme importance. As in the preceding example, drivers have to know how far away approaching vehicles are and how fast they are going so that they can avoid crashes. Snack bar servers have to know how close the soda machine spout is or they will have trouble refilling your cup. Baseball players have to know the distance to first base so that they can throw out the batter.

Countless factors affect visual depth perception. One factor is whether you use one eye or both. Most people guess correctly that depth perception is far better with two eyes open than one. This is because there are depth cues available to us when we use both eyes that are not available when we use only one. But can you estimate distances more accurately when you move your head or when you keep your head still? The obvious answer is that keeping your head stationary allows you to see sharper images and thereby estimate distances more accurately. However, this answer overlooks the fact that the relative motion of objects can be an important cue to their distance, as you can see when riding in a moving car. As you move, near objects appear to pass you at a faster rate than more distant objects. Therefore, moving your head may add an additional distance cue that can enhance the accuracy of your perception of depth.

Suppose you survived your near-collision with the train and you decide to enlist the aid of a psychology professor in studying some of the factors that led to your perceptual error. She designs an experiment in depth and motion perception using the two independent variables mentioned earlier: number of eyes open and movement/nonmovement of head. The first independent variable, number of eyes open, has two levels—one or two eyes. (You decide not to study the zero eyes condition for obvious reasons.) The second independent variable, head motion, has three levels—no motion, slow motion, and moderate motion. You measure the accuracy of each participant's depth perception by requiring him or her to align two small vertical rods from a distance of 6 meters. The dependent variable, then, is the distance (in millimeters) between the two rods.

In the previous two chapters, you saw how to analyze data from studies that had multiple levels of one independent variable. In this chapter, you will see how to analyze data from studies involving two independent variables, each having two or more levels. The study in the current example has two independent variables, one with two levels (one eye or two eyes open) and another with three levels (type of head motion). Now, you *could* separate the problem into two experiments. The first one could investigate the perception of depth using either one eye or two eyes open, and because it would involve one independent variable with only two levels, you could use a *t* test to analyze the data. The second experiment could investigate differences in perceived depth as a result of head motion, and because this would involve one independent variable with three different levels, you could use a one-way analysis of variance to analyze the data. This approach is certainly feasible and reasonable, but it is more intriguing, as well as easier, to investigate the two independent variables in the same experiment. That way, you can explore the effects of each independent variable on the dependent variable, as well as any effects of the *combination* of the two independent variables on the dependent variable.

An experiment with two or more independent variables is called a **factorial experiment.** The simplest of these is a two-way factorial in which there are only two independent variables (a three-way factorial design would be used when there are three independent variables, and so on). In this chapter, only the analysis of two-way factorial experiments is discussed.

The design of a factorial experiment is represented in a matrix, with the first independent variable displayed in the columns and the second independent variable displayed in the rows. The matrix for the depth perception experiment is illustrated in Table 14.1. Because there are two levels of the first independent variable and three levels of the second, the design is known as a two-by-three (2×3) factorial. This type of completely randomized factorial design was discussed in Chapter 11. In such an experiment, each person participates in only one level of the first independent variable and in only one level of the second independent variable. As you can see in Table 14.1, there are six (2×3) separate independent conditions or cells in this experiment.

If you want to have five people participate in each cell, you will need a total of 30 participants. Table 14.2 displays the information gathered from our sample

Table 14.1   The Design of the Depth Perception Experiment

Table 14.2   Data From the Depth Perception Experiment

	Independent Variable 1		
	One Eye Open	Two Eyes Open	
	X	X	
	8	5	
	10	4	
No Head Movement	8	1	$\overline{X}_{row} = 6$
	6	2	
	13	3	
	$\Sigma X = 45$	$\Sigma X = 15$	
	$\overline{X}_{cell} = 9$	$\overline{X}_{cell} = 3$	
	X	X	
	4	4	
	6	1	
Slow Head Movement	3	2	$\overline{X}_{row} = 3.7$
	5	3	
	7	2	
	$\Sigma X = 25$	$\Sigma X = 12$	
	$\overline{X}_{cell} = 5$	$\overline{X}_{cell} = 2.4$	
	X	X	
	2	3	
	2	0	
Moderate Head Movement	3	3	$\overline{X}_{row} = 2.7$
	4	2	
	6	2	
	$\Sigma X = 17$	$\Sigma X = 10$	
	$\overline{X}_{cell} = 3.4$	$\overline{X}_{cell} = 2$	
	$\overline{X}_{col} = 5.8$	$\overline{X}_{col} = 2.467$	

Independent Variable 2

experiment. In addition to the data from the individual participants, the table includes the individual cell means (the means of all the scores within each cell), the column means (the mean of each column), and the row means (the mean of each row). The row and column means give an indication of the effects of the two independent variables (the main effects), as well as the interaction between the two independent variables. To analyze these data, you need to conduct a two-way analysis of variance.

Main Effects

As you may recall, in a one-way analysis of variance, the total variance in the collected data is separated into two different variance estimates, between groups and within groups, which are compared in the F ratio. In a two-way analysis of variance, the between groups variance is further partitioned into three separate variance estimates, two of which are known as the *main effects* and the other as the *interaction*. The effect of one independent variable on the dependent variable is called a **main effect.** In the depth perception experiment, there are two independent variables and therefore two main effects: (1) the effect of the number of eyes open on the perception of depth (as measured by the distance between the vertical rods), and (2) the effect of the type of head motion on the perception of depth. The main effect for number of eyes open is represented by the columns in Table 14.2. When the mean for the one-eye-open column (5.8-mm error) is compared to the mean for the two-eyes-open column (2.467-mm error), it seems obvious that participants are more accurate with two eyes open than with one. The other main effect, type of head motion, is represented by the rows in Table 14.2. When the means for no head motion (6 mm error), slow head motion (3.7 mm error), and moderate head motion (3.7 mm error) are compared, there is a systematic difference.

By this point in your study of statistics, you should know that even though it looks obvious from the data that there are differences among the samples, you don't know whether the differences are due to chance or whether each of the samples in each main effect came from a different population. Thus, it is necessary to test one null hypothesis for each of the main effects (the rows and the columns). The null hypothesis for the columns is

$$H_{0_{col}} : \mu_{col_1} = \mu_{col_2} = \cdots = \mu_{col_k}$$

The null hypothesis for the rows is

$$H_{0_{row}} : \mu_{row_1} = \mu_{row_2} = \cdots = \mu_{row_k}$$

Here are the corresponding research hypotheses:

$H_{1_{col}}$:   At least one of the samples represented by the columns comes from a different population distribution than the others.

$H_{1_{row}}$:   At least one of the samples represented by the rows comes from a different population distribution than the others.

In the depth perception example, the research hypothesis for the columns states that there is a difference in the accuracy of depth perception when a participant views the display with one eye instead of two eyes. The research hypothesis for the rows states that the type of head motion—none, slow, or moderate—affects the participants' perception of depth. After running an experiment to test these hypotheses, you must conduct a two-way analysis of variance to analyze the results. First, however, is a little more about the interaction.

Interaction

In a two-way factorial analysis of variance, the **interaction** is the effect of the *combination* of the two independent variables on the dependent variable. Graphing the cell means from the experiment (see Figure 14.1) will help you understand what is meant by the interaction. In the graph of an interaction, the dependent variable is always represented along the *Y* axis, and in most cases the independent variable with the greatest number of levels is represented along the *X* axis. Separate lines are used to represent different levels of the other independent variable.

To decipher Figure 14.1, you need some additional explanation. To begin with, as mentioned, the dependent variable (amount of error, in millimeters) is represented along the *Y* axis, whereas the independent variable with the most levels (degree of motion) is represented along the *X* axis. The independent variable with the fewest levels (number of eyes open) is represented by separate lines on the graph. You can see from Figure 14.1 that the two lines have different slopes. Although both lines slope down to the right, the line for one eye open has a much steeper slope than the line for two eyes open. *Whenever there is an interaction,* the lines on this type of graph have different slopes, as is in Figure 14.2. The separation between the lines is of no consequence; the only significant factor is the difference in the slopes of the two lines. If there is *no interaction,* as in Figures 14.3 and 14.4, the lines are parallel at all points. (When one line goes up, the other also goes up, and when one line goes down, the other also goes down.)

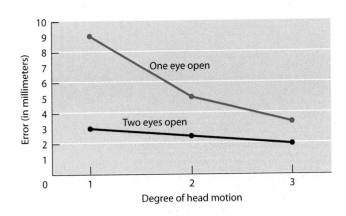

Figure 14.1
A graph of the cell means from the depth perception experiment illustrates the interaction.

Figure 14.2
Intersecting lines with different slopes indicate an interaction between the two independent variables.

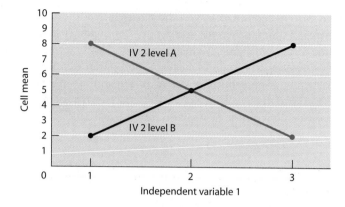

Figure 14.3
These parallel lines indicate that there is no interaction between the two independent variables.

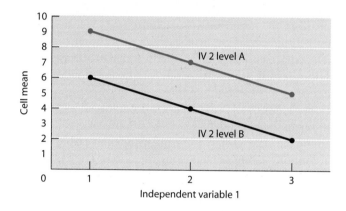

Figure 14.4
These nonintersecting lines indicate that there is no interaction between the two independent variables.

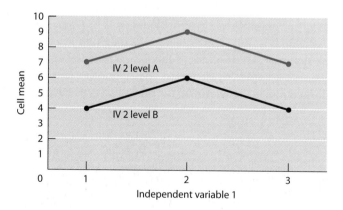

When an interaction exists, it is often more interesting than any of the main effects. For instance, look at Figure 14.1. It appears that the head motion drastically reduced the error rate in the one-eye-open condition but had very little effect on the errors made when participants had two eyes open. Thus, even though the main effect of head motion may be significant, the interaction effect indicates that head motion is most effective when people use only one eye. Remember: It is the pattern of the responses that is important when we investigate interaction. Parallel lines indicate no interaction, whereas nonparallel or intersecting lines usually indicate an interaction.

> **Question:** Does that mean, then, that if the cell means are graphed and even a slight difference in the slopes is found, there is a significant interaction?

Not necessarily. Slight differences in the slopes could be due to chance variability between the participants in the different conditions. Even though you notice an apparent interaction on the graph, you must conduct a two-way analysis of variance to know whether the interaction is significant. Below are the hypotheses for the interaction. (Note that the notation used for the interaction is $r \times c$, which means row by column interaction.):

$H_{0_{r \times c}}$: The effect of one independent variable on the dependent variable is unaffected by the other independent variable(s).

$H_{1_{r \times c}}$: The effect of one independent variable on the dependent variable is affected by the other independent variable(s).

In the depth perception experiment, the research hypothesis for the interaction states that the interaction between the number of eyes and the type of head motion will affect the subjects' perception of depth. Basically, this means that the effect of head motion depends on the number of eyes used to view the display. The rejection of the null hypothesis by the two-way analysis of variance will not *explain* the interaction effects; it will only confirm that the interaction is significant. You, as the experimenter, are responsible for the explanation of any interaction effects.

Concept Quiz

What information do we get from a handshake? In Chaplin, Phillips, Brown, Clanton, and Stein's (2000) experiment, participants filled out personality questionnaires and had their hands shaken twice by trained men and women coders. Coders recorded the characteristics of the handshake in terms of grip strength, vigor, eye contact, and so on, and their first impression of the participant. Among their findings: Firm handshakes were evaluated more positively in first impressions and were more frequent for male participants. A firm handshake was also related positively to extraversion and emotional expressiveness and negatively to shyness and neuroticism among both male and female participants. Suppose Dr. Vickman wanted to see whether the length of handshake time differed between gender (male versus female) depending on the gender of the other person (male versus female). Dr. Vickman assigns each participant to be in only one of four possible conditions. If the participant is female, she only shakes hands with one female or with one male. If the participant is male, he only shakes hands with one female or with one male.

1. Dr. Vickman's study is called a _____ design.

2. A main effect is the effect of _____ on the dependent variable, and an interaction is the effect of _____ on the dependent variable.

3. In Vickman's proposed study, how many main effects and interactions are possible?

4. In a two-way analysis of variance, the between-groups variance estimate is partitioned into three separate variance estimates. These are known as the _____ and the _____.

5. In a two-way analysis of variance, the main effects are represented by the _____ and the _____.

6. In Vickman's study, if gender of participant (male versus female) is the *row* independent variable, the research hypothesis states that at least _____ of the samples represented by the rows comes from a different population distribution.

7. If gender of the other person (male versus female) is the *column* independent variable, the research hypothesis for the columns states that at least _____ of the samples represented by the columns comes from a different population distribution.

8. When interactions are graphed, which means are used? Suppose there were three levels of one independent variable and two levels of the other independent variable. Which would be graphed on the *X* axis?

9. When lines representing a significant interaction are graphed, their slopes are _____.

10. Lines on a graph that represent no interaction are _____.

Answers

1. 2 × 2 factorial
2. one independent variable; a combination of two independent variables
3. two main effects; one interaction
4. main effects; interaction
5. rows; columns
6. one
7. one
8. the cell means for each level of the independent variables
   are used; the three levels of the first independent variable would be graphed on the *X* axis
9. different
10. parallel

Computation of Sums of Squares for Two-Way Analysis of Variance

In a two-way analysis of variance, you are testing two main effects and the interaction, so you need to compute four sums of squares—columns, rows, interaction, and within—plus the total sum of squares, along with the corresponding degrees of freedom, mean squares, and F ratios. The values needed for these computations are shown in a source table, Table 14.3. The formulas for the sum of squares within groups (SS_{wg}) and the sum of squares total (SS_{total}) are the same as the computational formulas used in a one-way analysis of variance. They are slightly rewritten because we now have rows (no, slow, or moderate head motion), columns (one or two eyes open), and cells rather than only different samples. Because in a two-way analysis of variance the between-groups sum of squares (SS_{bg}) has been partitioned into rows, columns, and interaction, the formulas for these sum of squares values are new. These new sums of squares and the resulting mean squares represent the amount of variance that is due only to the manipulation of the two different independent variables, as well as the amount of variance that is due only to the interaction of the two independent variables.

Before looking at the formulas, it is important to take time out to clarify some new notation. As you can see in Table 14.3, the sum of squares total is still represented by SS_{total} and the sum of squares within groups by SS_{wg}. The sum of squares for rows is represented by SS_r, the sum of squares for columns is represented by SS_c, and the sum of squares for the interaction is represented by $SS_{r \times c}$. All the formulas used to compute these values require some sum of scores. The following is a list of the summation notation that is used in those formulas:

$\Sigma\Sigma X^2$ = the sum of the sums of the X^2 for all the cells in the entire analysis. You square each score, add up the scores in each cell, and then add all the cells together. In the depth perception example, the result is 752 (see Table 14.4).

$\Sigma\Sigma X$ = the sum of the sum of the X values for all cells in the entire analysis. You add up all the scores in each cell and then add

Table 14.3 Source Table for Two-Way Factorial Analysis of Variance

Source of Variation	Sum of Squares	Degrees of Freedom	Mean Square	F
Rows	SS_r	df_r	MS_r	F_r
Columns	SS_c	df_c	MS_c	F_c
Interaction	$SS_{r \times c}$	$df_{r \times c}$	$MS_{r \times c}$	$F_{r \times c}$
Within	SS_{wg}	df_{wg}	MS_{wg}	
Total	SS_{total}	df_{total}		

up all the cells in the analysis. In the depth perception example, the result is 124 (see Table 14.4).

$\Sigma(\Sigma X_{cell})^2$ = the sum of the square of the sum of the X values for each cell. You compute the sum of the scores within each cell, square that value, and then add up these squared values from all the cells. In the depth perception example, the values are $45^2 + 15^2 + 25^2 + 12^2 + 17^2 + 10^2$ (see Table 14.4).

$\Sigma(\Sigma X_{row})^2$ = the sum of the square of the sum of the X values for each row. You compute the sum of the scores within each row, square that value, and then add up these squared values for all the rows. In the depth perception example, the values are $60^2 + 37^2 + 27^2$ (see Table 14.4).

$\Sigma(\Sigma X_{col})^2$ = the sum of the square of the sum of the X values for each column. You compute the sum of the scores within each column, square that value, and then add up these squared values for all the columns. In the depth perception example, the values are $87^2 + 37^2$ (see Table 14.4).

There are also several types of Ns.

N_{total} = the total number of scores in all the samples combined. In the depth perception experiment, there are a total of 30 scores (see Table 14.4).

n_{cell} = the number of scores in an individual cell. In the depth perception experiment, there are 5 scores per cell (see Table 14.4).

n_{row} = the number of scores in each row. In the depth perception experiment, there are 10 scores in each row (see Table 14.4).

n_{col} = the number of scores in each column. In the depth perception experiment, there are 15 scores in each column (see Table 14.4).

Here are the formulas needed to calculate the various sums of squares. The formula for sum of squares total for a two-way analysis of variance is

$$SS_{total} = \Sigma\Sigma X^2 - \frac{(\Sigma\Sigma X)^2}{N_{total}} \tag{14.1}$$

The formula for sum of squares within is

$$SS_{wg} = \Sigma\Sigma X^2 - \frac{\Sigma(\Sigma X_{cell})^2}{n_{cell}} \tag{14.2}$$

Table 14.4   Sums Needed to Compute Two-Way Analysis of Variance for Depth Perception Experiment

<table>
<tr><td></td><td colspan="4" align="center">**Independent Variable 1**</td><td></td></tr>
<tr><td></td><td colspan="2" align="center">One Eye Open</td><td colspan="2" align="center">Two Eyes Open</td><td></td></tr>
<tr>
<td rowspan="7">No
Head
Movement</td>
<td>X</td><td>X^2</td><td>X</td><td>X^2</td><td></td>
</tr>
<tr><td>8</td><td>64</td><td>5</td><td>25</td><td></td></tr>
<tr><td>10</td><td>100</td><td>4</td><td>16</td><td>$\overline{X}_{row} = 6$</td></tr>
<tr><td>8</td><td>64</td><td>1</td><td>1</td><td>$\Sigma X_{row} = 60$</td></tr>
<tr><td>6</td><td>36</td><td>2</td><td>4</td><td>$\Sigma X^2_{row} = 488$</td></tr>
<tr><td>13</td><td>169</td><td>3</td><td>9</td><td></td></tr>
<tr><td>$\Sigma X = 45$</td><td>$\Sigma X^2 = 433$</td><td>$\Sigma X = 15$</td><td>$\Sigma X^2 = 55$</td><td></td></tr>
<tr><td></td><td>$\overline{X}_{cell} = 9$</td><td></td><td>$\overline{X}_{cell} = 3$</td><td></td><td></td></tr>
<tr>
<td rowspan="7">Slow
Head
Movement</td>
<td>X</td><td>X^2</td><td>X</td><td>X^2</td><td></td>
</tr>
<tr><td>4</td><td>16</td><td>4</td><td>16</td><td></td></tr>
<tr><td>6</td><td>36</td><td>1</td><td>1</td><td>$\overline{X}_{row} = 3.7$</td></tr>
<tr><td>3</td><td>9</td><td>2</td><td>4</td><td>$\Sigma X_{row} = 37$</td></tr>
<tr><td>5</td><td>25</td><td>3</td><td>9</td><td>$\Sigma X^2_{row} = 169$</td></tr>
<tr><td>7</td><td>49</td><td>2</td><td>4</td><td></td></tr>
<tr><td>$\Sigma X = 25$</td><td>$\Sigma X^2 = 135$</td><td>$\Sigma X = 12$</td><td>$\Sigma X^2 = 34$</td><td></td></tr>
<tr><td></td><td>$\overline{X}_{cell} = 5$</td><td></td><td>$\overline{X}_{cell} = 2.4$</td><td></td><td></td></tr>
<tr>
<td rowspan="7">Moderate
Head
Movement</td>
<td>X</td><td>X^2</td><td>X</td><td>X^2</td><td></td>
</tr>
<tr><td>2</td><td>4</td><td>3</td><td>9</td><td></td></tr>
<tr><td>2</td><td>4</td><td>0</td><td>0</td><td>$\overline{X}_{row} = 2.7$</td></tr>
<tr><td>3</td><td>9</td><td>3</td><td>9</td><td>$\Sigma X_{row} = 27$</td></tr>
<tr><td>4</td><td>16</td><td>2</td><td>4</td><td>$\Sigma X^2_{row} = 95$</td></tr>
<tr><td>6</td><td>36</td><td>2</td><td>4</td><td></td></tr>
<tr><td>$\Sigma X = 17$</td><td>$\Sigma X^2 = 69$</td><td>$\Sigma X = 10$</td><td>$\Sigma X^2 = 26$</td><td></td></tr>
<tr><td></td><td>$\overline{X}_{cell} = 3.4$</td><td></td><td>$\overline{X}_{cell} = 2$</td><td></td><td></td></tr>
<tr><td></td><td colspan="2" align="center">$\overline{X}_{col} = 5.8$</td><td colspan="2" align="center">$\overline{X}_{col} = 2.467$</td><td></td></tr>
<tr><td></td><td colspan="2" align="center">$\Sigma X_{col} = 87$</td><td colspan="2" align="center">$\Sigma X_{col} = 37$</td><td>$\Sigma\Sigma X = 124$</td></tr>
<tr><td></td><td colspan="2" align="center">$\Sigma X^2_{col} = 637$</td><td colspan="2" align="center">$\Sigma X^2_{col} = 1,157$</td><td>$\Sigma\Sigma X^2 = 752$</td></tr>
</table>

Independent Variable 2

The formula for sum of squares rows is

$$SS_r = \frac{\Sigma(\Sigma X_{row})^2}{n_{row}} - \frac{(\Sigma\Sigma X)^2}{N_{total}} \tag{14.3}$$

The formula for sum of squares columns is

$$SS_c = \frac{\Sigma(\Sigma X_{col})^2}{n_{col}} - \frac{(\Sigma\Sigma X)^2}{N_{total}} \tag{14.4}$$

Finally, the sum of squares for the interaction is arrived at by subtraction:

$$SS_{r \times c} = SS_{total} - (SS_{wg} + SS_r + SS_c) \tag{14.5}$$

Question: If the outcome is a negative sum of squares, does that mean the results are opposite to the research hypothesis?

No, it means that you have made a mistake. Sums of squares can never be negative. If you look carefully at Formulas 14.1–14.5, you will note that all of them involve adding or subtracting squared values. All the squared values will, of course, be positive. Also, you will always subtract a smaller value from a larger value; therefore, the result can never be negative. If you compute a negative value for any sum of squares, you need to go back and find where you made the error.

Computing the sum of squares for the depth perception experiment is simply a matter of finding the appropriate values of sums from Table 14.4 and then using Formulas 14.1–14.5. You can begin by computing the sum of squares total using Formula 14.1.

$$SS_{total} = \Sigma\Sigma X^2 - \frac{(\Sigma\Sigma X)^2}{N_{total}} = 752 - \frac{124^2}{30} = 752 - \frac{15,376}{30}$$

$$= 752 - 512.533 = 239.467$$

Next, compute sum of squares within using Formula 14.2:

$$SS_{wg} = \Sigma\Sigma X^2 - \frac{\Sigma(\Sigma X_{cell})^2}{n_{cell}}$$

$$= 752 - \frac{45^2 + 15^2 + 25^2 + 12^2 + 17^2 + 10^2}{5}$$

$$= 752 - \frac{2,025 + 225 + 625 + 144 + 289 + 100}{5}$$

$$= 752 - \frac{3,408}{5} = 752 - 681.6$$

$$= 70.4$$

Now compute the sum of squares for the rows using Formula 14.3. Remember that the rows represent no head motion, slow head motion, and moderate head motion:

$$SS_r = \frac{\Sigma(\Sigma X_{row})^2}{n_{row}} - \frac{(\Sigma\Sigma X)^2}{N_{total}} = \frac{60^2 + 37^2 + 27^2}{10} - \frac{124^2}{30}$$

$$= \frac{3,600 + 1,369 + 729}{10} - \frac{15,376}{30} = \frac{5,698}{10} - 512.533$$

$$= 569.8 - 512.533 = 57.267$$

Then compute the sum of squares for columns with Formula 14.4. Remember that the columns represent the number of eyes used to view the depth perception apparatus:

$$SS_c = \frac{\Sigma(\Sigma X_{col})^2}{n_{col}} - \frac{(\Sigma\Sigma X)^2}{N_{total}} = \frac{87^2 + 37^2}{15} - \frac{124^2}{30}$$

$$= \frac{7,569 + 1,369}{15} - \frac{15,376}{30}$$

$$= \frac{8,938}{15} - 512.533 = 595.867 - 512.533 = 83,334$$

Finally, compute the sum of squares for the interaction by using Formula 14.5 and the preceding results from Formulas 14.1–14.4:

$$SS_{r \times c} = SS_{total} - (SS_{wg} + SS_r + SS_c)$$

$$= 239.467 - (70.4 + 57.267 + 83.334)$$

$$= 239.467 - 211.001 = 28.466$$

After computing all the sums of squares, create a source table like Table 14.5. Enter the sums in the table. The next step is to compute the degrees of freedom.

Table 14.5 Source Table for Two-Way Factorial Analysis of Variance Showing the Computed Sums of Squares

Source of Variation	Sum of Squares	Degrees of Freedom	Mean Square	F
Rows	57.267			
Columns	83.334			
Interaction	28.466			
Within	70.400			
Total	239.467			

Concept Quiz

Think back to the handshake study described in the previous concept quiz (Chaplin, Phillips, Brown, Clanton, & Stein, 2000) and Dr. Vickman's proposed modification. Recall that Dr. Vickman wanted to see whether the length of handshake time differed between gender (male versus female) depending on the gender of the other person (male versus female). Assume that Dr. Vickman has completed this study and is now ready to analyze data, and answer the following procedural questions.

1. List the sums of squares that must be computed for a two-way analysis of variance.

2. The computational formulas for sum of squares _____ and sum of squares _____ are the same as the computational formulas used in a one-way analysis of variance.

3. In a two-way analysis of variance, the sum of squares between is partitioned into what three different sums of squares?

4. Express each of the following in words:
   a. $\Sigma\Sigma X^2$ f. N_{total}
   b. $\Sigma\Sigma X$ g. n_{cell}
   c. $\Sigma(\Sigma X_{cell})^2$ h. n_{row}
   d. $\Sigma(\Sigma X_{row})^2$ i. n_{col}
   e. $\Sigma(\Sigma X_{col})^2$

5. Which sum of squares is arrived at by subtraction?

Answers

1. Sum of squares rows (SS_r); sum of squares columns (SS_c); sum of squares interaction ($SS_{r \times c}$); sum of squares within (SS_{wg}); sum of squares total (SS_{total})
2. within groups; total
3. Sum of squares rows, sum of squares columns, and sum of squares interaction
4. a. The sum of the sums of the X^2 for all the cells in the entire analysis

   b. The sum of the sums of the X-values for all cells in the entire analysis. You add up all the scores from all the cells in the analysis.

   c. The sum of the square of the sum of the X-values for each cell. You compute the sum of

   the scores within each cell, square that value, and then add up all these squared values across all cells.

   d. The sum of the square of the sum of the X-values for each row. You compute the sum of the scores within each row, square that value, and then add up these squared values across all rows.

e. The sum of the square of the sum of the X-values for each row. You compute the sum of the scores within each row, square that value, and then

add up these squared values across all rows.

f. The total number of scores in all the samples

g. The number of scores in an individual cell

h. The number of scores in each row

i. The number of scores in each column

5. Sum of squares interaction

Computation of Degrees of Freedom for Two-Way Analysis of Variance

In referring to the source table, Table 14.5 or Table 14.6, you can see that there are five different types of degrees of freedom in a two-way analysis of variance: rows (df_r), columns (df_c), interaction $(df_{r \times c})$, within groups (df_{wg}), and total (df_{total}). The number of degrees of freedom of the rows is equal to the number of rows minus 1:

$$df_r = \text{number of rows} \ - \ 1 \tag{14.6}$$

Similarly, the number of degrees of freedom for the columns is equal to the number of columns minus 1:

$$df_c = \text{number of columns} \ - \ 1 \tag{14.7}$$

The degrees of freedom for the interaction are equal to the degrees of freedom for the rows times the degrees of freedom for the columns:

$$df_{r \times c} = df_r \cdot df_c = (\text{number of rows} - 1) \cdot (\text{number of columns} - 1) \tag{14.8}$$

The degrees of freedom within are equal to the sum of the separate degrees of freedom for each cell or the number of scores in all the samples minus the number of cells:

$$df_{wg} = (n_{cell_1} - 1) + (n_{cell_2} - 1) + \cdots + (n_{cell_k} - 1)$$

or

$$df_{wg} = N_{total} - \text{number of cells} \tag{14.9}$$

The final degrees of freedom, the degrees of freedom total, equals the total number of scores minus 1:

$$df_{total} = N_{total} - 1 \tag{14.10}$$

Table 14.6 Source Table for Two-Way Factorial Analysis of Variance Showing the Computed Sums of Squares and Degrees of Freedom

Source of Variation	Sum of Squares	Degress of Freedom	Mean Square	F
Rows	57.267	2		
Columns	83.334	1		
Interaction	28.466	2		
Within	70.400	24		
Total	239.467	29		

Now use these formulas to compute the degrees of freedom for the depth perception experiment and enter the values in Table 14.6. Because three different types of motion are represented by the rows, the number of degrees of freedom for rows is

$$df_r = \text{number of rows} - 1 = 3 - 1 = 2$$

The columns represent two conditions, one eye open and two eyes open; therefore, the number of degrees of freedom for columns is

$$df_c = \text{number of columns} - 1 = 2 - 1 = 1$$

From Formula 14.8, the number of degrees of freedom for the interaction is

$$df_{r \times c} = df_r \cdot df_c = (\text{number of rows} - 1) \cdot (\text{number of columns} - 1) = 2 \cdot 1 = 2$$

There are 30 participants and six different cells in our experiment, so the number of degrees of freedom within is equal to

$$df_{wg} = N_{total} - \text{number of cells} = 30 - 6 = 24$$

Finally, the number of degrees of freedom total is equal to the 30 total participants minus 1.

$$df_{total} = N_{total} - 1 = 30 - 1 = 29$$

Computation of the Mean Squares for Two-Way Analysis of Variance

After the sums of squares and the degrees of freedom have been computed, the mean squares can be computed in the same way as in the one-way analysis of variance. The mean square is equal to the sum of squares divided by the degrees of freedom. The computations for all the mean squares are as follows:

$$MS_r = \frac{SS_r}{df_r} \tag{14.11}$$

$$= \frac{57.267}{2} = 28.634$$

$$MS_c = \frac{SS_c}{df_c} \tag{14.12}$$

$$= \frac{83.334}{1} = 83.3344$$

$$MS_{r \times c} = \frac{SS_{r \times c}}{df_{r \times c}} \tag{14.13}$$

$$= \frac{28.466}{2} = 14.233$$

$$MS_{wg} = \frac{SS_{wg}}{df_{wg}} \tag{14.14}$$

$$= \frac{70.400}{24} = 2.993$$

Once you have completed the mean squares computations, you will need to plug the values into the source table. Table 14.7 contains all the values you just computed. Now you can calculate the F ratios.

Table 14.7 Source Table for Two-Way Factorial Analysis of Variance Showing the Computed Sums of Squares, Degrees of Freedom, and Mean Squares

Source of Variation	Sum of Squares	Degrees of Freedom	Mean Square	F
Rows	57.267	2	28.634	
Columns	83.334	1	83.334	
Interaction	28.466	2	14.233	
Within	70.400	24	2.933	
Total	239.467	29		

Computation of the *F* Ratios for Two-Way Analysis of Variance

In the two-way analysis of variance, three sets of null hypotheses are being tested; thus, it is necessary to compute three different *F* ratios. Compute one *F* ratio to test the rows, one to test the columns, and one to test the interaction. All *F* ratios are computed in the same way as in the one-way analysis of variance: Divide the mean square for the source of variation being tested by the mean square within groups. The formulas and computations of each *F* for the depth perception data follow. Keep in mind that the rows represent the main effect of the type of motion on the dependent variable, the columns represent the main effect of the number of eyes open on the dependent variable, and the interaction represents the effect of both independent variables on the dependent variable:

$$F_r = \frac{MS_r}{MS_{wg}} \tag{14.15}$$

$$= \frac{28.634}{2.933} = 9.763$$

$$F_c = \frac{MS_c}{MS_{wg}} \tag{14.16}$$

$$= \frac{83.334}{2.933} = 28.413$$

$$F_{r \times c} = \frac{MS_{r \times c}}{MS_{wg}} \tag{14.17}$$

$$= \frac{14.233}{2.933} = 4.853$$

With the computation of these *F* ratios, the source table can now be completed (see Table 14.8).

Table 14.8   Completed Source Table for Two-Way Factorial Analysis of Variance Showing the Computed Sums of Squares, Degrees of Freedom, Mean Squares, and *F* Ratios

Source of Variation	Sum of Squares	Degrees of Freedom	Mean Square	F
Rows	57.267	2	28.634	9.763
Columns	83.334	1	83.334	28.413
Interaction	28.466	2	14.233	4.853
Within	70.400	24	2.933	
Total	239.467	29		

VISUAL SUMMARY

Two-Way Analysis of Variance

Before You Begin: Compute $\Sigma\Sigma X^2$, $\Sigma\Sigma X$, $\Sigma(\Sigma X_{cell})^2$, $\Sigma(\Sigma X_{row})^2$, $\Sigma(\Sigma X_{col})^2$, N_{total}, n_{cell}, n_{row}, n_{col}.

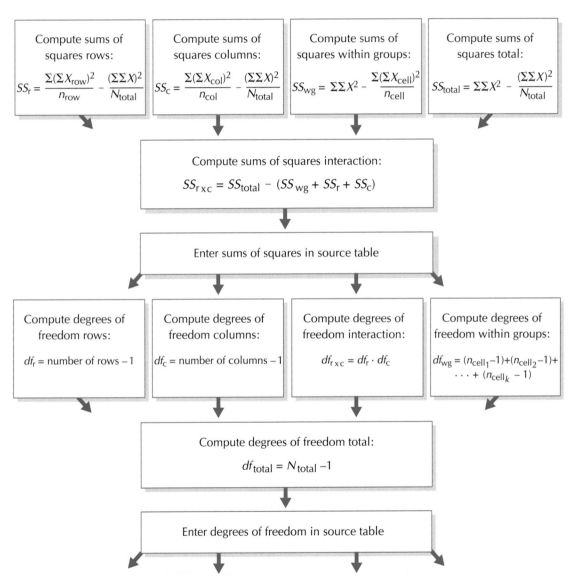

Compute sums of squares rows:

$$SS_r = \frac{\Sigma(\Sigma X_{row})^2}{n_{row}} - \frac{(\Sigma\Sigma X)^2}{N_{total}}$$

Compute sums of squares columns:

$$SS_c = \frac{\Sigma(\Sigma X_{col})^2}{n_{col}} - \frac{(\Sigma\Sigma X)^2}{N_{total}}$$

Compute sums of squares within groups:

$$SS_{wg} = \Sigma\Sigma X^2 - \frac{\Sigma(\Sigma X_{cell})^2}{n_{cell}}$$

Compute sums of squares total:

$$SS_{total} = \Sigma\Sigma X^2 - \frac{(\Sigma\Sigma X)^2}{N_{total}}$$

Compute sums of squares interaction:

$$SS_{r \times c} = SS_{total} - (SS_{wg} + SS_r + SS_c)$$

Enter sums of squares in source table

Compute degrees of freedom rows:

df_r = number of rows − 1

Compute degrees of freedom columns:

df_c = number of columns − 1

Compute degrees of freedom interaction:

$df_{r \times c} = df_r \cdot df_c$

Compute degrees of freedom within groups:

$df_{wg} = (n_{cell_1}-1)+(n_{cell_2}-1)+ \cdots + (n_{cell_k} - 1)$

Compute degrees of freedom total:

$df_{total} = N_{total} - 1$

Enter degrees of freedom in source table

(continued)

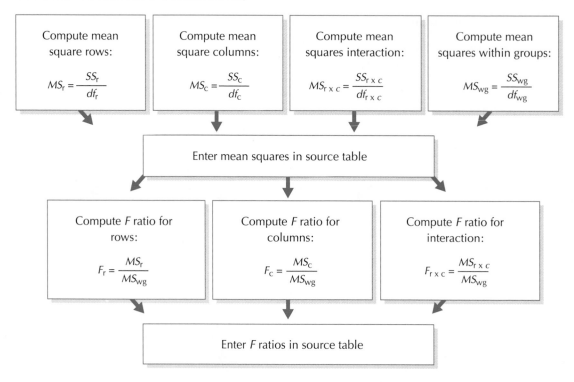

Question: Do these *F* ratios still have to be looked up in Table F to see whether they are significant?

Yes. You still need to compare each computed *F* ratio to the appropriate value in Table F, and you do this the same way as for a one-way analysis of variance. You enter Table F by using the degrees of freedom of the numerator and the denominator in the *F* ratio. The first step is to compare the critical value in Table F to your computed *F* ratio for the main effect of rows (type of motion), which is 9.763. Looking in the table, you find the computed values of 2 degrees of freedom for the numerator and 24 degrees of freedom for the denominator, and you find the critical value to be 3.40. Because the computed value for *F* is greater than the critical value, reject the null hypothesis and accept the research hypothesis for the rows. This means that it is pretty certain that at least one of the rows came from a different population than the other rows, and that head motion makes a difference in the accuracy of depth perception.

Significance of the Main Effects

When there are three or more levels of an independent variable, as is the case with the types of head motion, a significant F ratio tells you that there is a real difference, but you cannot be sure which sample means are significantly different from one another. Therefore, you must use the HSD test, as in Chapter 13. The HSD is computed in the same way as it was for the one-way analysis of variance using Formula 13.15:

$$HSD = q \cdot \sqrt{\frac{MS_{wg}}{n}} \qquad\qquad (13.15)$$

Look up the value of q in Table Q in Appendix A using the number of means to be compared, 3, and the degrees of freedom within groups, 24, and find a q value of 3.53. The value for n is equal to the number of participants in *each* level being compared; in this case, it is equal to n_{row}, or 10. Thus,

$$HSD = q \cdot \sqrt{\frac{MS_{wg}}{n}} = 3.53 \cdot \sqrt{\frac{2.933}{10}} = 3.53 \cdot \sqrt{.293}$$

$$= 3.53 \cdot .541 = 1.910$$

This result tells you that any difference of 1.910 millimeters between means is an honestly significant difference. The means for the three different levels of head motion are

$$\overline{X}_{no} = 6.0 \text{ mm}$$

$$\overline{X}_{slow} = 3.7 \text{ mm}$$

$$\overline{X}_{moderate} = 2.7 \text{ mm}$$

The differences, then, are

$$\overline{X}_{no} - \overline{X}_{slow} = 6.0 - 3.7 = 2.3 \text{ mm}$$

$$\overline{X}_{no} - \overline{X}_{moderate} = 6.0 - 2.7 = 3.3 \text{ mm}$$

$$\overline{X}_{slow} - \overline{X}_{moderate} = 3.7 - 2.7 = 1.0 \text{ mm}$$

Compare these three differences to the HSD and you will find that the difference between the means for the no-motion and slow-motion conditions is significantly different, as is the difference between the no-motion and moderate-motion conditions. On the other hand, the difference between the slow- and moderate-motion conditions is not significant. It is clear from these data, then, that the perception of depth is significantly better when participants move their heads than when there is no movement.

Similar comparisons must be done with the computed F ratio for the columns (number of eyes open). Try to think this through on your own before reading the discussion. If you are still fuzzy on this concept, review the procedures used for the rows. What do you do first? You look up the critical value for the F ratio in Table F using 1 degree of freedom for the numerator (columns) and 24 degrees of freedom for the denominator (within groups). Next, you compare the computed F ratio, 28.413, to the critical value, 4.26. Because your computed F ratio is greater than the critical value, you then reject the null hypothesis and accept the research hypothesis. Next, you need to decide whether you are required to conduct an HSD test. Remember that you only need to do an HSD if you are comparing three or more columns (or rows). Because there are only two columns, you do not need to do the HSD. Therefore, the mean error of 5.8 millimeters in the one-eye-open condition is significantly greater than the mean error of 2.6 millimeters in the two-eyes-open condition, which confirms what we suspected from the beginning: Two eyes are better than one.

Significance of the Interaction

The computed F ratio for the interaction is tested by comparing it to the value in Table F for 2 degrees of freedom in the numerator and 24 degrees of freedom in the denominator. Your computed F ratio for the interaction is 4.853, whereas the critical value from Table F is 3.40. Because the computed value is greater than the critical value, you can reject the null hypothesis for the interaction and accept the research hypothesis, which states that the interaction of the independent variables represented by the columns and rows has an effect on the dependent variable. As mentioned at the beginning of the chapter, merely knowing that a significant interaction exists does not explain the reason for the interaction or its implications. These explanations are up to the researcher, and they are often quite difficult to make. Graphing the means of the different experimental cells (shown in Figure 14.1, which is repeated here) indicates that head motion drastically reduces the

Figure 14.1
A graph of the cell means from the depth perception experiment illustrates the interaction.

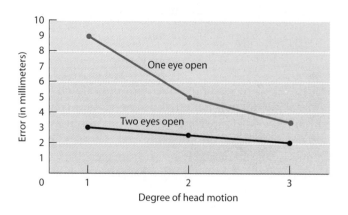

error rate in the one-eye-open condition, whereas it has a minimal effect when participants use both eyes. By using these data, you can recommend that people who have the use of only one eye can improve their depth perception by moving their head. This movement will greatly enhance their depth perception and make them almost as accurate as people who have the use of both eyes.

Concept Quiz

Dr. Vickman completed the experiment, a 2 (gender of participant) $\times$ 2 (gender of other) factorial design with handshake time as the dependent variable. A partially completed source table is shown here because all the analyses are not completed.

Source Table for Handshake Experiment

Source of Variation	Sum of Squares	Degrees of Freedom	Mean Square	F
Rows	57.80			
Columns	62.20			
Interaction	26.10			
Within	95.60			
Total	241.70			

1. List the five different types of degrees of freedom in a two-way analysis of variance, and give the general formulas for computing them.

2. Assume that there were 60 participants in Vickman's study, 15 in each condition, and calculate each of the types of degrees of freedom.

3. In a two-way analysis of variance, as in a one-way analysis of variance, the mean square is equal to the _____ divided by the

   _____.

4. Use the degrees of freedom calculated in Problem 2 and calculate the mean square for rows, columns, interaction, and within for Vickman's study.

5. The *F* ratio is computed by dividing the mean square of interest (rows, columns, or interaction) by the mean square _____.

6. Calculate the *F* ratio for rows, columns, and the interaction for Vickman.

7. For our computed F ratio to be significant, it must be _____ the critical value from Table F.

8. Which, if any, of the F ratios in Vickman's study are significant?

9. If the F ratio for a main effect—columns or rows—with three or more levels is significant, you can use the _____ to determine which means are significantly different from one another.

10. The effects of a significant interaction are usually easier to see in a

    _____.

Answers

1. rows (df_r), columns (df_c), interaction ($df_{r \times c}$), within (df_{wg}), total (df_{total})
    df_r = number of rows − 1
    df_c = number of columns − 1
    $df_{r \times c} = df_r \cdot df_c$
    $df_{wg} = \Sigma(n_{cell} - 1)$
    $df_{total} = N_{total} - 1$

2. $df_r = 2 - 1 = 1$
    $df_c = 2 - 1 = 1$

    $df_{r \times c} = (1)(1) = 1$
    $df_{wg} = (15-1) +$
    $(15-1) + (15-1) +$
    $(15-1) = 56$
    $df_{total} = 60 - 1 = 59$

3. sum of squares; degrees of freedom

4. $MS_r = 57.80$;
    $MS_c = 62.20$;
    $MS_{r \times c} = 26.10$;
    $MS_{wg} = 1.707$

5. within

6. $F_r = 33.861$; $F_c = 36.438$; $F_{r \times c} = .273$

7. greater than or equal to

8. main effect of gender of participant, main effect of gender of other person, no interaction

9. HSD

10. graph

Summary

Experiments that have two independent variables can be analyzed using two-way analysis of variance. In a two-way analysis of variance, four separate mean squares are computed. Two of these are called the main effects and are represented by the mean square rows and mean square columns. In addition to the main effects, there is a mean square for the interaction of the two variables being tested, as well as a mean square within groups. Each main effect represents the effect of only one of the independent variables on the dependent variable. The interaction is the effect of the combination of both independent variables on the dependent variable. The easiest way to illustrate an interaction is to graph the independent variables on the same axes and to compare the slopes of the resulting lines. If the slopes are similar, there is little or no interaction, but if the slopes are very different or opposite, an interaction exists.

The mean square for each element in the analysis consists of the sum of squares divided by the corresponding degrees of freedom. F ratios for the two main effects and the interaction are then computed by dividing the appropriate mean squares by the mean square within groups. The resulting *F* ratios are compared to a critical value found in Table F. If the computed *F* ratio is greater than or equal to the critical value, you can reject the null hypothesis. If there are three or more levels of one of your main effects, then you need to conduct an HSD test to determine which means are different from one another.

Key Terms

factorial experiment   main effect   interaction

Formulas

$$SS_{total} = \Sigma\Sigma X^2 - \frac{(\Sigma\Sigma X)^2}{N_{total}} \tag{14.1}$$

$$SS_{wg} = \Sigma\Sigma X^2 - \frac{\Sigma(\Sigma X_{cell})^2}{n_{cell}} \tag{14.2}$$

$$SS_r = \frac{\Sigma(\Sigma X_{row})^2}{n_{row}} - \frac{(\Sigma\Sigma X)^2}{N_{total}} \tag{14.3}$$

$$SS_c = \frac{\Sigma(\Sigma X_{col})^2}{n_{col}} - \frac{(\Sigma\Sigma X)^2}{N_{total}} \tag{14.4}$$

$$SS_{r \times c} = SS_{total} - (SS_{wg} + SS_r + SS_c) \tag{14.5}$$

$$df_r = \text{number of rows} - 1 \tag{14.6}$$

$$df_c = \text{number of columns} - 1 \tag{14.7}$$

$$df_{r \times c} = df_r \cdot df_c = (\text{number of rows} - 1) \cdot (\text{number of columns} - 1) \tag{14.8}$$

$$df_{wg} = (n_{cell_1} - 1) + (n_{cell_2} - 1) + \cdots + (n_{cell_k} - 1) \text{ or}$$

$$df_{wg} = N_{total} - \text{number of cells} \tag{14.9}$$

$$df_{total} = N_{total} - 1 \tag{14.10}$$

$$MS_r = \frac{SS_r}{df_r} \tag{14.11}$$

$$MS_c = \frac{SS_c}{df_c} \tag{14.12}$$

$$MS_{r \times c} = \frac{SS_{r \times c}}{df_{r \times c}}$$ (14.13)

$$MS_{wg} = \frac{SS_{wg}}{df_{wg}}$$ (14.14)

$$F_r = \frac{MS_r}{MS_{wg}}$$ (14.15)

$$F_c = \frac{MS_c}{MS_{wg}}$$ (14.16)

$$F_{r \times c} = \frac{MS_{r \times c}}{MS_{wg}}$$ (14.17)

Problems

The problems for Chapter 14 are all examples of possible experiments. Complete the following steps for each problem using the data presented.

a. Write down each null hypothesis and each research hypothesis for the two main effects and for the interaction.

b. Create a two-way analysis of variance source table, including the source of variation, sums of squares, degrees of freedom, mean squares, and F ratios.

c. Look up the critical value for each F ratio in Table F in Appendix A and determine whether the F ratio is significant.

d. If one of the main effects is significant and it contains three or more levels, compute an HSD, compare the means, and determine which levels are significantly different from one another.

e. Graph the interaction if it is significant and, using your knowledge of the problem, attempt to explain the significant interaction.

f. State in a few sentences what you can conclude from this experiment.

1. Your computer company is about to market a new palm computer and you are asked to determine which of two screens should be used with the computer. One screen's display has black letters on a white background, and the other screen has white letters on a blue background. In addition, you are asked to evaluate the visibility of the screen in three different lighting conditions: incandescent light, fluorescent light, and sunlight. You design an experiment in which 30 people are divided into six different groups: those using the black and white screen under incandescent light, those using the black and white screen under fluorescent lights, those using the black and white screen in sunlight, those using the white and blue screen under incandescent light, those using the white and blue screen under fluorescent lights, and those using the

white and blue screen in sunlight. The dependent variable, listed in the table, is the number of seconds each person takes to read 1,000 words displayed on the palm computer screen.

Type of Light

	Fluorescent	Incandescent	Sunlight
Black/White	130	132	147
	129	117	152
	118	123	149
	113	129	138
	125	122	157
White/Blue	144	147	148
	139	143	147
	145	141	154
	139	134	150
	139	140	145

2. A memory experiment is conducted to determine whether the type of task—recognition or free recall—is affected by the type of word list used—meaningful or nonsense. Both meaningful and nonsense lists are made up of three-letter consonant-vowel-consonant combinations. Participants are briefly shown a list of "words" and are then asked to remember the list using either recognition (identifying whether the word was on the list) or recall (generating the entire list from memory without prompting). The dependent variable is the number of correct words recognized or recalled from a 50-word list. The data are listed in the table.

Type of Word

	Nonsense	Meaningful
Recall	23	36
	18	39
	20	33
	16	35
Recognition	27	34
	29	37
	28	38
	32	35

3. The Diagnostic and Statistical Manual (DSM) of the American Psychiatric Association is an attempt to classify all mental disorders. Unfortunately, or fortunately, depending on your point of view, every few years the DSM must be revised to account for new research on psychopathology. Every change in the DSM requires that all psychologists and psychiatrists learn the new classification system. You are a state government researcher who works with the psychology and psychiatry licensing board. The board has ruled that all clinical psychologists and all psychiatrists must complete a continuing education course that teaches the new version of the DSM. In the past, two different kinds of courses have been offered by your office: lecture and television. This year, for convenience, the board would like to add an Internet class to the other two methods of instruction. You are asked to determine the relative effectiveness of these methods of instruction for both psychiatrists and psychologists. Therefore,

you design an experiment with two independent variables: type of instruction (lecture, television, or Internet) and type of license (psychologist or psychiatrist). The dependent variable is the number of correct items on a test that measures knowledge of the new DSM. The test scores are given in the table.

Type of Instruction

	Lecture	Television	Internet
Psychologist	75	88	96
	94	93	94
	81	63	97
Psychiatrist	74	82	74
	93	95	63
	82	99	79

4. As a psychobiologist, you are interested in the effect of two new drugs on the electrical charge of a neuron membrane. In addition to observing general differences between the two drugs, you want to see whether their effects vary at different temperatures. Therefore, you design an experiment whereby you inject the drugs into a giant squid's large neurons that have been kept alive in a saline solution. You inject each drug into four separate neurons at 20°C (normal room temperature) and then again at 37°C (normal human body temperature). For each presentation of the drug, you measure the change in the electrical charge (in millivolts) of the neuronal membrane. For a total of 16 neurons, the table lists the results for the four conditions.

Temperature

	20°C	37°C
Drug A	4	3
	−2	7
	1	9
	2	11
Drug B	9	13
	8	12
	7	14
	8	15

5. As a budding psychologist, you wonder whether you can teach old dogs new tricks. So you go to the pound and adopt five old dogs and five puppies, and you attempt to teach all the dogs three of the old standards: "sit," "shake," and "roll over." Teaching only one trick to each dog, you keep a record of how many days it takes before they learn the tricks. The results of your experiment are listed in the table.

Type of Trick

	"Sit"	"Shake"	"Roll Over"
Young Dog	2	4	6
	1	5	9
	3	4	7
	1	6	8
	2	7	10
Old Dog	2	9	13
	5	10	12
	2	11	15
	4	13	17
	3	7	13

6. An expert on proofreading is interested in the effect of two separate variables on proofreading. She develops three 10-page manuscripts, one having no errors in the first 7 pages and then 20 errors over the last 3 pages, one having 5 errors per page in the first 7 pages and the same 20 errors over the last 3 pages, and one having 10 errors per page in the first 7 pages and the same 20 errors over the last 3 pages. Her experiment has two independent variables. One is the number of errors in the first 7 pages, and the other is the method of displaying the manuscript: on a 17-inch computer screen, a small hand-held computer screen, or paper. The first independent variable has three levels: no errors, an average of 5 errors per page in the first 7 pages, or an average of 10 errors per page in the first 7 pages. The second also has three levels: paper, a 17-inch computer screen, or a hand-held computer screen. The dependent variable is the number of errors detected on the last 3 pages. Data are in the table.

Errors on the First 7 Pages

	None	5 per Page	10 per Page
Paper	18	19	18
	19	17	17
	17	20	16
	15	16	18
17" Computer Screen	11	12	16
	12	14	17
	16	16	19
	14	18	20
Hand-Held Computer Screen	9	11	14
	9	12	16
	11	15	17
	10	15	16

7. Although the vast majority of psychology research participants are human, animal rights have become a major concern for psychology. Because of the importance of animal rights issues, a group of researchers has designed an experiment to determine the effectiveness of various animal rights measures. The researchers want to determine whether participants perceive animal research differently depending on whether they know where the research is being conducted and whether they can form some sort of empathy with the researcher by seeing his or her photograph. Thus, there are two independent variables, the first being whether or not the institution is mentioned, and the second being the presence or absence of the experimenter's photo. The dependent variable is the participant's rating of the effectiveness of the message on a 10-point interval scale. The results of this 2×2 factorial experiment are given in the table.

Institution Mentioned

	Yes	No
Photograph	6	9
	7	9
	4	7
	8	6
No Photograph	4	4
	5	2
	3	1
	4	5

Problems From the Literature

The following problems refer to actual results from research studies that are cited at the end of the

Victim's Sexual Orientation

	Heterosexual	Homosexual	Bisexual
Heterosexual	20 18 20 22	15 17 14 16	14 18 15 15
Homosexual	25 28 24 30	10 11 8 7	11 9 10 9
Bisexual	20 24 19 19	5 8 10 9	10 10 8 5

Defendant's Sexual Orientation

chapter. However, the data used to generate the problem sets are hypothetical.

8. When jurors hear sexual assault cases, does the victim's or defendant's sexual orientation make a difference on the outcome of the case? Hill (2000) examined this question and found that homosexuals were treated differently than heterosexuals. In some cases the treatment was more lenient, and in other cases it was more harsh. Suppose another researcher conducted a similar sexual assault study to see whether the length of prison sentence differed depending on the sexual orientation of the victim (heterosexual, homosexual, bisexual) and/or the sexual orientation of the defendant (heterosexual, homosexual, bisexual). Participants were told they were to imagine themselves as jurors assigned to the penalty phase of a sexual assault trial. They were randomly assigned to read a scenario describing the sexual assault case in one of nine experimental conditions and then indicated the number of years in prison they would sentence the defendant. The gender of victim and defendant were held constant. Data for this 3×3 factorial experiment are shown in the table.

9. In Giuliano, Popp, and Knight's (2000) study examining differences in childhood play experiences between college women varsity athletes and nonathletes, it was revealed that the women athletes played more masculine games, such as "Army," as children than nonathletes. However, women

athletes did not play more with masculine toys than the nonathletic women. Imagine that another researcher extended this area of research and conducted a study to determine whether these groups valued masculine and feminine games differently. Both college women athletes and nonathletes were randomly assigned to read a short scenario involving a young girl playing either a masculine or feminine game with friends. After reading the scenario, the participants indicated how valuable the play experience was for the girl on a scale from 1 (not valuable) to 7 (very valuable). Data are shown in the table.

	Type of Game	
	Masculine	Feminine
Women Athletes	6	2
	4	1
	5	3
	6	1
Women Nonathletes	3	6
	2	5
	2	6
	1	4

References

Chaplin, W. F., Phillips, J. B., Brown, J. D., Clanton, N. R., & Stein, J. L. (2000). Handshaking, gender, personality, and first impressions. *Journal of Personality and Social Psychology, 79,* 110–117.

Giuliano, T. A., Popp, K. E., & Knight, J. L. (2000). Footballs versus Barbies: Childhood play activities as predictors of sports participation by women, *Sex Roles, 42,* 159–181.

Hill, J. M. (2000). The effects of sexual orientation in the courtroom: A double standard. *Journal of Homosexuality, 39,* 93–111.

Liebowitz, H. W. (1985). Grade crossing accidents and human factors engineering. *American Scientist, 73,* 558–562.

Meeker, F., Fox, D., & Weber, C. (1997). A comparison of driver behavior at railroad grade crossings with two different protection systems. *Accident Analysis and Prevention, 29,* 11–16.

Raslear, T. G. (1996). *Driver behavior at rail-highway crossings: A signal detection theory analysis.* U.S. Department of Transportation (Monograph). DOT/FRA/ORD-95/14.2, 2–46.

Tenkink, E., & van der Horst, R. (1990). Car driver behavior at flashing light railroad grade crossings. *Accident Analysis and Prevention, 22,* 229–239.

Witte, K., & Donohue, W. A. (2000). Preventing vehicle crashes with trains at grade crossings: The risk seeker challenge. *Accident Analysis and Prevention, 32,* 127–139.

15

Chi-Square and Other Nonparametric Statistics

- Chi-Square
  VISUAL SUMMARY: Chi-Square
- The Mann–Whitney *U* Test
  VISUAL SUMMARY: The
  Mann–Whitney *U* Test
- The Wilcoxon *T* Test
  VISUAL SUMMARY: The
  Wilcoxon *T* Test
- The Kruskal–Wallis Test
  VISUAL SUMMARY: The
  Kruskal–Wallis Test
- Summary
  VISUAL SUMMARY: Chi-Square
  and Other Nonparametric
  Statistics
- Key Terms
- Formulas
- Problems
  Problems From the Literature
- References

One out of every four Americans can expect to be diagnosed as having some type of cancer during his or her lifetime. One out of every four! How many people are in your immediate family? Two? Four? Five? How many are in your extended family? Twenty? Thirty? More? With these numbers in mind, you can appreciate the extreme importance of cancer research, not only in finding cures for the more than 100 different types of cancer but also in exploring ways to minimize your chances of getting cancer. These ways often involve behavioral changes that diminish our exposure to carcinogens, such as moving away from a chemical plant or stopping smoking. Several researchers in health psychology have been investigating other, less obvious factors related to cancer, such as personality, exercise, and social support networks (Brady & Helgeson, 1999; Manne & Miller, 1998; Turner-Cobb, Sephton, Koopman, Blake-Mortimer, & Spiegel, 2000).

In a study of social connections conducted by Kaplan and Reynolds in 1988, women who reported that they were socially isolated were significantly more likely to die of cancer than their same-age peers who had many social connections. Based on this study, it is logical to propose that the extent of a person's social network may be a factor in the development of terminal cancer. Suppose you decide to conduct a hypothetical study to try to confirm this research hypothesis. You spend months recruiting women for your study and create three nearly identical groups of 1,000 women each, the only difference being that all the women in

Table 15.1   Number of Cancer Deaths per Thousand Women for Three Types of Social Networks

Type of Social Network

Poor	Moderate	Good
45	34	20

the first group have a poor social network (they are socially isolated with no close friends or relatives), all the women in the second group have a moderate social network (they have only one or two close friends or relatives), and all the women in the third group have a good social network (they have more than two close friends or relatives). Over the next 5 years, you keep in touch with the people in the three groups and record the number of cancer deaths for each group. Table 15.1 shows what these hypothetical data might look like.

Of the 99 women who died of cancer, 45 had a poor social network, 34 had a moderate social network, and 20 had a good social network. Of course, you would like to know whether the death rates were significantly different from one another. The question is: How do you analyze these data? There is one variable, the type of social network, that has three levels: poor, moderate, and good.

> **Question:** Isn't this a multilevel experimental design that can be analyzed using a one-way analysis of variance?

This does resemble the experimental design requiring a one-way analysis of variance, except that in a one-way analysis of variance there is a separate interval or ratio score for each participant, rather than a table listing merely the number of participants in each condition. Do you remember reading in Chapter 1 about the different scales of measurement? Well, the analysis of variance analyzes data from interval or ratio scales. The data in Table 15.1 are different. They are **nominal data;** that is, they are reported only as a list of the numbers of people who fit into certain categories. Analysis of variance is not appropriate for such data, but there is an appropriate statistic for analyzing nominal data. It is known as chi-square (χ^2).

Chi-Square

Chi-square (χ^2) is a statistical technique that enables you to compare the observed frequencies in different categories (the actual numbers obtained) with the frequencies expected from some theory or hypothesis. An **observed frequency** is represented by the symbol f_o, and an **expected frequency** by the symbol f_e. The formula for χ^2 is

$$\chi^2 = \sum \frac{(f_o - f_e)^2}{f_e} \tag{15.1}$$

Chi-square, then, is computed by subtracting the expected frequency from the observed frequency, squaring this difference and dividing this squared value by the expected frequency, and then summing these terms over all the cells.

> **Question:** The observed frequency is the data collected, but how do you come up with the expected frequency?

In our cancer study, you would, as before, have two different hypotheses: the null hypothesis stating that cancer rates are the same for all types of social networks and the research hypothesis stating that cancer rates are not the same for all the types. If the null hypothesis were true and cancer death rates were the same for each type, you would expect that the 99 cancer deaths would be spread evenly across all the types and there would be 33 deaths in each category. Thus, the expected frequency for each category would be 33. Table 15.2 shows the observed frequency as well as the expected frequency for each category. It is obvious from these data that the number of deaths in the poor and good conditions are different from the expected frequency, but the χ^2 test indicates whether the pattern of responses is significantly different from what is expected, given the null hypothesis.

Using Formula 15.1 to compute χ^2 from the data in Table 15.2 results in the following:

$$\chi^2 = \sum \frac{(f_o - f_e)^2}{f_e} = \frac{(45 - 33)^2}{33} + \frac{(34 - 33)^2}{33} + \frac{(20 - 33)^2}{33}$$

$$= \frac{12^2}{33} + \frac{1^2}{33} + \frac{-13^2}{33} = \frac{144}{33} + \frac{1}{33} + \frac{169}{33} = 4.364 + .030 + 5.0121$$

$$= 9.515$$

Table 15.2 Observed Frequency and Expected Frequency for the Social Networks Research Project

	Type of Social Network		
	Poor	Moderate	Good
	$f_o = 45$	$f_o = 34$	$f_o = 20$
	$f_e = 33$	$f_e = 33$	$f_e = 33$

Question: Is a χ^2 of 9.515 good or bad?

If good or bad means significant or not significant, then the next step is to determine whether the χ^2 is significant. It is certain that the larger the χ^2, the more likely it will be significant. You can see this by taking a look at Formula 15.1. Because χ^2 is a comparison of the observed frequency to the expected frequency, a larger discrepancy between the observed frequency and the expected frequency results in a larger χ^2. Another interesting point about the χ^2 distribution is that χ^2 is likely to become larger as additional cells are added to the analysis.

Now, to determine the significance of the χ^2. Just as you would for a computed t value or a computed F value, compare your computed χ^2 to a critical value that you get from a table in the appendix to see whether it is significant. Use Table X in Appendix A, the chi-square distribution table, a small portion of which is reproduced in Table 15.3. As with Tables T and F, you need to know the degrees of freedom in order to enter Table X. The degrees of freedom for a chi-square with only one row is the number of cells minus 1. (The computation of the number of degrees of freedom changes slightly when additional rows are added.) The study of the effect of social networks on cancer rates has only one row and three cells. Therefore, the number of degrees of freedom for this χ^2 is 3 cells minus 1, or 2 degrees of freedom.

Take a look at Table 15.3, which is a small portion of Table X, and find the critical value of χ^2. To enter the table, find the degrees of freedom in the left-hand column and look across the row until you reach the .05 column. (This is the column where the critical values represent an $\alpha = .05$.) Here you should find the value 5.991. If the computed χ^2 with 2 degrees of freedom is greater than or equal to 5.991, then you can reject the null hypothesis and accept the research hypothesis. In the cancer/social network study, the computed χ^2 equals 9.515. Because this is greater than the critical value of 5.991, you reject the null hypothesis and accept the research hypothesis. Your project confirms that cancer rates are not the same for the different types of social networks.

Question: This seems easy enough, but previously it was said that the degrees of freedom computation is different for two rows. What does that mean? And is chi-square much more complicated when there are two rows?

Table 15.3 A Portion of Table X, The χ^2 Distribution

df	.25	.10	.05	.025	.01	.005
1	1.323	2.706	3.841	5.024	6.635	7.879
2	2.773	4.605	5.991	7.378	9.210	10.597
3	4.108	6.251	7.815	9.348	11.345	12.838
4	5.385	7.779	9.448	11.143	13.277	14.860
5	6.626	9.236	11.071	12.833	15.086	16.750

Source: Owen, 1962.

Table 15.4   Number of Cancer Deaths per Thousand Women for Three Types of Social Networks and for Smokers and Nonsmokers

	Type of Social Network			
	Poor	Moderate	Good	Total
Smoker	25	26	18	69
Nonsmoker	20	8	2	30
Total	45	34	20	99

The reference was to additional rows in the experimental design matrix. When there are two variables, there are two or more rows in the matrix. Computing χ^2 for a matrix with two or more rows is exactly the same as computing χ^2 with only one row. You must calculate an observed frequency and an expected frequency for each cell and then use Formula 15.1 to compute χ^2. To illustrate, this study will be extended to include an additional variable.

As you might already know, smoking is the single most preventable cause of death and disease in the United States, according to the U.S. Department of Health and Human Services. So now examine the relationship between cancer deaths and smoking behavior as well as social support networks. Now your table should look like Table 15.4, which is a 2 × 3 table with two rows and three columns. Note that the number of cancer deaths is still 99, but each deceased woman has been further identified by whether or not she smoked.

Formula 15.1 will still be used to compute the χ^2, but first an f_o and f_e must be identified for each cell. The observed frequencies are shown in Table 15.4, but you need to compute the expected frequencies based on the null hypothesis of no difference in the rate of deaths caused by cancer. This computation would be easy if the numbers of women were equal in all conditions, but in this case it is necessary to correct for the fact that more than twice as many smokers as nonsmokers die from cancer. A relatively simple formula compensates for differences in either row totals or in column totals, or in both, and enables you to compute the expected frequency for each cell:

$$f_e = \frac{(\text{row total}) \cdot (\text{column total})}{\text{grand total}} \tag{15.2}$$

Because this particular χ^2 has two rows and three columns, six different expected frequencies must be computed using Formula 15.2. Thus, the expected frequency for row 1, column 1 is

$$f_e = \frac{(\text{row total}) \cdot (\text{column total})}{\text{grand total}} = \frac{69 \cdot 45}{99} = \frac{3{,}105}{99} = 31.36$$

The expected frequency for row 1, column 2 is

$$f_e = \frac{(\text{row total}) \cdot (\text{column total})}{\text{grand total}} = \frac{69 \cdot 345}{99} = \frac{2{,}346}{99} = 23.70$$

The expected frequency for row 1, column 3 is:

$$f_e = \frac{(\text{row total}) \cdot (\text{column total})}{\text{grand total}} = \frac{69 \cdot 20}{99} = \frac{1{,}380}{99} = 13.94$$

The expected frequency for row 2, column 1 is

$$f_e = \frac{(\text{row total}) \cdot (\text{column total})}{\text{grand total}} = \frac{30 \cdot 45}{99} = \frac{1{,}350}{99} = 13.64$$

The expected frequency for row 2, column 2 is

$$f_e = \frac{(\text{row total}) \cdot (\text{column total})}{\text{grand total}} = \frac{30 \cdot 34}{99} = \frac{1{,}020}{99} = 10.30$$

The expected frequency for row 2, column 3 is

$$f_e = \frac{(\text{row total}) \cdot (\text{column total})}{\text{grand total}} = \frac{30 \cdot 20}{99} = \frac{600}{99} = 6.06$$

These expected frequencies, along with the corresponding observed frequencies, are listed in Table 15.5.

Table 15.5   Observed Frequencies and Expected Frequencies for Three Types of Social Networks and for Smokers and Nonsmokers

Type of Social Network

	Poor	Moderate	Good	Total
Smoker	$f_o = 25$ $f_e = 31.36$	$f_o = 26$ $f_e = 23.70$	$f_o = 18$ $f_e = 13.94$	69
Nonsmoker	$f_o = 20$ $f_e = 13.64$	$f_o = 8$ $f_e = 10.30$	$f_o = 2$ $f_e = 6.06$	30
Total	45	34	20	99

Now Formula 15.1 can be used to compute the χ^2.

$$\chi^2 = \sum \frac{(f_o - f_e)^2}{f_e} = \frac{(25 - 31.36)^2}{31.36} + \frac{(26 - 23.70)^2}{23.70} +$$

$$\frac{(18 - 13.94)^2}{13.94} + \frac{(20 - 13.64)^2}{13.64} + \frac{(8 - 10.30)^2}{10.30} + \frac{(2 - 6.063)^2}{6.06}$$

$$= \frac{-6.36^2}{31.36} + \frac{2.30^2}{23.70} + \frac{4.06^2}{13.94} + \frac{6.36^2}{13.64} + \frac{-2.30^2}{10.30} + \frac{-4.06^2}{6.06}$$

$$= \frac{40.45}{31.36} + \frac{5.29}{23.70} + \frac{16.48^2}{13.94} + \frac{40.45}{13.64} + \frac{5.29}{10.30} + \frac{16.48}{6.06}$$

$$= 1.29 + .22 + 1.18 + 2.97 + .51 + 2.72$$

$$= 8.89$$

The χ^2 is 8.89, but Table X must still be used to determine significance. Earlier it was said that the number of degrees of freedom is the number of cells minus 1 if there is only one row. When there is more than one row, the formula for degrees of freedom is

$$df = (\text{number of rows} -1) \cdot (\text{number of columns} - 1) \qquad (15.3)$$

Because there are two rows and three columns in the cancer study, the number of degrees of freedom is

$$df = (2 \text{ rows} -1) \cdot (3 \text{ columns} - 1) = 1 \cdot 2 = 2$$

Now you need to look in Table X for 2 degrees of freedom and then compare your computed χ^2 value of 8.89 to the critical value of 5.99. Your computed value is greater than the critical value from the table, so you reject the null hypothesis and accept the research hypothesis that there is a difference between the frequencies in the various cells. On inspection of Table 15.5, it is evident that of the cancer victims with good social networks, most were smokers. The same result holds true for those with poor and moderate social networks.

The chi-square test is straightforward and easy to use. However, there are a few assumptions and limitations that you need to be aware of when you consider using it:

1. It is assumed that the sample is randomly selected from the population.
2. It is assumed that all observations are independent. (This assumption is usually met if only one observation is made for each participant.)
3. The χ^2 test is limited to nominal data.
4. The χ^2 test tends to be less accurate with very small expected frequencies. (This is especially true with expected frequencies of less

than 5. A good rule is not to conduct the χ^2 test on data with expected frequencies of less than 5.)

5. The χ^2 test tends to be less accurate for small degrees of freedom and a small N. (A correction is available for $df = 1$. See, for example, Minimum, 1978.)

VISUAL SUMMARY

Chi-Square

Before You Begin: State H_0 and H_1.

Collect observed frequencies (f_o).
Compute number of rows; number of columns.

Compute expected frequency (f_e):

$$f_e = \frac{\text{(row total)} \cdot \text{(column total)}}{\text{grand total}}$$

Compute chi-square (χ^2):

$$\chi^2 = \Sigma \frac{(f_o - f_e)^2}{f_e}$$

Compute degrees of freedom (df):

$$df = \text{(number of rows} - 1) \cdot \text{(number of columns} - 1)$$

Find the critical value in Table X

If χ^2 is greater than the critical value, then reject H_0

Concept Quiz

SBC Communications (2001) conducted a survey of Digital Subscriber Line (DSL) users in the United States and found that 96% of their sample viewed high-speed access to the Internet as the most important technology in their home. A large number of these respondents also said they would be willing to give up their morning coffee, newspaper, radio, or cable television to keep DSL. Given the increase in the use of caffeine by college students, suppose a concerned researcher does a similar study. The researcher asks male and female students to answer if they would be willing to give up coffee to keep access to the Internet by circling yes, no, or maybe. Do you think male and female students would differ in their answer? Think about this research scenario and answer the following questions.

1. Chi-square can be used only on _____ data.

2. If you analyzed the data collected in this study, using chi-square, which of the following would be possible χ^2 values?

   -2.7 $.37$ 10.38 -4.77 -10.83 $-.47$

3. To conduct the χ^2 test, it is inadvisable to have expected frequencies of less than _____.

4. For this 2 × 3 study, there are _____ rows and _____ columns.

5. What would be the degrees of freedom in this study?

6. If the researcher decided to see whether students attending only day classes, only night classes, or a combination of day and night classes differed as to their willingness to give up coffee to keep the Internet, what would be the degrees of freedom and the critical value for χ^2?

Answers

1. nominal
2. .37 and 10.38 (χ^2 values are always positive because you always square the

differences between the expected and observed frequencies.)
3. 5
4. 2; 3

5. $(2-1) \cdot (3-1) = 2$
6. $df = (3-1) \cdot (3-1) = 4$; critical $\chi^2 = 9.488$

The Mann–Whitney *U* Test

Suppose that you are hired as a statistical consultant for a manufacturing company to evaluate the effectiveness of a job-training program. The managers of the company want to know whether people who went through a training program designed and administered by the local community college are significantly better workers than those who did not participate in the program. Unfortunately, you were not hired until after the data from the first group of workers had been collected, so you have no control over how the data were gathered. The data are shown in Table 15.6.

> **Question:** Can't the data just be separated into people with training and people with no training and then a *t* test be conducted to see whether there is any difference between the two groups?

The data you must work with, as you can see in Table 15.6, are not scores on a job proficiency test but *rankings* based on supervisors' evaluations of workers' job performance. A *t* test requires an interval or a ratio scale of measurement. When you use rankings, the data are ordered by size, but there is no guarantee that

Table 15.6   Job Performance Rankings of 20 Workers

Worker	Rank	Training Program	
T. D.	1	No	**Explanation:** The best
M. K.	2	No	worker gets a rank of
D. C.	3	Yes	20, and the poorest
R. K.	4	No	worker gets a rank
C. T.	5	No	of 1.
M. O.	6	Yes	
P. H.	7	No	
B. S.	8	Yes	
G. S.	9	No	
A. G.	10	Yes	
B. W.	11	No	
H. D.	12	Yes	
K. T.	13	No	
M. S.	14	Yes	
D. O.	15	Yes	
A. H.	16	Yes	
T. H.	17	No	
M. V.	18	Yes	
Z. S.	19	Yes	
K. H.	20	Yes	

the intervals between the ranks are equal. Therefore, these data represent an ordinal scale of measurement, and it is inappropriate to use a t test to analyze ordinal data. You must use a nonparametric test such as the Mann–Whitney U.

> **Question:** The title of this chapter uses the term "Nonparametric Statistics," and the Mann–Whitney U is a nonparametric test, but what does that mean? What is a nonparametric test?

As discussed in Chapter 1, statistics are generally classified as descriptive or inferential, and inferential statistics can be further divided into parametric and nonparametric statistics. **Parametric statistics** are those that are stated in terms of and make assumptions about population parameters (the characteristic elements of a population under study, such as the population mean and population standard deviation). For example, the hypotheses for the t test and the analysis of variance are stated in terms of the population mean, μ, and it is assumed that the variances of the populations being compared are equal and the scores are normally distributed. It is impossible to compare such parameters as population means when the data are ranked, and often it is impossible to guarantee equality of variances or normality, especially when the samples are small. **Nonparametric statistics** do not compare population parameters, and they make fewer assumptions than parametric statistics. The major advantages of most nonparametric statistics are that they work quite well with data that are ranked or skewed, as well as with small samples. The disadvantage of nonparametric tests is that, on average, they are less powerful and therefore less likely than parametric tests to reject the null hypothesis when the null hypothesis is false.

Just as with parametric tests, nonparametric tests are based on a null hypothesis and a research hypothesis, but the hypotheses are not presented in terms of population parameters. The null hypothesis simply states that the two independent samples come from the same population distribution. When the research hypothesis is two-tailed and nondirectional, it merely states that the two independent samples come from different population distributions. When the research hypothesis is one-tailed and directional, it states that one of the samples comes from a population comprised of ranks that are smaller than the population of the other sample. The nonparametric test used to analyze two independent samples is the **Mann–Whitney U.**

To compute the Mann–Whitney U, you actually compute two separate statistics called U_1 and U_2. The formulas for U_1 and U_2 are as follows:

$$U_1 = (n_1 \cdot n_2) + \frac{n_1(n_1 + 1)}{2} - \Sigma R_1 \tag{15.4}$$

$$U_2 = (n_2 \cdot n_1) + \frac{n_2(n_2 + 1)}{2} - \Sigma R_2 \tag{15.5}$$

n_1 and n_2 are the number of participants in Sample 1 and Sample 2, respectively. The only new terms are ΣR_1 and ΣR_2. ΣR_1 is the sum of the ranks for Sample 1;

Table 15.7   Job Performance Rankings of 20 Workers Separated Into Training and No-Training Samples

No Ranks (R_1)	Yes Ranks (R_2)
	Training
3	1
6	2
8	4
10	5
12	7
14	9
15	11
16	13
18	17
19	$\Sigma R_2 = 69$
20	$n_2 = 9$
$\Sigma R_1 = 141$	
$n_1 = 11$	

ΣR_2 is the sum of the ranks for Sample 2. To conduct a Mann–Whitney U test with the data in Table 15.6, you first need to separate the data into two samples; one is the workers who took the training program and the other is those who did not participate. The reorganized data are shown in Table 15.7.

Once the data are separated, sum the ranks for each sample and then compute U_1 and U_2:

$$U_1 = (n_1 \cdot n_2) + \frac{n_1(n_1 + 1)}{2} - \Sigma R_1 = (11 \cdot 9) + \frac{11(11 + 1)}{2} - 141$$

$$= 99 + \frac{11 \cdot 12}{2} - 141 = 99 + \frac{132}{2} - 141 = 99 + 66 - 141$$

$$= 24$$

$$U_2 = (n_2 \cdot n_1) + \frac{n_2(n_2 - 1)}{2} - \Sigma R_2 = (9 \cdot 11) + \frac{9(9 + 1)}{2} - 69$$

$$= 99 + \frac{9 \cdot 10}{2} - 69 = 99 + \frac{90}{2} - 69 = 99 + 45 - 69$$

$$= 75$$

Having computed both U values, you can swiftly verify their accuracy because their sum must always equal the product of n_1 and n_2; that is,

$$U_1 + U_2 = n_1 \cdot n_2 \tag{15.6}$$

Now verify the accuracy of your calculations. You know that n_1 is equal to 11 and n_2 is equal to 9, and you calculated that U_1 is 24 and U_2 is 75, so

$$U_1 + U_2 = n_1 \cdot n_2$$

$$24 + 75 = 11 \cdot 9$$

$$99 = 99$$

It checks.

Question: Now that these two U values have been correctly computed, what do I do with them? Do I compare them to each other, compute a ratio, or compare them to a critical value from a table?

First, compare your computed U_1 and U_2 values to each other and determine which is smaller. Henceforth, refer to this smaller value as U. So, if

$$U_1 = 24 \text{ and } U_2 = 75$$

then

$$U = 24$$

Next, you need to compare U to the appropriate values in Table U in Appendix A, a portion of which is reprinted in Table 15.8. You need both n_1 and n_2 to enter this table. Because your n_1 equals 11 and n_2 equals 9, go over to column 11 and then down to row 9. At the junction of column 11 and row 9, find the following numbers:

27   Regular type for a directional (one-tailed) hypothesis at the .05 level of significance

and

23   **Bold type** for a nondirectional (two-tailed) hypothesis at the .05 level of significance

For U to be significant, it must be *less than* or *equal to* the number listed in the table. (All the tests discussed so far require the computed statistic to be larger than the critical value. For the Mann–Whitney U, you want the computed value to be smaller than the critical value.) The research hypothesis is one-tailed: It states that the sample of people who did not take the training program is from a population comprised of lower rankings than the population of people who went through the training. (Remember that the better workers got higher rankings.) Thus, the U of 24 is significant because it is less than the 27 that the table lists as the critical value for a one-tailed hypothesis. Had your research hypothesis been

Table 15.8   A Portion of Table U—Critical Values of the Mann–Whitney *U* Test

n_2 \ n_1	1	2	3	4	5	6	7	8	9	10	11	12	13	14	15	16	17	18	19	20
1	—	—	—	—	—	—	—	—	—	—	—	—	—	—	—	—	—	—	0	0
																			—	—
2	—	—	—	—	0	0	0	1	1	1	1	2	2	2	3	3	3	4	4	4
					—	—	—	0	0	0	0	1	1	1	1	1	2	2	2	2
3	—	—	0	0	1	2	2	3	3	4	5	5	6	7	7	8	9	9	10	11
	—	—	—	—	0	1	1	2	2	3	3	4	4	5	5	6	6	7	7	8
4	—	—	0	1	2	3	4	5	6	7	8	9	10	11	12	14	15	16	17	18
	—	—	—	0	1	2	3	4	4	5	6	7	8	9	10	11	11	12	13	13
5	—	0	1	2	4	5	6	8	9	11	12	13	15	16	18	19	20	22	23	25
	—	—	0	1	2	3	5	6	7	8	9	11	12	13	14	15	17	18	19	20
6	—	0	2	3	5	7	8	10	12	14	16	17	19	21	23	25	26	28	30	32
	—	—	1	2	3	5	6	8	10	11	13	14	16	17	19	21	22	24	25	27
7	—	0	2	4	6	8	11	13	15	17	19	21	24	26	28	30	33	35	37	39
	—	—	1	3	5	6	8	10	12	14	16	18	20	22	24	26	28	30	32	34
8	—	1	3	5	8	10	13	15	18	20	23	26	28	31	33	36	39	41	44	47
	—	0	2	4	6	8	10	13	15	17	19	22	24	26	29	31	34	36	38	41
9	—	1	3	6	9	12	15	18	21	24	27	30	33	36	39	42	45	48	51	54
	—	0	2	4	7	10	12	15	17	20	23	26	28	31	34	37	39	42	45	48

Source: Kirk, 1978.

two-tailed, you would not have been able to reject the null hypothesis because your computed *U* of 24 is greater than the table value of 23.

Question: It isn't clear: When can the Mann–Whitney *U* be used?

Because the Mann–Whitney *U* requires fewer assumptions than the *t* test, you can use it on any independent two-sample data sets that can be ranked. Take a look at the data in Table 15.9. These data are scores on an algebra readiness test given to two math classes. Each class participated in a different math program during the past year. One class used a traditional program involving lots of paper/pencil and book work, and the other used a hands-on program with lots of tokens and objects that the students were required to move about in order to solve the problems. Put yourself in the place of one of the school district's math teachers who would like to determine whether there is any difference in the test scores of the two types of classes. This is a two-tailed research hypothesis because it asks only whether there will be a difference; it does not specify in which direction the difference will lie. When you examine closely the data from the two classes, you will notice that the distribution of scores from the traditional class seems to be relatively flat, whereas the

Table 15.9 Scores on an Algebra Readiness Test Given to Two Sixth-Grade Math Classes

Traditional Class	Hands-on Class
96	100
91	99
89	98
88	95
88	94
85	93
84	92
79	90
76	88
73	86
72	82
71	80
70	78
70	
70	
67	
65	
60	

distribution of scores from the hands-on class appears to be skewed toward the high end of the scale. Neither sample is normally distributed, so it is unwise to assume that their populations are normally distributed. This means that the basic assumptions for the *t* test cannot be met, and it is therefore best to use the nonparametric Mann–Whitney *U* to test the research hypothesis.

Question: The data in Table 15.9 are not ranked. How is a Mann–Whitney *U* conducted on data that have not been ranked?

The answer is simple enough. You *create* ranks by ranking the data. When ranking any data set, *always give the lowest score a rank of 1;* when ranking the scores for a Mann–Whitney *U* test, assign ranks as if the two samples have been combined. It is very important to remember to combine the samples when ranking and then separate the samples when computing ΣR_1 and ΣR_2. If you take another look at Table 15.9, you can see that the 10 lowest scores (60 through 76) are all from the traditional class, but the 11th score (78) is from the hands-on class. Thus, scores 60 through 76 get ranks 1 through 10, 78 gets a rank of 11, and you continue to rank the scores in this manner until all scores have ranks.

Question: This seems easy enough, but how are the three scores of 70 ranked?

Table 15.10   Ranks for Scores on an Algebra Readiness Test Given to Two Sixth-Grade Math Classes

Traditional Class	R_1	Hands-on Class	R_2
96	28	100	31
91	23	99	30
89	21	98	29
88	19	95	27
88	19	94	26
85	16	93	25
84	15	92	24
79	12	90	22
76	10	88	19
73	9	86	17
72	8	82	14
71	7	80	13
70	5	78	$\underline{11}$
70	5		$\Sigma R_2 = 288$
70	5		$n_2 = 13$
67	3		
65	2		
60	$\underline{1}$		
	$\Sigma R_1 = 208$		
	$n_1 = 18$		

Each tied score is assigned the same rank. You compute the average of the ranks that would have been assigned to the scores and assign that average rank to each score. Here is how to rank the three scores of 70: The previous score of 67 was assigned a rank of 3. The next three scores would typically receive the ranks of 4, 5, and 6, but because they are tied, they must all be assigned the same rank. The average of 4, 5, and 6 is 5, so you assign the rank of 5 to each score of 70. Assign the next score, 71, the rank of 7, and then proceed to rank the remaining scores, dealing with ties in the same manner. (Large numbers of tied scores are a bit of a problem in the Mann–Whitney *U* test, but a few tied scores should not affect the outcome of the test.)

Table 15.10 shows the two samples with their corresponding assigned ranks. Now you can use the sum of the ranks for the traditional math class (ΣR_1) and the sum of the ranks for the hands-on math class (ΣR_2) to compute U_1 and U_2:

$$U_1 = (n_1 \cdot n_2) + \frac{n_1(n_1 + 1)}{2} - \Sigma R_1 = (18 \cdot 13) + \frac{18(18 + 1)}{2} - 208$$

$$= 234 + \frac{18 \cdot 19}{2} - 208 = 234 + \frac{342}{2} - 208 = 234 + 171 - 208$$

$$= 197$$

VISUAL SUMMARY

The Mann–Whitney U Test

Before You Begin: State H_0 and H_1.

Compute n_1 and n_2.

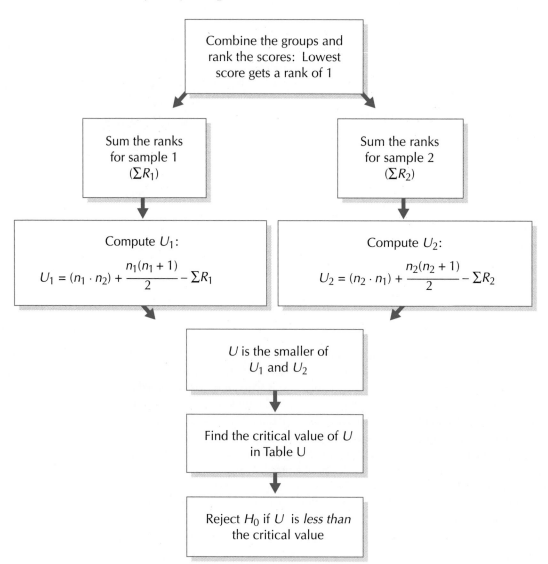

Combine the groups and
rank the scores: Lowest
score gets a rank of 1

Sum the ranks
for sample 1
(ΣR_1)

Sum the ranks
for sample 2
(ΣR_2)

Compute U_1:

$$U_1 = (n_1 \cdot n_2) + \frac{n_1(n_1 + 1)}{2} - \Sigma R_1$$

Compute U_2:

$$U_2 = (n_2 \cdot n_1) + \frac{n_2(n_2 + 1)}{2} - \Sigma R_2$$

U is the smaller of
U_1 and U_2

Find the critical value of U
in Table U

Reject H_0 if U is *less than*
the critical value

$$U_2 = \left(n_2 \cdot n_1\right) + \frac{n_2\left(n_2 + 1\right)}{2} - \Sigma R_2 = \left(13 \cdot 18\right) + \frac{13\left(13 + 1\right)}{2} - 288$$

$$= 234 + \frac{13 \cdot 14}{2} - 288 = 234 + \frac{182}{2} - 288 = 234 + 91 - 288$$

$$= 37$$

Using Formula 15.6 to check your computation of the two U values gives

$$U_1 + U_2 = n_1 \cdot n_2$$

$$197 + 37 = 18 \cdot 13$$

$$234 = 234$$

It checks out, and because U is the smaller of U_1 and U_2,

$$U = 37$$

Next, compare this computed value of U to the value found in Table U. Because the research hypothesis is two-tailed, you must use the two-tailed portion of Table U to determine the critical value of U. Using $n_1 = 18$ and $n_2 = 13$, you find a critical value of 67. You can reject the null hypothesis and accept the research hypothesis because your computed U is less than the critical value. There is a difference between the two classes on the algebra readiness test.

Concept Quiz

Hope is important in athletic performance and academic achievement (Curry, Snyder, Cook, Ruby, & Rehm, 1997). Suppose a researcher developed a positive thinking training program for children and predicts that children learning these skills will be better in sports than those without the training. The researcher recruits a Little League Baseball team and randomly assigns half to the training condition and the other to a control condition. Afterward, a sports scout watches the children play baseball and ranks the performance of all players on the team.

1. Because data in this study are _____ and the samples are _____, the requirements to use the Mann–Whitney U test are met.

2. If there were 12 children on the team, when ranking the data, the poorest performance gets a rank of _____ and the best performance gets a rank of _____.

3. If any scores are tied, then they are given the _____ rank.

4. $U_1 + U_2$ is always equal to _____.

5. If U_1 equals 35 and U_2 equals 55, then U is equal to _____.

6. When comparing your computed U to the value in Table U, your U will be significant if it is _____ than the table value.

Answers

1. ranked; independent   3. same   5. 35
2. 1; 12   4. $n_1 \cdot n_2$ 6. equal to or less

The Wilcoxon *T* Test

> **Question:** The Mann–Whitney U test requires independent samples. Is there a nonparametric test that can be used on correlated samples?

Yes. The Wilcoxon T test is a nonparametric statistical test that can be used to determine whether there is a significant difference between two correlated samples. Just like the Mann-Whitney U, the Wilcoxon T makes very few assumptions about the raw data that have been collected. The only major requirements for this test are that (1) the samples must be correlated and (2) it must be possible to rank the differences between the two samples. The following example illustrates when it is appropriate to use the Wilcoxon T.

As traffic congestion and air pollution become more and more pressing problems for large cities in the world, researchers and government representatives continue to search for solutions. The reason for traffic congestion is that too many cars are on the road at the same time. Anyone who lives near a large city is aware that traffic is at its worst during the morning and evening rush hours. The rush-hour phenomenon occurs because nearly all business and industry workers arrive at their jobs between 7 and 10 A.M., and they leave their jobs between 3 and 6 P.M. One obvious solution to this problem is to stagger the arrival and departure times of workers throughout the day rather than concentrate them into a few hours in the morning and the afternoon. Ideally, if 1/24th of the workforce began work at, say, 6 A.M., another 24th began work at 7 A.M., and so on throughout the 24-hour day, traffic congestion would be significantly reduced.

In compliance with appeals from environmental groups and the traffic commission, a large accounting firm is considering staggering its workers' beginning and ending times throughout the day. As an initial step, the company hires you as a consultant to study whether work productivity is affected when working hours are changed from the traditional 9 A.M. to 5 P.M. to an earlier 6 A.M. to 2 P.M. shift. That is, you are to test the two-tailed research hypothesis that different work schedules will result in different productivity ratings.

To begin your research, you ask management to assign 10 accountants to be participants in a small experiment. The accountants will have their productivity measured for 1 month on the regular 9-to-5 schedule, and then have their pro-

Table 15.11 Productivity Measures for 10 Accountants

	Schedule	
Accountant	Regular	Early
M. P.	2.0	1.7
D. Q.	1.7	1.6
O. D.	1.3	1.3
P. H.	.6	.8
D. M.	.6	.5
A. D.	.5	.4
W. A.	.4	.3
N. M.	.4	.9
C. L.	.3	.1
Z. Z.	.3	.1

ductivity measured, after a 2-week adjustment period, for 1 month on the earlier 6-to-2 schedule. Productivity is measured by the number of dollars produced for the company by each accountant, divided by the mean number of dollars produced by all company accountants. Thus, an accountant who has a productivity measure of 2.0 is twice as productive as the typical accountant at the company, and someone who has a productivity measure of .5 is half as productive as the typical accountant. The productivity measure of the 10 accountants on the two different work schedules are listed in Table 15.11.

Because it appears that the intervals within these data are not equal, these data do not meet the minimum data type requirements for the *t* test. Consequently, a nonparametric test must be used to analyze these data. Moreover, because the same participants were used in both conditions, the two samples should be correlated. The **Wilcoxon *T* test** is the most appropriate to analyze these data.

So far, all of the statistical tests discussed in this book can be represented by one or more formulas. However, the Wilcoxon *T* test is best described as a procedure rather than a formula. When you conduct a Wilcoxon *T* test, you find the differences between the paired scores and then compare the ranks of those differences. Therefore, the first step in the procedure requires that you compute differences between the paired scores, just as for the parametric correlated *t*. See Table 15.12.

Next, see whether there are any zero differences. All pairs that result in a zero difference are excluded from further analysis. Accountant O. D. had a zero difference, so her scores were not used in calculating the ranks. This leaves you with the nine pairs of scores in Table 15.13.

Now rank the differences according to absolute value; that is, ignore the sign and give a +.2 the same rank as a −.2. Remember that when you rank the differences, you give the smallest difference, according to absolute value, a rank of 1, and you give any tied differences the average of the ranks they typically would have received. Table 15.14 shows the final ranks for the accountants' productivity measures.

Table 15.12 Differences Between Productivity Measures for 10 Accountants

	Schedule		
Accountant	Regular	Early	Difference
M. P.	2.0	1.7	.3
D. Q.	1.7	1.6	.1
O. D.	1.3	1.3	.0
P. H.	.6	.8	−.2
D. M.	.6	.5	.1
A. D.	.5	.4	.1
W. A.	.4	.3	.1
N. M.	.4	.9	−.05
C. L.	.3	.1	.2
Z. Z.	.3	.1	.2

Table 15.13 Exclude Zero Differences

	Schedule		
Accountant	Regular	Early	Difference
M. P.	2.0	1.7	.3
D. Q.	1.7	1.6	.1
~~O. D.~~	~~1.3~~	~~1.3~~	~~.0~~
P. H.	.6	.8	−.2
D. M.	.6	.5	.1
A. D.	.5	.4	.1
W. A.	.4	.3	.1
N. M.	.4	.9	−.05
C. L.	.3	.1	.2
Z. Z.	.3	.1	.2

Having ranked the differences, you then **sign the ranks**. This is a process whereby each rank is assigned to a category based on the arithmetic sign of the difference score for that rank. If the difference score is negative, assign the rank to the minus category; if the difference score is positive, assign the rank to the plus category. Table 15.15 lists the signed ranks for the nine remaining accountants.

Next, sum the plus ranks (ΣR_+) and sum the minus ranks (ΣR_-), as shown in Table 15.16.

Question: Shouldn't the sum of the minus ranks be −15, rather than 15?

Table 15.14 Ranked Differences

Accountant	Schedule Regular	Early	Difference	Rank
M. P.	2.0	1.7	.3	8
D. Q.	1.7	1.6	.1	2.5
~~O. D.~~	~~1.3~~	~~1.3~~	~~.0~~	
P. H.	.6	.8	−.2	6
D. M.	.6	.5	.1	2.5
A. D.	.5	.4	.1	2.5
W. A.	.4	.3	.1	2.5
N. M.	.4	.9	−.05	9
C. L.	.3	.1	.2	6
Z. Z.	.3	.1	.2	6

Table 15.15 Signed Ranks

Accountant	Schedule Regular	Early	Difference	+ Ranks (R_+)	− Ranks (R_-)
M. P.	2.0	1.7	.3	8	
D. Q.	1.7	1.6	.1	2.5	
~~O. D.~~	~~1.3~~	~~1.3~~	~~.0~~		
P. H.	.6	.8	−.2		6
D. M.	.6	.5	.1	2.5	
A. D.	.5	.4	.1	2.5	
W. A.	.4	.3	.1	2.5	
N. M.	.4	.9	−.05		9
C. L.	.3	.1	.2	6	
Z. Z.	.3	.1	.2	6	

No. You must remember that plus and minus are now *categories.* All the ranks have a positive value, no matter what category they are in. After adding up the ranks, you determine the Wilcoxon *T,* which is the smaller of the ΣR_+ and ΣR_-. Therefore, if the sum of the plus ranks equals 30 and the sum of the minus ranks equals 15, then the Wilcoxon *T* equals 15:

$$\Sigma R_+ = 30$$

$$\Sigma R_- = 15$$

Wilcoxon $T = 15$

Table 15.16   Sum of the Plus Ranks (ΣR_+) and Sum of the Minus Ranks (ΣR_-)

Accountant	Schedule Regular	Early	Difference	+ Ranks (R_+)	− Ranks (R_-)
M. P.	2.0	1.7	.3	8	
D. Q.	1.7	1.6	.1	2.5	
~~O. D.~~	~~1.3~~	~~1.3~~	~~.0~~		
P. H.	.6	.8	−.2		6
D. M.	.6	.5	.1	2.5	
A. D.	.5	.4	.1	2.5	
W. A.	.4	.3	.1	2.5	
N. M.	.4	.9	−.05		9
C. L.	.3	.1	.2	6	
Z. Z.	.3	.1	.2	6	
				$\Sigma R_+ = 30$	$\Sigma R_- = 15$

Table 15.17   A Portion of Table W, Critical Values of the Wilcoxon T Test

	Level of Significance for a One-Tailed Test			
	.05	.025	.01	.005
	Level of Significance for a Two-Tailed Test			
n	.10	.05	.02	.01
5	0	—	—	—
6	2	0	—	—
7	3	2	0	—
8	5	3	1	0
9	8	5	3	1
10	10	8	5	3

Source: Kirk, 1978.

To determine whether a T of 15 is significant, use Table W in Appendix A, a portion of which is shown in Table 15.17. To enter Table W, you need to know whether the research hypothesis is directional (one-tailed) or nondirectional (two-tailed). You also need to know the number of signed ranks (n), which is the number of original pairs minus the number of pairs that have a zero difference. In the example, the research hypothesis is nondirectional and $n = 9$ because there

VISUAL SUMMARY

The Wilcoxon *T* Test

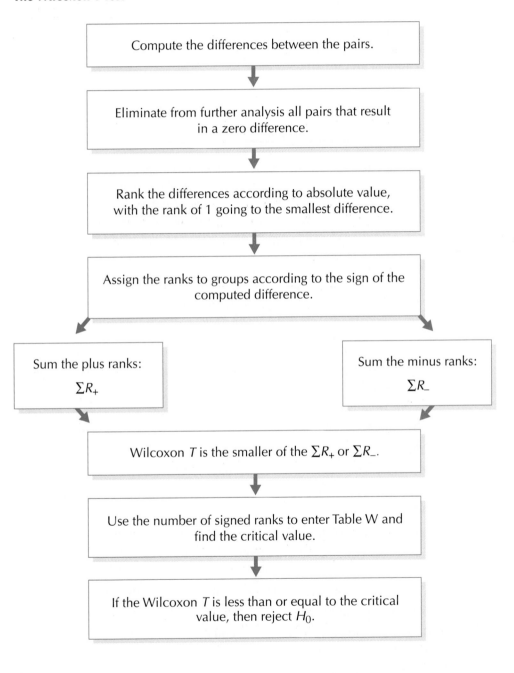

Compute the differences between the pairs.

Eliminate from further analysis all pairs that result in a zero difference.

Rank the differences according to absolute value, with the rank of 1 going to the smallest difference.

Assign the ranks to groups according to the sign of the computed difference.

Sum the plus ranks:

$$\Sigma R_+$$

Sum the minus ranks:

$$\Sigma R_-$$

Wilcoxon *T* is the smaller of the ΣR_+ or ΣR_-.

Use the number of signed ranks to enter Table W and find the critical value.

If the Wilcoxon *T* is less than or equal to the critical value, then reject H_0.

were 10 original pairs and only one of those had a zero difference. So the critical value of the Wilcoxon T that corresponds to 9 signed ranks for a nondirectional (two-tailed) test is 5. To be significant, the Wilcoxon T must be equal to or less than the critical value. Your Wilcoxon T value of 15 is greater than the critical value. It is not significant and you fail to reject the null hypothesis. According to this bogus research, shifting the work schedule back 3 hours earlier has no significant effect on productivity.

Concept Quiz

Killen et. al. (2000) conducted a study to determine the effectiveness of the transdermal nicotine system (patch) with the combination of different dosage levels of an additional medication or a placebo in helping smokers quit the habit and also reduce their nicotine craving and depression symptoms. Findings indicated that when participants were compliant, the transdermal nicotine patch with medication was significantly more effective than the patch with placebo. Imagine you conducted a similar study but used a counterbalanced design. Each participant wore a nicotine patch with medication for 1 week and a nicotine patch with a placebo for 1 week. At the end of each week, they rated the subjective quality of their anxiety on a scale from 0 to 30, with higher numbers indicating higher anxiety. Thus, each participant wore both patches for a week and evaluated the quality of their anxiety twice. Because the measurement scale is subjective, the intervals cannot be presumed to be equal; thus, a nonparametric test must be used to analyze the data.

1. In this study, a Wilcoxon T test is used because it is _____ and it compares the difference between two _____ samples.

2. The evaluations made by smokers are subjective, and intervals in these data are not _____, so a nonparametric test must be used.

3. Pairs with a difference of _____ are eliminated from further analysis.

4. In the Wilcoxon T procedure, all differences are ranked according to _____, with the rank of 1 going to the_____ score.

5. After the differences are ranked, they are separated into two different categories according to _____.

6. Next, both the _____ and the _____ must be computed.

7. The Wilcoxon T is equal to _____.

8. The Wilcoxon T must be _____ the critical value from Table W to be significant.

9. Which of the following are possible Wilcoxon T values?

    24   -24 2 -6 $-.03$ 2.5

10. Is there a significant difference between the transdermal patches if the Wilcoxon T is 26 for a two-tailed test with 15 signed ranks?

Answers

1. nonparametric; correlated
2. equal
3. zero
4. absolute value; smallest
5. the sign of the difference score
6. sum of the plus ranks; sum of the minus ranks

7. whichever is smaller, the sum of the plus ranks or the sum of the minus ranks
8. equal to or less than
9. All the positive values are possible Ts: 24, 2, and 2.5. Even though we sum the minus ranks, the ranks themselves are

positive; therefore, T is always positive.
10. No. According to Table W, with 15 signed ranks and two-tailed nondirectional hypothesis, the T-value must be equal to or less than 25 in order to be significant.

The Kruskal–Wallis Test

Having discussed the nonparametric substitutions for the t tests, it is time to turn to the nonparametric counterpart of the one-way analysis of variance. Known as the **Kruskal–Wallis test,** it is essentially an extension of the Mann–Whitney U test to more than two groups. One of the examples used when explaining the Mann–Whitney U test involved scores on an algebra readiness test given to two sixth-grade classes, one that had participated in a traditional math program and another that had used manipulatives in a nontraditional, hands-on program. Suppose that the school district adds still another level to the independent variable. In addition to the traditional and hands-on classes, another sixth-grade class, known as the prealgebra class, is introduced to basic algebraic terminology, notation, and exercises. To compare the programs, instead of including all the students from the three classes, the math committee decides to choose 21 similar students and randomly assign them to one of the three classes (7 to each class) and then give them the algebra readiness test at the completion of the class. The data from this test for all 21 students are shown in Table 15.18. The research hypothesis using these data states that the populations producing these three samples are different from one another.

Table 15.18   Scores on an Algebra Readiness Test for Samples From Three Classes

Traditional	Hands-On	Prealgebra
95	98	100
94	96	99
89	82	97
84	91	83
83	86	90
81	85	88
80	82	87

As mentioned earlier, the Kruskal–Wallis test is basically the same as the Mann–Whitney U, but it is used with more than two samples. With this in mind, what do you think is the first step in conducting a Kruskal–Wallis test? You should combine the scores and rank them. The 21 scores from the algebra readiness test in the example are ranked in Table 15.19.

You can refer to these rankings as you use Formula 15.7 to compute the Kruskal–Wallis test statistic, which is called H:

$$H = \left[\frac{12}{N_{\text{total}} \cdot (N_{\text{total}} + 1)} \right] \cdot \left[\frac{(\Sigma R_1)^2}{n_1} + \frac{(\Sigma R_2)^2}{n_2} + \cdots + \frac{(\Sigma R_k)^2}{n_k} \right] - \left[3 \cdot (N_{\text{total}} + 1) \right]$$

(15.7)

The symbols in Formula 15.7 should be familiar to you:

$\Sigma R_1 = $ the sum of the ranks for Sample 1 $= 53$

$\Sigma R_2 = $ the sum of the ranks for Sample 2 $= 77$

$\Sigma R_3 = $ the sum of the ranks for Sample 3 $= 101$

$n_1 = $ the number of scores in Sample 1 $= 7$

$n_2 = $ the number of scores in Sample 2 $= 7$

$n_3 = $ the number of scores in Sample 3 $= 7$

$N_{\text{total}} = $ the total number of scores in all the samples $= 21$

$k = $ the number of groups $= 3$

Table 15.19   Scores on an Algebra Readiness Test and Ranks for Samples From Three Classes

Traditional	R_1	Hands-On	R_2	Prealgebra	R_3
95	16	98	19	100	21
94	15	96	17	99	20
89	10	82	13	97	18
84	5	91	12	83	14
83	4	86	7	90	11
81	2	85	6	88	9
80	1	82	3	87	8
	$\Sigma R_1 = 53$		$\Sigma R_2 = 77$		$\Sigma R_3 = 101$
	$n_1 = 7$		$n_2 = 7$		$n_3 = 7$

Substituting these values into Formula 15.7 gives

$$H = \left[\frac{12}{N_{total} \cdot (N_{total} + 1)} \right] \cdot \left[\frac{(\Sigma R_1)^2}{n_1} + \frac{(\Sigma R_2)^2}{n_2} + \frac{(\Sigma R_3)^2}{n_3} \right] -$$

$$\left[3 \cdot (N_{total} + 1) \right]$$

$$= \left[\frac{12}{21 \cdot (21 + 1)} \right] \cdot \left[\frac{(53)^2}{7} + \frac{(77)^2}{7} + \frac{(101)^2}{7} \right] - \left[3 \cdot (21 + 1) \right]$$

$$= \left[\frac{12}{21 \cdot (22)} \right] \cdot \left[\frac{2,809}{7} + \frac{5,929}{7} + \frac{10,201}{7} \right] - \left[3 \cdot (22) \right]$$

$$= \left[\frac{12}{462} \right] \cdot \left[401.286 + 847 + 1,457.286 \right] - 66$$

$$= \left[0.026 \cdot 2,705.572 \right] - 66 = 70.345 - 66$$

$$= 4.345$$

Question: Is the next step to look up the H value in Table H?

Actually, there's no need for a separate table for H values because the χ^2 distribution is a very close estimate of the distribution of H. Therefore, you can look in the χ^2 table, Table X in Appendix A, and find the critical value of H for $k - 1$, or 2 degrees of freedom.

The critical value in Table X at the .05 level of significance and 2 degrees of freedom is 5.99. For H to be significant, it must be *equal to or greater than* the critical value from the table (note that this is different from the Mann–Whitney U and the Wilcoxon T). Your computed H is 4.345, which is less than the table value, so you would fail to reject the null hypothesis. There is no significant difference between the samples drawn for the three different classes. In cases where the H is significant, the Mann–Whitney U is used to make comparisons between pairs of samples.

VISUAL SUMMARY

The Kruskal–Wallis Test

Before You Begin: State H_0 and H_1.

Compute $n_1, n_2, \ldots, n_k$, and N_{total}.

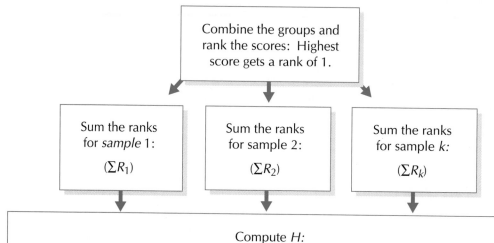

Combine the groups and rank the scores: Highest score gets a rank of 1.

Sum the ranks for *sample* 1: (ΣR_1)	Sum the ranks for sample 2: (ΣR_2)	Sum the ranks for sample *k:* (ΣR_k)

Compute H:

$$H = \left[\frac{12}{N_{total} \cdot (N_{total} + 1)} \right] \cdot \left[\frac{(\Sigma R_1)^2}{n_1} + \frac{(\Sigma R_2)^2}{n_2} + \cdots + \frac{(\Sigma R_k)^2}{n_k} \right] - [3 \cdot (N_{total} + 1)]$$

Find the critical value of H in the chi-square table, Table X, using $k - 1$ degrees of freedom.

Reject H_0 if H is *greater than or equal to* the critical value.

Concept Quiz

In the previous concept quiz, we mentioned the Killen et. al. (2000) study, which found that the transdermal nicotine patch, when combined with either medication, was more effective in helping smokers abstain from smoking and in reducing their nicotine craving and depression symptoms. Suppose you conducted another study and wanted to compare how smokers evaluated three different smoking cessation treatments. In your study, you recruit smokers hoping to quit the habit and, using a seminar format, present each smoker with details of one of three different therapy programs. Participants are then asked to rate subjectively the quality of the therapy on a scale from 1 to 20 for overall qualities as cost, treatment time, expected effectiveness, ability to relieve cravings, and so on.

1. The Kruskal–Wallis test is essentially an extension of the _____ to more than two samples.

2. In the Kruskal–Wallis test, all scores are _____ and then ranked, with the _____ score receiving the rank of 1.

3. The Kruskal–Wallis statistic is called _____, and its distribution is very closely approximated by the _____ distribution.

4. In this study, the number of degrees of freedom for the H statistic is equal to _____.

Answers

1. Mann–Whitney U test   3. H; χ^2 4. $k - 1$ (the number of
2. combined; lowest   samples minus 1) = 2

Summary

Parametric statistics are those that are stated in terms of and make assumptions about population parameters, whereas nonparametric statistics do not compare population parameters and have fewer assumptions than parametric statistics. This chapter describes four nonparametric statistical tests that can be used with nominal or ranked data. Chi-square is used to analyze nominal data. The Mann–Whitney U is used to analyze ranked data from two independent samples. The Wilcoxon T is a nonparametric test that can be used to determine any significant difference between two correlated samples. The Kruskal–Wallis test is used to analyze ranked data from three or more independent samples.

The visual summary that follows is designed to help you choose the proper nonparametric statistic based on the type of data and the design of your research project. First, determine whether the data are nominal or ordinal. If the data are nominal, the appropriate test is chi-square. If the data are ordinal, you have to determine the number of samples. If there are three or more samples, you can conduct a Kruskal–Wallis test. If there are two samples, you must determine whether the samples are independent or correlated. If the samples are independent, you can use the Mann–Whitney U test. If the samples are correlated, you can use the Wilcoxon T.

VISUAL SUMMARY

Chi-Square and Other Nonparametric Statistics

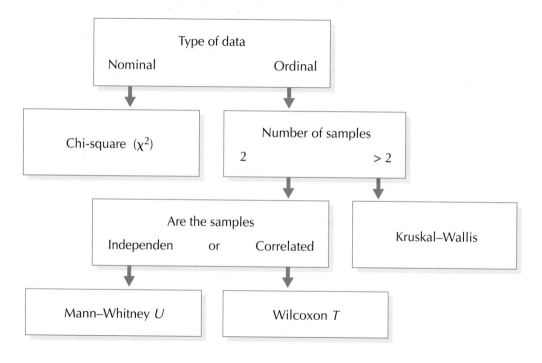

Key Terms

nominal data
chi-square (χ^2)
observed frequency (f_o)
expected frequency (f_e)

parametric statistics
nonparametric
   statistics
Mann–Whitney U

Wilcoxon T
sign the ranks
Kruskal–Wallis test
   (H)

Formulas

$$\chi^2 = \sum \frac{(f_o - f_e)^2}{f_e} \tag{15.1}$$

$$f_e = \frac{(\text{row total}) \cdot (\text{column total})}{\text{grand total}} \tag{15.2}$$

$$df = (\text{number of rows} - 1) \cdot (\text{number of columns} - 1) \tag{15.3}$$

$$U_1 = (n_1 \cdot n_2) + \frac{n_1(n_1 + 1)}{2} - \Sigma R_1 \tag{15.4}$$

$$U_2 = (n_2 \cdot n_1) + \frac{n_2(n_2 + 1)}{2} - \Sigma R_2 \tag{15.5}$$

$$U_1 + U_2 = n_1 \cdot n_2 \tag{15.6}$$

$$H = \left[\frac{12}{N_{\text{total}} \cdot (N_{\text{total}} + 1)} \right] \cdot \left[\frac{(\Sigma R_1)^2}{n_1} + \frac{(\Sigma R_2)^2}{n_2} + \cdots + \frac{(\Sigma R_k)^2}{n_k} \right] - \left[3 \cdot (N_{\text{total}} + 1) \right] \tag{15.7}$$

Problems

1. A major fast-food chain has hired you to do some marketing research. Given ecological and environmental concerns, they want to know whether the general public prefers their hamburgers wrapped in aluminum foil, foam plastic boxes, or paper. You have collected the following data from 3,000 people. Analyze the data and tell whether there is a significant difference between the three categories.

Foil	Foam	Paper
1,230	740	1,030

2. As a clinical psychologist, you have been testing three types of talk therapies on a group of 120 patients who have schizophrenia. Using the following data, compute a χ^2 to determine whether there is a difference among the outcomes of the three types of therapy.

Outcome of Therapy

	Poor	Moderate	Good
Therapy 1	5	12	23
Therapy 2	20	12	8
Therapy 3	13	13	14

3. You are a sociologist, and your current interest is people's behavior in relation to petty theft. In a crowded student union, your accomplice leaves his books and electronic calculator on a table while he gets a soft drink. When the accomplice is away, another person walks up and takes the calculator. You want to see how many people will stop the thief and whether it makes a difference if your accomplice asks a student sitting nearby to watch his things. Using the data given here, compute a χ^2 and state your conclusions based on the data.

Asked for Help

	Yes	No
Stopped thief	25	8
Did not stop thief	7	24

4. A psychologist interested in interpersonal attraction asked 80 undergraduate students whether they prefer to date blonds, brunettes, or redheads. The data from that project are given here. Analyze the data using χ^2 and give your conclusions.

Blonds	Brunettes	Redheads
23	34	23

5. Suppose you ask 150 people whether they ever had an experience that they would classify as supernatural. At the same time, you ask them about their school experience and assign them to one of four groups: those who did not graduate from high school, those who graduated from high school, those who graduated from college, and those who have a graduate degree. Use χ^2 to analyze the following data and tell whether they are significant.

Supernatural Experience

	Yes	No
No high school diploma	23	3
High school diploma	25	20
College degree	15	35
Graduate degree	2	27

6. In the process of revamping its curriculum, the sociology department at a small college surveyed its 200 sociology majors to see whether they preferred to have fewer required courses, keep the same number of required courses, or add more required courses for the sociology major. The results, grouped according to the respondents' year in school, are listed here. Analyze the data and tell whether there is any significance. If you were a member of the sociology faculty at this college, what conclusions could you draw from the data?

Number of Courses

	Fewer	Same	More
Freshman	35	15	10
Sophomore	25	10	20
Junior	15	15	15
Senior	10	20	10

7. The chairperson of the Learning College psychology department is interested in determining whether the length of professors' teaching experience affects

student rankings of the professors' teaching effectiveness. Based on student evaluations, the department chair assigns ranks to the 20 professors in the department based on student evaluations. Then he separates the faculty into two categories, those with fewer than 5 years of teaching experience and those with 5 or more years. Use the appropriate nonparametric test and the data in the table to tell whether there is a difference between the rankings of the two groups of professors.

Rankings of Professors	
Less than 5 Years of Experience	5 or More Years of Experience
20	6
2	8
19	12
18	7
9	11
16	5
14	3
15	17
	13
	1
	4
	10

8. Use the Mann–Whitney U test to see whether there is a difference between the visual acuity of a randomly chosen group of seven children and that of a randomly chosen group of nine adults. The vision test scores are listed here.

Children	Adults
22	19
23	16
13	22
16	19
21	17
14	25
24	20
	18
	15

9. An experiment was designed to compare the short-term memory capacity of 21 participants randomly assigned to one of two conditions. In one condition, the participants were asked to remember a list of words, and in the other condition, the participants were asked to remember a list of numbers. The table lists the number of words or numbers each participant remembered. Generate a null hypothesis and a research hypothesis for this experiment, and then use the Mann–Whitney U to determine whether there is a significant difference between the two samples. Given the computed U value and the significance level for this problem, what conclusions can you reach about the experiment?

Words	Numbers
5	4
7	6
5	6
4	3
3	7
8	5
3	8
7	9
8	7
8	7
5	

10. A psychologist who is a proofreading expert has developed two 10-page manuscripts for an experiment. One manuscript has no errors on the first 7 pages and then 20 errors on the last 3 pages; the other manuscript has an average of 5 errors per page on the first 7 pages and then the identical 20 errors on the last 3 pages of the manuscript. The dependent variable in this experiment is the number of errors detected by each reader on the last 3 pages of the manuscript assigned. The researcher predicts that the manuscript with the errors throughout will lead to more errors being noticed on the last 3 pages. Using the

data in the table, compute a Mann–Whitney U and determine whether it is significant. Remember to include the null hypothesis, the research hypothesis, and any conclusions that you can draw from this experiment.

Errors in First 7 Pages	No Errors in First 7 Pages
13	10
18	12
7	6
15	10
14	6
12	8
17	3
19	9
15	10

11. A researcher studying human factors related to computer screens decides to conduct an experiment to compare the picture clarity of two different types of computer monitors: the typical CRT-type monitors and the newer flat-panel monitors. The researcher sets up 20 monitors with identical displays in a large room, 10 CRT-type and 10 flat-panel, and then asks an art critic to rank the monitors according to clarity. The critic's ranks are given in the table. Use the data to determine whether there is a difference in ranking between the two types of monitors.

CRT-Type	Flat-Panel
3	1
6	2
9	4
10	5
11	7
14	8
15	12
16	13
19	17
20	18

12. Use the Mann–Whitney U to determine whether there is a difference between the numbers of positive social responses per hour that are given by children with autism who are undergoing two different types of therapy. One is a sensory deprivation approach known as "restricted environmental stimulation therapy (REST), and the other is a traditional behavior modification approach. The data are given in the table.

Number of Positive Social Responses	
REST Technique	Behavior Modification
6	9
0	1
4	12
5	8
7	21
3	6
2	13
7	15

13. Ten pairs of identical twin rats were used in a study to determine whether diet affects brain development. The two members of each pair of twins were fed a different diet for 10 weeks after they were weaned. One group received a protein-rich diet and the other a protein-deficient diet. At the end of the 10-week period, the brains of the rats were examined to see whether there was any difference in the brain mass (measured in grams) between the two groups. Use the appropriate nonparametric test to analyze the data in the table and determine whether there is a significant difference between the two groups of rats.

	Diet	
Pair	Protein Rich	Protein Deficient
1	23	20
2	26	23
3	21	21
4	17	19
5	15	16
6	29	21
7	27	22
8	33	20
9	21	17
10	28	19

14. Ivan Pavlov IV decides to replicate one of his great-grandfather's experiments. He classically conditions 12 dogs to salivate to a 1,000 cycle-per-second tone by pairing the tone with a Tastie Bite Dog Yummie. (Ivan IV works for the Tastie Bite Dog Yummie Company.) He plays the tone and then gives the dog the Yummie, thereby eliciting the salivation. Eventually, the dog salivates to the tone alone. Now Ivan predicts that his dogs are more likely to salivate to a similar but higher tone, rather than a similar but lower tone. To test this hypothesis, he presents a 900-cycle and a 1,100-cycle tone and measures the amount of salivation (in milliliters). Use the Wilcoxon T to test this hypothesis using the amounts given in the table.

Dog	900-Cycle Tone	1,100-Cycle Tone
1	8.7	8.8
2	8.9	9.2
3	12.8	7.2
4	19.7	18.3
5	11.9	15.6
6	12.6	12.6
7	21.9	16.3
8	31.6	16.5
9	8.7	22.6
10	9.8	9.3
11	15.6	16.1
12	4.6	3.8

15. Use the Wilcoxon T to determine whether there is a difference between the pretest and posttest scores of nine patients who have schizophrenia and are undergoing a new drug therapy. The table lists the numbers of delusional responses given in a structured interview before and after the drug is administered.

Patient	Pretest	Posttest
P. J.	10	7
O. C.	22	12
D. J.	18	19
S. R.	15	7
M. P.	22	21
D. T.	9	3
M. M.	4	0
L. N.	16	17
D. H.	8	2

16. Thirteen participants underwent an assertiveness training program. Before and after completing the program, they were rated on their aggressiveness by an impartial observer. Use the Wilcoxon T to tell whether there is a difference between the before ratings and the after ratings.

Participant	Before	After
1	70	81
2	55	66
3	36	47
4	56	53
5	77	76
6	93	99
7	37	48
8	22	47
9	82	93
10	83	81
11	84	92
12	77	88
13	47	84

17. Eight laboratory rats were trained to run a maze in the dark. Two weeks later, each was tested in the maze, once in the dark and once in the light. The dependent variable in this experiment is the number of errors the rat makes running the maze. The data for each rat are given in the table. Use the Wilcoxon T to determine whether there is a difference between the ability of the rats to run the maze in the dark and to run the maze in the light.

Rat	Dark	Light
1	23	18
2	18	28
3	14	14
4	22	21
5	33	35
6	27	29
7	9	12
8	22	17

18. Twenty-one participants are divided into three groups of seven in a study of jealousy. Each group is asked to read a paragraph that describes a spouse flirting with another one, two, or three different people at a party. The participants are asked to pretend that the paragraph describes their spouses and to evaluate how jealous they feel on a 10-point scale, with 10 being very jealous and 1 being not very jealous. The table lists the data from this experiment. Use a nonparametric test to determine whether there is a significant difference among the groups.

One Flirt	Two Flirts	Three Flirts
6	7	5
4	6	9
5	6	10
1	7	9
3	8	10
2	5	6
4	4	5

19. If a person is deprived of REM (dream) sleep, he or she tends to spend more time in REM sleep when the deprivation period is over. Use the Kruskal–Wallis test to determine whether the amount of time spent in REM sleep the first night after the end of sleep deprivation is significantly different for people who have spent one, two, three, or four nights being deprived of REM sleep. The number of minutes spent in REM sleep for the 20 participants is given here.

One Night	Two Nights	Three Nights	Four Nights
100	120	140	160
122	137	145	173
97	129	147	158
110	122	151	151
109	121	139	144

20. Suppose you are interested in studying humor. You ask three comedians to tell the same joke to several different people. Each person listens to only one comedian and then rates the "funniness" of the joke on a scale from 1 to 100. A rating of 1 means that the joke is not at all funny, and a rating of 100 means that the joke is the funniest the person has ever heard. Use the Kruskal–Wallis test to determine whether there is a difference among the three different comedians based on the data listed in the table.

Comedian 1	Comedian 2	Comedian 3
75	62	56
68	66	2
99	45	46
86	65	54
76	69	55
69	59	
73		

21. The following data were gathered from three groups of eight people who participated in an experiment comparing long-term memory for three types of items: words, nonwords, and numbers. The dependent variable in this experiment was the number of items remembered out of a list of 50 items. Generate a null hypothesis and a research hypothesis for this experiment, and then use the Kruskal–Wallis test to determine whether there is a difference among the three conditions.

Words	Nonwords	Numbers
28	15	6
29	14	6
37	15	5
30	16	7
29	23	5
18	15	6
28	14	7
17	13	7

22. Three separate groups of randomly assigned participants were asked to list the number of words they recognized from a 100-word list spoken by a man, a woman, or a computer. State a null hypothesis and a research hypothesis, and then use the table data to conduct a Kruskal–Wallis test. Is it significant?

Man	Woman	Computer
97	99	86
96	94	80
93	92	88
94	97	80
93	92	81
92	94	80
95	96	82
95	96	87
93	94	79

Problems From the Literature

The following problems refer to actual results from research studies that are cited at the end of the chapter. However, the data used to generate problem sets are hypothetical. Unless stated otherwise, use the .05 significance level for all analyses.

23. What does shoe size have to do with delivering a baby? Gorman, Noble, and Andrews (1997) looked at the association between small shoe sizes and vaginal and cesarean section childbirth delivery. They found no relationship between the two. Suppose another researcher wanted to extend this unusual line of research to men's shoe size and the mode of delivery of their first child. The researcher collected and classified shoe size data on 600 first-time fathers into three groups: large (size 10 and above), average (size 8 and 9), and small (size 7 and smaller). Use the appropriate nonparametric test to analyze the following data and tell whether there is a significant difference in mode of a first-born child's delivery relative to the father's shoe size.

First-Time Father's Shoe Size

	Small	Average	Large
Vaginal Delivery	103	105	92
Cesarean Section	115	85	100

24. Social phobia is a psychological disorder in which the patient is very anxious in social settings and tends to avoid social situations and interactions. A study done by Beidel, Turner, and Morris (2000) evaluated the effectiveness of a behavioral treatment compared to a control group in reducing social anxiety among young children. The behavioral treatment involved social skills

training followed by interactions with other children in group activities like bowling, a fear exposure activity, and lessons about social phobia. Children in the behavioral treatment had significantly more gains in their fight against social phobia than those in the control condition. Moreover, these gains were still apparent 6 months later. Suppose you recruited a sample of 12-year-old children with social phobia and asked them to subjectively evaluate their social phobia on a scale from 1 (extremely low social phobia) to 20 (extremely high social phobia) before and after their treatment. Use the appropriate nonparametric test to determine whether there is a difference between the before and after evaluations of social phobia.

Child	Before Treatment	After Treatment
1	18	10
2	20	14
3	17	15
4	20	19
5	17	17
6	16	19
7	16	14
8	20	18
9	19	15
10	14	17
11	13	13
12	8	10

25. Barling, Kelloway, and Cheng (1996) examined the importance of time management in predicting achievement performance. Among their findings was a significant relationship between short-range planning and achievement striving. In particular, data from 102 car salespersons indicated that when motivation was high, time management could predict car sale performance. Suppose you conducted a study of your own and ranked salespeople according to the number of automobiles they sold in the past 6 months. The rankings of the top 20 salespeople were separated into two groups: those that valued time management and those that did not value time management. Use the appropriate nonparametric test to determine whether the groups are significantly different.

Rankings of Salespeople	
Time Management Important	Time Management Not Important
3	18
2	4
12	20
6	19
9	11
16	7
1	13
10	15
5	14
	17
	8

26. Researchers Detweiler, Bedell, Salovey, Pronin, and Rothman (1999) found that a sun-protection brochure with skin cancer statistics and a gain-message describing the increased chances of living a longer life with protection from the sun was an effective way to promote the use of waterproof sunscreen with a sun protection factor (SPF) of 15+ among college students. Suppose you wanted to examine skin cancer fears or losses to see what aspects college students feared most so you could develop a different sun-protection brochure. You recruit 21 students and ask them to subjectively rate one of three potential consequences of skin cancer using a scale from 1 to 20 in terms of fear, impact on self-esteem, changes in life, ease of adjustment, and so on. Data are shown here, with higher

numbers indicating a more negative rating. Use the appropriate nonparametric test to determine whether there are significant differences between conditions.

Ratings

Melanoma on Face	Chemotherapy Treatments	Reduce Life Span
1	5	14
3	8	12
1	10	9
6	7	2
9	6	10
2	5	4
5	12	1

27. As mentioned in Problem 25, Barling, Kelloway, and Cheng (1996) found that when car salespeople were highly motivated and valued the importance of time management, their job performance could be predicted. Suppose ABC Auto Sales decided to send all their employees to a time management class. Two months afterward, ABC asked full-time and part-time employees whether they were using time management. Data collected from a survey of their employees are shown here. Use this data to conduct a χ^2 test.

Use Time Management

	Yes	No
Full-Time	21	14
Part-Time	8	13

28. Mohr and colleagues (2001) explored positive and negative experiences and different social and solitary drinking

contexts along with the daily drinker's neuroticism levels. They found an association between negative experiences and solitary drinking and positive experiences and social drinking among those in their sample. Moreover, they found that individuals who scored high compared to low on neuroticism drank more in solitary contexts when there were negative experiences. Suppose a group of researchers recruited a sample of college students and asked them to complete several questionnaires, including the neuroticism scale. Participants evaluated the benefits of a solitary drinking environment on a scale from 0 to 30 following both negative and positive experiences. The participants were divided so that half first imagined the positive experience and then the negative experience. The remaining half imagined the negative experience followed by the positive experience. Evaluations for both conditions were divided between participants scoring high and low on neuroticism. Data are listed here. Use the appropriate nonparametric test to determine whether there is a significant difference between conditions.

Student	Negative Experience	Positive Experience
J. G.	21	10
L. M.	18	16
D. K.	30	17
M. V.	21	13
J. V.	15	15
J. W.	18	19
K. K.	29	14
A. R.	27	18
C. P.	18	18

29. Bruck, Ceci, and Francoeur (2000) conducted a study of the accuracy of children's use of anatomical dolls to

demonstrate their experience during a routine medical exam in one of two experimental conditions. Half of the three- and four-year-olds in the study had a medical exam that included a genital examination, and the other half did not. After the exam, the children were asked to use the anatomical dolls and demonstrate the events of the medical examination. Among their findings, data indicated age differences in the number of accurate displays of how the doctor used different instruments but no age differences in the children's reports of genital touching. However, among the girls there were more errors, with some children falsely showing insertions into the anal or genital cavity of the anatomical dolls. Thus, this research indicates that the reliability of reports using anatomical dolls may be limited to older children. Suppose another researcher does the same study but this time also included older children, ages 4, 5, and 6 years old. The researcher recorded whether or not the child was accurate in his or her display of the medical exam using the anatomical doll. Data are listed here. Use the appropriate nonparametric test to determine whether there is a significant difference between conditions.

Medical Demonstration

	Accurate	Not Accurate
4-Year-Olds	18	26
5-Year-Olds	51	28
6-Year-Olds	47	26

30. Researchers Recarte and Nunes (1996) did an experiment on the perception of speed in an automobile to see if it varied depending

on actual speed, previous acceleration, driving experience, and sex of driver. They found that overall participants tended to underestimate the speed of an automobile. Suppose another researcher thought the type of automobile might make a difference in speed estimations. In this study, participants were randomly assigned to sit in the front seat of one of four types of cars—(1) a sports car, (2) a compact car, (3) a mid-size sedan, or (4) a large sedan— and then estimate the speed of the car when asked. The color and amenities of the car were all very similar. Each car was hooked up to a driving/road test simulator so driving, road course, and weather conditions were the same in all conditions. Ten minutes after the car started on the road course, a horn beeped and the participant said aloud the estimated speed in miles per hour. The difference between actual and estimated speed was the dependent variable. Positive scores indicated overestimation, and negative scores indicated underestimation of speed compared to the actual speed of the auto. Because normal distribution cannot be assumed, use the data shown here to calculate the appropriate nonparametric test. Did the participants estimations differ between car conditions?

Type of Car			
Sports Car	Compact Car	Mid-Size Sedan	Large Sedan
2.7	−5.8	−7.9	−11.4
5.2	−6.2	−4.7	−8.7
−1.8	−10.7	−1.1	4.1
−4.3	4.6	2.3	6.2
5.9	−8.4	−8.5	−12.6
−6.6	5.1	6.0	−5.3
−2.8	−4.1	−10.8	−2.8
−1.5	−3.9	−9.6	−7.9

31. Albarracin and colleagues (2000) studied beliefs associated with condom use outcomes. Included were beliefs about the pros and cons of condom use and whether there was more of a self- or social concern linked to the belief. For example, beliefs about whether condoms protect you from AIDS, make you feel clean, make you worry less, are a lot of trouble, decrease pleasure, and so on, were assessed. The researchers found that protection had little influence on actual condom use and intentions to use condoms. Instead, they found that self-concept and pleasure were strongly related to attitudes of using condoms and both intentions and actual use of condoms. Given this information, suppose another group of researchers want to see whether there are gender differences in self-concept concerns if sexual partners wouldn't have sex with them without a condom. Participants were asked to evaluate this situation in terms of how this would make them feel about themselves, worries that they were dirty or sexually risky looking, and so on, on a scale from 1 (not much concern) to 20 (a lot of concern). Data are listed here. Determine the appropriate nonparametric test and see whether there is a self-concept concern difference between men and women.

Self-Concept Concern	
Women	Men
17	10
14	14
19	18
12	10
11	10
14	12
12	9
16	10
14	6
19	11
	12
	11

References

Albarracin, D., McNatt, P. S., Williams, W. R., Hoxworth, T., Zenilman, J., Ho, R. M., Rhodes, F., Malotte, C. K., Bolan, G. A., & Iatesta, M. (2000). Structure of outcome beliefs in condom use. *Health Psychology, 19,* 458–468.

Barling, J., Kelloway, E. K., & Cheng, D. (1996). Time management and achievement striving interact to predict car sales performance. *Journal of Applied Psychology, 81,* 821–826.

Beidel, D. C., Turner, S. M., & Morris, T. L. (2000). Behavioral treatment of childhood social phobia. *Journal of Consulting and Clinical Psychology, 68,* 1072–1080.

Brady, S. S., & Helgeson, V. S. (1999). Social support and adjustment recurrence of breast cancer. *Journal of Psychosocial Oncology, 17*(2), 37–55.

Bruck, M., Ceci, S. J., & Francoeur, E. (2000). Children's use of anatomically detailed dolls to report genital touching in a medical examination: Developmental and gender comparisons. *Journal of Experimental Psychology: Applied, 6,* 74–83.

Curry, L. A., Snyder, C. R., Cook, D. L., Ruby, B. C., & Rehm, M. (1997). Role of hope in academic and sports achievement. *Journal of Personality and Social Psychology, 73,* 1257–1267.

Detweiler, J. B., Bedell, B. T., Salovey, P., Pronin, E., & Rothman, A. J. (1999). Message framing and sunscreen use: Gain-framed messages motivate beachgoers. *Health Psychology, 18,* 189–196.

Gorman, R. E., Noble, A., & Andrews, C. M. (1997). The relationship of shoe size and mode of delivery. *Midwifery Today Childbirth Education, 41,* 70–71.

Kaplan, G. A., & Reynolds, P. (1988). Depression and cancer mortality and morbidity: Prospective evidence from the Alameda County Study. *Journal of Behavioral Medicine, 11,* 1–13.

Killen, J. D., Fortmann, S. P., Schatzberg, A. F., Hayward, C., Sussman, L., Rothman, M., Strausberg, L., & Varady, A. (2000). Nicotine patch and paraxetine for smoking cessation. *Journal of Consulting and Clinical Psychology, 68,* 883–889.

Kirk, R. E. (1978). *Introductory statistics.* Pacific Grove, CA: Brooks/Cole.

Manne, S., & Miller, D. (1998). Social support, social conflict, and adjustment among adolescents with cancer. *Journal of Pediatric Psychology, 23,* 121–130.

Minimum, E. W. (1978). *Statistical reasoning in psychology and education.* New York: Wiley.

Mohr, C. D., Armeli, S., Tennen, H., Carney, M. A., Affleck, G., & Hromi, A. (2001). Daily interpersonal experiences, context, and alcohol consumption: Crying in your beer and toasting good times. *Journal of Personality and Social Psychology, 80,* 489–500.

Owen, D. B. (1962). *Handbook of statistical tables.* Boston: Addison Wesley Longman.

Recarte, M. A., & Nunes, L. M. (1996). Perception of speed in an automobile: Estimation and production. *Journal of Experimental Psychology: Applied, 2,* 291–304.

SBC Communications, Inc. (2001). *Broadband Watch 2001 national survey fact sheet.* Retrieved April 10, 2001, from the World Wide Web: http://www.sbc.com/Products_Services/BW/National_Fact_Sheetx.doc.

Turner-Cobb, J. M., Sephton, S. E., Koopman, C., Blake-Mortimer, J., & Spiegel, D. (2000). Social support and salivary cortisol in women with metastatic breast cancer. *Psychosomatic Medicine, 62,* 337–345.

Tables

■ Table F:
The *F* Distribution

■ Table N:
Random Numbers

■ Table P:
Values of *z* Corresponding to the Larger or Smaller Proportion

■ Table Q:
The Studentized Range Statistic

■ Table R:
Critical Values of the Correlation Coefficient

■ Table T:
Critical Values of the *t* Distribution

■ Table U:
Critical Values of the Mann–Whitney *U* Test

■ Table W:
Critical Values of the Wilcoxon *T* Test

■ Table X:
The χ^2 Distribution

■ Table Z:
Areas Under the Normal Curve

Table F The F Distribution

α = .05

df_D \ df_N	1	2	3	4	5	6	7	8	9	10	12	15	20	24	30	40	60	120	∞
1	161.4	199.5	215.7	224.6	230.2	234.0	236.8	238.9	240.5	241.9	243.9	245.9	248.0	249.1	250.1	251.1	252.2	253.3	254.3
2	18.51	19.00	19.16	19.25	19.30	19.33	19.35	19.37	19.38	19.40	19.41	19.43	19.45	19.45	19.46	19.47	19.48	19.49	19.50
3	10.13	9.55	9.28	9.12	9.01	8.94	8.89	8.85	8.81	8.79	8.74	8.70	8.66	8.64	8.62	8.59	8.57	8.55	8.53
4	7.71	6.94	6.59	6.39	6.26	6.16	6.09	6.04	6.00	5.96	5.91	5.86	5.80	5.77	5.75	5.72	5.69	5.66	5.63
5	6.61	5.79	5.41	5.19	5.05	4.95	4.88	4.82	4.77	4.74	4.68	4.62	4.56	4.53	4.50	4.46	4.43	4.40	4.36
6	5.99	5.14	4.76	4.53	4.39	4.28	4.21	4.15	4.10	4.06	4.00	3.94	3.87	3.84	3.81	3.77	3.74	3.70	3.67
7	5.59	4.74	4.35	4.12	3.97	3.87	3.79	3.73	3.68	3.64	3.57	3.51	3.44	3.41	3.38	3.34	3.30	3.27	3.23
8	5.32	4.46	4.07	3.84	3.69	3.58	3.50	3.44	3.39	3.35	3.28	3.22	3.15	3.12	3.08	3.04	3.01	2.97	2.93
9	5.12	4.26	3.86	3.63	3.48	3.37	3.29	3.23	3.18	3.14	3.07	3.01	2.94	2.90	2.86	2.83	2.79	2.75	2.71
10	4.96	4.10	3.71	3.48	3.33	3.22	3.14	3.07	3.02	2.98	2.91	2.85	2.77	2.74	2.70	2.66	2.62	2.58	2.54
11	4.84	3.98	3.59	3.36	3.20	3.09	3.01	2.95	2.90	2.85	2.79	2.72	2.65	2.61	2.57	2.53	2.49	2.45	2.40
12	4.75	3.89	3.49	3.26	3.11	3.00	2.91	2.85	2.80	2.75	2.69	2.62	2.54	2.51	2.47	2.43	2.38	2.34	2.30
13	4.67	3.81	3.41	3.18	3.03	2.92	2.83	2.77	2.71	2.67	2.60	2.53	2.46	2.42	2.38	2.34	2.30	2.25	2.21
14	4.60	3.74	3.34	3.11	2.96	2.85	2.76	2.70	2.65	2.60	2.53	2.46	2.39	2.35	2.31	2.27	2.22	2.18	2.13
15	4.54	3.68	3.29	3.06	2.90	2.79	2.71	2.64	2.59	2.54	2.48	2.40	2.33	2.29	2.25	2.20	2.16	2.11	2.07
16	4.49	3.63	3.24	3.01	2.85	2.74	2.66	2.59	2.54	2.49	2.42	2.35	2.28	2.24	2.19	2.15	2.11	2.06	2.01
17	4.45	3.59	3.20	2.96	2.81	2.70	2.61	2.55	2.49	2.45	2.38	2.31	2.23	2.19	2.15	2.10	2.06	2.01	1.96
18	4.41	3.55	3.16	2.93	2.77	2.66	2.58	2.51	2.46	2.41	2.34	2.27	2.19	2.15	2.11	2.06	2.02	1.97	1.92
19	4.38	3.52	3.13	2.90	2.74	2.63	2.54	2.48	2.42	2.38	2.31	2.23	2.16	2.11	2.07	2.03	1.98	1.93	1.88
20	4.35	3.49	3.10	2.87	2.71	2.60	2.51	2.45	2.39	2.35	2.28	2.20	2.12	2.08	2.04	1.99	1.95	1.90	1.84
21	4.32	3.47	3.07	2.84	2.68	2.57	2.49	2.42	2.37	2.32	2.25	2.18	2.10	2.05	2.01	1.96	1.92	1.87	1.81
22	4.30	3.44	3.05	2.82	2.66	2.55	2.46	2.40	2.34	2.30	2.23	2.15	2.07	2.03	1.98	1.94	1.89	1.84	1.78
23	4.28	3.42	3.03	2.80	2.64	2.53	2.44	2.37	2.32	2.27	2.20	2.13	2.05	2.01	1.96	1.91	1.86	1.81	1.76
24	4.26	3.40	3.01	2.78	2.62	2.51	2.42	2.36	2.30	2.25	2.18	2.11	2.03	1.98	1.94	1.89	1.84	1.79	1.73
25	4.24	3.39	2.99	2.76	2.60	2.49	2.40	2.34	2.28	2.24	2.16	2.09	2.01	1.96	1.92	1.87	1.82	1.77	1.71
26	4.23	3.37	2.98	2.74	2.59	2.47	2.39	2.32	2.27	2.22	2.15	2.07	1.99	1.95	1.90	1.85	1.80	1.75	1.69
27	4.21	3.35	2.96	2.73	2.57	2.46	2.37	2.31	2.25	2.20	2.13	2.06	1.97	1.93	1.88	1.84	1.79	1.73	1.67
28	4.20	3.34	2.95	2.71	2.56	2.45	2.36	2.29	2.24	2.19	2.12	2.04	1.96	1.91	1.87	1.82	1.77	1.71	1.65
29	4.18	3.33	2.93	2.70	2.55	2.43	2.35	2.28	2.22	2.18	2.10	2.03	1.94	1.90	1.85	1.81	1.75	1.70	1.64
30	4.17	3.32	2.92	2.69	2.53	2.42	2.33	2.27	2.21	2.16	2.09	2.01	1.93	1.89	1.84	1.79	1.74	1.68	1.62
40	4.08	3.23	2.84	2.61	2.45	2.34	2.25	2.18	2.12	2.08	2.00	1.92	1.84	1.79	1.74	1.69	1.64	1.58	1.51
60	4.00	3.15	2.76	2.53	2.37	2.25	2.17	2.10	2.04	1.99	1.92	1.84	1.75	1.70	1.65	1.59	1.53	1.47	1.39
120	3.92	3.07	2.68	2.45	2.29	2.17	2.09	2.02	1.96	1.91	1.83	1.75	1.66	1.61	1.55	1.50	1.43	1.35	1.25
∞	3.84	3.00	2.60	2.37	2.21	2.10	2.01	1.94	1.88	1.83	1.75	1.67	1.57	1.52	1.46	1.39	1.32	1.22	1.00

Source: From *Biometrika Tables for Statisticians*, Vol. 1. Third Edition, edited by E. S. Pearson and H. O. Hartley, 1966, pp. 171 and 173. Reprinted by permission of the Biometrika Trustees.

Table N   Random Numbers

24483	69647	24743	47325	91484	65438	40410	19209	66040	07336
55115	52788	63353	79385	99841	09039	79424	18900	54835	13192
78889	30435	68614	30981	62425	27889	60019	70207	04655	99728
45519	73480	03054	15411	34884	54035	57401	53172	78233	79048
65864	46289	03918	45376	80824	29437	81784	02749	18282	84189
36242	07308	67374	26574	80255	08058	20295	16041	01730	99304
78808	93258	22275	53594	40710	85067	68822	75412	41821	44602
99713	25076	97829	71678	97090	83687	48072	22145	93745	45550
59872	54369	79905	11491	16150	25307	85173	60238	76114	49311
53104	93300	55899	09603	32591	07156	66500	41276	00223	12682
48183	05389	11811	33781	95532	60559	76722	31156	45395	57629
91287	02779	64560	61047	54621	21072	25367	88578	98179	77593
73246	01192	81080	31504	48219	99909	44353	00536	63943	39475
91640	26925	50204	31859	38620	55718	02794	35024	00123	62576
64168	01945	24039	88922	05474	61924	66817	57246	51442	07277
50543	93393	04173	22806	47616	15719	93589	39927	13782	18723
90141	73368	99843	57475	77670	77813	82486	70834	39483	89162
88309	49559	02168	71179	11128	48848	13072	83781	69933	54171
50390	23556	12846	98722	01933	43433	87200	64651	27027	45562
68176	13514	82571	75940	00584	15786	59245	08720	89771	65606
22398	59779	22158	31364	29353	04533	50603	11530	22965	12813
31569	82262	31442	31350	76936	65029	12557	73810	75280	21615
97085	99017	68415	04704	19542	18358	63044	11028	48639	70205
51138	95399	02665	29551	12468	04793	11574	87288	98715	22039
28487	41186	22062	39748	35194	00054	11539	40367	93178	70035
77361	80511	23872	23768	04595	72294	78828	66226	21903	65215
50545	39002	56941	13042	93781	22444	46939	98420	74848	20140
02255	70355	15985	22300	53448	39101	44818	21404	28334	36643
76232	94410	04562	90230	25718	26144	31841	13189	45321	37933
77963	02032	48836	16550	16299	26160	34531	13959	03453	42437
89188	82741	74054	17693	34826	10423	34497	24042	04560	63990
34565	90604	52324	31749	01537	87840	24819	51175	86140	96059
41679	13067	75648	05828	87538	62162	85443	61156	77113	50132
27993	19385	10849	28667	42680	79842	34626	68201	87605	78575
34860	28281	91603	35590	15733	53073	37833	30389	13958	22059
01248	33549	80899	21943	62125	05684	79941	63953	70796	06071
99241	52891	20877	94660	02104	63178	09400	40076	28858	86346
88684	00717	65757	28115	55195	50651	00550	28971	74981	03843
41214	31334	60752	79907	85751	22153	31213	05799	00295	28045
25417	84610	69412	32876	12606	42529	99107	26526	37224	69405

Table P   Values of *z* Corresponding to the Larger or Smaller Proportion

(Read *z* as a positive number)   (Read *z* as a negative number)

The Larger Area 1	z 2	The Smaller Area 3	The Larger Area 1	z 2	The Smaller Area 3
.500	0.0000	.500	.625	0.3186	.375
.505	0.0125	.495	.630	0.3319	.370
.510	0.0251	.490	.635	0.3451	.365
.515	0.0376	.485	.640	0.3585	.360
.520	0.0502	.480	.645	0.3719	.355
.525	0.0627	.475	.650	0.3853	.350
.530	0.0753	.470	.655	0.3989	.345
.535	0.0878	.465	.660	0.4125	.340
.540	0.1004	.460	.665	0.4261	.335
.545	0.1130	.455	.670	0.4399	.330
.550	0.1257	.450	.675	0.4538	.325
.555	0.1383	.445	.680	0.4677	.320
.560	0.1510	.440	.685	0.4817	.315
.565	0.1637	.435	.690	0.4959	.310
.570	0.1764	.430	.695	0.5101	.305
.575	0.1891	.425	.700	0.5244	.300
.580	0.2019	.420	.705	0.5388	.295
.585	0.2147	.415	.710	0.5534	.290
.590	0.2275	.410	.715	0.5681	.285
.595	0.2404	.405	.720	0.5828	.280
.600	0.2533	.400	.725	0.5978	.275
.605	0.2663	.395	.730	0.6128	.270
.610	0.2793	.390	.735	0.6280	.265
.615	0.2924	.385	.740	0.6433	.260
.620	0.3055	.380	.745	0.6588	.255

Table P Values of z *(continued)*

The Larger Area 1	z 2	The Smaller Area 3	The Larger Area 1	z 2	The Smaller Area 3
.750	0.6745	.250	.900	1.2816	.100
.755	0.6903	.245	.905	1.3106	.095
.760	0.7063	.240	.910	1.3408	.090
.765	0.7225	.235	.915	1.3722	.085
.770	0.7388	.230	.920	1.4051	.080
.775	0.7554	.225	.925	1.4395	.075
.780	0.7722	.220	.930	1.4757	.070
.785	0.7892	.215	.935	1.5141	.065
.790	0.8064	.210	.940	1.5548	.060
.795	0.8239	.205	.945	1.5982	.055
.800	0.8416	.200	.950	1.6449	.050
.805	0.8596	.195	.955	1.6954	.045
.810	0.8779	.190	.960	1.7507	.040
.815	0.8965	.185	.965	1.8119	.035
.820	0.9154	.180	.970	1.8808	.030
.825	0.9346	.175	.975	1.9600	.025
.830	0.9542	.170	.980	2.0537	.020
.835	0.9741	.165	.985	2.1701	.015
.840	0.9945	.160	.990	2.3263	.010
.845	1.0152	.155	.995	2.5758	.005
.850	1.0364	.150	.996	2.6521	.004
.855	1.0581	.145	.997	2.7478	.003
.860	1.0803	.140	.998	2.8782	.002
.865	1.1031	.135	.999	3.0902	.001
.870	1.1264	.130	.9995	3.2905	.0005
.875	1.1503	.125			
.880	1.1750	.120			
.885	1.2004	.115			
.890	1.2265	.110			
.895	1.2536	.105			

Source: From *Fundamental Statistics in Psychology and Education,* 4th Ed., by J. P. Guilford, McGraw-Hill, Inc., 1965, Appendix B, Table C.

Table Q The Studentized Range Statistic

Upper 5% Points

df_{wg} \ k	2	3	4	5	6	7	8	9	10	11	12	13	14	15	16	17	18	19	20
1	17.97	26.98	32.82	37.08	40.41	43.12	45.40	47.36	49.07	50.59	51.96	53.20	54.33	55.36	56.32	57.22	58.04	58.83	59.56
2	6.08	8.33	9.80	10.88	11.74	12.44	13.03	13.54	13.99	14.39	14.75	15.08	15.38	15.65	15.91	16.14	16.37	16.57	16.77
3	4.50	5.91	6.82	7.50	8.04	8.48	8.85	9.18	9.46	9.72	9.95	10.15	10.35	10.52	10.69	10.84	10.98	11.11	11.24
4	3.93	5.04	5.76	6.29	6.71	7.05	7.35	7.60	7.83	8.03	8.21	8.37	8.52	8.66	8.79	8.91	9.03	9.13	9.23
5	3.64	4.60	5.22	5.67	6.03	6.33	6.58	6.80	6.99	7.17	7.32	7.47	7.60	7.72	7.83	7.93	8.03	8.12	8.21
6	3.46	4.34	4.90	5.30	5.63	5.90	6.12	6.32	6.49	6.65	6.79	6.92	7.03	7.14	7.24	7.34	7.43	7.51	7.59
7	3.34	4.16	4.68	5.06	5.36	5.61	5.82	6.00	6.16	6.30	6.43	6.55	6.66	6.76	6.85	6.94	7.02	7.10	7.17
8	3.26	4.04	4.53	4.89	5.17	5.40	5.60	5.77	5.92	6.05	6.18	6.29	6.39	6.48	6.57	6.65	6.73	6.80	6.87
9	3.20	3.95	4.41	4.76	5.02	5.24	5.43	5.59	5.74	5.87	5.98	6.09	6.19	6.28	6.36	6.44	6.51	6.58	6.64
10	3.15	3.88	4.33	4.65	4.91	5.12	5.30	5.46	5.60	5.72	5.83	5.93	6.03	6.11	6.19	6.27	6.34	6.40	6.47
11	3.11	3.82	4.26	4.57	4.82	5.03	5.20	5.35	5.49	5.61	5.71	5.81	5.90	5.98	6.06	6.13	6.20	6.27	6.33
12	3.08	3.77	4.20	4.51	4.75	4.95	5.12	5.27	5.39	5.51	5.61	5.71	5.80	5.88	5.95	6.02	6.09	6.15	6.21
13	3.06	3.73	4.15	4.45	4.69	4.88	5.05	5.19	5.32	5.43	5.53	5.63	5.71	5.79	5.86	5.93	5.99	6.05	6.11
14	3.03	3.70	4.11	4.41	4.64	4.83	4.99	5.13	5.25	5.36	5.46	5.55	5.64	5.71	5.79	5.85	5.91	5.97	6.03
15	3.01	3.67	4.08	4.37	4.59	4.78	4.94	5.08	5.20	5.31	5.40	5.49	5.57	5.65	5.72	5.78	5.85	5.90	5.96
16	3.00	3.65	4.05	4.33	4.56	4.74	4.90	5.03	5.15	5.26	5.35	5.44	5.52	5.59	5.66	5.73	5.79	5.84	5.90
17	2.98	3.63	4.02	4.30	4.52	4.70	4.86	4.99	5.11	5.21	5.31	5.39	5.47	5.54	5.61	5.67	5.73	5.79	5.84
18	2.97	3.61	4.00	4.28	4.49	4.67	4.82	4.96	5.07	5.17	5.27	5.35	5.43	5.50	5.57	5.63	5.69	5.74	5.79
19	2.96	3.59	3.98	4.25	4.47	4.65	4.79	4.92	5.04	5.14	5.23	5.31	5.39	5.46	5.53	5.59	5.65	5.70	5.75
20	2.95	3.58	3.96	4.23	4.45	4.62	4.77	4.90	5.01	5.11	5.20	5.28	5.36	5.43	5.49	5.55	5.61	5.66	5.71
24	2.92	3.53	3.90	4.17	4.37	4.54	4.68	4.81	4.92	5.01	5.10	5.18	5.25	5.32	5.38	5.44	5.49	5.55	5.59
30	2.89	3.49	3.85	4.10	4.30	4.46	4.60	4.72	4.82	4.92	5.00	5.08	5.15	5.21	5.27	5.33	5.38	5.43	5.47
40	2.86	3.44	3.79	4.04	4.23	4.39	4.52	4.63	4.73	4.82	4.90	4.98	5.04	5.11	5.16	5.22	5.27	5.31	5.36
60	2.83	3.40	3.74	3.98	4.16	4.31	4.44	4.55	4.65	4.73	4.81	4.88	4.94	5.00	5.06	5.11	5.15	5.20	5.24
120	2.80	3.36	3.68	3.92	4.10	4.24	4.36	4.47	4.56	4.64	4.71	4.78	4.84	4.90	4.95	5.00	5.04	5.09	5.13
∞	2.77	3.31	3.63	3.86	4.03	4.17	4.29	4.39	4.47	4.55	4.62	4.68	4.74	4.80	4.85	4.89	4.93	4.97	5.01

k: The number of groups (or number of rows or number of columns)

df_{wg}: Degrees of freedom within groups

Source: From Biometrika Tables for Statisticians, Vol. 1, Third Edition, edited by E. S. Pearson and H. O. Hartley, 1966, p. 192. Reprinted by permission of the Biometrika Trustees.

Table R Critical Values of the Correlation Coefficient

	Levels of Significance for a One-Tailed Test			
	.05	.025	.01	.005
	Levels of Significance for a Two-Tailed Test			
df	.10	.05	.02	.01
1	.988	.997	.9995	.9999
2	.900	.950	.980	.990
3	.805	.878	.934	.959
4	.729	.811	.882	.917
5	.669	.754	.833	.874
6	.622	.707	.789	.834
7	.582	.666	.750	.798
8	.549	.632	.716	.765
9	.521	.602	.685	.735
10	.497	.576	.658	.708
11	.476	.553	.634	.684
12	.458	.532	.612	.661
13	.441	.514	.592	.641
14	.426	.497	.574	.623
15	.412	.482	.558	.606
16	.400	.468	.542	.590
17	.389	.456	.528	.575
18	.378	.444	.516	.561
19	.369	.433	.503	.549
20	.360	.423	.492	.537
21	.352	.413	.482	.526
22	.344	.404	.472	.515
23	.337	.396	.462	.505
24	.330	.388	.453	.496
25	.323	.381	.445	.487
26	.317	.374	.437	.479
27	.311	.367	.430	.471
28	.306	.361	.423	.463
29	.301	.355	.416	.456
30	.296	.349	.409	.449
32	.287	.339	.397	.436
34	.279	.329	.386	.424
36	.271	.320	.376	.413
38	.264	.312	.367	.403
40	.257	.304	.358	.393
42	.251	.297	.350	.384

(continued)

Table R   Critical Values of the Correlation Coefficient
           (continued)

	Levels of Significance for a One-Tailed Test			
	.05	.025	.01	.005
	Levels of Significance for a Two-Tailed Test			
df	.10	.05	.02	.01
44	.246	.291	.342	.376
46	.240	.285	.335	.368
48	.235	.279	.328	.361
50	.231	.273	.322	.354
55	.220	.261	.307	.339
60	.211	.250	.295	.325
65	.203	.240	.284	.313
70	.195	.232	.274	.302
75	.189	.224	.265	.292
80	.183	.217	.256	.283
85	.178	.211	.249	.275
90	.173	.205	.242	.267
95	.168	.200	.236	.260
100	.164	.195	.230	.254
120	.150	.178	.210	.232
150	.134	.159	.189	.208
200	.116	.138	.164	.181
300	.095	.113	.134	.148
400	.082	.098	.116	.128
500	.073	.088	.104	.115
1000	.052	.062	.073	.081

Source: From *The Handbook of Statistical Tables,* by D. B. Owen, p. 510.
Copyright © 1962 Addison Wesley Longman Publishing Co. Reprinted by
permission of Addison Wesley Longman.

Table T   Critical Values of the *t* Distribution

df	One-Tail = .4 Two-Tail = .8	.25 .5	.1 .2	.05 .1	.025 .05	.01 .02	.005 .01	.0025 .005	.001 .002	.0005 .001
1	0.325	1.000	3.078	6.314	12.706	31.821	63.657	127.32	318.31	636.62
2	0.289	0.816	1.886	2.920	4.303	6.965	9.925	14.089	22.327	31.598
3	0.277	0.765	1.638	2.353	3.182	4.541	5.841	7.453	10.214	12.924
4	0.271	0.741	1.533	2.132	2.776	3.747	4.604	5.598	7.173	8.610
5	0.267	0.727	1.476	2.015	2.571	3.365	4.032	4.773	5.893	6.869
6	0.265	0.718	1.440	1.943	2.447	3.143	3.707	4.317	5.208	5.959
7	0.263	0.711	1.415	1.895	2.365	2.998	3.499	4.029	4.785	5.408
8	0.262	0.706	1.397	1.860	2.306	2.896	3.355	3.833	4.501	5.041
9	0.261	0.703	1.383	1.833	2.262	2.821	3.250	3.690	4.297	4.781
10	0.260	0.700	1.372	1.812	2.228	2.764	3.169	3.581	4.144	4.587
11	0.260	0.697	1.363	1.796	2.201	2.718	3.106	3.497	4.025	4.437
12	0.259	0.695	1.356	1.782	2.179	2.681	3.055	3.428	3.930	4.318
13	0.259	0.694	1.350	1.771	2.160	2.650	3.012	3.372	3.852	4.221
14	0.258	0.692	1.345	1.761	2.145	2.624	2.977	3.326	3.787	4.140
15	0.258	0.691	1.341	1.753	2.131	2.602	2.947	3.286	3.733	4.073
16	0.258	0.690	1.337	1.746	2.120	2.583	2.921	3.252	3.686	4.015
17	0.257	0.689	1.333	1.740	2.110	2.567	2.898	3.222	3.646	3.965
18	0.257	0.688	1.330	1.734	2.101	2.552	2.878	3.197	3.610	3.922
19	0.257	0.688	1.328	1.729	2.093	2.539	2.861	3.174	3.579	3.883
20	0.257	0.687	1.325	1.725	2.086	2.528	2.845	3.153	3.552	3.850
21	0.257	0.686	1.323	1.721	2.080	2.518	2.831	3.135	3.527	3.819
22	0.256	0.686	1.321	1.717	2.074	2.508	2.819	3.119	3.505	3.792
23	0.256	0.685	1.319	1.714	2.069	2.500	2.807	3.104	3.485	3.767
24	0.256	0.685	1.318	1.711	2.064	2.492	2.797	3.091	3.467	3.745
25	0.256	0.684	1.316	1.708	2.060	2.485	2.787	3.078	3.450	3.725
26	0.256	0.684	1.315	1.706	2.056	2.479	2.779	3.067	3.435	3.707
27	0.256	0.684	1.314	1.703	2.052	2.473	2.771	3.057	3.421	3.690
28	0.256	0.683	1.313	1.701	2.048	2.467	2.763	3.047	3.408	3.674
29	0.256	0.683	1.311	1.699	2.045	2.462	2.756	3.038	3.396	3.659
30	0.256	0.683	1.310	1.697	2.042	2.457	2.750	3.030	3.385	3.646
40	0.255	0.681	1.303	1.684	2.021	2.423	2.704	2.971	3.307	3.551
60	0.254	0.679	1.296	1.671	2.000	2.390	2.660	2.915	3.232	3.460
120	0.254	0.677	1.289	1.658	1.980	2.358	2.617	2.860	3.160	3.373
∞	0.253	0.674	1.282	1.645	1.960	2.326	2.576	2.807	3.090	3.291

Table U   Critical Values of the Mann–Whitney U Test

n_2 \ n_1	1	2	3	4	5	6	7	8	9	10	11	12	13	14	15	16	17	18	19	20
1	—	—	—	—	—	—	—	—	—	—	—	—	—	—	—	—	—	—	0	0
	—	—	—	—	—	—	—	—	—	—	—	—	—	—	—	—	—	—	**—**	**—**
2	—	—	—	—	0	0	0	1	1	1	1	2	2	2	3	3	3	4	4	4
	—	—	—	—	—	—	—	**0**	**0**	**0**	**0**	**1**	**1**	**1**	**1**	**1**	**2**	**2**	**2**	**2**
3	—	—	0	0	1	2	2	3	3	4	5	5	6	7	7	8	9	9	10	11
	—	—	—	—	**0**	**1**	**1**	**2**	**2**	**3**	**3**	**4**	**4**	**5**	**5**	**6**	**6**	**7**	**7**	**8**
4	—	—	0	1	2	3	4	5	6	7	8	9	10	11	12	14	15	16	17	18
	—	—	—	**0**	**1**	**2**	**3**	**4**	**4**	**5**	**6**	**7**	**8**	**9**	**10**	**11**	**11**	**12**	**13**	**13**
5	—	0	1	2	4	5	6	8	9	11	12	13	15	16	18	19	20	22	23	25
	—	—	**0**	**1**	**2**	**3**	**5**	**6**	**7**	**8**	**9**	**11**	**12**	**13**	**14**	**15**	**17**	**18**	**19**	**20**
6	—	0	2	3	5	7	8	10	12	14	16	17	19	21	23	25	26	28	30	32
	—	—	**1**	**2**	**3**	**5**	**6**	**8**	**10**	**11**	**13**	**14**	**16**	**17**	**19**	**21**	**22**	**24**	**25**	**27**
7	—	0	2	4	6	8	11	13	15	17	19	21	24	26	28	30	33	35	37	39
	—	—	**1**	**3**	**5**	**6**	**8**	**10**	**12**	**14**	**16**	**18**	**20**	**22**	**24**	**26**	**28**	**30**	**32**	**34**
8	—	1	3	5	8	10	13	15	18	20	23	26	28	31	33	36	39	41	44	47
	—	**0**	**2**	**4**	**6**	**8**	**10**	**13**	**15**	**17**	**19**	**22**	**24**	**26**	**29**	**31**	**34**	**36**	**38**	**41**
9	—	1	3	6	9	12	15	18	21	24	27	30	33	36	39	42	45	48	51	54
	—	**0**	**2**	**4**	**7**	**10**	**12**	**15**	**17**	**20**	**23**	**26**	**28**	**31**	**34**	**37**	**39**	**42**	**45**	**48**
10	—	1	4	7	11	14	17	20	24	27	31	34	37	41	44	48	51	55	58	62
	—	**0**	**3**	**5**	**8**	**11**	**14**	**17**	**20**	**23**	**26**	**29**	**33**	**36**	**39**	**42**	**45**	**48**	**52**	**55**
11	—	1	5	8	12	16	19	23	27	31	34	38	42	46	50	54	57	61	65	69
	—	**0**	**3**	**6**	**9**	**13**	**16**	**19**	**23**	**26**	**30**	**33**	**37**	**40**	**44**	**47**	**51**	**55**	**58**	**62**
12	—	2	5	9	13	17	21	26	30	34	38	42	47	51	55	60	64	68	72	77
	—	**1**	**4**	**7**	**11**	**14**	**18**	**22**	**26**	**29**	**33**	**37**	**41**	**45**	**49**	**53**	**57**	**61**	**65**	**69**
13	—	2	6	10	15	19	24	28	33	37	42	47	51	56	61	65	70	75	80	84
	—	**1**	**4**	**8**	**12**	**16**	**20**	**24**	**28**	**33**	**37**	**41**	**45**	**50**	**54**	**59**	**63**	**67**	**72**	**76**
14	—	2	7	11	16	21	26	31	36	41	46	51	56	61	66	71	77	82	87	92
	—	**1**	**5**	**9**	**13**	**17**	**22**	**26**	**31**	**36**	**40**	**45**	**50**	**55**	**59**	**64**	**67**	**74**	**78**	**83**
15	—	3	7	12	18	23	28	33	39	44	50	55	61	66	72	77	83	88	94	100
	—	**1**	**5**	**10**	**14**	**19**	**24**	**29**	**34**	**39**	**44**	**49**	**54**	**59**	**64**	**70**	**75**	**80**	**85**	**90**
16	—	3	8	14	19	25	30	36	42	48	54	60	65	71	77	83	89	95	101	107
	—	**1**	**6**	**11**	**15**	**21**	**26**	**31**	**37**	**42**	**47**	**53**	**59**	**64**	**70**	**75**	**81**	**86**	**92**	**98**
17	—	3	9	15	20	26	33	39	45	51	57	64	70	77	83	89	96	102	109	115
	—	**2**	**6**	**11**	**17**	**22**	**28**	**34**	**39**	**45**	**51**	**57**	**63**	**67**	**75**	**81**	**87**	**93**	**99**	**105**
18	—	4	9	16	22	28	35	41	48	55	61	68	75	82	88	95	102	109	116	123
	—	**2**	**7**	**12**	**18**	**24**	**30**	**36**	**42**	**48**	**55**	**61**	**67**	**74**	**80**	**86**	**93**	**99**	**106**	**112**
19	0	4	10	17	23	30	37	44	51	58	65	72	80	87	94	101	109	116	123	130
	—	**2**	**7**	**13**	**19**	**25**	**32**	**38**	**45**	**52**	**58**	**65**	**72**	**78**	**85**	**92**	**99**	**106**	**113**	**119**
20	0	4	11	18	25	32	39	47	54	62	69	77	84	92	100	107	115	123	130	138
	—	**2**	**8**	**13**	**20**	**27**	**34**	**41**	**48**	**55**	**62**	**69**	**76**	**83**	**90**	**98**	**105**	**112**	**119**	**127**

Source: From *Introductory Statistics,* by R. E. Kirk, pp. 423 and 424, Brooks/Cole Publishing, 1978. Reprinted by permission of the author, Roger E. Kirk.

Explanation: Critical values for a one-tailed test at $\alpha = .05$ (regular type) and $\alpha = .025$ (**boldface type**) and for a two-tailed test at $\alpha = .10$ (regular type) and $\alpha = .05$ (**boldface type**)

Table W   Critical Values of the Wilcoxon *T* Test

	Level of Significance for a One-Tailed Test					Level of Significance for a One-Tailed Test			
	.05	.025	.01	.005		.05	.025	.01	.005
	Level of Significance for a Two-Tailed Test					Level of Significance for a Two-Tailed Test			
n	.10	.05	.02	.01	*n*	.10	.05	.02	.01
5	0	—	—	—	28	130	116	101	91
6	2	0	—	—	29	140	126	110	100
7	3	2	0	—	30	151	137	120	109
8	5	3	1	0	31	163	147	130	118
9	8	5	3	1	32	175	159	140	128
10	10	8	5	3	33	187	170	151	138
11	13	10	7	5	34	200	182	162	148
12	17	13	9	7	35	213	195	173	159
13	21	17	12	9	36	227	208	185	171
14	25	21	15	12	37	241	221	198	182
15	30	25	19	15	38	256	235	211	194
16	35	29	23	19	39	271	249	224	207
17	41	34	27	23	40	286	264	238	220
18	47	40	32	27	41	302	279	252	233
19	53	46	37	32	42	319	294	266	247
20	60	52	43	37	43	336	310	281	261
21	67	58	49	42	44	353	327	296	276
22	75	65	55	48	45	371	343	312	291
23	83	73	62	54	46	389	361	328	307
24	91	81	69	61	47	407	378	345	322
25	100	89	76	68	48	426	396	362	339
26	110	98	84	75	49	446	415	379	355
27	119	107	92	83	50	466	434	397	373

The symbol *T* denotes the smaller sum of ranks associated with differences that are all of the same sign. For any given *n* (number of ranked differences), the obtained *T* is significant at a given level if it is *equal to or less than* the value shown in the table.

Source: From *Introductory Statistics,* by R. E. Kirk, p. 425, Brooks/Cole Publishing, 1978. Reprinted by permission of the author, Roger E. Kirk.

Table X The χ^2 Distribution

df	.25	.10	.05	.025	.01	.005
1	1.323	2.706	3.841	5.024	6.635	7.879
2	2.773	4.605	5.991	7.378	9.210	10.597
3	4.108	6.251	7.815	9.348	11.345	12.838
4	5.385	7.779	9.488	11.143	13.277	14.860
5	6.626	9.236	11.071	12.833	15.086	16.750
6	7.841	10.645	12.592	14.449	16.812	18.548
7	9.037	12.017	14.067	16.013	18.475	20.278
8	10.219	13.362	15.507	17.535	20.090	21.955
9	11.389	14.684	16.919	19.023	21.666	23.589
10	12.549	15.987	18.307	20.483	23.209	25.188
11	13.701	17.275	19.675	21.920	24.725	26.757
12	14.845	18.549	21.026	23.337	26.217	28.299
13	15.984	19.812	22.362	24.736	27.688	29.819
14	17.117	21.064	23.685	26.119	29.141	31.319
15	18.245	22.307	24.996	27.488	30.578	32.801
16	19.369	23.542	26.296	28.845	32.000	34.267
17	20.489	24.769	27.587	30.191	33.409	35.718
18	21.605	25.989	28.869	31.526	34.805	37.156
19	22.718	27.204	30.144	32.852	36.191	38.582
20	23.828	28.412	31.410	34.170	37.566	39.997
21	24.935	29.615	32.671	35.479	38.932	41.401
22	26.039	30.813	33.924	36.781	40.289	42.796
23	27.141	32.007	35.172	38.076	41.638	44.181
24	28.241	33.196	36.415	39.364	42.980	45.559
25	29.339	34.382	37.652	40.646	44.314	46.928
26	30.435	35.563	38.885	41.923	45.642	48.290
27	31.528	36.741	40.113	43.194	46.963	49.645
28	32.620	37.916	41.337	44.461	48.278	50.993
29	33.711	39.087	42.557	45.722	49.588	52.336
30	34.800	40.256	43.773	46.979	50.892	53.672
31	35.887	41.422	44.985	48.232	52.191	55.003
32	36.973	42.585	46.194	49.480	53.486	56.328
33	38.058	43.745	47.400	50.725	54.776	57.648
34	39.141	44.903	48.602	51.966	56.061	58.964
35	40.223	46.059	49.802	53.203	57.342	60.275
36	41.304	47.212	50.998	54.437	58.619	61.581
37	42.383	48.363	52.192	55.668	59.892	62.883
38	43.462	49.513	53.384	56.896	61.162	64.181
39	44.539	50.660	54.572	58.120	62.428	65.476
40	45.616	51.805	55.758	59.342	63.691	66.766
41	46.692	52.949	56.942	60.561	64.950	68.053
42	47.766	54.090	58.124	61.777	66.206	69.336
43	48.840	55.230	59.304	62.990	67.459	70.616
44	49.913	56.369	60.481	64.201	68.710	71.893
45	50.985	57.505	61.656	65.410	69.957	73.166

Source: From *The Handbook of Statistical Tables,* by D. B. Owen, p. 50. Copyright © 1962 Addison Wesley Longman Publishing Co. Reprinted by permission of Addison Wesley Longman.

Table Z   Areas Under the Normal Curve

Column 2 gives the proportion of the area under the entire curve that is between the mean ($z = 0$) and the positive value of z. Areas for negative values of z are the same as for positive values because the curve is symmetrical.

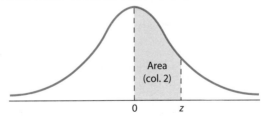

Column 3 gives the proportion of the area under the entire curve that falls beyond the stated positive value of z. Areas for negative values of z are the same because the curve is symmetrical.

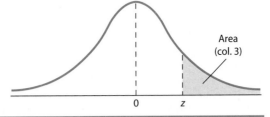

z 1	Area Between Mean and z 2	Area Beyond z 3	z 1	Area Between Mean and z 2	Area Beyond z 3
0.00	.0000	.5000	0.20	.0793	.4207
0.01	.0040	.4960	0.21	.0832	.4168
0.02	.0080	.4920	0.22	.0871	.4129
0.03	.0120	.4880	0.23	.0910	.4090
0.04	.0160	.4840	0.24	.0948	.4052
0.05	.0199	.4801	0.25	.0987	.4013
0.06	.0239	.4761	0.26	.1026	.3974
0.07	.0279	.4721	0.27	.1064	.3936
0.08	.0319	.4681	0.28	.1103	.3897
0.09	.0359	.4641	0.29	.1141	.3859
0.10	.0398	.4602	0.30	.1179	.3821
0.11	.0438	.4562	0.31	.1217	.3783
0.12	.0478	.4522	0.32	.1255	.3745
0.13	.0517	.4483	0.33	.1293	.3707
0.14	.0557	.4443	0.34	.1331	.3669
0.15	.0596	.4404	0.35	.1368	.3632
0.16	.0636	.4364	0.36	.1406	.3594
0.17	.0675	.4325	0.37	.1443	.3557
0.18	.0714	.4286	0.38	.1480	.3520
0.19	.0753	.4247	0.39	.1517	.3483

(continued)

Table Z   Areas Under the Normal Curve *(continued)*

z 1	Area Between Mean and z 2	Area Beyond z 3	z 1	Area Between Mean and z 2	Area Beyond z 3
0.40	.1554	.3446	0.75	.2734	.2266
0.41	.1591	.3409	0.76	.2764	.2236
0.42	.1628	.3372	0.77	.2794	.2206
0.43	.1664	.3336	0.78	.2823	.2177
0.44	.1700	.3300	0.79	.2852	.2148
0.45	.1736	.3264	0.80	.2881	.2119
0.46	.1772	.3228	0.81	.2910	.2090
0.47	.1808	.3192	0.82	.2939	.2061
0.48	.1844	.3156	0.83	.2967	.2033
0.49	.1879	.3121	0.84	.2995	.2005
0.50	.1915	.3085	0.85	.3023	.1977
0.51	.1950	.3050	0.86	.3051	.1949
0.52	.1985	.3015	0.87	.3078	.1922
0.53	.2019	.2981	0.88	.3106	.1894
0.54	.2054	.2946	0.89	.3133	.1867
0.55	.2088	.2912	0.90	.3159	.1841
0.56	.2123	.2877	0.91	.3186	.1814
0.57	.2157	.2843	0.92	.3212	.1788
0.58	.2190	.2810	0.93	.3238	.1762
0.59	.2224	.2776	0.94	.3264	.1736
0.60	.2257	.2743	0.95	.3289	.1711
0.61	.2291	.2709	0.96	.3315	.1685
0.62	.2324	.2676	0.97	.3340	.1660
0.63	.2357	.2643	0.98	.3365	.1635
0.64	.2389	.2611	0.99	.3389	.1611
0.65	.2422	.2578	1.00	.3413	.1587
0.66	.2454	.2546	1.01	.3438	.1562
0.67	.2486	.2514	1.02	.3461	.1539
0.68	.2517	.2483	1.03	.3485	.1515
0.69	.2549	.2451	1.04	.3508	.1492
0.70	.2580	.2420	1.05	.3531	.1469
0.71	.2611	.2389	1.06	.3554	.1446
0.72	.2642	.2358	1.07	.3577	.1423
0.73	.2673	.2327	1.08	.3599	.1401
0.74	.2704	.2296	1.09	.3621	.1379

Table Z Areas Under the Normal Curve *(continued)*

z 1	Area Between Mean and z 2	Area Beyond z 3	z 1	Area Between Mean and z 2	Area Beyond z 3
1.10	.3643	.1357	1.45	.4265	.0735
1.11	.3665	.1335	1.46	.4279	.0721
1.12	.3686	.1314	1.47	.4292	.0708
1.13	.3708	.1292	1.48	.4306	.0694
1.14	.3729	.1271	1.49	.4319	.0681
1.15	.3749	.1251	1.50	.4332	.0668
1.16	.3770	.1230	1.51	.4345	.0655
1.17	.3790	.1210	1.52	.4357	.0643
1.18	.3810	.1190	1.53	.4370	.0630
1.19	.3830	.1170	1.54	.4382	.0618
1.20	.3849	.1151	1.55	.4394	.0606
1.21	.3869	.1131	1.56	.4406	.0594
1.22	.3888	.1112	1.57	.4418	.0582
1.23	.3907	.1093	1.58	.4429	.0571
1.24	.3925	.1075	1.59	.4441	.0559
1.25	.3944	.1056	1.60	.4452	.0548
1.26	.3962	.1038	1.61	.4463	.0537
1.27	.3980	.1020	1.62	.4474	.0526
1.28	.3997	.1003	1.63	.4484	.0516
1.29	.4015	.0985	1.64	.4495	.0505
1.30	.4032	.0968	1.65	.4505	.0495
1.31	.4049	.0951	1.66	.4515	.0485
1.32	.4066	.0934	1.67	.4525	.0475
1.33	.4082	.0918	1.68	.4535	.0465
1.34	.4099	.0901	1.69	.4545	.0455
1.35	.4115	.0885	1.70	.4554	.0446
1.36	.4131	.0869	1.71	.4564	.0436
1.37	.4147	.0853	1.72	.4573	.0427
1.38	.4162	.0838	1.73	.4582	.0418
1.39	.4177	.0823	1.74	.4591	.0409
1.40	.4192	.0808	1.75	.4599	.0401
1.41	.4207	.0793	1.76	.4608	.0392
1.42	.4222	.0778	1.77	.4616	.0384
1.43	.4236	.0764	1.78	.4625	.0375
1.44	.4251	.0749	1.79	.4633	.0367

(continued)

Table Z   Areas Under the Normal Curve *(continued)*

z 1	Area Between Mean and z 2	Area Beyond z 3	z 1	Area Between Mean and z 2	Area Beyond z 3
1.80	.4641	.0359	2.15	.4842	.0158
1.81	.4649	.0351	2.16	.4846	.0154
1.82	.4656	.0344	2.17	.4850	.0150
1.83	.4664	.0336	2.18	.4854	.0146
1.84	.4671	.0329	2.19	.4857	.0143
1.85	.4678	.0322	2.20	.4861	.0139
1.86	.4686	.0314	2.21	.4864	.0136
1.87	.4693	.0307	2.22	.4868	.0132
1.88	.4699	.0301	2.23	.4871	.0129
1.89	.4706	.0294	2.24	.4875	.0125
1.90	.4713	.0287	2.25	.4878	.0122
1.91	.4719	.0281	2.26	.4881	.0119
1.92	.4726	.0274	2.27	.4884	.0116
1.93	.4732	.0268	2.28	.4887	.0113
1.94	.4738	.0262	2.29	.4890	.0110
1.95	.4744	.0256	2.30	.4893	.0107
1.96	.4750	.0250	2.31	.4896	.0104
1.97	.4756	.0244	2.32	.4898	.0102
1.98	.4761	.0239	2.33	.4901	.0099
1.99	.4767	.0233	2.34	.4904	.0096
2.00	.4772	.0228	2.35	.4906	.0094
2.01	.4778	.0222	2.36	.4909	.0091
2.02	.4783	.0217	2.37	.4911	.0089
2.03	.4788	.0212	2.38	.4913	.0087
2.04	.4793	.0207	2.39	.4916	.0084
2.05	.4798	.0202	2.40	.4918	.0082
2.06	.4803	.0197	2.41	.4920	.0080
2.07	.4808	.0192	2.42	.4922	.0078
2.08	.4812	.0188	2.43	.4925	.0075
2.09	.4817	.0183	2.44	.4927	.0073
2.10	.4821	.0179	2.45	.4929	.0071
2.11	.4826	.0174	2.46	.4931	.0069
2.12	.4830	.0170	2.47	.4932	.0068
2.13	.4834	.0166	2.48	.4934	.0066
2.14	.4838	.0162	2.49	.4936	.0064

Table Z Areas Under the Normal Curve *(continued)*

z	Area Between Mean and z	Area Beyond z		z	Area Between Mean and z	Area Beyond z
1	2	3		1	2	3
2.50	.4938	.0062		2.85	.4978	.0022
2.51	.4940	.0060		2.86	.4979	.0021
2.52	.4941	.0059		2.87	.4979	.0021
2.53	.4943	.0057		2.88	.4980	.0020
2.54	.4945	.0055		2.89	.4981	.0019
2.55	.4946	.0054		2.90	.4981	.0019
2.56	.4948	.0052		2.91	.4982	.0018
2.57	.4949	.0051		2.92	.4982	.0018
2.58	.4951	.0049		2.93	.4983	.0017
2.59	.4952	.0048		2.94	.4984	.0016
2.60	.4953	.0047		2.95	.4984	.0016
2.61	.4955	.0045		2.96	.4985	.0015
2.62	.4956	.0044		2.97	.4985	.0015
2.63	.4957	.0043		2.98	.4986	.0014
2.64	.4959	.0041		2.99	.4986	.0014
2.65	.4960	.0040		3.00	.4987	.0013
2.66	.4961	.0039		3.01	.4987	.0013
2.67	.4962	.0038		3.02	.4987	.0013
2.68	.4963	.0037		3.03	.4988	.0012
2.69	.4964	.0036		3.04	.4988	.0012
2.70	.4965	.0035		3.05	.4989	.0011
2.71	.4966	.0034		3.06	.4989	.0011
2.72	.4967	.0033		3.07	.4989	.0011
2.73	.4968	.0032		3.08	.4900	.0010
2.74	.4969	.0031		3.09	.4990	.0010
2.75	.4970	.0030		3.10	.4990	.0010
2.76	.4971	.0029		3.11	.4991	.0009
2.77	.4972	.0028		3.12	.4991	.0009
2.78	.4973	.0027		3.13	.4991	.0009
2.79	.4974	.0026		3.14	.4992	.0008
2.80	.4974	.0026		3.15	.4992	.0008
2.81	.4975	.0025		3.16	.4992	.0008
2.82	.4976	.0024		3.17	.4992	.0008
2.83	.4977	.0023		3.18	.4993	.0007
2.84	.4977	.0023		3.19	.4993	.0007

(continued)

Table Z Areas Under the Normal Curve *(continued)*

z	Area Between Mean and z	Area Beyond z	z	Area Between Mean and z	Area Beyond z
1	2	3	1	2	3
3.20	.4993	.0007	3.30	.4995	.0005
3.21	.4993	.0007	3.40	.4997	.0003
3.22	.4994	.0006	3.50	.4998	.0002
3.23	.4994	.0006	3.60	.4998	.0002
3.24	.4994	.0006	3.70	.4999	.0001

Source: Values calculated by Myron L. Braunstein. Reprinted by permission.

Solutions to
Odd-Numbered Problems

Chapter 1

1. 23,345.5678 is rounded up to 23,345.568 because the digit in the fourth decimal place is 5 or greater.
3. .24
5. 3.00
7. Answers will vary. An example of a correct answer is as follows:
   Null hypothesis: The speed at which children learn language using a new teaching technique will be the same as the speed using the current teaching technique.
   Research hypothesis: The speed at which children learn language with the new teaching technique will be greater than the speed using the current teaching technique.
9. Answers will vary. An example of a correct answer is as follows:
   Null hypothesis: There will be no difference in the recovery time of knee surgery patients released from the hospital 3 days after surgery compared to the recovery time released 5 days after surgery.
   Research hypothesis: There will be a faster recovery time for knee surgery patients released from the hospital 3 days after surgery than for those released 5 days after surgery.
11. Answers will vary. An example of a correct answer is as follows:
    Null hypothesis: Couples living together and couples married will not differ in romantic behavior.
    Research hypothesis: Couples living together and couples married will differ in romantic behavior.
13. The independent variable is the different concentrations of the nerve-blocking agent. The dependent variable is the change in the number of impulses.
15. The independent variable is the type of punishment (suspension versus physical punishment). The dependent variable is the number of disruptive acts exhibited in the 3-day period.
17. Interval
19. Ordinal
21. Nominal
23. Ratio
25. Ratio
27. Ratio

Problems From the Literature

29. Null hypothesis: There will be no differences in judgments of the applicant's ability when she is depicted with brunette, blonde, or red hair.
    Research hypothesis: There will be a difference in the judgment of the applicant's ability when she is depicted with brunette, blonde, or red hair.
31. The data came from a sample.
33. The photograph was an extraneous variable. The goal of controlling extraneous variables is to keep everything in the different experimental conditions the same except for the varying independent variable. Thus, if a different picture is used, it is possible that something might be different in the picture, such as her expression or lighting, that might also vary between conditions. If that happened, then these researchers would not know whether it was something that differed in the pictures or hair color that influenced the judgments of ability (dependent variable).
35. The independent variable is the type of treatment for dental phobia. The dependent variable is the dental anxiety reported by patients.
37. a. ordinal; b. interval; c. ratio; d. ordinal
39. Null hypothesis: There are no differences in reported pain, blood pressure, and heart rate between people incidentally touched and people not touched during a cold pressor test.
    Research hypothesis: There are differences in reported pain, blood pressure, and heart rate between people incidentally touched and people not touched during a cold pressor test.
41. The data came from a sample.
43. The answers will vary. Here is an example of an answer. Null hypothesis: Patients will not be more relaxed during a medical examination when the doctor greets them with a handshake than if they are greeted with no handshake.
    Research hypothesis: Patients will be more relaxed during a medical examination when the doctor greets them with a handshake than if they are greeted with no handshake.
45. The independent variable is the sun symbol on the coffee bill. The dependent variables are the frequency and amount of the tips.
47. Answers will vary. Examples of correct answers are as follows:
    a. *Nominal scale questions:*
       Does the sun make you feel good?   Yes   No
       Do you pay attention to what is written on your coffee bill?   Yes   No
       Did you order regular or decaffeinated coffee?   Yes   No
    b. *Ordinal scale questions:*
       Circle your favorite flavored coffee.   Vanilla   Mocha   French roast
       Imagine you are outside looking up at the sky; which would you like to see the most? (circle one)   Moon   Sun   Stars   Clouds
       What most influences the size of the tip you leave a food server? (circle one)
       Quality food/drink   Friendly server   My mood   Nothing
    c. *Interval scale questions:*
       How pleased were you with the coffee service today? (circle one)
            1   2   3   4   5
       Not pleased   Very pleased

To what extent is the percentage of your tip based on the personality of the server?

| 1 | 2 | 3 | 4 | 5 |

Not at all   Very much

   d. *Ratio scale questions:*

How many times a week do you come to this coffee bar? _____

On average, what percentage of the food/coffee bill do you leave as a tip for a food or beverage server? _____

Chapter 2

1. The ranked distribution for third-born children who graduated from 25 high schools in Escuela Nueva County last year: 86, 77, 77, 71, 70, 67, 63, 61, 59, 56, 55, 55, 54, 54, 54, 52, 50, 49, 46, 46, 43, 41, 39, 34, 33.

3. The ranked distribution for the number of targets missed by 20 radar operators over a 5-day period: 23, 21, 18, 17, 16, 16, 13, 8, 7, 7, 6, 6, 5, 5, 5, 4, 3, 2, 2, 0.

5. The range of prices of new automobiles at a local dealer is \$42,275. \$52,298 − \$10,023 = \$42,276.

7. The range of reaction times for participants in the experiment is 679 milliseconds: 876 milliseconds − 197 milliseconds = 679 milliseconds.

9. With a 60 as the range of test, 12 class intervals would be produced by a class interval of 5. $i \approx \dfrac{\text{range}}{\text{number of class intervals}} \approx \dfrac{60}{12} \approx 5$

11. The number of class intervals for a grouped frequency distribution for mental rotation time for each interval size is as follows:

   a. First, calculate the range, then the number of class intervals.

   Range = high score − low score; 623 − 235 = 388

   $$\text{Number of class intervals} \approx \dfrac{\text{range}}{i} = \dfrac{388}{25} = 15.5, \text{ or 16 class intervals}$$

   b. $\dfrac{388}{15} = 25.87$, or 26 class intervals

   c. $\dfrac{388}{20} = 19.4$, or 20 class intervals

   d. $\dfrac{388}{50} = 7.76$, or 8 class intervals

13. The rank order of raw scores: 32, 31, 31, 29, 29, 29, 29, 28, 25, 25, 22, 22, 22, 21, 21, 21, 19, 19, 19, 19, 18, 18, 16, 16, 15, 15, 14, 14, 13, 13, 12, 12, 11, 11, 9, 8, 7, 6, 4, 3, 3, 3, 2, 1, 1.

   Range = high score − low score; 32 − 1 = 31

   $$\text{Number of class intervals} \approx \dfrac{\text{range}}{i}; \dfrac{31}{3} = 10.33, \text{ or 11 class intervals}$$

   $$\text{Midpoint} = \dfrac{\text{lower limit} + \text{upper limit}}{2}; \dfrac{30 + 32}{2} = 31$$

	Grouped Frequency Distribution of the Number of Negative Statements		
Real Limits	Apparent Limits	Frequency	Midpoint
29.5–32.5	30–32	3	31
26.5–29.5	27–29	5	28
23.5–26.5	24–26	2	25
20.5–23.5	21–23	6	22
17.5–20.5	18–20	6	19
14.5–17.5	15–17	4	16
11.5–14.5	12–14	6	13
8.5–11.5	9–11	3	10
5.5–8.5	6–8	3	7
2.5–5.5	3–5	4	4
0–2.5	0–2	3	1

15. Range = high score − low score = 229 − 155 = 74

$$i \approx \frac{\text{range}}{\text{number of class intervals}} = \frac{74}{15} \approx 4.93$$

$$\text{Midpoint} = \frac{\text{lower limit} + \text{upper limit}}{2}; \quad \frac{225 + 229}{2} = 227$$

			Grouped Frequency Distribution of Heart Rates With New Drug			
Real Limits	Apparent Limits	Frequency	Midpoint	Cumulative Frequency	Relative Frequency	Cumulative Relative Frequency	Cumulative Percent
224.5–229.5	225–229	2	227	40	.050	1.00	100
219.5–224.5	220–224	3	222	38	.075	.95	95
214.5–219.5	215–219	1	217	35	.025	.875	87.5
209.5–214.5	210–214	3	212	34	.075	.85	85
204.5–209.5	205–209	1	207	31	.025	.775	77.5
199.5–204.5	200–204	1	202	30	.025	.75	75
194.5–199.5	195–199	2	197	29	.05	.725	72.5
189.5–194.5	190–194	2	192	27	.05	.675	67.5
184.5–189.5	185–189	0	187	25	.00	.625	62.5
179.5–184.5	180–184	5	182	25	.125	.625	62.5
174.5–179.5	175–179	2	177	20	.05	.50	50
169.5–174.5	170–174	3	172	18	.075	.45	45
164.5–169.5	165–169	2	167	15	.05	.375	37.5
159.5–164.5	160–164	6	162	13	.15	.325	32.5
154.5–159.5	155–159	7	157	7	.175	.175	17.5

17. Range = high score − low score = 123 − 17 = 106

Number of class intervals $\approx \dfrac{\text{range}}{i} = \dfrac{106}{10} \approx 10.6$

Midpoint $= \dfrac{\text{lower limit} + \text{upper limit}}{2}; \dfrac{120 + 129}{2} = 124.5$

				Grouped Frequency Distribution of Number of Aggressive Acts			
Real Limits	Apparent Limits	Frequency	Midpoint	Cumulative Frequency	Relative Frequency	Cumulative Relative Frequency	Cumulative Percent
119.5–129.5	120–129	2	124.5	30	.067	1.00	100
109.5–119.5	110–119	4	114.5	28	.133	.933	93.3
99.5–109.5	100–109	5	104.5	24	.167	.800	80.0
89.5–99.5	90–99	4	94.5	19	.133	.633	63.3
79.5–89.5	80–89	0	84.5	15	.000	.500	50.0
69.5–79.5	70–79	2	74.5	15	.067	.500	50.0
59.5–69.5	60–69	2	64.5	13	.067	.433	43.3
49.5–59.5	50–59	2	54.5	11	.067	.366	36.6
39.5–49.5	40–49	3	44.5	9	.100	.299	29.9
29.5–39.5	30–39	3	34.5	6	.100	.199	19.9
19.5–29.5	20–29	2	24.5	3	.067	.099	9.9
9.5–19.5	10–19	1	14.5	1	.033	.033	3.3

19. These two studies can be compared using relative frequencies, cumulative relative frequencies, or cumulative percentages. Half the children in the first study displayed between 70 and 90 aggressive acts over the 2-week period. Yet half the children in the second study displayed only 40–49 aggressive acts. This indicates that the children in the second study were less aggressive during the study period.

21. Range = high score − low score = 23 − 1 = 22

Number of class intervals $\approx \dfrac{\text{range}}{i} = \dfrac{22}{2} \approx 11$

Midpoint $= \dfrac{\text{lower limit} + \text{upper limit}}{2}; \dfrac{22 - 23}{2} = 22.5$

Grouped Frequency Distribution of Number of Items Feared

Real Limits	Apparent Limits	Frequency	Midpoint	Cumulative Frequency	Relative Frequency	Cumulative Relative Frequency	Cumulative Percent
21.5–23.5	22–23	3	22.5	50	.06	1.00	100
19.5–21.5	20–21	3	20.5	47	.06	.94	94
17.5–19.5	18–19	4	18.5	44	.08	.88	88
15.5–17.5	16–17	3	16.5	40	.06	.80	80
13.5–15.5	14–15	3	14.5	37	.06	.74	74
11.5–13.5	12–13	4	12.5	34	.08	.68	68
9.5–11.5	10–11	5	10.5	30	.10	.60	60
7.5–9.5	8–9	5	8.5	25	.10	.50	50
5.5–7.5	6–7	8	6.5	20	.16	.40	40
3.5–5.5	4–5	6	4.5	12	.12	.24	24
1.5–3.5	2–3	5	2.5	6	.10	.12	12
0–1.5	0–1	1	.5	1	.02	.02	2

23. Range = high score − low score = 74 − 7 = 67

$$\text{Number of class intervals} \approx \frac{\text{range}}{i} = \frac{67}{5} \approx 13.4$$

$$\text{Midpoint} = \frac{\text{lower limit} + \text{upper limit}}{2}; \quad \frac{70 + 74}{2} = 72$$

Grouped Frequency Distribution of Decision of Recall Data

Real Limits	Apparent Limits	Frequency	Midpoint	Cumulative Frequency	Relative Frequency	Cumulative Relative Frequency	Cumulative Percent
69.5–74.5	70–74	1	72	60	.017	1.00	100
64.5–69.5	65–69	2	67	59	.033	.983	98.3
59.5–64.5	60–64	3	62	57	.050	.95	95
54.5–59.5	55–59	2	57	54	.033	.90	90
49.5–54.5	50–54	4	52	52	.067	.867	86.7
44.5–49.5	45–49	2	47	48	.033	.799	79.9
39.5–44.5	40–44	2	42	46	.033	.766	76.6
34.5–39.5	35–39	3	37	44	.050	.733	73.3
29.5–34.5	30–34	9	32	41	.150	.683	68.3
24.5–29.5	25–29	9	27	32	.150	.533	53.3
19.5–24.5	20–24	6	22	23	.100	.383	38.3
14.5–19.5	15–19	6	17	17	.100	.283	28.3
9.5–14.5	10–14	5	12	11	.083	.183	18.3
4.5–9.5	5–9	6	7	6	.100	.100	10

Problems From the Literature

25. Range $=$ high score $-$ low score $= 664 - 511 = 153$

$$i \approx \frac{\text{range}}{\text{number of class intervals}} = \frac{153}{16} \approx 9.56$$

$$\text{Midpoint} = \frac{\text{lower point} + \text{upper limit}}{2}; \ \frac{510 + 519}{2} = 514.5$$

Grouped Frequency Distribution of Positive and Negative Feedback Data

Real Limits	Apparent Limits	Frequency	Midpoint	Cumulative Frequency	Relative Frequency	Cumulative Relative Frequency	Cumulative Percent
659.5–669.5	660–669	1	664.5	60	.017	1.00	100
649.5–659.5	650–659	3	654.5	59	.050	.983	98.3
639.5–649.5	640–649	8	644.5	56	.133	.933	93.3
629.5–639.5	630–639	8	634.5	48	.133	.800	80.0
619.5–629.5	620–629	3	624.5	40	.050	.667	66.7
609.5–619.5	610–619	3	614.5	37	.050	.617	61.7
599.5–609.5	600–609	2	604.5	34	.033	.567	56.7
589.5–599.5	590–599	2	594.5	32	.033	.534	53.4
579.5–589.5	580–589	0	584.5	30	.000	.501	50.1
569.5–579.5	570–579	1	574.5	30	.017	.501	50.1
559.5–569.5	560–569	0	564.5	29	.000	.484	48.4
549.5–559.5	550–559	6	554.5	29	.100	.484	48.4
539.5–549.5	540–549	8	544.5	23	.133	.384	38.4
529.5–539.5	530–539	6	534.5	15	.100	.251	25.1
519.5–529.5	520–529	4	524.5	9	.068	.151	15.1
509.5–519.5	510–519	5	514.5	5	.083	.083	8.3

27. Range $=$ high score $-$ low score $= 664 - 590 = 74$

$$i \approx \frac{\text{range}}{\text{number of class intervals}} = \frac{74}{13} \approx 5.69$$

$$\text{Midpoint} = \frac{\text{lower limit} + \text{upper limit}}{2}; \ \frac{588 + 593}{2} = 590.5$$

| | | | | | | Cumulative | |
Real Limits	Apparent Limits	Frequency	Midpoint	Cumulative Frequency	Relative Frequency	Relative Frequency	Cumulative Percent

Grouped Frequency Distribution of Positive Feedback Only Data

Real Limits	Apparent Limits	Frequency	Midpoint	Cumulative Frequency	Relative Frequency	Cumulative Relative Frequency	Cumulative Percent
659.5–665.5	660–665	1	662.5	30	.033	1.00	100
653.5–659.5	654–659	2	656.5	29	.067	.967	96.7
647.5–653.5	648–653	4	650.5	27	.133	.900	90.0
641.5–647.5	642–647	4	644.5	23	.133	.767	76.7
635.5–641.5	636–641	1	638.5	19	.033	.634	63.4
629.5–635.5	630–635	8	632.5	18	.267	.601	60.1
623.5–629.5	624–629	0	626.5	10	.000	.334	33.4
617.5–623.5	618–623	4	620.5	10	.133	.334	33.4
611.5–617.5	612–617	1	614.5	6	.033	.201	20.1
605.5–611.5	606–611	2	608.5	5	.067	.168	16.8
599.5–605.5	600–605	1	602.5	3	.033	.100	10.0
593.5–599.5	594–599	1	596.5	2	.033	.067	6.7
587.5–593.5	588–593	1	590.5	1	.033	.033	3.3

29. Range = high score − low score; 34 − 2 = 32

$$\text{Number of class intervals} \approx \frac{\text{range}}{i} = \frac{32}{3} \sim 10.67$$

$$\text{Midpoint} = \frac{\text{lower limit} + \text{upper limit}}{2}; \quad \frac{0 + 2}{2} = 1$$

Grouped Frequency Distribution of Life Experience Data

Real Limits	Apparent Limits	Frequency	Midpoint	Cumulative Frequency	Relative Frequency	Cumulative Relative Frequency	Cumulative Percent
32.5–35.5	33–35	3	34	50	.06	1.00	100
29.5–32.5	30–32	1	31	47	.02	.94	94
26.5–29.5	27–29	1	28	46	.02	.92	92
23.5–26.5	24–26	2	25	45	.04	.90	90
20.5–23.5	21–23	3	22	43	.06	.86	86
17.5–20.5	18–20	4	19	40	.08	.80	80
14.5–17.5	15–17	11	16	36	.22	.72	72
11.5–14.5	12–14	7	13	25	.14	.50	50
8.5–11.5	9–11	8	10	18	.16	.36	36
5.5–8.5	6–8	4	7	10	.08	.20	20
2.5–5.5	3–5	4	4	6	.08	.12	12
0–2.5	0–2	2	1	2	.04	.04	4

31. Subtract the cumulative frequency of participants below the upper real limit of the class interval 12–14 from the total participants. Thus, $50 - 25 = 25$ participants recalled more than 14 events. The cumulative relative frequency below the lower real limit of the class interval 12–14 is .36. Therefore, .36 of the participants recalled fewer than 12 events.

Chapter 3

1. Range = high score − low score; $83 - 8 = 75$

   Number of class intervals $\approx \dfrac{\text{range}}{i}$; $\dfrac{75}{5} \approx 15$ class intervals

   Midpoint $= \dfrac{\text{lower limit} + \text{upper limit}}{2}$; $\dfrac{80 + 84}{2} = 82$

Grouped Frequency Distribution of UPAY Swimming Lap Data

Real Limits	Apparent Limits	f	Cumulative f	Midpoint	Relative f	Cumulative Relative f	Cumulative Percent
79.5–84.5	80–84	1	100	82	.01	1.00	100
74.5–79.5	75–79	4	99	77	.04	.99	99
69.5–74.5	70–74	8	95	72	.08	.95	95
64.5–69.5	65–69	17	87	67	.17	.87	87
59.5–64.5	60–64	9	70	62	.09	.70	70
54.5–59.5	55–59	11	61	57	.11	.61	61
49.5–54.5	50–54	3	50	52	.03	.50	50
44.5–49.5	45–49	7	47	47	.07	.47	47
39.5–44.5	40–44	13	40	42	.13	.40	40
34.5–39.5	35–39	7	27	37	.07	.27	27
29.5–34.5	30–34	5	20	32	.05	.20	20
24.5–29.5	25–29	2	15	27	.02	.15	15
19.5–24.5	20–24	4	13	22	.04	.13	13
14.5–19.5	15–19	4	9	17	.04	.09	9
9.5–14.5	10–14	2	5	12	.02	.05	5
4.5–9.5	5–9	3	3	7	.03	.03	3

3.

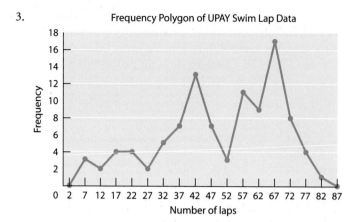

Frequency Polygon of UPAY Swim Lap Data

5.

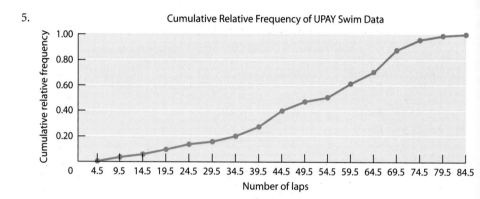

Cumulative Relative Frequency of UPAY Swim Data

7.

Stem-and-Leaf Diagram of UPAY Swim Lap Data

Stem	Leaf
0	8 9 9
1	1 4 6 8 8 9
2	0 0 0 2 7 9
3	1 3 4 4 4 5 6 6 8 8 9 9
4	0 0 0 0 1 2 2 2 2 3 3 4 4 5 5 5 5 6 6 8
5	0 1 4 5 5 6 6 6 7 8 8 8 9 9
6	1 3 3 3 3 4 4 4 4 5 5 5 6 6 7 7 7 7 8 8 8 9 9 9 9 9
7	0 0 0 0 1 1 4 4 5 5 6 7
8	3

9.

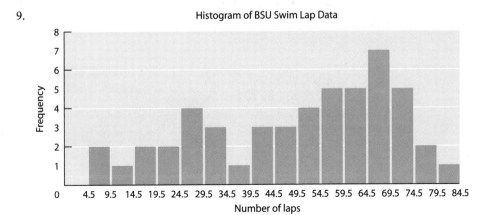

Histogram of BSU Swim Lap Data

11.

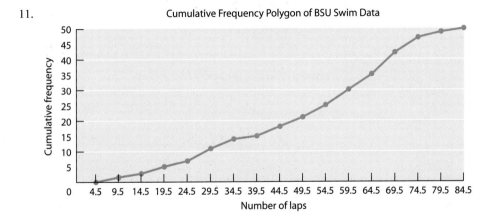

Cumulative Frequency Polygon of BSU Swim Data

13.

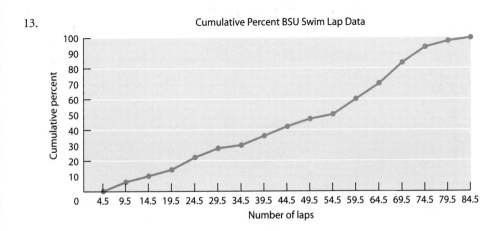

Cumulative Percent BSU Swim Lap Data

15.

Stem	Leaf
0	9 9
1	4 7 7
2	0 3 7 9 9 9
3	3 4 4 5
4	0 4 4 6 8 9
5	0 1 2 3 5 6 7 9 9
6	0 1 2 2 4 5 6 8 7 9 9 9
7	0 0 1 2 3 5 7
8	2

17. To plot the frequency polygon, midpoints need to be calculated.

$$\text{Midpoint} = \frac{\text{lower limit} + \text{upper limit}}{2}; \quad \frac{50 + 99}{2} = 74.5 = \text{the midpoint of the}$$

lowest class interval of the grouped frequency distribution.

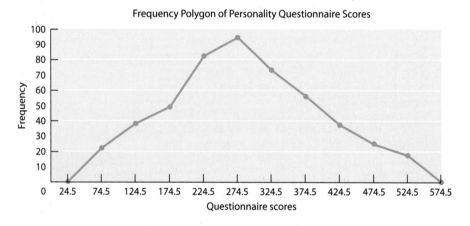

19.

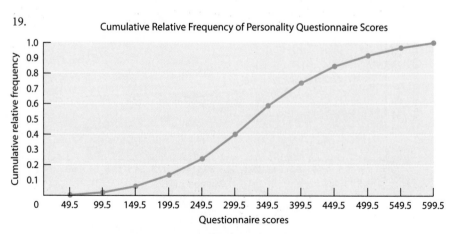

21.

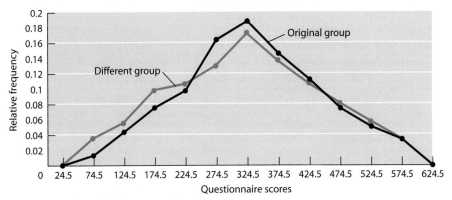

Relative Frequency Comparison of Personality Questionnaire Scores Between Groups

23. $\text{Midpoint} = \dfrac{\text{lower limit} + \text{upper limit}}{2}$

Real Limits	Apparent Limits	Frequency	Midpoints
89.5–99.5	90–99	10	94.5
79.5–89.5	80–89	16	84.5
69.5–79.5	70–79	28	74.5
59.5–69.5	60–69	34	64.5
49.5–59.5	50–59	49	54.5
39.5–49.5	40–49	25	44.5
29.5–39.5	30–39	39	34.5
19.5–29.5	20–29	32	24.5
9.5–19.5	10–19	17	14.5

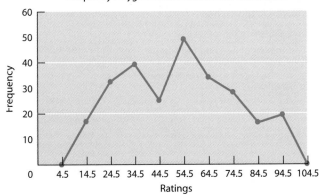

Frequency Polygon of Student Services Evaluations

25. $\text{Cumulative percent} = \dfrac{\text{cumulative frequency}}{n} \times 100.$ The cumulative percent for the lowest class intervals is $\dfrac{17}{250} \times 100 = 6.8.$

Real Limits	Apparent Limits	Frequency	Cumulative Frequency	Cumulative Percent
89.5–99.5	90–99	10	250	100
79.5–89.5	80–89	16	240	96.0
69.5–79.5	70–79	28	224	89.6
59.5–69.5	60–69	34	196	78.4
49.5–59.5	50–59	49	162	64.8
39.5–49.5	40–49	25	113	45.2
29.5–39.5	30–39	39	88	35.2
19.5–29.5	20–29	32	49	19.6
9.5–19.5	10–19	17	17	6.8

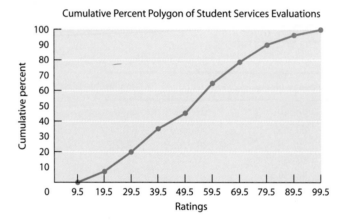

Cumulative Percent Polygon of Student Services Evaluations

27. The frequency polygon is plotted using midpoints. The interval between midpoints is 25, the same as the class interval size. The midpoint just below the lowest class interval is 512, which is the midpoint for the class interval 500–524. On this basis, the re-created grouped frequency is shown here.

Grouped Frequency Distribution of Aptitude Test Scores

Apparent Limits	Frequency
750–774	2
725–749	4
700–724	6
675–699	5
650–674	7
625–649	9
600–624	6
575–599	4
550–574	2
525–549	1

29. Stem and Leaf Diagram of Statistics Exam Grades

Stem	Leaf
2	0 1 2 9 6 9
3	0 5 6 9 9 9
4	0 1 2 4 5 7 8 9 9
5	0 4 4 6 8 8
6	1 3 5 7
7	2 6 7 8
8	4 4 7 8 8 9 9
9	1 2 3 4 5 6 7 9

Problems From the Literature

31.

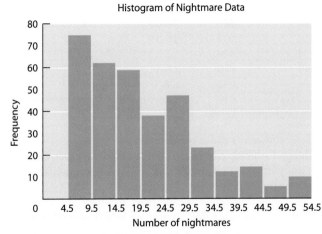

33.

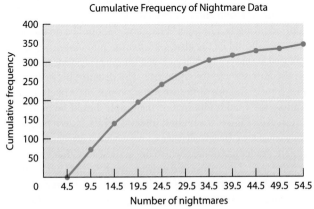

35. Drs. Good and Night should use a relative frequency polygon, cumulative relative frequency polygon, or a cumulative relative percent polygon.

37. Histograms cannot be used to directly compare distributions of data when the sample sizes are different. Histograms compare the mere frequency; since there were more participants in the high school sample than the college sample, the distributions of data would be different regardless. The students should have used one of the relative frequency graphs.

39.

Female-Valued Words			Male-Valued Words		
Apparent Limits	Frequency	Relative Frequency	Apparent Limits	Frequency	Relative Frequency
52–55	7	.037	44–47	4	.020
48–51	19	.100	40–43	20	.102
44–47	11	.058	36–39	27	.138
40–43	34	.178	32–35	41	.209
36–39	47	.246	28–31	34	.173
32–35	19	.100	24–27	26	.133
28–31	28	.147	20–23	14	.071
24–27	12	.063	16–19	6	.031
20–23	4	.020	12–15	12	.061
16–19	2	.010	8–11	7	.036
12–15	6	.031	4–7	5	.026
8–11	2	.010			

41. The graph has the following errors and corrections needed.
    a. Most likely the Internet self-help treatment group and control group did not have the same number of participants. A simple frequency polygon comparison is not meaningful. A relative frequency polygon should be used.
    b. The graph is not properly titled. The two lines represent the frequency of headaches for participants in either the Internet self-help treatment group or the control group. Because the ordinate has whole numbers, the graph is most likely a frequency polygon. An appropriate title could be "Headaches Reported by the Internet Self-Help Treatment Group and Control Group."
    c. The axes are not labeled properly. The label "Frequency" should be on the ordinate. "Number of Headaches" should be the abscissa label.
    d. The data are not plotted at midpoints of the class interval. Midpoints must be used.
    e. The midpoints on the abscissa are not equal size. The distance between the midpoints 10.5 and 14.5 is twice the size of the other midpoints. Most likely a midpoint is missing. In addition, the final midpoints of the graph should be plotted at the midpoint of the interval just above the highest interval, which is zero frequency for both distributions.
    f. A legend is missing. The reader has no idea which line represents either group. Identification by either a color legend or arrows and written words would correct this error.
43. To present a comparison of the number of headaches between the Internet self-help group and the control group, a relative frequency polygon should be used because it is unlikely there were an equal number of participants in each condition. Otherwise, the comparison has no meaning.
45. There is not enough information on the graph to tell whether the distributions are similar or not. The lines are marked so that it's impossible to tell which is cooperation

before and after the therapy. Because the title isn't clear and the axes are not properly labeled, it is impossible to know what the graph represents. Further statistical analysis must be done to determine whether there is a statistical difference. Finally, without a comparison group, there are many factors besides music therapy that could explain either a difference or the lack of a difference in cooperativeness.

Chapter 4

1. The mean IQ score $= \dfrac{\Sigma X}{n} = \dfrac{2{,}549}{24} = 106.208$. To calculate the median, arrange the IQ scores in rank order:

$$\dfrac{\left[\dfrac{24 + 2}{2}\right]\text{th score} + \left[\dfrac{24}{2}\right]\text{th score}}{2} = \dfrac{13\text{th score} + 12\text{th score}}{2} = \dfrac{100 + 106}{2} = 103$$

The IQ scores are multimodal: 92, 106, 129, and 134. All four of these scores have the same frequency.

3. The mean number of items answered correctly on the memory test $=$

$$\dfrac{\Sigma X}{n} = \dfrac{1{,}228}{30} = 40.933. \quad \text{Median}_{\text{even number of scores}} = \dfrac{\left[\dfrac{n + 2}{2}\right]\text{th score} + \left[\dfrac{n}{2}\right]\text{th score}}{2}$$

$$\dfrac{16\text{th score} + 15\text{th score}}{2} = 40.5. \text{ The mode is 38.}$$

5. The mean reaction time $= \dfrac{\Sigma X}{n} = \dfrac{5{,}198}{11} = 472.545$ milliseconds.

$$\text{Median}_{\text{odd number of scores}} = \left[\dfrac{n + 1}{2}\right]\text{th score} = \left[\dfrac{11 + 1}{2}\right]\text{th score} =$$

6th score $= 356$ milliseconds. These data are bimodal, 277 and 456.

7. The mean capacity of short-term memory $= \dfrac{\Sigma X}{n} = \dfrac{126}{18} = 7.$

$$\text{Median}_{\text{even number of scores}} = \dfrac{\left[\dfrac{n + 2}{2}\right]\text{th score} + \left[\dfrac{n}{2}\right]\text{th score}}{2} =$$

$$\dfrac{\left[\dfrac{18 + 2}{2}\right]\text{th score} + \left[\dfrac{18}{2}\right]\text{th score}}{2} =$$

$$\dfrac{10\text{th score} + 9\text{th score}}{2} = \dfrac{7 + 7}{2} = 7. \text{ The mode is 7.}$$

9. The mean number of days patients remained drug-free $= \dfrac{\Sigma X}{n} = \dfrac{1{,}578}{20} = 78.90.$

$$\text{Median}_{\text{even number of scores}} = \dfrac{\left[\dfrac{n + 2}{2}\right]\text{th score} + \left[\dfrac{n}{2}\right]\text{th score}}{2} =$$

$$\frac{\left[\dfrac{20+2}{2}\right]\text{th score} + \left[\dfrac{20}{2}\right]\text{th score}}{2} = \frac{11\text{th score} + 10\text{th score}}{2} = \frac{78+78}{2} = 78.$$

The mode is 78.

11. The mean performance ratings $= \dfrac{\Sigma X}{n} = \dfrac{120}{18} = 6.667.$

$$\text{Median}_{\text{even number of scores}} = \frac{\left[\dfrac{n+2}{2}\right]\text{th score} + \left[\dfrac{n}{2}\right]\text{th score}}{2} =$$

$$\frac{\left[\dfrac{18+2}{2}\right]\text{th score} + \left[\dfrac{18}{2}\right]\text{th score}}{2} = \frac{10\text{th score} + 9\text{th score}}{2} = \frac{6+6}{2} = 6.$$

The mode is 6.

13. Estimated mean IQ scores is $\overline{X} = \dfrac{\Sigma(\text{Frequency} \cdot \text{midpoint})}{n} = \dfrac{17,878.5}{173} = 103.34.$

The total n of the distribution is 173, and the class interval that contains the median (the middle score) is 100–109. The estimated median of the frequency distribution =

$$L + \left[\frac{(n/2) - CF_b}{F_i}\right] \cdot i = 99.5 + \left[\frac{(173/2) - 76}{36}\right] \cdot 10 =$$

$$99.5 + \left[\frac{86.5 - 76}{36}\right] \cdot 10 = 99.5 + \left[\frac{10.5}{36}\right] \cdot 10 = 99.5 + .292 \cdot 10 = 102.42.$$

The estimated mode is 104.5.

	Real Limits	Apparent Limits	f		Cumulative Frequency		Midpoint	Frequency · Midpoint
		150–159	3		173		154.5	463.5
		140–149	5		170		144.5	722.5
		130–139	9		165		134.5	1,210.5
		120–129	18		156		124.5	2,241.0
		110–119	26		138		114.5	2,977.0
	99.5–109.5	100–109	36	F_i	112		104.5	3,762.0
		90–99	34		76	CF_b	94.5	3,213.0
L		80–89	23		42		84.5	1,943.5
		70–79	13		19		74.5	968.5
		60–69	5		6		64.5	322.5
		50–59	1		1		54.5	54.5

$$\Sigma \text{ (frequency} \cdot \text{midpoint)} = 17,878.5$$

15. The estimated mean number of items answered correctly is

$$\overline{X} = \frac{\Sigma(\text{frequency} \cdot \text{midpoint})}{n} = \frac{2,329}{58} = 40.155.$$ The total n of the distribution is

58, and the class interval that contains the median (the middle score) is 40–41. The estimated median of the frequency distribution $= L + \left[\dfrac{(n/2) - CF_b}{F_i}\right] \cdot i = 39.5 +$

$$\left[\frac{(58/2) - 25}{13}\right] \cdot 2 = 39.5 + \left[\frac{29 - 25}{13}\right] \cdot 2 = 39.5 + \left[\frac{4}{13}\right] \cdot 2 = 39.5 +$$

$.308 \cdot 2 = 40.115.$ The estimated mode is 40.5.

Real Limits	Apparent Limits	f		Cumulative Frequency		Midpoint	Frequency · Midpoint
	48–49	2		58		48.5	97.0
	46–47	4		56		46.5	186.0
	44–45	5		52		44.5	222.5
	42–43	9		47		42.5	382.5
39.5–41.5	40–41	13	F_i	38		40.5	526.5
L	38–39	11		25	CF_b	38.5	423.5
	36–37	8		14		36.5	292.0
	34–35	3		6		34.5	103.5
	32–33	2		3		32.5	65.0
	30–31	1		1		30.5	30.5

Σ (frequency · midpoint) = 2,980

17. The estimated mean of annual salaries (in dollars) is $\overline{X} = \dfrac{\Sigma(\text{frequency} \cdot \text{midpoint})}{n} =$

$\dfrac{6,065,924.50}{161} = \$37,676.55.$ The total n of the distribution is 161, and the class interval that contains the median (the middle score) is 36,000–39,999. The estimated median of the frequency distribution $= L + \left[\dfrac{(n/2) - CF_b}{F_i}\right] \cdot i = 35,999.5 +$

$\left[\dfrac{(161/2) - 67}{35}\right] \cdot 4,000 = 35,999.5 + \left[\dfrac{80.5 - 67}{35}\right] \cdot 4,000 = 35,999.5 + \left[\dfrac{13.5}{35}\right] \cdot$

$4,000 = 35,999.5 + .386 \cdot 4,000 = \$37,542.357.$ The estimated mode is \$37,999.50.

Real Limits	Apparent Limits	F		Cumulative Frequency		Midpoint	Frequency · Midpoint
	56,000–59,999	2		161		57,999.5	115,999.00
	52,000–55,999	5		159		53,999.5	269,997.50
	48,000–51,999	11		154		49,999.5	549,999.50
	44,000–47,999	14		143		45,999.5	643,993.00
	40,000–43,999	27		129		41,999.5	1,133,986.50
35,999.5–39,999.5	36,000–39,999	35	F_i	102		37,999.5	1,329,982.50
	32,000–35,999	29		67	CF_b	33,999.5	985,985.50
L	28,000–31,999	18		38		29,999.5	539,991.00
	24,000–27,999	14		20		25,999.5	363,993.00
	20,000–23,999	6		6		21,999.5	131,997.00

Σ (frequency · midpoint) = 6,065,924.50

19. The estimated mean number of errors made by student drivers is

$$\bar{X} = \frac{\Sigma(\text{frequency} \cdot \text{midpoint})}{n} = \frac{12{,}768}{294} = 43.429.$$ The total n of the distribution

is 294, and the class interval that contains the median (the middle score) is 42–48. The

estimated median of the frequency distribution $= L + \left[\dfrac{(n/2) - CF_b}{F_i} \right] \cdot i =$

$41.5 + \left[\dfrac{(294/2) - 136}{56} \right] \cdot 7 = 41.5 + \left[\dfrac{147 - 136}{56} \right] \cdot 7 = 41.5 + \left[\dfrac{11}{56} \right] \cdot 7 =$

$41.5 + .196 \cdot 7 = 42.872.$ The estimated mode is 45.

	Real Limits	Apparent Limits	f		Cumulative Frequency		Midpoint	Frequency · Midpoint
		70–76	12		294		73	876
		63–69	23		282		66	1,518
		56–62	24		259		59	1,416
		49–55	43		235		52	2,236
L	41.5–48.5	42–48	56	F_i	192		45	2,520
		35–41	54		136	CF_b	38	2,052
		28–34	44		82		31	1,364
		21–27	23		38		24	552
		14–20	12		15		17	204
		7–13	3		3		10	30

$\Sigma\,(\text{frequency} \cdot \text{midpoint}) = 12{,}768$

21. Mean: The mean is the average of all scores. By adding a score of 37, which is considerably higher than the mean in a symmetrical distribution, the mean (15) will sharply
increase because there are so few scores in the distribution. Thus, each score has
a tremendous effect on the mean, with extreme scores pulling the mean in their
direction.
Median: The median is the middle score with half the scores above and half the scores
below. Thus, adding an additional score will shift the median slightly higher, but there
are not sufficient data to determine the amount of the decrease.
Mode: The distribution is symmetrical with the mode of the most frequent score. Because there are few scores in this distribution, adding an additional score may add an
additional mode.

23. This distribution is negatively skewed because the mean (34) is less than the median
(50) and the median is less than the mode (75). Considering that the distribution of
ratio or interval data is best represented by either the median or mode and that this is
a negatively skewed distribution, the best choice is the median.

25. This distribution is described as negatively skewed because the mean (123) is less
than the median (124) and the median is less than the mode (125). The measure of
central tendency that best represents a distribution of ratio or interval data is either
the median or mode. Considering this is a negatively skewed distribution, the median best represents the distribution. The mode is not usually the best choice with

this measurement scale, particularly if there is a small n, because the mode can drastically change with the addition of a score.

27. A distribution with very few scores at the high end has a positive skew.

Problems From the Literature

29. The mean performance ratings $= \dfrac{\Sigma X}{n} = \dfrac{492}{30} = 16.40.$

$$\text{Median}_{\text{even number of scores}} = \frac{\left[\dfrac{n+2}{2}\right]\text{th score} + \left[\dfrac{n}{2}\right]\text{th score}}{2} =$$

$$\frac{\left[\dfrac{30+2}{2}\right]\text{th score} + \left[\dfrac{30}{2}\right]\text{th score}}{2} = \frac{16\text{th score} + 15\text{th score}}{2} = \frac{17+17}{2} = 17.$$

The mode is 17.

31. The mean, median, and mode are almost the same. There is very little skew.

33. The data are positively skewed because the mean is greater than the median and the mode is smaller than the median. There were a few exceptionally high scores that moved the mean in that direction. The cultural sensitivity program should use either the median or mode. Considering the importance of the program, a conservative approach might be wise. Thus, the program would be conducted in more classes if the mode were used.

35. Briefly Touch:

$$Q_2 \text{ is the median. } \text{Median}_{\text{even number of scores}} = \frac{\left[\dfrac{10+2}{2}\right]\text{th score} + \left[\dfrac{10}{2}\right]\text{th score}}{2} =$$

5.5th score. Rank order data shows and computes the average for the sum of 31% +

34% tips. Thus, Q_2 is a 32.5% tip. $Q_1 = \left[\dfrac{\left(\dfrac{10+1}{2}\right)+1}{2}\right]\text{th score} = \dfrac{5.5}{2}\text{th score,}$

or the average of the 5th and 6th score, which is 32.50. To find Q_3, start at the highest score and count to the score that is halfway between the 5th and 6th score, which is 35. Q_1 is the score halfway between Q_2, and the lowest score is 25.

No Touch: $Q_1 = 13$, $Q_2 = 15.5$, and $Q_3 = 21$.

37. The median tip would be the best average to tell the new server. The mode would underestimate the tip, and the mean would overestimate the tip.

39. The estimated mean number of words recognized is

$$\overline{X} = \frac{\Sigma(\text{frequency} \cdot \text{midpoint})}{n} = \frac{961.5}{71} = 13.54.$$ The total n of the distribution is

71, and the class interval that contains the median (the middle score) is 14–15. The

estimated median of the frequency distribution $= L + \left[\dfrac{(n/2) - CF_b}{F_i}\right] \cdot i =$

$13.5 + \left[\dfrac{(71/2) - 35}{5}\right] \cdot 2 = 13.5 + \left[\dfrac{35.5 - 35}{5}\right] \cdot 2 = 13.5 + \left[\dfrac{.5}{5}\right] \cdot 2 =$

$13.5 + .1 \cdot 2 = 13.7.$ The estimated mode is 14.5.

Real Limits	Apparent Limits	f	Cumulative Frequency		Midpoint	Frequency · Midpoint
	22–23	18	71		22.5	405.0
	20–21	4	53		20.5	82.0
	18–19	3	49		18.5	55.5
	16–17	6	46		16.5	99.0
L 13.5–15.5	14–15	5 F_i	40		14.5	72.5
	12–13	5	35	CF_b	12.5	62.5
	10–11	5	30		10.5	52.5
	8–9	5	25		8.5	42.5
	6–7	7	20		6.5	45.5
	4–5	6	13		4.5	27.0
	2–3	7	7		2.5	17.5

$$\Sigma \,(\text{frequency} \cdot \text{midpoint}) = 961.5$$

41. The tail points in the negative direction, which indicates a negative skew.

Chapter 5

1. The mean, variance, and the standard deviation of IQ scores:

$$\bar{X} = \frac{\Sigma X}{n} = \frac{2{,}549}{24} = 106.208$$

$$S^2 = \frac{\Sigma X^2 - \dfrac{(\Sigma X)^2}{n}}{n-1} = \frac{280{,}297 - \dfrac{2{,}549^2}{24}}{24-1} = \frac{280{,}297 - \dfrac{64{,}974.01}{24}}{23} = 416.17$$

$$S = \sqrt{S^2} = \sqrt{41.617} = 20.40$$

3. The mean, variance, and standard deviation of the number of items on the memory test:

$$\bar{X} = \frac{\Sigma X}{n} = \frac{1{,}228}{30} = 40.933 \text{ items}$$

$$S^2 = \frac{\Sigma X^2 - \dfrac{(\Sigma X)^2}{n}}{n-1} = \frac{50{,}822 - \dfrac{1{,}228^2}{30}}{30-1} = \frac{50{,}822 - 50{,}266.133}{29} = 19.168$$

$$S = \sqrt{S^2} = \sqrt{19.168} = 4.378 \text{ items}$$

5. The mean, variance, and standard deviation of reaction time in milliseconds:

$$\bar{X} = \frac{\Sigma X}{n} = \frac{5{,}198}{11} = 472.545 \text{ milliseconds}$$

$$S^2 = \frac{\Sigma X^2 - \dfrac{(\Sigma X)^2}{n}}{n-1} = \frac{3{,}105{,}882 - \dfrac{5{,}198^2}{11}}{11-1} =$$

$$\frac{125{,}316 - 2{,}456{,}291.273}{10} = 64{,}959.073$$

$$S = \sqrt{S^2} = \sqrt{64{,}959.073} = 254.871 \text{ milliseconds}$$

7. The mean, variance, and standard deviation for the capacity of short-term memory:

$$\overline{X} = \frac{\Sigma X}{n} = \frac{126}{18} = 7$$

$$S^2 = \frac{\Sigma X^2 - \dfrac{(\Sigma X)^2}{n}}{n-1} = \frac{972 - \dfrac{126^2}{18}}{18-1} = \frac{972 - 882}{17} = 5.294$$

$$S = \sqrt{S^2} = \sqrt{5.294} = 2.301$$

9. The mean, variance, and standard deviation of days patients remained drug-free:

$$\overline{X} = \frac{\Sigma X}{n} = \frac{1{,}578}{20} = 78.90 \text{ days}$$

$$S^2 = \frac{\Sigma X^2 - \left(\dfrac{\Sigma X^2}{n}\right)}{n-1} = \frac{157{,}808 - \dfrac{1{,}578^2}{20}}{20-1} = \frac{157{,}808 - 124{,}504.2}{19} = 1{,}752.832$$

$$S = \sqrt{S^2} = \sqrt{1{,}752.832} = 41.867 \text{ days}$$

11. The mean, variance, and standard deviation of work performance ratings:

$$\overline{X} = \frac{\Sigma X}{n} = \frac{120}{18} = 6.667$$

$$S^2 = \frac{\Sigma X^2 - \dfrac{(\Sigma X)^2}{n}}{n-1} = \frac{872 - \dfrac{120^2}{18}}{18-1} = \frac{872 - 800}{17} = 4.235$$

$$S = \sqrt{S^2} = \sqrt{4.235} = 2.058$$

13. The estimated mean, variance, and standard deviation of the frequency distribution of IQ scores are as follows: $\overline{X} = 103.344$; $S^2 = 395.167$; $S = 19.878$

Apparent Limits	Frequency	Midpoint	Frequency · Midpoint	x	x^2	$F \cdot x^2$
150–159	3	154.5	463.5	51.156	2,616.936	7,850.808
140–149	5	144.5	722.5	41.156	1,693.816	8,469.080
130–139	9	134.5	1,210.5	31.156	970.696	8,736.264
120–129	18	124.5	2,241.0	21.156	447.576	8,056.368
110–119	26	114.5	2,977.0	11.156	124.456	3,235.856
100–109	36	104.5	3,762.0	1.156	1.336	48.096
90–99	34	94.5	3,213.0	−8.844	78.216	2,659.344
80–89	23	84.5	1,943.5	−18.844	355.096	8,167.208
70–79	13	74.5	968.5	−28.844	831.976	10,815.688
60–69	5	64.5	322.5	−38.844	1,508.856	7,544.280
50–59	1	54.5	54.5	−48.844	2,385.736	2,385.736

$$n = 173 \qquad \Sigma(F \cdot \text{midpoint}) = 17{,}878.5 \qquad \Sigma(F \cdot x^2) = 67{,}968.728$$

$$\overline{X} = \frac{17{,}878.5}{173} = 103.344 \qquad S^2 = \frac{67{,}968.728}{173 - 1} = 395.167$$

$$S = \sqrt{395.167} = 19.878$$

15. The estimated mean, variance, and standard deviation of the grouped frequency distribution of the number of items answered correctly are as follows: $\overline{X} = 40.155$ items; $S^2 = 15.598$; $S = 3.949$ items.

Apparent Limits	Frequency	Midpoint	Frequency · Midpoint	x	x^2	$F \cdot x^2$
48–49	2	48.5	97.0	8.345	69.639	139.278
46–47	4	46.5	186.0	6.345	40.259	161.036
44–45	5	44.5	222.5	4.345	18.879	94.395
42–43	9	42.5	382.5	2.345	5.499	49.491
40–41	13	40.5	526.5	.345	.119	1.547
38–39	11	38.5	423.5	−1.655	2.739	30.129
36–37	8	36.5	292.0	−3.655	13.359	106.872
34–35	3	34.5	103.5	−5.655	31.979	95.937
32–33	2	32.5	65.0	−7.655	58.599	117.198
30–31	1	30.5	30.5	−9.655	93.219	93.219

$n = 58$ $\Sigma(F \cdot \text{midpoint}) = 2{,}329$ $\Sigma(F \cdot x^2) = 889.102$

$$\overline{X} = \frac{2{,}329}{58} = 40.155 \qquad S^2 = \frac{889.102}{58 - 1} = 15.598$$

$$S = \sqrt{15.598} = 3.949$$

17. The mean, variance, and standard deviation of the grouped frequency distribution of professors' annual salaries are as follows: $\overline{X} = \$37{,}676.519$; $S^2 = \dfrac{\Sigma(F \cdot x^2)}{n - 1} = 63{,}395{,}031.056$; $S = \$7{,}962.10$.

Apparent Limits	Frequency	Midpoint	Frequency · Midpoint	x	x^2	$F \cdot x^2$
56,000–59,999	2	57,999.5	115,999.0	20,322.981	413,023,556.726	826,047,113.453
52,000–55,999	5	53,999.5	269,997.5	16,322.981	266,439,708.726	1,332,198,543.632
48,000–51,999	11	49,999.5	549,994.5	12,322.981	151,855,860.726	1,670,414,467.990
44,000–47,999	14	45,999.5	643,993.0	8,322.981	69,272,012.726	969,808,178.169
40,000–43,999	27	41,999.5	1,133,986.5	4,322.981	18,688,164.726	504,580,447.612
36,000–39,999	35	37,999.5	1,329,982.5	322.981	104,316.726	3,651,085.423
32,000–35,999	29	33,999.5	985,985.5	−3,677.019	13,520,468.726	392,093,593.064
28,000–31,999	18	29,999.5	539,991.0	−7,677.019	58,936,620.726	1,060,859,173.075
24,000–27,999	14	25,999.5	363,993.0	−11,677.019	136,352,772.726	1,908,938,818.169
20,000–23,999	6	21,999.5	131,997.0	−15,677.019	245,768,924.726	1,474,613,548.358

$n = 161$ $\Sigma(F \cdot \text{midpoint}) = 6{,}065{,}919.5$ $\Sigma(F \cdot x^2) = 10{,}143{,}204{,}968.944$

$$\overline{X} = \frac{6{,}065{,}919.5}{161} = 37{,}676.519 \qquad S^2 = \frac{10{,}143{,}204{,}968.944}{161 - 1} = 63{,}395{,}031.056$$

$$S = \sqrt{63{,}395{,}031.056} = 7{,}962.10$$

19. The mean, variance, and standard deviation of the grouped frequency distribution of student driver errors are as follows:

$$\overline{X} = 43.429; \; S^2 = \frac{\Sigma(F \cdot x^2)}{n - 1} = 205.229; \; S = 14.326$$

Apparent Limits	Frequency	Midpoint	Frequency · Midpoint	x	x^2	$F \cdot x^2$
70–76	12	73	876	29.571	874.444	10,493.328
63–69	23	66	1,518	22.571	509.450	11,717.350
56–62	24	59	1,416	15.571	242.456	5,818.945
49–55	43	52	2,236	8.571	73.462	3,158.868
42–48	56	45	2,520	1.571	2.468	138.210
35–41	54	38	2,052	−5.429	29.474	1,591.598
28–34	44	31	1,364	−12.429	154.480	6,797.122
21–27	23	24	552	−19.429	377.486	8,682.179
14–20	12	17	204	−26.429	698.492	8,381.904
7–13	3	10	30	−33.429	1,117.498	3,352.494

$$n = 294 \quad \Sigma(F \cdot \text{midpoint}) = 12,768 \quad \Sigma(F \cdot x^2) = 60,132.00$$

$$\overline{X} = \frac{12,768}{294} = 43.429 \qquad S^2 = \frac{60,132.00}{294 - 1} = 205.229$$

$$S = \sqrt{205.229} = 14.326$$

Problems From the Literature

21. Course 1: $\overline{X} = \dfrac{145}{30} = 4.833$; Course 2: $\overline{X} = \dfrac{104}{30} = 3.467$

23. Course 1: Variance $= S^2 = \dfrac{801 - \dfrac{(145)^2}{30}}{30 - 1} = 3.44;$

Course 2: Variance $= S^2 = \dfrac{432 - \dfrac{(104)^2}{30}}{30 - 1} = 2.464$

25. There is a larger standard deviation in scores for Course 1 ($s = 1.858$) compared to Course 2 ($s = 1.57$). The larger standard deviation means the distribution of scores in Course 1 are not clustered as close to the mean as they are in Course 2. There is not a huge difference between the two standard deviations, but it does indicate that the mean of Course 2 has less error than that of Course 1.

27. Range = high score − low score; 48 − 9 = 39.

29. $S = \sqrt{\dfrac{\Sigma X^2 - \dfrac{(\Sigma X)^2}{n}}{n - 1}} = \sqrt{\dfrac{19,817 - \dfrac{(561)^2}{18}}{18 - 1}} =$

$$\sqrt{\dfrac{19,817 - 17,484.5}{17}} = \sqrt{137.206} = 11.713$$

31. Estimated mean number of words recognized is $\overline{X} = \dfrac{\Sigma(\text{frequency} \cdot \text{midpoint})}{n} = \dfrac{961.5}{71} = 13.542$.

Apparent Limits	Frequency	Midpoint	Frequency · Midpoint
22–23	18	22.5	405.0
20–21	4	20.5	82.0
18–19	3	18.5	55.5
16–17	6	16.5	99.0
14–15	5	14.5	72.5
12–13	5	12.5	62.5
10–11	5	10.5	52.5
8–9	5	8.5	42.5
6–7	7	6.5	45.5
4–5	6	4.5	27.0
2–3	7	2.5	17.5
	$n = 71$		$\Sigma(\text{frequency} \cdot \text{midpoint}) = 961.5$

$$\overline{X} = \frac{961.5}{71} = 13.542$$

Chapter 6

1. $\overline{X}_{\text{new}} = \overline{X}_{\text{original}} + \text{constant} = 100 + 10 = 110$. $S_{\text{new}} = S_{\text{original}} = 20$
3. $\overline{X}_{\text{new}} = \overline{X}_{\text{original}} + \text{constant} = 100 + 25 = 125$. $S_{\text{new}} = S_{\text{original}} = 20$
5. $\overline{X}_{\text{new}} = \overline{X}_{\text{original}} - \text{constant} = 100 - 10 = 90$. $S_{\text{new}} = S_{\text{original}} = 20$
7. $\overline{X}_{\text{new}} = \overline{X}_{\text{original}} - \text{constant} = 100 - 25 = 75$. $S_{\text{new}} = S_{\text{original}} = 20$
9. $\overline{X}_{\text{new}} = \overline{X}_{\text{original}} \times or \div \text{constant} = 100 \times 7 = 700$
   $S_{\text{new}} = S_{\text{original}} \times or \div \text{constant} = 20 \times 7 = 140$
11. $\overline{X}_{\text{new}} = \overline{X}_{\text{original}} \times or \div \text{constant} = 100 \times 5 = 500$
   $S_{\text{new}} = S_{\text{original}} \times or \div \text{constant} = 20 \times 5 = 100$
13. $\overline{X}_{\text{new}} = \overline{X}_{\text{original}} \times or \div \text{constant} = 100 \div 7 = 14.286$
   $S_{\text{new}} = S_{\text{original}} \times or \div \text{constant} = 20 \div 7 = 2.857$
15. $\overline{X}_{\text{new}} = \overline{X}_{\text{original}} \times or \div \text{constant} = 100 \div 10 = 10$
   $S_{\text{new}} = S_{\text{original}} \times or \div \text{constant} = 20 \div 10 = 2$

17. $\bar{X}_{new} = \bar{X}_{original} \times or \div constant = 100 \div 20 = 5$
    $S_{new} = S_{original} \times or \div constant = 20 \div 20 = 1$

19. The mean and standard deviation for the saliva are as follows:

$$\bar{X} = \frac{\Sigma X}{n} = \frac{2,310}{10} = 231 \quad S = \sqrt{\frac{\Sigma X^2 - \frac{(\Sigma X)^2}{n}}{n-1}} =$$

$$\sqrt{\frac{553,900 - \frac{2,310^2}{10}}{10-1}} = 47.481 \quad z = \frac{X - \bar{X}}{S}$$

Calculations for each are shown in the right-hand column of the following table.

Dog	Amount of Saliva (in milliliters)	Calculations for z-scores
Spot	250	$z = \frac{250 - 231}{47.481} = .40$
Rover	240	$z = \frac{240 - 231}{47.481} = .19$
Blackie	280	$z = \frac{280 - 231}{47.481} = 1.032$
Ginger	190	$z = \frac{190 - 231}{47.481} = -.864$
Gus	300	$z = \frac{300 - 231}{47.481} = 1.453$
Scruffy	200	$z = \frac{200 - 231}{47.481} = -.653$
Digger	230	$z = \frac{230 - 231}{47.481} = -.021$
Muffin	180	$z = \frac{180 - 231}{47.481} = -1.074$
Amber	160	$z = \frac{160 - 231}{47.481} = -1.495$
Tiger	280	$z = \frac{280 - 231}{47.481} = 1.032$

21. $z = \frac{X - \bar{X}}{S}$; a. $z = \frac{94 - 84}{4} = 2.5$; b. $z = \frac{97 - 84}{4} = 3.25$;

c. $z = \frac{88 - 84}{4} = 1.00$; d. $z = \frac{84 - 84}{4} = 0$; e. $z = \frac{80 - 84}{4} = -1.00$;

f. $z = \frac{77 - 84}{4} = -1.75$; g. $z = \frac{74 - 84}{4} = -2.5$; h. $z = \frac{76 - 84}{4} = -2.00$

23. $z = \dfrac{X - \overline{X}}{S}$; a. $z = \dfrac{700 - 825}{186} = -.672$; b. $z = \dfrac{1{,}000 - 825}{186} = .941$;

c. $z = \dfrac{1{,}200 - 825}{186} = 2.016$; d. $z = \dfrac{850 - 825}{186} = .134$;

e. $z = \dfrac{623 - 825}{186} = -1.086$; f. $z = \dfrac{245 - 825}{186} = -3.118$;

g. $z = \dfrac{975 - 825}{186} = .806$; h. $z = \dfrac{832 - 825}{186} = .038$;

i. $z = \dfrac{469 - 825}{186} = -1.914$

Problems From the Literature

25. College 1: $\overline{X}_{new} = \overline{X}_{original} + \text{constant} = 43.2 + 15 = 58.2$. $S_{new} = S_{original} = 11.7$
College 2: $\overline{X}_{new} = \overline{X}_{original} + \text{constant} = 57.1 + 15 = 72.1$. $S_{new} = S_{original} = 22.4$
The means increased the amount of the constant, but the standard deviation remained the same because the dispersion of scores in the distribution did not change.

27. Calculations for each score are shown in the following table.

	College One	
Student	Estimated Risk	z score
Puff	23	$z = \dfrac{23 - 43.2}{11.7} = -1.726$
Cough	31	$z = \dfrac{31 - 43.2}{11.7} = -1.043$
Gasp	33	$z = \dfrac{33 - 43.2}{11.7} = -.872$
Smokie	27	$z = \dfrac{27 - 43.2}{11.7} = -1.385$
Flick	15	$z = \dfrac{15 - 43.2}{11.7} = -2.410$

29. Flossy Mae: $z = \dfrac{X - \overline{X}}{S} = z = \dfrac{31 - 57.1}{22.4} = -1.165$

Billy Bob: $z = \dfrac{31 - 43.2}{11.7} = -1.043$

Flossy Mae estimated she had less risk of getting lung cancer than did Billy Bob.

31. Statistics Class A: $\overline{X}_{new} = \overline{X}_{original} \times or \div \text{constant} = 39.9 \times 4 = 159.6$
$S_{new} = S_{original} \times or \div \text{constant} = 17.1 \times 4 = 68.4$
Statistics Class B: $\overline{X}_{new} = \overline{X}_{original} \times or \div \text{constant} = 39.9 \times 4 = 159.6$

$S_{new} = S_{original} \times or \div constant = 21.95 \times 4 = 87.6$. Because each score is 4 times higher, the means increase the same. The spread of the scores changed also. Scores that may have been 2 numbers apart are now 8 numbers apart. Thus, the standard deviations now are 4 times greater, but the relative dispersion of scores around the mean remains the same.

33. For student in Class A, $z = \dfrac{X - \overline{X}}{S} = z = \dfrac{45 - 39.9}{17.1} = .298$; for student in Class B,

$z = \dfrac{45 - 39.9}{21.9} = .233$. The student in Class B had the lower risk estimation.

Chapter 7

1. $z = 3.00$; area beyond $z = .0013$
   $z = 1.00$; area beyond $z = .1587$
   $z = -.50$; area beyond $z = .3085$
   $z = -.25$; area beyond $z = .4013$
   $z = -1.37$; area beyond $z = .0853$
   $z = -2.75$; area beyond $z = .0030$
3. $z = 3.00$; area between the mean and $z = .4987$
   $z = 1.00$; area between the mean and $z = .3413$
   $z = .50$; area between the mean and $z = .1915$
   $z = -.25$; area between the mean and $z = .0987$
   $z = -1.37$; area between the mean and $z = .4147$
   $z = -2.75$; area between the mean and $z = .4970$
5. $z = \dfrac{X - \overline{X}}{S} = \dfrac{140 - 150}{25} = -.40$. Table Z area between the mean and $z = .1554$.
   $.1554 + .50 = .6554$, the proportion of people taking the test who had a reaction time longer than 140 msec.
7. $z = \dfrac{X - \overline{X}}{S} = \dfrac{115 - 150}{25} = -1.40$. Table Z area between the mean and $z = .4192$.
   $.4192 + .50 = .9192$, the proportion of people taking the test who had a reaction time longer than 115 msec.
9. $z = \dfrac{X - \overline{X}}{S} = \dfrac{99 - 150}{25} = -2.04$. Table Z area beyond $z = .0207$, the proportion of people taking the test who had a reaction time shorter than 99 msec.
11. $z = \dfrac{X - \overline{X}}{S} = \dfrac{127 - 150}{25} = -.92$. Table Z area beyond $z = .1788$, the proportion of people taking the test who had a reaction time shorter than 127 msec.
13. $z = \dfrac{X - \overline{X}}{S} = \dfrac{128 - 150}{25} = -.88$. Table Z area beyond $z = .1894$.

   $z = \dfrac{X - \overline{X}}{S} = \dfrac{112 - 150}{25} = -1.52$. Table Z area beyond $z = .0643$.
   Both scores are below the mean, $.1894 - .0643 = .1251$, the proportion of people with reaction times between 128 and 112 msec.

15. $z = \dfrac{X - \overline{X}}{S} = \dfrac{113 - 150}{25} = -1.48$. Table Z area beyond $z = .0694$.

$z = \dfrac{X - \overline{X}}{S} = \dfrac{105 - 150}{25} = -1.80$. Table Z area beyond $z = .0359$.

Both scores are below the mean, $.0694 - .0359 = .0335$, the proportion of people with reaction times between 113 and 105 msec.

17. $z = \dfrac{X - \overline{X}}{S} = \dfrac{137 - 150}{25} = -.52$. Table Z area beyond $z = .3015$.

$z = \dfrac{X - \overline{X}}{S} = \dfrac{142 - 150}{25} = -.32$. Table Z area beyond $z = .3745$.

Both scores are below the mean. $.3015 - .3745 = .073$, the proportion of people with reaction times between 137 and 142 msec.

19. Convert the 75th percentile to proportion $75/100 = .75$. Table P column 1 proportion $.75 = z$ score of $.6745$. $X = \mu + (z \cdot \sigma) = 150 + (.6745 \cdot 25) = 150 + 16.863 = 166.86$.

21. Convert the 45th percentile to proportion $45/100 = .45$. Table P column 3 proportion $.45 = z$ score of $-.1257$. $X = \mu + (z \cdot \sigma) = 150 + (-.1257 \cdot 25) = 150 - 3.143 = 146.857$.

23. $z = \dfrac{X - \overline{X}}{S} = \dfrac{36 - 42}{5} = -1.20$. Table Z area between the mean and $z = .3849$.

$z = \dfrac{X - \overline{X}}{S} = \dfrac{48 - 42}{5} = -1.20$. Table Z area between the mean and $z = .3849$.

Add these together to determine the proportion of the target sales population: $.3849 + .3849 = .7698$.

25. $z = \dfrac{X - \overline{X}}{S} = \dfrac{36 - 42}{5} = -1.20$. Table Z area beyond $z = .1151$, the proportion of the target sales population too short to safely use this product.

27. $Q_1 = $ 75th percentile. Convert the 75th percentile to proportion $75/100 = .75$. Table P column proportion 1 $.75 = z$ score of $.6745$. $X = \mu + (z \cdot \sigma) = 42 + (.6745 \cdot 5) = 42 + 3.373 = 45.37$ inches.

29. $z = \dfrac{X - \overline{X}}{S} = \dfrac{43{,}000 - 68{,}000}{17{,}000} = -1.471$. Table Z area from the mean to $z = .4292$. $.4292 + .50 = .9292$, the proportion of families in Uppityton that make more than $43,000 per year.

31. $z = \dfrac{X - \overline{X}}{S} = \dfrac{54{,}000 - 68{,}000}{17{,}000} = -.824$. Table Z area beyond $z = .2061$, the proportion of the families in Uppityton that make less than $54,000 per year.

33. $z = \dfrac{X - \overline{X}}{S} = \dfrac{80{,}000 - 68{,}000}{17{,}000} = .706$. Table Z area between the mean and $z = .2611$. $z = \dfrac{X - \overline{X}}{S} = \dfrac{70{,}000 - 68{,}000}{17{,}000} = .1176$. Table Z area between the mean and $z = .0478$. Both scores are above the mean, $.2611 - .0478 = .2133$, the proportion of families in Uppityton who make between $70,000 and $80,000 per year.

35. $z = \dfrac{X - \overline{X}}{S} = \dfrac{47,000 - 68,000}{17,000} = -1.236$. Table Z area between the mean and

$z = .3925$. $z = \dfrac{X - \overline{X}}{S} = \dfrac{58,000 - 68,000}{17,000} = -.5882$. Table Z area between the

mean and $z = .2224$. Both scores are below the mean, $.3925 - .2224 = .1701$, the proportion of families who make between \$47,000 and \$58,000 annual income.

37. Convert the 15th percentile to proportion $15/100 = .15$. Table P column 3 proportion $.15 = z$ score of -1.0364. $X = \mu + (z \cdot \sigma) = \$68,000 + (-1.0364 \cdot \$17,000) = \$68,000 - 17,618.80 = \$50,381.20$.

Problems From the Literature

39. $z = \dfrac{X - \overline{X}}{S} = \dfrac{150,000 - 70,617}{41,373} = 1.919$. Table Z area beyond $z = .0281$, the proportion of sports psychologists who make more than \$150,000 per year.

41. $z = \dfrac{X - \overline{X}}{S} = \dfrac{35,000 - 70,617}{41,373} = -.861$. Table Z area beyond $z = .1949$, the proportion of sports psychologists who make less than \$35,000 per year.

43. $z = \dfrac{X - \overline{X}}{S} = \dfrac{150,000 - 70,617}{41,373} = 1.919$. Table Z area between the mean and

$z = .4726$. $z = \dfrac{X - \overline{X}}{S} = \dfrac{200,000 - 70,617}{41,373} = 3.127$. Table Z area between the mean

and $z = .4991$. Both scores are above the mean, $.4991 - .4726 = .0265$, the proportion of sports psychologists who make between \$150,000 and \$200,000 per year.

45. Convert the 25th percentile to proportion $25/100 = .25$. Table P column 1 proportion $.25 = z$ score of $-.6745$. $X = \mu + (z \cdot \sigma) = \$70,617 + (-.6745 \cdot \$41,373) = \$70,617 - \$27,906.089 = \$42,710.91$.

47. Convert the 10th percentile to proportion $10/100 = .10$. Table P column 1 proportion $.10 = z$ score of -1.2816. $X = \mu + (z \cdot \sigma) = \$70,617 + (-1.2816 \cdot \$41,373) = \$70,617 - \$53,023.637 = \$17,593.36$.

49. $z = \dfrac{X - \overline{X}}{S} = \dfrac{15 - 19.41}{3.17} = -1.391$. Table Z area beyond $z = .0823$, the proportion of participants that recalled fewer than 15 names.

51. $z = \dfrac{X - \overline{X}}{S} = \dfrac{30 - 19.41}{3.17} = 3.341$. Table Z area beyond $z = .0004$, the proportion of participants that recalled more than 30 names.

53. $z = \dfrac{X - \overline{X}}{S} = \dfrac{10 - 19.41}{3.17} = -2.968$. Table Z area between the mean and $z = .4985$.

$z = \dfrac{X - \overline{X}}{S} = \dfrac{20 - 19.41}{3.17} = .186$. Table Z area between the mean and $z = .073$. One score is above the mean and the other is below the mean, $.4985 + .073 = .572$, the proportion of participants that recalled between 10 and 20 names.

55. Convert 20th percentile to proportion 20/100 = .20. Table P column 1 proportion .20 = z score of −.8416. $X = \mu + (z \cdot \sigma) = 19.41 + (−.8416 \cdot 3.17) = 19.41 − 2.668 = 16.74$.

57. Convert the 90th percentile to proportion 90/100 = .90. Table P column 1 proportion .90 = z score of 1.2816. $X = \mu + (z \cdot \sigma) = 19.41 + (1.2816 \cdot 3.17) = 19.41 + 4.063 = 23.47$.

Chapter 8

1. The scatterplot reveals a negative correlation between birth order and SAT verbal scores in that as birth order increases, the SAT verbal score decreases.

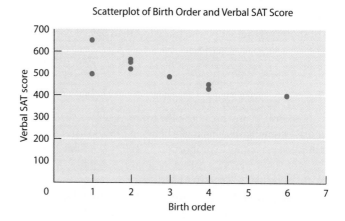

Scatterplot of Birth Order and Verbal SAT Score

3. $$r_{xy} = \frac{(n \cdot \Sigma XY) - (\Sigma X \cdot \Sigma Y)}{\sqrt{[(n \cdot \Sigma X^2) - (\Sigma X)^2] \cdot [(n \cdot \Sigma Y^2) - (\Sigma Y)^2]}}$$

$$= \frac{(10 \cdot 13{,}195) - (28 \cdot 5{,}020)}{\sqrt{[(10 \cdot 100) - (28)^2] \cdot [(10 \cdot 256{,}900) - (5{,}020)^2]}}$$

$$= \frac{(131{,}950) - (140{,}560)}{\sqrt{[(1{,}000) - (784)] \cdot [(25{,}690{,}000) - (25{,}200{,}400)]}}$$

$$= \frac{-8{,}610}{\sqrt{150{,}753{,}600}} = -.837$$

$df = n - 2 = 10 - 2 = 8$. The critical value in Table R = .6215. $r_{xy} = -.837$ is significantly greater than 0.

Participant	Birth Order (X)	X^2	Verbal SAT Score (Y)	Y^2	XY
1	1	1	650	422,500	650
2	2	4	550	302,500	1,100
3	4	16	450	202,500	1,800
4	1	1	500	250,000	500
5	3	9	475	225,625	1,425
6	4	16	425	180,625	1,700
7	2	4	565	319,225	1,130
8	2	4	525	275,625	1,050
9	6	36	400	160,000	2,400
10	3	9	480	230,400	1,440

$$\Sigma X = 28 \quad \Sigma X^2 = 100 \quad \Sigma Y = 5,020 \quad \Sigma Y^2 = 2,569,000 \quad \Sigma XY = 13,195$$

5. $cov_{xy} = \dfrac{\Sigma XY - \dfrac{\Sigma X \cdot \Sigma Y}{n}}{n-1} = \dfrac{11,334 - \dfrac{219 \cdot 490}{12}}{12 - 1} = \dfrac{11,334 - 8,942.5}{11} = 217.409$

Student	Number of Pages Typed (X)	X^2	Typing Speed (Y)	Y^2	XY
Chris	37	1,369	73	5,329	2,701
Mary	6	36	24	576	144
Paul	12	144	36	1,296	432
Juan	24	576	72	5,184	1,728
Marcel	16	256	50	2,500	800
Olga	7	49	19	361	133
Ni	22	484	49	2,401	1,078
Nima	4	16	6	36	24
Sari	34	1,156	48	2,304	1,632
Jarrod	32	1,024	59	3,481	1,888
Kevin	17	289	38	1,444	646
Lisa	8	64	16	256	127

$$\Sigma X = 219 \quad \Sigma X^2 = 5,463 \quad \Sigma Y = 490 \quad \Sigma Y^2 = 25,168 \quad \Sigma XY = 11,334$$

7. The coefficient of determination $= r^2 = .8695^2 = .756$, or 75.6%. This means that 75.6% of the variance in the number of pages typed can be explained by the variance in the typing speed of the students.

9. The scatterplot reveals a zero relationship between test A and test B.

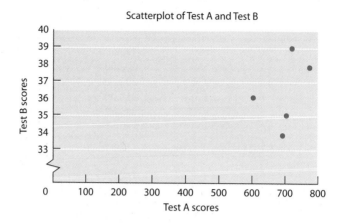

Scatterplot of Test A and Test B

11. $r_{xy} = \dfrac{(n \cdot \Sigma XY) - (\Sigma X \cdot \Sigma Y)}{\sqrt{[(n \cdot \Sigma X^2) - (\Sigma X)^2] \cdot [(n \cdot \Sigma Y^2) - (\Sigma Y)^2]}}$

$= \dfrac{(5 \cdot 127,365) - (3,493 \cdot 182)}{\sqrt{[(5 \cdot 2,454,875) - (3,493)^2] \cdot [(5 \cdot 6,642) - (182)^2]}}$

$= \dfrac{(636,825) - (635,726)}{\sqrt{[(12,274,375) - (12,201,049)] \cdot [(33,210) - (33,124)]}}$

$= \dfrac{1,099}{\sqrt{6,306,036}} = .4376$

$df = n - 2 = 5 - 2 = 3$. The critical value in Table R = .9877. $r_{xy} = .4376$ is not greater than the critical value. Therefore, the correlation coefficient is not significantly greater than zero.

Participant	Test A (X)	X^2	Test B (Y)	Y^2	XY
1	700	490,000	35	1,225	24,500
2	772	595,984	38	1,444	29,336
3	605	366,025	36	1,296	21,780
4	721	519,841	39	1,521	28,119
5	695	483,025	34	1,156	23,630

$\Sigma X = 3,493 \quad \Sigma X^2 = 2,454,875 \quad \Sigma Y = 182 \quad \Sigma Y^2 = 6,642 \quad \Sigma XY = 127,365$

13. $\text{cov}_{xy} = \dfrac{\Sigma XY - \dfrac{\Sigma X \cdot \Sigma Y}{n}}{n - 1} = \dfrac{1,120 - \dfrac{88 \cdot 93}{5}}{5 - 1} = \dfrac{1,120 - 1,636.8}{4} = -129.2$

15. The coefficient of determination $= r^2 = .956^2 = .9145$, or 91.45%. This means that 91.4% of the variance in aptitude test score can be explained by the variance in the number of assembly line errors.

17. $\text{cov}_{xy} = \dfrac{\Sigma XY - \dfrac{\Sigma X \cdot \Sigma Y}{n}}{n-1} = \dfrac{2{,}127 - \dfrac{341 \cdot 33}{7}}{7-1} = \dfrac{2{,}127 - 1{,}607.57}{6} = 86.571$

19. The coefficient of determination $= r^2 = .9276^2 = .8604$, or 86.0%. This means the 86% of the variance in assembly line errors can be explained by the variance in aptitude test scores.

21. Although there appears to be a positive correlation between birth control usage and the number of electrical appliances owned, it doesn't make statistical sense for the government to begin giving toasters to teenage girls to help in the fight against teen pregnancy. This is primarily because correlation does not imply causation. Therefore, it cannot be assumed that increasing the number of appliances is the cause of the increase in birth control usage. This is most likely a spurious relationship where two variables appear to be highly related but, in fact, are not. Some third variable, such as socioeconomic status, or a combination of variables could contribute to the correlation between the two variables.

23. $-.77$

25. The scatterplot reveals a positive relationship between the male and female twins.

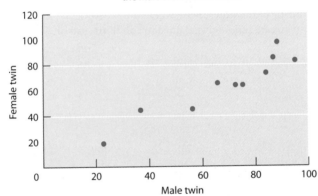

Scatterplot of Personality Test Scores for the Male and Female Twins

27. $r_{xy} = \dfrac{(n \cdot \Sigma XY) - (\Sigma X \cdot \Sigma Y)}{\sqrt{\left[(n \cdot \Sigma X^2) - (\Sigma X)^2\right] \cdot \left[(n \cdot \Sigma Y^2) - (\Sigma Y)^2\right]}}$

$= \dfrac{(10 \cdot 49{,}401) - (687 \cdot 650)}{\sqrt{\left[(10 \cdot 52{,}487) - (687)^2\right] \cdot \left[(10 \cdot 47{,}080) - (650)^2\right]}}$

$= \dfrac{(494{,}010) - (446{,}550)}{\sqrt{\left[(524{,}870) - (471{,}969)\right] \cdot \left[(470{,}800) - (422{,}500)\right]}}$

$= \dfrac{47{,}460}{\sqrt{2{,}555{,}118{,}300}} = .9389$

$df = n - 2 = 10 - 2 = 8$. The critical value in Table R $= .6215$. $r_{xy} = .9389$ is significantly greater than 0.

Male Twin (X)	X^2	Female Twin (Y)	Y^2	XY
88	7,744	86	7,396	7,568
76	5,776	65	4,225	4,940
96	9,216	84	7,056	8,064
36	1,296	47	2,209	1,692
54	2,916	48	2,304	2,592
66	4,356	66	4,356	4,356
73	5,329	65	4,225	4,745
85	7,225	72	5,184	6,120
90	8,100	99	9,801	8,910
23	529	18	324	414
$\Sigma X = 687$	$\Sigma X^2 = 52{,}487$	$\Sigma Y = 650$	$\Sigma Y^2 = 47{,}080$	$\Sigma XY = 49{,}401$

29. High

31. A high correlation means the strength of association between the two variables is great. Even though the correlation is high, causation cannot be implied because there are many variables not measured that could be responsible for the relationship. Only by conducting a true experiment, where the experimenter manipulates a variable and participants are randomly assigned to condition, can cause be inferred from the results.

33. Using 13 degrees of freedom, the critical value = .4762.

Problems From the Literature

35. $\displaystyle \text{cov}_{xy} = \frac{\Sigma XY - \dfrac{\Sigma X \cdot \Sigma Y}{n}}{n-1} = \frac{1{,}850 - \dfrac{65 \cdot 306}{12}}{12 - 1} = \frac{1{,}850 - 1{,}657.5}{11} = 17.5$

37. $\displaystyle r_{xy} = \frac{(n \cdot \Sigma XY) - (\Sigma X \cdot \Sigma Y)}{\sqrt{\left[(n \cdot \Sigma X^2) - (\Sigma X)^2\right] \cdot \left[(n \cdot \Sigma Y^2) - (\Sigma Y)^2\right]}}$

$\displaystyle = \frac{(12 \cdot 1{,}850) - (65 \cdot 306)}{\sqrt{\left[(12 \cdot 419) - (65)^2\right] \cdot \left[(12 \cdot 8{,}658) - (306)^2\right]}}$

$\displaystyle = \frac{(22{,}200) - (19{,}890)}{\sqrt{\left[(5{,}028) - (4{,}225)\right] \cdot \left[(103{,}896) - (93{,}636)\right]}}$

$\displaystyle = \frac{2{,}310}{\sqrt{8{,}238{,}780}} = .805$

$df = n - 2 = 12 - 2 = 10$. The critical value in Table R = .5493. $r_{xy} = .805$ is significantly greater than 0.

Student	Grip Strength (X)	X^2	Introversion/ Extroversion (Y)	Y^2	XY
Jamie	3	9	16	256	48
Carrie	4	16	21	441	84
Bob	7	49	35	1,225	245
Jorge	5	25	30	900	150
Olga	3	9	19	361	57
Robin	6	36	36	1,296	216
Linso	2	4	15	225	30
Nima	3	9	11	121	33
Yukari	6	36	28	784	168
Mark	8	64	36	1,296	288
Harrison	9	81	32	1,024	288
Anna	9	81	27	729	243
	$\Sigma X = 65$	$\Sigma X^2 = 419$	$\Sigma Y = 306$	$\Sigma Y^2 = 8,658$	$\Sigma XY = 1,850$

39. Don't agree with Dr. Strong because his statement infers cause. These results are based on the relationship between two variables. Correlation is not causation because any number of third variables can be responsible for the observed relationship.

41. The scatterplot shows a positive linear relationship between these variables.

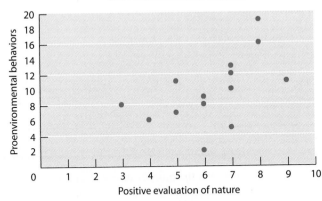

Scatterplot for Nature Evaluation and Proenvironmental Behavior

43. The coefficient of determination = $r^2 = .577^2 = .333$, or 33.3%. This means that 33% of the variance in participant's proenvironmental behaviors can be explained by the variance in knowledge of the environment.

45. The researcher expects a negative relationship. As the number of friendships increases, the number of times people are sick should be reduced.

47. $r_{xy} = \dfrac{(n \cdot \Sigma XY) - (\Sigma X \cdot \Sigma Y)}{\sqrt{[(n \cdot \Sigma X^2) - (\Sigma X)^2] \cdot [(n \cdot \Sigma Y^2) - (\Sigma Y)^2]}}$

$$= \frac{(18 \cdot 235) - (256 \cdot 22)}{\sqrt{[(18 \cdot 4{,}306) - (256)^2] \cdot [(18 \cdot 58) - (22)^2]}}$$

$$= \frac{(4{,}230) - (5{,}632)}{\sqrt{[(77{,}508) - (65{,}536)] \cdot [(1{,}044) - (484)]}}$$

$$= \frac{-1{,}402}{\sqrt{6{,}704{,}320}} = -.541$$

$df = n - 2 = 18 - 2 = 16$. The critical value in Table R = .4259. $r_{xy} = -.541$ is significantly greater than 0.

Participant ID	Friends (X)	X^2	Times Sick (Y)	Y^2	XY
1	7	49	5	25	35
2	11	121	1	1	11
3	13	169	0	0	0
4	5	25	3	9	15
5	19	361	0	0	0
6	28	784	1	1	28
7	6	36	3	9	18
8	21	441	0	0	0
9	17	289	1	1	17
10	20	400	2	4	40
11	17	289	0	0	0
12	9	81	2	4	18
13	9	81	1	1	9
14	16	256	0	0	0
15	22	484	1	1	22
16	14	196	0	0	0
17	12	144	1	1	12
18	10	100	1	1	10
	$\Sigma X = 256$	$\Sigma X^2 = 4{,}306$	$\Sigma Y = 22$	$\Sigma Y^2 = 58$	$\Sigma XY = 235$

49. There is a negative relationship between the number of friendships participants reported and the times they were sick. This is an association, and causal inferences can't be made. It is a causal statement if one says the number of friendships buffered or protected these participants from illness.

Chapter 9

1.

Birth Order Average X	X^2	SAT Verbal Score Y	Y^2	XY
2.5	6.25	485	235,225	1,212.5
2.6	6.76	480	230,400	1,248
2.6	6.76	480	230,400	1,248
2.6	6.76	475	225,625	1,235
2.7	7.29	475	225,625	1,282.5
2.7	7.29	470	220,900	1,269
2.8	7.84	470	220,900	1,316
2.8	7.84	465	216,225	1,302
2.8	7.84	460	211,600	1,288
2.9	8.41	455	207,025	1,319.5

$\Sigma X = 27 \qquad \Sigma X^2 = 73.04 \qquad \Sigma Y = 4,715 \qquad \Sigma Y^2 = 2,223,925 \quad \Sigma XY = 12,720.5$

$\bar{X} = \dfrac{27}{10} = 2.7 \qquad\qquad \bar{Y} = \dfrac{4,715}{10} = 471.5$

$S_x = .118 \qquad\qquad\qquad S_Y = 8.958$

$$\text{cov}_{xy} = \frac{\Sigma XY - \dfrac{\Sigma X \cdot \Sigma Y}{n}}{n-1} = \frac{12,720.5 - \dfrac{27 \cdot 4,715}{10}}{10-1}$$

$$= \frac{12,720.5 - 12,730.5}{9} = \frac{-10}{9} = -1.111$$

$$r_{xy} = \frac{(n \cdot \Sigma XY) - (\Sigma X \cdot \Sigma Y)}{\sqrt{\left[(n \cdot \Sigma X^2) - (\Sigma X)^2\right] \cdot \left[(n \cdot \Sigma Y^2) - (\Sigma Y)^2\right]}}$$

$$= \frac{(10 \cdot 12,720.5) - (27 \cdot 4,715)}{\sqrt{\left[(10 \cdot 73.04) - (27)^2\right] \cdot \left[(10 \cdot 2,223,925) - (4,715)^2\right]}}$$

$$= \frac{(127,205) - (127,305)}{\sqrt{\left[(730.4) - (729)\right] \cdot \left[(22,239,250) - (22,231,225)\right]}}$$

$$= \frac{-100}{\sqrt{1.4 \cdot 8,025}} = \frac{-100}{105.995} = -.9434$$

3. $S_{YX} = S_Y \cdot \sqrt{1 - r^2} = S_{YX} = .118 \cdot \sqrt{1 - .9434^2} = .118\sqrt{1 - .890} =$
   $.118 \cdot .335 = .0391.$

5. $z_Y = \dfrac{Y - \bar{Y}}{S_Y} = \dfrac{495 - 471.5}{8.958} = \dfrac{23.5}{8.958} = 2.623$

7. $\hat{Y} = bX + a = \hat{Y} = -71.618X + 664.87$

9. $\hat{Y} = bX + a \qquad \hat{Y} = -71.618(3.0) + 664.87 \qquad \hat{Y} = -214.8552 + 664.87$
   $\hat{Y} = 450.015$

11. $S_{YX} = S_Y \cdot \sqrt{1 - r^2}$ $\quad$ $S_{YX} = 6.5 \cdot \sqrt{1 - (.55)^2}$ $\quad$ $S_{YX} = 6.5 \cdot \sqrt{.6975^2}$
$\quad$ $S_{YX} = S_Y \cdot \sqrt{1 - r^2}$ $\quad$ $S_{YX} = 6.5 \cdot .8352$ $\quad$ $S_{YX} = 5.429$

13. $\hat{X} = bY + a = .3808Y + 25.1984 = .3808(44) + 25.1984 = 41.9536$

15. $\hat{X} = bY + a = .3808(52) + 25.1984 = 45$

17. $\hat{X} = bY + a = .3808(53) + 25.1984 = 20.1824 + 25.1984 = 45.3808$

19. $\hat{Y} = bX + a = .7944(46) + 16.252 = 36.5424 + 16.252 = 52.7944$

21. $\hat{Y} = bX + a = .7944(39) + 16.252 = 30.9839 + 16.252 = 47.2336$

23. $b = r_{xy} \cdot \dfrac{S_x}{S_y} = (-.880) \cdot \dfrac{.580}{1.836} = (-.880) \cdot (.3159) = -.278$

$\quad$ $a = \overline{X} - (b \cdot \overline{Y}) = 1.70 - (-.278) \cdot (2.950) = 1.70 - (-.8201) = 2.5201$
$\quad$ $\hat{X} = bY + a = (-.278)(2.8) + 2.5201 = (-.7784) + 2.5201 =$
$\quad$ $1.7417 \pm .2755$ hours each day
$\quad$ $Sxy = Sx \cdot \sqrt{1 - r^2} = .58 \cdot \sqrt{1 - .88^2} = .2755$

25. $\hat{X} = bY + a = (-.278)(3.2) + 2.5201 = (-.890) + 2.5201 =$
$\quad$ $1.6305 \pm .2755$ hours per day

27. $\hat{X} = bY + a = (-.278)(2.95) + 2.5201 = (-.8201) + 2.5201 =$
$\quad$ $1.7 \pm .2755$ hours each day

29. $b = r_{xy} \cdot \dfrac{S_y}{S_x} = (-.880) \cdot \dfrac{1.836}{.580} = (-.880) \cdot (3.1655) = -2.7856$

$\quad$ $a = \overline{Y} - (b \cdot \overline{X}) = 2.95 - (-2.7856) \cdot (1.700) = 2.950 - (-4.7355) = 7.6855$
$\quad$ $\hat{Y} = bX + a = (-2.7856)(3) + 7.6855 = (-8.3568) + 7.6855 = -.6713$ GPA

31. $\hat{Y} = bX + a = (-2.7856)(1.5) + 7.6855 = (-4.1784) + 7.6855 = 3.5071$ GPA

Problems From the Literature

33. $b = r_{xy} \cdot \dfrac{S_y}{S_x} = (-.680) \cdot \dfrac{1.15}{1.76} = (-.680) \cdot (.6534) = -.4443$

$\quad$ $a = \overline{Y} - (b \cdot \overline{X}) = 2.88 - (-.4443) \cdot (12.700) = 2.88 - (-5.6426) = 8.5226$
$\quad$ $\hat{Y} = bX + a = (-.4443)(8.2) + 8.5226 = (-3.6433) + 8.5226 = 4.879 \pm .8432$
$\quad$ perceived control
$\quad$ $Syx = Sy \cdot \sqrt{1 - r^2} = 1.15 \cdot \sqrt{1 - (-.68)^2} = .8432$

35. $\hat{Y} = bX + a = (-.4443)(9.5) + 8.5226 = (-4.2209) + 8.5226 = 4.3017 \pm .8432$
$\quad$ perceived control

37. $b = r_{xy} \cdot \dfrac{S_x}{S_y} = (-.680) \cdot \dfrac{1.76}{1.15} = (-.680) \cdot (1.5304) = -1.0407$

$\quad$ $a = \overline{X} - (b \cdot \overline{Y}) = 12.70 - (-1.0407) \cdot (2.88) = 12.70 - (-2.9972) = 15.6972$
$\quad$ $\hat{X} = bY + a = (-1.0407)(6) + 15.6972 = (-6.2442) + 15.6975 = 9.4533 \pm$
$\quad$ 1.2904 ASD symptoms
$\quad$ $Sxy = Sx \cdot \sqrt{1 - r^2} = 1.76 \cdot \sqrt{1 - (-.68)^2} = 1.2904$

39. $\hat{X} = bY + a = (-1.0407)(2) + 15.6972 = (-2.0814) + 15.6975 = 13.6161 \pm$
$\quad$ 1.2904 ASD symptoms

41. $b = r_{xy} \cdot \dfrac{S_y}{S_x} = (.811) \cdot \dfrac{1.79}{2.15} = (.811) \cdot (.8326) = .6752$

$\quad$ $a = \overline{Y} - (b \cdot \overline{X}) = 4.15 - (.6752) \cdot (5.33) = 4.15 - 3.599 = .5512$

$\hat{Y} = bX + a = (.6752)(6) + .5512 = 4.0512 + .5512 = 4.6022 \pm 1.0472$ competitive activity need score

$Syx = Sy \cdot \sqrt{1 - r^2} = 1.79 \cdot \sqrt{1 - (.811)^2} = 1.0472$

43. $\hat{Y} = bX + a = (.6752)(2) + .5512 = 1.3504 + .5512 = 1.9016 \pm 1.0472$
competitive activity need score

45. $b = r_{xy} \cdot \dfrac{S_x}{S_y} = (.811) \cdot \dfrac{2.15}{1.79} = (.811) \cdot (1.2011) = .9741$

$a = \overline{X} - (b \cdot \overline{Y}) = 5.33 - (.9741) \cdot 4.15 = 5.33 - (4.0425) = 1.2875$

$\hat{X} = bY + a = (.9741)(3) + 1.2875 = 2.9223 + 1.2875 = 4.2098 \pm 1.2578$
enjoyment score

$Sxy = Sx \cdot \sqrt{1 - r^2} = 2.15 \cdot \sqrt{1 - (.811)^2} = 1.2578$

47. $\hat{X} = bY + a = (.9741)(6) + 1.2875 = 5.8446 + 1.2875 = 7.1321 \pm 1.2578$
enjoyment score

49. $b = r_{xy} \cdot \dfrac{S_y}{S_x} = (.591) \cdot \dfrac{.83}{2.39} = (.591)(.347) = .2052$

$a = \overline{Y} - (b \cdot \overline{X}) = 2.64 - (.2052) \cdot (4.92) = 2.64 - (1.0096) = 1.6304$

$\hat{Y} = bX + a = (.2052)(6) + 1.6304 = (1.2312) + 1.6304 = 2.8616 \pm 66.95$
perceived control

$Syx = Sy \cdot \sqrt{1 - r^2} = .83 \cdot \sqrt{1 - (.591)^2} = .6695$

51. $\hat{Y} = bX + a = (.2052)(1) + 1.6304 = 1.8356 \pm .6695$
perceived control

53. $b = r_{xy} \cdot \dfrac{S_x}{S_y} = (.591) \cdot \dfrac{2.39}{.83} = (.591) \cdot (2.8795) = 1.7018$

$a = \overline{X} - (b \cdot \overline{Y}) = 4.92 - (1.7018) \cdot (2.64) = 4.92 - (4.4928) = .4272$

$\hat{X} = bY + a = (1.7018)(2) + .4272 = (3.4036) + .4272 = 3.8308 \pm 1.9281$
health status score

$Sxy = Sx \cdot \sqrt{1 - r^2} = 2.39 \cdot \sqrt{1 - (.591)^2} = 1.9281$

55. $\hat{X} = bY + a = (1.7018)(6) + .4272 = (10.2108) + .4272 = 10.638 \pm 1.9281$
health status score

Chapter 10

1. $p(A) = \dfrac{n(A)}{n} = p(\text{psych major}) = \dfrac{900}{12,000} = .075$

3. $p(A \text{ or } B) = p(A) + p(B);\ p(\text{psych major}) = \dfrac{900}{12,000} = .075;\ p(\text{soc major}) =$

$\dfrac{500}{12,000} = .042;\ p(\text{psych major or soc major}) = .075 + .042 = .117$

5. $p(A \text{ or } B) = p(A) + p(B) - p(A \text{ and } B);\ p(\text{psych major}) = \dfrac{900}{12,000} = .075;$

$p(\text{soc major}) = \dfrac{500}{12,000} = .042;\ p(\text{psych and soc major}) = \dfrac{50}{12,000} = .0042;$

$p(\text{psych major or soc major}) = .075 + .042 - .0042 = .113$

7. $p(A) = \dfrac{n(A)}{n} = p(\text{highly introverted}) = \dfrac{106}{1,117} = .095$

9. $p(A) = \dfrac{n(A)}{n} = p(\text{highly extroverted}) = \dfrac{213}{1,117} = .191$

11. $p(A \text{ or } B) = p(A) + p(B) = p(\text{highly introverted or average}) = .095 + .714 = .809$

13. $p(A \text{ or } B) = p(A) + p(B) = p(\text{employed by government or unemployed}) =$
    $.25 + .10 = .35$

15. $p(A \text{ and } B) = p(A) \cdot p(B) = p(\text{employed by government}) \cdot p(\text{schizophrenia}) =$
    $.25 \cdot .01 = .0025$

17. $p(A \text{ and } B) = p(A) \cdot p(B) = p(\text{employed by government}) \cdot$
    $p(\text{high sensation seeker}) = .25 \cdot .20 = .05$

19. $p(A) = \dfrac{n(A)}{n} = p(\text{type A}) = \dfrac{123}{500} = .246$

21. $p(A) = \dfrac{n(A)}{n} = p(\text{average}) = \dfrac{200}{500} = .40$

23. $p(A \text{ or } B) = p(A) + p(B) = p(\text{type B or average}) = .354 + .40 = .754$

25. $p(A \text{ or } B) = p(A) + p(B) = p(\text{type A or average}) = .246 + .40 = .646$

Problems From the Literature

27. $p(A \text{ or } B) = p(A) + p(B) = \dfrac{95}{250} + \dfrac{89}{250} = \dfrac{184}{250} = .736$

29. $p(A \text{ or } B) = p(A) + p(B) = \dfrac{66}{1,440} + \dfrac{294}{1,440} = \dfrac{360}{1,440} = .25$

31. $p(A \text{ or } B) = p(A) + p(B) = \dfrac{45}{1,440} + \dfrac{32}{1,440} = \dfrac{77}{1,440} = .053$

33. $p(A \text{ or } B) = p(A) + p(B) = p(\text{female and socializing})$ or $p(\text{female and playing video games})$. First calculate the $p(A)$ and $p(B)$ separately using the multiplication rule for each computation. Then apply the addition rule. $p(\text{female and socializing}) = \dfrac{115}{250} \cdot \dfrac{45}{1,440} = .46 \cdot .031 = .014$; $p(\text{female and playing video games}) = \dfrac{115}{250} \cdot \dfrac{125}{1,440} = .46 \cdot .087 = .04$; $.014 + .04 = .054$.

35. The representativeness of the sample is important. Suppose the sample consisted of children raised by single parents. It is possible that the results could differ for children raised by two parents. There are many variables, such as working status of parents, number of siblings, and so forth. When researchers use a sample to make estimations of the population values, the selection technique is very important. If they do not use random sampling, then they should do their best to carefully select the sample to be as representative as possible of the population of interest.

37. $p(A \text{ and } B) = p(A) \cdot p(B) = p(\text{male}) \cdot p(\text{very urgent need}) = .68 \cdot .57 = .388$

39. $p(A \text{ or } B) = p(A) + p(B) = p(\text{woman and Asian American})$ or $p(\text{man and Asian American})$. First calculate the $p(A)$ and $p(B)$ separately using the multiplication rule for each computation. Then apply the addition rule. $p(\text{woman and Asian American}) = .32 \cdot .08 = .026$); $p(\text{man and Asian American}) = .68 \cdot .08 = .054$; $.026 + .054 = .08$.

41. p(A and B) = p(A) · p(B) = p(moderately urgent need) · p(receiving poor quality kidney) = .15 · .31 = .047.

43. p(A or B) = p(A) + p(B) = p(semi-urgent need and excellent quality kidney) or p(semi-urgent need and average quality kidney). First calculate the p(A) and p(B) separately using the multiplication rule for each computation. Then use the addition rule. p(semi-urgent need and excellent quality kidney) = .28 · .21 = .059; p(semi-urgent need and average quality kidney) = .28 · .48 = .134; .059 + .134 = .193.

45. p(A or B) = p(A) + p(B) = p(moderately urgent need and poor quality kidney) or p(moderately urgent need and average quality kidney). First calculate the p(A) and p(B) separately using the multiplication rule for each computation. Then use the addition rule. p(moderately urgent need and poor quality kidney) = .15 · .31 = .465; p(semi-urgent need and average quality kidney) = .15 · .48 = .072; .465 + .072 = .119.

47. p(A or B or C) = p(A) + p(B) + p(C) = p(woman and Hispanic) or p(woman and African American) or p(woman and Asian American). First calculate the p(A), p(B), and p(C) separately using the multiplication rule for each computation. Then use the addition rule. p(woman and Hispanic) = .32 · .10 = .032; p(woman and African American) = .32 · .26 = .083; p(woman and Asian American) = .32 · .08 = .026; .032 + .083 + .026 = .141.

49. p(A or B) = p(A) + p(B) = p(average quality) + p(poor quality) = .48 + .31 = .79

Chapter 11

1. hypothesis
3. independent
5. dependent
7. a. Research hypothesis (H_1): Stroke victims with language impairment will communicate better through sign language than oral speech. b. The independent variable is the type of treatment (spoken word or gestured sign). c. The dependent variable is the number of correct photograph identification responses.
9. The problem with Dr. Hilo's research design is that height is a subject variable. Because there cannot be random assignment of a subject variable, the results cannot provide a causal explanation for the differences in self-assuredness between tall and short people.
11. In between-subjects experimental design, each person participates in one level of the independent variable in the experiment.
13. It is a within-subjects experimental design.
15. The major drawback for between-subjects designs is that they require more participants because each participant only participates in one level of the independent variable.
17. a. Type of design: completely randomized between-subjects experimental design.
    b. Research hypothesis (H_1): Infants will look longer at a card with an organized array of lines pattern than a regular pattern of horizontal lines.
    c. The independent variable is type of pattern organization on a card (organized versus random).
    d. The dependent variable is the amount of time the infant spends looking at the card.
    e. There are many extraneous variables that need to be held constant. These variables include noise level in the room, room illumination, the time of day the sessions are conducted, the distance the card is placed in front of the infant, the color of the

lines and background color of the card, the presentation of card and whether it's by an experimenter or automated (if automated it must be the same computer program, etc.).

19. Dr. Bambino's design is a factorial experimental design, and it is in the form of a 2 × 2 factorial design because there are two independent variables (pattern organization and familiarity of pattern) with two levels (random arrangement and organized arrangement).

21. Whenever possible, all extraneous variables should be held constant so that they don't interfere with the identification of the variables that are the true cause(s) of the behavior being studied. They should be held constant because the experimenter wants only the independent variable to vary between conditions.

23. Demand characteristics occur when participants figure out the hypothesis and try to "help" by providing responses that they think support that hypothesis.

25. Researchers need to test their results for statistical significance to determine how likely it is that the observed differences are real or are due to chance.

27. In Dr. Pena's experiment, the null hypothesis (H_0): For chronic headache patients the severity of headaches will be the same for those using biofeedback and not using biofeedback.

29. Null hypothesis H_0: Stroke victims with language impairment will communicate the same through sign language as through oral speech.

31. .05

33. One-tailed

Problems From the Literature

35. Null hypothesis (H_0): Speech anxiety for oral communication students will not differ with or without the presence of a pet in the class.
Research hypothesis (H_1): Speech anxiety for oral communication students will be less with the presence of a pet than it will with no pet in the class.

37. The dependent variable is speech anxiety.

39. Answers will vary. Examples of extraneous variables are type of dog, size of dog, distance dog is from speaker, etc.

41. This is a nonexperimental design because gender of participant cannot be randomly assigned.

43. Type II.

45. The independent variable is the type of sensory stimulus with three levels: (1) odor only, (2) sound only, and (3) odor and sound combined.

47. a. This is a within-subjects randomized design. Each participant participated in each level (condition) of the independent variable. b. No, this is not completely randomized because participants were not randomly selected to participate in the study. However, it is a true experiment and a randomized design because participants were randomly assigned to the condition.

49. a. This would be a mixed randomized factorial design. All participants would participate in each level of the sensory stimulus, but half would be presented the stimuli in a dark room and the other half would be presented the stimuli in a lighted room. It is a randomized design because Dr. D proposed randomly assigning participants to the presence of light conditions.
b. 30

Chapter 12

1. a. Null hypothesis: The sonar trainees using the new sonar training system will identify the same or fewer targets than the population of sonar operators.
      $H_0: \overline{X} \leq \mu$
   b. Research hypothesis: The new sonar trainees using the new sonar training system will identify more targets than the population of sonar operators.
      $H_1: \overline{X} > \mu$
   c. $\sigma_x = \dfrac{\sigma}{\sqrt{n}} = \dfrac{12}{\sqrt{15}} = \dfrac{12}{3.873} = 3.098; \quad t = \dfrac{\overline{X} - \mu}{\sigma_X} = \dfrac{87 - 82}{3.098} = 1.614$
   d. $df = n - 1 = 15 - 1 = 14$
   e. Critical $t_{(df = 14,\, p = .05,\, \text{one-tailed})} = 1.761$
   f. Fail to reject the null hypothesis. The t statistic is not significant. Therefore, in this sample, the trainees using the new sonar training system did not identify targets at a significantly better rate than the population of sonar operators.

3. a. Null hypothesis: The sample mean will be lower or less than the population mean.
      $H_0: \overline{X} \leq \mu$
   b. Research hypothesis: The sample mean will be greater than the population.
      $H_1: \overline{X} > \mu$
   c. Estimated $\sigma_x = \dfrac{S}{\sqrt{n}} = \dfrac{5.4}{\sqrt{64}} = \dfrac{5.4}{8} = .675;$

   $t = \dfrac{\overline{X} - \mu}{\text{estimated } \sigma_X} = \dfrac{82 - 80}{.675} = 2.963$
   d. $df = n - 1 = 64 - 1 = 63$
   e. Critical $t_{(df = 63,\, p = .05,\, \text{one-tailed})} = 1.67$
   f. Reject the null hypothesis. The t statistic is significant. The mean of the sample was significantly higher than the population mean.

5. a. Null hypothesis: There will be no difference in the number of words typed per minute between participants using keyboard A and those using keyboard B.
      $H_0: \mu_1 = \mu_2$
   b. Research hypothesis: There will be a difference in the number of words typed per minute between participants using keyboard A and those using keyboard B.
      $H_0: \mu_1 \neq \mu_2$
   c. Estimated $\sigma_{\text{diff}} = \sqrt{\left(\text{estimated } \sigma_{\overline{X}_1}\right)^2 + \left(\text{estimated } \sigma_{\overline{X}_2}\right)} =$

   $\sqrt{(2.992)^2 + (2.909)^2} = \sqrt{8.952 + 8.463} = \sqrt{17.415} = 4.173 \text{ or}$

   $\sqrt{\dfrac{S_1^2}{n_1} + \dfrac{S_2^2}{n_2}} = \sqrt{\dfrac{10.366^2}{12} + \dfrac{10.077^2}{12}} = \sqrt{17.417} = 4.173$

   Estimated $\sigma_{\overline{X}_1} = \dfrac{S_1}{\sqrt{n_1}} = \dfrac{10.366}{\sqrt{12}} = \dfrac{10.366}{3.464} = 2.992$

   Estimated $\sigma_{\overline{X}_2} = \dfrac{S_2}{\sqrt{n_2}} = \dfrac{10.077}{\sqrt{12}} = \dfrac{10.077}{3.464} = 2.909$

   $t = \dfrac{\overline{X}_1 - \overline{X}_2}{\text{estimated } \sigma_{\text{diff}}} = \dfrac{64.00 - 53.917}{4.173} = 2.416$

d. $df = (n_1 - 1) + (n_2 - 1) = (12 - 1) + (12 - 1) = 11 + 11 = 22$

e. Critical $t_{(df = 22, p = .05, \text{two-tailed})} = 2.074$

f. Reject the null hypothesis. The t statistic is significant. There were significantly more words typed per minute by participants using Keyboard A ($\mu = 64.00$, $SD = 10.37$) compared to those using Keyboard B ($\mu = 53.92$, $SD = 10.08$).

7. a. Null hypothesis: There will be no difference between the pretest and posttest results.

   $H_0: \mu_1 = \mu_1$

   b. Research hypothesis: There will be a significant difference between the pretest and posttest results.

   $H_1: \mu_1 \neq \mu_2$

   c. Estimated $\sigma_{\bar{X}_1} = \sqrt{\dfrac{S_1^2}{n_1}} = \sqrt{\dfrac{52^2}{25}} = 10.4$

   Estimated $\sigma_{\bar{X}_2} = \sqrt{\dfrac{S_2^2}{n_2}} = \sqrt{\dfrac{85^2}{25}} = 17.0$

   $\sigma_{\text{diff}} = \sqrt{(\text{estimated } \sigma_{\bar{X}_1})^2 + (\text{estimated } \sigma_{\bar{X}_2})^2 - (2 \cdot r \cdot \text{estimated } \sigma_{\bar{X}_1} \cdot \text{estimated } \sigma_{\bar{X}_2})} =$

   $\sqrt{(10.4)^2 + (17.0)^2 - (2 \cdot 77 \cdot 10.4 \cdot 17.0)} =$

   $\sqrt{(108.16 + 289.0 - 272.272} = \sqrt{124.888} = 11.175$

   $t = \dfrac{\bar{X}_1 - \bar{X}_2}{\text{estimated } \sigma_{\text{diff}}} = \dfrac{235 - 342}{11.175} = -9.575$

   d. $df_{\text{correlated samples}} = \text{number of pairs} - 1; df = 25 - 1 = 24$

   e. Critical $t_{(df = 24, p = .05, \text{two-tailed})} = 2.064$

   f. Reject the null hypothesis. There was a significant difference between the pretest and posttest reaction time scores.

9. a. Null hypothesis: The number of brake pedal errors will be less for the new compared to the old gas pedal location.

   $H_0: \mu_{\text{old}} \geq \mu_{\text{new}}$

   b. Research hypothesis: The number of brake pedal errors will differ between the new and old gas pedal locations.

   $H_1: \mu_{\text{old}} < \mu_{\text{new}}$

   c. Estimated $\sigma_{\text{diff}} = \sqrt{\dfrac{\dfrac{\Sigma D^2}{n} - \bar{D}^2}{n - 1}} = \sqrt{\dfrac{\dfrac{45}{10} - 1.5^2}{n - 1}} =$

   $\sqrt{\dfrac{4.5 - 2.25}{9}} = \sqrt{.25} = .5$

   $t = \dfrac{\bar{D}}{\text{estimated } \sigma_{\text{diff}}} = \dfrac{-1.5}{.5} = -3.00$

   d. $df_{\text{correlated samples}} = \text{number of pairs} - 1; df = 20 - 1 = 19$

   e. Critical $t_{(df = 19, p = .05, \text{one-tailed})} = 1.729$

   f. Reject the null hypothesis. Participants made significantly fewer brake pedal errors in the new ($\mu = 5.70$, $SD = 3.56$) compared to the old ($\mu = 7.20$, $SD = 3.52$) location arrangement.

11. a. Null hypothesis: There will be no difference between the number of words and the number of letters that participants remember in the short-term memory task.

   $H_0: \mu_1 = \mu_1$

b. Research hypothesis: There will be a difference between the number of words and the number of letters that participants remember in the short-term memory task.
$H_1: \mu_1 \neq \mu_2$

c. Estimated $\sigma_{\text{diff}} = \sqrt{\dfrac{S_1^2}{n_1} + \dfrac{S_2^2}{n_2}} = \sqrt{\dfrac{1.90^2}{12} + \dfrac{1.96^2}{12}} = \sqrt{.301 + .320} = .788$

$t = \dfrac{(\overline{X}_1 - \overline{X}_2)}{\sigma_{\text{diff}}} = \dfrac{5.833 - 6.25}{.788} = \dfrac{-.417}{.788} = -.529$

d. $df_{\text{independent samples}} = (n_1 - 1) + (n_2 - 1) = (12 - 1) + (12 - 1) = 22$

e. Critical $t_{(df = 22, \, p = .05, \, \text{two-tailed})} = 2.074$

f. Fail to reject the null hypothesis. There was no significant difference between the number of words ($\mu = 5.83$, $SD = 1.90$) and the number of letters ($\mu = 6.25$, $SD = 1.96$) participants remembered.

13. a. Null hypothesis: The amount of the hormone in the bloodstream of the sample of rats under stress will be the same or less than the amount in the bloodstream of the population of rats not under stress.
$H_0: \overline{X} \leq \mu$

b. Research hypothesis: The amount of hormone in the bloodstream of the sample of rats under stress will be higher than the amount in the bloodstream of the population of rats not under stress.
$H_1: \overline{X} > \mu$

c. Estimated $\sigma_x = \dfrac{S}{\sqrt{n}} = \dfrac{25}{\sqrt{25}} = 5;$

$t = \dfrac{\overline{X} - \mu}{\text{estimated } \sigma_X} = \dfrac{267 - 250}{5.00} = \dfrac{17}{5.00} = 3.4$

d. $df_{\text{single sample}} = n - 1 = 25 - 1 = 24$

e. Critical $t_{(df = 24, \, p = .05, \, \text{one-tailed})} = 1.711$

f. Reject the null hypothesis. The t statistic is significant. The hormone in the bloodstream of the sample of rats under stress was significantly higher than in the population of rats not under stress.

Problems From the Literature

15. a. Null hypothesis: The amount of waste generated by this sample of adults will be the same or less than the amount of waste generated by the population.
$H_0: \overline{X} \leq \mu$

b. Research hypothesis: The amount of waste generated by this sample of adults will be less than the amount of waste generated by the population.
$H_1: \overline{X} > \mu$

c. Estimated $\sigma_x = \dfrac{S}{\sqrt{n}} = \dfrac{1.3}{\sqrt{60}} = .168;$ $t = \dfrac{\overline{X} - \mu}{\text{estimated } \sigma_X} = \dfrac{4.9 - 4.5}{.168} = 2.381$

d. $df_{\text{single sample}} = n - 1 = 60 - 1 = 59$

e. Critical $t_{(df = 59, \, p = .05, \, \text{one-tailed})} = 1.671$

f. Reject the null hypothesis. Participants in the sample generated significantly more waste than the population reported by the U.S. Environmental Protection Agency (1999).

17. a. Null hypothesis: Diners will leave the food server the same or lower percentage of tip when their food bill tray has a credit card insignia than when there is no insignia on the food bill tray.

$H_0: \mu_1 \le \mu_1$

b. Research hypothesis: Diners will leave the food server a higher percentage of tip when their food bill tray has a credit card insignia than when it has no insignia.

$H_1: \mu_1 > \mu_2$

c. Estimated $\sigma_{\text{diff}} = \sqrt{\dfrac{S_1^2}{n_1} + \dfrac{S_2^2}{n_2}} = \sqrt{\dfrac{4.675^2}{10} + \dfrac{3.089^2}{10}} = \sqrt{2.186 + .954} = 1.772$

$t = \dfrac{(\overline{X}_1 - \overline{X}_2)}{\sigma_{\text{diff}}} = \dfrac{20.361 - 16.669}{1.772} = \dfrac{3.692}{1.772} = 2.084$

d. $df_{\text{independent samples}} = (n_1 - 1) + (n_2 - 1) = (10 - 1) + (10 - 1) = 18$

e. Critical $t_{(df = 18, \, p = .05, \, \text{one-tailed})} = 1.734$

f. Reject the null hypothesis. Diners left significantly higher percentages of tips when their food bill was presented with a credit card insignia ($\mu = \$20.36, SD = 4.68$) than when there was no insignia on the tray ($\mu = \$16.67, SD = 3.09$).

19. a. Null hypothesis: The cognitive functioning of participants will be the same before and after the vitamin program.

$H_0: \mu_{\text{before}} = \mu_{\text{after}}$

b. Research hypothesis: The cognitive functioning of participants will improve after tne vitamin program.

$H_1: \mu_{\text{before}} < \mu_{\text{after}}$

c. Estimated $\sigma_{\text{diff}} = \sqrt{\dfrac{\dfrac{\Sigma D^2}{n} - \overline{D}^2}{n - 1}} = \sqrt{\dfrac{\dfrac{483}{10} - (-2.70)^2}{10 - 1}} =$

$\sqrt{\dfrac{48.3 - 7.29}{9}} = \sqrt{4.557} = 2.135$

$t = \dfrac{\overline{D}}{\text{estimated } \sigma_{\text{diff}}} = \dfrac{-2.70}{2.135} = -1.265$

d. $df_{\text{correlated samples}} = \text{number of pairs} - 1; df = 10 - 1 = 9$

e. Critical $t_{(df = 9, \, p = .05, \, \text{one-tailed})} = 1.833$

f. Fail to reject the null hypothesis. There was no significant difference in the cognitive functioning of participants after ($\mu = 29.20, SD = 13.77$) compared to their cognitive functioning before ($\mu = 26.50, SD = 10.16$) the vitamin program.

21. a. Null hypothesis: The number of words remembered will be the same for the participants memorizing a word list while skipping and those memorizing a word list while hopping.

$H_0: \mu_1 = \mu_2$

b. Research hypothesis: The number of words remembered will differ between the participants memorizing a word list while skipping and those memorizing a word list while hopping.

$H_1: \mu_1 \ne \mu_2$

c. Estimated $\sigma_{\text{diff}} = \sqrt{\dfrac{S_1^2}{n_1} + \dfrac{S_2^2}{n_2}} = \sqrt{\dfrac{1.899^2}{12} + \dfrac{1.960^2}{12}} = \sqrt{.301 + .320} = .788$

$\dfrac{(\overline{X}_1 - \overline{X}_2)}{\sigma_{\text{diff}}} = \dfrac{5.833 - 6.25}{.788} = -.529$

d. $df_{\text{independent samples}} = (n_1 - 1) + (n_2 - 1) = (12 - 1) + (12 - 1) = 22$

e. Critical $t_{(df = 22, \, p = .05, \, \text{two-tailed})} = 2.074$

f. Fail to reject the null hypothesis. There was no significant difference in the number of words remembered by participants skipping ($\mu = 5.833$, $SD = 1.90$) while memorizing a word list compared to participants hopping ($\mu = 6.25$, $SD = 1.96$) while memorizing the list.

23. a. Null hypothesis: Patients using the progressive muscle relaxation technique will have the same or more dental anxiety before they meet the dentist as patients not using the technique.

$H_0: \mu_1 \geq \mu_1$

b. Research hypothesis: Patients using the progressive muscle relaxation technique will have less dental anxiety before they meet the dentist than patients not using the technique.

$H_1: \mu_1 < \mu_2$

c. Estimated $\sigma_{\text{diff}} = \sqrt{\dfrac{S_1^2}{n_1} + \dfrac{S_2^2}{n_2}} = \sqrt{\dfrac{2.21^2}{7} + \dfrac{2.41^2}{7}} = \sqrt{1.527} = 1.236$

$t = \dfrac{(\overline{X}_1 - \overline{X}_2)}{\sigma_{\text{diff}}} = \dfrac{8.286 - 10.857}{1.236} = \dfrac{-2.571}{1.236} = -2.08$

d. $df_{\text{independent samples}} = (n_1 - 1) + (n_2 - 1) = (7 - 1) + (7 - 1) = 12$

e. Critical $t_{(df = 12, \, p = .05, \, \text{one-tailed})} = 1.782$

f. Reject the null hypothesis. Patients that used the music-assisted progressive muscle relaxation technique ($\mu = 8.29$, $SD = 2.21$) reported significantly less dental anxiety than patients not using the technique ($\mu = 10.86$, $SD = 2.41$).

Chapter 13

1. The written hypotheses are as follows.

Null hypothesis: The number of authors will not affect the amount of negative comments received on the research paper submitted to journals.

Research hypothesis: The number of authors will affect the amount of negative comments received on the research paper submitted to journals.

Statistical hypotheses:

$H_0: \mu_1 = \mu_2 = \mu_3 = \mu_4$
$H_1: \mu_1 \neq \mu_2 \neq \mu_3 \neq \mu_4$

Source	Sums of Squares	df	Mean Square	F	p
Between	188.75	3	62.917	2.459	> .05
Within	307.00	12	25.583		
Total	495.75	15			

$SS_{\text{bg}} = \left[\dfrac{(\Sigma X_1)^2}{n_1} + \dfrac{(\Sigma X_2)^2}{n_2} + \dfrac{(\Sigma X_3)^2}{n_3} + \dfrac{(\Sigma X_4)^2}{n_4} \right] -$

$\left[\dfrac{(\Sigma X_1 + \Sigma X_2 + \Sigma X_3 + \Sigma X_4)^2}{N_{\text{total}}} \right] =$

$$\left[\frac{(90)^2}{4} + \frac{(74)^2}{4} + \frac{(58)^2}{4} + \frac{(56)^2}{4}\right] - \left[\frac{(90 + 74 + 58 + 56)^2}{16}\right] =$$

$$\left[\frac{8,100}{4} + \frac{5,476}{4} + \frac{3,364}{4} + \frac{3,136}{4}\right] - \left[\frac{(278)^2}{16}\right] =$$

$2,025 + 1,369 + 841 + 784 - 4,830.25 = 5,019 - 4,830.25 = 188.75$

$$SS_{wg} = \left[\Sigma X_1^2 + \Sigma X_2^2 + \Sigma X_3^2 + \Sigma X_4^2\right] -$$

$$\left[\frac{(\Sigma X_1)^2}{n_1} + \frac{(\Sigma X_2)^2}{n_2} + \frac{(\Sigma X_3)^2}{n_3} + \frac{(\Sigma X_4)^2}{n_4}\right] =$$

$$(2,098 + 1,428 + 900 + 900) - \left[\frac{(90)^2}{4} + \frac{(74)^2}{4} + \frac{(58)^2}{4} + \frac{(56)^2}{4}\right] =$$

$$(2,098 + 1,428 + 900 + 900) - \left[\frac{8,100}{4} + \frac{5,476}{4} + \frac{3,364}{4} + \frac{3,136}{4}\right] =$$

$5,326 - 5,019 = 307$

$SS_{total} = SS_{bg} + SS_{wg} = 188.75 + 307.00 = 495.75$

$df_{bg} = k - 1 = 4 - 1 = 3$

$df_{wg} = (n_1 - 1) + (n_2 - 1) + (n_3 - 1) + (n_4 - 1) =$
$(4 - 1) + (4 - 1) + (4 - 1) + (4 - 1) = 12$

$df_{total} = N - 1 = 16 - 1 = 15$

$$MS_{bg} = \frac{SS_{bg}}{df_{bg}} = \frac{188.75}{3} = 62.917; \quad MS_{wg} = \frac{SS_{wg}}{df_{wg}} = \frac{307}{12} = 25.583$$

$$F = \frac{MS_{bg}}{MS_{wg}} = \frac{62.917}{25.583} = 2.459$$

From Table F, the critical $F_{(3, 12, \alpha = .05)} = 3.49$. Calculated $F_{(3, 12, \alpha = .05)}$ $2.459 < 3.49$. Conclusion: Fail to reject the null hypothesis.

Interpretation: There were no significant differences in the amount of negative comments received from journals on the manuscripts submitted with one ($\mu = 22.50$, $SD = 4.93$), two ($\mu = 18.50$, $SD = 4.43$), three ($\mu = 14.50$, $SD = 4.43$), and four ($\mu = 17.38$, $SD = 5.75$) authors ($F_{(2, 12)} = 2.46$, $p > .05$).

3. The written hypotheses are as follows.

Null hypothesis: The type of scholarship does not affect students' grades.
Research hypothesis: The type of scholarship affects students' grades.
Statistical hypotheses:
$H_0: \mu_1 = \mu_2 = \mu_3$
$H_1: \mu_1 \neq \mu_2 \neq \mu_3$

Source	Sums of Squares	df	Mean Square	F	p
Between	.149	2	.075	0.146	> .05
Within	6.144	12	.512		
Total	6.293	14			

$$SS_{bg} = \left[\frac{(\Sigma X_1)^2}{n_1} + \frac{(\Sigma X_2)^2}{n_2} + \frac{(\Sigma X_3)^2}{n_3}\right] - \left[\frac{(\Sigma X_1 + \Sigma X_2 + \Sigma X_3)^2}{N_{total}}\right] =$$

$$\left[\frac{13.7^2}{5} + \frac{14.5^2}{5} + \frac{13.3^2}{5}\right] - \left[\frac{(13.7 + 14.5 + 13.3)^2}{15}\right] =$$

$$(37.538 + 42.05 + 35.378) - 114.817 = 114.966 - 114.817 = 0.149$$

$$SS_{wg} = \left[\Sigma X_1^2 + \Sigma X_2^2 + \Sigma X_3^2\right] - \left[\frac{(\Sigma X_1)^2}{n_1} + \frac{(\Sigma X_2)^2}{n_2} + \frac{(\Sigma X_3)^2}{n_3}\right] =$$

$$\left[39.65 + 44.01 + 37.45\right] - \left[\frac{13.7^2}{5} + \frac{14.5^2}{5} + \frac{13.3^2}{5}\right] = 121.11 - 114.966 = 6.144$$

$$SS_{total} = SS_{bg} + SS_{wg} = 0.149 + 6.144 = 6.293$$

$$df_{bg} = k - 1 = 3 - 1 = 2$$

$$df_{wg} = (n_1 - 1) + (n_2 - 1) + (n_3 - 1) = (5 - 1) + (5 - 1) + (5 - 1) = 12$$

$$df_{total} = N - 1 = 15 - 1 = 14$$

$$MS_{bg} = \frac{SS_{bg}}{df_{bg}} = \frac{.149}{2} = .0745; \; MS_{wg} = \frac{SS_{wg}}{df_{wg}} = \frac{6.144}{12} = .512$$

$$F = \frac{MS_{bg}}{MS_{wg}} = \frac{.0745}{.512} = .0146$$

From Table F, the critical $F_{(2, 12, \alpha = .05)} = 3.89$. Calculated $F_{(2, 12, \alpha = .05)} .146 < 3.89$. Conclusion: Fail to reject the null hypothesis.

Interpretation: There were no significant differences in the grades of student's with full scholarships ($\mu = 2.74$, $SD = .73$), partial scholarships ($\mu = 2.90$, $SD = .70$), and no scholarships ($\mu = 2.66$, $SD = .72$) in this sample ($F_{(2, 12)} = .15$, $p > .05$).

5. The written hypotheses are as follows.

Null hypothesis: Interns assigned to different medical specialty fields during a 3-month rotation will not differ in their moral development.

Research hypothesis: Interns assigned to different medical special fields during a 3-month rotation will differ in their moral development.

Statistical hypotheses:

$H_0: \mu_1 = \mu_2 = \mu_3$

$H_1: \mu_1 \neq \mu_2 \neq \mu_3$

Source	Sums of Squares	df	Mean Square	F	p
Between	1,708.286	2	854.143	2.486	> .05
Within	6,184.857	18	343.603		
Total	7,893.143	20			

$$SS_{bg} = \left[\frac{(\Sigma X_1)^2}{n_1} + \frac{(\Sigma X_2)^2}{n_2} + \frac{(\Sigma X_3)^2}{n_3}\right] - \left[\frac{(\Sigma X_1 + \Sigma X_2 + \Sigma X_3)^2}{N_{total}}\right] =$$

$$\left[\frac{390^2}{7} + \frac{543^2}{7} + \frac{486^2}{7}\right] - \left[\frac{(390 + 543 + 486)^2}{21}\right] =$$

$$(21,728.571 + 42,121.286 + 33,742.286) - 95,883.857 =$$

$$97,592.143 - 95,883.857 = 1,708.286$$

$$SS_{wg} = \left[\Sigma X_1^2 + \Sigma X_2^2 + \Sigma X_3^2\right] - \left[\frac{(\Sigma X_1)^2}{n_1} + \frac{(\Sigma X_2)^2}{n_2} + \frac{(\Sigma X_3)^2}{n_3}\right] =$$

$$\left[24{,}566 + 44{,}161 + 35{,}050\right] - \left[\frac{390^2}{7} + \frac{543^2}{7} + \frac{486^2}{7}\right] =$$

$103{,}777 - 97{,}592.143 = 6{,}184.857$

$SS_{total} = SS_{bg} + SS_{wg} = 1{,}708.286 + 6{,}184.857 = 7{,}893.143$

$df_{bg} = k - 1 = 3 - 1 = 2$

$df_{wg} = (n_1 - 1) + (n_2 - 1) + (n_3 - 1) = (7 - 1) + (7 - 1) + (7 - 1) = 18$

$df_{total} = N - 1 = 21 - 1 = 20$

$$MS_{bg} = \frac{SS_{bg}}{df_{bg}} = \frac{1{,}708.286}{2} = 854.143; \quad MS_{wg} = \frac{SS_{wg}}{df_{wg}} = \frac{6{,}184.857}{18} = 343.603$$

$$F = \frac{MS_{bg}}{MS_{wg}} = \frac{854.143}{343.603} = 2.486$$

From Table F, the critical $F_{(2, 18, \alpha = .05)} = 3.55$. Calculated $F_{(2, 18, \alpha = .05)}$ $2.486 < 3.55$. Conclusion: Fail to reject the null hypothesis.

Interpretation: There were no statistical differences in interns' moral development between those assigned to orthopedics ($\mu = 55.71$, $SD = 21.75$), pediatrics ($\mu = 77.571$, $SD = 18.44$), and oncology ($\mu = 69.43$, $SD = 14.76$) during their 3-month rotation ($F_{(2, 18)} = 2.486$, $p > .05$).

7. The written hypotheses are as follows.

Null hypothesis: Participants' blood pressure will not decrease any differently between the four different biofeedback methods.

Research hypothesis: Participants' blood pressure will decrease differently between the four different biofeedback methods.

Statistical hypotheses:

H_0: $\mu_1 = \mu_2 = \mu_3 = \mu_4$
H_1: $\mu_1 \neq \mu_2 \neq \mu_3 \neq \mu_4$

Source	Sums of Squares	df	Mean Square	F	p
Between	578.55	3	192.85	9.097	< .05
Within	339.20	16	21.20		
Total	917.75	19			

$$SS_{bg} = \left[\frac{(\Sigma X_1)^2}{n_1} + \frac{(\Sigma X_2)^2}{n_2} + \frac{(\Sigma X_3)^2}{n_3} + \frac{(\Sigma X_4)^2}{n_4}\right] -$$

$$\left[\frac{(\Sigma X_1 + \Sigma X_2 + \Sigma X_3 + \Sigma X_4)^2}{N_{total}}\right] = \left[\frac{(43)^2}{5} + \frac{(105)^2}{5} + \frac{(48)^2}{5} + \frac{(39)^2}{5}\right] -$$

$$\left[\frac{(43 + 105 + 48 + 39)^2}{20}\right] = \left[\frac{1{,}849}{5} + \frac{11{,}025}{5} + \frac{2{,}304}{5} + \frac{1{,}521}{5}\right] - \left[\frac{(235)^2}{20}\right] =$$

$369.8 + 2{,}205 + 460.8 + 304.2 - 2{,}761.25 = 3{,}339.8 - 2{,}761.25 = 578.55$

$$SS_{wg} = \left[\Sigma X_1^2 + \Sigma X_2^2 + \Sigma X_3^2 + \Sigma X_4^2\right] - \left[\frac{(\Sigma X_1)^2}{n_1} + \frac{(\Sigma X_2)^2}{n_2} + \frac{(\Sigma X_3)^2}{n_3} + \frac{(\Sigma X_4)^2}{n_4}\right] =$$

$$(463 + 2{,}255 + 552 + 399) - \left[\frac{(43)^2}{5} + \frac{(105)^2}{5} + \frac{(48)^2}{5} + \frac{(39)^2}{5}\right] =$$

$$(463 + 2{,}255 + 552 + 399) - \left[\frac{1{,}849}{5} + \frac{11{,}025}{5} + \frac{2{,}304}{5} + \frac{1{,}521}{5}\right] =$$

$3{,}679 - 3{,}339.8 = 339.2$

$SS_{total} = SS_{bg} + SS_{wg} = 578.55 + 339.20 = 917.75$

$df_{bg} = k - 1 = 4 - 1 = 3$

$df_{wg} = (n_1 - 1) + (n_2 - 1) + (n_3 - 1) + (n_4 - 1) = (5 - 1) + (5 - 1) +$
$(5 - 1) + (5 - 1) = 16$

$df_{total} = N - 1 = 20 - 1 = 19$

$$MS_{bg} = \frac{SS_{bg}}{df_{bg}} = \frac{578.55}{3} = 192.85; \quad MS_{wg} = \frac{SS_{wg}}{df_{wg}} = \frac{339.20}{16} = 21.20$$

$$F = \frac{MS_{bg}}{MS_{wg}} = \frac{192.85}{21.20} = 9.097$$

From Table F, the critical $F_{(3, 16, \alpha = .05)} = 3.24$. Calculated $F_{(3, 16, \alpha = .05)}$ $9.097 > 3.49$. Conclusion: Reject the null hypothesis and continue with Tukey HSD post-hoc analysis.

$$HSD = q \cdot \sqrt{\frac{MS_{wg}}{n}} = 4.05 \cdot \sqrt{\frac{21.20}{5}} = 3.95 \cdot \sqrt{4.24} = 3.95 \cdot 2.059 = 8.133$$

*The difference between means must be greater than 8.133 to be statistically different.

$\overline{X}_1 - \overline{X}_2 = 8.60 - 21.00 = -12.40\mathbf{*}; \overline{X}_1 - \overline{X}_3 = 8.60 - 9.60 = 1.0$
$\overline{X}_1 - \overline{X}_4 = 8.60 - 7.80 = .80; \overline{X}_2 - \overline{X}_3 = 21.00 - 9.60 = 11.4\mathbf{*}$
$\overline{X}_2 - \overline{X}_4 = 21.00 - 7.80 = 13.20\mathbf{*}; \overline{X}_3 - \overline{X}_4 = 9.60 - 7.80 = 1.80$

Interpretation: There was a significant difference in the blood pressure change as a function of the biofeedback method. Participants using method B ($\mu = 21.00$, $SD = 3.54$) had a significantly greater decrease in their blood pressure than those taught method A ($\mu = 8.60$, $SD = 4.83$), method C ($\mu = 9.60$, $SD = 5.03$), and method D ($\mu = 7.80$, $SD = 4.87$) in this study ($F_{(3, 16)} = 9.097$, $p < .05$). Methods A, C, and D did not significantly differ from each other.

9. The written hypotheses are as follows.
Null hypothesis: The percentage of letters correctly identified will not differ between threshold levels.
Research hypothesis: The percentage of letters correctly identified will differ between threshold levels.
Statistical hypotheses:
H_0: $\mu_1 = \mu_2 = \mu_3$
H_1: $\mu_1 \neq \mu_2 \neq \mu_3$

Source	Sums of Squares	df	Mean Square	F	p
Between	23,286.667	2	11,643.333	523.950	< .05
Within	600.00	27	22.222		
Total	23,886.667	29			

$$SS_{bg} = \left[\frac{(\Sigma X_1)^2}{n_1} + \frac{(\Sigma X_2)^2}{n_2} + \frac{(\Sigma X_3)^2}{n_3} \right] - \left[\frac{(\Sigma X_1 + \Sigma X_2 + \Sigma X_3)^2}{N_{total}} \right] =$$

$$\left[\frac{880^2}{10} + \frac{490^2}{10} + \frac{200^2}{10} \right] - \left[\frac{(880 + 490 + 200)^2}{30} \right] = (77,440 +$$

$24,010 + 4,000) - 82,163.33 = 105,450 - 82,163.33 = 23,286.67$

$$SS_{wg} = \left[\Sigma X_1^2 + \Sigma X_2^2 + \Sigma X_3^2 \right] - \left[\frac{(\Sigma X_1)^2}{n_1} + \frac{(\Sigma X_2)^2}{n_2} + \frac{(\Sigma X_3)^2}{n_3} \right] =$$

$$\left[77,700 + 24,250 + 4,100 \right] - \left[\frac{880^2}{10} + \frac{490^2}{10} + \frac{200^2}{10} \right] =$$

$106,050 - 105,450 = 600.00$

$SS_{total} = SS_{bg} + SS_{wg} = 23,286.667 + 600.00 = 23,886.667$

$df_{bg} = k - 1 = 3 - 1 = 2;\ df_{wg} = (n_1 - 1) + (n_2 - 1) + (n_3 - 1) =$
$(10 - 1) + (10 - 1) + (10 - 1) = 27$

$df_{total} = N - 1 = 30 - 1 = 29$

$$MS_{bg} = \frac{SS_{bg}}{df_{bg}} = \frac{23,286.667}{2} = 11,643.333;\ MS_{wg} = \frac{SS_{wg}}{df_{wg}} = \frac{600.00}{27} = 22.222$$

$$F = \frac{MS_{bg}}{MS_{wg}} = \frac{11,643.333}{22.222} = 523.95$$

From Table F, the critical $F_{(2, 27, \alpha = .05)} = 3.35$. Calculated $F_{(2, 27, \alpha = .05)}$ 523.95 > 3.35. Conclusion: Reject the null hypothesis and continue with Tukey HSD.

$$HSD = q \cdot \sqrt{\frac{MS_{wg}}{n}} = 3.53 \cdot \sqrt{\frac{22.222}{10}} = 3.53 \cdot \sqrt{2.222} = 3.53 \cdot 1.491 = 5.263$$

*The difference between means must be greater than 5.263 to be statistically different.

$\overline{X}_1 - \overline{X}_2 = 88.00 - 49.00 = 39.00^\star;\ \overline{X}_1 - \overline{X}_3 = 88.00 - 20.00 = 68.00^\star$
$\overline{X}_2 - \overline{X}_3 = 49.00 - 20.00 = 29.0^\star$

Interpretation: The percentage of letters participants identified differed significantly between all three threshold levels ($F_{(2, 27)} = 523.95$, $p < .05$). Participants identified the highest percentage of letters correctly when the letters were presented above threshold ($\mu = 88.00$, $SD = 5.37$), followed by at threshold ($\mu = 49.00$, $SD = 5.16$) and below threshold ($\mu = 20.00$, $SD = 3.33$). For this sample, subliminal perception was the least effective in identification of letters.

11. The written hypotheses are as follows.
Null hypothesis: Participants' blood level of the hormone will not differ between the stress conditions.
Research hypothesis: Participants' blood level of the hormone will differ between the stress conditions.

Statistical hypotheses:

$H_0: \mu_1 = \mu_2 = \mu_3 = \mu_4$

$H_1: \mu_1 \neq \mu_2 \neq \mu_3 \neq \mu_4$

Source	Sums of Squares	df	Mean Square	F	p
Between	1,071.750	3	357.25	39.475	< .05
Within	144.800	16	9.05		
Total	1,216.550	19			

$$SS_{bg} = \left[\frac{(\Sigma X_1)^2}{n_1} + \frac{(\Sigma X_2)^2}{n_2} + \frac{(\Sigma X_3)^2}{n_3} + \frac{(\Sigma X_4)^2}{n_4}\right] -$$

$$\left[\frac{(\Sigma X_1 + \Sigma X_2 + \Sigma X_3 + \Sigma X_4)^2}{N_{total}}\right] =$$

$$\left[\frac{(1,338)^2}{5} + \frac{(1,334)^2}{5} + \frac{(1,331)^2}{5} + \frac{(1,250)^2}{5}\right] -$$

$$\left[\frac{(1,338 + 1,334 + 1,331 + 1,250)^2}{20}\right] =$$

$$\left[\frac{1,790,244}{5} + \frac{1,779,556}{5} + \frac{1,771,561}{5} + \frac{1,562,500}{5}\right] - \left[\frac{(5,253)^2}{20}\right] =$$

$$358,048.8 + 355,911.2 + 354,312.2 + 312,500 - 1,379,700.45 =$$

$$1,380,772.20 - 1,379,700.45 = 1,071.75$$

$$SS_{wg} = \left[\Sigma X_1^2 + \Sigma X_2^2 + \Sigma X_3^2 + \Sigma X_4^2\right] -$$

$$\left[\frac{(\Sigma X_1)^2}{n_1} + \frac{(\Sigma X_2)^2}{n_2} + \frac{(\Sigma X_3)^2}{n_3} + \frac{(\Sigma X_4)^2}{n_4}\right] =$$

$$(358,078 + 355,982 + 354,319 + 312,538) -$$

$$\left[\frac{(1,338)^2}{5} + \frac{(1,334)^2}{5} + \frac{(1,331)^2}{5} + \frac{(1,250)^2}{5}\right] =$$

$$(358,078 + 355,982 + 354,319 + 312,538) -$$

$$\left[\frac{1,790,244}{5} + \frac{1,779,556}{5} + \frac{1,771,561}{5} + \frac{1,562,500}{5}\right] =$$

$$1,380,917.00 - 1,380,772.20 = 144.80$$

$$SS_{total} = SS_{bg} + SS_{wg} = 1,071.75 + 144.80 = 1,216.55$$

$$df_{bg} = k - 1 = 4 - 1 = 3$$

$$df_{wg} = (n_1 - 1) + (n_2 - 1) + (n_3 - 1) + (n_4 - 1) = (5 - 1) + (5 - 1) +$$

$$(5 - 1) + (5 - 1) = 16$$

$$df_{total} = N - 1 = 20 - 1 = 19$$

$$MS_{bg} = \frac{SS_{bg}}{df_{bg}} = \frac{1{,}071.75}{3} = 357.25; \quad MS_{wg} = \frac{SS_{wg}}{df_{wg}} = \frac{144.80}{16} = 9.05$$

$$F = \frac{MS_{bg}}{MS_{wg}} = \frac{357.25}{9.05} = 39.475$$

From Table F, the critical $F_{(3, 16, \alpha = .05)} = 3.24$. Calculated $F_{(3, 16, \alpha = .05)}$ $39.475 > 3.49$. Reject the null hypothesis and continue with Tukey HSD post-hoc analysis.

$$HSD = q \cdot \sqrt{\frac{MS_{wg}}{n}} = 3.24 \cdot \sqrt{\frac{9.05}{5}} = 3.24 \cdot \sqrt{3.008} = 3.24 \cdot 1.734 = 5.618$$

*The difference between means must be greater than 5.618 to be statistically different.
$\overline{X}_1 - \overline{X}_2 = 267.60 - 266.80 = .80$; $\overline{X}_1 - \overline{X}_3 = 267.60 - 266.20 = 1.4$
$\overline{X}_1 - \overline{X}_4 = 267.60 - 250.00 = 17.60*$; $\overline{X}_2 - \overline{X}_3 = 266.80 - 266.20 = .60$
$\overline{X}_2 - \overline{X}_4 = 266.8 - 250.00 = 16.80*$; $\overline{X}_3 - \overline{X}_4 = 266.20 - 250.00 = 16.20*$
Interpretation: The blood level of the hormone significantly differed depending on the stress situation condition of the animals ($F_{(3, 16)} = 39.475, p < .05$). In the control condition ($\mu = 250.00, SD = 3.08$), the animals' blood level of the hormone was significantly lower compared to swimming ($\mu = 267.60, SD = 2.70$), being shocked in ice water ($\mu = 266.80, SD = 4.21$), and being dropped from 10 feet in the air ($\mu = 266.20, SD = 1.31$). However, animals in the experimental stress situations did not differ in the blood level of the hormone.

Problems From the Literature

13. The written hypotheses are as follows.
    Null hypothesis: The number of on-the-job accidents will be the same for locations where employees' perceive the safety awareness program was implemented by either top-level management, immediate supervisors, or control conditions.
    Research hypothesis: The number of on-the-job accidents will differ between locations as a function of employees' perception that the safety awareness program was implemented by either top-level management, immediate supervisors, or control conditions.
    Statistical hypotheses:
    $H_0: \mu_1 = \mu_2 = \mu_3$
    $H_1: \mu_1 \neq \mu_2 \neq \mu_3$

Source	Sums of Squares	df	Mean Square	F	p
Between	81.17	2	40.58	4.16	$< .05$
Within	321.58	33	9.75		
Total	402.75	35			

$$SS_{bg} = \left[\frac{(\Sigma X_1)^2}{n_1} + \frac{(\Sigma X_2)^2}{n_2} + \frac{(\Sigma X_3)^2}{n_3} \right] - \left[\frac{(\Sigma X_1 + \Sigma X_2 + \Sigma X_3)^2}{N_{total}} \right] =$$

$$\left[\frac{90^2}{12} + \frac{46^2}{12} + \frac{65^2}{12} \right] - \left[\frac{(90 + 46 + 65)^2}{36} \right] =$$

$$(675 + 176.333 + 352.083) - 1{,}122.25 = 1{,}203.416 - 1{,}122.25 = 80.96$$

$$SS_{wg} = \left[\Sigma X_1^2 + \Sigma X_2^2 + \Sigma X_3^2\right] - \left[\frac{(\Sigma X_1)^2}{n_1} + \frac{(\Sigma X_2)^2}{n_2} + \frac{(\Sigma X_3)^2}{n_3}\right] =$$

$$\left[792.00 + 278 + 455\right] - \left[\frac{90^2}{12} + \frac{46^2}{12} + \frac{65^2}{12}\right] =$$

$1,525.00 - 1,203.416 = 321.58$

$SS_{total} = SS_{bg} + SS_{wg} = 321.58 + 81.17 = 402.75$

$df_{bg} = k - 1 = 3 - 1 = 2; df_{wg} = (n_1 - 1) + (n_2 - 1) + (n_3 - 1) =$
$(12 - 1) + (12 - 1) + (12 - 1) = 33; df_{total} = N - 1 = 36 - 1 = 35$

$MS_{bg} = \dfrac{SS_{bg}}{df_{bg}} = \dfrac{81.17}{2} = 40.58; MS_{wg} = \dfrac{SS_{wg}}{df_{wg}} = \dfrac{321.58}{33} = 9.75;$

$F = \dfrac{MS_{bg}}{MS_{wg}} = \dfrac{40.58}{9.75} = 4.15$

From Table F, the critical $F_{(2, 33, \alpha = .05)} = 3.32$. Calculated $F_{(2, 33, \alpha = .05)}$ $4.15 > 3.32$.
Conclusion: Reject the null hypothesis and continue with Tukey HSD.

$$HSD = q \cdot \sqrt{\frac{MS_{wg}}{n}} = 3.50 \cdot \sqrt{\frac{9.75}{12}} = 3.50 \cdot \sqrt{.813} = 3.50 \cdot .903 = 3.161$$

*The difference between means must be greater than 3.161 to be statistically different.
$\overline{X}_1 - \overline{X}_2 = 7.80 - 3.833 = 3.667^*$; $\overline{X}_1 - \overline{X}_3 = 7.80 - 5.417 = 2.383$
$\overline{X}_2 - \overline{X}_3 = 3.83 - 5.417 = -1.587$

Interpretation: There were significant differences in the number of annual accidents on the job depending on workers' perceptions of the source of the safety awareness program ($F_{(2, 33)} = 4.15, p < .05$). Significantly more minor accidents were reported at the location in which employees perceived the safety program to be implemented by top-level management ($\mu = 7.50, SD = 3.26$) compared to locations where it was perceived to be implemented by their immediate supervisors ($\mu = 3.83, SD = 3.04$). There were no significant differences in the number of accidents at locations where employees perceived the safety program to be implemented by immediate supervisors or a control condition ($\mu = 5.42, SD = 3.06$) or when it was believed to be implemented by top-level management compared to a control condition.

15. Both of these studies cannot make causal inferences based on the findings. The study examining perceptions of the source of implementations for a safety awareness program did not have random assignment. The study examining body self-esteem and sexual behavior did not have a manipulated independent variable or random assignment. Thus, statistical interpretation should not imply causation based on this study.

Chapter 14

1. Null hypothesis: There will be no difference between the fluorescent, incandescent, and sunlight lighting conditions in the time it takes participants to read 1,000 words on the computer screen. ($H_{0_1}: \mu_1 = \mu_2 = \mu_3$)
Research hypothesis: There will be a difference between the fluorescent, incandescent, and sunlight lighting conditions in the time it takes participants to read 1,000 words on the computer screen. ($H_1: \mu_1 \neq \mu_2 \neq \mu_3$)

Null hypothesis: There will be no difference in the time it takes participants to read 1,000 words on the computer screen that has a blue background with white letters compared to the screen that has a white background with black letters. ($H_{0_2}: \mu_1 = \mu_2$) Research hypothesis: There will be a difference in the time it takes participants to read 1,000 words on the computer screen that has a blue background with white letters compared to the screen that has a white background with black letters. ($H_2: \mu_1 \neq \mu_2$) Null hypothesis: There will be no interaction of lighting and screen conditions. Research hypothesis: There will be an interaction of lighting and screen conditions.

Source of Variation	Sums of Squares	Degrees of Freedom	Mean Square	F	p
Rows (type of screen)	1,009.200	1	1,009.20	33.362	< .05
Columns (type of light)	1,762.867	2	881.433	29.138	< .05
Interaction (screen × light)	491.40	2	245.70	8.122	< .05
Within	726.00	24	30.25		
Total	3989.467	29			

Summary data are as follows:

	Fluorescent	Incandescent	Sunlight	
Black/White	$\Sigma X = 615$ $\Sigma X^2 = 75,859$ $\overline{X} = 123, n = 5$	$\Sigma X = 623$ $\Sigma X^2 = 77,767$ $\overline{X} = 124.60, n = 5$	$\Sigma X = 743$ $\Sigma X^2 = 110,607$ $\overline{X} = 148.60, n = 5$	$\Sigma X_{row1} = 1,981$ $\Sigma X^2_{row1} = 264,233$ $n_{row1} = 15$
White/Blue	$\Sigma X = 706$ $\Sigma X^2 = 99,724$ $\overline{X} = 141.20, n = 5$	$\Sigma X = 705$ $\Sigma X^2 = 99,495$ $\overline{X} = 148.50, n = 5$	$\Sigma X = 744$ $\Sigma X^2 = 110,754$ $\overline{X} = 148.60, n = 5$	$\Sigma X_{row2} = 2,155$ $\Sigma X^2_{row2} = 309,973$ $n_{row2} = 15$
	$\Sigma X_{col1} = 1,321$ $\Sigma X^2_{col1} = 175,583$ $n_{col1} = 10$	$\Sigma X_{col2} = 1,328$ $\Sigma X^2_{col2} = 177,262$ $n_{col2} = 10$	$\Sigma X_{col3} = 1,487$ $\Sigma X^2_{col3} = 221,361$ $n_{col3} = 10$	$\Sigma\Sigma X = 4,136$ $\Sigma\Sigma X^2 = 574,206$ $N_{total} = 30$

$$SS_{total} = \Sigma\Sigma X^2 - \frac{(\Sigma\Sigma X)^2}{N_{total}} = 574,206 - \frac{4,136^2}{30} = 574,206 - \frac{17,106,496}{30} =$$

$$574,206 - 570,216.533 = 3,989.467$$

$$SS_{wg} = \Sigma\Sigma X^2 - \frac{\Sigma(\Sigma X_{cell})^2}{n_{cell}} = 574,206 -$$

$$\frac{615^2 + 623^2 + 743^2 + 706^2 + 705^2 + 744^2}{5} = 574,206 -$$

$$\frac{378,225 + 388,129 + 552,049 + 498,436 + 497,025 + 553,536}{5} =$$

$$574,206 - \frac{2,867,400}{5} = 574,206 - 573,480 = 726$$

$$SS_r = \frac{\Sigma(\Sigma X_{row})^2}{n_{row}} - \frac{(\Sigma\Sigma x)^2}{N_{total}} = \frac{1,981^2 + 2,155^2}{15} - \frac{4,136^2}{30} =$$

$$\frac{3,924,361 + 4,644,025}{15} - \frac{17,106,496}{30} = \frac{8,568,386}{15} -$$

$$570,216.533 = 571,225.733 - 570,216.533 = 1,009.20$$

$$SS_c = \frac{\Sigma(\Sigma X_{col})^2}{n_{col}} - \frac{(\Sigma\Sigma X)^2}{N_{total}} = \frac{1,321^2 + 1,328^2 + 1,487^2}{10} - \frac{4,136^2}{30} =$$

$$\frac{5,719,794}{10} - \frac{17,106,496}{30} = 571,979.4 - 570,216.533 = 1,762.867$$

$$SS_{r \times c} = SS_{total} - (SS_{wg} + SS_r + SS_c) = 3,989.467 -$$
$$(726 + 1,009.20 + 1,762.87) = 3,989.467 - 3,498.07 = 491.40$$

$$df_r = \text{number of rows} - 1 = 2 - 1 = 1$$

$$df_c = \text{number of columns} - 1 = 3 - 1 = 2$$

$$df_{r \times c} = df_r \cdot df_c = (\text{number of rows} - 1) \cdot (\text{number of columns} - 1) =$$
$$(2 - 1) \cdot (3 - 1) = 2$$

$$df_{wg} = N_{total} - \text{number of cells} = 20 - 6 = 24$$

$$df_{total} = N_{total} - 1 = 30 - 1 = 29$$

$$MS_r = \frac{SS_r}{df_r} = \frac{1,009.20}{1} = 1,009.20; \; MS_c = \frac{SS_c}{df_c} = \frac{1,762.867}{2} = 881.433$$

$$MS_{r \times c} = \frac{SS_{r \times c}}{df_{r \times c}} = \frac{491.40}{2} = 245.70; \; MS_{wg} = \frac{SS_{wg}}{df_{wg}} = \frac{726}{24} = 30.25$$

$$F_r = \frac{MS_r}{MS_{wg}} = \frac{1,009.20}{30.25} = 33.362; \; F_c = \frac{MS_c}{MS_{wg}} = \frac{881.433}{30.25} = 29.138$$

$$F_{r \times c} = \frac{MS_{r \times c}}{MS_{wg}} = \frac{245.70}{30.25} = 8.122$$

Comparison of computed F ratios to critical values:

Source of Variation	Computed F Ratio	Critical F Value, $\alpha = .05$	Decision
Type of Screen	33.362	$(df = 1, 24) = 4.26$	Reject null hypothesis
Type of Lighting	29.138	$(df = 2, 24) = 3.40$	Reject null hypothesis
Interaction S × L	8.122	$(df = 2, 24) = 3.40$	Reject null hypothesis

Post-hoc Tukey HSD for type of lighting:

$$HSD = q \cdot \sqrt{\frac{MS_{wg}}{n}} = 3.53 \cdot \sqrt{\frac{30.25}{5}} = 3.53 \cdot \sqrt{6.05} = 3.53 \cdot 2.46 = 8.683$$

*The difference is significant.

$\overline{X}_{Fluor} - \overline{X}_{Incand} = 132.10 - 132.80 = -.7$ seconds; $\overline{X}_{Fluor} - \overline{X}_{Sun} =$
$132.10 - 148.7 = -16.6$ seconds*; $\overline{X}_{Incand} - \overline{X}_{Sun} = 132.80 - 148.70 =$
-15.9 seconds*

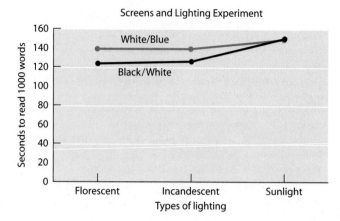

Participants read significantly faster on the screen that had a white background with black letters than on the screen with a blue background with white letters. It also took significantly less time to read the words under fluorescent lighting than under incandescent lighting and sunlight. There was no significant difference detected in the time it took to read the words between incandescent and sunlight conditions. There was an interaction of screen and lighting conditions, in that participants had the fastest speed when they read from a screen that had the white background with black letters under fluorescent lights.

3. Null hypothesis: Participants completing either a lecture, television, or Internet DSM continuing education course will not differ in the number of items answered correctly on the new DSM knowledge test. ($H_{0_1}: \mu_1 = \mu_2 = \mu_3$)

Research hypothesis: Participants completing either a lecture, television, or Internet DSM continuing education course will differ in the number of items answered correctly on the new DSM knowledge test. ($H_1: \mu_1 \neq \mu_2 \neq \mu_3$)

Null hypothesis: There will be no difference between licensed psychologists and licensed psychiatrists in the number of items correctly answered on the new DSM knowledge test. ($H_{0_2}: \mu_1 = \mu_2$)

Research hypothesis: There will be a difference between licensed psychologists and licensed psychiatrists in the number of items correctly answered on the new DSM knowledge test. ($H_2: \mu_1 \neq \mu_2$)

Null hypothesis: There will be no interaction of type of continuing education instruction and the type of professional license.

Research hypothesis: There will be an interaction of type of continuing education instruction and the type of professional license.

Source of Variation	Sums of Squares	Degrees of Freedom	Mean Square	F	p
Rows (type of instruction)	88.889	1	88.889	.901	> .05
Columns (type of license)	41.444	2	20.722	.210	> .05
Interaction (instruction × license)	922.111	2	461.056	4.673	< .05
Within	1,184.000	12	98.667		
Total	2,236.444	17			

Summary data are as follows:

	Lecture	Television	Internet	
Psychologist	$\Sigma X = 250$ $\Sigma X^2 = 21,022$ $\overline{X} = 83.333, n = 3$	$\Sigma X = 244$ $\Sigma X^2 = 20,362$ $\overline{X} = 81.333, n = 3$	$\Sigma X = 287$ $\Sigma X^2 = 27,461$ $\overline{X} = 95.667, n = 3$	$\Sigma X_{row1} = 781$ $\Sigma X_{row1}^2 = 62,085$ $n_{row1} = 9$
Psychiatrist	$\Sigma X = 249$ $\Sigma X^2 = 20,849$ $\overline{X} = 83.00, n = 3$	$\Sigma X = 276$ $\Sigma X^2 = 25,550$ $\overline{X} = 92.00, n = 3$	$\Sigma X = 216$ $\Sigma X^2 = 15,686$ $\overline{X} = 72.00, n = 3$	$\Sigma X_{row2} = 741$ $\Sigma X_{row2}^2 = 68,845$ $n_{row2} = 9$
	$\Sigma X_{col1} = 499$ $\Sigma X_{col1}^2 = 41,871$ $n_{col1} = 6$	$\Sigma X_{col2} = 520$ $\Sigma X_{col2}^2 = 45,912$ $n_{col2} = 6$	$\Sigma X_{col3} = 503$ $\Sigma X_{col3}^2 = 43,147$ $n_{col3} = 6$	$\Sigma\Sigma X = 1,522$ $\Sigma\Sigma X^2 = 130,930$ $N_{total} = 18$

$$SS_{total} = \Sigma\Sigma X^2 - \frac{(\Sigma\Sigma X)^2}{N_{total}} = 130,930 - \frac{1,522^2}{18} = 130,930 - \frac{2,316,484}{18} =$$

$$130,930 - 128,693.556 = 2,236.444$$

$$SS_{wg} = \Sigma\Sigma X^2 - \frac{\Sigma(\Sigma X_{cell})^2}{n_{cell}} = 130,930 -$$

$$\frac{250^2 + 244^2 + 287^2 + 249^2 + 276^2 + 216^2}{3} = 130,930 -$$

$$\frac{62,500 + 59,536 + 82,369 + 62,001 + 76,176 + 46,656}{3} =$$

$$130,930 - \frac{389,238}{3} = 130,930 - 129,746 = 1,184$$

$$SS_r = \frac{\Sigma(\Sigma X_{row})^2}{n_{row}} - \frac{(\Sigma\Sigma X)^2}{N_{total}} = \frac{781^2 + 741^2}{9} - \frac{1,522^2}{18} =$$

$$\frac{609,961 + 549,081}{9} - \frac{2,316,484}{18} = \frac{1,159,042}{9} -$$

$$128,693.556 = 128,782.444 - 128,693.556 = 88.889$$

$$SS_c = \frac{\Sigma(\Sigma X_{col})^2}{n_{col}} - \frac{(\Sigma\Sigma X)^2}{N_{total}} = \frac{499^2 + 520^2 + 503^2}{6} - \frac{1,522^2}{30} =$$

$$\frac{772,410}{6} - \frac{2,316,484}{18} = 128,735 - 128,693.556 = 41.444$$

$SS_{r \times c} = SS_{total} - (SS_{wg} + SS_r + SS_c) = 2,236.444 -$
$(1,184 + 41.444 + 88.889) = 2,236.444 - 1,314.333 = 922.111$
df_r = number of rows $- 1 = 2 - 1 = 1$
df_c = number of columns $- 1 = 3 - 1 = 2$
$df_{r \times c} = df_r \cdot df_c = (\text{number of rows} - 1) \cdot (\text{number of columns} - 1) =$
$(2 - 1) \cdot (3 - 1) = 2$
$df_{wg} = N_{total} -$ number of cells $= 18 - 6 = 12$
$df_{total} = N_{total} - 1 = 18 - 1 = 17$

$$MS_r = \frac{SS_r}{df_r} = \frac{88.889}{1} = 88.889; \; MS_c = \frac{SS_c}{df_c} = \frac{41.444}{2} = 20.722$$

$$MS_{r \times c} = \frac{SS_{r \times c}}{df_{r \times c}} = \frac{922.111}{2} = 461.056; \; MS_{wg} = \frac{SS_{wg}}{df_{wg}} = \frac{1,184}{12} = 98.667$$

$$F_r = \frac{MS_r}{MS_{wg}} = \frac{88.889}{98.667} = .901; \; F_c = \frac{MS_c}{MS_{wg}} = \frac{20.722}{98.667} = .210$$

$$F_{r \times c} = \frac{MS_{r \times c}}{MS_{wg}} = \frac{461.056}{98.667} = 4.673$$

Comparison of computed F ratios to critical values:

Source of Variation	Computed F Ratio	Critical F Value, $\alpha = .05$	Decision
Type of Instruction	.901	$(df = 1,12) = 4.75$	Fail to reject
Type of License	.210	$(df = 2,12) = 3.89$	Fail to reject
Interaction I × L	4.673	$(df = 2,12) = 3.89$	Reject null hypothesis

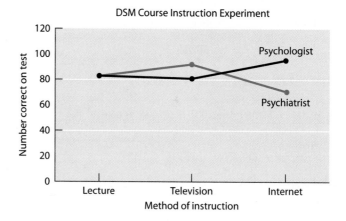

The number of items answered correctly on the new DSM test did not differ significantly between the three types of continuing education instruction or between the two types of licenses. However, there was a significant interaction of type of instruction and type of license. As shown in the figure, when course instruction was via the Internet, psychologists got the most items correct and psychiatrists got the least correct. The opposite happened with televised instruction, in that psychiatrists got the most correct and psychologists got the least correct. Thus, the most effective type of instruction differs as a function of the license type.

5. Null hypothesis: There will be no difference in the number of days it takes to learn new tricks between old and young dogs. ($H_{0_1}: \mu_1 = \mu_2 = \mu_3$)
Research hypothesis: There will be a difference in the number of days it takes to learn new tricks between old and young dogs. ($H_1: \mu_1 \neq \mu_2 \neq \mu_3$)
Null hypothesis: There will be no difference in the number of days it takes dogs to learn to either sit, shake, or roll over. ($H_{0_2}: \mu_1 = \mu_2$)

Research hypothesis: There will be a difference in the number of days it takes dogs to learn to either sit, shake, or roll over. ($H_2: \mu_1 \neq \mu_2$)
Null hypothesis: There will be no interaction of type of trick and age of dog.
Research hypothesis: There will be an interaction of type of trick and age of dog.

Source of Variation	Sums of Squares	Degrees of Freedom	Mean Square	F	p
Rows (age of dog)	124.033	1	124.033	47.705	< .05
Columns (type of trick)	366.067	2	183.033	70.397	< .05
Interaction (dog × trick)	28.467	2	14.233	5.473	< .05
Within	62.400	24	2.600		
Total	580.967	29			

Summary data are as follows:

	Sit	Shake	Roll Over	
Young Dog	$\Sigma X = 9$ $\Sigma X^2 = 19$ $\overline{X} = 1.8, n = 5$	$\Sigma X = 26$ $\Sigma X^2 = 142$ $\overline{X} = 5.2, n = 5$	$\Sigma X = 40$ $\Sigma X^2 = 330$ $\overline{X} = 8, n = 5$	$\Sigma X_{\text{row1}} = 75$ $\Sigma X^2_{\text{row1}} = 491$ $n_{\text{row1}} = 15$
Old Dog	$\Sigma X = 16$ $\Sigma X^2 = 58$ $\overline{X} = 3.2, n = 5$	$\Sigma X = 50$ $\Sigma X^2 = 520$ $\overline{X} = 10, n = 8$	$\Sigma X = 70$ $\Sigma X^2 = 996$ $\overline{X} = 14, n = 5$	$\Sigma X_{\text{row2}} = 136$ $\Sigma X^2_{\text{row2}} = 1574$ $n_{\text{row2}} = 15$
	$\Sigma X_{\text{col1}} = 25$ $\Sigma X^2_{\text{col1}} = 77$ $n_{\text{col1}} = 10$	$\Sigma X_{\text{col2}} = 76$ $\Sigma X^2_{\text{col2}} = 662$ $n_{\text{col2}} = 10$	$\Sigma X_{\text{col3}} = 110$ $\Sigma X^2_{\text{col3}} = 1,326$ $n_{\text{col3}} = 10$	$\Sigma\Sigma X = 211$ $\Sigma\Sigma X^2 = 2,065$ $N_{\text{total}} = 30$

$$SS_{\text{total}} = \Sigma\Sigma X^2 - \frac{(\Sigma\Sigma X)^2}{N_{\text{total}}} = 2,065 - \frac{211^2}{30} = 2,065 - \frac{44,521}{30} =$$

$$2,065 - 1,484.033 = 580.967$$

$$SS_{\text{wg}} = \Sigma\Sigma X^2 - \frac{\Sigma(\Sigma X_{\text{cell}})^2}{n_{\text{cell}}} = 2,065 -$$

$$\frac{9^2 + 26^2 + 40^2 + 16^2 + 50^2 + 70^2}{5} = 2,065 -$$

$$\frac{81 + 676 + 1,600 + 256 + 2,500 + 4,900}{5} =$$

$$2,065 - \frac{10,013}{5} = 2,065 - 2,002.6 = 62.4$$

$$SS_r = \frac{\Sigma(\Sigma X_{\text{row}})^2}{n_{\text{row}}} - \frac{(\Sigma\Sigma X)^2}{N_{\text{total}}} = \frac{75^2 + 136^2}{15} - \frac{211^2}{30} =$$

$$\frac{5{,}625 + 18{,}496}{15} - \frac{44{,}521}{30} = \frac{24{,}121}{15} -$$

$$1{,}484.033 = 1{,}608.066 - 1{,}484.033 = 124.033$$

$$SS_c = \frac{\Sigma(\Sigma X_{col})^2}{n_{col}} - \frac{(\Sigma\Sigma X)^2}{N_{total}} = \frac{25^2 + 76^2 + 110^2}{10} - \frac{211^2}{30} =$$

$$\frac{18{,}501}{10} - \frac{44{,}521}{30} = 1{,}850.10 - 1{,}484.033 = 366.067$$

$$SS_{r \times c} = SS_{total} - (SS_{wg} + SS_r + SS_c) = 580.967 -$$

$$(62.40 + 124.033 + 366.067) = 580.967 - 552.5 = 28.467$$

df_r = number of rows $- 1 = 2 - 1 = 1$

df_c = number of columns $- 1 = 3 - 1 = 2$

$df_{r \times c} = df_r \cdot df_c = (\text{number of rows} - 1) \cdot (\text{number of columns} - 1) =$

$(2 - 1) \cdot (3 - 1) = 2$

$df_{wg} = N_{total} - \text{number of cells} = 30 - 6 = 24$

$df_{total} = N_{total} - 1 = 30 - 1 = 29$

$$MS_r = \frac{SS_r}{df_r} = \frac{124.033}{1} = 124.033; \ MS_c = \frac{SS_c}{df_c} = \frac{366.067}{2} = 183.033$$

$$MS_{r \times c} = \frac{SS_{r \times c}}{df_{r \times c}} = \frac{28.467}{2} = 14.233; \ MS_{wg} = \frac{SS_{wg}}{df_{wg}} = \frac{62.40}{24} = 2.60$$

$$F_r = \frac{MS_r}{MS_{wg}} = \frac{124.033}{2.60} = 47.705; \ F_c = \frac{MS_c}{MS_{wg}} = \frac{183.033}{2.60} = 70.397$$

$$F_{r \times c} = \frac{MS_{r \times c}}{MS_{wg}} = \frac{14.23}{2.60} = 5.473$$

Comparison of computed F ratios to critical values:

Source of Variation	Computed F Ratio	Critical F Value, $\alpha = .05$	Decision
Age of Dog	47.705	$(df = 1, 24) = 4.26$	Reject null hypothesis
Type of Trick	70.397	$(df = 2, 24) = 3.40$	Reject null hypothesis
Interaction D × T	5.473	$(df = 2, 24) = 3.40$	Reject null hypothesis

Post-hoc Tukey HSD for type of trick:

$$HSD = q \cdot \sqrt{\frac{MS_{wg}}{n}} = 3.53 \cdot \sqrt{\frac{2.60}{5}} = 3.53 \cdot \sqrt{.52} = 3.53 \cdot .721 = 2.545$$

*The difference is significant.

$\overline{X}_{Sit} - \overline{X}_{Shake} = 2.5 - 7.6 = -5.1 \text{ days}^*$

$\overline{X}_{Sit} - \overline{X}_{Roll} = 2.5 - 11.0 = -8.5 \text{ days}^*$

$\overline{X}_{Shake} - \overline{X}_{Roll} = 7.6 - 11.0 = -3.4 \text{ days}^*$

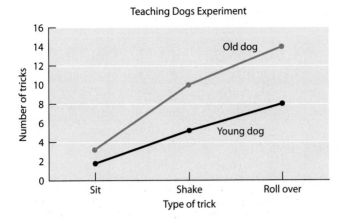

There was a significant difference in the number of days it took dogs to learn each type of trick. It took dogs the longest to learn to roll over, followed by shake and sit. Also, there may be some truth to the saying, "You can't teach old dogs new tricks," as these results showed young dogs learned significantly faster than old dogs. There was also an interaction of the type of trick and age of dog. As shown in the figure, all conditions varied significantly from each other.

7. Null hypothesis: There will be no difference in the effectiveness ratings of the animal rights message when the institution is mentioned compared to when it is not mentioned. $(H_{0_1}: \mu_1 = \mu_2)$
Research hypothesis: There will be a difference in the effectiveness ratings of the animal rights message when the institution is mentioned compared to when it is not mentioned. $(H_1: \mu_1 \neq \mu_2)$
Null hypothesis: There will be no difference in the effectiveness ratings of the animal rights message when a photograph of the researcher is present compared to when it is not present. $(H_{0_2}: \mu_1 = \mu_2)$
Research hypothesis: There will be a difference in the effectiveness ratings of the animal rights message when a photograph of the researcher is present compared to when it is not present. $(H_2: \mu_1 \neq \mu_2)$
Null hypothesis: There will be no interaction of institution and photograph conditions on the effectiveness ratings of the animal rights message.
Research hypothesis: There will be an interaction of institution and photograph conditions on the effectiveness ratings of the animal rights message.

Source of Variation	Sums of Squares	Degrees of Freedom	Mean Square	F	p
Rows (photograph presence)	.250	1	.250	.109	$> .05$
Columns (institution mentioned)	49.000	1	49.000	21.378	$< .05$
Interaction (photo × institution)	6.250	1	6.250	2.727	$> .05$
Within	27.500	12	2.292		
Total	83.000	15			

Summary data are as follows:

	Yes	No	
Photograph	$\Sigma X = 25$ $\Sigma X^2 = 165$ $\overline{X} = 6.25, n = 4$	$\Sigma X = 31$ $\Sigma X^2 = 247$ $\overline{X} = 7.75, n = 4$	$\Sigma X_{row1} = 56$ $\Sigma X^2_{row1} = 412$ $n_{row1} = 8$
No Photograph	$\Sigma X = 16$ $\Sigma X^2 = 66$ $\overline{X} = 4.00, n = 4$	$\Sigma X = 12$ $\Sigma X^2 = 46$ $\overline{X} = 3, n = 4$	$\Sigma X_{row2} = 28$ $\Sigma X^2_{row2} = 112$ $n_{row2} = 8$
	$\Sigma X_{col1} = 41$ $\Sigma X^2_{col1} = 231$ $n_{col1} = 8$	$\Sigma X_{col2} = 43$ $\Sigma X^2_{col2} = 293$ $n_{col2} = 8$	$\Sigma\Sigma X = 84$ $\Sigma\Sigma X^2 = 524$ $N_{total} = 16$

$$SS_{total} = \Sigma\Sigma X^2 - \frac{(\Sigma\Sigma X)^2}{N_{total}} = 524 - \frac{84^2}{16} = 524 - \frac{7,056}{16} =$$

$$524 - 441 = 83.00$$

$$SS_{wg} = \Sigma\Sigma X^2 - \frac{\Sigma(\Sigma X_{cell})^2}{n_{cell}} = 524 - \frac{25^2 + 31^2 + 16^2 + 12^2}{4} =$$

$$524 - \frac{625 + 961 + 256 + 144}{4} = 526 - \frac{1,986}{4} = 524 - 496.5 = 27.50$$

$$SS_r = \frac{\Sigma(\Sigma X_{row})^2}{n_{row}} - \frac{(\Sigma\Sigma X)^2}{N_{total}} = \frac{56^2 + 28^2}{8} - \frac{84^2}{16} = \frac{3,136 + 784}{8} - \frac{7,056}{16} =$$

$$\frac{3,920}{8} - 441 = 490 - 441 = 49.00$$

$$SS_c = \frac{\Sigma(\Sigma X_{col})^2}{n_{col}} - \frac{(\Sigma\Sigma X)^2}{N_{total}} = \frac{41^2 + 43^2}{8} - \frac{84^2}{16} = \frac{1,681 + 1,849}{8} - \frac{7,056}{16} =$$

$$\frac{3,530}{8} - 441 = 441.25 - 441.00 = .250$$

$SS_{r \times c} = SS_{total} - (SS_{wg} + SS_r + SS_c) = 83.00 - (27.50 + .250 + 49.00) = 83.00 - 76.75 = 6.25$

df_r = number of rows $- 1 = 2 - 1 = 1$

df_c = number of columns $- 1 = 2 - 1 = 1$

$df_{r \times c} = df_r \cdot df_c = ($number of rows $- 1) \cdot ($number of columns $- 1) = (2 - 1) \cdot (2 - 1) = 1$

$df_{wg} = N_{total} -$ number of cells $= 16 - 4 = 12$

$df_{total} = N_{total} - 1 = 16 - 1 = 15$

$$MS_r = \frac{SS_r}{df_r} = \frac{.25}{1} = .25; \quad MS_c = \frac{SS_c}{df_c} = \frac{49.00}{1} = 49.00$$

$$MS_{r \times c} = \frac{SS_{r \times c}}{df_{r \times c}} = \frac{6.25}{1} = 6.25; \quad MS_{wg} = \frac{SS_{wg}}{df_{wg}} = \frac{27.50}{12} = 2.292$$

$$F_r = \frac{MS_r}{MS_{wg}} = \frac{.25}{2.292} = .109; F_c = \frac{MS_c}{MS_{wg}} = \frac{49.00}{2.292} = 21.378$$

$$F_{r \times c} = \frac{MS_{r \times c}}{MS_{wg}} = \frac{6.250}{2.292} = 2.727$$

Comparison of computed F ratios to critical values:

Source of Variation	Computed F Ratio	Critical F Value, $\alpha = .05$	Decision
Institution Mentioned	.10	$(df = 1, 12) = 4.75$	Fail to reject
Presence of Photograph	21.378	$(df = 1, 12) = 4.75$	Reject the null
Interaction 1 $\times$ P	2.727	$(df = 1, 12) = 4.75$	Fail to reject

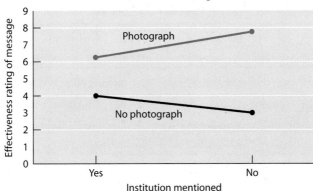

Effectiveness of Animal Rights Issues

There was no significant effect detected on the effectiveness ratings of the animal rights message when the institution was or was not mentioned. However, when the photograph of the researcher was present, the message was rated significantly more effective than when the photograph was absent. As shown in the figure, there was no interaction of the institution being mentioned or the presence or absence of the researcher's photograph on the effectiveness ratings of the message.

Problems From the Literature

9. Null hypothesis: There will be no difference in the number of years the defendant is sentenced when the victim's sexual orientation is heterosexual, homosexual, or bisexual. ($H_{0_1}: \mu_1 = \mu_2 = \mu_3$)
   Research hypothesis: There will be a difference in the number of years the defendant is sentenced when the victim's sexual orientation is heterosexual, homosexual, or bisexual. ($H_1: \mu_1 \neq \mu_2 \neq \mu_3$)
   Null hypothesis: There will be no difference in the number of years sentenced when the defendant's sexual orientation is heterosexual, homosexual, or bisexual. ($H_{0_2}: \mu_1 = \mu_2 = \mu_3$)
   Research hypothesis: There will be a difference in the number of years sentenced when the defendant's sexual orientation is heterosexual, homosexual, or bisexual. ($H_2: \mu_1 \neq \mu_2 \neq \mu_3$)

Null hypothesis: There will be no interaction of the victim's sexual orientation and the defendant's sexual orientation on the number of years the defendant is sentenced. Research hypothesis: There will be an interaction of the victim's sexual orientation and the defendant's sexual orientation on the number of years the defendant is sentenced.

Source of Variation	Sums of Squares	Degrees of Freedom	Mean Square	F	p
Rows (victim's orientation)	1,043.389	2	521.695	133.837	< .05
Columns (defendant's orientation)	137.722	2	68.861	17.666	< .05
Interaction (VSO × DSO)	225.278	4	56.320	14.448	< .05
Within	105.250	27	3.898		
Total	1,511.639	35			

Summary data are as follows:

	Heterosexual (V)	Homosexual (V)	Bisexual (V)	
Heterosexual (D)	$\Sigma X = 80$ $\Sigma X^2 = 1,608$ $\bar{X} = 20, n = 4$	$\Sigma X = 62$ $\Sigma X^2 = 966$ $\bar{X} = 15.5, n = 4$	$\Sigma X = 62$ $\Sigma X^2 = 970$ $\bar{X} = 15.5, n = 4$	$\Sigma X_{row1} = 204$ $\Sigma X^2_{row1} = 3,544$ $n_{row1} = 12$
Homosexual (D)	$\Sigma X = 107$ $\Sigma X^2 = 2,885$ $\bar{X} = 26.7, n = 4$	$\Sigma X = 36$ $\Sigma X^2 = 334$ $\bar{X} = 9, n = 4$	$\Sigma X = 39$ $\Sigma X^2 = 383$ $\bar{X} = 9.75, n = 4$	$\Sigma X_{row2} = 182$ $\Sigma X^2_{row2} = 3,602$ $n_{row2} = 12$
Bisexual (D)	$\Sigma X = 82$ $\Sigma X^2 = 1,698$ $\bar{X} = 20.5, n = 4$	$\Sigma X = 32$ $\Sigma X^2 = 270$ $\bar{X} = 8.0, n = 4$	$\Sigma X = 33$ $\Sigma X^2 = 289$ $\bar{X} = 8.25, n = 4$	$\Sigma X_{row3} = 147$ $\Sigma X^2_{row3} = 2,257$ $n_{row3} = 12$
	$\Sigma X_{col1} = 269$ $\Sigma X^2_{col1} = 6,191$ $n_{col1} = 10$	$\Sigma X_{col2} = 130$ $\Sigma X^2_{col2} = 1,570$ $n_{col2} = 10$	$\Sigma X_{col3} = 134$ $\Sigma X^2_{col3} = 1,642$ $n_{col3} = 10$	$\Sigma\Sigma X = 533$ $\Sigma\Sigma X^2 = 9,403$ $N_{total} = 36$

$$SS_{total} = \Sigma\Sigma X^2 - \frac{(\Sigma\Sigma X)^2}{N_{total}} = 9,403 - \frac{533^2}{36} = 9,403 - \frac{284,089}{36} =$$

$$9,403 - 7,891.361 = 1,511.639$$

$$SS_{wg} = \Sigma\Sigma X^2 - \frac{\Sigma(\Sigma X_{cell})^2}{n_{cell}} = 9,403 -$$

$$\frac{80^2 + 62^2 + 62^2 + 107^2 + 36^2 + 39^2 + 82^2 + 32^2 + 33^3}{4} = 9,403 -$$

$$\frac{6,400 + 3,844 + 3,844 + 11,449 + 1,296 + 1,521 + 6,724 + 1,024 + 1,089}{4} =$$

$$9,403 - \frac{37,191}{4} = 9,403 - 9,297.75 = 105.25$$

$$SS_r = \frac{\Sigma(\Sigma X_{row})^2}{n_{row}} - \frac{(\Sigma\Sigma X)^2}{N_{total}} = \frac{204^2 + 182^2 + 147^2}{12} - \frac{533^2}{36} =$$

$$\frac{41,616 + 33,124 + 21,609}{12} - \frac{284,089}{36} = \frac{96,349}{12} -$$

$$7,891.361 = 8,029.083 - 7,891.361 = 137.722$$

$$SS_c = \frac{\Sigma(\Sigma X_{col})^2}{n_{col}} - \frac{(\Sigma\Sigma X)^2}{N_{total}} = \frac{269^2 + 130^2 + 134^2}{12} - \frac{533^2}{36} =$$

$$\frac{107,217}{12} - \frac{284,089}{36} = 8,934.75 - 7,891.36 = 1,043.389$$

$$SS_{r \times c} = SS_{total} - (SS_{wg} + SS_r + SS_c) = 1,511.639 -$$
$$(105.250 + 1,043.389 + 137.722) = 1,511.639 - 1,286.361 = 225.278$$

df_r = number of rows $- 1 = 3 - 1 = 2$

df_c = number of columns $- 1 = 3 - 1 = 2$

$df_{r \times c} = df_r \cdot df_c$ = (number of rows $- 1$) $\cdot$ (number of columns $- 1$) =
$(3 - 1) \cdot (3 - 1) = 4$

$df_{wg} = N_{total}$ $-$ number of cells $= 36 - 9 = 27$

$df_{total} = N_{total} - 1 = 36 - 1 = 35$

$$MS_r = \frac{SS_r}{df_r} = \frac{1,043.389}{2} = 521.695; \quad MS_c = \frac{SS_c}{df_c} = \frac{137.722}{2} = 68.861$$

$$MS_{r \times c} = \frac{SS_{r \times c}}{df_{r \times c}} = \frac{225.278}{4} = 56.320; \quad MS_{wg} = \frac{SS_{wg}}{df_{wg}} = \frac{105.250}{27} = 3.898$$

$$F_r = \frac{MS_r}{MS_{wg}} = \frac{521.695}{3.898} = 133.837; \quad F_c = \frac{MS_c}{MS_{wg}} = \frac{68.861}{3.898} = 17.666$$

$$F_{r \times c} = \frac{MS_{r \times c}}{MS_{wg}} = \frac{56.320}{3.898} = 14.448$$

Comparison of computed F ratios to critical values:

Source of Variation	Computer F Ratio	Critical F Value, $\alpha = .05$	Decision
Victim's Sexual Orientation	133.837	$(df = 2, 27) = 3.35$	Reject null hypothesis
Defendant's Sexual Orientation	17.666	$(df = 2, 27) = 3.35$	Reject null hypothesis
Interaction VSO $\times$ DSO	14.448	$(df = 4, 27) = 2.73$	Reject null hypothesis

Post-hoc Tukey HSD for victim's sexual orientation:

$$HSD = q \cdot \sqrt{\frac{MS_{wg}}{n}} = 3.49 \cdot \sqrt{\frac{3.898}{4}} = 3.53 \cdot \sqrt{.9745} = 3.49 \cdot .987 = 3.445$$

*The difference is significant.

$\overline{X}_{Hetero} - \overline{X}_{Homo} = 22.417 - 10.833 = 11.584$ years*

$\overline{X}_{Hetero} - \overline{X}_{Bisex} = 22.417 - 11.167 = 11.25$ years*

$\overline{X}_{Homo} - \overline{X}_{Bisex} = 10.833 - 11.167 = -.334$ years

Post-hoc Tukey HSD for defendant's sexual orientation:

$$\text{HSD} = q \cdot \sqrt{\frac{MS_{\text{wg}}}{n}} = 3.49 \cdot \sqrt{\frac{3.898}{4}} = 3.53 \cdot \sqrt{.9745} = 3.49 \cdot .987 = 3.445$$

*The difference is significant.

$\overline{X}_{\text{Hetero}} - \overline{X}_{\text{Homo}} = 17.00 - 15.167 = 1.833$ years

$\overline{X}_{\text{Hetero}} - \overline{X}_{\text{Bisex}} = 17.00 - 12.25 = 4.75$ years*

$\overline{X}_{\text{Homo}} - \overline{X}_{\text{Bisex}} = 15.167 - 12.25 = 2.917$ years

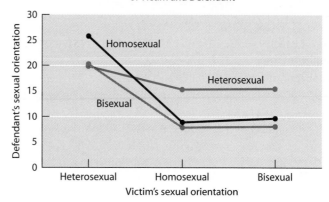

Interaction of Sexual Orientation
of Victim and Defendant

Participants sentenced the defendant to significantly more years in jail when the victim's sexual orientation was heterosexual than when it was homosexual or bisexual. However, there was no significant difference in the number of years the defendant was sentenced when the victim's sexual orientation was homosexual compared to bisexual.

When the defendant's sexual orientation was depicted as heterosexual compared to bisexual, participants sentenced the defendant to significantly more years in jail. There was no significant difference in the number of years sentenced when the defendant was depicted as heterosexual compared to homosexual or homosexual compared to bisexual.

There was a significant interaction of the victim's sexual orientation and defendant's sexual orientation in the number of years participants sentenced the defendant. In particular, participants assigned the most years in jail when the defendant's and victim's sexual orientation were both homosexual. On the other hand, when the victim's sexual orientation was homosexual and the defendant's was bisexual, the least number of years were given to the defendant.

Chapter 15

1. $\chi^2 = \sum \dfrac{(f_o - f_e)^2}{f_e} = \dfrac{(1{,}230 - 1{,}000)^2}{1{,}000} + \dfrac{(740 - 1{,}000)^2}{1{,}000} + \dfrac{(1{,}030 - 1{,}000)^2}{1{,}000} =$

$\dfrac{230^2}{1{,}000} + \dfrac{(260)^2}{1{,}000} + \dfrac{(30)^2}{1{,}000} = \dfrac{52{,}900}{1{,}000} + \dfrac{67{,}600}{1{,}000} + \dfrac{900}{1{,}000} =$

$52.90 + 67.60 + .90 = 121.4$

$df = $ number of cells $- 1 = 2$; critical value $= 5.99$

There was a statistical difference between the three categories of burger wrapping materials. Significantly more people preferred foil over paper and foam.

3. $f_e = \dfrac{(\text{row total}) \cdot (\text{column total})}{\text{grand total}} = \dfrac{(33 \cdot 32)}{64} = \dfrac{1{,}056}{64} = 16.5; \dfrac{(33 \cdot 32)}{64} =$

$\dfrac{1{,}056}{64} = 16.5; \dfrac{(31 \cdot 32)}{64} = \dfrac{992}{64} = 15.5; \dfrac{(31 \cdot 32)}{64} = \dfrac{992}{64} = 15.5$

$\chi^2 = \sum \dfrac{(f_o - f_e)^2}{f_e} = \dfrac{(25 - 16.5)^2}{16.5} + \dfrac{(8 - 16.5)^2}{16.5} + \dfrac{(7 - 15.5)^2}{15.5} + \dfrac{(24 - 15.5)^2}{15.5} =$

$\dfrac{72.25}{16.5} + \dfrac{72.25}{16.5} + \dfrac{72.25}{15.5} + \dfrac{72.25}{15.5} = 4.379 + 4.379 + 4.661 + 4.661 = 18.08$

$df = (\text{number of rows} - 1) \cdot (\text{number of columns} - 1) = 2 - 1 \cdot 2 - 1 = 1$; critical value = 3.841.

There were significantly more people who stopped the thief when a student was asked to help watch the items, and more people did not stop the thief when the belongings were left unattended.

5. $f_e = \dfrac{(\text{row total}) \cdot (\text{column total})}{\text{grand total}} = \dfrac{(26 \cdot 65)}{150} = \dfrac{(1{,}690)}{150} = 11.267; \dfrac{(26 \cdot 85)}{150} =$

$\dfrac{(2{,}210)}{150} = 14.733; \dfrac{(45 \cdot 65)}{150} = \dfrac{(2{,}925)}{150} = 19.5; \dfrac{(45 \cdot 85)}{150} =$

$\dfrac{(3{,}825)}{150} = 25.5; \dfrac{(50 \cdot 65)}{150} = \dfrac{(3{,}250)}{150} = 21.667; \dfrac{(50 \cdot 85)}{150} =$

$\dfrac{(4{,}250)}{150} = 28.333; \dfrac{(29 \cdot 65)}{150} = \dfrac{(1{,}885)}{150} = 12.567; = \dfrac{(29 \cdot 85)}{150} =$

$\dfrac{(2{,}465)}{150} = 16.43$

$\chi^2 = \sum \dfrac{(f_o - f_e)^2}{f_e} = \dfrac{(23 - 11.27)^2}{11.27} + \dfrac{(3 - 14.73)^2}{14.733} + \dfrac{(25 - 19.5)^2}{19.5} +$

$\dfrac{(20 - 25.5)^2}{25.5} + \dfrac{(20 - 25.5)^2}{25.5} + \dfrac{(15 - 21.667)^2}{21.667} + \dfrac{(35 - 28.333)^2}{28.333} +$

$\dfrac{(2 - 12.567)^2}{12.567} + \dfrac{(27 - 16.433)^2}{16.433} = \dfrac{137.593}{11.27} + \dfrac{137.663}{14.733} + \dfrac{30.25}{19.5} +$

$\dfrac{30.25}{25.5} + \dfrac{44.449}{21.667} + \dfrac{44.449}{28.333} + \dfrac{111.661}{12.567} + \dfrac{111.661}{16.433} = 12.2088 + 9.348 +$

$1.551 + 1.186 + 2.051 + 1.569 + 8.885 + 6.795 = 43.59$

$df = (\text{number of rows} - 1) \cdot (\text{number of columns} - 1) =$
$4 - 1 \cdot 2 - 1 = 3$; critical value = 7.815.

There were significant differences in the number of people reporting supernatural experiences depending on the level of educational attainment.

7. $U_1 = (n_1 \cdot n_2) + \dfrac{n_1(n_1 + 1)}{2} - \Sigma R_1 = (8 \cdot 12) + \dfrac{8(8 + 1)}{2} - 113 =$

$96 + \dfrac{72}{2} - 113 = 96 + 36 - 113 = 19$

$$U_2 = (n_2 \cdot n_1) + \frac{n_2(n_2 + 1)}{2} - \Sigma R_2 = (12 \cdot 8) + \frac{12(12 + 1)}{2} - 97 =$$

$$96 + \frac{156}{2} - 97 = 96 + 78 - 97 = 77$$

U_1 is smaller and is used to determine statistical significance. Critical value = 22. There is a statistical difference between the rankings of the two groups of professors. Professors with 5 or more years experience were ranked higher than their colleagues with less experience.

9. $$U_1 = (n_1 \cdot n_2) + \frac{n_1(n_1 + 1)}{2} - \Sigma R_1 = (11 \cdot 10) + \frac{11(11 + 1)}{2} - 63 =$$

$$110 + \frac{132}{2} - 63 = 110 + 66 - 63 = 113$$

$$U_2 = (n_2 \cdot n_1) + \frac{n_2(n_2 + 1)}{2} - \Sigma R_2 = (10 \cdot 11) + \frac{10(10 + 1)}{2} - 62 =$$

$$110 + \frac{110}{2} - 62 = 110 + 55 - 62 = 103$$

U_2 is smaller and is used to determine statistical significance. Critical value = 26. Not significant.

11. $$U_1 = (n_1 \cdot n_2) + \frac{n_1(n_1 + 1)}{2} - \Sigma R_1 = (10 \cdot 10) + \frac{10(10 + 1)}{2} - 123 =$$

$$100 + \frac{110}{2} - 123 = 100 + 55 - 123 = 32$$

$$U_2 = (n_2 \cdot n_1) + \frac{n_2(n_2 + 1)}{2} - \Sigma R_2 = (10 \cdot 10) + \frac{10(10 + 1)}{2} - 87 =$$

$$100 + \frac{110}{2} - 87 = 100 + 55 - 87 = 68$$

U_1 is smaller and is used to determine statistical significance. Critical value = 23. Not significant.

13.

			Diet			
Pair	Protein Rich	Protein Deficient	Difference	Rank	+ Rank	− Rank
1	23	20	3	3.5	3.5	
2	26	23	3	3.5	3.5	
3	21	21	Out	Out		
4	17	19	−2	2		2
5	15	16	−1	1		1
6	29	21	8	7	7	
7	27	22	5	6	6	
8	33	20	13	9	9	
9	21	17	4	5	5	
10	28	19	9	8	8	
					Σ + rank = 42	Σ − rank = 3

$T = 3$; nondirectional with $n = 9$, T critical value $= 5$. $T = 3$ is significant. There was a statistically significant difference in ranking between the CRT-type and flat-panel monitors.

15.

Patient	Pretest	Posttest	Difference	Rank	+ Rank	− Rank
P. J.	10	7	3	4	4	
O. C.	22	12	10	9	9	
D. J.	18	19	−1	3.5		2
S. R.	15	7	8	8	8	
M. P.	22	21	1	3.5	2	
D. T.	9	3	6	6.5	6.5	
M. M.	4	0	4	5	5	
L. N.	16	17	−1	3.5		2
D. H.	8	2	6	6.5	6.5	

$$\Sigma + \text{rank} = 41.0 \quad \Sigma - \text{rank} = 7$$

$T = 4$; nondirectional with $n = 9$, T critical value $= 5$. T of 4 is significant.

17.

Rat	Dark	Light	Difference	Rank	+ Rank	− Rank
1	23	18	5	5.5	5.5	
2	18	28	−10	7		7
3	14	14	Out	Out		
4	22	21	1	1	1	
5	33	35	−2	2.5		2.5
6	27	29	−2	2.5		2.5
7	9	12	−3	4		4
8	22	17	5	5.5	5.5	

$$\Sigma + \text{rank} = 12 \quad \Sigma - \text{rank} = 16$$

$T = 12$; nondirectional with $n = 7$, T critical value $= 2$. Not significant.

19. Data were first combined and then ranked. Results are as follows:

One Night	R_1	Two Nights	R_2	Three Nights	R_3	Four Nights	R_4
100	2	120	5	140	12	160	19
122	7.5	137	10	145	14	173	20
97	1	129	9	147	15	158	18
110	4	122	7.5	151	16.5	151	16.5
109	3	121	6	139	11	144	13

$n_1 = 5 \quad \Sigma R_1 = 17.5 \quad n_2 = 5 \quad \Sigma R_2 = 37.5 \quad n_3 = 5 \quad \Sigma R_3 = 68.5 \quad n_4 = 5 \quad \Sigma R_4 = 86.5$

$$H = \left[\frac{12}{N_{total} \cdot (N_{total} + 1)} \right] \cdot \left[\frac{(\Sigma R_1)^2}{n_1} + \frac{(\Sigma R_2)^2}{n_2} + \cdots + \frac{(\Sigma R_k)^2}{n_k} \right] -$$

$$[3 \cdot (N_{total} + 1)] = \left[\frac{12}{20 \cdot (20 + 1)} \right] \cdot \left[\frac{(17.5)^2}{5} + \frac{(37.5)^2}{5} + \frac{(68.5)^2}{5} + \frac{(86.5)^2}{5} \right] -$$

$$[3 \cdot (20 + 1)] = \left[\frac{12}{20 \cdot (21)} \right] \cdot \left[\frac{306.25}{5} + \frac{1,406.25}{5} + \frac{4,692.25}{5} + \frac{7,482.25}{5} \right] -$$

$$63 = \frac{12}{420} \cdot (61.25 + 281.25 + 938.45 + 1,496.45) - 63 = (.0286) \cdot 2,777.4 -$$

$63 = 79.434 - 63 = 16.434$

$df = k - 1 = 4 - 1 = 3$

Critical value of $H = 7.815$. H is significant. Reject the null hypothesis.

21. Data were first combined and then ranked. Results are as follows:

Words	R_1	Nonwords	R_2	Numbers	R_3
28	19.5	15	13	6	4
29	21.5	14	10.5	6	4
37	24	15	13	5	1.5
30	23	16	15	7	7
29	21.5	23	18	5	1.5
18	17	15	13	6	4
28	19.5	14	10.5	7	7
17	16	13	9	7	7
$n_1 = 8$	$\Sigma R_1 = 162$	$n_2 = 8$	$\Sigma R_2 = 102$	$n_3 = 8$	$\Sigma R_3 = 36$

$$H = \left[\frac{12}{N_{total} \cdot (N_{total} + 1)} \right] \cdot \left[\frac{(\Sigma R_1)^2}{n_1} + \frac{(\Sigma R_2)^2}{n_2} + \cdots + \frac{(\Sigma R_k)^2}{n_k} \right] -$$

$$[3 \cdot (N_{total} + 1)] = \left[\frac{12}{24 \cdot (24 + 1)} \right] \cdot \left[\frac{(162)^2}{8} + \frac{(102)^2}{8} + \frac{(36)^2}{8} \right] -$$

$$[3 \cdot (24 + 1)] = \left[\frac{12}{24 \cdot (25)} \right] \cdot \left[\frac{26,244}{8} + \frac{10,404}{8} + \frac{1,296}{8} \right] - 75 =$$

$$\frac{12}{600} \cdot (3,280.5 + 1,300.5 + 162) - 75 = (.02) \cdot 4,743 -$$

$75 = 94.86 - 75 = 19.86$

$df = k - 1 = 3 - 1 = 2$

Critical value of $H = 5.99$. H is significant. Reject the null hypothesis. There was a significant difference in the number of words remembered between the words, nonwords, and numbers conditions.

Problems From the Literature

23. $f_e = \dfrac{(\text{row total}) \cdot (\text{column total})}{\text{grand total}} = \dfrac{(300 \cdot 218)}{600} = \dfrac{65,400}{600} = 109; \dfrac{(300 \cdot 190)}{600} =$

$$\frac{57{,}000}{600} = 95; \quad \frac{(300 \cdot 192)}{600} = \frac{57{,}600}{600} = 96$$

The second row is identical.

$$\chi^2 = \sum \frac{(f_o - f_e)^2}{f_e} = \frac{(103 - 109)^2}{109} + \frac{(105 - 95)^2}{95} + \frac{(92 - 96)^2}{96} +$$

$$\frac{(115 - 109)^2}{109} + \frac{(85 - 95)^2}{95} + \frac{(100 - 96)^2}{96} + \frac{(115 - 109)^2}{109} = \frac{36}{109} +$$

$$\frac{100}{95} + \frac{16}{96} + \frac{36}{109} + \frac{100}{95} + \frac{16}{96} = .3303 + 1.0526 + .1667 + .3303 +$$

$1.0526 + .1667 = 3.099$

$df = $ (number of rows -1) $\cdot$ (number of columns $- 1$) $= 3 - 1 \cdot 2 - 1 = 2$
Critical value $= 5.99$. Fail to reject the null hypothesis.

25. $U_1 = (n_1 \cdot n_2) + \dfrac{n_1(n_1 + 1)}{2} - \Sigma R_1 = (9 \cdot 11) + \dfrac{9(9 + 1)}{2} - 64 =$

$$99 + \frac{90}{2} - 64 = 99 + 45 - 64 = 80$$

$$U_2 = (n_2 \cdot n_1) + \frac{n_2(n_2 + 1)}{2} - \Sigma R_2 = (11 \cdot 9) + \frac{11(11 + 1)}{2} - 146 =$$

$$99 + \frac{132}{2} - 64 = 99 + 66 - 146 = 19$$

U_2 is smaller and is used to determine statistical significance. Critical value $= 23$. There are significant differences in the rankings between salespeople that use and don't use time management.

27. $f_e = \dfrac{(\text{row total}) \cdot (\text{column total})}{\text{grand total}} = \dfrac{(35 \cdot 29)}{56} + \dfrac{(35 \cdot 27)}{56} + \dfrac{(21 \cdot 29)}{56} + \dfrac{(21 \cdot 27)}{56}$

$$\chi^2 = \sum \frac{(f_o - f_e)^2}{f_e} = \frac{(21 - 18.125)^2}{18.125} + \frac{(14 - 16.875)^2}{16.875} + \frac{(8 - 10.875)^2}{10.875} +$$

$$\frac{(13 - 10.125)^2}{10.125} = \frac{8.2656}{18.125} + \frac{8.2656}{16.875} + \frac{8.2656}{16.875} + \frac{8.2656}{10.875} = .456 + .490 +$$

$.76 + .816 = 2.522$

$df = $ (number of rows -1) $\cdot$ (number of columns $- 1$) $= 2 - 1 \cdot 2 - 1 = 1$
Critical value $= 3.841$. Fail to reject the null hypothesis.

29. $f_e = \dfrac{(\text{row total}) \cdot (\text{column total})}{\text{grand total}} = \dfrac{(44 \cdot 116)}{196} = \dfrac{5{,}104}{96} = 26.041$

$$\frac{(44 \cdot 80)}{196} = \frac{3{,}520}{196} = 17.959; \quad \frac{(79 \cdot 116)}{196} = \frac{9{,}164}{196} = 46.755$$

$$\frac{(79 \cdot 80)}{196} = \frac{6{,}320}{196} = 32.245; \quad \frac{(73 \cdot 116)}{196} = \frac{8{,}468}{196} = 43.204$$

$$\frac{(73 \cdot 80)}{196} = \frac{5{,}840}{196} = 29.80$$

$$\chi^2 = \sum \frac{(f_o - f_e)^2}{f_e} = \frac{(18 - 26.041)^2}{26.041} + \frac{(26 - 17.959)^2}{17.959} + \frac{(51 - 46.755)^2}{46.755} +$$

$$\frac{(28 - 32.245)^2}{32.245} + \frac{(47 - 43.204)^2}{43.204} + \frac{(26 - 29.80)^2}{29.80} = \frac{64.658}{26.041} + \frac{64.658}{17.959} +$$

$$\frac{18.02}{46.755} + \frac{18.02}{32.245} + \frac{14.44}{43.204} + \frac{14.44}{29.80} = 2.483 + 3.60 + .385 + .559 + .334 +$$

$.485 = 7.84$

$df = (\text{number of rows} - 1) \cdot (\text{number of columns} - 1) = (3 - 1) \cdot (2 - 1) = 2$
Critical value $= 5.991$. There were significant age differences in the number of accurate displays of the medical exam using the anatomical doll.

31. $U_1 = (n_1 \cdot n_2) + \dfrac{n_1(n_1 + 1)}{2} - \Sigma R_1 = (10 \cdot 12) + \dfrac{10(10 + 1)}{2} - 160 =$

$120 + \dfrac{110}{2} - 160 = 120 + 55 - 160 = 15$

$U_2 = (n_2 \cdot n_1) + \dfrac{n_2(n_2 + 1)}{2} - \Sigma R_2 = (12 \cdot 10) + \dfrac{12(12 + 1)}{2} - 133 =$

$120 + \dfrac{156}{2} - 130 = 120 + 78 - 130 = 65$

U_1 is smaller and is used to determine statistical significance. Critical value $= 29$. This is significant.

Index

abscissa, 52–54
accuracy of calculations, 6–7
adding a constant, 138–139
addition rule of probability, 235
alpha (α), 272, 275–276, 328
analysis of variance, 328. *See also*
  one-way analysis of variance;
  two-way analysis of variance
apparent limits, 29
areas under normal curve, 159–162
  above *z*, 162–164
  below *z*, 164–166
  visual summaries, 166, 171
  between *z* scores, 168–171
arithmetic mean. *See* mean
average. *See* measures of central
  tendency
average mean deviation (*AMD*),
  114–115
axes, 52–54

bar graphs. *See* histograms
bell curve. *See* normal curve
beta (β), 275–276
between-groups variance estimate,
  331–332
between-subjects design, 259,
  260–261
bimodal distribution, 87
boxplots, 92–94

calculators
  purchasing decision, 5–6
  rounding answers, 6–7
causation, 196–197, 198, 257, 258
central limit theorem, 243–244, 290

chi-square test, 387–393, 416
  assumptions of, 392
  limitations of, 392–393
  with two variables, 390–392
  visual summary, 394
class intervals, 24–29
  apparent and real limits, 29–30
  midpoints, 30–32
  visual summary, 33
coefficient of determination,
  197–198, 210
control group, 296
correlated samples
  t test, 302–308, 309, 310
  Wilcoxon *T* test, 404–409, 410, 416
correlation, 180–184
  causation and, 196–197, 198, 258
correlation coefficient (*r*), 184, 188
  computational formula, 191–193
  regression line and, 214–221
  significance of, 193–197
  visual summary, 190
covariance, 184–188
  computational formula, 191–192
  regression line and, 214
  visual summary, 190
critical value, 195–196
cumulative frequency, 34–36
cumulative frequency polygon,
  63–64
cumulative percent, 39
  See also percentiles
cumulative percent polygon, 65
cumulative relative frequency, 38–39
cumulative relative frequency
  polygon, 64–65

data. *See* ranked data; raw data;
  skewed data
deception, 268
degrees of freedom (*df*)
  for chi-square test, 389, 392, 393
  for correlation coefficient, 195
  meaning of, 293–294
  for one-way analysis of variance,
  336
  for *t* test, correlated-sample,
  304–305
  for *t* test, single-sample, 292–293
  for *t* test, two-sample, 298
  for two-way analysis of variance,
  369–370
demand characteristics, 267–268
dependent variable, 9, 52, 54,
  256–257
descriptive statistics, 396
deviation scores, 114–115
difference method, 306–307
discarding data, 268
distributions
  comparisons of, 36–39, 59–61,
  136–137
  of differences between means,
  296–299
  graphs of, 52–54
  probability and, 234
  ranked, 23–24
  of sample means, 241–244,
  271–272, 290
  scaling of, 137–141
  simple frequency, 24
  skew of, 89–94
  of *t* scores, 290

distributions *(continued)*
  of *z* scores, 144
  See also grouped frequency
    distributions; normal curve
dividing by constant, 139, 141

effect size, 197, 310
error. *See* standard error of difference;
  standard error of estimate;
  standard error of mean; Type I
  error; Type II error
estimates
  defined, 15
  See also prediction
expected frequency, 388, 390–391,
  392–393
experimenter bias, 267
experiments
  causation and, 196–197, 198, 258
  control of, 265–268, 296
  designs of, 259–264, 356–358
  literature search and, 255, 274
  See also hypotheses; variables
extraneous variables, 9, 266–267,
  268

factorial experiment, 264, 356–358
falsifiability, 256
F ratio
  one-way analysis of variance, 332,
    336–337, 339–342, 343
  two-way analysis of variance,
    372–373, 374, 375, 376
frequency, 24
  in class interval, 27–28
  cumulative, 34–36
  cumulative relative, 38–39
  expected, 388, 390–391, 392–393
  observed, 387–388
  relative, 36–39, 234
frequency distributions. *See* grouped
  frequency distributions
frequency histogram, 55–58
frequency polygon, 58–59
  cumulative, 63–64
  relative, 59–61
  of sampling distribution,
    242–243
  skew of, 89

graphs
  basic construction of, 51–54
  boxplots, 92–94
  changing shape of, 67–69
  critical evaluation of, 49–51, 67–69
  histograms, 55–58
  polygons, 55, 58–61, 63–65
  of regression equation, 216–221
  stem-and-leaf diagrams, 66–67
grouped frequency distributions,
  24–33
  comparisons of, 36–39, 59–61
  frequency polygons of, 58–61,
    63–65
  histograms of, 55–58
  mean, 95–98
  median, 99–100, 101
  mode, 100
  standard deviation, 124–127
  variance, 124–127
  visual summary, 32

H. See Kruskal–Wallis test
H_0. *See* null hypothesis
H_1. *See* research hypothesis
histograms, 55–58
homoscedasticity, 222
HSD test
  one-way analysis of variance, 342,
    344
  two-way analysis of variance,
    375–376
hypotheses, 7–8, 255–256, 269–276
  for analysis of variance, 328–329
  for nonparametric test, 396

independent events, 236
independent-group design, 259,
  260–261
independent variables, 9
  experimental designs and, 256,
    257, 258, 259–264
  on graph, 52, 54
  one-way analysis of variance, 328,
    331
  two-way analysis of variance,
    355–356
inferential statistics, 396
inner fence, 92

interaction, 359–361, 376–377
interval scales, 11, 12–13, 14
  analysis of variance and, 387
  measure of central tendency for,
    92

Kruskal–Wallis test, 411–414

line, equation for, 213
linear regression. *See* regression;
  regression equations
linear relationship, 208
literature search, 255, 274

main effects, 358–359, 375–376
Mann–Whitney *U* test, 395–403
  with more than two groups, 411,
    413
  visual summary, 402
mean, 78–80
  of grouped frequency distribution,
    95–98
  of normal distribution, 156
  of population, 79, 80, 240, 241,
    243–244
  regression toward, 209–210
  of sample, 79–80, 239–240
  of sample means, 241, 244–245
  of scaled scores, 138, 139, 141
  of skewed distribution, 89–90
  standard error of, 241–243,
    244–245, 246, 288
  visual summary, 81
  when to use, 90–91, 92
  of *z*-score distribution, 144
  See also sample means
mean deviation, 114–115
mean square (*MS*), 330
  one-way analysis of variance,
    331–332, 333–336, 339–344
  two-way analysis of variance,
    370–372, 374, 375
measurement scales, 11–14, 92
measures of central tendency, 78
  of frequency distribution, 95–102
  misleading use of, 77–78
  summary, 103–104
  which to use, 89–92
  See also mean; median; mode

measures of variability, 112–113
  average mean deviation, 114–115
  of frequency distribution,
    124–127
  range, 113–114
  See also standard deviation;
    variance
median, 82–84
  of grouped frequency distribution,
    99–100, 101
  of normal distribution, 156
  quartiles and, 84–86
  of skewed distribution, 89–90, 91
  when to use, 91, 92
midpoint, of class interval, 30–32
mixed design, 259, 261–262
mode, 86–87
  of grouped frequency distribution,
    100
  of normal distribution, 156
  of skewed distribution, 89–90, 91
  when to use, 91–92
MS. *See* mean square
multimodal distribution, 87
multiplication rule of probability,
    236
multiplying by constant, 139
mutually exclusive events, 234–235

N (size of population), 14
n (size of sample), 15
negative correlation, 182, 184, 188
negative skew, 89
nominal scales, 11–12, 14
  chi-square test and, 387, 392
  mode and, 92
nonexperimental research, 258
nonlinear relationship, 208
nonparametric statistics, 396,
    415–416
  chi-square test, 387–393, 394, 416
  with correlated samples, 404–409,
    410, 416
  Kruskal–Wallis test, 411–414
  Mann–Whitney *U* test, 395–402,
    403, 411, 413
  visual summary, 416
  Wilcoxon *T* test, 404–410, 416
normal curve, 154–177

areas under, 159–166, 168–171
characteristics of, 155–158
percentages under, 160, 162
percentiles and, 172–175
probabilities and, 160, 162, 236–237
scientific data and, 154–155
normal distribution, 155
  of sample means, 243–244,
    271–272, 290
notation, 6
null hypothesis (H_0), 8, 269–271,
    275–276
  for analysis of variance, 328–329
  for nonparametric test, 396

observed frequency, 387–388
ogive, 64
one-group experimental design, 263
one-tailed tests, 272, 274
  with *t* score, 292–293
  with *z* score, 289
one-way analysis of variance,
    326–347
  basic principles, 328–332
  computational formulas, 339–344
  degrees of freedom, 336
  F test in, 332, 336–337, 339–342,
    343
  HSD test with, 342, 344
  mean squares, 330, 331–332,
    333–336, 339–344
  nonparametric counterpart of, 411
  scales of measurement and, 387
  sums of squares, 339–341, 343
  visual summary, 337
ordinal scales, 11, 12, 14
  Mann–Whitney *U* test and, 396
  median and, 92
ordinate, 52–54
outliers, 92, 93

parameters, defined, 15
parametric statistics, 276, 396
percentages, 160, 162
percentiles, 39, 65, 172–175
pie graph, 50–51
pilot study, 268
polygons, 55, 58–61, 63–65
population, 14–15

estimated variance of, 330–332
  mean of, 79, 80, 240, 241, 243–244
  parametric statistics and, 276,
    396
  standard deviation of, 118, 120
  variance of, 117, 120, 123
positive correlation, 181–182, 184, 188
positive skew, 89
post-hoc tests, 342, 344, 375–376
power, 275–277
  of *t* tests, 309–310
prediction
  coefficient of determination and,
    197–198, 210
  with regression equation,
    213–221, 223
  standard error of estimate, 221–223
  with *z*-score method, 206–212
probability, 160, 162, 232–237
p value, 341, 342

q (Studentized Range Statistic), 344,
    435
qualitative variables. *See* nominal
    scales
quartiles, 84–86
  on boxplot, 92–94
  of normal distribution, 175

r. See correlation coefficient
randomized experimental design,
    263–264
random number table, 239, 431
random sampling, 238–240
range, 113–114
  of grouped frequency distribution,
    26
  interquartile, 92
ranked data, 12, 14, 23–24
  Mann–Whitney *U* test and,
    395–402, 403
  Wilcoxon *T* test and, 405–410
ratio scales, 11, 13, 14
  analysis of variance and, 387
  measure of central tendency for,
    92
raw data, 23
  reconstruction of, 96
  visual display of, 65–67

real limits, 29
regression
    toward mean, 209–210
    z-score method, 207–212
regression coefficients, 214
regression equations, 213–221
    standard error of estimate, 221–223
    visual summary, 223
regression lines, 216–221
relative frequency, 36–39
    cumulative, 38–39
    probability and, 234
relative frequency polygon, 59–61
    cumulative, 64–65
repeated-measures design, 259
representative sample, 238
research hypothesis (H_1), 8, 255–256,
    269–276
    for analysis of variance, 329
    for nonparametric test, 396
rounding numbers, 7

sample, 15
    random, 238–240
    representative, 238
    standard deviation of, 118–120,
        240–241
    variance of, 117, 120, 121, 123
sample means, 79–80, 239–240
    distribution of, 241–244, 271–272,
        290
    mean of, 241, 244–245
    standard error of, 241–243,
        244–245, 246, 288
    standard error of difference,
        297–298, 302–304, 306–308
    statistical significance and, 269,
        270, 271–274
sample size
    critical values and, 195–196
    nonparametric tests and, 396
    power and, 276, 310
    t tests and, 290
sampling, 238–241
scaled scores, 137–141
scales of measurement, 11–14, 92
scatterplots, 182–184, 208
semi-interquartile range, 92
signed ranks, 406–409

simple frequency distribution, 24
single-sample t tests, 290–295, 309
skewed data, 89–91
    boxplot of, 92–94
    tests with, 396, 400
slope of regression line, 214–221
source table
    one-way analysis of variance,
        341–342
    two-way analysis of variance, 363,
        367, 371, 372
standard deviation, 118–120
    computational formula, 120–122,
        123
    of population, 118, 120
    of sample, 118–120, 240–241
    of sample means, 241–243,
        244–245, 246
    of scaled scores, 139, 141
    of z-score distribution, 144
standard error of difference
    correlated samples, 302–304,
        306–308
    independent samples, 297–298
standard error of estimate, 221–223
standard error of mean, 241–243,
    244–245, 246
    estimated, 288
standard scores. See z scores
statistical significance, 269–275,
    286
statistics, 2, 396. See also
    nonparametric statistics
stem-and-leaf diagrams, 66–67
Studentized Range Statistic (q), 344,
    434
study tips, 4–6
subject variables, 257–258, 266
subtracting a constant, 138–139
sums of squares
    one-way analysis of variance,
        339–341, 343
    two-way analysis of variance,
        363–367
symmetrical distribution, 89, 91

tails of distribution, 89
t distribution, 290
T test, 404–409, 410, 416

t tests, 290
    vs. analysis of variance,
        328–329
    correlated samples, 302–308, 309,
        310
    independent samples, 296–299,
        300, 309, 310
    multiple samples, 327–328
    ordinal data and, 395–396
    power of, 309–310
    sign of t, 305–306
    single-sample, 290–295, 309
two-group design, 263
two-tailed tests, 274
    with t score, 305
    with z score, 289
two-way analysis of variance,
    354–380
    degrees of freedom, 369–370
    experimental design and,
        354–358
    F test in, 372–373, 374, 375, 376
    HSD test with, 375–376
    interaction, 359–361, 376–377
    main effects, 358–359, 375–376
    mean squares in, 370–372, 374,
        375
    sums of squares in, 363–367
    visual summary, 373–374
Type I error, 271, 272
    F test and, 342
    with multiple t tests, 328
Type II error, 271, 275

U test, 395–402, 403, 411, 413

variability. See measures of
    variability
variables, 8–9, 256–258
    extraneous, 9, 266–267, 268
    on graph, 52, 54
    See also independent variables
variance, 117–118, 120
    coefficient of determination and,
        197–198, 210
    computational formula, 120–122,
        123
    of scaled scores, 139
    See also analysis of variance